The American Judicial Tradition THIRD EDITION

ALSO BY G. EDWARD WHITE

The Eastern Establishment and the Western Experience (1968)

Patterns of American Legal Thought (1978)

Tort Law in America: An Intellectual History (1980)

Earl Warren: A Public Life (1982)

The Marshall Court and Cultural Change (1988)

Justice Oliver Wendell Holmes: Law and the Inner Self (1993)

Intervention and Detachment: Essays in Legal History and Jurisprudence (1994)

Creating the National Pastime: Baseball Transforms Itself, 1903–1953 (1996)

The Constitution and the New Deal (2000)

Alger Hiss's Looking-Glass Wars (2004)

Oliver Wendell Holmes, Jr. (2006)

History and the Constitution: Collected Essays (2007)

The American Judicial Tradition

Profiles of Leading American Judges

THIRD EDITION

G. Edward White

UNIVERSITY PRESS

2007

OXFORD
UNIVERSITY PRESS

Oxford University Press, Inc., publishes works that further
Oxford University's objective of excellence
in research, scholarship, and education.

Oxford New York
Auckland Cape Town Dar es Salaam Hong Kong Karachi
Kuala Lumpur Madrid Melbourne Mexico City Nairobi
New Delhi Shanghai Taipei Toronto

With offices in
Argentina Austria Brazil Chile Czech Republic France Greece
Guatemala Hungary Italy Japan Poland Portugal Singapore
South Korea Switzerland Thailand Turkey Ukraine Vietnam

First published 1976 by Oxford University Press, Inc.
200 Madison Avenue, New York, New York 10016

www.oup.com

First issued as an Oxford University Press paperback, 1978

Oxford is a registered trademark of Oxford University Press

Library of Congress Cataloging-in-Publication Data
White, G. Edward.
The American judicial tradition : profiles of
leading American judges / by G. Edward White.—3rd ed.
p. cm.
Includes bibliographical references and index.
ISBN-13 978-0-19-513962-4; 978-0-19-513963-1 (pbk.)
ISBN 0-19-513962-3; 0-19-513963-1 (pbk.)
1. Judges—United States—Biography. 2. United States.
Supreme Court—History. I. Title.
KF8744.W5 2007
347.73'2634—dc22 2006017230

10 9 8 7 6 5 4 3

Printed in the United States of America
on acid-free paper

for Elisabeth McCafferty Davis White

Preface to the Third Edition

Holmes once wrote that all ideas are dead after twenty years,[1] and it has been more than thirty since the publication of the first edition of this book. Although I have retained a good deal of the material in the first edition, I have omitted two of its chapters, one on Justices Samuel Miller, Joseph Bradley, and Stephen Field and the other on the "Four Horsemen" of the Taft and Hughes Courts (Willis Van Devanter, James McReynolds, George Sutherland, and Pierce Butler), on the ground that the perspective taken toward them in earlier editions has become historiographically obsolete.[2] I could have used the same criterion to omit the chapter on James Kent, Joseph Story, and Lemuel Shaw, but two of those three judges remain underresearched figures,[3] so I have resolved to retain it in the hope it might serve as a foil for some forthcoming revisionist work.[4]

In the chapter on the Rehnquist Court that serves as the focal point of this edition, I have adopted the approach employed in the Burger Court chapter rather than that on the Warren Court. Instead of using a few Justices as figures representing a Court's tendencies, I have offered brief sketches of all the Rehnquist Court's members and presented the Court through an analysis of its internal atmosphere, some of its important lines of decisions, and its jurisprudential orientation. My approach is not intended to suggest that none of the Justices on the Burger or Rehnquist Courts is worthy of more extended treatment, but it is arguably more difficult to gain a sense of a judge's importance in the history of the American judicial tradition without more historical distance from the judge's tenure. Another reason I have not chosen to single out individual Rehnquist Court Justices for particular emphasis is to underscore the importance, in understanding that Court's tendencies, of the fact that its personnel did not change for over a decade, resulting in the collegial dimensions of its work being very important.

This edition continues the emphasis of the first two on the constraints that affect the performance of Justices of the Supreme Court of the United States, notwithstanding their very considerable power to make significant policy decisions in the guise of constitutional interpretation. In this edition, however, the nature of the perceived constraints on Justices as consitutional interpreters has somewhat shifted since the close of the Burger Court, and that shift requires some comment.

The thematic organization of this book derives from posited continuities and contrasts about the role of American appellate judges over time. The overriding continuity affecting the role of judges over the course of American history has been the belief that judges, especially Supreme Court Justices, may not legitimately equate their interpretations of law with their ideological preferences. The belief has partly rested on the perception that law transcends human partisanship and partly on the fact that Supreme Court Justices have life tenure and are subjected to few political checks when making decisions. Thus from Marshall through Rehnquist, American Justices have been expected to demonstrate that their decisions, despite often having major political consequences, are faithful to law as opposed to partisan ideology.

The consistency of that expectation over time, however, has been accompanied by quite different perceptions about the appropriate justifications for meeting it. The book has been organized around the evolution of those different perceptions. In the period in which the "oracular" theory of judging was in place, which stretched from the time of the framing of the Constitution through the nineteenth century, the dominant understanding of judicial decision-making treated it as an exercise in "finding" rather than "making" law, with "law" being conceived as a body of finite and immutable principles that existed independent of its interpreters. Marshall captured that understanding in a distinction he made between "the will of the judge" and the "will of the law."[5] The former "will" referred to the partisan interests of a judge as a human being, the latter to a body of transcendent principles. The obligation of judges was to demonstrate that their decisions followed law rather than personal agendas.

The same distinction, put in slightly different terms, was made by Brewer in his 1893 address, in which he claimed that judges "make no laws," "establish no policy," and "never enter into the domain of public action." Their functions, he maintained, were "limited to seeing that popular action does not trespass on right and justice as it exists in written constitutions and natural law."[6] The distinction presupposed that "right and justice" were finite concepts, independent of political ideology, and that judges simply discerned the meaning of those concepts by reading the Constitution against a backdrop of natural law principles.

The oracular theory of judging thus assumed that "law" itself was a constraint on judges. Judicial decisions achieved legitimacy when the opinions accompanying them demonstrated that judges were merely discerning finite and transcendent legal principles and applying them to cases. This was why Marshall's opinions took pains to elucidate the meaning of provisions in the Constitution, and to identify them with natural law principles, such as the principle that a legislature could not take property from A and give it to B without adequate compensation. His elucidations were offered as proof that he was following the "will of the law," not his partisan inclinations.

Judicial elucidation was particularly important because many provisions of the Constitution included terms, such as "contracts," "commerce," "speech," "due process," and "equal protection," whose meaning in individual cases was not self-evident. In those cases the technique of the oracular judge was to infuse the terms with background assumptions drawn from principles of natural law, political economy, or social organization. This meant that when the commerce clause was interpreted as governing some transactions, and not others, or when the "liberties" in the due process clauses were adjudged to protect some activities, and not others, the justifications for the uneven applications were thought of as being drawn from the foundational political, social, and economic assumptions of American republican ideology. The "law" that constrained judges thus included, as Brewer put it, background principles of "right and justice" that Americans shared. It was therefore not synonymous with the particularistic ideologies of the judges who discerned it.

The understanding that authoritative sources of law (common law principles, as embodied in judicial decisions, or provisions of the Constitution) were interpreted against a backdrop of foundational political and social assumptions enabled American common and constitutional law to change its content over time. In particular, as assumptions about the content of principles such as liberty or equality, or of constitutionally significant terms such as "contract" or "commerce," changed over the course of the nineteenth century, judicial interpretations of sources embodying those principles reflected the changes. A vivid illustration came in the period between the 1840s and 1880s, when the contracts clause, which had been interpreted by Marshall Court decisions to be an absolute bar to legislation divesting propertyholders of property conveyed to them by a prior legislature, ceased to be a bar once states were permitted to reserve the right to modify the terms of their charters to private corporations or individuals in the original grant. The "liberty" of private enterprises to conduct their business free of state oversight was thus significantly curtailed for a brief period.[7] But after the passage of the Fourteenth Amendment in 1868, courts came to intepret its due process clause as a restriction on state interference with property comparable to the earlier interpretation of the Contracts Clause. Both interpretations were bottomed on the assumption that republican political theory placed limits on the ability of government to interfere with the property rights of individuals.

Both those interpretations had been made at a time when the oracular theory of judging remained dominant, and thus both were treated as the judicial application of preexisting principles of law and political economy rather than the fostering of a judicial ideology, such as "laissez-faire capitalism." But as the nineteenth century drew to a close, the oracular theory itself came under pressure. The most vulnerable element of that theory had been its posited distinction between the will of the judge and the will of the law, and over time, as judicial glosses on constitutional provisions produced changing applications of those provisions, and as common law judges often distinguished and sometimes overruled prior judicial interpretations of legal principles, it became more difficult to maintain a radical separation between legal sources and the interpreters of those sources.

The eventual collapse of the distinction between the will of the law and the will of the judge was a product of fundamentally altered conceptions of human agency that emerged in the first three decades of the twentieth century. The emergence of those altered conceptions was part of an epistemological response to modernity, which had unambiguously established itself in America by the years before World War I. Modernist epistomology replaced the external causal agents of a premodern worldview—God, nature, the cycles of history, stratified social roles, the "iron laws" of political economy, and "law" as a collection of immanent and timeless principles—with human will and power. Humans could control their destinies, make their futures qualitatively better than their pasts, arrive at a scientific understanding of the natural and physical worlds, and thereby end the inevitable degeneration of republican institutions into tyranny and corruption. Humans simply needed to shake off their belief that they were buffeted by inexorable external forces in the universe and harness the scientifically inspired techniques of secular higher learning toward progressive and beneficent ends. Law, just like science, history, political economy, and the natural and physical sciences, could be a vehicle for human policy-making.[8]

With the onset of modernist epistemology in the early twentieth century came the new "schools" of American jurisprudence, Sociological Jurisprudence and legal Realism. With it came, as well, an approach to constitutional interpretation that identified the Constitution as a "living document" whose meaning changed with the times and was created by human judges. Finally, with modernist epistemology came the collapse of a distinction between the sources of law and its interpreters: law was "made," in the view of modernist commentators, as much by judges as by legislators. A new group of Supreme Court Justices, the most eminent of whom were Holmes and Brandeis, came to occupy their positions against a backdrop of altered definitions of the role of a judge. Instead of judges being thought of as persons who discerned and applied preexisting principles of law, they were thought of as persons who had the power to equate the meaning of the Constitution with their interpretations of it.[9]

The collapse of the distinction between the will of the law and the will of the judge meant that the primary set of justifications advanced by judges for their interpretations of authoritative legal sources came to be seen by twentieth-century critics as largely meaningless. Instead of the interpretations being seen as simply the extractions of legal principles and their application to cases, they were seen as more purposive, more creative, and more ideological in nature. Late-nineteenth- and early-twentieth-century Justices had identified their function, in due process cases, as marking out the boundary between the police power and private rights in accordance with foundational principles of republican political economy. Twentieth-century commentators were unconvinced that this meant any more than the convictions of those Justices that the Constitution embodied laissez-faire economic theory.[10]

Once twentieth-century commentors characterized the principal interpretive justifications of a line of Justices from Marshall through Brewer as largely ideological in nature, the perceived obligation of American judges to disassociate their legal decisions from their partisan concerns returned with a vengeance. If judges "made" law, transforming the meaning of the Constitution in accordance with their interpretations, what constrained them in their decision-making? This is the background question that has affected all Supreme Court Justices since Holmes. With modernity and the elevation of modernist conceptions of human-centered causal agency to a position of orthodoxy, all Supreme Court Justices have needed to develop a set of justifications for their decisions that, while implicitly acknowledging that judicial interpretation is a creative process akin to lawmaking, preserves the legitimacy of the decisions by disassociating them from partisanship.

The twentieth-century Justices featured in the first and second editions of this book devoted their energy to the working out of what might be called modernist-driven interpretive justifications for their decisions, and successive chapters devote attention to the varying interpretive approaches of particular judges. But there has been an overarching similarity in the justifications employed by Justices from Holmes through Burger. In the place of the premodern constraints incorporated within the oracular theory of judging, with their emphasis on the nature of "law" as an external, immanent, timeless causal agent in the universe, judges for most of the twentieth century have emphasized modernist-driven institutional constraints

The theory of institutional constraints on the judiciary begins with the assumptions that America is a democracy and that judges, especially Supreme Court Justices, are not "democratic" officials in the sense of being subjected to the political checks affecting elected officeholders. They have life tenure, and thus do not have to run for office, and their decisions are rarely countermanded by Congress, the Executive, or state legislatures. Even when the Court's decisions are countermanded, as when Congress passes a statute that seeks to reverse the outcome reached in a Supreme Court case, such action is subject to constitutional review by the Court, and the Court's judgment, on review, is authoritative. These dimensions of the office of Supreme Court Justice arguably create a "countermajoritarian difficulty," in that a conspicuously nondemocratic institution has the power to displace the policy judgments of governmental branches more accountable to the public at large. The "difficulty" was made more acute, for modernist-inspired commentators, by their belief that judges were another species of lawmakers whose interpretations of authoritative legal sources amounted to policy judgments.

The "countermajoritarian difficulty" was not a concern for judges or commentators working within the assumptions of the oracular theory of judging because "law," as a body of foundational, timeless principles, was treated as a constraint on the actions of the lawmaking branches. In Brewer's formulation of the role of judges, that role was to ensure that "popular action," by which he meant legislative or executive policies, did not "trespass on right and justice" as embodied in the law. As such the judiciary was a "countermajoritarian" force: there was no "difficulty." Brewer's formulation was buttressed by the belief that "law" embodied foundational principles of republican political theory, and by the associated belief that republicanism was designed to impose structural checks on the power of democratically elected branches to forestall tyranny and corruption. When judges sought to prevent legislatures from trespassing on "right and justice," they were protecting American citizens against the demagogic tendencies of popular bodies.

By the twentieth century a more robust conception of democracy had replaced republicanism as the dominant political ideology in America, and the idea of the judiciary as a countermajoritarian force had become more problematic. The idea of institutional constraints on judges followed from those developments.[11] The idea surfaced, progressively, in various tendencies in early-twentieth-century constitutional commentary that are reviewed in the chapters discussing the careers of judges from Holmes through the Burger Court. The first of the tendencies was a recharacterization of the Court's severe scrutiny of legislation under the due process clauses, particularly the "liberty of contract" doctrine. The oracular theory of judging treated that scrutiny as a routine part of the obligation of judges to see that popular action did not "trespass" on foundational "liberties"; modernist-inspired jurisprudential theories saw the Court's "liberty of contract" decisions as representing the judicial imposition of a particular economic ideology on more democratic institutions.

In order to prevent inappropriate judicial usurpations of the prerogatives of democratically elected branches, commentators, and subsequently judges, established the canon of "judicial self-restraint," which operationalized itself in a presumption that courts, when engaging in constitutional review of the policies of other branches, would validate those policies unless they directly contravened an express provision of the Constitution. Holmes in particular, and subsequently Brandeis, were judicial pioneers in developing an approach to constitutional review that emphasized deference to other branches. At the same time, however, they developed an exception to that approach in cases, predominantly those involving legislative restrictions on speech, where more aggressive judicial review could be justified as consistent with democratic theory because the "liberty" of speaking freely on public issues was a foundational principle of democratic government.

Over time additional judges made contributions to the refinement of a stance toward constitutional review that maintained the presumption of deference to other branch policies but preserved exceptions for instances in which aggressive constitutional scrutiny of certain types of legislation furthered the goals of democratic theory. A case decided by the Stone Court in 1938, *United States v. Carolene Products,*[12] provided a tentative roadmap for what amounted to a system of bifurcated review, alternating deferential with aggressive scrutiny depending on the kinds of "rights," or the kinds of persons, being affected by the statutes or policies being subjected to constitutional challenge. By the Warren Court, "Carolene Products" review had become the norm, with the Court, in areas such as race relations, legislative reapportionment, and school prayers, reviving its role as a countermajoritarian force, this time on the ground that its intervention checked the antidemocratic tendencies of legislatures.

For an interval of more than three decades, then, debates in American constitutional jurisprudence centered on the institutional constraints on judges, and the exceptions to those constraints, allegedly mandated by democratic theory. The debates reached their highest level of intensity on the Warren Court, when many of its major decisions, such as those involving racial discrimination and reapportionment, were attacked by commentators who maintained that although they agreed with the outcomes the Court had reached, they disapproved, on institutional competence grounds, of its aggressive review stance. The interplay of what I call "substantive" and "process liberalism" during the years of Warren's tenure captured the debates. The Warren Court's critics were, on the whole, supportive of eliminating racial discrimination, apportioning legislatures on the basis of population, and secularizing American public education. But they believed that the Court was not the appropriate institution to mandate those policies.

By the end of the Warren Court it was clear that "judicial activism," a posture deplored by critics of the Court who believed in the canon of self-restraint, had established itself as an alternative to deference in many cases. The Burger Court, several of whose appointees had been expected, for ideological reasons, to endorse the restraint canon, showed little sign of doing so. More significantly, Justices and commentators seemed to be paying increasingly less attention to institutional constraints as the Burger Court evolved. By the time Rehnquist replaced Burger as Chief Justice, scholars had characterized the Court's approach as one of "rootless activism," in which shifting judicial majorities selectively scrutinized or deferred to the policies of other branches, apparently largely on ideological grounds.[13]

Despite the belief among commentators, by the 1980s, that the debate between judicial activists and subscribers to the canon of restraint was no longer central to the Court's constitutional jurisprudence, the very characterization of the Burger Court as a collection of rootless activists testified to the fact that the principal constraints on American judges continued to be seen as institutional in nature. Despite the apparent indifference of Burger Court Justices to canons of deference, they remained part of a long list of twentieth-century American judges whose interpretive approaches were fashioned from the starting assumption that the legitimacy of judicial decisions was intimately tied to their ability to confront, and surmount, the countermajoritarian difficulty. No influential Justice from Holmes through the Burger Court sought to locate the constraints on judges in essentialist conceptions of "law" or in the foundational assumptions of American republicanism; they took for granted the obligation of judges to square their decisions with democratic theory and their own role as a species of lawmakers.

Thus the first two editions of this book sought to narrate the interaction of a continuously perceived obligation on the part of American judges to disassociate their decisions from partisan concerns with shifting conceptions of the central constraints on judges as interpreters of authoritative legal sources. In the nineteenth-century portions of the book, judges seek to advance justifications for their decisions that reflect an oracular theory of judging and thus emphasize constraints derived from "law" itself; in the twentieth-century portions, the justifications take a different form, centering on institutional constraints related to the countermajoritarian difficulty.

If one thinks of the narrative of an "American judicial tradition" as evolving in that fashion, the Rehnquist Court can be seen as presenting a new phase in that narrative. For it is clear that the central jurisprudential debates of the Rehnquist Court did not center on the countermajoritarian difficulty or related institutional constraints on judges as interpreters. They centered on opposing approaches to constitutional interpretation that reflected radically different conceptions of that process. One approach, primarily exemplified in the opinions of Justices Scalia and Thomas, posited that the chief constraints on judges as constitutional interpreters were those of history, the text of the Constitution, and the "original understanding" of constitutional provisions by their framers and contemporaries. Under this approach, typically known as "originalism," Justices emphasized historical research and linguistic analysis to ascertain the "original understanding" of provisions they were called upon to interpret. Once they determined that "understanding," they treated it as controlling their interpretations. Under that approach the meaning of the Constitution did not change with time; judges were bound to follow the understandings of provisions held by their framers and peers. The chief constraints on judges as constitutional interpreters were the constitutional text and history.[14]

The alternative approach rejected the assumption of originalists that the Constitution's meaning remained fixed in time. Instead it adopted the "living Constitution" theory of constitutional adaptivity, which posited that when new cases posed new applications of constitutional provisions, those applications resulted in a change in the meaning of the provisions. If, for example, the equal protection clause of the Fourteenth Amendment had not been understood by its framers to apply to discriminations on the basis of gender because differences between men and women were understood to be natural and necessary, that understanding could change when gender discrimination was judged, in some contexts, to perpetuate antiquated and invidious stereotypes about the sexes. When the Court employed the equal protection clause to strike down legislation embodying such stereotypes, it was changing the meaning of the clause.

The two approaches are thus quite far apart on some basic questions of constitutional interpretation. One is the aforementioned question of whether the meaning of the Constitution changes as judges interpret it over time. A second is the status of accumulated judicial glosses on a provision of the Constitution. An example is the succession of judicial decisions interpreting the free speech clause of the First Amendment. It is clear from those decisions that constitutional protection for "speech" does not include every form of utterance in any set of circumstances: urging the immediate murder of a government official would not be protected. At the same time it is clear that protected "speech" extends to certain forms of symbolic conduct, such as wearing clothing with a political message or burning a flag as a form of protest. It would seem apparent that an investigation of the current "meaning" of the free speech clause would need to take into account judicial decisions that have interpreted it.

Originalist and "living Constitution" theories of constitutional interpretation treat lines of judicial decisions glossing a provision quite differently. Although historical evidence suggests that the framers of the First Amendment did not intend protection for "speech" to extend to exhortations to murder public officials, it also suggests that they did not equate symbolic communicative conduct with "speech." It may even have been the case, as courts and commentators once believed, that the First Amendment was not designed to restrict the opportunity of the federal government to punish individuals for speech thought to be inconsistent with public order or otherwise offensive, but merely to prevent the government from censuring speech in advance. If the "orginal understanding" of the free speech clause limited it to protection against "prior restraints," a thoroughgoing originalist would need to regard a long line of twentieth-century cases as wrongly decided. A devotee of the "living Constitution" approach, in contrast, would treat that line of cases as illustrative of the changing "meaning" of the free speech clause over time.

The different attitudes of the two approaches toward accumulated judicial glosses illustrate quite different perspectives on the weight to be given to judicial precedents in constitutional interpretation. For originalists, precedents deserve weight only if they reflect the original understandings of a constitutional provision; if they depart from those understandings they amount to flawed interpretations. Originalism thus has the potential to spawn deeply revisionist analyses of existing constitutional doctrine. To the extent that established doctrine can be seen to be the product of successive judicial glosses that depart from the original understanding of provisions, it appears illegitimate from an originalist perspective. Since fidelity to the original understandings of the constitutional text is the primary constraint on judges as interpreters, glosses that depart from those understandings amount simply to judicial preferences for particular interpretations and outcomes. As such, to originalists, they amount to unconstrained judicial decisions, undermining their legitimacy. They are also vulnerable to being discarded, root and branch, as doctrinal guideposts for the interpretation of constitutional provisions.

In contrast, advocates of a "living Consitititution" perspective treat successive judicial glosses on provisions as part of the inevitable process by which the Constitution "adapts" itself to changing cultural contexts. Far from being susceptible to being discarded as illegitimate if exposed as unfaithful to original understandings, judicial glosses are part of the changing "meaning" of constitutional provisions: they signal how a provision has been applied in different contexts. A line of glosses can even serve to create established constitutional doctrine on which persons come to rely, adding to the weight to be accorded them in subsequent cases. The plurality opinion in *Planned Parenthood v. Casey*[15] made a version of this argument in concluding that *Roe v. Wade*, as a precedent, should be retained: countless persons, it argued, had conducted their affairs with the expectation that there was a limited constitutional right to terminate a pregnancy.

Thus to the extent that shifting the primary constraints on judges to the Constitution's text and history may require the overruling of whole lines of cases, the originalist approach to constitutional interpretation would seem to be comparatively disadvantaged. But the "living Constitution" approach would seem to be comparably vulnerable, for a different reason. If the major disadvantage of originalism is that it is either a radically revisionist or an otherworldly approach, the major disadvantage of "living Constitution" jurisprudence is that once one concedes that judges are free to help change the meaning of the Constitution to fit the times, it is hard to see what constraints exist on judges.

"Living Constitution" jurisprudence is not an approach that necessarily focuses on institutional constraints. Its concern is with the capacity of constitutional language to adapt itself to new situations. If one were to conclude that the use of a constitutional provision to prevent another branch from enacting a policy that most current Americans thought reprehensible was precluded by originalist concerns, that would represent an institutionalist judgment of a kind. The court that felt bound not to invoke the provision to invalidate the noxious policy would implicitly be appealing to other branches to do so or to the people to amend the Constitution. But if one were to conclude that the provision, despite its "original intent," could be read by the courts, given contemporary concerns, to invalidate the policy, that would represent an institutionalist judgment of another kind: courts need not defer to the decisions of other branches when they make particularly bad policies.

The latter approach would seem to raise all the concerns about subjective, unconstrained judging that have been part of the American judicial tradition from its origin. It is thus no small matter that the "living Constitution" approach rapidly runs into the problem of how judicially created changes in the meaning of constitutional provisions can be justified. Surely the argument that the changes result in "good" policy outcomes is not a reassuring one for those attempting to maintain a line between judging and partisan politics. So the debate between originalists and "living Constitution" advocates would seem to pit theorists whose insistence on a certain set of historical and linguistic constraints on judges sometimes borders on the myopic against theorists who would seem to have difficulty articulating the constraints that "living Constitution" judicial interpreters live under.

The most significant feature of the debate, for the purposes of this book, is that neither of the competing approaches is centered on the institutional considerations related to the countermajoritarian difficulty. As noted, originalist and "living Constitution" approaches are both capable of being radically activist. Neither is necessarily supportive of the canon of deference to other branch actors. Both are capable of supporting decisively "countermajoritarian" interventions by the Supreme Court. The approaches, in short, appear to be moving beyond the central concerns of American constitutional jurisprudence for most of the twentieth century. It seems much too soon to predict that another major phase in the history of the American judicial tradition has begun. But there are signs of a jurisprudential passage of a sort, and the

Rehnquist Court has clearly been involved with that passage. Hence the end of Chief Justice Rehnquist's tenure may illustrate more than the close of a chapter in the history of the Supreme Court of the United States. It may also illustrate the beginning of new conceptions of the role of judges in America.

It is never an unalloyed pleasure to revist one's earlier scholarship, and the successive prefaces to this work give testimony to the extent to which I have modified my perspective on its central issues over the years. In the interval between the second edition and this one the interest of scholars, students, and judges in the historical dimensions of law has grown dramatically, with the result that I have many more colleagues, both at the University of Virginia and at other institutions, working on projects in legal and constitutional history. Their presence has been a great benefit to me in direct and indirect ways, and I hope the trend continues.

As usual, my secretary Karen Spradlin and the reference desk at the University of Virginia Law School library have been a great help with research and production issues. My love to Susan Davis White, Alexandra Valre White, Bruce Arendt, Lucas Davis James Arendt, and the dedicatee Elisabeth McCafferty Davis White. Having missed the first two editions, it is their chance to get acquainted with this version.

Charlottesville
May 2006

Preface to the Expanded Edition

In the first edition of this book I indicated that it had been inspired by Richard Hofstadter's *The American Political Tradition*. My interest was in presenting the sweep of American judicial history in a series of portraits of important individual actors, an approach similar to that employed by Hofstadter. There are, of course, significant differences between judges and politicians. I nonetheless began the first edition assuming that, just as the careers of politicians could be made to symbolize larger political movements in the course of American history, the careers of judges could be seen as representing broader currents in American law and jurisprudence. When I was writing the first edition I sensed that there were considerable complexities in the process of linking individual judicial careers to themes in American jurisprudence, but the complexities I then chose to emphasize are not necessarily the ones I would choose to emphasize now. If one looks at the subtitles of the successive chapters, hints of the nature of the complexities that then engaged me surface. I was, to be sure, interested in the relationship of appellate judging to central ideological issues, such as property and race, and to political perspectives, such as liberalism. But I was primarily interested in what might be called institutional complexities. Among the issues suggested by the title subchapters were the limits of judicial power to make moral pronouncements, the difficulties of accommodating federal and state judicial systems, the relationship between professional norms of conduct and political values, the sources of a judge's reputation, and the meaning and role of "rationality" in judicial opinions.

In the first edition I disclaimed any particular approach to historiographical issues. In particular, I indicated that my delineation of a "tradition" of American appellate judging should not be taken as evidence of a "consensus" approach to history. In retrospect, I think the institutional emphasis of the chapter subtitles may undermine that claim. I do want to say, however, that at the time of the first edition the connection between "consensus history" and an institutionally oriented approach to appellate judging was not clear in my mind, so that if I held a "consensus" perspective it was unconscious. That, of course, does not make the perspective any less significant: indeed, it now seems to me that I was more imprisoned by the structures of Process Jurisprudence, with its emphasis on the relative competence of various institutional decision-makers in American society, than I would have cared to admit.

Put another way, what then seemed to me to be very important about the calculus of appellate judging in America was the extent to which judges were *constrained* in their decisions, and the constraints that I found most significant were those that seemed to stem from the nature of judging itself. Judges had an obligation to give reasons for their results; judges had an obligation not to usurp the powers of other branches of government; judges were required not to deviate too far from the consensual values of their times. Judges, thus, were not like politicians because they were constrained by the obligations of judicial reasoning. Not only must judges give reasons for their results, those reasons must at least make an effort to persuade not only those inclined to support the results but those not inclined to. Reasoning, viewed in this fashion, becomes the vehicle by which the judge seeks to convince his or her audience that more than naked subjectivity explains the result. The reasoning offered is intended itself to serve as a constraint on that subjectivity.

The above characterization, needless to say, is not free from difficulty. How does a judge's audience know whether the reasoning offered is wholly in a service of a predetermined result, an elaborate rationalization of a decision reached for other reasons? There are numerous responses to that question, one brief one being that after the reasoning is offered nothing else matters; the result becomes synonymous with the reasoning on which it is based. I am not sure that response is definitive, since the capacity of words and arguments to expand and shrink in the hands of those who reuse them suggests that reasoning can never be definitive. The motivation of the next user may be crucial and may also be undisclosed. But I think it is fair to say that the appellate judiciary in America is constrained from naked subjectivity at least in a "weak" sense: judges have to try to convince us that they are not being subjective. Other decision-makers do not. That fact alone gives some sense of the identity of the office.

The associated belief that legislators are more likely to represent the views of the public, and therefore that judges should defer to legislatures on "political" issues or "policy-making" questions seems equally problematic. The federal judiciary is hardly a representative institution in the sense of being directly accountable to an electorate. But Congress and the state legislatures are not all that representative either. Incumbent legislators are elected overwhelmingly at both the federal and the state levels; single-issue voting and lobbying allegedly dominate legislative sessions; and the ostensible wisdom of legislators as policy-makers may be nothing more than a recognition of the fact that legislators make policy quite regularly. So, by the way, do judges: does *Brown v. Board of Education* somehow become a decision of "principle" and not one of "policy" because the Court and not Congress decided it? In short, the twin bases of the institutional competence assumption—that judges are competent to decide some kinds of issues (those of "principle") and that legislators are competent to decide others (those of "policy")—seem unsubstantiated.

To the extent, then, that I assumed in the first edition that American appellate judges have had an *inherent* obligation to convince their audience that they did not transgress their appropriate institutional sphere of decision-making and thereby enter into areas in which they were not competent, that assumption needs to be restated here. There have surely been times throughout the course of American judicial history when judges have been constrained in their decision-making by one version or another of the institutional competence assumption. But that constraint has been *ideologically derived:* that is, it has been a result of a version of the institutional competence assumption occupying a position of stature in jurisprudential theory. Judges have not "had to" defer to the decisions of legislatures on "political" questions simply because they were judges; they have "had to" defer because to do otherwise would violate the assumptions of an established jurisprudential orthodoxy. While it is easy to see that orthodoxy firmly in place for much of the time period covered by this study, it is also possible to see it yielding to other pressures. Institutional competence theory called for the Court to decide *Brown* other than it did. There was no clear constitutional doctrine suggesting that racial segregation violated the equal protection clause; there was some doctrine suggesting that it did not; and Congress had taken no action on the question of segregated schools. The Court nonetheless decided *Brown* and radically altered its role as a decision-maker, not only with respect to racial issues but with respect to other pressing social issues as well. In so doing it was implicitly claiming that it could fashion policies as competently as could legislators. That claim represented a clear abandonment of institutional competence theory.

To the extent, then, that several justices in this study are identified as facing dilemmas associated with the facilitation of liberal policy results and the maintenance of a "restrained" theory of judging, those dilemmas should be seen as the products of the strength of the orthodoxy of institutional competence theory, not as something inherent in the nature of twentieth-century judging. When the oracular theory of judging was attacked and lost stature in the early decades of the twentieth century, judges could no longer be seen as constrained merely by the presence of the "law." Since it was clear that judges, being mortal and politically unaccountable, needed to be constrained by something, various theories were offered emphasizing the fact that nakedly subjective judicial decision-making is inconsistent with the expectations of impartiality that accompany the role of judge. One such theory stressed the subordination of subjectivity by suggesting that judges were not legislators and thus could not follow their "legislative" instincts. Many early- and mid-twentieth-century judges, some of whose careers are sketched in this study, took that theory sufficiently seriously to develop their stance toward constitutional adjudication around a perceived tension between the values of the judge and the obligation of judicial self-restraint. The response of those judges tells us a good deal about the history of early- and mid-twentieth-century jurisprudence. We should be cautious in attributing more significance to that response. We should be particularly cautious in concluding that the dilemmas of those judges will always be the dilemma of a judge who functions in a non-oracular world.

Were I writing this book anew, then, I might well phrase the elements of an American judicial tradition differently. But I have not chosen to undertake that rewriting in this edition, in part because I believe that my framing of the elements, while perhaps not the identical formulation I would use today, captured the important variables affecting appellate judging in America. The tradeoff between independence and accountability still seems central to defining the appellate judicial role. Appellate judges maintain a delicate relationship to American political culture, as the successive nominations of Judges Scalia and Bork to the Supreme Court amply demonstrate. The ideological differences between those two nominees were comparatively slight; the nominating President the same. But the political culture in which Bork's nomination was considered was dramatically different from that in which Scalia's was, and thus Scalia's non-answers to questions seeking to extract his ideology were replaced by Bork's forthright but shifting answers, with disastrous consequences for Bork's nomination. Politics dictated the choice of both Scalia and Bork; politics dictated the result of both nominations. Yet no one, not even the persons who nominated those judges, could predict with any degree of assurance what their future stance would be as Supreme Court Justices. Appellate judging in America is of politics but never identical to politics.

Finally, despite my earlier comments, I would not revise my claim that the American judicial tradition has been composed, in part, of a recurrent series of tradeoffs between "freedoms" in the judge and constraints on his or her behavior. I have listed the "freedoms" in Chapter 15, and see no reason to alter that list. I have suggested above some constraints that I believe will continue to adhere in the office. Reduced to their lowest terms, the constraints dictate that judges cannot be like politicians: should their decisions be perceived as merely the end products of their ideology, others will find those decisions unreasoned or usurpatious.

I continue to think that judges are significantly constrained in their decision-making. But I am less sure that they are constrained because they are judges than because they are, like other actors in a culture at a phase in its history, imprisoned by the unexpressed but deeply held premises that set the boundaries of an ideological agenda. The inability of judges wholly to make-over "the law" in their own image is not so much a product of their institutional role as it is a function of the ideological universe in which their decisions are made. If they hold views that are sufficiently extreme to be outside the boundaries of established discourse at a point in time, their inability to infuse those views into the law is principally a consequence of the fact that arguments for such views, in whatever form, will be "unacceptable" because the views themselves are "unacceptable."

I would like to close this recognition of the passage of time between editions of this book by thanking Professors A. E. Dick Howard and Yale Kamisar, who read earlier drafts of the expanded edition, Rachel Toor of Oxford Press, who helped edit it, and the numerous persons who have reviewed it, commented upon it, used it in classrooms, and sometimes given me the impression that they have profited from it. A special thanks to my father, George L. White, who first thought of an expanded edition.

Authors change as well as subjects, and it is not always pleasant for an author to confront the "dated" qualities of his own work. But if I have changed my mind about some of the emphasis in the first edition, and winced from time to time about some of its erroneous or dubious interpretations (some of which have been corrected but others of which perhaps remain), I have not changed my conviction, which surfaced before I first began writing, that this was a book that would meet a need, a need to make celebrated American judges more accessible. Twelve years later that need seems not to have diminished. Hence this expanded second edition.

Charlottesville
March 1988

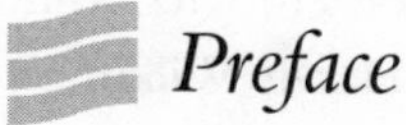

Preface

This book did not actually take shape during the years I participated in an informal legal history group at Harvard Law School, but its genesis was there. As with several other people currently teaching in law schools and history departments across the country, my interest in legal history can be traced to that experience. Jerome Cohen was the founder and moving spirit of that group; he has been a catalyst to the emergence of modern scholarship in American legal history.

I never met the late Richard Hofstadter, whose *American Political Tradition* served as a point of reference for this study. I am not certain that Hofstadter and I would necessarily have agreed on historiographical issues. I find Hofstadter's scholarship to be provocative in the best sense of the word, and I appreciate his willingness to synthesize or theorize and his concern with stylistic elegance. This present book, however, is about a judicial, as distinguished from a political, tradition and about judges as distinguished from politicians. I take those distinctions to be real, profound, and worth writing about.

A somewhat revised version of Chapter 6 appeared in the January 1975 issue of the *American Journal of Legal History,* and I am grateful to the editors for permission to reprint it.

Daniel Flanigan, William H. Harbaugh, Stanley N. Katz, Daniel J. Meador, William E. Nelson, and Calvin Woodard have read the entire manuscript in various drafts and improved it with their suggestions. Morton Horwitz, A. E. Dick Howard, John C. McCoid, Harvey S. Perlman, and J. Harvie Wilkinson III have read portions of it and given me the benefit of their critical comments. Roger J. Traynor has been kind enough to react to an early draft of the chapter on his career, although that essay is in no sense authorized. Merrill D. Peterson was supportive of the work and helpful to me in early stages. Linda Carroll Moore has been an outstanding research assistant, and the book has benefited considerably from her editorial suggestions. The secretarial staff of Virginia Law School, notably Sandy Durham, has been a great help throughout its composition. Grants from the American Council of Learned Societies and the Virginia Law School Foundation facilitated its progress. The last stages of publication have profited by the incisiveness of Susan Rabiner and the conscientiousness of Mary Ellen Evans of Oxford University Press.

Alexandra Valre White and especially Susan Davis White have immeasurably enriched my life while I have been working on the book. They would have done so had the book not existed.

Charlottesville
December 1975

Contents

The American Judicial Tradition THIRD EDITION

Introduction

The relation between the title and the subtitle of this book requires a preliminary comment. The title is intended to suggest a generalized argument that there has been and is a tradition of American appellate judging; that it contains, at a minimum, certain identifiable elements; and that it has persisted, in a complex and variegated fashion, through time. The subtitle suggests, however, that this tradition is here being examined through a series of individual and group portraits of leading judges. The portraits are not intended to be complete or definitive. They stress themes and traits I found central to an understanding of the subjects and their times; they seek to capture essences. The book, then, is intended to communicate on varying levels of abstraction and concreteness, some levels involving broad generalizations about the judicial role in American history and others involving anecdotal or analytical comments on the life and work of a particular judge.

Given the length of the book, a summary of its central generalized argument may be useful. I begin by maintaining that the American judicial tradition, as I define it, did not exist at the formation of the nation, but was created during the tenure of John Marshall, and largely through his efforts. The tradition Marshall passed on at his retirement contained three identifiable elements, which I describe and analyze at various points in the narrative. The elements can be summarized here as a tension between independence and accountability, a delicate and unique relation to politics, and a recurrent trade-off between acknowledged powers and freedoms in the individual judge, and acknowledged constraints on the institution of the judiciary.

The first eight chapters describe, through profiles of leading judges, the course of the tradition in the nineteenth century. Central to that description is an argument that judging was not regarded in the nineteenth century as an exercise in making law. Rather, law was conceived of as a mystical body of permanent truths, and the judge was seen as one who declared what those truths were and made them intelligible—as an oracle who "found" and interpreted the law. The core elements of the tradition were derived from the oracular theory of judging and its interaction with politics in America. The oracular theory, I argue, persisted throughout the great part of the nineteenth century, despite important shifts in American jurisprudential attitudes.

The final seven chapters follow the path of the American judicial tradition in the twentieth century. Here the argument shifts. The characterization of the judge as an oracle came to be discredited in the early years of this century, I maintain; judges were acknowledged to be lawmakers, not law-finders. But the central elements of the tradition remained intact. This continuity was made possible by a series of successive jurisprudential theories that supplied various checks on judicial performance. Judicial reasoning was transformed from an exercise in law declaration to an exercise in justifying autocratic power in a democratic society. A nineteenth-century contrast between the "will of the judge" and the "will of the law" was replaced by a twentieth-century contrast between the results a judge reached and the reasons he gave for them. I conclude by suggesting that despite the dramatic changes in the posture of the appellate judiciary during Earl Warren's Chief Justiceship, and despite current jurisprudential ferment, the experience of contemporary American judges has some continuity with that of their predecessors in the tradition.

A work that presents a broad sweep of history through profiles of individuals necessarily presents problems of inclusion and exclusion. The judges selected for treatment have not been chosen arbitrarily, although some readers may quarrel with their presence. One criterion used in the selection process has been termination of service: no judges active at the time of the writing of the book were included. Although this criterion has resulted in the omission of some interesting and influential careers, such as that of recently retired Justice William O. Douglas of the United States Supreme Court, or those of Chief Justice Walter V. Schaefer of the Supreme Court of Illinois and Judge Henry Friendly of the Court of Appeals for the Second Circuit, it rests on the premise that a judge's impact is not entirely perceptible until his retirement.

A second criterion has been historical interest. Here more than one individual might have served to embody a theme or represent an attitude, and a further refinement has been necessary; or a less well-known individual has been thought deserving of attention for his historical significance. Utilization of this criterion has eliminated Chief Justice John Bannister Gibson, who served on the Supreme Court of Pennsylvania in the early nineteenth century, and Thomas Ruffin, Chief Justice of the Supreme Court of North Carolina at the same time. Other judges, such as James Kent, Joseph Story, and Roger Taney, were thought to personify points of view roughly similar to those of Gibson or Ruffin. In the same fashion Thomas McIntyre Cooley of the Supreme Court of Michigan has been chosen over John Forrest Dillon of the Supreme Court of Iowa, whose jurisprudential attitudes greatly resembled Cooley's.

Where two men could be said to personify a similar point of view and to have made a roughly comparable impact on history, a third criterion has been employed, that of availability of information on a prospective subject's personal life. One function of a biographical-essay format is to sketch the character and personality of a subject; and since judges do not always reveal themselves in their decisions, additional information is generally necessary to flesh out the portrait. In the case of Ruffin and Dillon the relative paucity of such information contributed to their exclusion. Only in the treatment of Roger Traynor, the one living judge studied, has personal information been underemphasized.

Finally, perceptions of the current state of knowledge on various subjects has affected the breadth of their coverage. Justices Holmes and Brandeis, for example, are contained in a single chapter, though Justices Jackson and Traynor receive separate treatment. These judgments on coverage were based not on an implicit ranking of the stature or importance of the subjects but on a desire to provide fresh perspectives on the mind-set of individual judges, thereby avoiding as often as possible the repetition of familiar information or conventional analysis. In some instances I sought a new perspective in a group portrait; in others, through a more detailed focus on an individual character.

A far more systematic set of criteria than the above would still not insure an infallible selection process. Indeed, the use of the biographical-essay format as a means of writing history presents obvious difficulties. The format sacrifices exhaustiveness of detail for distillations and syntheses; it seeks, as used herein, to capture habits of mind, impulses of thought and feeling, style and influence. History as biography also overemphasizes individual contributions: no "great man" theory is advanced here, and care has been taken to point out the cultural imperatives of time and place that confine human influence within prescribed channels.

Identifying and describing a "tradition" of American appellate judging assumes a certain cohesiveness and continuity in the process of appellate adjudication over time. This study does not go so far as to suggest, as Roscoe Pound once did, that social and economic conditions are merely pieces of evidence fitted in to the workings of a "taught legal tradition."[1] It suggests, rather, that judging is bound to reflect the governing social and intellectual assumptions of various periods in American history, and that its relation to its social context is one of total integration. But in examining appellate judging in America one cannot ignore its distinctive institutional characteristics, which have remained relatively constant over the years and which have affected judicial behavior.

This study's emphasis on continuity and tradition is not intended to identify it with a "consensus" view of American history or with any alternative view. Conflict and consensus are not terms that lend themselves readily to judicial history. Adjudication has as its essential function the resolution of social conflict, but it performs that function in part through appeals to consensual attitudes as they have manifested themselves in past legal decisions, whether by judges or legislatures. It is not the purpose of this study to assess the validity of treating American history from one theoretical perspective or another; its purpose is rather to try to convey, in a broad sense, an understanding of what it has meant to be an American appellate judge.

Throughout this work, judging and a judicial tradition are identified with courts of appeal rather than with trial courts. In this sense its focus is narrower than its title might perhaps imply. It emphasizes a more abstract component of judging, one with an emphasis on the content and meaning of legal doctrine, than that which is often emphasized at the trial-court level. Nothing is said here about the functions of examining witnesses, charging juries, making rulings on points of evidence, or creating a trial record, all of which form in part the business of trial judging. This is not to minimize the importance of those functions: they simply do not lend themselves as well to jurisprudential or historical analysis as does the work of appellate courts, nor, from one perspective, are they as significant.

Not all the subjects portrayed here have been treated with admiration. No effort has been made to perpetuate a mystique of judges as being innately wise and dignified human beings. Still, a tinge of respect has suffused the portraits, respect not only for many of the individuals involved but also for the institution of the appellate judiciary. As a professional ideal it demands balanced judgment and honesty from those who personify it; it attempts to make complex adjustments in human relations and yet requires intelligence and rationality in the undertaking. It can serve, in its finest performances, as a solidifying force in our culture.

I 

John Marshall and the Genesis of the Tradition

In pre-Revolutionary America the specific responsibilities of the appellate judge varied from colony to colony, but judges generally served in two capacities: as intermediaries between colonial executives and local communities and as leadership figures in the localities. The judges of the Superior Court of Massachusetts, for example, passed on the validity of tax assessments and entertained damage suits against sheriffs, jailers, customs officials, and moderators of town meetings. As such, they were agents of the provincial government, functioning as executive bureaucrats. Being men of high status, they were usually pillars of their local communities. They were also asked to use their power and prestige to preserve local order and tranquility.[1]

The specific responsibilities of colonial judges assured them of a wide range of petty powers but of little independence. They were accountable to those who appointed them and to those affected by their decisions. They could not entirely ignore their administrative responsibilities, and neither could they enforce distasteful judgments. In addition, colonies such as Massachusetts sought to limit judicial power further by giving great weight to jury verdicts while restricting the power of judges to influence juries—through trial court instructions—or to modify jury findings on appeal.[2] Finally, the independence of the appellate judiciary in the colonies was limited by the predominant jurisprudential assumption that judges merely "found" the law, mechanically applying existing rules to new situations. This assumption fostered an image of judges as oracles who could discover the law's technical mysteries but who could not influence the content of law itself.

The advent of the Revolution and the introduction of the Constitution changed the structure of the appellate court system in America but did not dramatically change the status of judges. The history of the Supreme Court from 1789 to 1801, the year of John Marshall's appointment as Chief Justice, was marked by three phenomena: the minimal extent of Court business; the disorganization and disunity of the Court itself—most notably with regard to the question of its authority to pass on the constitutionality of Congressional legislation—and the increasing involvement of the Court in partisan politics.[3]

Between February 1790, when the Court began its first term, and February 1793, it heard only five cases. From 1790 to 1801 it decided only fifty-five. The Court had two Chief Justices during this period. The first, John Jay, felt so little burdened by his office that he remained active in Federalist party politics while on the bench, and finally resigned in 1795 to run for Governor of New York. His successor, Oliver Ellsworth, was ill much of the time and spent most of the rest of his tenure in the diplomatic corps.[4] The Court membership numbered six until 1801, and five between 1801 and the 1803 term.[5] Justices often gave separate opinions for their decisions, and they revealed themselves divided on, among other things, their own power to construe, and possibly invalidate, acts of Congress in light of the Constitution. The most notable case decided in this first decade of the Court, *Chisholm v. Georgia*,[6] which allowed a citizen of one state to sue another state in a federal court, was overruled by the 11th Amendment in 1798.

Worst of all, the passage of the Alien and Sedition Acts of 1798 embroiled the justices in partisan politics.[7] The Court failed to declare that controversial legislation unconstitutional; in response, the Virginia and Kentucky Resolutions, which argued that state legislatures, not the Court, were the ultimate interpreters of the Constitution, were drafted. After Jefferson's election in 1800, the outgoing Federalists "packed" the federal judiciary with party supporters; their opponents, the Republicans, responded by bringing impeachment charges against several judges, including Justice Samuel Chase of the Supreme Court. John Jay, who was again offered appointment to the Court, this time in 1800 by President John Adams, characterized the state of judicial affairs in his respectful but firm rejection of the position. The Court, he told Adams, labored "under a system so defective" that it could not possibly "obtain the energy, weight, and dignity which were essential to its affording due support to the National Government, nor acquire the public confidence and respect which, as the last resort of the justice of the nation, it should possess."[8] This was the branch of government John Marshall was named to head in 1801.

The genesis of the American judicial tradition was the transformation of the office of appellate judge under John Marshall. This tradition has, since its origins, contained certain core elements: a measure of true independence and autonomy for the appellate judiciary from the other two branches of government; the extension, within limits, of judicial authority to questions of politics in addition to technical questions of law; and the presence of a set of internalized constraints upon the office of judge that circumscribe judicial freedom of choice and give the office an identity discrete from the personalities of the individuals who occupy it at any specific time. Since Marshall the appellate judiciary in America has been consciously aloof from direct participation in politics and an active and weighty political force; at once the least regulated and the most constrained branch of American government. Marshall was the primary creator of this unique institutional role.

Each of the tradition's central elements can be seen as having been derived by Marshall in response to the particular difficulties the judiciary faced at the opening of the nineteenth century. In response to the problems of excessive accountability and uncertain status, Marshall declared the independence of judges in *Marbury v. Madison*,[9] making the appellate judiciary the final interpreter of the supreme law of the land. In response to the limiting effects of an oracular theory of judging, which sought to divorce "law" from community values, Marshall developed a technique of decision-making that retained an oracular style but grounded decisions on appeals to the first principles of American civilization. And while entangling the Court in the resolution of questions of social, economic, and philosophical importance—questions that were political in the grander sense of the term—Marshall took steps, in response to the problem of partisanship, to disassociate the Justices of the Supreme Court from orthodox political affairs and to secure unanimity among them. Out of Marshall's efforts came the distinctive blend of independence, sensitivity to political currents, and appearance of impartiality that has since constituted the challenge of excellence in appellate judging in America.

I

Any attempt to understand Marshall must take into account his extraordinary personality, a central trait of which was inoffensiveness. After three and a half volumes, Marshall's first major biographer, Albert Beveridge, lamented that his subject remained "so surpassingly great and good" that Beveridge virtually despaired of finding "some human frailty [to identify] his hero with mankind." The discovery of personal weakness in Marshall would have been "most welcome" for Beveridge, but he confessed to have uncovered only "some small and gracious defects."[10] On Marshall's death the attorneys and officers who had served before him testified to his "equanimity," "benignity of temper," and "amenity of manners," which were said to be so pronounced that "none of the judges who sat with him on the bench, . . . no member of the bar, no officer of the court, no juror, no witness, no suitor, in a single instance, ever found or imagined, in any thing said or done, or omitted by him, the slightest cause of offence."[11]

Part of Marshall's inoffensiveness may be traced to his informality and lack of pretension: Americans have long admired modesty and humility in their public servants. Although his age prided itself on style and dress and made them badges of status, Marshall did not conform to such conventions. Numerous contemporary observers commented on his unkempt hair, his dangling knee buckles, the mud on his boots; his appearance was more than once described as awkward or slovenly. He spoke freely to strangers on the street and regularly performed menial domestic tasks, such as marketing or carrying firewood, which seemed inconsistent with his station. "In his whole appearance, and demeanour, dress, attitudes, gesture, sitting, standing, or walking," wrote a contemporary, "he is as far removed from the idolized graces of Lord Chesterfield, as any other gentleman on earth."[12]

If Marshall was a "simple, unaffected man," unconcerned with his personal appearance, contemptuous of "studied manners,"[13] and given to humor at his own expense, he was also aware of his mental capabilities and was self-confident in his exercise of them. Justice Joseph Story, who sat on the Supreme Court with Marshall for twenty-four years, said that "no one ever possessed a more entire sense of his own extraordinary talents."[14] In an oral argument as a lawyer, Marshall would begin tentatively and awkwardly, then appear to pick up confidence from his own argument, to become almost magisterial at the end. He preferred to make closing arguments so that he could draw information and ammunition from his opponents' presentations.[15] At the Supreme Court it was said that he encouraged lengthy oral arguments, using them to educate himself on the particulars of a case. During his Chief Justiceship there was no limit on the length of arguments, and lawyers sometimes spoke continuously for four or five days. Yet Marshall had the gift, contemporaries wrote, "of developing a subject by a single glance of his mind, and detecting at once the very point on which every controversy depends."[16] His mind "possessed the rare faculty of condensation; he distilled an argument down to its essence."[17]

The ability to "master the most complicated subjects with facilty" was joined in Marshall with a certain disinclination toward academic learning and "some little propensity for indolence."[18] His legal education consisted of a six-week lecture course given by George Wythe at William & Mary College in 1780, during which, if Marshall's notebook may be trusted, he devoted at least as much thought to the pursuit of his future wife, Polly Ambler (whose name was scrawled at prominent places throughout his law notes), as to the offerings of Mr. Wythe.[19] As a lawyer in Virginia, and later as a judge, he was not prone to the use of legal authorities, and on several occasions his arguments in Virginia rested on no precedents at all.[20] On the Supreme Court his "original bias," according to his colleague Story, "was to general principles and comprehensive views, rather than to technical or recondite learning."[21] His greatest strength both as a lawyer and as a judge was not technical expertise, but the ability, as a contemporary remarked, to lay "his premises so remotely from the point directly in debate, or else in terms so general and so spacious, that the hearer . . . was just as willing to admit them as not."[22] Once Marshall's premises were conceded, his opponents were at a distinct disadvantage, for his skill in reasoning syllogistically downward from premises to results was so pronounced that Thomas Jefferson reportedly said, "When conversing with Marshall, I never admit anything. So sure as you admit any position to be good, no matter how remote from the conclusion he seeks to establish, you are gone."[23]

Marshall was generally regarded as being far fonder of leisure than of work. A French visitor to Virginia in 1796 reported that Marshall was perceived as "being a little lazy . . . but that does not prevent him from being a most superior person when he sits down to his work."[24] He unquestionably did not like legal research, preferring to prepare himself by refuting or accepting the insights of others while incorporating them. It was not his custom to work long hours either as a lawyer or as Chief Justice. In Richmond he often walked the streets in search of conversation, gave luncheons or dinners, or played quoits at his club. After he was appointed Chief Justice in 1801 he divided his time among Richmond, Raleigh, Washington, and his estate in Fauquier County, Virginia. In February the Supreme Court opened its term in Washington, with the entire term lasting no more than six weeks from 1801 until 1827, and no more than ten weeks until Marshall's death in 1835. After the Court adjourned, Marshall left for Richmond, where he held Circuit Court there for approximately three weeks, beginning in the third week of May. In the middle or at the end of June he left Richmond for Raleigh, where he held court for no more than a week. He then retired to Fauquier County, where he often remained through October. The third week in November he reopened court in Richmond for another three-week period; after New Year's he returned to Raleigh for another brief stay. At the end of January he returned to Washington.[25]

Even allowing for time in transit, which was not inconsiderable, this represents a working year of no more than twenty weeks, and in most years closer to fifteen. But Marshall wrote some opinions over the summer, and, at any rate, the working day of a Supreme Court Justice cannot be measured by the amount of time he sits in court. Between 1801 and 1807 Marshall wrote only twenty-seven opinions for the Supreme Court, but he wrote an additional fifty-six while sitting on circuit, and in addition produced a five-volume biography of George Washington. During the thirty-four years of Marshall's tenure as Chief Justice, the Supreme Court decided 1,215 cases, 1,006 by written individual opinion. In 519 of these 1,006 cases Marshall spoke for the Court.[26] Marshall thus wrote an average of fifteen opinions a year during his tenure. This figure can be contrasted with the approximately ninety-eight opinions a year issued by the Court from 1950 to 1970—an average of eleven opinions per Justice.[27] Although there is abundant evidence that Marshall sought out and enjoyed leisure (he was continually regretting his inability to work on the Washington biography because of the necessity to remain on his summer estate),[28] the impression he creates is that of a man with a peculiarly quick, penetrating, and facile mind, able to take a variety of intellectual short cuts.

As a businessman Marshall was less than totally successful in his ventures. He seemed to be incapable of giving business transactions his full attention. Between 1790 and 1800 he engaged in land speculation ventures that resulted in extended litigation and that, in one instance—the ill-fated purchase of the Fairfax Estate in Northern Virginia—left him with a due note of £14,000 and nearly ruined him financially. These difficulties first led him to accept an appointment as an envoy to France and later to undertake the biography of Washington, from which he expected to earn $50,000 eventually.[29] He initially set aside one year to complete the biography, which he planned as a four- or five-volume work, each volume to be 400-to-500 pages. He was two years into the project before he wrote a word.[30]

The intellectual acuteness, the disorderliness, the amiability, and the unpretentiousness of Marshall blended admirably in the performance of his office. He assumed the office of Chief Justice at a time when the Court was beleaguered by partisan strife and internal doubts about its role in the emerging American government. Marshall was confident enough of his philosophical premises and skillful enough in the use of his intellectual powers to assert and justify an active, expansive role for the federal judiciary. But he was also sufficiently acute in his understanding of human nature and sufficiently likable and admirable as a human being to make palatable, in his own person, the judicial power he asserted. Consequently under Marshall's guidance the Court became not only an increasingly important force in national politics but also a source of pride and inspiration to the men appointed to its bench. Its blossoming was tied not only to Marshall's personal impact but also to the manner in which he infused into the jurisprudence of his time his own philosophical premises.

II

Marshall's social thought, like that of many of his contemporaries, rested on the assumption that man held inalienable natural rights in the abstract, and these he brought with him into society. In a hypothetical state of nature, human beings possessed, merely by virtue of their humanity, such rights as life, liberty, property, and the pursuit of their own happiness. Social organizations reflected the common opinion of mankind that some measure of ordered co-operation was necessary for the full enjoyment of these rights, but they did not reflect any judgment that the exercise of the rights could arbitrarily be limited by society. In an abstract sense, society existed not to circumscribe natural rights but to preserve and promote them.

At the more concrete level of specific social interactions between persons, however, certain circumscriptions were inevitable. A right to liberty did not mean freedom to kill one's neighbor with impunity, nor did a right to life mean that one could never forfeit that right. A right to hold and enjoy property was likewise not absolute, but could, on specific occasions, be interfered with, the test of the legitimacy of the interference being whether it promoted natural rights in the aggregate. Those such as Marshall who began their observations of society by making such assumptions tended to have many of their intellectual disputes over the status of natural rights in practice: which individual rights could be infringed upon by society in order for society to survive, and how extensively could society infringe upon these rights in order to promote the general good?[31] Marshall found himself often more inclined to support particular infringements on rights than did some of his contemporaries, such as Jefferson.

Thus, although as a Congressional candidate he could criticize the Alien and Sedition Acts, which suppressed certain forms of speech critical of the national government, as a Supreme Court Justice Marshall held that these same Acts were constitutional. And since he conceived of the Constitution as being grounded in natural rights theory, the Alien and Sedition Acts were, moreover, philosophically justifiable. But the particular occasions on which he tolerated the confinement of natural rights were matched with occasions in which he believed that the extent of such confinement should be severely limited. In the trial of Aaron Burr, for example, Marshall gave a very narrow reading of the extent of governmental power to punish for treason. He believed that criminal statutes should be construed strictly; that the writ of habeas corpus, which allowed an individual to challenge his incarceration, was a necessary mechanism for an enlightened society; and that governmental interference with the holding or use of private property was presumptively suspect.[32]

On balance, Marshall had a strong and consistent commitment to the general inalienability of natural rights. To that commitment was joined, however, an acute perception of the need to have in society a set of governing institutions exercising real and extensive supervisory power, even though those institutions were ultimately controlled by their constituents. Men might have natural rights, but they did not always perceive or execute them sensibly. Although one could build a society on the reasonable assumption that man was self-interested and would seek to promote his own interests, this was not to assume that the behavior of the individual subject could be left unregulated, for man was also passionate and given to excesses.

Implicit in this formulation was a presupposition, held by Marshall throughout his life, that there was a distinction between an enlightened elite and the masses at large; between men of "character" and the common man. This paternalistic belief served to justify for Marshall the existence of government itself and the need for governmental power. Discounting the moderation and wisdom of the common man as a social being, Marshall supported Virginia's system of county courts, whose membership was entirely appointive and self-perpetuating; opposed vigorously the election of Andrew Jackson, whom Marshall felt to embody in his person the incarnation of unchecked common passions; and distinguished sharply between a republican form of government, which he identified with "order," and a democratic form, which he associated with "chaos."[33]

If Marshall was an elitist and a paternalist, he was by no means an aristocrat. The central organizing principles of society for him were not social status, not breeding, intelligence, or culture, but self-interest and acquisitiveness. He began with a suspicion of communal organizations that required men to subordinate their self-interest to the general welfare—at least where that subordination involved self-deprivation of one's tangible physical possessions. Society was better off, he felt, when individuals were encouraged to pursue their own interests; ultimately such pursuits would benefit all. Trade, commerce, and industry were inevitably profitable undertakings in a nation with abundant resources and a growing population, and were to be encouraged.[34] Property rights were to be protected if they symbolized the freedom to make use of one's acquisitive skills, but not if they represented simply the fruits of inheritance. Thus, primogeniture could be summarily abolished by the state, but the right to make use of the fruits of one's labor could not be so cavalierly curtailed.[35] The relatively free acquisition of wealth and status through enterprise was a prime ingredient of Marshall's social thought; class lines could give way to the acquisitive impulse. Yet a certain hierarchical structure remained. The masses were encouraged to be industrious, but remained in another sense the masses.

For Marshall the other side of the coin of acquisitiveness was tolerance and humanitarianism. As one encouraged individual men to pursue self-interest, so one respected their idiosyncrasies and responded in some measure to their unique demands upon society. But humanitarian policies were implemented in the light of their social utility. One might recognize the original right of Indians to the possession of lands in the New World, but one also conceded the right of American settlers to self-preservation and took into account the powers that flowed from conquest. At some point, then, the property claimed by Indians, although indisputably theirs in the natural-rights sense, became part of the indistinguishable mass of property held by the citizens of the American nation, and its appropriation by settlers became justifiable.[36] Similarly, slavery was, in the abstract, a clear violation of the natural right of man to the fruits of his own labor; yet an economic system resting on the classification of slaves as property could be sanctioned (at least on a short-run basis) because it allowed *slaveowners* the free and secure use of their own property. Marshall tended to regard slavery as a pernicious institution, but primarily, although not exclusively, because it threatened security.[37]

The intricate and sometimes strained devices to which Marshall resorted to reconcile natural rights with the legitimate demands of an ordered society were characteristic of the arguments and rationales of other social planners of his time. The public men of the Revolutionary generation derived a good share of their creativity from the fusion of two contradictory social insights. Man was fit to govern himself, but he could not be trusted to exercise self-government in a moderate and disinterested fashion. The question was how to design a society incorporating organizations in which these contradictions could be reconciled or, alternatively, contained. At some point, as Marshall and others saw, orderly government led to tyranny, oppression, and a frozen status system; at another point, alternatively, popular sovereignty led to violence, chaos, and mob rule. The ultimate search of statecraft was therefore a search for balance and moderation. Where the points of equilibrium lay was a matter of individual temperament, depending upon the extent to which one feared or trusted the common masses, the degree to which one was willing to circumscribe the rights of his fellow man in order to obtain some security and tranquility, and how deeply one was convinced of the wisdom and beneficence of a class of educated gentlemen. On these issues Marshall's viewpoint, in the context of the late eighteenth century, was middle-of-the-road. He stood with Washington against the tyranny of monarchy and the comparable tyranny of mob rule.

III

Law and legal institutions, as conceived by the Revolutionary generation, were aids in the process of balancing the virtues and excesses of the sovereign people against the virtues and excesses of their government. A first premise of the Founding Fathers, including Marshall, was that the sovereign people were not above the laws, although they had the power to change them. Considerable time and thought were devoted by Marshall and his contemporaries to operationalizing this principle in the form of a national government. Their solution was the creation of a series of balanced but often ambiguous power relations between the branches of the government and between those branches and their sovereign constituency. The term federalism has been characteristically used to describe this solution, but the term has difficulties.

When applied to the late eighteenth and early nineteenth centuries, federalism has two distinct connotations. It may refer either to a constitutional frame of government, with its emphasis on a union as distinguished from a confederation, or to the ideas of a political party that came to be known as Federalists. Marshall's jurisprudence complemented federalism in the first sense but not always in the second. If he was a nominal Federalist before becoming Chief Justice, he ceased being one while on the Court; on the other hand, he remained a thoroughgoing advocate of the federal union form of government. In the latter posture, however, he was in the mainstream of his generation: as Jefferson said, the framers of the new nation were all federalists and all republicans. Marshall staked out a distinguishable position and quarreled with others among the Founding Fathers primarily over the role of the judiciary in a federal union. He believed that federalism required the presence of an independent federal judiciary; others, such as Jefferson, could concede the desirability of a federal system without seeing any necessity for judicial independence of the kind Marshall advocated. An independent judiciary was logically the ultimate necessity in Marshall's jurisprudence, the culmination of his beliefs about law and government. He sought to show that judicial independence was not merely a side effect of federalism but a first principle of American civilization.

The principle of judicial independence was derived from a series of jurisprudential inquiries made by Marshall that began with a cataloguing of the appropriate sources of law. One source, he believed, was the principles of natural rights. In coming to America, Englishmen had brought their natural rights with them; in codifying certain rights for themselves in the Constitution, however, American citizens had not given up those other rights conferred upon man in his original state. Hence, certain "vested" property rights were protected from state interference not only by the Constitution's obligation of contracts clause but also by their permissibility in a state of nature. Marshall held thereby that he was free to ground his decisions alternatively in "general principles which are common to our free institutions," or in "the particular provisions of the Constitution of the United States";[38] on occasion he resorted to both when each alone seemed insufficient.

Precedents laid down by past courts, an important source of the law in England and in colonial America, were diminished in value by Marshall's jurisprudence, especially in cases of constitutional interpretation. Several conditions combined to insure the degraded status of precedent: first, the sparsity of reports of English decisions in America; second, the divergence of the new American nation from England in its governmental structure and, apparently, in its philosophical assumptions; third, Marshall's own penchant for reasoning on the level of broad generalities; fourth, the relative absence, especially in the early years of Marshall's Chief Justiceship, of judicial interpretations of the Constitution. When, in the course of his career, Marshall had the opportunity to reason from his own precedents, he tended to treat a precedent not only as an authority in itself but also as an illustration of a fundamental principle of American government, which he then reaffirmed anew. Thus, his decisions in *Gibbons v. Ogden*[39] and *McCulloch v. Maryland*[40] had announced, respectively, the federal government's power to regulate commerce and its immunity from state taxation; his subsequent decision in *Brown v. Maryland*[41] explicitly made both those principles the basis for holding that foreign goods imported into a state could not be taxed by the state while they were held by the importer in the "original package."

In sum, Marshall's sources of law were arranged in a hierarchy, with the first principles of American civilization, in abstract and generalized form, given a higher ranking than specific manifestations of those principles. Wherever possible, Marshall sought to justify a particular decision in the broadest terms possible, so that it could be regarded as an unassailable manifestation of fundamental American beliefs.

Among the first principles Marshall articulated were four concerning the functions of American governmental institutions and the relations of these institutions with one another. The first principle concerned the discretionary powers of a government. The fact that government existed to protect individual rights did not mean that its officials were precluded from making the judgment that infringement of some rights was necessary for the protection of others. On this principle Marshall based his justifications for government suppression of such acts as seditious speech and domestic violence. The people's possession of natural rights in the abstract did not preclude the restriction of these rights in specific instances once the people had consented to be governed.

The second and third principles were derived from Marshall's understanding of the particular meaning of sovereignty to federalism. In establishing the Constitution, Marshall believed, the people of the states had consented not only to be governed but to be united as well. A dual delegation of power had been made by individual citizens of the Republic: a grant of sovereignty to their respective states, then a further grant to the federal government of a more inclusive but limited set of sovereign powers. The sovereign power of the federal government transcended state boundaries and was thus superior to the sovereign power of the states, but only with respect to the federal powers enumerated in the Constitution. Where the scope of federal sovereignty was unclear, a court, in resolving the controversy, could resort to constitutional interpretation in the broadest sense of the term. It could, for example, ask itself whether the area in dispute was "national" or "local" in its nature, and in making that inquiry consider the extent to which local interests had surrendered their parochial concerns or had chosen to remain autonomous when they ratified the national government. Using this approach, Marshall found that the states had surrendered to the national government the power to regulate coastal navigation for commercial purposes,[42] but had retained for themselves the power to dam up navigable creeks that eventually spilled into coastal waterways.[43]

The third principle likewise dealt with the consequences of the people's tacit surrender of sovereignty to their national government. Although the people were the ultimate sovereign, in consenting to be governed they had chosen a particular form of governmental control, the republican form. That form, in Marshall's view, constrained the people as much as it allowed them self-government. Against the potential chaos attendant on mass participatory democracy, republicanism erected the institutional buffers of legislative representatives and an independent judiciary. The excesses of the people were moderated by representation, a process by which their passionate demands were reformulated by an enlightened and reasonable class of public servants. The need of the populace for an articulation of their individual rights under law was met by the presence of a body of judges not beholden to the masses in any immediate, partisan sense. One purpose of such buffers was to preclude mass lawmaking.

These first three principles envisaged delicate interactions between the various branches of the national government, between that government and the states, and between governments at large and their popular constituencies. The effective functioning of government in America appeared to rest on a precise knowledge of the limits of federal power, of the points at which state sovereignty was to be supplanted by federal sovereignty, of the degree to which discretionary authority could be used by governmental institutions, and of the limitations on popular rule. Marshall's fourth principle underscored the balancing processes at the core of American government and entrusted these processes primarily to the judiciary.

According to this principle the Constitution granted the branches of the national government discretionary powers, but also created in them reciprocal obligations. Intertwined with the untrammeled authority possessed by Congress or by the Executive within the limits of their respective jurisdictions was a duty not to transgress these limits. The laws of the nation were the source of the power of government officials; and such officials had to obey those laws. They had been given powers in connection with the assignment of particular tasks oriented toward the achievement of great national objectives; governmental powers were hence inseparable from governmental obligations. Whether particular branches of government had met their obligations or ignored them, whether they had appropriately exercised their powers or gone beyond them, whether they had utilized discretion strictly within the limits of their jurisdiction or usurped the province of another branch—those were questions involving interpretations of the laws and, as such, were proper questions for consideration and resolution by the judicial branch of government. Judicial consideration of such questions was proper even though the judiciary did not make laws but merely construed them as they applied to individuals.

The role of the judiciary, in this view, was founded on a paradox. Courts were second-line institutions; they merely carried through the general commands of the legislature in particular instances, and could not alter the form of those commands. Yet in the process of construing generalized law in its particulars, the courts could decide whether the branch of government issuing the general command—the legislature or its delegate, the executive—had been constitutionally authorized to issue it. The courts, then, were bound by the Constitution, but they determined what it meant in specific instances. They were obliged to defer to the lawmaking authority of other branches but were empowered to decide the constitutional limits of that authority. Marshall's view of the special role of the national judiciary in America, and (by implication) of the office of judge at large, attempted to make this paradox intelligible.

Despite his broad mandate for judicial interpretation, Marshall did not think of judges as exercising discretion in the modern sense of the term. He did not believe that "interpreting" the law could be seen as synonymous with "making" it, or that determinations by judges of the limits of judicial power could be seen as representing an unwarranted exercise of that power. He saw legal principles as omnipresent and immutable. Over time the enumerated powers in the Constitution were to remain fixed; the social ends (the great objects) to which those powers were related were also fixed. The meaning of the Constitution was hence *not* intended to change with time. Once a particular passage had been interpreted, that interpretation was to remain until the people chose to amend the document itself. The notion that different generations of Americans might attach different meanings to constitutional language was alien to Marshall.

The apparent inconsistency between this static, constrained, passive view of the function of the judiciary and the increasingly active and dominant role played by the Supreme Court in national politics during Marshall's tenure becomes readily apparent. Yet Marshall did not find the two inconsistent. For although courts were bound only to "interpret" laws and to decide only "legal" questions, yet in their search for fundamental principles on which to rest their decisions courts were empowered to go beyond the letter of the law to the general set of philosophical beliefs on which the law was founded. Where, for example, a question arose as to the limits of the powers of the general government or one of its branches, that question, although in one sense a question of "politics," was in another sense a question compelling recourse to the fundamental principles inherent in the creation of the American nation. If those principles constituted the foundations of the law governing the nation, and the jurisdiction of courts to interpret the law was as broad as the law itself, then consideration of questions involving those principles was a proper task of the judiciary.

Marshall's celebrated argument on behalf of judicial review of the constitutionality of Congressional legislation in *Marbury v. Madison* was a variant on this theme. As has frequently been pointed out,[44] Marshall's opinion in *Marbury v. Madison* tended to assume away the very issue in dispute: whether an independent judicial consideration of the constitutionality of acts passed by Congress was permissible. *Marbury v. Madison* raised the question whether the Secretary of State could choose not to deliver a Justice of the Peace commission once the designate of that commission had been confirmed by the Senate, and his commission signed and sealed. The designate in question, William Marbury, applied to the Supreme Court for a writ of mandamus to compel the President to show cause why his commission had not been delivered, basing his appeal on a 1789 Act of Congress that gave the judiciary authority to issue writs of mandamus to "persons holding office under the authority of the United States." Marshall's opinion decided that the Court had jurisdiction to consider Marbury's case since, although the President had unlimited discretion to appoint federal officials, he could not arbitrarily remove them once appointed; that the Executive should therefore show cause why the commission had not been delivered; but that the Supreme Court lacked power to issue the writ of mandamus because the 1789 Act violated the section of Article III in the Constitution conferring original jurisdiction on the Court. Thus, in the process of construing a U.S. law, Marshall decided at least three arguably "political" questions: first, that the President had discretion to appoint federal officers at his will; second, that once appointed, he could not arbitrarily remove them; and third, and most celebrated, that the Court had the authority to decide that an act of Congress violated the Constitution.

In *Marbury v. Madison* the portion of Marshall's opinion authorizing judicial review of Congressional legislation made use of the following syllogism:

major premise, the laws of a nation were to be interpreted by its courts;
minor premise, the Constitution was a law of the United States;
conclusion, the Constitution was to be interpreted by the federal courts, the Supreme Court being the ultimate interpreter.

This syllogism, of course, turned on a definition of "law" that blinked the distinction between "political" and "legal" questions, thereby suggesting that the Constitution was an exclusively legal rather than a political document. Under this formulation a power in the judiciary to interpret "laws" necessarily involved a further power to decide whether a dispute arising out of the construction of a law raised "legal" or "political" questions.

Even if Marshall's opinion in *Marbury v. Madison* tended to assume away the central point in dispute, the case should not necessarily be viewed as an exercise in judicial subterfuge. The power of judicial review, though not explicitly sanctioned until *Marbury*, had been widely championed at the time of the framing of the Constitution and was a respectable intellectual position in the climate of late eighteenth-century jurisprudence.[45] If the theoretical framework of the Constitution was one of natural rights, and if the Constitution was not the exclusive source of those rights but merely an important one, then the lines between "law," philosophy, and politics were not always clear. There is evidence that certain of the Founding Fathers, notably Hamilton, envisaged judicial review as an exercise in politics through which an independent judicial elite could temper the democratic excesses of legislatures by affirming the republican political balances inherent in the Constitution.[46] In this view the role of the judiciary was explicitly political, and law and politics were virtually inseparable. Marshall's opinion in *Marbury v. Madison* rejected this position for one that conferred "political" powers on the judiciary only insofar as principles of fundamental law could be said to subsume basic political judgments.

The national judiciary, then, could play a role in the political process, but a role of a specially conceived kind. The judicial branch of government could fashion, through its power to search for fundamental principles of law, the locus and scope of institutional authority, and could intervene to protect certain "fundamental" private rights against governmental interference. In its interpretations of the Constitution, for example, it could define the scope of

Congress's power to regulate commerce as against competing power claims by the states; it could, more generally, determine the points where state sovereignty gave way to national sovereignty; and it could carve out the areas in which vested private rights were to be protected against infringements by government.

The court's constituency, in this view, was twofold: the educated professional elites who served as buffers between government and the people, and the people themselves. If the judgments of courts, in Marshall's jurisprudence, were, in terms of their language and reasoning, directed at an elite rather than at a common audience, the judiciary was nonetheless ultimately the servant of the people, being at the mercy of political change as manifested in the current whims of the multitude. This was true not only because the people, through their elected representatives, staffed the courts, but also because the changing social views of the public affected the kinds of controversy brought to the courts. Thus, when Andrew Jackson's election seemed imminent in 1828, Marshall, who had anticipated retirement, decided to stay on as Chief Justice in order to deprive Jackson of the ability to name his successor, whom Marshall felt would undoubtedly be a man far less distressed than he about the increasing demands of democratic mobs for political change. Hence the dependence of an "independent" judiciary upon the political branches of government was inescapable. Although this sense of dependence frustrated Marshall in his last years on the bench, it was conceptually consistent with his jurisprudence.

IV

Marshall's intellectual abilities, social and philosophical assumptions, and jurisprudential premises were all manifested in the rhetoric of his opinions. The rhetorical outlines of his opinions roughly resembled the following pattern:

first, broad formulation of an abstract and seemingly innocuous general principle of law and government, with little effort to tie this principle in a precise way to the case before him;

second, investigation of the particular legal language, whether constitutional or statutory, whose interpretation was in question, and consequent refinement of that language;

third, the statement of a secondary principle based on Marshall's refinement of the language;
fourth, the setting forth of a series of implications that necessarily followed from the secondary principle;
fifth, decision of the case on the basis of those implications, but in terms incorporating the initial general principle, so that the decision had immense potential significance for future cases.

This pattern was not exclusively followed, nor its order always adhered to, but its presence was common enough to be distinctive. Three examples will suffice.

The case of *Fletcher v. Peck*, which Marshall decided in 1810, was a dispute feigned to elicit a judicial resolution of a controversy involving the sale of land claims in Georgia. The background of the case was heavy with corruption, fraud, and politics. At one point Marshall confided to the Court reporter that he had been reluctant to decide it because of the patently spurious character of the lawsuit.[47] The central question was whether a state could rescind title to land previously granted to private persons if the state itself had been the original grantor.

Marshall began his opinion with a characteristically artful tactic. He underscored the absence of power in the national judiciary to scrutinize the actions of a state legislature.[48] In examining the constitutional validity of legislative activity, he found that the courts could not inquire into the motives of a legislature. Even the motive of corruption, present in *Fletcher v. Peck*, did not permit judicial involvement. Having made this bow to legislative authority, Marshall then announced that "certain great principles of justice" ought "not to be entirely disregarded" in the case. Those included the "rules of property," which were "common to all the citizens of the United States," and the "principles of equity," which were "acknowledged in all our courts."[49] Under these principles innocent purchasers of land titles were entitled to protection of their rights, and a legislature could ignore them only by nakedly asserting its sovereign power. "The nature of society and of government" as well suggested "some limits to the legislative power." Where were those limits, Marshall asked, "if the property of an individual, fairly and honestly acquired, may be seized without compensation"?[50]

This general principle of inviolate "natural" private rights against the state was not, however, explicitly made applicable to the case, for Georgia, Marshall argued, was not "a single, unconnected sovereign power" but a member of the American Union, and hence restrictions on the states imposed by that Union's Constitution were relevant. Among those was the clause declaring that no state could pass a law impairing the obligation of contracts, and Marshall turned to an interpretation of the language of that clause in the circumstances of *Fletcher v. Peck*. In the course of his interpretation he made the refinement that a grant was a "contract" within the meaning of the Constitution, since every grant contained within it an implied contract by the grantor not to reassert his rights to the property granted. If a grant was a contract, Marshall then reasoned, the next question was whether the Constitution distinguished between types of contracts, either "executory or executed" or private or public, in its obligation of contracts clause. He found that it did not: "the words are general, and are applicable to contracts of every description."[51] Hence the Constitution included a general prohibition against impairing the obligation of contracts.

By means of implications following from his reading of "contract," Marshall had by this point in the opinion reached the desired result that Georgia could not rescind title to a deed previously granted. He then proceeded to ground that result on the broadest possible principle: Georgia was restrained "either by general principles which are common to our free institutions" or by "the particular provisions of the constitution of the United States."[52] The decision in *Fletcher v. Peck*, then, appeared to affirm the absolute inviolability of "vested" private rights against interference by state governments. Yet this broad principle was not essential to the decision of the case, for the result actually turned on the secondary principle that the impairment of contracts clause in the Constitution was to be read to cover "grants" as well as "contracts" and public grants as well as private grants. Jefferson, in an 1823 letter to Justice William Johnson, called this technique a "practice . . . of travelling out of [the] case to proscribe what the law would be in a moot case not before the court."[53]

Nine years after *Fletcher v. Peck* came the most controversial of Marshall's decisions, *McCulloch v. Maryland*. It considered the constitutionality of a state law enacting a tax on notes issued by a branch of the Bank of the United States in Baltimore, and, preliminarily, the constitutionality of the Bank's charter itself. The constitutional position of the Bank had been discussed at length, Hamilton and Jefferson having issued contrasting opinions on the validity of a national bank at the time of the Bank's original charter in 1791. There has been speculation[54] that Marshall had written portions of his opinion in *McCulloch v. Maryland* prior to the arguments in the case; the suit, another arranged controversy, had been pending for a year before being argued before the Court, and Marshall was known to be thoroughly versed in the issue of national versus state sovereignty that it raised.

Marshall's opinion considered first the constitutionality of the Bank's charter. He began by asking, rhetorically, whether the Constitution was a creation of the sovereign states or of the people who made up those states. This was a question to which he and republicans of his time knew the answer. The ultimate sovereignty rested in the people, and the fact that they had delegated powers to state governments did not preclude their delegating powers to the federal government. Indeed, a primary purpose of the Constitution was to delegate particular powers to a central government. Once delegated, those enumerated powers prevailed over competing state powers. If the federal government was "emphatically, and truly, a government of the people," whose "powers [were] granted by them, and [were] to be exercised directly on them, and for their benefit," then (Marshall maintained) that government was "the government of all" and "act[ed] for all." And thus "the nation, on those subjects on which it can act, must necessarily bind its component parts." That is to say, the federal government was "supreme within its sphere of action": this "would seem to result necessarily from its nature."[55]

At this point Marshall was merely restating a familiar tenet of his, that of the locus of sovereignty in a republican government and its implications for a federal system. But he subsequently made effective use of this general principle. First he formulated a derivative principle, and then put it to work in an interpretation of constitutional language. A constitution, being an instrument for the delegation of certain powers toward the achievement of certain "great objects," was not meant to resemble a code: it designated only "its great outlines" and "its important objects," leaving "the minor ingredients which compare these objects [to] be deduced from the nature of the objects themselves." Otherwise "it would probably never be understood by the public."[56] If this view of the Constitution's "nature" were accepted, then its necessary and proper clause was to be read as meaning not that Congress could only enact legislation "absolutely" necessary to the exercise of its enumerated powers, but that Congress had wide discretion to choose the means by which "great objects" were to be achieved. The necessary and proper clause, then, authorized Congress to enact legislation incidental to the purposes for which it had been granted specific powers. If it had the power to lay and collect taxes, borrow money, and regulate commerce, it could charter a bank to help effectuate those goals. "The power being given," argued Marshall, "it is the interest of the nation to facilitate its execution. It can never be their interest, and cannot be presumed to have been their intention, to clog and embarrass its execution by withholding the most appropriate means."[57]

By means of his secondary principle concerning the "nature" of the Constitution and his reading of the necessary and proper clause, then, Marshall had reached the result of upholding the constitutionality of the Bank's charter. He then tied this result back to his original sovereignty dictum with the celebrated phrase,

> Let the end be legitimate, let it be within the scope of the Constitution, and all means which are appropriate, which are plainly adapted to that end, which are not prohibited, but consistent with the letter and spirit of the Constitution, are constitutional.[58]

In other words, the theory of sovereignty implicit in the Constitution's framing gave to the federal government unlimited discretionary power within the scope of its enumerated powers. If one accepts this reading, the significance of *McCulloch v. Maryland* becomes extraordinarily vast.

That Marshall intended the opinion to be read broadly can be seen from his treatment of the second issue in the case: whether, assuming that the Bank was constitutional, Maryland could tax it. He began by conceding that the delegation of a power of taxation to the federal government did not preclude concurrent taxing power in the states. But he then asserted that if a state's use of its taxing power was incompatible with the objects for which the federal government's powers were created, the taxing power of the state could be abridged, even though state taxation of the particular subject in question was not expressly prohibited by the Constitution.

Marshall next established this assertion in the context of the *McCulloch* case. The assertion rested, he maintained, on the "great principle . . . that the constitution and the laws made in pursuance thereof are supreme; that they control the constitution and laws of the respective states, and cannot be controlled by them."[59] From that principle were "deduced" certain "corollaries" relevant to the taxation issue in *McCulloch*. Thus, a power to create implied a power to preserve; a power to destroy, "if wielded by a different hand," was incompatible with the powers to create and preserve; and where this "repugnancy" existed, "that authority which is supreme must control." It was "too obvious to be denied" that Maryland could "destroy" the Bank if allowed to tax it. The state's power to destroy might thereby defeat the power in Congress to create a bank; consequently conflict existed, and the principle of national supremacy came into play. Therefore not only could the State of Maryland not tax a national bank (result in *McCulloch*); the states, moreover, had "no power, by taxation or otherwise, to retard, impede, burden, or in any manner control the operations of the constitutional laws enacted by Congress to carry into execution the powers vested in the general government."[60] With this statement Marshall returned to his original principle of unlimited discretionary power in the federal government within the scope of its enumerated powers.

In *McCulloch v. Maryland* Marshall seemed to be saying not only that the states could not tax any operations of the federal government, but also that it was unclear whether they could retard those operations by any means at all, provided the operations could be tied to the "great objects" envisaged by the Constitution. This was, of course, an extraordinary claim, and contemporary critics were not unaware of its being so or of the devices used by Marshall to arrive at such conclusion. Judge Spencer Roane of the Virginia Court of Appeals, writing under a pseudonym, declared that the *McCulloch* decision tended "to strip [the states] of some of the most important attributes of their sovereignty." If Congress, Judge Roane observed, "should think proper to legislate to the full extent upon the principles now adjudicated by the Supreme Court, it is difficult to say how small [will be] the remnant of powers left in the hands of the State authorities." James Madison's criticism took a different tack. "The occasion [of *McCulloch v. Maryland*]," he wrote to Judge Roane, "did not call for the general and abstract doctrine interwoven with the decision of the particular case. I have always supposed that the meaning of a law, and for a like reason, of a Constitution, so far as it depends on judicial interpretation, was to result from a course of particular decisions, and not . . . from a previous and abstract comment on the subject. The example in this instance tends to reverse the rule."[61]

If Marshall's opinion in *McCulloch* was his most controversial—ultimately resulting in his responding anonymously to the criticism it incurred[62]—his opinion in *Gibbons v. Ogden* was probably his most widely read.[63] *Gibbons* was of particular interest and magnitude in that it combined the political question of state sovereignty with the economic question of monopolistic control of navigation. At issue was the constitutionality of a grant from New York State to Robert Livingston, Robert Fulton, and their successors and licensees (of whom Ogden was one), of the exclusive right to operate steamboats on New York waters. The grant had been challenged by one Gibbons, who had chosen to operate coastal steamers on the Hudson River between New York and New Jersey in defiance of the Livingston-Fulton monopoly. The existence of the monopoly had long been an object of controversy: in 1812 the New York courts had sustained its constitutionality,[64] and in 1818 and 1822 New Jersey, Connecticut, and Ohio had passed retaliatory statutes forbidding the Livingston steamboats from using their waters.

Marshall opened his opinion in *Gibbons v. Ogden* with one of the most useful of all his starting general principles: the notion that the enumerated powers delegated to the federal government in the Constitution could be liberally construed. A liberal construction of the Constitution was possible, Marshall maintained, because the framers, and, ultimately, the people, intended to use words "in their natural sense"; and if, over time, that sense had become imperfect, then it was to be clarified by resort to the purposes of the document itself. Under this formulation language in the Constitution was to be read as in ordinary usage; the meaning of language was its common and "natural" one.[65]

From this starting point Marshall quickly deduced the working principle of his opinion—that the word "commerce" in the Constitution comprehended navigation. Commerce, in its natural sense, was more than "traffic," it was "intercourse"; [a]ll America" understood it to comprehend navigation; a power "to regulate navigation [had been] expressly granted [to Congress] as if that term had been added to the word 'commerce.' "[66] And if navigation was included in the term "commerce," then the power granted to Congress to regulate commerce "among" the several states meant that Congress had power over navigation within the limits of each state as far as that navigation could be connected with interstate or foreign trade.[67]

But the question remained whether there was not a concurrent power in the states to regulate commerce, analogous to the taxing power that Marshall had conceded to the states in *McCulloch*. Here again Marshall's refinements of language proved helpful. If Congress had been granted a power to regulate interstate navigation, and had exercised that power, its power was exclusive, so that if states attempted simultaneously to regulate trade that made use of interstate navigable waterways, they could not do so under any concurrent "commerce" power. They did, of course, have certain powers to affect interstate commerce, such as the power to establish health standards on vessels using their waters or the power to charge tolls for ferries. These, however, were "internal police" powers; in the field of regulatory interstate commerce Congress remained supreme, and might "control State laws [based on internal police powers] so far as it [might] be necessary to control them, for the regulation of commerce."[68]

There was a conflict, then, between the coastal license granted Gibbons by Congress and the New York grant to Livingston, first, because the New York grant ultimately regulated interstate navigation; second, because the coastal license, in Marshall's reading, conferred not only the right to engage in "foreign" coastal commerce but also the right to navigate the waters of the United States. And in this conflict the federal statute inevitably prevailed. Its supremacy did not rest on the character of the monopoly in question, for whether sailboats or steamboats were involved was unimportant since "the act of a State inhibiting the use of [its waters] to any vessel having a license under the act of Congress" came in "direct collision with that act."[69] The implications of the decision were thus clear: the powers expressly granted to the federal government could not "be contracted, by construction, into the narrowest possible compass," nor could "the original powers of the States [be] retained, if any possible construction will retain them."[70] In Marshall's judgment the decision in *Gibbons v. Ogden* rested ultimately on "the safe and fundamental principles" of dual sovereignty in a federal republic.

As in *McCulloch v. Maryland*, contemporary commentators understood the aim of Marshall's rhetoric in *Gibbons*. John Randolph wrote to a friend, in reference to the decision, that "[a] judicial opinion should decide nothing and embrace nothing that is not before the Court." Marshall could have rested the decision, Randolph pointed out, on the narrow ground of conflict between a coastal license and a state navigation monopoly in those areas where conflict patently existed. Instead he had used the occasion to carve out an exclusive power in Congress to regulate navigation that seemed massively broad in its scope. "No one admires more than I do," Randolph confessed, "the extraordinary powers of Marshall's mind; no one respects more his amiable deportment in private life. He is the most unpretending and unassuming of men." But Marshall's long experience as an advocate, Randolph thought, had perhaps "injured . . . the tone of his perception . . . of truth or falsehood."[71]

Randolph was perceptive in his appraisal of Marshall's rhetoric if not necessarily fair in his judgment about the effects on Marshall of his career as a practitioner. It was Marshall's supreme mastery of the existing rhetorical techniques of his time that gave his admittedly partisan results their unassailable quality. He understood the axioms of republican political theory and the steps of syllogistic reasoning, but, above all, he knew how to use them in dazzling combination, so that techniques of language construction were interwoven with appeals to "fundamental" political principles to produce the impression that the results reached were inevitable. Grant Marshall his starting principles, however vague and bland, and swiftly those principles, in refined form, led him to his desired outcome. Grant him that outcome, and it was made illustrative of a general principle of government that, if followed, decided countless other cases. "[W]rong, all wrong," Randolph allegedly said on reading one Marshall opinion, "but no man in the United States can tell why or wherein."[72]

In Marshall's hands the judiciary, while remaining aloof from politics, allegedly deciding legal, not political questions, and only interpreting and declaring the law, became a political force comparable in stature to the other branches of government. Marshall's tenure saw the genesis of a judicial tradition in America, and that tradition consequently has borne the marks of his personal interpretations of eighteenth-century social philosophy, jurisprudence, and politics. Under Marshall's guidance, judging in America became a technique of exercising power through the use of institutional constraints, themselves derived from broader jurisprudential assumptions. Since judges were obligated to discover and follow the laws made by other branches of government, they could and should be politically independent. Since the law was discoverable and, as manifested in the Constitution, "sacred," the idiosyncrasies of individual judges were necessarily subordinated to higher principles. Politics in the narrow partisan sense was thus incompatible with judging, and consequently a tyrannical judiciary was not to be feared, for judges could only follow the laws, and the people could change their content.

The legitimacy of the judiciary, from Marshall on, rested on its ability to persuade the people that its members had indeed been subject to these constraints in reaching their decisions. The source of judicial authority, then, was the process of judicial reasoning. Reasoning illustrated the extent to which judges merely "followed" the law; reasoning illuminated the fundamental principles of American government at stake in a case. Rhetoric, in a judicial opinion, had thus a dual function: that of interpreting the law and that of justifying the exercise of the judicial function in a politically independent manner. But rhetoric necessitated an audience, and that audience could fail to be persuaded by it. Implicit in Marshall's blueprint for the American judiciary was the possibility of violent public reaction against the implications of a decision.

2 

Kent, Story, and Shaw: The Judicial Function and Property Rights

The legacy handed down by Marshall to his judicial successors had been a considerable one. Appointed to a court that could easily have become and nearly did become a resting place for minor political officials, Marshall gave to succeeding judges a national judiciary able to stand as an equal alongside the other two branches of the federal government. While maintaining that judges were aloof from politics, he had made the judiciary a national political force. While asserting that "judicial power is never exercised for the purpose of giving effect to the will of the judge, always for the purpose of giving effect . . . to the will of the law,"[1] he had made judging an exercise in statecraft, a high form of applied political theory. He had more closely associated the art of judging with the positive qualities of impartiality and disinterestedness, and yet he had made his office a vehicle for the expression of his views about the proper foundations of American government. And through the artistry of his reasoning and the acuteness of his political judgments, he had linked the public image of the judiciary to his own formidable self. The strides made by the judiciary during Marshall's Chief Justiceship were considerable. By his death in 1835 the federal judiciary had become a dynamic force in American government.

Although Marshall's legacy was broad in one sense, it was still narrow in another. Marshall's primary concern as Chief Justice had been to demonstrate the relevance of an independent, powerful judiciary to an eighteenth-century model of balanced government, and in this he had succeeded almost beyond all expectations. He had concentrated on the high political issues of his day, and his decisions survive as impressively broad statements of the principles on which the American Republic was founded. His opinions became and remain important guidelines for future relations among the institutions of American government. But as the delicate equilibrium envisaged by the eighteenth-century model of government was upset by new pressures of nineteenth-century America—a surging economy and the increased prominence, especially in the states, of political movements in mass democracy—the Marshall legacy showed some limitations. It rested on fixed assumptions about the nature of man and the manner in which society was ordered; as these assumptions came to be challenged, social and legal problems surfaced that Marshall had not and perhaps could not have considered.

In particular, two situations evolved that called for judicial attention of a different character. The first was the need within the states for a set of coherent, accessible legal authorities as guidelines for ordinary private activity: a corpus of jurisprudence. The second, closely tied to the first though more specific in nature, was the need for a body of law defining and regulating the new forms of private and semiprivate enterprise, such as internal improvement franchises, utilities, and corporations, that had emerged with the expanded economy of nineteenth-century America. Marshall had helped sketch the broad outlines of state sovereignty in the new republic, and had underscored the importance of private enterprise and property rights to the framers of the Constitution. That importance was to be re-evaluated several times during the nineteenth century as those two concepts took on new dimensions.

Three early-nineteenth-century judges distinguished themselves in their efforts to modify the Marshallian legacy in the light of the circumstances of their time. James Kent, Chief Judge of the New York Supreme Court and later Chancellor of New York, Joseph Story, Associate Justice of the Supreme Court from Massachusetts, and Lemuel Shaw, Chief Justice of the Supreme Court of Massachusetts, were members of the post-Revolutionary generation of American judges. Although their careers, especially Kent's, overlapped that of Marshall, they were not his contemporaries. They had been too young to serve in the Revolutionary War; they had not been party to the framing of the Constitution; their concern was not so much with establishing the fundamental bases of American law as with elaborating legal doctrine and adapting it to a rapidly changing environment. Their attention centered on the development and consequent use of a body of judicially interpreted law (the "common" law) to meet a variety of new social problems. One major set of problems was spawned by the interaction of state governments and private entrepreneurs in an atmosphere of rapid and turbulent economic growth.

I

The careers of Kent, Story, and Shaw possessed a rough similarity that illustrates the close connection of the nineteenth-century judicial profession to state politics. Before being appointed to the bench all three men served in their respective state legislatures—Kent as a Federalist in the New York General Assembly from 1790 to 1793, Story as a Republican in the Massachusetts General Court from 1805 to 1808, and Shaw as a Federalist in that same body from 1811 to 1815, from 1820 to 1822, and from 1829 to 1830. In each man's case, experience as a state legislator formed a prelude to service on the bench. Kent's closeness to Governor John Jay, for whom he had worked as a legislator, secured him a nomination to the State Supreme Court in 1798; Story's service in the Massachusetts legislature helped put him in a position to secure a nomination to Congress in 1808, where he met James Madison, who appointed him to the Supreme Court in 1811; through Shaw's involvement in Federalist party politics he met Daniel Webster, who was influential in persuading him to accept the Chief Justiceship of Massachusetts in 1830.

As state politicians and rising lawyers all three demonstrated a concern for the interests of established men of means and a degree of resistance to political or economic change. Kent, according to his biographer, was "true to all the traditions—and prejudices— . . . of the complacent class to which by fortune he belonged";[2] Story, though nominally a Republican, was by 1807 being characterized by Federalist Harrison Gray Otis as "a young man . . . who commenced Democrat a few years since and was much fondled by his party," but who "acted on several occasions with a very salutary spirit of independence." "[A] little attention from the right sort of people," Otis added, "will be very useful to him and to us."[3] Shaw, in 1815, on celebrating the end of the War of 1812, hoped "that the day of idle theory, of frivolous experiment, and of dangerous trifling with our great national interests, which commenced with the Administration of Mr. Jefferson, has passed away."[4]

But if there were parallels in their backgrounds and early social views, the three men also had marked dissimilarities of temperament and developed contrasting interpretations of their judicial office. Kent was diffident, shy, and austere. As a young man, his lack of gregariousness and his apparent disdain for the common man kept him from attracting much business for his law practice and from becoming a successful legislator. He did not particularly enjoy advocacy, being an indifferent speaker and disinclined to engage in heated debate.[5] His ambition (which was marked) was channeled primarily into intellectual pursuits; he early identified professional success with a thorough grounding in the historical antecedents of English common law and in the classics generally.[6] His eventual high reputation as a practitioner was acquired on the basis of his skill at marshaling and presenting ancient authorities.[7]

Kent's ultimate goal, a judicial career, was eventually attained in his thirty-fifth year, when Governor Jay appointed him to the New York Supreme Court. He remained on that Court, first as Puisne Justice and then as Chief Justice, until 1814, when he was named Chancellor of the system of equity courts (which in New York remained separate from law courts). The office of judge was compatible with Kent's temperament. Its field of inquiry was as much that of scholarly research as of contemporary affairs, and Kent was essentially the judge as scholar. Yet the office of judge still retained a certain political aspect, not so much in the active partisan sense as in the realm where social philosophy and politics came together, and Kent had from his youth possessed strong political views, and in adulthood continued to exhibit a certain rigidity and zeal in his efforts to promote them. But it also cloaked its adherents in a mantle of austerity that appealed to Kent's pride and diffidence: the story is told[8] that one time Kent's son found his father, then in his eighties, sitting astride a cherry tree branch on his farm in New Jersey. On being advised to take care in coming down from the tree, Kent replied: "My son, I am used to elevated stations, and know how and when to descend with dignity."

At his maturity Kent was a leading jurist of his day. He had come to dominate the Supreme Court of New York to such an extent that Marshall felt compelled, on overruling him in *Gibbons v. Ogden*, to praise his reputation. He had single-handedly revolutionalized equity practice in New York, transforming it from a haphazard, unorganized collection of random decisions to a system with its own rather rigid and technical rules and procedures; and with the publication between 1826 and 1830 of his *Commentaries* he had emerged as the first of the great treatise writers of the early nineteenth century.

He was also identified—especially in the latter portion of his judicial career—as a judge whose doctrines tended to erect barriers to the broadening of economic or political power. For this reason he had become anathema to radical Democrats in the New York legislature, who were delighted to invoke a mandatory retirement statute for state judges when Kent reached the age of 60.[9] Kent, for his part, responded in kind: his political convictions were fierce, and he did not temper his passions with a sense of humor. He vociferously damned advocates of universal suffrage and opponents of established property rights, and attempted to show, in his *Commentaries on American Law*, the fallacy of these doctrines. His political friendships, such as those with Jay and Alexander Hamilton, were of long standing, as were his animosities. Aaron Burr, who had run unsuccessfully for Governor of New York in 1804, fell into the second category. Kent, in fact, was named by Burr in the complaint that served as a starting point for his 1804 duel with Hamilton. Ten years after that incident, Kent encountered Burr on Nassau Street in Lower Manhattan, and, shaking his cane in Burr's face, blurted out: "You are a scoundrel, sir!—a scoundrel!" Burr allegedly replied that the opinions of the learned Chancellor of New York were always entitled to the highest consideration.[10]

Joseph Story came to be one of Kent's first friends. The two held remarkably similar political views, mirrored each other in many respects in their professional careers, and found companionship in their later years through a correspondence in which they railed against the outrages of President Jackson and his judicial appointees. But where Kent was rigid in his approach to ideas and people, Story was mercurial; where Kent was distant and remote, Story was approachable and convivial.

Story's outstanding characteristic was his remarkable nervous energy. A bombastic, pugnacious child, a restlessly ambitious youth, an adult dogged by misfortunes, among them the loss of his first wife six months after their wedding, and the death of most of his children before their adolescence, Story found constant activity a respite from his anxieties. "[M]y cheerfulness," he confessed, "is the effect of labor and exertion to fly from melancholy recollections, and to catch at momentary joy."[11] His exuberance not only endowed him with a reputation as one of the great monologuists in an age when travel induced lengthy conversation, it resulted in a staggering number of professional accomplishments as well. Between 1811, when he was appointed to the Supreme Court, and 1845, the year of his death, Story performed the duties of a Justice (which included circuit riding in New England as well as sitting in Washington), wrote nine multi-volumed commentaries on legal subjects, served for sixteen years as a full-time professor of law at Harvard and for over twenty years as president of a Massachusetts branch of the National Bank, produced a volume's worth of speeches and addresses and a larger number of letters, and engaged in a great deal of behind-the-scenes political activity, at both state and national levels.

This last interest stemmed from Story's life-long concern with politics. From an early age he had sought out and engaged in political controversy, needling his acquaintances, and occasionally, in his youth, becoming involved in fist fights.[12] He subsequently learned, however, to suppress overt hostilities and to moderate his political stances. As a law professor he advised his students "[a]lways [to] have in readiness," in legal or political debate, "some of those unmeaning but respectful formularies [such as] 'the learned gentleman.' "[13] His approach to politics rested on the belief that "[h]e who lives a long life and never changes his opinions may value himself upon his consistency; but rarely can be complimented for his wisdom."[14]

Political activity for Story was not at all inconsistent with the office of judge. He viewed his office as a forum from which he could give unofficial advice on any number of political subjects. The specter of judicial conflicts of interest did not loom large to nineteenth-century Americans, and Story seems to have given such issues only indifferent attention. Although he once went on record as declining "to avail myself of my judicial station . . . to affect the opinion of others,"[15] he repeatedly attempted to use his influence with Treasury Department officials to secure large bank deposits in the branch bank of which he was president;[16] he sat in judgment of cases involving the Bank of the United States while retaining his bank presidency, and helped Daniel Webster draft a reply to President Jackson's message vetoing the National Bank's charter in 1832; and he also participated in the decision in the famous *Charles River Bridge* case of 1837, notwithstanding the fact that Harvard University, of which he was both a member of the faculty and a Fellow of the Corporation, received annual income from one of the litigants.

Story's energetic participation in contemporary affairs and his combative temperament provoked animosities in spite of his acknowledged wit and charm. With Justice William Johnson he carried on a protracted feud that occasionally erupted in open sniping by both parties in the United States Reports.[17] After Johnson's death Story clashed repeatedly with Justice Henry Baldwin.[18] He eventually became estranged from his friend Henry Wheaton, Court Reporter during much of Story's tenure, who in 1837 called Story a prevaricator and a hypocrite.[19] When Thomas Jefferson, no admirer of Story during his lifetime, was alleged posthumously to have referred to Story as a "pseudo-republican," Story responded by stating that that term was employed for "every one . . . who dared to venture upon a doubt of [Jefferson's] infallibility."[20]

Kent and Story had both been precocious in their professional development. Both were admitted to practice at twenty-two; both were serving in their state legislatures by twenty-seven; at twenty-nine Story was a Congressman, at thirty Kent was Professor of Law at Columbia; at thirty-two Story was on the U.S. Supreme Court, and at thirty-five Kent was on the New York Supreme Court. In contrast, Shaw was a late bloomer. At twenty-four, after his first year in practice, he earned approximately $200. He did not argue a case before the Supreme Court of Massachusetts until he was twenty-nine. At thirty he was a Justice of the Peace for Suffolk County. But after 1811, when he was elected to the Massachusetts legislature, Shaw began to prosper. In the interval between that year and 1830, when he was appointed Chief Justice of the Massachusetts Supreme Court, he married an affluent merchant's daughter, served as a member of the Massachusetts Constitutional Convention of 1820, became chief counsel to and a director of a bank, developed a thriving law practice, declined nomination to a judgeship on the Court of Common Pleas, and was elected president of the elite Suffolk Bar Association. By 1830 he was earning over $15,000 a year and had to be strongly persuaded before accepting the Chief Justiceship.[21]

In considering whether to undertake a judicial career, Shaw indicated that he was "conscious that I cannot . . . discharge the duties [with distinction]." Others, he noted, had assured him that he could, but the prospect gave him "apprehension and alarm."[22] There was a rational basis for Shaw's fears. He was not a legal technician; as a practitioner he had been impatient with legal research, relying on others to search for authorities.[23] His skill lay in counseling clients, where his honesty, straightforwardness, and common sense served him well. He associated judging with "patient research and persevering investigation"; his disinclination for those tasks nearly resolved him against accepting the position of Chief Justice, giving way at the eleventh hour to his sense that he had harbored similar doubts of his abilities with regard to "other arduous undertakings," and yet had "upon trial . . . found my strength equal to the occasion."[24]

Shaw, as a judge, appeared to contemporaries as a formidable, even awesome, figure. His physical appearance, short and massive, with a huge head and lined face, suggested strength in homeliness; his demeanor in the courtroom was ponderous, deliberate, bluff, and grave; he suffered no levity or disturbance and was capable of abusing counsel or peremptorily dismissing him;[25] he scrupulously avoided participation in political activity, considering his judicial office to be "quite aloof from political controversy";[26] he so dominated his Court that he wrote only one dissent in thirty years and had the unanimous approval of his fellow judges in forty-seven of his fifty opinions in constitutional law. His austerity and his accomplishments as Chief Justice were coupled with a striking lack of vanity, and this, as one contemporary noted, "gave a grandeur to his mind." Another stated that members of the Massachusetts bar were wont to speculate whether Shaw was "a divine institution or a human contrivance."[27]

In writing opinions, Shaw de-emphasized precedents, as Marshall had, preferring arguments based on what he called "the plain dictates of natural justice."[28] His greatest ability was in modifying existing legal doctrine in the context of the demands of contemporary society. He could see the policy implications in legal rules, he was receptive to change, and he had few partisan convictions that prevented his taking a detached view of a legal problem. In consequence, the tone of his opinions differed markedly from that of Kent or of Story. To some extent the difference was a function of time, for Shaw began his judicial career after Kent had completed his, and Shaw continued in service until 1860.

In the period in which Shaw wrote, the empty spaces of American jurisprudence had begun to be filled in, thanks largely to the work of Kent and Story themselves. The judicial task of undertaking a painstaking review of the historical antecedents of a problem had been greatly simplified by the publication of Kent's and Story's treatises. Moreover, judges in America had come, in the early years of the nineteenth century, to give increasing attention to the policy implications of legal doctrines.[29] But even in this context Shaw's work was distinctive. Where Kent or Story might rest a decision on a technical distinction, Shaw grounded it on rough common sense. Where Kent and Story might string together sets of authorities, Shaw completely ignored them. And where Kent and Story might pursue a legal principle to its consistent, logical conclusion, Shaw emphasized its ambivalences and suggested that it could lead to contradictory results in diverse instances.

III

The judicial world that Kent, Story, and, later, Shaw confronted was still shaped by the semiprimitive conditions of life on the American continent. Judges literally brought the law to the people—a task filled with physical and intellectual obstacles. Circuit riding to county courthouses in back-country settlements was a lonely and arduous practice: time in transit—if the circuit was extensive—often matched time in court. The judge carried his law books with him, since there were no public law libraries. There were few law books at best: until 1775 only forty-eight had been published in America,[30] and until 1790 there were few published reports of judicial decisions. During the first decade of the nineteenth century only the Supreme Court and a handful of state courts had printed records of their earlier cases. Under such circumstances judges were accustomed to deciding cases on an impressionistic basis and to seeing their decisions rapidly vanish into obscurity. The informality of the process was augmented in post-Revolutionary America by a popular prejudice against English common law and lawyers themselves, an attitude manifesting itself in the toleration of rough, *ad hoc* justice meted out without resort to technicalities. "It is our duty to do justice between parties," an early-nineteenth-century judge from New Hampshire announced, "not by any quirk out of Coke and Blackstone—books that I never read and never will."[31]

To Kent and Story, men with an inclination toward scholarship, an exalted image of their profession, and a certain class consciousness, such conditions were intolerable. "The progress of jurisprudence," Kent noted, "was nothing in New York prior to 1793."[32] What was most particularly absent, for Kent and Story, was a body of established authorities from which judges could derive rules for the resolution of cases coming before them. Marshall, faced with this void, had created his own body of working principles, but Marshall's task had been the initial formulation of the jurisprudence of the American Revolution, not its preservation and maintenance. Moreover, for the most part Marshall had not been called on to decide ordinary cases, but cases that raised issues of high politics. Kent, in his role as a state judge, and Story, who spent much of his time deciding lower-level federal cases for the New England circuit, needed more practical guidance.

Confronted with an absence of established American law, Kent and Story sought to create it themselves. A first step in that process was to secure publication and dissemination of court decisions, and, as a secondary goal, to ensure that the reporter charged with overseeing the publication would be sympathetic toward one's jurisprudential views. In William Johnson and Henry Wheaton, Kent and Story found two such men.

Johnson, who was appointed reporter of the New York Supreme Court in 1804, was a life-long personal and political friend of Kent. In 1814, when Kent was named Chancellor, he brought Johnson with him as reporter of equity decisions; by 1821 a speaker at the New York constitutional convention asserted that Johnson's reports were quoted "from Maine to New Orleans."[33] Johnson's *Chancery Reports* were dedicated to Kent and helped to make Kent's reputation. Chief Justice Isaac Parker of the Massachusetts Supreme Court commented, also in 1821, that the bench of New York, "ever since we have been enabled to judge of its character by the masterly reports of Mr. Johnson, has been distinguished by great learning and uncommon legal acumen."[34] No English chancery decisions, noted the *London Law Magazine* in 1834, were "more frequently or more respectfully cited in the courts of South Carolina than the seven volumes of Mr. Johnson's reports of Kent's decisions."[35]

Story had ingratiated himself with Wheaton, shortly after Wheaton was named the Supreme Court's reporter, by helping draft a statute—the Reporter's Act of 1817—providing an annual salary for the office. From that point on, at least, Story found Wheaton receptive to the use of Court reports as a vehicle for Story's essays and also inclined to promote the distribution of Story's Court opinions. Story assisted Wheaton in his summaries of the Court's decisions,[36] contributed anonymous notes to Wheaton's early volumes,[37] planned to collaborate in a digest of Court decisions to be published under Wheaton's name,[38] and lobbied through Wheaton for publication in the several states of his own opinions.[39] Wheaton, for his part, was a willing participant in all these ventures, including the last. Thus, after Story had urged him to disseminate an opinion from which Justice William Johnson, Story's ardent foe, had dissented, Wheaton wrote, "Mr. Justice Johnson places the decision of the Court on a quicksand—yours on a rock. And I am therefore the more anxious to see it before the public."[40]

Reportage was but one means employed by Kent and Story to further their goal of developing American jurisprudence; another was the use of historical scholarship. For Kent and Story the canvassing of historical authorities served three functions simultaneously. It was, first of all, an exercise congenial to their temperaments. They were not only interested in scholarship for its own sake, they strongly pursued an ideal of cultivated gentility that had as one of its components intellectual exposure to history and the classics. They spoke, read, and wrote Latin, corresponding with each other in it; they immersed themselves in the civil law treatises of Europe; through Blackstone they were lead to Mansfield, Coke, Bacon, Glanvil, Bracton, and finally to Roman law. From these readings came the formidable succession of authorities that documented their judicial decisions. Behind an announced principle of law, in their analyses, lay the collective wisdom of the ages.

The personal and social fulfillment Kent and Story found in canvassing authorities was matched by professional pride. They saw the law as the vocation of gentlemen, requiring not only that its practitioners be learned, but that they be, in early nineteenth-century terms, "liberal"—that is to say, wide-ranging and imaginative in their intellectual pursuits. A dash of the classics or a smidgin of the ancient common law forms uplifted the quality of professional discourse. In this belief Kent and Story were not unique; one of the striking characteristics of nineteenth-century advocacy in America was a tendency on the part of appellate lawyers to project the gist of their arguments in Latin maxims.

There was another, less esoteric justification for historical research: the need to present American lawyers with a corpus of source material from which they could derive arguments. The more thorough the foray into the ancient authorities, the wider the range of possible precedents for an advocate; the more extensive that foray, the less the need for subsequent excursions. Scholarly exegesis, if full enough, thus came to serve as a form of lawmaking itself, as practitioners relied on Kent's or Story's canvasses rather than making their own. Since the purpose of Kent's and Story's digests was not merely to declare legal principles but implicitly, to argue for their existence, their synopses in a sense became modest exercises in making law.

This was the central function of the celebrated treatises of Kent and Story, first appearing in 1826 with the publication of the first volume of Kent's *Commentaries*, and continuing until Story's death in 1845. The treatises constituted an American version of small codes. They were not, technically, regarded as "authorities" in the same sense as were decisions of courts or statutes, but at a time when other published resources were scarce, they became for countless practitioners the starting points for research. The "law" of bailments, as Story would have been the first to admit, was not synonymous with *Story on Bailments*, which was published in 1832; yet the treatise's synopsis of legal principles was, practically speaking, a sufficient surrogate for the law itself. As such, the writings of Kent and Story, ostensibly collections of and glosses on "the authorities," became authoritative in themselves.

In addition to the personal and professional functions served by the historical scholarship of Kent and Story, there was a third function, one that might fairly be called political, in a broad sense of the term. Kent and Story used historical authorities not simply to bring additional information to bear on a legal problem, but also to prove the universality of certain propositions by demonstrating the ubiquity of their presence. Hence the appearance, in their decisions or commentaries, of a procession of ancients endorsing a particular legal proposition served as a means of indicating its truth. A practice of Roman law, commented on by Bracton, was seen to be duplicated in a common law rule, as explicated by Coke; and when an analogous civil law practice could be shown by reading the civilian commentators, the phenomenon took on the dimensions of a universal law of nature.

But the technique could work backward in time as well as forward. A theory of contemporary politics, assumed *arguendo* to be sound, could be shown to have such wide and deep historical antecedents as to constitute a social truth. One example of this was the universality of property rights: history showed for Kent "the gradual enlargement and cultivation of [the] sense [of property] from feeble force in the savage state to its full vigour and maturity among polished nations."[41] The demonstration of such a truth had a certain inevitability once one assumed, as did Kent and Story, that "a question of the highest moment" for statesmen was "how the property-holding part of the community may be sustained against the inroads of poverty and vice."[42]

IV

The role of the judiciary in demonstrating the inviolability of property rights and in preserving their sanctity had been an important concern of Marshall; maintaining this aspect of the judicial function was a central, self-designated task of Kent and Story. Associated with the protection of property rights, in Marshall's jurisprudence, had been an oracular theory of judging. Since the judiciary only "found" rather than "made" law, it could not be accused of protecting property rights for partisan or idiosyncratic reasons; alternatively, since an intention to secure autonomy for property could be found in sources of law such as the Constitution, the natural truth of that proposition was self-evident. But whereas Marshall harmonized protection of property rights with an allegedly nonpartisan role for the judiciary, maintenance of that harmony was to become a source of difficulty for Kent and Story. Ultimately, issues involving the place of property rights in the American legal system were to result in a modification not only of Marshall's view of property but of his theory of the judicial function as well. By the time Shaw became Chief Justice of the Massachusetts Supreme Court in 1830, the groundwork for that modification had already been laid.

Protection for property had been linked, in Marshall's jurisprudence, with the notion that security of property had been one of the original rights conferred upon man in a state of nature and brought with him into society. But this conception did not respond to the problem of determining which kinds of property should be protected when two property rights were in conflict. In one instance of conflict Marshall made a clear choice. He argued that property rights acquired by primogeniture or entail, being incompatible with a republican form of government, could be usurped by states at their pleasure; but by contrast, property that represented one's right to the fruits of his labor, such as lands acquired by contract, either with a state or with a private person, could not likewise be usurped.

This distinction between types of property rights was congenial to the dissolution of certain fixed badges of status that had prevailed in England and were considered anathema by Marshall's generation. Abolishing primogeniture and entail was comparable to abolishing titles or supplanting the monarchy with the Presidency: it participated in the self-definition of the new American nation. For Kent's and Story's generation, however, the task of ascertaining which property rights deserved protection became more complicated. A phalanx of vested property rights in the Revolutionary sense of the term had sprung up. During and after the Revolution, states had granted lands to entrepreneurs for various purposes, and in many instances those grants had resulted in the monopolization of large tracts of land or of certain public facilities, such as bridges, ferries, or turnpikes. As the American population grew and the national economy expanded, these property rights came to be regarded, in occasional instances, as barriers to further social or economic development. But a body of law, which Marshall had helped to create, apparently held that these rights could not be interfered with. Hence two competing conceptions of property emerged, one that emphasized its dynamic aspects, associating it with economic growth, and another that emphasized its static character, associating it with security from too rapid change. The inevitable clash between these two conceptions was not resolved with Marshall's decision in *Fletcher v. Peck*, but recurred again and again throughout the nineteenth century.

Kent was prepared to concede the inapplicability in America of English methods of restricting the transfer of property. "Entailments are recommended in monarchical governments," he wrote, "as a protection to the power and influence of the landed aristocracy; but such a policy has no application to republican establishments . . . under which every individual of every family has his equal rights, and is equally invited, by the genius of the institutions, to depend upon his own merit and exertions."[43] But to doubt the appropriateness of a form of preventing transfers of land was not to deny the principle that family influence and property, once acquired, could be preserved and perpetuated.[44] For Kent, the "sense of property" was bestowed on mankind for the "purpose of rousing us from sloth, and stimulating us to action." It pervaded "the foundations of social improvement"; it lead to the creation of governments and the establishment of justice. Legislatures had no right to limit the extent to which property could be acquired; a state of equality as to property, in fact, was "impossible to be maintained," as being "against the laws of our nature."[45]

For Kent this conception of property rights translated itself into four legal propositions: first, the powerlessness of legislatures to disturb previously vested contract rights; second, the requirement that if a legislature took private property for public purposes it must compensate fully all those whose property was either appropriated or damaged in consequence of the appropriation; third, a power in legislatures to regulate the use of property in accordance with the safety or health of the community, subject to judicial approval; fourth, a power in courts to define what constituted "public purposes," to determine the amounts required by full compensation, and to ascertain in which kinds of cases the regulation of property use was permissible.[46]

These propositions were not altogether bound to a static theory of property. The second and third, in fact, were early statements of the eminent domain and police powers of state governments, powers that emerged as important grounds for the promotion of new economic enterprises by states throughout the century. But Kent's formulation as a whole envisaged the judiciary, through its protection of vested rights and its ability to determine the conditions permitting legislative abrogations of property holdings, as a buffer between established property holders and the people. In Kent's view, judges could fairly find that a state grant of a monopoly in steamboat traffic to one entrepreneur prevented it from later granting a steamboat license to another;[47] that a state franchise to a bridge company could be used to prohibit subsequent bridge companies from competing with it;[48] and, in general, that the legislative grant of a franchise to a private corporation implicitly gave the corporation a privilege to enjoin its prospective competitors.[49]

Kent thus envisaged a peculiar relation between the legislature, the judiciary, and private entrepreneurs. To promote economic development, states had conceived the practice of granting lands or franchises to private entrepreneurs to pursue certain goals, such as making internal improvements. Under Kent's doctrines nothing prevented a state legislature from making these original grants or indeed from simply appropriating the property of its citizens for public purposes. Moreover, the state could insist that property be used one way rather than another if the public health or safety required it. But once the state granted away its lands, it could not regain them unless it had expressly reserved the right to do so. Nor could it permit subsequent potential grantees to pursue the very same economic objectives for which it had subsidized its original grantee. At some point, then, in Kent's view, property rights, having vested and created necessary attendant privileges in their owners, became static, and were guarantees of security against encroachment except under unusual circumstances.

The chief institutional protector of security and ultimate apologist for a static view of property was the judiciary. Ultimately, judges were to side with those who held property against those who sought to obtain it—and this was perfectly acceptable to Kent. "Society," he announced in 1821, "is an association for the protection of property as well as of life, and the individual who contributes only one cent to the common stock ought not to have the same power and influence in directing the property concerns of the partnership as he who contributes his thousands."[50]

Kent's concern that economic expansion be stimulated yet not allowed to undermine the security of property led him to look favorably on forms of business enterprise that appeared to foster both those goals. One such form was the corporation, which simultaneously provided for the free, advantageous exertion of "industry, skill and enterprise,"[51] and afforded "security to the persons of the members, and to their property."[52] Kent, however, regarded indiscriminate expansion of the corporate form as unwise, believing that it was best suited to high-risk public-service enterprises that required large capitalizations. Used indiscriminately it might tend to lessen competition.[53]

If Kent was cautious in his endorsement of the corporation, Story was not. Like Kent, Story was interested in maintenance of support for static property rights amidst a climate of economic expansion. He believed that "the sacred rights of property" were "to be granted at every point";[54] that whenever legislation rendered "the possession or enjoyment of property precarious," it was "in its essence tyranny";[55] that there could be "no freedom" where there was "no safety to property";[56] and that government could "scarcely be deemed to be free [when] the rights of property [were] left solely dependent upon the will of a legislative body, without any restraint."[57] Accordingly, he sustained vested rights against legislative interference, either through use of the contracts clause of the Constitution,[58] a state constitution's prohibition against "retrospective laws,"[59] or, when pressed, the principles of natural law themselves.[60] But Story did not see a static theory of property rights as necessarily incompatible with economic expansion. In his concurring opinion in the *Dartmouth College* case, for example, he simultaneously upheld the sanctity of vested rights against legislative infringement, and suggested a means by which legislatures could in subsequent charters to private enterprises reserve the right to repeal grants they had made.[61]

Story's concurrence in *Dartmouth College* was more important, however, for its effect upon the status of corporations. Corporate entities had existed in America since colonial times, but not primarily as business enterprises. Most colonial corporations were churches or municipalities; after 1800 the corporate form became associated with transportation companies chartered by legislatures to undertake special projects. Originally such charters conferred only limited discretionary powers, required special acts of the legislature for their implementation, and were not thought of as assuring limited liability for the corporation's stockholders. Perpetual charters, incorporation certificates, and limited liability were features evolving in the later nineteenth century, when the corporation began to assume its modern identification with business enterprise.

Dartmouth College approximated the colonial model of a corporation more than the later model. It was an organization that had been chartered not to pursue an economic venture but to provide education for the public. In the eighteenth and early nineteenth centuries, however, the close relations between state governments and private enterprise had spawned a legal doctrine that threatened to conflict with the notion of vested private rights: the theory that property rights "in the public domain" or "affected by a public interest" could be infringed by the state. This doctrine was made a basis for state involvement in cases such as those involving claims to riparian rights on the grounds that certain types of property, even if private in their ownership, were public in their use.[62]

A college corporation also seemed subject to public-interest restrictive legislation. Colleges functioned to educate the public; the state had an arguable interest in the nature and quality of the education a college provided. Hence the *Dartmouth College* case appeared to raise squarely the issue of whether a previous grant of a charter to a "public" corporation could be subsequently amended by the state in the light of the construction of the obligation of contracts clause advanced in *Fletcher v. Peck*. The issue seemed in doubt, despite the *Fletcher* decision, because of the public domain doctrine and because even the most tenacious defenders of the sanctity of property had conceded that some state restraints on its use were permissible. Marshall's opinion, however, seemed to draw a bright line between "private" and "public" corporations—a stance unresponsive to the subtleties of the case. In a literal sense Dartmouth College was a private institution, not an administrative wing of the state.[63] But in another sense it was surely "public"; Marshall's opinion simply chose to deemphasize that aspect of its character.

Story's concurrence, however, spoke both to the relation of the *Dartmouth College* case to the public domain doctrine and to the political ramifications of the decision, which were quickly perceived by contemporaries.[64] The decision created for any arguably "private" corporation an umbrella of protection against state interference with the terms of its charter, despite the ability of states to interfere with property that was in the public domain or affected with a public interest. There were, Story maintained, two meanings of the term "public": a "popular" meaning and a "strictly legal" one. Any corporation serving the populace was public in the former sense, but its legal responsibilities flowed from the latter. If the "foundation" of a corporation was private, it was immune from state interference regardless of the uses to which it was put. Only corporations that remained actual governmental entities, such as municipalities, were "public" in the legal sense. Banks, insurance companies, transportation franchises, and educational institutions were private corporations, even though their "objects and operations" might "partake of a public nature." The phase "affected with a public interest" was to be strictly construed.[65]

But the freedom from state interference ascribed to private corporations, Story maintained, rested not on universal natural rights principles but on the more limited basis of the contracts clause in the Constitution. State or even royal charters to corporations were clearly "contracts," but nothing prevented states from reserving by the terms of its contracts a power to amend charters and thereby affect the rights of a corporation's members. Thus, while Story's concurrence in *Dartmouth College* served to limit the applicability of the public domain doctrine on a theoretical level, it also suggested a practical means by which states could control the expansion of private enterprises.

State legislatures were highly receptive to the practical proposal Story had advanced, and reservation of an amendment power became a common ingredient of incorporation charters in the nineteenth century.[66] But Story's suggestion that theory be tempered with practice was not so readily received. The public domain doctrine was not easily curbed; it revived itself in a variety of ways in the courts, and in 1837, in the *Charles River Bridge* case,[67] it captured a majority of the Supreme Court, to Story's "humiliation" and Kent's utter disgust.[68]

The revival of the doctrine was symptomatic of the emerging conceptions of property use associated with the century's second wave of economic expansion. From the Revolution through the first thirty-odd years of the nineteenth century, the internal development of the nation's economy was largely tied to ventures in transportation, and the form of the ventures was often that of partnerships between states and private groups organized around a single project. The turnpikes, ferries, bridges, and canals that made possible mercantile exchange between the seacoast and the interior were built primarily by state-chartered private monopolies. The original theory of state franchises for effecting internal improvements assumed that what the state could give it could take away, since the duration of monopolistic franchises was at state sufferance.

The contracts clause cases, such as *Fletcher* and *Dartmouth College*, served to modify the original partnership theory. State charters once created could not, absent an expressly reserved amendment power in the grantor, be abolished; temporary, risky internal improvement ventures were made into permanent, monopolistic enterprises. The owners of bridges or turnpikes could impose tolls to take advantage of the traffic in commerce their facilities had stimulated. In a few years, if they were well situated geographically, they could count on securing a return on their original investment and making monopoly profits besides.

With the continued growth of population in the nation's interior and the consequent rise in trade between the seacoast and the backcountry, the demand for additional transportation routes became irresistible, and the enormous entrepreneurial potential of internal improvement franchises became widely perceived. At this point (occurring at different times in different localities), pressures toward a second wave of economic expansion mounted—a wave that treated ventures in transportation less as public service operations than as profitable business undertakings, and responded not so much to incentives created by a state to foster development of its resources as to demands of private persons for easy freight and passenger service between the interior and the seacoast. Consequently internal improvement schemes became focal points for the demands of a variety of interests: shippers who wanted an abundance of fast, cheap transportation; existent franchise holders who wanted a profitable return for their risk-takings; potential competing groups who wanted to enter the transportation services market; passengers who wanted safe, reliable, inexpensive transportation to previously inaccessible regions.

The theory of property rights advanced by Marshall and generally supported by Kent and Story was responsive to only one of these interest groups—established franchise holders. It suggested that a second wave of expansion in the transportation area could not take place if the first wave, that marked by state-private partnerships, had resulted in unreserved grants to private monopolies. The rights originally granted had now "vested." Competitive franchises could be enjoined, monopoly prices could be set, and subsequent expansion of transportation facilities was to be at the pleasure of the original franchise holders. In the view of Kent and Story the new expansionists, as Chief Justice Taney said in the *Charles River Bridge* case, were "obliged to stand still, until the claims of the old turnpike corporations shall be satisfied."[69]

That too many interests favored further expansion in the transportation sector to tolerate the continued primacy of the vested-rights doctrine was apparent by the 1830s. The Court majority in *Charles River Bridge* only codified the inevitable when it refused to enjoin a new bridge over the Charles River despite its obvious infringement on the vested rights of the existing bridge's stockholders. Less apparent were the legal theories to be utilized in developing protection for the emerging expansionist interests and their effects on the role of the judiciary, which had been conceived by Kent and Story as a buffer between those who held property and those who sought to acquire it.

Shaw began his judicial career at the crest of the expansionist wave. His thirty years on the bench witnessed a transformation of the status of vested property rights from an absolute bar to legislative activity to one of several ingredients that were balanced in a legislature's determination of the "public interest." This transformation served to resolve the tension between static and dynamic theories of property—and largely in favor of the dynamic theory. In helping to effectuate this change, Shaw utilized a breed of judicial activism whose audacity and originality were reminiscent of that of Marshall. Paradoxically, the result of his activism was to prescribe a far more passive role for the judiciary than that prescribed by Kent or Story.

In his reconsideration of the place of property rights in the society of his time, Shaw developed new usages for four existing legal doctrines: that of delegation of legislative powers, that of a public use, that of eminent domain, and that of state police powers. The doctrines were not original with Shaw, but in his hands they became the foundation for a new set of relations among private entrepreneurs, the legislature, and the judiciary.

The partnership form characterizing early-nineteenth-century economic ventures had been based on a particular interpretation of the powers of a state government. Governments, the theory assumed, had a power to control the use of private property if the common welfare so required. Although that power could be delegated to private persons, the state implicitly reserved the right to attach conditions to its delegation. An early application of this theory was the Massachusetts mill acts. Gristmills ran on water power, and thus required access to water and also tended to discharge water on adjacent farmland. At common law the owner of lands flooded by a nearby mill could enjoin the operation of the mill as a nuisance or sue the mill owner for damages. These sanctions acted as a deterrent to the development of mills; so in the mill acts Massachusetts delegated to mill owners its theoretical power to affect the use of private property, thereby allowing them to flood adjacent lands with impunity, but retained the right to oversee the rates they charged and the services they provided. The original justification for this legislative alteration of the common law was that the owners whose land was flooded, being farmers, received economic benefits from the presence of the mills, which helped to make their products marketable.

In the course of Shaw's tenure, several cases arose involving extension of the mill acts beyond gristmills to other kinds of enterprises. Iron mills or cotton mills, after 1830, were arguably not so similar to their earlier counterparts as to merit the same protection. They were merely one type of manufacturing enterprise in a diversifying state economy, and not necessarily indispensable requirements for economic health. Shaw, however, was prepared to sustain legislative delegations of an appropriation power to manufacturers. The "public interest," he maintained, was furthered by "the establishment of a great mill-power for manufacturing purposes . . . especially since manufacturing has come to be one of the great public industrial pursuits of the commonwealth."[70] And the same argument could be made in behalf of manufacturing enterprises that did not rely on water, such as factories and railroads. Shaw's test was whether, in a broad sense, the activity receiving special privileges constituted a benefit to the public.

This interpretation of the relation between state power and private enterprise was not, however, essentially designed to promote the interests of new forms of private enterprise at the expense of those injured by their operations. It also functioned to maintain the state's ability to continue regulation of private enterprise on the grounds of its "public" character. For if the justification for delegating privileges to certain enterprises was that they furthered the public interest, that same justification might be used for subsequent legislative control of their operations. Under this view the concept of vested rights became only one of a number of variables affecting the propriety of legislative regulation of private enterprise. If the public interest, on balance, was promoted by statutory infringements on vested rights, courts would not generally invalidate those infringements.

Shaw's approach to cases involving property rights entailed a delicate interweaving of the doctrines of eminent domain, public use, and police power. The doctrine of eminent domain, which had been recognized by Kent,[71] conceded to legislatures a power to appropriate land within their domain and tolerated delegation of that power to private enterprises to achieve certain "public" objects. The mill acts were early examples of delegations of this power. Its most extensive use, however, was in connection with the development of railroads.

The railroad industry required for its development the right to cut swaths of land for roadbeds out of existent property, and this need raised a series of questions involving the eminent domain doctrine. The first was whether the state could delegate its power of eminent domain to railroads. Shaw answered this affirmatively in *Boston Water Power Co. v. Boston & Worcester R.R.* and *Fuller v. Dame*.[72] The justification for an eminent domain power in railroads was that they were, like turnpikes, bridges, and mills, "public works," inasmuch as they were established by public authority for public use even though their construction was financed by private individuals. The second question was, assuming an eminent domain power in railroads, What was the effect of that power on vested contract rights? In a second case involving the Boston and Worcester Railroad and the Boston Water Power Company,[73] Shaw held that appropriation of land under the eminent domain power did not violate contract rights stemming from the original grant of that land. He distinguished between ordinary and extra-ordinary legislative powers, locating eminent domain in the latter category, since it rested on the demands of "public necessity." Original legislative grants to private individuals were assumed to benefit the public, since those "contracts," while creating rights in the grantees, implicitly reserved power in the grantors to recalculate the benefits of the arrangement. If on balance the public benefited from subsequent legislative infringement on existing rights based on the eminent domain power, the infringement was permissible.

Determining the proper relations between vested rights and eminent domain in any particular case was a matter, then, of ascertaining where the public interest lay. In certain instances, the public was aided by the maintenance of prerogatives for vested private interests, and existing contract rights could be protected. Hence the legislature could create a monopoly of railroad traffic along a certain route, and subsequent challenges to that monopoly by potential competitors could be overriden by the courts.[74] This was because the public was better served by a regulated monopoly than by competition in that particular situation, since competition between railroads over short routes fostered a waste of resources. Moreover, the possibility of subsequent competitors provided a disincentive for investors in the original railroad enterprise, and the public relied on private capital to subsidize the railroad industry.[75]

This resolution of the third question raised by the eminent domain doctrine—whether that doctrine created a presumption that vested rights were vulnerable to subsequent encroachment—left existing property holders a degree of autonomy. Competitors of railroads, or railroads themselves, could not infringe vested rights of others merely by showing proof of their incorporation by the legislature, for, if they had not expressly been granted specific eminent domain powers, they could not claim them by implication. Hence, railroads could not appropriate the existing roadbeds of turnpikes unless specifically authorized,[76] nor could they claim that a power to appropriate land exempted them from compensating owners of land not appropriated but damaged.[77]

There were, then, a series of judicially enforced limitations on delegation of the eminent domain power. Thus appropriation of land by eminent domain required compensation; the power extended only to those circumstances for which it had been expressly and unambiguously granted. The test in every instance was whether the object for which use of the power was employed constituted a benefit to the public or was merely a vehicle for private gain. In the first case, vested rights gave way to eminent domain; in the second, there was no need to disturb them, since their presence was assumed to benefit the public and their infringement only enhanced the economic position of certain private interests.

In short, private exercise of the eminent domain power was justified if the "use" to which it was being put was "public." And the presence of a public use justified the continued protection of the public interest in the relevant private enterprise. That protection could be effectuated through regulation: the legislature could set rates for railroads and mills and control their profits.[78] It could also be effectuated by outright prohibition of certain economic activity on the grounds that it was injurious to the public health. During Shaw's tenure the Massachusetts legislature moved from selective regulation of the liquor industry to more extensive regulation to outright prohibition. Shaw sustained each successive infringement,[79] limiting the legislature only by requiring that its regulations provide procedural safeguards for those persons whose property was being appropriated.

The eminent domain doctrine thus implied a "public use" of private enterprises that in turn implied the vulnerability of those enterprises to state regulation under the police powers. The concept of police power entered American jurisprudence during the years coincident with Shaw's tenure. It was a product of the partnership theory of state-private relations, the Tenth Amendment of the Constitution, and the eighteenth-century principle that all property, being "derived directly or indirectly from the government," was held "subject to those general regulations which are necessary to the common good and general welfare."[80] It implanted in the states the ability to restrict the use of property on the ground that a particular use jeopardized the general welfare; as Shaw put it, "the nature of well ordered civil society" required that "every holder of property, however absolute and unqualified may be his title, holds it under the implied liability that his use of it may be so regulated, that it shall not be injurious . . . to the rights of the community."[81]

Restriction of property through the police power was not a "taking," and hence did not require compensation.[82] The test of the constitutionality of a police power regulation was its "reasonableness," and regulations justified on the basis of state police powers were presumed to be valid; when found unconstitutional, they were voided only insofar as they affected the particular parties challenging them.[83] Under its police powers Massachusetts could suppress the liquor traffic,[84] regulate banks,[85] control the building of wharves,[86] and condemn buildings used as houses of prostitution.[87]

In sum, private property under Shaw was considered primarily with respect to its social usefulness. The public, through the legislature, was given considerable freedom to decide to what extent the impairment of particular property rights benefited the public at large. In tolerating this legislative calculus, Shaw was not only modifying the place of property rights in American jurisprudence, he was altering the Kent-Story conception of the function of the judiciary as well. Kent and Story had envisaged the judicial branch as an aristocratic barrier against the excesses of democratic legislatures, with the protection of existent property rights one of its major tasks. Under Shaw the judiciary became a partner with the legislature in shaping public policy. Individual cases were conceived of as manifestations of principles of civilized living and, as such, each new case could test the continued applicability of the principles it symbolized. "It is one of the great merits and advantages of the common law," Shaw wrote, "that instead of a series of detailed practical rules . . . [it] consists of a few broad and comprehensive principles founded on reason, natural justice, and enlightened public policy modified and adapted to the circumstances of all the particular cases which fall within it."[88] When new cases arose, they were to "be governed by the general principle . . . , modified and adapted to new circumstances by considerations of fitness and property, of reason and justice."[89]

Under this theory of the judicial function, great weight was given to the policy implications of a legal dispute. There were two primary sources of wisdom on matters of public policy: the decisions of prior courts (which were manifestations of "general principles" of reason and justice) and the enactments of legislatures (the principal expositors of public sentiment). Hence judges had a good deal of freedom to modify precedents in the light of changed circumstances, extracting their principles and reasoning by analogy, but little freedom to modify the decisions of legislators. Constitutional limitations on legislative activity were few, and judicial review of the actions of legislatures was narrow in its scope. The constitutionality of statutes was presumed; where alternative readings of a statute were possible, the one preserving its constitutionality was to be preferred; the invalidity of part of a statute did not void the whole; and the parties challenging the constitutionality of a statute had to prove its adverse effect on them.[90] Although the contracts clause of the federal Constitution was acknowledged by Shaw to be a limitation on state legislative activity, it was used to strike down statutes only three times in his thirty-year tenure.[91] Established property rights were considered as deserving of judicial protection only when their presence furthered the public interest[92] or they were being infringed in a shockingly arbitrary fashion.[93]

V

In one of the nation's most influential states, then, property rights had by 1860 lost their specially protected status and were subject to usurpation in the public interest. Shaw had supported and furthered this transformation of status; Kent and Story had opposed it. The transformation could be seen as a triumph for aspiring entrepreneurs and property holders as against established landowners. Insofar as the expanding character of the American economy required judicial tolerance of new uses of property, such transformation was progressive as opposed to reactionary. But identifying Shaw's approach to property rights issues as "liberal" and that of Kent and Story as "conservative" is not particularly useful. For one thing, it offends against the parlance of the time, under which Kent and Story regarded their views as representative of a liberal frame of mind.[94] Further, it de-emphasizes Shaw's use of the eminent-domain doctrine to promote corporate interests and maintain the security of stockholders of transportation ventures. And it leads to a distortion of the legal history of the post-Civil War period, where the theories of Kent and Story were revived not to protect "vested" interests but to preclude further governmental regulation of corporate entities, such as railroads, which had greatly expanded their operations under state control and now wanted further room to expand.

A more appropriate contrast between Kent and Story and Shaw involves their interpretation of the Marshallian view of the judicial function in the light of the exigencies of nineteenth-century America. Marshall's legacy, in this respect, had four features: an active judiciary, distrust of the popular will and its manifestation in acts of legislatures, sympathy toward entrepreneurial as opposed to static uses of property, and a method of deciding cases by appeal to principles of high politics. In the nineteenth century, continuing economic expansion—supervised and encouraged by state legislatures—created a tension between certain aspects of this legacy, most particularly between its preference for dynamic uses of property and its distrust of the popular will. Since this tension ultimately involved basic assumptions about the nature of man and his place in society, it affected the Marshallian method of decision-making, which rested on the assertion of shared principles of social organization in America. Consequently judges who followed Marshall were faced with a troublesome choice. They could develop either a method of decision-making that identified the judiciary with economic expansion and made it a tacit partner of the legislature, or a method that retained the judicial branch as a check on legislative activity and a protector of static uses of property. Shaw chose the former method, and with it Marshall's belief that judicial interpretation was a matter of returning to first principles; Kent and Story chose the latter, making it an exercise in partisan historical scholarship.

In a transitory fashion history supported Shaw's choice, so that a passive, although free-wheeling, conception of the judicial function supplanted the more active and rigid view of Kent and Story for a time. It would be inaccurate, however, to state that consequently Shaw made a greater contribution to the development of the American judicial tradition than Kent or Story. The latter two men provided their profession, through their scholarship, with a synthetic body of "law" with which to work, and with it a perspective in which emerging legal problems could be viewed. Masterfully broad in some respects, that perspective was narrowly partisan in others, and it was in those areas, such as property rights, that it first came to be abandoned. Shaw's form of abandonment, which created a new way of thinking about property rights, was particularly responsive to new features of the nineteenth-century American economy, and thereby enormously influential. But Shaw built on Kent and Story as much as he moved beyond them. On Shaw's retirement in 1860 a group of lawyers who had practiced before his court remarked that "[i]t was the task of those who went before you, to show that the principles of the common and the commercial law were available to the wants of communities which were far more recent than the origin of those systems. It was for you to adapt those systems to still newer and greater exigencies."[95] Both efforts were part of the function of the judge in nineteenth-century America, so that in praising Shaw the Massachusetts Bar was praising Kent and Story as well.

A conception of law as a body of shared principles was decisive in determining the judicial approach of Kent and Story and also the contrasting approach of Shaw. Kent and Story saw what they had once perceived as common American values revealed as class values; and having come upon that insight, they retreated into history to find the sources of legal doctrine. In so doing they rendered their pronouncements vulnerable to changed circumstances. A historical definition of property rights, however once universalized, could become anti-utilitarian and obsolete. Principles of law, in the sense used by Kent and Story, could be modified with time. Shaw, who had the benefit of Kent's and Story's scholarship, also saw its impermanence: to him principles of law meant something closer to contemporary communal values. In defining principles in that fashion and in appealing to them in his opinions Shaw was reminiscent of Marshall, but with an important difference. Marshall had appealed to principles he thought immutable as well as incontrovertible. Shaw's appeal was to the public utilitarian calculus of the moment. In his hands judges were not so much oracles as public servants. What, then, if a judge misread public sentiment; what if the first principles on which he grounded his opinions were politically unacceptable? That difficulty, avoided by Shaw, was to haunt his contemporary Roger Taney.

3 Roger Taney and the Limits of Judicial Power

In a surviving portrait of Roger Taney his disheveled hair and pained, meditative expression create an ascetic appearance more appropriate to a saint than to the man who has come to be called the judicial defender of racism and human bondage. His reputation has been resurrected several times by scholars, who have pointed out that he was a judge of considerable talent and stature and that his association with the infamous *Dred Scott* decision[1] needs to be viewed in the context of his other accomplishments.[2] Yet he remains a symbol of the moral nadir of the American judicial tradition, when the Supreme Court of the United States publicly declared the "degraded status" of blacks in America and the inherent inferiority of their race, and gave legal sanction to the enslavement of blacks by whites. With *Dred Scott* to remind us of the ignorance and viciousness long embedded in American culture, Taney's reputation may never be completely vindicated. He forces us to see the extent to which our institutions of government and our system of laws can become, even while administered by the educated and well-intentioned, affronts against humanity.

Taney was representative of educated professional Americans of his generation. Confronted with a rapidly expanding economy, changing political alignments, and the growth of cultural schizophrenia of which the system of black slavery was a root cause, he sought to adjust the nation's institutions so that they might survive in the new conditions created by these phenomena. Like many other statesmen of his day, Taney tried and failed to solve the slavery problem, but his response to the problem, no more unsuccessful than any other response, has become particularly offensive with time. The tension between the humanitarian and egalitarian ideals associated with the founding of the American nation and the presence of black slavery was simply too debilitating and pervasive to admit of peaceful consensual solution; moreover, it occurred at a time when consensual values were noticeably lacking throughout American civilization. The internal conflicts, of which the slavery issue was the most dramatic example, were never truly resolved, but engendered a forced reconciliation of the nation, with one set of attitudes summarily superimposed on another. Taney can hardly be faulted for failing to provide a set of fundamental constitutional principles by which the question of slavery could be amicably settled. Indeed, given the ideological context of his time, none existed. But he can, from another perspective, be faulted for the political and moral choices he made in attempting to settle the question.

Between 1836, the year when Taney replaced Marshall as Chief Justice, and 1857, the year of the *Dred Scott* decision, an affirmative justification for racially based enslavement was developed and refined in America. On the Court, Taney provided legal support for that justification. His intention was benign; he was concerned not with preserving slavery as such but with maintaining peaceful coexistence between competing ideologies in the nation. One cannot, however, ignore the fact that, despite his motives, Taney attempted to use the power of the judicial branch of government to further the existence of a subculture in which persons of one race were considered the property of persons of another. In this use of his office Taney demonstrated the moral and political limits of judicial power in America.

I

Taney served on the Court in a period of striking change, diffusion, and ambiguity in American civilization. Competing models of social organization existed in numerous areas of life in early-nineteenth-century America: static versus dynamic theories of property-holding; a stratified, restrictive system of political participation as opposed to successive movements appealing to the rhetoric of mass democracy; humanitarian reform in contrast to slavery. Taney reflected these contradictory impulses himself. The son of an established propertyholder, he was first elected to the Maryland legislature in 1799 largely because of the prominence of his father, and in his first term resisted a series of efforts to restrict the influence of the landed gentry. Yet in the 1820s and 1830s he aligned himself with the Democratic Party, which advocated mass suffrage, and became a strong supporter of Andrew Jackson and a prominent figure in the Jacksonian campaign against the Second Bank of the United States, regarded by both supporters and opponents as an assault on social and economic privilege. Despite his close identification with the landed gentry of his region, he became a principal spokesman on the Court for doctrines curtailing the power of landowners in an expansionist economy. While a member of the Maryland legislature he had actively promoted the rights of black freedmen and slaves, calling slavery "a blot on our national character,"[3] and freeing his own slaves;[4] yet as attorney general under Jackson he gave his official opinion that "the African race in the United States" were "every where a degraded class," not endowed with inalienable rights and not entitled to political privileges.[5]

Throughout his life Taney was involved in politics, thus tempting one to attribute the contradictions in his thought to considerations of expediency. If such motivation existed, it was not generally noted by his contemporaries. Daniel Webster called Taney "cunning," but Webster was rarely dispassionate in his appraisal of his political opponents; a more representative comment described Taney as having "an air of so much sincerity in all he said that it was next to impossible to believe he was wrong."[6] The general impression Taney made was that of a gentle, moderate, and likable man, with a capacity to defuse through his person the passions his actions engendered. Story, who had deplored Taney's appointment, described him as one who in his judicial duties "conducted himself with great urbanity and propriety";[7] Justice Samuel Miller, who sat with Taney during the latter's final two years in office, was less grudging in his praise. "When I came to Washington," Miller recalled, "I had never looked upon the face of Judge Taney, but I knew of him. I remembered that he had attempted to throttle the Bank of the United States, and I hated him for it. . . . He had been the chief Spokesman of the Court in the Dred Scott case, and I hated him for that. But from my first acquaintance with him, I realized that these feelings toward him were but the suggestions of the worst elements of our nature; for before the first term of my service in the Court had passed, I more than liked him; I loved him."[8]

A striking feature of Taney's career was the relatively few personal attacks made on him by his enemies, especially in the light of his continued participation in controversial matters. Hostile contemporary commentators on his actions as a Maryland politician resorted only to standard mild caricature, and he escaped much of the calumny heaped on the Jackson administration, despite being the central figure in attacks on the Bank of the United States. Only after *Dred Scott* did he undergo savage public criticism.

Part of Taney's ability to avoid personal antagonisms can be traced to his ethereality. He was frail and withdrawn, preoccupied with his health and that of his family. He was not ambitious, although he never declined advancement to a higher office; and despite the sensitivity of his disposition, he was not upset by criticism and was scrupulously moderate when provoked. He retreated from work whenever his physical energies were taxed to their limit (which was frequently), and was often absent from the Court, but he persevered for twenty-eight years as Chief Justice and died in harness, as he had said he would. He was morbidly fearful of crowds, suffering from stage fright as an advocate, and his voice was variously described as feeble and hollow; yet he was markedly effective in argument. It was said that his presentations were so clear and created such an impression of conviction that his audience never focused on his unprepossessing appearance.[9]

In personal relations Taney's strong suits were subtlety and tact. He was neither a gregarious nor a dominating personality and was never able to mold the Court to his views as Marshall had been able to do. Under Taney's tenure two of the solidifying features of the Marshall Court—the absence of dissenting opinions and the practice of having the Justices live together during the Term—disappeared. Characteristic of Taney's approach to his office was his assignment of two[10] of the first three important cases of his first term to associates, keeping only the *Charles River Bridge*[11] opinion for himself. All three cases involved major issues and represented significant departures from the Marshall Court—types of cases Marshall had appropriated for the Chief Justiceship. Taney preferred to influence others through the power of suggestion rather than of persuasion, as a letter to President Jackson in 1833 indicates.

Taney's object was to induce Jackson to remove deposits from the National Bank and to appoint him Secretary of the Treasury. To that end he summarized the difficulties involved in the deposit policy, stating that although no man but Jackson was "strong enough to meet and destroy [the Bank],"[12] the risks were perhaps too great, and he (Taney) would understand if the effort were not made; and he indicated that he thought himself not well qualified to be Secretary of the Treasury, but was willing to defer to Jackson's wishes. The effect of the letter was to feed Jackson's competitive spirit, rouse him to action against the Bank, and secure Taney the Treasury nomination.

Taney's reticence and equanimity masked a capacity for passionate opinions, stubbornness, and irascibility, which as an adult he completely suppressed in public. Having once made his mind up on an issue, he was not apt to change it; and when he regarded the issue as a matter of principle, he was willing to go the limit in its defense. His early misgivings about slavery had been superseded by a conviction that the states had complete independence in dealing with the slave trade and that any interference with their sovereignty in this respect was intolerable. This judgment led him not only to declare the unconstitutionality of the Missouri Compromise,[13] but also, in a hypothetical opinion, that of Lincoln's Emancipation Proclamation.[14]

The tradition of judicial performance that Taney had inherited from Marshall assumed considerable participation by the judiciary in high affairs of state and a large measure of judicial freedom to interpret the Constitution in accordance with the changing "crisis of human affairs." Though Taney was to differ with Marshall on specific issues and on the extent of permissible judicial involvement in "political" questions, he essentially accepted Marshall's activist theory of the judicial function and attempted to adapt it to what he regarded as the peculiarly pressing social needs of his time. He sought, in this task, a technique of analyzing questions of commerce in order to resolve conflicts raised by economic expansion; a theory of sovereignty in a federal system in order to reflect the diffusion of political power in nineteenth-century America; and a judicial reconciliation of the divisive slavery issue. He pursued each goal in the activist tradition he had inherited from Marshall, but he was ultimately unable to make use of the principal justification for Marshallian activism: appeal to the common philosophical principles on which American civilization was founded. In Taney's tenure Americans were divided on first principles; denied that appeal, Taney turned cautious, then stubborn, leaving himself and his office unguarded.

II

The Marshall Court, in the course of its existence, had proved alternatively receptive and hostile to economic development. Its constructions of the contracts and commerce clauses of the Constitution had created major incentives, then barriers, to the unrestricted private use of property. The contracts clause, as interpreted in the vested rights doctrine, gave original property holders a right to "the fruits of their labor," and also allowed them to block further use of lands they had been granted. The doctrine of federal pre-emption of commerce had fostered traffic on the nation's waterways, but by the 1830s it apparently precluded state regulation of commercial enterprises, often an incentive for state subsidization of private entrepreneurial activity. Pressure on Marshall Court doctrines from the second wave of economic expansion in the early nineteenth century could be seen in the almost unprecedented dissension fostered in that Court by the *Charles River Bridge* case, first argued in 1830 and undecided for six years.[15]

Taney's opinion in *Charles River Bridge* represented an intermediate position between the primacy given vested rights by the Marshall Court and the eventual subordination by courts, such as the Supreme Judicial Court of Massachusetts under Shaw, of property rights to the public welfare. Taney rested his arguments on the assumption that a state had the power to "promote the happiness and property of the community" and could restrict private property rights in the process. Surrender of that power through grants of absolute monopolies was possible but should not be presumed unless the legislature had explicitly indicated such a purpose, for "the whole community" had an interest in reserving the power in the state. Unless a particular grant openly surrendered the power, then it should be construed as "preserving it undiminished." In *Charles River Bridge* the original grant was not explicit, and hence it was to be read in favor of the public. The rights of private property were to be "sacredly guarded," but only when intentionally immunized from legislative scrutiny, for "the community also [had] rights, and . . . the happiness and well being of every citizen depend[ed] on their faithful preservation."[16]

The interpretation of the contracts clause advanced in *Charles River Bridge* set the tone for subsequent treatments of vested rights by the Taney Court. Infringements by states of the rights of previous grantees were generally tolerated on the basis that certain powers, such as taxing[17] or eminent domain,[18] were implicit in state sovereignty and would be considered reserved by the states unless explicitly surrendered. This approach did not prevent the occasional protection of vested rights when they were affected by changes in state mortgage laws[19] or in laws taxing banks.[20] But in general the contracts clause barrier to state regulation of private economy activity was removed during Taney's tenure. This development did not, as Story feared, deter entrepreneurs from entering into risky new ventures; in fact it created incentives for state support of those ventures, since the states could rely on retaining control over the enterprises they subsidized. The massive growth of the railroad industry between 1850 and 1860 was a product of such thinking. Railroad proprietors were permitted to infringe the rights of competing transportation franchises but remained, under potential state control regarding the location of their routes and the pricing of their services.

A second potential constitutional barrier to economic expansion was the commerce clause, as interpreted by the Marshall Court. In *Gibbons v. Ogden,*[21] that Court had held that where a federal statute affecting commerce conflicted with a state statute, the federal regulation prevailed. The Court did not directly resolve the question whether the commerce clause prevented all state regulation of interstate commerce or merely those regulations that conflicted with existent federal statutes. At least one Justice, Johnson, had taken the position that the federal government had pre-empted the field so that no state regulation of interstate commerce was permissible even in the absence of federal activity. This view, if followed by the Taney Court, would have had profound effects on the commercial development of the nation, for it would have meant that any business engaged in interstate commerce would have been immune from state regulation. It also had implications for the growth of slavery, since by the 1830s several states had passed laws regulating the slave traffic and providing procedures for the capture and return of fugitive slaves. Pre-emption of that power by Congress would have immeasurably affected the investment of Southern states in the slave trade.

Taney quickly moved to dispel the notion of federal pre-emption, but had difficulty articulating an overriding rationale to which his whole Court could subscribe. *New York v. Miln*[22] tested the validity of a New York statute requiring the masters of ships entering the Port of New York to supply the state with information about the health and financial condition of immigrant passengers. The purpose of the statute was to enable New York to prevent impoverished immigrants from entering the state. The Court sustained the statute against a claim that it regulated interstate commerce, holding that persons were not articles of commerce and the act was a legitimate exercise of the state's police powers. In the *License Cases,*[23] however, that distinction was not possible, since the contested statutes regulated the sale of liquors. Taney, in a concurring opinion, attempted to set forth a new theory of federal-state relations under the commerce clause. His theory assumed a concurrent power in-states to regulate commerce within its borders, even if that commerce subsequently passed beyond the state, so long as the regulation of internal traffic did not conflict with an existing federal statute. In the case of liquor, Congress had sanctioned its importation; hence no state could prevent that. But the liquor traffic, having entered a state, had an internal commerce within it that the state could regulate in the absence of Congressional regulation. Taney's theory thus required a twofold inquiry under the commerce clause: whether the traffic regulated was "internal," and whether Congress had occupied the field. If the first question was answered in the affirmative and the second in the negative, state regulation was permissible.

Under this formula Taney had no difficulty distinguishing subjects that states could regulate from those they could not. States could tax immigrants entering their ports, but not American citizens;[24] they could authorize construction of bridges in the absence of Congressional action, even though the bridges obstructed navigation;[25] but they could not tax shipments for export, since Congress had pre-empted that field.[26] Further, a state could enact bankruptcy laws, even though Congress possessed that power—but such state laws had no force outside the state.[27] Similarly, a state could tax out-of-state legatees of property even if Congress attempted, through a treaty, to create a tax exemption for certain foreigners.[28] In short, the commerce clause did not preclude all state regulation of commerce; state sovereignty set limits on the exclusivity of federal regulatory power.

Taney's formulation nonetheless allowed a considerable range of federal autonomy. One decision of his greatly expanded the admiralty jurisdiction of the federal courts and thereby the federal control of navigation on the inland waterways;[29] another allowed the development of a uniform federal commercial law by holding that federal courts were not bound to follow the decisions of state courts in commercial cases involving citizens of more than one state;[30] still another broadened federal court jurisdiction over corporations.[31] This last case promoted the interests of corporations by making it easier for them to escape hostile state courts but, in general, Taney was not inclined to protect banks or corporations from state regulation unless the privileges they claimed, such as immunity from taxation[32] or the right freely to engage in business in a state other than that of its domicile,[33] had been explicitly granted.

By and large, Taney's views on constitutional issues affecting economic development reflected his own attitudes toward various forms of entrepreneurial activity. He remained sympathetic toward landholding, including mortgage-holding,[34] hostile toward banks, suspicious of corporations, tolerant of federal power in a few limited areas such as navigation, and zealously protective of state powers in most instances, especially where implicit or dormant federal powers were the basis of pre-empting state activity. His decisions reflected those views, but rested on narrow and subtle distinctions that did not bring to his side a majority of his Court and rarely secured unanimity. The distinctions indicated more than lawyers' artfulness and political caution. They reflected the contradictory impulses of economic life in early-nineteenth-century America, where the antinomies of security and progress, stability and expansionism, and order and efficiency maintained an uneasy coexistence.

III

Taney's re-evaluations of the commerce and contracts clauses rested on a novel theory of sovereignty designed to respond to the diffusion of political power in America, to the greater diversity of attitudes and interests manifested in its growing population, and, above all, to the need of the South to maintain and expand its unique system of labor. Taney's purpose was to recast the conceptions of sovereignty held by the Founding Fathers and assumed by Marshall in the light of the growing sectional character of nineteenth-century American civilization.

Taney's theory underscored the states' role in a federal system. His theory counterpointed Marshall's: it began with the same assumptions—that after the Revolution sovereignty rested in the people, who then delegated it in part to various governments—but then emphasized the powers reserved for the states rather than those surrendered to the general government. Taney conceded that the states had surrendered particular powers to the federal government, but maintained that they were otherwise "absolutely and unconditionally sovereign within their respective territories."[35] These two starting points spawned a series of "angry and irritating controversies between sovereignties,"[36] since the extent to which the federal government could disturb asserted state supremacy, by actions "necessary" to implement its own conceded powers, had not been determined. The limits of state and federal power were to be determined ultimately by the Supreme Court, which functioned not only to maintain the supremacy of the national government but also to protect the states from federal usurpation of their reserved powers.

The Court was an appropriate institution to resolve controversies between sovereignties because it was not like a state court, yet, unlike other federal courts, it was not solely the creation of Congress. It had been "erected," according to Taney, "and . . . powers . . . conferred upon it, not by the Federal government, but by the people of the States, who formed and adopted that Government."[37] It owed its allegiances neither to federal nor to state governments as such but to the people, in their capacity as citizens of both the nation and their respective states.

Since controversies between states and the federal government had recurred increasingly with the diffusion of political power in the early nineteenth century, Taney's view assumed, in some areas, the presence of an activist judiciary, upholding federal supremacy where necessary but emphasizing primarily the importance of the states in a federal system. In its reinterpretations of the commerce clause, the vested rights doctrine, admiralty jurisdiction, and the relations between state and federal law, the Taney Court proved itself as bold and free-wheeling as its predecessor. But in other respects his Court set limitations on its exercise of power. In cases between 1838 and 1854 Taney employed the "political questions" doctrine to preclude judicial determination of the legitimate composition of Rhode Island's state legislature[38] and of the right of a foreign government to recognition by the United States,[39] and maintained that the Court could not resolve state boundary disputes involving jurisdiction rather than physical property.[40] He also read narrowly the Constitution's requirement that courts decide only "cases and controversies," holding that the Court could not review the findings of a territorial court with regard to land claims of Spanish citizens against the United States,[41] and could not review judgments of the Court of Claims if those judgments were to be executed in the future.[42] In commercial law, by contrast, the Court, in the famous case of *Swift v. Tyson,*[43] claimed power to disregard the findings of state courts. By 1851 a commentator claimed that in commercial law both the state courts and the Supreme Court were "courts of final and coordinate jurisdiction."[44]

Despite these qualifications on the Court's power, Taney's conception of the judicial function assumed that the appellate judiciary would continue to be a source of political statesmanship. His theory of sovereignty was meaningless, in the face of Marshall Court precedents, without active participation by his Court to redress the balance between federal and state sovereignties. The theory rested in fact on the assumption that in matters of peculiarly sectional concern the states were the appropriate regulatory forum, and their judgments were presumptively entitled to respect. Taney's preference for state supremacy proved explosive in the area of slavery.

IV

The slavery controversy incorporated within itself the major themes of Taney's term of office. At one level it was an issue involving economic expansion in that it questioned whether a particular system of labor could be prohibited in new areas of the nation where conditions appeared favorable for its use. At another level it tested the extent to which political diffusion and sectional diversity would be tolerated in America by asking whether a region committed to the practice of slavery could remain an influential political force in the American nation, or even a part of that nation at all. Finally, it asked to what extent American society was grounded on ideological principles and to what extent those principles could be abandoned in practice. Were all men, or only white men, created equal? Were all men endowed with the rights of life and liberty, or could blacks be summarily deprived of those rights?

The extent to which the slavery issue raised these fundamental questions was not immediately perceived by nineteenth-century Americans. In the early years of the century there seems to have been a general belief, expressed by Taney as a Maryland state legislator, that slavery was an objectionable practice, that it was not flourishing and would gradually be abandoned, but that it should not forcibly be eradicated. The opening up of the trans-Mississippi

West, however, destroyed whatever consensus existed on slavery. Certain portions of the unsettled West appeared, in a geographical sense, capable of supporting an agricultural economy similar to that of the lower South, in which the economic importance of slave labor was inestimable. Moreover, even if cotton or rice or indigo were unsuited to the trans-Mississippi West, slavery might be useful in other areas, such as produce farming or even mining; and further expansion of the American nation might include areas of the Caribbean to which slavery was clearly adaptable.

Most important, the projected expansion of slavery highlighted the moral implications of the existing slave system. It was one thing to tell a Southerner how to manage his household, another to object in principle to a system that treated human beings as property and to deplore its emergence in new territories. But attacks on slavery at large invariably became attacks on the practices tolerated by particular Southern states, so that the South felt compelled to protest the most abstract form of criticism and to oppose the eradication of slavery even in territories, such as Oregon, in which it was apparently neither feasible nor desired by the residents. Increasingly in the 1840s and 1850s the slavery issue became a vehicle for pitting one region against another. The successive Congressional "compromises" on slavery, including the Missouri Compromise and the Compromise of 1850, rigorously preserved an absolute balance of power between North and South, as though a deviation from this equilibrium would result in the imposition of one region's ideology on the other.

By the time Taney replaced Marshall as Chief Justice it was clear that no easy or wholly satisfactory solution to the slavery issue was forthcoming, and the Court was reluctant to involve itself in the dispute. Issues of social controversy are often translated into appellate litigation, however, and in 1841 the case of *Groves v. Slaughter*[45] came before the Court. The case involved the constitutionality of a clause in the Mississippi Constitution prohibiting the introduction of slaves into Mississippi after 1833. A contract had been signed to bring slaves into the state after that year, and the question was whether the contract was voided by the state Constitution, and, if so, whether the state Constitution conflicted with the federal Constitution's commerce clause. Potentially at stake were the answers to the critical questions as to whether slaves were persons or articles of commerce, and whether, if they were persons, they were citizens of the United States.

The Taney Court, on that occasion, managed to avoid deciding both those questions by finding that the clause in the Mississippi Constitution required enabling legislation to be effective, and since no such legislation had been passed, the contract was valid. Justice McLean, however, wrote a concurring opinion in which he faced the commerce question and found that state sovereignty prevailed over the commerce clause with regard to the slave trade. McLean's intent was to show that antislavery states could prohibit the introduction of slavery, but his opinion was also read as conceding to the slave states a power to prohibit free blacks from entering their borders.[46]

Groves v. Slaughter hinted at divisions within the Taney Court on the slavery issue; they came to the surface in *Prigg v. Pennsylvania,*[47] decided in 1842. *Prigg* involved a Pennsylvania statute modifying the Fugitive Slave Act of 1793. The question it raised was whether the power of Congress to prescribe regulations for the return of fugitive slaves was exclusive. The Court found that it was, and so held the Pennsylvania statute unconstitutional. In the course of his opinion, however, Story maintained that this exclusive federal power over fugitive slaves prohibited the states not only from enacting laws modifying the effect of the Fugitive Slave Act, but even from enacting laws implementing it. Between 1843 and 1848, six Northern states enacted legislation forbidding compliance with the Act; in 1850 Congress responded with a more comprehensive fugitive slave law. Taney dissented from the latter portion of Story's opinion, maintaining that state noncompliance with the Fugitive Slave Act was impermissible.

Reaction to the *Prigg* decision demonstrated how inextricably the Court had been drawn into the politics of the slave issue. Northern newspapers denounced the Court for upholding the Act; a Southern senator called *Prigg* "one of the most unfortunate decisions in its effect upon the South of any that has ever been made."[48] While a new fugitive slave law was being debated in Congress, efforts were made to expose the Court's pro-Southern composition and to suggest that it would invariably support the South on slavery questions. Senator Charles Sumner of Massachusetts went so far as to suggest that Congress could ignore the decisons of the Court.[49]

In 1851 Taney delivered the opinion of the Court in *Strader v. Graham.*[50] That case involved the question whether slaves who had gone from Kentucky (a slave state) to Ohio (a free state) and then returned to Kentucky had lost their slave status. The Kentucky Court of Appeals had held that they had not.

The Supreme Court refused to decide the case, finding that the question was one of Kentucky law and that nothing in the Constitution was contrary to it. Thus, no federal question existed, and the Court was without jurisdiction to review the decision of the Kentucky Court of Appeals. Taney's opinion, grounded on the narrowest of holdings, had wider implications, however, since the individual determination of slave status in cases of this kind were left to slave-state courts. Characteristically, Taney's opinion was subtle and cautious, its broad ramifications made implicit rather than explicit.

If *Strader v. Graham* seemed to settle questions regarding the interchange of slaves between slave states and free states, it had not resolved the question of the effect of a slave's subsequent residence in one of the territories of the trans-Mississippi West. The status of slavery in those territories reappeared as a national issue after 1848, when the Mexican War vastly increased the western holdings of the United States. The Missouri Compromise has prohibited slavery in certain territories, but in 1854 it had been repealed by the Kansas-Nebraska Act, and the choice of slavery had been left to the settlers of the new territories. Meanwhile, the *Dred Scott* case had begun to work its way up to the Court. By 1852 the Missouri Supreme Court had held that Scott, originally a slave in Missouri, subsequently taken into the free state of Illinois and Wisconsin Territory and then returned to Missouri, had become a slave on return. Scott's lawyers, anxious to secure a disposition of the issue by the Supreme Court, then brought suit in federal circuit court against John F. A. Sanford, the brother-in-law of Scott's original owner, who may have been acting as the agent of Scott's owner's widow. Sanford was a resident of New York, and the case thus had the requisite diversity of citizenship. The trial judge ruled that Scott, who had alleged that he was a citizen of Missouri, was eligible to bring suit in the federal courts, but that because he had returned to Missouri he remained Sanford's property. The case then proceeded on a writ of error to the Supreme Court, being placed on the docket in the 1854 Term.

The *Dred Scott* case was remarkably similar to *Strader v. Graham,* and seemed dispositive on similar grounds. There were, however, two complicating factors: for one thing, Scott had gone from a slave state to a territory where Congress had outlawed slavery, not to a free state; further, Scott was claiming United States citizenship by virtue of his suit in a federal court. Potentially, then, the case raised three issues: first, whether a slave permanently lost his slave status when taken into a free territory; second, whether Congress could outlaw slavery in the Territories; and third, whether a black alleging himself to be free was a citizen of the United States. The first question was virtually on all fours with that decided in *Strader v. Graham*, and the latter two were politically so explosive that it was doubtful that the Court would decide them—or so commentators at the time thought.[51]

The Taney Court divided first on whether it could entertain the case at all because of the jurisdictional question raised by Scott's citizenship, and in May 1856 the case was set down for reargument. While it was pending, the Presidential election of 1856 was held. James Buchanan was elected, and was to assume the office in March of 1857. A series of extraordinary events then took place. *Dred Scott* was reargued in December 1856, and the Justices first considered it in conference in February 1857. There a majority of the Court decided, with two dissenters, to resolve the case by following *Strader v. Graham*—that is, holding that Missouri law determined Scott's status in Missouri and that since Scott was considered a slave in Missouri he could not bring suit in a federal court. This decision avoided passing either on the citizenship question or on the constitutionality of the Missouri Compromise. Taney, himself a member of the majority, assigned Justice Samuel Nelson (New York) the task of writing the Court's opinion. The dissenters, Justices John McLean (Ohio) and Benjamin Curtis (Massachusetts), resolved, however, to address in their opinions the constitutionality of the Missouri Compromise and to sustain the power of Congress to prohibit slavery in the territories.

Learning of this, the members of the majority reconsidered, and some, notably Justice James Wayne (Georgia), determined to counter the dissenters by reaching the constitutionality of the Missouri Compromise and declaring it void. Wayne persuaded four of the majority Justices, Taney among them, to abandon Nelson's opinion and replace it with one by Taney that would decide all the issues in the case. Nelson and Justice Robert Grier (Pennsylvania) tentatively refused to commit themselves to this procedure, so that a bare 5–4 majority now appeared to exist in behalf of a comprehensive disposition of the case.

At this point Justice John Catron (Tennessee) wrote a letter to President-elect Buchanan suggesting that he write Justice Grier and impress him with the necessity for settling all the points at issue in the case. Catron did not tell Buchanan the proposed outcome of the case, but Grier's position was particularly significant in that, whereas the other five Justices who had formed the new majority—Taney, Wayne, Catron, John Campbell (Alabama), and Peter Daniel (Virginia)—were all Southerners, Buchanan, like Grier, was a Pennsylvanian. Buchanan wrote Grier, and Grier responded by telling Buchanan the outcome of *Dred Scott,* agreeing to concur with Taney's opinion and informing Buchanan that the opinion would not be handed down before March 4, Buchanan's Inauguration Day. Having received that letter, Buchanan said in his Inaugural that the question of the permissibility of slavery in the territories was a judicial question to be decided by the Court, and he would "cheerfully submit" to the Court's decision, which he expected would "finally settle" the issue.[52]

The decision by the new majority to resolve all the issues raised by the *Dred Scott* case was all the more remarkable because by deciding the citizenship issue against Scott they made irrelevant the issue of the constitutionality of the Missouri Compromise and left themselves open to the charge that passing on its constitutionality was a gratuitous invasion by the Court into the political arena. Equally remarkable was the strong language used by Taney in his historical argument that Africans had not been considered American citizens. Taney said, among other things, that at the time of the framing of the Constitution blacks were considered "a subordinate and inferior class of beings"; that they "had been subjugated by the dominant race, and whether emancipated or not, yet remained subject to their authority"; that they "had no rights or privileges but such as those who held the power and the Government might choose to grant them"; and that they had "no rights which the white man was bound to respect."[53] Such attitudes Taney described as "universal[ly]" held. Contemporary critics of the *Dred Scott* opinion immediately asserted that this language represented Taney's own views rather than the views of most Americans at the time the word "citizen" was introduced into the Constitution.[54]

Finally, Taney's argument with regard to the constitutionality of the Missouri Compromise stretched his talent for subtle legal distinctions to its limits. He made a very narrow reading of the constitutional clause empowering Congress to make rules and regulations respecting the territories of the United States. He distinguished "rules and regulations" from more general legislation, proposed that the federal government merely held territories in trust for "the benefit of the people of the several states," and concluded that acts of Congress prohibiting slavery in territories prevented American citizens from bringing their property into these territories, thereby depriving them of property without due process of law.[55]

Few decisions of the Court have stimulated as much heated commentary as the *Dred Scott*. The striking aspect of the commentary was its tendency to regard the decision as a venture by the Court into politics rather than an ordinary opinion. Both friends and critics of the decision called it a "stump speech" and an attempt by the Court to "thrust itself into the political contests," making it "a mere party machine."[56] Opponents of the decision called for a remodeling of the Court,[57] and for civil disobedience;[58] supporters suggested that resistance to the decision was tantamount to treason.[59] Taney was called "subtle, ingenious, sophistical and false," a "tricky lawyer" rather than an "upright judge," and one who "walked with inverted and hesitating steps," his forehead "contracted," his eyes "sunken," and his face with "a sinister expression."[60] A commentator at the time summarized the impact of such characterizations. "The country," he wrote, "will feel the consequences of the decision more deeply and more permanently, in the loss of confidence in the sound judicial integrity and strictly legal character of their tribunals."[61] Among other things, the decision stimulated irreparable conflicts among the Court's members, and Taney became so estranged from Curtis over the early publication of his dissent that Curtis resigned at the close of the 1857 term. To the end of his life Taney resisted criticism of the decision. As he wrote Franklin Pierce in 1857, he had "an abiding confidence that this act of [his] judicial life will stand the test of time and the sober judgment of the country,"[62] and he persisted in believing that attempts by the federal government to interfere, even in wartime, with relations between slaves and their owners were unconstitutional.[63]

V

It is easy to criticize the Taney Court for deciding the *Dred Scott* case at all or for deciding it in the manner chosen, and the facts behind the decision suggest that it was one of the least detached exercises of judicial power in American history. To choose to resolve highly controversial questions in a format in which their resolution was hardly necessary for a decision was surely a tactical error, doubtless the effect of the passions the case generated among the justices. It is too much to say, however, that the case precipitated the Civil War; it merely represented another unacceptable attempt to resolve the essentially unresolvable dilemma of the presence of slavery in America. It was not the Taney

Court's failure to solve the problem of slavery that disgraced it, but the manner in which its attempt was made.

Taney's career, at its close, illustrated the inescapably political character of judging in America; yet it also demonstrated the limitations of the judiciary as a political force. Under Taney the Court had been sensitive to economic and political change and had reinterpreted existing constitutional doctrines to make them responsive to new features of nineteenth-century American society. Several of its decisions in the areas of economic development and federal-state relations had been "popular" in the sense of providing judicial interpretations that harmonized with prevailing social attitudes or responded to emergent economic and political interests. The very tentativeness of the Court's course in those areas can be seen as politically skillful. Although the pace of change was acute, its direction seemed uncertain, and Taney's subtle distinctions helped steer a middle course between inertia and frenzy. But in the *Dred Scott* decision, by contrast, Taney chose not to reflect the ambivalences in public sentiment but to attempt a permanent resolution of an issue that had become increasingly unresolvable. By the time it reached the Taney Court, the *Dred Scott* case had become a symbolic manifestation of a conflict in values. A sizable minority of the nation had a heavy social and economic investment in the "peculiar institution," slavery; another sizable minority found it morally offensive. When a conflict in social values becomes that pervasive and profound, judicial reasoning cannot assuage it; sublety becomes artificiality, and statesmanship partisan politics.

The judiciary in America has not proved to be suited to the resolution of controversies in such instances. The legitimacy of judicial decisions rests on the public's willingness to accept the expertise and authority of the judicial office, which is itself based on the ability of judges to persuade by a process of reasoning in their opinions. Judicial reasons are in essence articulations of values; they persuade by appealing to shared beliefs whose existence may be only dimly perceived by the public at large. A judicial decision is "right" not by virtue of some transcendent quality of logic or reason, but because the values it affirms and appeals to are perceived as important and worthwhile by the general public. When no set of first principles emerges from the analysis of a case—when in fact the case dramatizes either the absence of such principles or a deep disagreement as to the appropriate values to be affirmed—judicial reasons lose their impartiality. At this point the judiciary can no longer effectively function, for its legitimacy rests on its separation from and transcendence of partisan discourse. If a court may be judged to have entered the political arena and is criticized on that arena's terms, as the Taney Court was after *Dred Scott,* it cannot help but lose stature.

In the end, the infamy that Taney brought upon himself by his opinion in *Dred Scott* stemmed from the fact that he made the alleged inferiority of blacks a principle of law. As the subsequent history of the nation has shown, a good many Americans have not been particularly disturbed by the *practice* of racial discrimination, even if that practice has been at odds with national ideals of fairness and equality. What was disturbing in *Dred Scott* was the *open justification* of discrimination by the legal system—the announcement that in a constitutional sense blacks were not equal, not deserving of fair treatment, and not entitled to the full panoply of inalienable natural rights. If this were so, the principle of the Declaration of Independence that all men were created equal either was a mockery without moral force or had a special set of racially based limitations. Some Americans were prepared to go to war over the question of whether one race could treat another as subhuman, and many would not abide a judicial declaration that such treatment was legitimate. In attempting that declaration, Taney overstepped the limits of judicial power. Under the pressure of events, he departed from his usual practice and sought a ringing affirmation of overriding principles, in the Marshall tradition. But the first principles had vanished; available in their place were only opposing sets of deeply held values. His choice between those sets of values exacerbated tensions in his own time and has left him vulnerable to the moral censure of later generations.

4 

Political Ideologies, Professional Norms, and the State Judiciary in the Late Nineteenth Century: Cooley and Doe

I

The review functions of the federal appellate judiciary, as established by Marshall and refined by his successors, together with the potentially vast expansion in the jurisdiction of the federal courts augured by the Reconstruction Amendments, might have inclined one to predict, in the 1870s, that the resolution of significant legal issues by American appellate courts would henceforth take place primarily at the federal level. Such a prediction, however, would have ignored the intimate connection (already illustrated by the careers of Kent and Shaw) between state appellate judging and the regulation of the American economy.

Since state constitutions were patterned on the federal Constitution, with its tripartite division of powers, and since state legislatures were active in the area of economic regulation throughout the nineteenth century, delicate questions involving the allocation of power among governmental branches or the limits of legislative authority over private enterprise were regularly entrusted to the state judiciary before 1900. These cases represented ideological and political disputes of the first magnitude. Since Congress had tacitly allowed the states to take the lead in regulating entrepreneurial activity, the pattern of regulation tolerated by state courts came to serve as a pattern for the nation. The states became testing grounds for extensions of governmental power over the lives of individuals under the rubric of state "police powers"—powers derived from the perceived duty of the states to protect the health, welfare, safety, and morals of their citizens. The police powers doctrine had first been employed by state judges such as Shaw; its first major challenge was also to come in the state courts.

Closely tied to questions of legislative prerogative were separation-of-powers issues. Each time that a state court invalidated or tolerated legislative regulation of private activity it implicitly took a position on the scope of its own authority. If legislative control of a particular activity was impermissible, judicial control, through the evolutionary process of the common law, loomed as a possible alternative. A consequence of judicial invalidation of legislation, then, was the emergency of the judiciary as a protector of private economic or civil rights. Alternatively, judicial toleration of police power regulations suggested either a sympathy with the content of the regulation or a narrow view of the scope of judicial regulatory power. In each of these instances the decisions of state courts had political and ideological implications.

The state judiciary in nineteenth-century American was thus not isolated from matters of national political importance. Yet because of the nature of the decision-making process among state judges of that time and because of rapid and pervasive shifts in the political vocabulary of the nineteenth century, terms used traditionally to describe the ideological character of judicial decisions, such as "liberal" or "conservative," require special definition as applied to the late-nineteenth-century state judiciary. Twentieth-century perspectives on economic regulation, for example, confuse matters. If liberalism and conservatism are distinguished from one another in terms of a respective sympathy and antipathy toward rapid change and government regulation of private enterprise, then governmental policies from the New Deal through the 1960s can be considered liberal. On the other hand, belief in the autonomy of a system of "free enterprise" can be identified with conservatism. In the nineteenth century, however, American attitudes toward the issue of government regulation of private enterprise went through three phases, none of which can be categorized in twentieth-century terms.

In the first phase, which served as the ideological context for most of Kent's decisions, legislative promotion of entrepreneurial ventures, such as bridge and turnpike construction, was considered inimical to established landholding interests, since it prevented them from restricting the future use of their lands. Eminent domain, as conceived by Kent, was a device intended to insure compensation for established landholders, should portions of their property be confiscated by states to promote internal improvements. Under Shaw, however, eminent domain became a weapon for change. The state governments that granted franchises reserved the right to regulate them in the public interest; hence in this phase governmental regulation served to promote change and was resisted by existent elites.

As the effects of state promotion of privately financed internal improvements became clear, a reorientation of political attitudes took place. A turnpike or railroad charter, if interpreted to create an exclusive franchise in the grantee, was an immensely lucrative holding. Having secured a franchise, the builders of internal improvements naturally resisted competition, so that by the 1830s and 1840s economic liberty and equality became slogans of the Jacksonian Democrats. In the political alignments of that period, the Whigs, who favored government promotion and regulation of internal improvement ventures, could be said to have represented a conservative point of view.

The growth of the railroad industry and attendant industrialization after 1850 introduced yet another phase. In contrast to the older model of state-private partnership, railroad networks were built in the Midwest, South, and West with much less state participation. As extant railroad networks expanded, the federal government simply used its eminent domain power to grant swaths of state land for railroad beds. Interstate railroad traffic was within the regulatory ambit of the federal government, but Congress did not choose to exercise its regulatory powers. At the advent of the industrial revolution in America, then, the mode of transportation that helped engender that revolution was essentially free of government regulation.

In the absence of federal action, certain states attempted to reinstitute themselves as the regulators of transportation franchises. They were met by opposition from railroad interests and those industries whose shipping volume was sufficient to merit favorable treatment from the interstate railroads. Apologists for these groups articulated a philosophy of government that envisioned a free market without governmental interference. Although the groups they represented had become established elites with startling suddenness, they nonetheless were the "vested" interests of the post-Civil War years. In contrast, among the supporters of government regulation were farmers and small shippers, groups who were disadvantaged in a free-market situation.

The slogans of Jacksonian Democrats—free trade, economic liberty, equality of opportunity—were adopted by conservative political theorists of the late nineteenth century. The inviolability of private property came to be talked about in terms resembling those employed by Kent, but in a vastly different context. The ease with which Jacksonian concepts were employed to justify the dominant position of post-Civil War industrialists testified to the ambivalent character of the theories of economic equality and liberty advanced in the 1830s. On one hand, those theories constituted radical attacks on special privilege; on the other, they recalled notions of inviolate private property—notions that had originated in the eighteenth century. Updated, they made the principles of egalitarianism and libertarianism—when the reference was to economic issues—attractive to conservatives.

In a limited sense, then, judicial responses to state regulation of private enterprise in the nineteenth century may be seen as an index of political attitudes that were manifested in interpretations of the function of a judge. Kent viewed the judiciary as a buffer between established wealth and the excessively democratic legislature. Shaw tended to defer to legislative prerogatives—thereby circumscribing the role of the judiciary—but generally agreed with the regulatory policies expressed by the Massachusetts legislature during his tenure. Taney likewise applauded legislative attempts to curb corporate privilege and to maintain the prerogatives of slaveholders, and found support for them in the Constitution. Field, after sustaining paternalistic legislation while on the California Supreme Court, became one of the chief theorists of negative judicial activism, in which the judiciary was perceived as an omnipresent watchman against legislative usurpation of private property rights.

Justice Thomas Cooley of the Michigan Supreme Court and Chief Justice Charles Doe of the New Hampshire Supreme Court had as their collective period of service the years 1859–1896, in which nineteenth-century attitudes toward government regulation of private enterprise, notably railroads, were in their third phase. Each had discernible views about the value of government regulation and the proper role of the judiciary in that process. But the attitudes of Cooley and Doe toward the major political issues of their day do not altogether explain the impact of their careers or the source of their reputations. Cooley achieved prominence more as a treatise writer than as a judge, and some of his judicial decisions have been thought to deviate from the thrust of his scholarly writings.[1] Doe resists characterization in orthodox political terms: his reputation has been based primarily on his remarkably innovative approach to the process of judicial decision-making.

The careers of Cooley and Doe illustrate the presence of another set of variables affecting the work of appellate judges, especially at the state level. In addition to their political constituency of citizens who often directly elect them, state judges have a professional constituency: the lawyers who practice before them and the clients of those lawyers. In periods such as the late nineteenth century, when the function of state judges is essentially a common-law function of interpreting the meaning of existing judicial decisions in new factual circumstances, judicial innovation takes on an expanded meaning. It is more than "liberalism" or "conservatism"; it is, in most instances, a departure from established judicial practice. If prior judicial decisions may be thought of as guides of conduct to lawyers and their clients, the clearer and more unchanging the guideline the more certain can professional constituents be that actions they advise or undertake will not run counter to the law. Conversely, the less reliance a court places on its prior decisions, the less predictability it insures its professional constituents.

Opposed to the values of certainty and predictability in common law decision-making is that of flexibility. A prior decision is never an authoritative resolution of all future cases, unless those cases are identical to that previously decided. It is merely an analogy that may prove applicable in the next relatively similar case. It may not prove applicable, however, for any number of reasons, not the least being that considerations of public policy that lent support to the prior decision may not be operative in the next case or may have ceased to be thought important. If a court rigidly applies the prior decision to cover all succeeding similar cases, it may ultimately reach a result that in its particular context is thought unjust. Part of the value of common law decision-making, then, is that prior judicial decisions are regarded as persuasive but not conclusive; they can be distinguished or even overruled. In this manner a system of judge-made law responds to change.

At various times in American history, for reasons having to do with relations between ideology and changing social conditions, different theories of judicial decision-making have been in vogue.[2] Shaw, favoring flexibility, assumed in his adjudication calculus that previous decisions, being manifestations of larger principles, were always subject to modification. During the tenure of Cooley and of Doe the values of certainty and predictability came into fashion, primarily because of a perception of social chaos and widespread, rapid change that gripped late-nineteenth-century Americans, with a resultant need for intellectual theories that would lend stability and purpose to the universe. Law was not the only academic discipline affected by this need: rigid economic, sociological, and biological "laws" were created to afford stability at roughly the same time.[3] One class of persons particularly interested in achieving stability and predictability in their affairs was the large transportation and industrial interests. One way that state courts could respond to this concern was by slavishly following precedents.

An interest in achieving certainty or predictability through judicial decisions is not always the equivalent of conservatism, as a hypothetical example will illustrate. Assume that in the 1820s a state grants franchises to turnpike companies and supervises the rates charged by those companies. An 1830 decision of that state's highest court sustains the legislature's authority to ensure that the rates charged be "reasonable." Fifty years pass, and turnpikes are replaced by railroads as the major mode of transportation in the state. For a time the state legislature exercises no control over railroad rates, and the railroads make several types of price discriminations. In the 1880s protests against railroad rebates and other forms of price discrimination arise, and the state passes a law creating a commission empowered to fix railroad rates. The constitutionality of that law is challenged. In this situation the railroads could expect, in the face of the 1830 turnpike decision, that they would be treated like turnpikes and that the state's power to set rates would be sustained. This would be the predictable result. But the railroads would argue, in challenging the law, that railroads differed from turnpikes because of the economics of the industry, which necessitated price discriminations; or that new considerations of public policy that had emerged in the fifty-year period necessitated a distinction between turnpikes and railroads; or that the earlier decision had been an erroneous interpretation of legislative powers under the state constitution.

In advancing these arguments the railroads would be emphasizing the value of flexibility in the common law to secure a result in keeping with a conservative perspective. Since railroads had in the fifty years after 1830 become an entrenched elite in the transportation field in the state, and since they had achieved this position in the absence of state regulation, judicial support for the new regulatory statute would necessitate a radical change in their operations. But if they secured a decision distinguishing them from turnpikes, the railroads would be ensuring freedom for themselves to maintain their business as they had maintained it for the past fifty years.

To be sure, common law issues can be seen as having a political or ideological tinge: single plaintiffs sue large companies, landowners sue squatters, and some of those classes of litigants are more eager to resist sweeping political change than are others. But in the great range of state common law cases in the late nineteenth century the basic questions largely involved relations between the state court and its professional constituency. Thus, was the court innovative, or inclined to follow the decisions of its predecessors? was it interested in promulgating and maintaining a static system of legal rules, or did it consider responsiveness to change one of the chief responsibilities of interpreters of the common law? did it associate legal change with the judicial branch of government, or primarily confine innovation to the legislature? The response of leading state judges often turned not so much on their political affiliations or their preference for one social class or group over another as on their attitudes toward freedom and restraint in the use of their office, their respect for the pronouncements of prior courts, and their temperamental responsiveness to change.

II

Thomas Cooley shared with Joseph Story an appetite for scholarship, a clarity of expression, and an abundance of energy, but lacked Story's charm, conviviality, attraction to controversy, and flair. Both men were treatise writers of great influence, judges whose tenure surpassed twenty years, public officials, successful private practitioners, and the dominant professors at a generative period of a major law school. But where Story made a strong impression, for better or for worse, on his contemporaries, Cooley made a mild one. Story's students at Harvard remembered him as the teller of delightful anecdotes, whereas Cooley's at

Michigan recalled that he presented careful, clear lectures in a dry, measured monotone. Had Cooley not been a lawyer, a colleague speculated, he might have been a "great financier":[4] he was sound, meticulous, well-organized, moderate, and parsimonious. His tastes were simple, he never took a vacation, and he was a regular churchgoer. As a young practitioner, he was, like Kent, apparently too retiring in his manner to generate much business; as a trial advocate he was "not promine[n]t . . . and never could have [been]";[5] he allegedly never sought advancement to any of the offices he held; and his best-known treatise, *Constitutional Limitations*, which first appeared in 1868, was the product of a series of lectures that Cooley wrote only after his colleagues on the University of Michigan Law School faculty had declined to do so.

Cooley was born in upstate New York and had only a minimal formal education, attending grammar school before first reading law at the age of eighteen in a law office in Palmyra. As with Bradley, there are familiar boyhood stories indicating that Cooley was eager for an education and was an intellectual self-starter.

Evidence of these traits appeared also in his later life, when he became an amateur historian and produced a history of Michigan published in 1885. After a year at Palmyra, Cooley traveled westward, apparently heading for Chicago, but settled in Adrian, Michigan, and there continued reading law until 1846, when he was admitted to the Michigan bar. For the next eleven years he was a relatively successful itinerant small town practitioner. In 1847 he formed a partnership with another lawyer in Tecumseh, Michigan; dissolved that and returned to a law office in Adrian in 1848; moved to Toledo, Ohio, to set up his own practice in 1854; and returned to Adrian in 1855. During the same period he dabbled in newspaper writing, farming, and real estate, and was a county circuit court commissioner and a village recorder.

In 1857 the Democrat-controlled Michigan legislature created a state supreme court, and in 1858 Cooley, a loyal Democrat, was named court reporter. At that time the office of reporter, as witnessed by the careers of Henry Wheaton and William Johnson, was one of special influence. Reporters commonly argued cases before the judges whose decisions they published. Cooley argued over forty cases before the Supreme Court of Michigan in the seven years he served as reporter. The reportership not only greatly enhanced Cooley's career as a practitioner; it also made him a logical candidate for the faculty of the state law school, which was established in 1859.

In 1864, "as if by a sort of natural selection,"[6] Cooley was elected an Associate Justice of the Michigan Supreme Court on the Republican ticket. Like many other Democrats, he had changed parties during the Civil War (in several Northern states the Democratic party was impotent or discredited for several years after 1860). Cooley was closely acquainted with the Michigan Supreme Court justices (who were all Republicans until 1884), and particularly with James V. Campbell, who had been appointed with him as a charter member of the Michigan law faculty. Although Campbell may have been influential in securing Cooley's nomination in 1864, he was to clash continually with him on the bench until Cooley's resignation in 1885.

Cooley, after twenty years of service on the Supreme Court, was defeated for re-election by Allen B. Morse, a Democrat. Cooley's defeat has been attributed to his alienation of the growing labor movement in Michigan, his sympathy with the railroads and the general resurgence of the Democrats in the 1880s.[7] His retirement from the bench did not blunt his capacity for work, and he quickly found other outlets. Despite his intention to enter private practice, in 1886 he was appointed receiver of the bankrupt Wabash Railroad and in 1887 was named a commissioner of the newly created Interstate Commerce Commission, with which he remained until his retirement in 1891 for reasons of health.

Cooley rivaled Story in his ability to pursue several full-time jobs at once. In 1883, for example, in his sixtieth year, he wrote over 140 judicial opinions, heard 600 cases, gave 100 one-hour lectures in the law school and the political science department at the University of Michigan, published three scholarly articles and two new editions of treatises, was advisory counsel to the city of Ann Arbor (where he resided), managed his properties in Lansing and Bay City, served as President of the Michigan Law School Alumni Association, and planned and supervised an addition to his house. When his health finally broke in 1891, he attributed it to compulsive labors of this sort.

Early in his career Cooley identified himself as a social theorist of Jacksonian democracy and its antecedents, among them, notably, the free-trade stance. He opposed special privilege and favored open access for all to economic benefits, opposed internal improvement schemes if they tended to favor particularistic interests, believed that local bodies were the most efficient units of government, and supported universal public education.[8] He was an active Democrat as a newspaper editor in Adrian in the 1840s and 1850s, and ran unsuccessfully for the office of Judge of the Toledo Court of Common Pleas. In some circles, however, his reputation has been that of an apologist for private enterprise who provided railroads and other giant "special interests" of the late nineteenth century with a legal rationale for their operations. One commentator has suggested that his treatise *Constitutional Limitations* supplied "laissezfaire capitalism . . . with a legal ideology."[9]

The apparent conflict between Cooley the democrat and Cooley the capitalist is partially illusory. The transition from Jacksonian attacks on economic privilege to post-Civil War support for unregulated capitalism was a relatively painless one, requiring only the superimposition of an older value system on a new set of economic conditions. The Jacksonian reformers favored the abrogation of special relations between privileged elites and governments. They wanted the purported restoration of a mythic society in which true equality of economic opportunity existed and no person could take advantage of inherited or otherwise privileged wealth. Extending this ideology to other areas, they favored universal suffrage and education as well; but the focus of their reform was on centers of economic power, such as the Bank of the United States.[10] By the close of the Civil War the concept of equality of economic opportunity had become useful to new elites that had risen to power through a combination of technological development and government support, but now desired widespread autonomy to pursue their operations and feared that too-close government supervision might prevent the consolidation schemes they envisaged as buffers against economic instability. Equality of economic opportunity, restated as "laissez faire," became a congenial ideology to those groups; they favored a "free market" approach to markets they controlled.

Cooley's treatise *Constitutional Limitations*, from an ideological point of view, was a reaffirmation of his Jacksonian tenets. What made the treatise a national bestseller was the context in which his pronouncements were made. For one thing, his focus was not on the federal government but on the states. The treatise collected and synthesized the numerous ways in which states could potentially be restricted from passing legislation by their own constitutions or by the federal Constitution. As such it focused attention on the major source of regulatory legislation in the nineteenth century and gave state constitutions a new uniformity and life. Again, Cooley chose as his chief source of limitations the due process clauses of state constitutions rather than the obligation of contracts clauses, which had been emasculated by states through the technique of reserving amendment rights in franchise grants. Particularistic legislation benefiting a certain class of persons, and excessively vague general legislation, Cooley argued, were both violations of due process. From this insight late-nineteenth-century judges such as Field were eventually to instill a substantive meaning to the phrase "due process of law."

The use of the due process clause as a bar to excessive restrictions on private property had been anticipated by Taney in *Dred Scott*, and the other "limitations" emphasized by Cooley stemmed from orthodox Jacksonian social assumptions. Particularistic legislation was suspect because it violated the principle of equality of economic opportunity; overly general legislation was "arbitrary and unusual" in its nature and infringed the right of "the whole community . . . to demand the protection of the ancient principles which shield private rights against arbitrary interference."[11] Cooley's contribution was to give these principles a new and potentially widespread applicability. A due process clause or an equivalent "law of the land" clause was included in virtually all state constitutions; its content was impressively vague, and its relevance to state attempts to invade the "liberty" of private enterprises or to legislate against particular economic organization was apparent.

Cooley stopped short, however, of fashioning the limitations of the due process clause into dogmas such as the doctrine of liberty of contract, through which judges, by maintaining the fiction of equal bargaining power in industrial workers and their employers, invalidated much of the welfare legislation passed by states in the late nineteenth and early twentieth centuries. For Cooley constitutional limitations were two-edged: they functioned not only to protect private enterprise from undue legislative supervision but also to prevent it from securing special benefits. This second function was emphasized by Cooley in his 1870 opinion in *People v. Salem*.[12]

The *Salem* case gave Cooley an opportunity to express his views on particularistic state taxation legislation, one of the most common means by which nineteenth-century legislatures had financed internal improvement ventures. A common means of state aid to railroads after the Civil War was the purchase by municipalities of bonds funded through local taxation.[13] A special act of the Michigan Legislature in 1864 authorized certain townships, including Salem, to execute and issue municipal bonds in behalf of the Detroit and Howell Railroad. The constitutionality of the act was challenged on the ground that it represented taxation without a "public purpose." In defiance of numerous other state courts and in disregard of the convention that courts should not substitute their views for those of legislatures on questions of the "public" nature of taxation unless the purpose of a tax statute was plainly and palpably not public,[14] Cooley held that a railroad was not a public entity for the purpose of taxation. In the course of the decision, he referred to an economic "equality of right," "a maxim of state government" that was violated by laws favoring particular classes or occupations.[15]

Cooley's decision in *Salem* made him something of a favorite among Republican Party reform elements, who revived in the 1870s earlier Democratic attacks on concentrated capital and special privilege. A coalition of Liberal Republicans (who had emerged as a splinter party) and Democrats sought to nominate Cooley either for Governor of Michigan or as a candidate for Congress. Neither effort was successful; their only tangible effects were to identify Cooley as a dissident and to prevent his being considered for the United States Supreme Court when vacancies developed during the Grant Administration.

In some respects Cooley's judicial decisions were closer to those of Taney than to those of Field. He construed the obligation of contracts clause strictly and was suspicious of its use to protect corporate privilege.[16] He asserted the supremacy of legislative power against private claims: a municipality, he maintained, could not delegate its powers to some private individuals to seek redress against others.[17] He articulated a narrow theory of judicial review of legislative,[18] executive,[19] or administrative activity;[20] and in a celebrated case involving the Michigan Tax Commission in 1882, he not only upheld the autonomy of the Commission's operations, he also inveighed against judges who "assaulted" statutes because they "did not like the legislation."[21] Finally, despite the harmony of Cooley's interpretation of the role of due process clauses in state constitutions with the delegation to the judiciary of wide powers to review legislation, he apparently never intended this result.[22]

In the face of his rather limited view of the scope of judicial power and his animosity toward corporate privilege, how did Cooley come to be pictured as one of the builders of the late-nineteenth-century judiciary-capitalist complex? The answer is that Cooley was simultaneously an opponent of concentrated wealth and one of the intellectual founders of legal justifications for unregulated capitalism. He and the economic elites of the post-Civil War years had two things in common: first, a faith that equality of economic opportunity could be achieved merely by the absence of governmental participation in the affairs of private enterprise;[23] and second, a belief that certainty and predictability in the law were attainable and desirable.

With respect to the second of these beliefs, Cooley functioned on a different level from that of advocates for large corporations who made ample use of his treatises. He believed that painstaking research and clear-headed analysis could uncover general principles of law, and that such principles were timeless. As a treatise writer his function was to extract such principles and set them forth as guides to conduct; as a judge his function was to apply them, whether they suited his fancy or not. In 1887, in an address to the Georgia Bar Association entitled "The Uncertainty of the Law," Cooley sought to show that certainty could be achieved.[24] His methods were simple. Law was a science, governed by axioms; one discovered the axioms, articulated and synthesized them, then applied them to resolve controversies. Solutions were evident, lines could be drawn, rules could be made. With this technique, over time, one could truly know what the law "was." At the bottom of Cooley's rules and principles, of course, were his own predilections, which had stimulated his search in the various state constitutions for clauses that limited legislative power to support privilege. But that search, for reasons Cooley would have disapproved had he entirely perceived them, made him an unwilling patron of the railroads and trusts whose existence he feared. His career came to illustrate the close connection, in the late nineteenth century, between academic methodologies seeking for immutable intellectual principles, and the political ideologies that supported the continued primacy of elites.

III

If Cooley's approach to judging was ultimately congenial with the ideological perspectives of an influential segment of late-nineteenth-century Americans—albeit not for conventional reasons—Charles Doe's approach cannot be associated with any dominant nineteenth-century political theory or ideology: it was uniquely and idiosyncratically his own. It cannot be characterized in traditional political terms; it invites, rather, an alternative analysis of judicial behavior. It served to isolate Doe from the jurisprudential climate of his day and to make him the most creative state judge of the late nineteenth century.

Doe's approach, in simplest terms, revived the role of judges as dispensers of justice rather than as builders of a system of law. He believed, as had one of his eighteenth-century New Hampshire predecessors, that it was his business "to do justice between the parties . . . by common sense and common honesty as between man and man."[25] Doe assumed this role, however, not in a society that had no jurisprudence at all, as Kent had put it, but in one with a legacy of reported decisions, a congeries of well-established interest groups who looked to the law as a potential repository of security in their affairs, entrenched systems of procedural rules, and a scientific ideal of lawmaking. Among the jurists of his day, with their increasing fondness for formal rules and immutable principles, Doe was an anarchist. He found judicial remedies wherever he found a violation of individual rights, expanded the jurisdiction of his office whenever necessary to do justice, ignored precedents that stood in his way or procedures that tied his hand, and single-handedly reformed the common law of New Hampshire.

Doe's unconventional approach to his office was in keeping with his temperament. He was born into a moderately affluent and influential family, attended Exeter, Andover, Harvard, Dartmouth, and Harvard Law School, married a member of the Portsmouth aristocracy, and became independently wealthy. But he was unpretentious, entirely oblivious of social niceties, eccentric in his habits, and contemptuous of ostentation. "A vulgar notion of display and an affectation of social rank," he once wrote to John Wigmore, "are besetting sins, so universal and so ruinous, that an old man fails in his duty when he neglects a fair opportunity to warn every young person who is worthy of a high place in the world."[26] Doe practiced his teachings so painstakingly as to give the appearance of utter poverty. He dressed his children in cloth smocks and denim overalls, he wore woolen mittens instead of dress gloves, he traveled in circuit wearing a horse blanket and a cloth cap, he never shined his shoes, and he wore the same Prince Albert coat for over twenty years. He shunned social contacts almost altogether, hated publicity and public praise, continually attributed his judicial innovations to others, and held that judges should not be celebrated until after their deaths.

In the courtroom Doe was notably informal and eccentric. While a trial judge, he occasionally sat alongside counsel rather than on the bench, held hearings in his hotel room, fraternized with indicted murderers, dispensed with as many procedural formalities as he could, and refused to wear a robe. He also attempted to prevent lawyers from haranguing witnesses,[27] ignored rules of evidence, selected the jurors himself, examined and cross-examined witnesses, and gave charges to the jury in common idiom.

Doe's informality was symptomatic of his general impatience with legal tradition and ritual unless it had some functional significance. He regarded precedents, for example, as simply evidence of the current state of the law, having no particular persuasive value. He believed that "the maxim which, taken literally, requires courts to follow decided cases" was merely "a figurative expression requiring only a reasonable respect" for prior decisions.[28] The variables that chiefly concerned him in a judicial decision involved the rough justice of the fact situation before the court: whether an injury had been done to the complaining party; whether he had a right to complain; how Doe felt, intuitively, about the equities of the situation. With this emphasis, precedents became merely tools to be used or abandoned at the discretion of the judge; the real "law" lay in the circumstances of the dispute itself.

The methodology employed by Doe in making decisions thus tended to reduce questions of substantive law to questions of factual analysis, based on common sense and perceptions of justice. Legal doctrines in Doe's hands became generalized articulations of his perceptions; as such they could be revised or abandoned at will. Judging became an *ad hoc* process. No one case was ever precisely like another, no rule could be followed invariably, and the law abounded in artificialities and fictions that could be exposed and discarded at will. Continuity, certainty, predictability, and stability were desirable ends only if they conformed with reason and justice in the individual case; reform and innovation were inherent in the individualized process of judicial decision-making.

Despite Doe's disclaimers, he was the great common-law reformer of his generation. He broke down the custom of criminal lawyers of using their interrogations of witnesses as intimidation devices. He abolished the New Hampshire system of writ pleading—in which the success of a suit often turned on the particular phrasing of the complaint—by allowing complainants to amend their pleadings during a trial.[29] He allowed an error of law to be corrected at trial, rather than requiring a new trial;[30] he allowed suits in law to be converted to suits in equity in the course of a proceeding.[31] He converted the New Hampshire law of evidence from one based on artificial "presumptions" to one whose primary rule was that courts shall hear the "best evidence" available, the question of what evidence was "best" being one of fact.[32] He discarded the M'Naghten rules for criminal insanity, which presumed a defendant to be sane unless he could establish that he did not know the difference between right and wrong, and substituted a test whereby the jury considered all the available evidence with a view of determining, as a matter of fact, whether the crime had been an "offspring or product of mental disease."[33] He pioneered the development in torts of the "reasonableness" test for liability, in which the conduct of the defendant was evaluated against a hypothetical community standard of reason and prudence supplied by the jury, with liability resulting only if his conduct deviated from that standard.[34]

Doe did not confine his innovations to common law issues, although the bulk of his decisions were on common law subjects. He developed a theory of statutory and testamentary interpretation that tied the meaning of a document to the "intent" of its framers, the question of intent being one of fact to be determined by historical research.[35] Using such a test, he ignored the long-established "rule against perpetuities" in a case in which it functioned to defeat the intention of the maker of a will.[36] Complementing Doe's theory of interpretation was his belief that judges could fashion remedies out of necessity. He made available the writs of mandamus, quo warranto, and habeas corpus or injunctive relief—technical obstacles notwithstanding—if a plaintiff could show that he had been injured and was entitled to a remedy. Under his approach, judicial freedom to interpret laws enacted by legislatures was extensive, and judicial power to intervene in behalf of existing civil rights was wide-ranging.

Doe's inclination to regard legal doctrines as justifications for results based on common sense and natural justice, his unabashed interest in judicial "legislation," his disregard for formalities, his skepticism toward abstractions, and his conception of law as continually in flux link him with the legal realists of the twentieth century. Alongside other judges of his time, who solemnly maintained that the judicial branch merely "found" the laws and who seemingly accepted without question a conception of law as a science or a body of rules, Doe appears strikingly modern. Yet his theories of government were not of his own century, but of that which had preceded it. He regarded constitutions as social compacts and believed that individual rights were reserved by the people as conditions of their agreement to be governed.[37] He identified equality not with special treatment for oppressed minorities but with the right of all citizens to receive like economic or social[38] opportunities. He equated liberty with the protection of private property, and held that security in property was a foundation of all civil rights.[39]

Such views—which associate Doe with Marshall—led him to insist that state taxation not be imposed on one set of persons rather than another;[40] that local and state taxes be equally assessed within the appropriate governmental unit;[41] and that the practice of granting bondholders immunity from taxation be declared constitutionally invalid.[42] They also led him to oppose vigorously legislative attempts to control the assets of private corporations[43] or to regulate railroad rates.[44] In Doe's view, legislatures simply had no power to interfere with the use of private property.

Although the affairs of private enterprise were immune from legislative control, entrepreneurs were not absolved of any responsibility to the state. They were required to set "reasonable" rates, and the reasonableness of the rates was a question for the judiciary. Here Doe revived the older conception of enterprise regulation that had prevailed in such states as Massachusetts in the eighteenth and early nineteenth centuries, where mill owners and turnpike franchises were held accountable to the public to maintain rates at a reasonable level. In making the supervision of railroad rates part of the province of the judiciary, however, Doe was again being innovative. Shaw, a pioneer in developing the regulatory police powers of the states, had suggested that only the legislative branch of government could impose regulations. Doe entrusted this function to the judiciary simply by assuming that private rights had been violated by railroad price discriminations, and that the courts could supply a remedy.

The combination of Doe's radical disrespect for tradition and formality, zealous adherence to eighteenth-century constitutional principles, and broad conception of the powers of his office assured his status as the most unconventional judge of his era. Two jurisprudential principles of Taney's generation—judicial deference to the will of the legislature, and an expanded conception of the powers of states to regulate the private affairs of their citizens—were decisively repudiated by Doe. This repudiation linked him to late-nineteenth-century innovators such as Field, but Doe never shared Field's solicitude for large corporate interests, nor his sanctimonious assertion of immutable legal principles. Nor did Doe espouse the economic egalitarianism of Cooley. For him private enterprise, though secure from legislative control, was ultimately required to behave in an economically reasonable manner.

On balance, all attempts to link Doe with any nineteenth-century political philosophy or ideology only render him *sui generis.* His importance lies more in his relation to the professional norms of his time. His career was a testament to his belief that certainty and predictability in the law were values of very little importance in the face of the dictates of reason and justice, and that judicial precedents—those indices of legal continuity on which nineteenth-century jurisprudes hoped to build a science of law—were nothing but manifestations of a past court's conception of justice, to be followed or abandoned at another court's discretion. In an age in which tradition, stability, and regularity were looked upon as barriers against chaos, and judges were increasingly expected to be mechanical and predictable, Doe maintained and expanded an older conception of homespun justice.

IV

The careers of Cooley and Doe underscore a dimension of the process of American appellate adjudication that has not always been made apparent in portraits of leading judges, particularly those on the Supreme Court. This dimension involves the dual constituencies, professional and political, of an appellate judge. At one level, an appellate decision is a resolution of a controversy between individual litigants with potential meaning for similarly situated persons in the future. Here it can function as a guideline for private conduct, since like cases, in Anglo-American jurisprudence, are presumably treated alike. An appellate decision is at another level, however, a resolution of competing social issues, extending (when constitutional controversies of great magnitude come before the Supreme Court) to an attempted reconciliation of pervasive value conflicts in the nation. At this level a decision has important political and ideological significance, and the positions adopted by individual judges can be considered in that context.

Although the professional and political constituencies of courts overlap, they are also distinguishable. Political conservatism in a judge is not always allied with institutional conservatism, nor is political liberalism necessarily allied with institutional activism. Though in the contexts of their times neither Cooley nor Doe was easily classifiable as a political liberal or political conservative, Cooley was decidedly an institutional conservative, attempting as he did to achieve continuity and predictability in judicial decisions, and Doe was decidedly an institutional activist, emphasizing change. Yet Doe's vision of an ideal America was grounded in a more distant past than Cooley's.

The tradition of appellate judging in America has thus involved more than a delicate and ambivalent relation between the judiciary and a changing political and ideological climate of opinion. It has involved also determinations by individual judges as to how much freedom and restraint they associate with the performance of their office. These determinations are not always capable of being characterized in conventional political terms. Neither Cooley nor Doe fits nicely into a "liberal" or a "conservative" package; their jurisprudence was based more on an institutional than an ideological perspective. That perspective, though perhaps most marked in the state appellate judiciary, has been a longstanding part of the calculus of judging in America. A claimed power in appellate judges to decide questions of great political import engendered, in the nineteenth century, a search for fundamental principles of political theory to which judicial decisions could appeal. Judicial power begat a sense of its own limitations. Similarly, a strong judicial interest in perpetuating independence for the judiciary engendered a sense of institutional constraints. Judges, like other visible officials, were accountable to their constituents and to the other branches of government. Their being oracles of the law's wisdom did not change that fact.

5 

John Marshall Harlan I: The Precursor

After his death in 1911 he was virtually ignored by scholars for nearly forty years; in 1947 Justice Frankfurter called him an "eccentric exception" to the distinguished majority of judges, Frankfurter included, who had resisted making the Bill of Rights freedoms available to petitioning citizens against the states through the due process clause of the Fourteenth Amendment.[1] Two years later, however, a law review article predicted his "coming vindication";[2] in 1954 he was hailed by the *New York Times* as the progenitor of *Brown v. Board of Education;*[3] by the 1960s he was one of twelve Supreme Court Justices singled out as deserving of special biographical treatment;[4] and in a 1972 survey he was ranked as one of the twelve "great" Justices in the history of the Court.[5]

Thus has John Marshall Harlan I's reputation climbed from obscurity to prominence. Ironically, the same factors that alienated him from most of his peers and the scholarly public during his lifetime and long after his death have formed the basis of his reincarnation. More an ideologue than a jurist, he held views that were once distinctly out of phase; recently they have come into fashion. None of these slights or exaltations of history would have concerned Harlan, according to contemporaries. He allegedly went to sleep with one hand upon the Constitution and the other on the Bible, and thus secured the untroubled sleep of the just and the righteous.[6]

Harlan's career suggests that not all leading appellate judges can be classified by reference to theories of judicial performance. Two perspectives on federal appellate judging clashed during his tenure on the Supreme Court, one harmonious with antebellum economic and political theories and one responsive to the changes in late-nineteenth-century American life signified by Reconstruction and large-scale industrialization. The constitutional history of the Supreme Court in the latter part of the century exemplified the gradual replacement of the first perspective by the second. The first perspective, illustrated in the majority opinions in the *Slaughter-House* cases[7] and *Munn v. Illinois,*[8] tolerated state economic regulation, attempted to maintain concurrent sovereignty and an equilibrium between the federal and state systems, and read the Reconstruction Amendments as declaring that the existing civil rights of white American citizens now applied to blacks. The second perspective, illustrated by the majority opinions in the *Civil Rights* cases[9] and *Wabash v. Illinois,*[10] was suspicious of state economic regulation, read the Reconstruction Amendments as creating an increased role for the federal judiciary as protectors of private rights against the states, and distinguished between the kinds of rights protected, vindicating economic rights far more than civil rights. Many leading Justices of the late nineteenth century held one perspective or another: Waite, a prime advocate of the first; Field, the chief exponent of the second; Miller and Bradley, imperceptibly and irregularly sliding from the first to the second.

Harlan cannot be described in the same terms. He combined a passionate desire to vindicate the civil rights of blacks with a reverence for private property. He often opposed economic regulation by the states, but generally tolerated it when undertaken by the federal government. He had no affinity for the reform ideologies of the late nineteenth century—populism, syndicalism, and socialism. Yet he joined supporters of those movements in railing against and attempting to regulate the giant industrial enterprises of the period. Harlan's theory of judging was primarily designed to implement his individual convictions. It placed a premium on arriving at desirable results, not on internal consistency. It bound a judge only to his own intuitive sense of what was right. But Harlan's intuition that a paternalistic federal government could serve as a protector of the socially and economically disadvantaged struck fire with social reformers in the early and middle twentieth century. Once a maverick, Harlan has become a visionary prophet.

I

Harlan was deeply influenced throughout his judicial life by his early experiences as a Kentucky politician. His father was a Whig Congressman from Kentucky and a confidant of Henry Clay; and he himself adopted and maintained the Whig belief in a strong national government, never losing his sense of the Union's importance. He was also a Southern slaveowner, and the two affiliations proved increasingly difficult to reconcile. Before the Civil War he attempted to reconcile support for slavery with opposition to secession. During the war he chose nationalism over states' rights, repudiating his original position on slavery. In 1890 he declared that the Union could not exist "without a government of the whole" and that the "general government" was "supreme" with respect to its "objects," which he defined as those purposes for which "America has chosen to be . . . a nation."[11]

In the 1850s the Whig party in Kentucky found itself bankrupt as a result of the death of Clay and the ominous aspects of nationalism at a time when slaveholding seemed compatible only with states' rights. As the Kentucky Whigs disintegrated, Harlan sought other political bases from which he could simultaneously espouse slavery and support the Union: first the American party, whose chief positions were anti-Catholicism and opposition to immigration; then the Conservative Union party of the 1860s, which favored preservation of the Union but opposed emancipation and abolitionism. At various points from the 1850s to the 1870s Harlan spoke out against popular sovereignty, threatened secession if the war were made a mandate for emancipation, charged that the Emancipation Proclamation of 1862 was unconstitutional, opposed any grant of political privileges to blacks, called the proposed Reconstruction Amendments symbols of "a complete revolution in our Republican government," and maintained that blacks were socially inferior to whites and that segregation of the races was right and proper.[12]

Despite these efforts to defend the caste system of his youth, Harlan increasingly found himself prepared to support the Union even at the price of eradication of slavery. In 1868 he joined the Republican Party and in 1871 ran for Governor of Kentucky on that ticket. In the course of that campaign he publicly repudiated his earlier views. He stated that he had "acquiesced in the irreversible results of the war," expressed regret at his earlier championing of slavery, and claimed that "there is no man on this continent . . . who rejoices more than I do at the extinction of slavery."[13] He supported Reconstruction legislation such as the Ku Klux Klan Act of 1870 and the Civil Rights Act of 1871, and renounced his earlier views on immigration. Defeated, he ran again in 1875, reaffirming his support for Reconstruction and civil rights, and once again lost.

Harlan's conversion on the issue of black rights and his persistent faith in the federal government as a uniform and efficient distributor of economic benefits were to form the intellectual cornerstones of his approach to judging. In his 1871 gubernatorial campaign both beliefs were in evidence. In addition to supporting the civil rights legislation of Reconstruction, Harlan proposed an extension of "the powers of industry and national wealth" through the abolition of interstate railroad monopolies, a graduated income tax to avoid imposing burdens on the poor, and an equalization of school taxes, based on the principle that "the rich owed it to the poor to contribute to the education of the latter."[14] Six years after that campaign, Harlan was a power in Republican Party politics. When he successfully maneuvered to swing the Kentucky delegation to Rutherford Hayes in 1876, he was rewarded with an appointment to the Supreme Court the next year.

Personality traits that strongly influenced Harlan's interpretation of his judicial office had also been exhibited in his political campaigns. He had entered politics early in life, making speeches for the American Party in 1856 when he was twenty-three and rapidly acquiring self-confidence and a sureness of his convictions. After his first public speech he became conscious, he later wrote, "of a capacity to say what I desired to say, and to make myself understood."[15] His ample proportions and striking appearance perhaps contributed to this self-esteem: Harlan's wife remembered that when she first saw him, when he was twenty-one, he walked "as if the whole world belonged to him."[16] A religious fundamentalism augmented his self-righteousness. He believed that nothing that the Bible commanded could "be safely or properly disregarded" and nothing that "it condemn[ed] [could] be justified."[17] The taunts of opponents who reminded him of his conversion on black rights only strengthened his beliefs. He would rather be "right," he said in 1871, "than consistent."[18]

Strength of conviction combined in Harlan with an approach to judicial decision-making that emphasized the achievement of results. His troublesome division between the Union and slavery, once resolved in favor of the Union, produced a messianic commitment to black rights. Harlan almost never failed to uphold the civil rights of black plaintiffs, never invalidated civil rights legislation when it pertained to freed blacks, and regularly dissented from cases that left black petitioners without a remedy against either discrimination by states or attacks by private citizens. To achieve those results Harlan was prepared to read the Thirteenth and Fourteenth Amendments exceptionally broadly[19] or, if required, to ignore procedural irregularities.[20]

In cases involving government regulation of economic affairs, Harlan was equally result-oriented. He believed in broad federal regulatory powers, and complained that Court decisions emasculating or invalidating federal statutes constituted "judicial legislation."[21] On the other hand, he opposed state attempts at rate regulation, was suspicious of the powers of federal executive officers, and believed that federal regulatory powers, though broad in scope, were limited in nature. In espousing these positions he described the judiciary as a guardian of private property,[22] trumpeted the rights of individuals against the government,[23] and made use of orthodox laissez-faire precepts such as the liberty-of-contract doctrine.[24] At the same time that he tolerated state regulation of working hours, maintaining that the judiciary had no right to "enter the domain of legislation and . . . annul statutes that had received the sanction of the people's representatives,"[25] he invalidated a federal statute purporting to extend the commerce power to include private labor relations, claiming that it arbitrarily sanctioned an illegal invasion of personal liberty and property rights.[26]

Harlan's result-orientation testified to his sense that the law could be shaped to conform to a judge's personal convictions. He once stated to a group of students at George Washington University (where he taught constitutional law from 1889 until his death) that if Justices did not "like an act of Congress, we don't have much trouble to find grounds to declare it unconstitutional."[27] In his own case a basis for animosity or preference was often deep-seated, and he was rarely at a loss to justify it and rarely influenced by the views of his fellow Justices. Chief Justice White, speaking gingerly at a ceremony honoring Harlan, stated that Harlan's "methods of thought . . . led him to the broadest lines of conviction, and as those lines were by him discerned, . . . differences between himself and others became impossible of reconciliation."[28]

At least two disagreements between Harlan and his brethren provoked open confrontations. During the reading of his dissent in the case of *Pollock v. Farmers' Loan & Trust Co.,* which declared the income tax unconstitutional, Harlan was reported to have "pounded the desk, [shaken] his finger under the noses of Chief Justice [Fuller] and Mr. Justice Field," and to have "several times . . . turned his chair" to glare at Field, Fuller, and Justice Gray.[29] Harlan claimed that Field had whispered and shuffled papers during the reading of Harlan's dissent and had "acted like a mad man" throughout the Court's consideration of the *Income Tax* cases.[30] At the end of his career, Harlan became equally distressed at the *Standard Oil*[31] and *American Tobacco* decisions,[32] which gave power to the judiciary to construe the Sherman Act in the light of a "reasonableness" standard. The decision represented a personal blow to Harlan, since it modified his holding in the 1903 *Northern Securities* case,[33] in which a judicial "rule of reason" had specifically been repudiated. In his dissent in *Standard Oil* Harlan stated that "many things are intimated and said in the Court's opinion which will not be regarded otherwise than as sanctioning an invasion by the judiciary of the constitutional domain of Congress—an attempt by interpretation to soften or modify what some regard as a harsh public policy." He described this tendency toward "judicial construction" as "most harmful."[34] For Harlan, federal antitrust legislation was intended to ensure that the weak were not mastered by the strong—this being for him an essential part of rendering justice. In such circumstances he was intolerant of "mere metaphysical conceptions or distinctions of casuistry,"[35] and ill-disposed toward those who would employ them to reach unjust results.

II

Harlan's orientation toward results and individualized views on economic issues have made his opinions on government regulation difficult to characterize. He has been alternatively called a "liberal nationalist"[36] and a "complete reactionary,"[37] a "premature New Dealer"[38] and a "Whig-Progressive,"[39] and "both an economic liberal and conservative."[40] Central to an understanding of Harlan's decisions involving government regulation of the economy is a sense of their timing. He came to the Court with well-developed ideas about the role of government in promoting and regulating industrial enterprise, but those ideas originally had no apparent applicability to contemporary circumstances, and later suggested solutions that were not entirely consistent with other aspects of Harlan's thought.

In summary, Harlan began his service on the Court holding economic views that were already outmoded, persisted in those views despite their obsolescence, then saw them take on different implications in the late 1880s and 1890s with the advent of collectivist ideologies. The interaction of Harlan's attitudes with the changing intellectual climate of his years of service made him appear first as an economic reactionary and then as something of a radical, but he disdained either characterization. If he and those favoring nationalization of the American economy were united in their hatred of giant corporate interests, this did not, Harlan felt, make him a socialist;[41] if he was anxious to secure for entrepreneurs an adequate return on their investments, this did not affiliate him with the captains of industry.

In 1877, when he joined the Court, Harlan had revealed himself as an orthodox Whig. He favored a "strong national economy," by which was meant support for the free flow of interstate commerce against particularistic local interests. He supported active government promotion of entrepreneurial ventures and held to a Marshallian interpretation of the commerce clause, which emphasized plenary federal control of commerce in the interest of economic expansion. To these tenets Harlan added a personal sympathy for economically disadvantaged persons, manifested in his 1871 and 1875 economics-reform proposals for Kentucky, which advocated the use of tax policies as a means of alleviating the burdens of the poor. In the 1870's there was virtually no intellectual home for these positions. The states, rather than the federal government, had emerged as the chief promoters and regulators of industrial enterprise. The focus of controversy in questions involving governmental regulation was not whether the states or the nation should do the regulating, but whether governmental institutions had any right to regulate the use of private property. Pressure for federal regulation as a means of combating excessive market power, as exemplified in the legislation creating the Interstate Commerce Commission in 1887, had not yet emerged. Poverty had not yet been "discovered";[42] the costs of industrialism were not yet so apparent that policies intended to aid the victims of an industrial society had very widespread appeal.

In this purview, Harlan's earliest decisions on government regulation—decisions involving the responsibility of defaulting states and municipalities to their bondholders—indicated an appreciation of the risks taken by investors, and revealed a rigorous application of the impairment of contracts clause reminiscent of Marshall.[43] Recognition of the importance of capital investment in transportation ventures and a belief in the sanctity of contracts were antebellum Whig doctrines; Harlan persisted longer in use of the impairment of contracts clause than any other post-Civil War Justice with the possible exception of Field.[44]

A chief bugaboo of Harlan's, as manifested in the municipal bond cases, was the restrictive effects of local legislatures on the development of enterprises financed by out-of-state investment. Harlan resorted to a number of devices to try to protect investors. In addition to invoking the contracts and commerce clauses to invalidate state legislation adversely affecting their interests, he attempted to avoid the Eleventh Amendment's barrier to suits against a state by citizens of another state,[45] supported efforts to expand the diversity jurisdiction of the federal courts and to facilitate removal of cases from state courts,[46] and invoked the due process clause to invalidate state regulation of foreign corporations.[47] These were essentially negative decisions, linking him with an approach to judging represented by Field. But they did not imply opposition to all forms of government regulation; they were merely the obstructive half of a twofold policy designed to ensure uniform national flow of capital and commerce. The other half of the policy was positive federal action.

Other factors complicating an assessment of Harlan's attitudes toward governmental regulation include his distinction between state efforts to interfere with capitalization and to regulate the use of other goods and services, and his use of Marshall's distinction, in commerce-clause cases, between "local" and "national" objects. He was zealous to protect out-of-state insurance companies[48] and investors in railroads,[49] but he tolerated state regulation of liquor and oleomargarine.[50] He denied to states the authority to set railroad eates, but allowed them to prohibit railroad traffic on Sunday or control the points of stoppage on railroad lines.[51] He invalidated a Federal statute attempting to regularize hours for union employees,[52] but sustained New York and Kansas statutes fixing hours for bakers and state employees against a similar challenge.[53] His result-orientation was doubtless partially responsible for the uneven pattern of these decisions. Religious and moral convictions informed his attitude toward Sunday closing laws, temperance legislation, and questionable business practices, while at the same time his strong desire to provide entrepreneurs a return on their investments made him suspicious of legislation that jeopardized the security of investors.

Harlan's philosophy of government regulation developed an added dimension after 1887, when federal regulatory statutes creating the Interstate Commerce Commission and prohibiting monopolies and conspiracies in restraint of trade provided an outlet for his dormant Whig attitudes. In the regulatory policies of a newly assertive federal government he saw the personification of the older American system, with its emphasis on the even-handed promotion of economic growth nation-wide. "Aggregations of capital," he felt, threatened to impose "another kind of slavery" on the American people.[54] A vigorous federal regulatory commission and rigidly enforced antitrust laws would prevent large enterprises from unfairly controlling the nation's business.

Thus, the antebellum Whig became the late-century paternalist who saw the federal government as an ally of those discriminated against by large-scale industrial enterprises. The powers delegated to the Interstate Commerce Commission to set railroad rates were to be strictly upheld by the courts; Supreme Court decisions emasculating the Commission constituted blatant judicial legislation.[55] The Sherman Anti-Trust law meant what it said: any industrial combination formed for the purpose of restraining trade was illegal. Whether the restraint was "reasonable" was not a question for the courts.[56] Sophistical judicial distinctions between "manufacture" and "commerce" intended to defeat the purpose of the antitrust laws were equally illegitimate.[57] A federal income tax that placed the costs of national economic growth on those who could most easily bear them was compatible with views long held by Harlan. Invalidation of that tax by the Court seemed to him disastrous.[58]

Even while enthusiastically accepting paternalistic regulatory legislation, Harlan retained his older beliefs in the sanctity of individual rights. He decried "the effort of accumulated capital . . . to escape the burden of just taxation,"[59] and maintained that "the greatest injury to the integrity of our social organization comes from the enormous power of corporations";[60] yet he protested against arbitrary governmental interference with the property rights of citizens.[61] When these two beliefs came into conflict, such as when regulatory statutes infringed economic "liberties," Harlan resolved the tension by following his intuitions. He seemed to think that labor unions did not need special protection;[62] he accepted state regulation of wages and hours[63] more easily than state interference with creditor rights;[64] he did not usually maintain his general suspicion of state attempts to interfere with property rights in the area of taxation.[65] If this approach made Harlan unpredictable and inconsistent, it also prevented him from succumbing to the fear that gripped many American judges when collectivist doctrines began to be discussed in the late nineteenth century,[66] a fear often manifested by attempts to define the emerging problems of industrialization out of existence.

III

In civil rights cases the experience of Harlan's years in Kentucky immeasurably affected his stance. He had come to see the barbarity of a system in which whites treated blacks as chattels, and he could never look at cases involving the civil rights of blacks without invoking that vision. An incident from Harlan's domestic life is revealing of the symbolic meaning of the antebellum South for him. Shortly after his appointment to the Supreme Court, he had discovered in the Marshal's office at the Court an inkstand used by Taney in writing his decisions. On learning that Taney had used the inkstand to write *Dred Scott,* Harlan demonstrated such interest in it that he was given it as a present. After the inkstand had remained with Harlan for a time, he promised to give it to the wife of Senator George Pendleton of Ohio, who had expressed a desire to have it because Taney had been a relative of hers. Mrs. Harlan, believing that her husband would regret giving up the inkstand, secretly retrieved it from his study and hid it. Harlan told Mrs. Pendleton that the inkstand had inexplicably disappeared and subsequently forgot about it.

In 1883, when the *Civil Rights Cases* came before the Court, Harlan resolved to dissent, but was having difficulty writing a dissenting opinion. One Sunday morning, in the midst of his difficulties, Mrs. Harlan again intervened. Knowing that Harlan would not fail to attend services, she declined to accompany him, and while he was at church she retrieved Taney's inkstand, polished it and filled it with ink, placed it in a conspicuous spot in his study, and removed the other inkwells. When Harlan returned she called it to his attention and confessed her part in keeping it in the Harlan household. With the inkstand serving as a catalyst, Harlan began his dissent, the Reconstruction Amendments and the abolition of slavery linked in his mind. Out of those associations came sentences such as "I insist that the national legislature may, without transcending the limits of the Constitution, do for human liberty and the fundamental rights of American citizenship, what it did, with the sanction of this court, for the protection of slavery and the rights of the masters of fugitive slaves."[67]

Harlan's civil rights opinions were his representative performances. They brought together his emotional attachment to the plight of freed blacks, his broad reading of national power to protect citizenship rights under the Reconstruction Amendments, his willingness to shape legal doctrines to justify preferred results, the strength and stubbornness of his moral convictions, and his independence from the views of his colleagues. The cases, which were largely but not exclusively concerned with the rights of black plaintiffs, underscored for Harlan the federal government's responsibility to take affirmative action to protect the rights of disadvantaged minorities. In this area Harlan viewed the government's proper function as that of a benign despot continually intervening on the side of the underprivileged; and he would use whatever juristic tools were available to maintain the primacy of federal powers. The only extent to which he tolerated alleged racial discrimination was in matters of proof; if an affirmative case for discriminatory practices had not been made, Harlan would vote to deny a petitioner relief.[68] He was by all odds the leading judicial civil-libertarian of his time and the only nineteenth-century Justice whose approach to civil rights cases even faintly resembled that taken by the Warren Court.

Most of the civil rights cases considered by the Court in the early years of Harlan's tenure concerned federal legislation entitling blacks to trial by juries selected without racial discrimination, or preventing jurors from being excluded on account of race. Of all the black rights cases, the Court was most sympathetic to petitioners in this area. In 1880 Harlan joined three decisions sustaining federal legislation that gave blacks a right to be tried by juries selected without racial discrimination,[69] provided for indictments against state judges who excluded blacks from juries,[70] and permitted black petitioners to remove their cases to a federal court if a state did not allow nondiscriminatory jury selection.[71] In 1881 he wrote the opinion for the Court in a case in which the state of Delaware had systematically excluded blacks from juries, and a black petitioner had sued to have his conviction by an all-white jury reversed. Harlan read the 1880 jury cases as holding that the equal-protection clause of the Fourteenth Amendment itself prevented blacks from being tried by juries on which black jurors had been forbidden to serve on the basis of race. He maintained, however, that a prima-facie case of racial discrimination had to be made out; it could not merely be inferred from statistical evidence.[72]

For the remainder of his Court tenure, Harlan followed the approach to jury cases he had taken in the 1880s, with the continual support of a majority of the Justices. He invalidated state statutes excluding blacks from juries on the basis of race,[73] but only where real evidence of discrimination had been presented or where the states had not seriously entertained claims of proof.[74] In other instances, in which a prima-facie case of discrimination had not been made out, or where a state trial court had ruled the evidence insufficient,[75] Harlan denied relief. He also gave a relatively narrow scope to the right of removal from state courts in jury discrimination cases.[76] His jury decisions were unusual in that his position harmonized with that of most of his fellow Justices and in that they evidenced a relatively cautious attitude toward civil rights claims.

In Fifteenth Amendment cases Harlan's views gradually deviated from that of the Court. In 1884, in the case of *Ex parte Yarborough,*[77] the Court upheld federal legislation preventing private citizens from conspiring to deprive blacks of their right to vote in a federal election; Harlan joined the majority. Nineteen years later, however, at a high point in the Court's tolerance of racial discrimination, *Yarborough* was ignored by the majority in *James v. Bowman.*[78] That case involved the constitutionality of a federal statute preventing private citizens from interfering with Fifteenth Amendment rights through bribery or intimidation. Two citizens of Kentucky were convicted under the statute for harassing a black voter in Kentucky. The Court struck down as overbroad the statute's application to them, since the statute did not limit its reach to federal elections and since the Fifteenth Amendment did not prohibit private citizens, as opposed to states, from interfering with voting rights. Harlan, in dissent, rejected that reading of the Amendment.

In *Giles v. Harris,*[79] another 1903 case, the Court showed its then current tendency to avoid disturbing state schemes aimed at disenfranchising blacks. Alabama had established certain voting requirements that tended to prevent blacks from registering; a black petitioned for equitable relief in federal court, claiming that he and other blacks had been illegally prevented from registering. The Court denied relief, claiming that if Alabama's registration provisions were unconstitutional, the Court could not tolerate their presence by adding blacks to the registration rolls, and that since the Court could not enforce an equitable decree, it should not impose its views on state legislatures. Harlan, dissenting, maintained that the petitioner had made out a case for equitable relief and that the federal courts had the power to grant it.[80]

Harlan's reading of the Thirteenth Amendment also diverged from that of his peers. He believed, as he stated in the *Civil Rights Cases,* that the Amendment prevented not only "incidents" of slavery, such as compulsory labor or disqualification from holding property or making contracts, but also "badges" of slavery, such as exclusion of blacks from public accommodations. Harlan was willing to find evidence of "slavery" in acts of private creditors forcing black debtors to return to a state[81] or preventing blacks from working in a lumber mill,[82] in a state statute that made refusal to work prima-facie evidence of an intent to defraud an employer,[83] and in state statutes compelling seamen on private vessels to honor their contracts.[84] In this last case, Harlan maintained that "the condition of one who contracts to render personal services in connection with the private business of another becomes a condition of involuntary servitude *from the moment he is compelled against his will* to continue in such service."[85] A prior practice in America of permitting the forcible return of seamen to their vessels was for Harlan unjustifiable after the passage of the Thirteenth Amendment. In only one of these cases was Harlan's position eventually upheld by the Court.[86]

It was in cases involving the Fourteenth Amendment, however, that Harlan demonstrated his farthest isolation from the Court. He had begun this estrangement in the *Civil Rights* cases, where he had maintained that public accommodations and transportation franchises were instrumentalities of the states for purposes of the "state action" clause of the amendment, and that the amendment's enforcement clause, taken together with its broad grant of citizenship rights, meant that Congress could determine what legislation was necessary to protect rights that were "fundamental in citizenship in a free republican government."[87] This meant that, despite the apparent restriction of the Fourteenth's reach to discriminations by states, the federal government still had broad potential powers to prevent private discriminatory acts. From these positions stemmed Harlan's dissents in subsequent Fourteenth Amendment cases.

In the area of transportation Harlan steadfastly maintained that state-enforced segregation of blacks from whites was impermissible. The first major transportation case in his tenure was *Louisville, New Orleans, and Texas Ry. v. Mississippi,*[88] in which the Fuller Court showed its inclination to uphold Southern states in their efforts to prevent racial intermingling. In 1877 the Court, in a case in which Harlan did not participate, had invalidated a Louisiana law forbidding racial discrimination on interstate steamboats passing through the state, on the ground that such law constituted an undue usurpation of federal commerce powers.[89] The *Louisville* case presented an analogous situation, since it tested the constitutionality of a Mississippi statute requiring racial segregation during the Mississippi portion of interstate railroad trips. The Court distinguished the earlier case, claiming that compelling white passengers to share their steamboat cabins with blacks was a far greater burden on interstate commerce than compelling whites and blacks to have separate accommodations in Pullman cars. Harlan's dissent denounced the spuriousness of this reasoning and held the statute an interference with interstate commerce. Though technically he did not reach the equal protection issue, he intimated that the statute violated the Fourteenth Amendment as well.[90]

Louisville set the stage for *Plessy v. Ferguson,*[91] the notorious 1896 decision sustaining the constitutionality of a Louisiana statute requiring racially segregated railway cars against a Fourteenth Amendment challenge. For Americans of today the most striking aspect of Harlan's dissent in *Plessy v. Ferguson* has been the attitudes of racial toleration and the fears of racial antagonism that it expressed, as well as its conviction that "the destinies of the two races, in this country, are indissolubly linked."[92] But in a historical context those aspects of the opinion were overshadowed by Harlan's overriding assumption that the Fourteenth Amendment had radically equalized the status of all Americans. Inequality of citizenship rights, after the Reconstruction Amendments, was simply impermissible for Harlan. He admitted no distinctions between state and private action, between slavery and its vestiges, between reasonable and unreasonable governmental discrimination. He read the Reconstruction Amendments as creating a domain of protection for American citizens against inequitable treatment before the law and as making the federal government the supervisor of that domain. In his support for the civil rights conferred by the Amendments, his older beliefs in individual liberties against the government merged with his more recent sympathy for freed blacks, creating a phalanx of ideological and moral conviction.

Harlan went to extraordinary lengths to find support for his positions in the traditional authoritative sources of a judge. He read the Thirteenth Amendment as forbidding private actions that fostered incidents or badges of slavery despite strong evidence in the legislative history that its scope was confined to state activities.[93] He extended the scope of that amendment to reach areas, such as public accommodations, that it was very likely not intended to cover.[94] He interpreted the Fourteenth Amendment to apply to non-naturalized Indians who chose not to live on Indian reservations.[95] He believed that federal civil-rights legislation could be made to apply not only to protect citizens against attempted infringement of their rights by private persons, but to protect aliens as well.[96] Neither of these last two positions had the support of the Waite or Fuller Courts.

Most remarkable of all, in the context of his times, was Harlan's belief that the Fourteenth Amendment had assured that "not one of the fundamental rights of life, liberty or property, recognized by the Constitution of the United States, can be denied or abridged by a State in respect to any person within its jurisdiction."[97] Harlan meant by that statement that each of the first eight amendments to the Bill of Rights was incorporated in the Fourteenth Amendment's due process and equal protection clauses, and thus each applied against the states. He appears, in fact, to have meant even more than that, for he stated that fundamental U.S. citizenship rights were "principally" enumerated in the Bill of Rights, implying that others might be found and likewise applied as limitations on state conduct. In six cases between 1884 and 1908 involving the application of various Bill of Rights provisions to the states, Harlan affirmed this position.[98] No other member of the Court accepted it. Today, despite the long efforts of Justices Black and Douglas, "selective incorporation" of Bill of Rights provisions in the Fourteenth Amendment remains the majority doctrine. Yet for Harlan total incorporation was obvious: the Reconstruction Amendments had redefined the meaning of American citizenship and in the process had altered fundamentally the relation of the federal government to the states. United States citizens, after 1870, were wards of the nation.

IV

The dramatic turnabout in attitudes toward racial equality in the 1950s and 1960s seems to have been the chief catalyst in augmenting Harlan's reputation. The spectacle of a Southerner laying bare the prejudices and sophistries of his peers, appealing in his rhetoric to the same humanitarian feelings that lay at the base of the twentieth-century civil rights movement, demonstrating in his own person the zealousness that can be produced by a combination of insight and guilt, was an overwhelmingly attractive image to twentieth-century integrationists. Harlan's more general interest in the responsibilities of the federal government toward its citizens also contributed to his enhanced stature in a century in which national social-welfare legislation came into existence. But although he was the only late-nineteenth-century Justice to find paternalism at all congenial, he was a precursor of, rather than a spokesman for, judicial attitudes that later came into vogue. He had no integrated theory of judging, only his own convictions; he read the imperatives of his office only as a mandate to dispense his individualized kind of justice. Ultimately, his jurisprudence resists categorization, except as result-orientation, and his reputation becomes peculiarly vulnerable to changes in social attitudes. One generation's eccentric has become another's visionary, but his stature remains indeterminate. His currently high stature may be more transitory than it now appears.

Harlan's preoccupation with reaching results that satisfied his intuition and convictions raises a theme of great importance to the remaining judges in this study. In an age whose jurisprudence defined the judge as an oracle, result-orientation ostensibly never existed. Judging was an exercise in declaring the will of the law, not the will of the judge. But as Harlan's interpretative clashes with his colleagues revealed, the "law" was capable of being "declared" in a variety of ways for a variety of purposes.

The mystical, immutable principles of the law were the nineteenth-century judge's barrier against result-orientation. "The courts," Harlan's colleague David Brewer said in 1893, "hold neither purse nor sword; they cannot corrupt nor arbitrarily control. They make no laws. They establish no policy, they never enter into the domain of public action. They do not govern. Their functions . . . are limited to seeing that popular action does not trespass upon right and justice as it exists in written constitutions and natural law."[99] Not long after Brewer's statement the jurisprudential theory on which it rested was subjected to severe attack. The course of the American judicial tradition in the twentieth century was dramatically affected by that attack. A fear of unchecked result-orientation in the judiciary, covert for the most part throughout the nineteenth century, became starkly overt. The consequences of that development for twentieth-century judges require lengthy attention. First, however, a brief recapitulation of the tradition's course in the nineteenth century.

6 

The Tradition at the Close of the Nineteenth Century

With the end of Harlan's tenure, American appellate judging entered the twentieth century. Harlan's performance exemplified this development in a symbolic as well as a literal sense. While memories that influenced his decision-making resurrected experiences of an older America, his special concerns foreshadowed major areas of twentieth-century judicial activity. He therefore affords a stopping place for some general observations on the path of American appellate judging from the opening to the closing of the nineteenth century.

The elements of judging central to Marshall's conception of his office—independence and accountability; detachment from, yet involvement with politics; a sense that judicial power was a constraining as well as a liberating force—survived intact throughout the nineteenth century. The times when the Supreme Court seriously lowered its own stature through imprudent or misguided decisions, as in *Dred Scott* or the conflicting *Legal Tender* cases, served to strengthen Marshall's legacy. *Dred Scott* and the *Legal Tender* cases were instances in which judges had been too openly responsive to political pressures or too ambitious in the use of their power. The lesson of those "self-inflicted wounds"[1] was that judicial independence could be achieved only through the appearance of genuine detachment and restraint. Those qualities were somehow associated with appeals in opinions to "first principles," the consensual norms and values of American civilization. To avoid such an appeal, as in the *Legal Tender* cases, or to make it imperfectly, as in *Dred Scott,* was to summon up the specter of judicial tyranny and to threaten the concept of an independent judiciary. None of the leading judges of the nineteenth century was as successful as Marshall in making this appeal, either because their sense of first principles differed from that of a majority of their contemporaries, because they were unable to perceive or articulate the consensual norms of their times, or because no clear consensus of values existed. But the challenge of Marshall's legacy remained intact throughout the century.

The legacy passed down by Marshall helped write additional themes emerging out of the experience of nineteenth-century appellate judging. One involved the complex relations between ideological beliefs and interpretations of the office of judge. A strong set of ideological convictions influenced the way that certain judges, notably Harlan, interpreted their roles, but in other judges, such as Shaw, Cooley, or Doe, ideological positions were derivative of attitudes toward judicial performance. In still others, such as Marshall, Kent, and Story, political persuasions seemed to stimulate attitudes toward judging, and such attitudes, once independently developed, reinforced the judge's original political instincts. In addition, as the social context of judicial decisions altered during the course of the century, so did the implications of a particular theory of judging. Hence, to associate "activism" or "self-restraint" in nineteenth-century judges with "liberal" or "conservative" political views invites oversimplification unless the terms are used in context.

A second theme emerging in the nineteenth century involved the professional constituency of appellate judges and the related values of certainty, predictability, innovation, and flexibility. For certain judges, such as Shaw, Cooley, and Doe, a trade-off between certainty and innovativeness seemed more central to their decision-making process than any other variable. For others, such as Harlan, this variable seemed inconsequential. In some instances, professionalist values can aid attempts to characterize the performance of a judge. A seemingly bizarre pattern of performance may clarify itself, as in the case of Doe, if professionalist values are substituted for political ones. But an understanding that judges often respond to the expectations of those most immediately affected by their decisions can be stretched out of proportion. Not all judges are instrumentalists, and the law is more than a series of responses to the demands of professional elites.[2] The theme appeared most dramatically in the nineteenth century at the state court level, where issues of vast political significance appeared with less frequency; it was perhaps less decisive in the calculus of most Supreme Court Justices. But it serves to highlight the variegated pressures on the office of judge in nineteenth-century America.

Another element of the tradition of American judging, the delicate relation between the judiciary and politics, engendered a third theme of the nineteenth-century experience. The tacit assumption that judges could remain aloof from the political arena at one level and yet participate in it at another created an ambiguity in American jurisprudence. From Marshall to Harlan, judges conceived of themselves as oracles whose function was simply that of rendering intelligible an already existing body of legal principles. Even the innovative judges of the mid-nineteenth century, such as Taney and Shaw, who modified legal doctrines to respond to altered economic and social conditions, believed that they were not making law but merely discovering its continual applicability to changing events. Yet critics of the American judiciary, from Marshall's tenure on, preceived the ability of judicial decisions to influence the course of politics. They learned early to read opinions at two levels: one, the immediate practical result reached and its professional and political consequences; another, the reasoning justifying that result, this reasoning serving as a rationale for the use of power by an undemocratic branch of government.

Since the reasoning process in its opinions constituted the undemocratic judiciary's essential means of justifying its power in a democratic society, that process needed to emphasize constraints on the behavior of judges, so as to deflect fears of judicial tyranny. A conception of judges as passive oracles making already existing truths intelligible aided in that deflection, but because of the political ramifications of judicial decisions, it did not at any time in the century forestall scrutiny of judicial reasoning. On scrutiny, judicial opinions periodically revealed themselves as something other than mere declarations of the state of the law. They expressed political and social points of view; they advanced theories of governmental and societal relations. At times they seemed so transparently opinionated as to threaten the oracular theory of judging itself. Hence a tension developed between the conception of judges as lawfinders rather than lawmakers and the discernible impact of judicial decisions on political affairs. This tension ultimately resolved itself in a two-stage process in the early twentieth century: first, the articulation of a rigid version of the oracular theory, a version that denied any lawmaking function to judges at all; second, the exposure and eventual discrediting of the oracular theory itself. With the open concession that judges made law in some limited sense, the American judicial tradition began its twentieth-century phase.

7 

Holmes, Brandeis, and the Origins of Judicial Liberalism

A sharp distinction between "nineteenth-century" and "twentieth-century" phases of the American judicial tradition has some artificial features. Older jurisprudential attitudes and theories of judging persisted after 1900; their persistence, in fact, is one of the features of American judicial history in the twentieth century. The striking twentieth-century changes in the intellectual climate in which judicial decisions were made, discussed in this chapter and subsequent ones, should not create an inference that the nineteenth century, by contrast, was static in its jurisprudence; the difference is one of degree. Finally, the prominence given in this and succeeding chapters to modern liberalism as a force helping to redefine judicial attitudes cannot, in the face of previous chapters, be read as suggesting that an ideological dimension to judging in America is peculiar to the twentieth century.

Nonetheless, a major reorientation of the American judicial tradition did occur in the first decades of the twentieth century. The oracular theory of judging ceased to be regarded as a universal principle, eventually became a minority viewpoint, and subsequently lost academic respectability altogether. Although none of the basic challenges of appellate judging in America disappeared, the intellectual context in which they were faced was altered. That process of alteration was part of a more general re-examination of attitudes and values in America, out of which emerged the ideology of modern liberalism.

The standard referents for political thought during most of the twentieth century have been the terms "conservatism" and "liberalism." So ubiquitous has been their usage that they have ceased to function as sharp characterizations and have become symbolic instruments of rhetoric. The incorporation of the term "liberalism" into our contemporary vocabulary in this fashion has some historical significance, since the term had, at its modern origins, a precise and revolutionary meaning. It had suggested then a radically new ideological perspective, based on a rejection of longstanding assumptions about the way in which society ought to be organized and on the creation of a novel relation between the individual citizen and his government. "Liberalism" has lost its original meaning largely because its premises have become so widely and loosely accepted. Before the 1920s the term, in its modern sense, was barely known; by the 1950s it was academically respectable to argue that liberalism had been the dominant ideology in the history of American civilization.[1]

The origins of modern liberalism in America coincided with the Supreme Court tenures of Justices Oliver Wendell Holmes and Louis Brandeis. The coincidence was accidental but of great import. The social thought of Holmes and Brandeis was not decisively affected by the emergence of twentieth-century liberalism, nor were their interpretations of their office markedly influenced by any desire to act as models of modern liberal judges. But the advent of liberalism provided critics of the judiciary with a new perspective from which to evaluate judicial performance. This perspective revealed innovative and contemporary elements in the jurisprudence of Holmes and of Brandeis and led to their apotheosis as heroic liberal judges.

I

Modern liberalism began in America with an insight, which dawned around the outbreak of World War I and revived in the 1920s, that the cultural unity of American civilization was disintegrating. There were numerous diverse manifestations of this perception, ranging from nervous reaffirmations of the purity of Anglo-Saxon America to attacks upon traditional symbols of virtue and respectability.[2] Linking these myriad forms of protest was a feeling that the core values of American culture had become meaningless slogans, capable of countless self-serving interpretations and hence no longer capable of functioning as a code of honorable behavior. As though for the first time, skeptics of the period saw that every unifying value engendered its own countervalue: morality begat hypocrisy; progress, exploitation; religiosity, bigotry; refinement, snobbishness; democracy, philistinism. As older consensual values became tarnished, former success models became figures of irony and pathos. The captain of industry, the self-made man, and the supersalesman were each regarded as having had a part in creating the stock market crash of 1929 and the ensuing depression.

Another perception followed from the original consciousness of value disintegration. Mature industrialism had created inequities and left a residue of victims. While rewarding a large segment of the nation's citizens, it had ignored or hurt other segments. It had not, for instance, eradicated poverty, or measurably improved the welfare of industrial laborers, or helped the increased percentage of elderly persons, or improved the quality of rural life. For these groups, progress had not necessarily been beneficial; for them industrialization had not brought success.

Over time, the sense of a wholesale loss of consensual American values merged with the perception of the costs of industrial progress to produce an affirmative ideology that supplanted the scattered "reform" movements of the late nineteenth and early twentieth centuries. The chief catalyst in the appearance of modern liberalism as a positive social philosophy in America was the crisis produced by the Depression of the 1930s. That crisis gave an immediacy to reform proposals that had been articulated in the 1920s by persons such as the advocates of a welfare state in Great Britain.[3] The principal innovation of modern liberalism was its utilization of the state as an agent to fill the void left by consensual value disintegration. The state, in this role, became a permanent force for social planning, order, and enlightened progress, substituting its administrative procedures for the discredited set of traditional values. It articulated common national goals by fiat and conceived and executed social policies consistent with those goals. The goals were not elaborately linked to consensual values; they were more often the tentative formulations of those who managed the state. The pursuit of social goals represented a form of coerced coherence necessitated by crisis and the dissolution of a previous value consensus.

Liberalism, at the time of its origin, represented a modification of some of the tenets of preceding reform movements in the light of a twentieth-century crisis in values. It retained a belief in an active, positive government; it also supported expansion of the class of government wards and beneficiaries. But it modified many of the substantive assumptions of advocates of one or another form of paternalism, embodying them, if at all, in standards of fair procedure. A comparison of liberalism with populism and the early-twentieth-century reform movement of progressivism illustrates the modifications. The populists and progressives both supported legislation intended to benefit industrial laborers; so did the liberals of the New Deal. The rhetorical emphasis of the first two groups was on removing the conditions—such as excessive size in industrial corporations and exploitation of workers by employers—that prevented workers from achieving freedom and independence in their jobs. The rhetorical emphasis of liberalism was on securing for industrial workers a forum, through unionization and collective bargaining, in which their interests could be fairly and equally represented. For populists or progressives, reform often had a moral content, evidenced in idealized roles for its beneficiaries, such as that of free and independent yeomen for industrial workers. Liberal reformers were not so much concerned with the life-style or moral character of those whose causes they supported as with insuring them a fair opportunity to air their grievances and promote their own self-interests.[4]

Although the idea of professionals in government was first articulated in the twentieth century by progressives, liberals gave it a new interpretation. The progressives, borrowing notions advanced by late-nineteenth-century elite reformers, argued that the presence in government of persons of high social and economic status would stimulate a revival of moral values because such persons would be above corruption and beyond the influence of special interests.[5] Liberals, though retaining a belief that government should be managed by elites, equated elite status more with technical and administrative expertise than with wealth or social position. This modification was in keeping with the assumption of modern liberals that professionalism's essential impact was to be felt in efficient and fair governmental procedures.

At its inception liberalism was an ideology based less on a commitment to shared values than on a response to their perceived disintegration. But as it evolved, its constant attention to the plight of casualties of progress became itself a value, often articulated as humanitarianism. As the victims of twentieth-century life came to include not only economic minorities but also ethnic, religious, or racial groups, a paradox developed. Humanitarianism compelled support for those whose minority status was made manifest by usurpations of their civil rights and liberties. Yet policies conceived and implemented by governmental officials inevitably produced such usurpations. What was the proper liberal response to government suppression of dissident speech in wartime, to wartime incarceration of naturalized American citizens who had retained or previously held citizenship in an enemy nation, to the invasion of welfare recipients' privacy by government agencies? Liberalism had as its major premise the validity of positive governmental intervention to further individual rights; what happened when the state acted to suppress them?

The paradoxes in modern liberalism were reflected in its ideals for judicial performance. On one hand, liberalism asked judges to reach results in keeping with the substantive values it cherished, such as those that sustained affirmative governmental action to alleviate economic and social inequalities or to help disadvantaged persons. On the other hand, liberalism asked judges to interpret their office in a professional manner—and by the 1920s judicial professionalism had taken on a new meaning. The model of judging embodied by Field had encountered strong criticism from legal scholars. The model permitted (so critics charged) an unwarranted imposition of the social and economic views of judges on the public at large. The apparent refusal of many members of the judiciary to respond to changed social conditions only exacerbated the situation.[6] Indeed some states, thwarted by the courts in their attempts to enact social welfare legislation, had responded by imposing elective checks, such as recall, on the performance of their judges. Two early-twentieth-century jurisprudential theories, Sociological Jurisprudence and a then nameless one that was eventually called Realism, had gained prominence on the strength of arguments that judging was a highly politicized and idiosyncratic process and that effective judicial performance could come only from constant attention to the social context of decisions, a full recognition by judges of the role that bias played in decision-making, and serious efforts on the part of the judiciary to confine the scope of its powers.[7]

The stunning effect of this criticism, in terms of the history of appellate judging, was its discrediting of the oracular theory of judicial decision-making.

Deference by the judiciary to legislative activity was required (the critique maintained) for the reason that law could be shaped in the process of judicial interpretation to harmonize with the predilections of the judge. To claim that judicial theories of social organization or economics were outmoded was to imply that the law could be made synonymous with the social attitudes of judges. The vast majority of nineteenth-century jurists had not ignored the fact that judges had social attitudes, but they had insisted on a separation of those attitudes from the fabric of the law itself. Discovering the law remained a process independent of one's personal convictions, despite the social ramifications of discoveries. Sociological Jurisprudence and Realism found the separation between "law" and the interpretations of its officials to be artificial. Realism eventually took the step of equating law with the idiosyncratic judgments of judges and other lawmakers, but this step was not necessary to discredit the oracular theory of judging. All that was needed was the triumph of the belief that judges were, even in a limited sense, lawmakers rather than simply law finders.

All these factors combined to make what came to be called judicial self-restraint an important professional value. Competent professionalism, as defined by a set of academic critics in the early twentieth century, demanded that judges abandon the use of their office to bar "excessively democratic" legislation. Such a response was grounded simply on bias and was therefore intellectually unjustifiable. The appellate judiciary should not substitute its views on social issues for those of the legislature; the latter branch was far better suited to perceive and respond to social change. Judicial professionalism, if not humanitarianism, thus dictated deference on the part of judges to the affirmative governmental actions supported by liberals.

From the time of Holmes's appointment to the Court in 1902 through Brandeis's appointment in 1916 to Holmes's retirement in 1932, the general tenets of liberalism and its double-edged mandate for the judiciary gained increasing acceptance. At the same time a large number of appellate judges, including a shifting majority of the Justices on the Supreme Court, continued to scrutinize and invalidate social welfare legislation, often using language that suggested a continued belief in the oracular theory of judging. In most instances the scrutinized legislation constituted an intervention in behalf of disadvantaged groups or individuals. From a liberal perspective, judicial self-restraint in such cases facilitated desirable results. For reasons primarily related to their approach to judging, Holmes and Brandeis both protested against judicial involvement in the great majority of such cases and were subsequently hailed as modern liberals.[8] In a smaller set of cases, the limits of government power to suppress individual rights were tested. Here the Holmes-Brandeis hegemony broke down, and differences between their jurisprudential views were revealed. In this latter group of cases their images as liberals became somewhat clouded, and some of the inherent contradictions in judicial liberalism were first exposed.

II

The conspicious advantages of Holmes's youth—his family being socially prominent, economically confortable, and at the center of Boston's intellectual community—only served to fire his ambition to divorce himself from his heritage and to distinguish himself in his own right. His father was not merely a competent physician and well-known poet but also a leading public figure of his time; he loved publicity, social companionship, and good conversation, and his public reputation was thereby so deeply entrenched that when the younger Holmes was appointed to the Supreme Court in 1902, at age sixty-one, he was chiefly described as Dr. Holmes's son.[9] Holmes reacted early and sharply against the stature and impact of his father. He was as solitary and self-preoccupied as his father was garrulous; as serious and introspective as his father was effervescent and glib. Dr. Holmes thought his son given to "looking at life as a solemn show where he is only a spectator";[10] William James, less charitable, found in him a "cold-blooded, conscious egotism and conceit."[11] For his part, Holmes thought his father "largely distracted into easy talk and occasional verse": had Dr. Holmes been "less popular," said his son, "he might have produced a great work."[12]

In Holmes's college years he seemed eager to arrive at some organizing ideological or philosophical principle that would isolate his way of thinking from that of his family circle. He rejected his father's religious views and at one point believed that "an all-comprehending science has embraced the universe . . . generalizing and systematizing . . . every vagary of the human mind."[13] In the 1850's, as the gap between North and South widened, Holmes became a rabid abolitionist and, when war came, enlisted in a regiment of Massachusetts volunteers in the Union army. Once at war, however, he found that life resisted a neat intellectual ordering and that the rightness or wrongness of beliefs was largely irrelevant. From these experiences came the celebrated paradoxes on which Holmes built his mature philosophic stance. Searching for general principles was the ultimate in intellectual satisfaction, but no generalization was worth a damn; fighting for ideals was heroic, but ideals were meaningless in themselves.

One can see the presence of these paradoxes in Holmes's scholarship, written largely in the nineteenth century; in his general attitude toward the relation of governmental institutions to social change; and in his interpretation of his judicial office. In his most extensive and impressive piece of scholarship, *The Common Law* (1880), he adopted an analytical technique that was to become characteristic: exposure of the fallacies of a prevailing system of thought, substitution of a counter-system, denial of the "truth" of that counter-system. In *The Common Law* the discarded system was nineteenth-century "logic," by which Holmes meant the formalistic, religion-based logic that reasoned downward syllogistically from assumed truths about the universe; the proposed counter-system was "experience," the changing "felt necessities" that reflected current social values and were altered by time and circumstances. Yet experience did not always produce wisdom, and change was not always for the better; so Holmes's system was not a model for lawmaking but merely a fatalistic acceptance that law was not so much the embodiment of reason as a manifestation of dominant beliefs at a given time.

Similar messages were conveyed in his two other major contributions to legal scholarship of the nineteenth century. In an essay, "The Path of the Law," he denied that the law was "a system of reason" or a series of "deduction[s] from principles of ethics";[14] it was simply an embodiment of the ends and purposes of a society at a given point in its history. One could study current social purposes and, by referring legal rules to them, better understand the course of legal development. One could not, however, treat some purposes as invariably true or timeless and erect a logical jurisprudence on them. In another essay, "Law in Science and Science in Law," he argued, in fact, that one could even measure, through the techniques of statistics and economics, the intensity of the "competing social desires" that clashed in a lawsuit and, having made that measurement, arrive at a decision that kept law "in accord with the wishes and feelings of the community." But science, though a helpful tool, could not be thought of as an ultimate organizing principle. There would probably never be,

Holmes felt, a "commonwealth in which science [was] everywhere supreme." It was only "an ideal—but "without ideals what is life worth?"[15]

Holmes apparently never read a newspaper (at least in his later life), and kept informed on contemporary events mainly through correspondence and conversation. Although he once said that academic life was half-life, his lifestyle while a judge, particularly during his tenure on the Supreme Court, was cloistered, focused on intellectual pursuits, and entirely isolated from national government and politics. Yet Holmes had no difficulty forming opinions on current political issues and resolving, as a judge, delicate questions of government. So integrated and flexible was his philosophic stance that it could absorb new issues, ideals, and events without disturbing its essential balance.

Life, Holmes assumed, was in constant flux, ideals gaining and losing primacy; one could not alter this process, however devoted one was to a particular viewpoint. The temporary triumph or defeat of ideas was determined by the unregulated intellectual marketplace. Hence there was no harm in tolerating the expression of ideas but no guarantee that any idea could survive for all time. Since America was a republic, majority opinion determined the acceptability of views, and a majority had the right to impose its beliefs on minorities. The principal vehicle for majoritarian expression was the lawmaking branch of the government; legislative power, grounded on majoritarian sentiment, was therefore limitless. But a majoritarian power to suppress minority viewpoints could be exercised only when the activities or viewpoints of a minority could reasonably be said to subvert social goals espoused by the prevailing majority. Up to that point, dissenting actions or opinions were protected, since they had a right to enter the intellectual marketplace to become "popular" or to be confined to oblivion.

Accordingly, the legislative branch of government could suppress speech, but only if the speech in question were clearly subversive of majoritarian social goals.[16] It could sterilize imbeciles if the ultimate eradication of mental defectives from the population were an end receiving majority support and if sterilization could reasonably be said to further that end.[17] It could prevent aliens from owning guns if the belief of a majority that aliens were inclined more than citizens to violence could be deemed reasonable.[18] A citizen might nonetheless campaign all his life against a war, in behalf of imbeciles, for equal treatment for aliens, or for the broader ideal of freedom to act and speak in a dissenting vein. American society had long recognized the latter ideal, and Holmes believed that he would be as willing as others had been to die for it.[19] But at some point civilized living in America required the recognition that unpopular views were ultimately impotent because the sentiments of the majoritarians determined the path of the law; and short of revolution, the laws of a majority were to be obeyed.

If Holmes's polity worked smoothly, dissenting actions and viewpoints continually beat against the wall of majoritarianism, the majority acted against them, and clashes in "social desires" resulted. The resolution of these clashes was the task of the courts, which held the "sovereign prerogative of choice."[20] But their freedom of choice was severely limited. To some extent, courts were bound by the choices of their predecessors; it was not generally the province of judges to "undertake to renovate the law."[21] Even on those occasions when precedents gave no guidelines, a series of institutional constraints derived from Holmes's notion of majoritarian sovereignty limited judicial freedom. The judiciary, not being elected representatives of the majority, was [not] to substitute its views for those of legislatures. The judiciary did not necessarily protect even constitutional rights against legislative infringement. All individual rights, for Holmes, were ultimately held at majority sufferance. Vindication of a right that the majority chose to circumscribe required a revolution and the forcible installation of a new majority.

Over and over, in his years on the Supreme Court, Holmes sounded these themes. Paternalistic social-welfare legislation was challenged before the Court; Holmes, who liked to play the cranky Social Darwinist, muttered about the frivolity or foolishness of the legislation but upheld the legislature's power to enact it. This interpretation of the judicial function came to be called tolerant or self-restrained or even statesmanlike by Holmes's admirers. Holmes, professing disdain for the last appellation, privately coveted it.[22]

In the end Holmes's intellectual vantage point was compatible with the opposing impulses that lurked, unarticulated, within him. He felt pride in the democratic and egalitarian consciousness of Americans, yet he was an intellectual and social snob, contemptuous of the "crowd." His personal relations were marked by barriers and distance. The archetypal Holmes friendship was a correspondence friendship, with the other participant being inaccessible to Holmes except for occasional visits. Even the most persistent of his correspondents, such as Harold Laski, rarely got beyond a certain level of intimacy.

When Laski proposed, after many years of letters, that he call Holmes by his first name, he was summarily rebuffed.

Although much of Holmes's communication with others was at the level of intellectual abstraction, he also had an earthy, bawdy side, which punctuated his talk and occasionally his writings and revealed itself in his covert private life. Much of the distinctiveness of Holmes's style came from his juxtaposition of earthy or homely language with abstract ideas; although he held the two impulses apart in his activities, in his thoughts they easily intermeshed. "I wonder," he once said, "if cosmically an idea is any more important than the bowels."[23]

The internal tensions in Holmes ultimately led him to a fatalistic dependence on paradox and impotence, and this formed the basis of his jurisprudence. Consciously or unconsciously, he perceived the opposing impulses in himself, and gave up attempting to reconcile them. Whether man was inherently evil or perfectible, whether change ever constituted progress, even whether he himself existed—a question he took seriously—were unanswerable riddles. The easy solution was to acknowledge "ultimate facts"—power, force, and change—and let the "goodness or badness of laws" turn on "what the crowd wants," even though the crowd, "if it knew," would not want what it did.[24]

III

Late in his career Holmes came increasingly to parallel Brandeis, who had joined Holmes on the Court in 1916, in his voting record on certain constitutional issues. Chief Justice William Howard Taft, who was never enthusiastic about Brandeis as a colleague, said that in his later years Holmes was "so completely under the control" of Brandeis that it gave Brandeis two votes instead of one.[25] A 1927 press comment claimed that Holmes and Brandeis had "achieved a spiritual kinship that mark[ed] them off as a separate liberal chamber" of the Court.[26] The kinship of Holmes and Brandeis was one of the accidents of history. Neither their temperaments nor their philosophies were similar; the congruence of their views was largely a matter of time and circumstance.

As a young man Brandeis coveted the symbols of Holmes's inheritance: social prestige, affluence, and access to the Boston intelligentsia. The son of German immigrants who had settled in Kentucky, he entered Harvard Law School at eighteen in 1875 and rapidly became entranced by the intellectual atmosphere of Cambridge, determining for himself the "rising lights" among his professors[27] and "carefully not[ing] the names and addresses of eminent people."[28] He felt, as a Southerner, a Jew, and not a college graduate, that gaps existed between himself and his peers; he strove to narrow those gaps by adopting the life-styles of those about him. He was successful enough in this endeavor to lay the groundwork for a prospective law partnership in Boston with Samuel Warren, a wealthy socialite, and to secure for himself and his wife, a Jew from New York, a moderate degree of acceptance on the part of Boston society.[29]

Once economically and socially comfortable, however, Brandeis did not blend into Holmes's world. He was mindful, as he said to a close friend, that "whatever I have achieved, or may achieve is my own, pure and simple, unassisted by the fortuitous circumstances of family influence or social position,"[30] and he retained a distance from the life in the trappings of which he surrounded himself. He joined clubs in order to "captivate" potential clients,[31] insisted that his wife adopt conventional upper-class dress standards, and dabbled in gentlemanly politics, such as civil service reform; yet in 1891 he attributed "the little successes I may have had" to "pressure from within" that stemmed from "a deep sense of obligation" rather than from "the allurement of a possible distinction."[32] Obligation for Brandeis meant adherence to a code of rigid personal standards, which included the tenets of self-denial, distaste for excess in any form, and moral righteousness. It was as though he were compelled by his conscience to follow these standards, with success following naturally upon them.

The Brandeis code justified, among other things, low heat in his law office to save expense, a short working day (to keep one's mind fresh), disdain for drinking, dancing, and like pursuits, the zealous molding of the lives of the underprivileged so that paupers might achieve "moral growth,"[33] distaste for sloppy and inefficient business practices, and eventually, in his maturity, adoption of the public as his client in a series of lawsuits designed to dissolve the monopolistic positions held by gas utilities, life insurance companies, banks, and the New Haven Railroad. It was not important to Brandeis that in those suits he actually represented competitors of the various industries rather than their consumers. What was important was that his clients recognize the value of moderation, efficiency, and social responsibility in their business practices. The proper task of the legal profession was to aid them in that recognition. Lawyers at large should occupy the position Brandeis had carved out for himself: one of "independence between the wealthy and the people, prepared to curb the excesses of either."[34]

By the time of Brandeis's appointment to the Court, against the protests of an influential segment of the Boston legal and commercial community, who felt that the combination of an economic reformer and a Jew was too much to tolerate, the eligible beneficiaries of his wisdom were numerous. He had scrutinized business trusts and concluded that excessive size produced economic waste. The trust-busting aspects of Woodrow Wilson's New Freedom were largely his creation.[35] Scientific management, the efficiency-oriented program created by the engineer Frederick Taylor, had become one of his causes, even though it was opposed by labor unions whose members he wanted to liberate from their industrial slavery. The moral fervor of Zionism and its passion for social planning attracted him, and he began to deplore assimilation on the part of American Jews, calling it "national suicide."[36] He lobbied for reform of the banking industry and was one of the draftsmen of the Federal Reserve Act, which initiated national control over the distribution of currency and credit. Even institutions of government became objects of Brandeisian crusades. As counsel for *Collier's Weekly*, which had exposed mismanagement of Interior Department resources, Brandeis publicized the cause of a middle-level employee of Interior who had been muzzled for uncovering inefficiency and corruption in his superiors.

As with Holmes, a juxtaposition of competing impulses formed the core of Brandeis's philosophy. In his case the impulses were those of freedom and self-restraint. Excess size, inequities, or inefficiencies choked or stifled individual initiative, he believed, but success and accomplishment were ascribed to self-abnegation and a conservation of human resources. Brandeis found industrial laborers his "most congenial company,"[37] and regarded the industrious among them as heroes (but was infuriated to see them smoking cigarettes). For him they were to be a counterpoint to the "intense materialism and luxuriousness"[38] of economic royalists. Freedom came, as it had in his case, from self-denial. In countless attempts to ingratiate himself with the eminent in Boston, in endless chilly days with overcoats substituted for radiators, in the husbanding of his early savings bonds, the moderation of pleasures, and the renunciation of luxuries were found the bits and pieces of Brandeis's eventual independence. When he joined the Court he was financially secure and beholden to no class or interest group. He was also convinced of his own righteousness, and zealous to impose his life-style on others.

The cosmic reach of Brandeis's philosophy suggested that he might come to the Court with developed views on the proper function of the judiciary. In actuality he had given little thought to the specific task of appellate judging, tending to include judges within his general observations on the legal profession. Two themes were central to his interpretation of law practice: the importance of empirical observation, and the lawyer's duty to be an intermediary between his clients and the public. Confronted with a legal problem, Brandeis sought to gather "the facts," and his great powers of organization and synthesis made fact analysis one of his special arts.

The facts having been collected and sifted, a course of action emerged. Each problem, he felt, formed the evidentiary basis of its own solution, since a sufficient supply of empirical data clarified the costs and benefits of various legal approaches. With the solution at hand, the next task was to persuade a client of its virtue. Here again, a grasp of "facts," including an understanding of the client's temperament, was a lawyer's best weapon. Empirical analysis, then, led to an inductive reasoning process in which costs were weighed against benefits; the process yielded a strategy with independent validity; a lawyer proceeded to persuade his client to adopt that strategy; in so doing, he not only gave good advice but influenced social policy and preserved his independence as well.

Judging, for Brandeis, was simply another exercise in this method. It was not a process of "reasoning from abstract conception," but one of "reasoning from life," taking "notice of facts."[39] In his first years on the Court, Brandeis seemed to make almost no distinction between his opinions and the briefs he had written as an advocate. He set forth the factual basis of his inquiry, undertook an extensive empirical investigation (complete with technical references), made a cost-benefit analysis of the effects of various policy choices made by a lower court or a legislature, chose the most efficient solution, and lobbied for it. In a case in his first year on the Court, *Adams v. Tanner*,[40] which considered the constitutionality of a Washington statute prohibiting employment agencies from charging fees, Brandeis asked himself what was "the evil which the people of Washington sought to correct," why had they chosen "the particular remedy embodied in the statute," and what had been "the experience . . . of other states or countries in this connection."[41] Fifteen pages of labor statistics provided the answers. Private employment agencies had been corrupt and inefficient. It was reasonable for the people of Washington to want to eradicate corruption and inefficiency, and just for the Court to promote their cause.

For Holmes, this sort of partisan documentation was out of place in a judicial opinion[42]—and tedious as well. Holmes was not concerned with showing the positive value of paternalistic or regulatory legislation, but merely that its basis was reasonable. Therein lay a vital difference between him and Brandeis. Both men, as judges, believed that a legislative majority could infringe upon individual rights. "Above all rights," Brandeis said in one opinion, "rises duty to the community."[43] But whereas Holmes simply accepted the ultimate logic of that view, Brandeis needed to be personally convinced of the rightness of the majority's action. He was not receptive to, indeed was suspicious of, governmental power in the abstract, but when that power was being used for a moral purpose, he welcomed it. For example, Brandeis believed that economic independence and political democracy were interrelated. Excess size in enterprises was not only wasteful, he felt, but posed a threat to individual self-reliance, since the enterprise, as a unit, came to wield power over its own employees and other American citizens. Hence the use of governmental power to reduce the size of giant corporations amounted to a crusade for individual freedom. There was nothing inherently attractive in governmental power, however; "Big Government" was as much a potential threat to the individual as "Big Business."

Holmes, in contrast, recognized the "fact" of majority sovereignty and suggested to oppressed minorities that they consider revolution. In the historic struggles between the increasingly omnipotent governments of the twentieth century and various sets of individual rights, Holmes's reaction to government intervention—if he thought it anything but arbitrary—was generally passive; Brandeis's selectively enthusiastic or hostile. Consequently Holmes was almost uniformly indifferent to individual rights or liberties, whether economic or civil, whereas Brandeis, despite his view that all rights were ultimately subsumed in a broad obligation to society, occasionally approximated the stance of a civil libertarian.

IV

Of the thousands of opinions written by Holmes and Brandeis during their tenure on the Court, perhaps the most revealing, if not necessarily the most influential, were those in which they considered the effect of governmental regulation on two sets of liberties—first, the Fifth and Fourteenth Amendments' alleged guarantees of "liberty of contract"; second, the First and Fourteenth Amendments' guarantees of free speech.

The doctrine of liberty of contract, originally hinted at by Cooley in *Constitutional Limitations*, was developed in state courts in the 1880s,[44] was slowly and obliquely incorporated in Supreme Court decisions in the late 1880s and 1890s,[45] and was explicitly, though irregularly, accepted by a Court majority between 1905 and 1923.[46] Its advocates postulated an inalienable right in employers and employees to buy and sell their goods or services on terms they chose, deriving this right, originally, from the Fourteenth Amendment's protection against state interference with liberty and property. Later a similar gloss was made on the Fifth Amendment's protection of liberty and property rights from interference by the federal government, making liberty of contract a philosophical principle as well as a constitutional doctrine. In its most extreme form, liberty of contract declared that any governmental attempt to regulate private contractual relations was presumptively invalid. It was that presumption that jeopardized much of the welfare legislation of the early twentieth century.

Judicial use of the liberty-of-contract doctrine to invalidate paternalistic legislation became an object of controversy in the first decade of the twentieth century. Opponents of the doctrine, among them Roscoe Pound and Theodore Roosevelt, suggested that it was unsound for two reasons: it ignored "new conceptions of the relation of property to human welfare,"[47] and it exemplified an artificial process of judicial reasoning in which predetermined beliefs were developed pseudologically "in the teeth of the actual facts."[48] If every man held his property subject to the general right of the community to regulate its use, property and contract rights were not inalienable. To exaggerate their importance in judicial formulas such as liberty of contract, which ignored the disadvantaged position of industrial workers in modern America, was to fail to adjust "[legal] principles and doctrines to human conditions."[49] This failure invited a characterization of judges as reactionaries or antiquarians.

Holmes identified himself with the opponents of liberty of contract in his first Supreme Court opinion, but his opposition stemmed from a different source. The case, *Otis v. Parker*,[50] tested the constitutionality of a California statute prohibiting sales of stock shares on margin. Holmes dismissed a claim that the statute limited unduly the freedom of adult persons to make contracts, by invoking his view on the proper allocation of institutional power in America. The fact that a statute could be said in a general way to violate the Constitution did not end the inquiry, he maintained, for "general propositions do not carry us far." The appropriate question for the Court in cases involving legislative infringement of "liberties" was not whether judges thought the statute "excessive, unsuited to its ostensible end, or based on [disagreeable] conceptions of morality," but whether it had a rational purpose and could be said to be a reasonable exercise of legislative power.[51]

At the outset of his career on the Court, then, Holmes indicated that his opposition to the liberty-of-contract doctrine could not be grounded on any enthusiasm for the paternalistic legislation that he sustained against its challenge. He thought that hours-and-wages laws merely "shift[ed] the burden to a different point of incidence";[52] he professed indifference toward "legislation to make other people better";[53] he did not believe that "wholesale regeneration" could be achieved "by tinkering with the institution of property."[54] He simply acquiesced in the apparent fact that "the liberty of a citizen to do as he likes" was "interfered with . . . by every state or municipal institution which takes his money for purposes thought desirable, whether he likes it or not."[55] When a legislative majority believed that an "important ground of public policy" called for restraint of individual liberties, Holmes felt that the Constitution permitted that restraint. "[T]he right to make contracts at will that has been derived from the word liberty in the [Fifth and Fourteenth] Amendments," he observed, had "been stretched to its extreme."[56]

From *Lochner v. New York* through *Adair v. U.S.* to *Adkins v. Children's Hospital*, the last a 1923 case invalidating the constitutionality of a minimum-wage law in the District of Columbia as an undue interference with the liberty to contract, Holmes protested against the use of the doctrine and all such "general propositions of law" to decide "concrete cases." But his protest stemmed from a general proposition of his own: "the scope of state sovereignty" was "a question of fact."[57] By this phrase Holmes meant that governmental interference with individual liberties was permissible in circumstances in which that interference could be shown to be grounded on some rational basis or tied to the achievement of some important public purpose. Whether it could be so shown or so tied was a matter of quasi-empirical proof, proof of the seriousness and rationality of the legislature's purpose. The importance and seriousness of a given purpose varied with time, but the test of its rationality was majority sentiment. A majority might behave irrationally, however, and not every interference with liberties was justifiable. The mere fact that legislation infringing individual rights furthered a public purpose did not prevent judicial inquiry into its reasonableness. Such inquiries, however, could only be made on an *ad hoc* basis.

Nowhere in Holmes's approach was there an attempt to demonstrate the particular worth of a piece of legislation. He would support a paternalistic statute only to the extent of conceding that an economic or social inequality existed and that the disadvantaged group could fairly convince a majority that the inequality ought to be alleviated. Thus, in his dissent in *Coppage v. Kansas*,[58] a 1915 case that struck down a Kansas statute prohibiting employers from preventing their employees from joining labor unions, Holmes stated that "in present conditions a workingman not unnaturally might believe that only by belonging to a union can he secure a contract that shall be fair to him,"[59] but stopped well short of endorsing the value of labor unions.

In contrast to this fatalism and indifference was the righteousness and zeal of Brandeis. Liberty of contract arguments stimulated Brandeis to demonstrate the value of the legislation being challenged. His interest was not so much in exposing the sterility of judicial decisions that reasoned downward from preconceived beliefs as in showing that the preconceptions themselves were unsound in light of the "facts" of twentieth-century life in America. The liberty-of-contract doctrine was inadequate, he felt, not so much because it represented the inappropriate judicial promulgation of a particular economic theory, but because it assumed an equality of bargaining power between employees and employers when it did not actually exist, or because it failed to recognize that, in modern life, considerations of social welfare could transcend the exercise of individual rights.

For Brandeis there were good theories and bad theories, purposes that were noble and purposes that were illegitimate. A Washington statute forbidding employment agencies from receiving fees for their services had been passed in response to a number of "evils" incumbent upon that practice, including waste, inefficiency, and corruption.[60] An Arizona law forbidding the use of injunctions in labor disputes had been partially motivated by the inequitable and heavy-handed use of the practices and by the divided state of public opinion as to its efficacy.[61] A Nebraska statute fixing maximum weights for loaves of bread was attempting to eradicate unfair competition among bakers and frauds on the public.[62]

Brandeis's support for legislative infringements on individual rights, in short, varied with his enthusiasm for the goals envisaged by the legislation. In certain areas of life he believed firmly that persons should be protected against their own self-destructive tendencies, requiring not only moral guidance but a degree of coercion. Consumption of alcoholic beverages was one of these areas. For Brandeis "evil [was] sure to flow from the appetite of men for stimulating liquors."[63] He supported prohibition legislation and, as a judge, he granted to the federal government and the states a wide scope of power to implement it. A provision of the War-Time Prohibition Act of 1918 preventing the sale of liquors in bond was not an unconstitutional taking of property.[64] Congress and the states had power to enact legislation designed to suppress traffic in intoxicating liquors even if that legislation regulated alleged nonintoxicants such as beer and malt liquor.[65] The presence of intoxicating liquor in a car rendered it forfeitable to the government regardless of whether the car's owner knew of the liquor's presence.[66] The amount of liquor dispensed by physicians for medicinal purposes could be limited by Congress.[67]

Brandeis did not apply uniformly his belief that a paternalistic government should protect members of the public against themselves. In the area of free speech he seemed to move, in the course of his career in the Court, toward a stricter standard of judicial scrutiny for regulatory legislation than he advocated in cases involving property and contract rights. Holmes, as well, appeared in free speech cases to be giving greater deference to individual rights than his theory of majoritarian sovereignty would allow.

Free-speech cases in the early twentieth century underscored the anxieties that centered around the place of consensual norms and values in American civilization. Freedom to express dissident and unpopular sentiments had been a traditional American value, part of the nation's revolutionary heritage. But World War I, an increasingly diverse and heterogeneous population, and the international success of alternative ideologies to capitalism and democracy combined to produce a perception that dissident attitudes and values could threaten national security. As the ethnic and cultural heritage of American citizens became more diffuse, pressures for national unity against outside threats increased. The result was a strident reaffirmation of the values and norms that allegedly unified Americans in the face of their disintegration. Dissident speech raised the troublesome problem of defining what beliefs early twentieth-century Americans still held in common.

Holmes came to free-speech cases with an attitude he once expressed by saying "I see no meaning in the rights of man except what the crowd will fight for."[68] There were no such things as natural rights for Holmes, only the right of majorities to impose their opinions on minorities and the correlative right of minorities to overthrow the majority. But exchange of ideas, in a democratic society, was an essential part of the continual replacement of majorities by other majorities. Little as Holmes believed in the inalienability of free speech, he said, he hoped he would die for it; although time had "upset many fighting faiths," the "ultimate good desired" was best achieved by "free trade in ideas."[69]

Holmes thus appears to have accepted, in addition to the "ultimate fact" of force on which governmental power rested, an intermediate basis of legitimacy. In democratic societies, at any rate, one way in which majorities held power was by convincing citizens of the rightness of their beliefs. They imposed their views on others and suppressed dissenting opinions, but they also attempted to justify their own actions. Quite often in America, Holmes believed, majorities "doubt[ed] [their] power or [their] premises."[70] There was something about American civilization that lent an uneasy status to the naked use of power. Holmes did not go on record as applauding this uneasiness. He took pains, in fact, to stress that power was the essential rationale for governmental acts. But he recognized it and built his analysis of free-speech questions upon it.

Holmes began his free-speech decisions by stressing the power in legislatures to suppress speech and, having established that premise, attempted to work out an accommodation between majoritarian sovereignty and the First Amendment. In *Patterson v. Colorado*,[71] a 1907 decision, he allowed the Colorado Supreme Court to hold in contempt a man who had published articles criticizing its motives, announcing in the process that the First Amendment's protection extended primarily to prior restraints on speech, not to speech that had been published. In the 1915 case of *Fox v. Washington*,[72] which sustained the constitutionality of a statute punishing any speech that had a tendency to encourage or incite the commission of a crime, he made no inquiry into the actual consequences of the speaker's words.

But in *Schenck v. United States*[73] and *Abrams v. United States*, two 1919 cases, he appeared to be moving toward a practical compromise between governmental power and free expresssion, embodied in the "clear and present danger" test articulated in *Schenck*. The proper judicial inquiry in speech cases, Holmes maintained, was "whether the words used are used in such circumstances and are of such a nature as to create a clear and present danger that they will bring about the substantive evils that Congress has a right to prevent."[74] Under this test, circulars urging persons subject to the draft to resist conscription could be suppressed and their authors punished, but circulars urging munitions workers to support the Russian Revolution of 1917 were constitutionally protected.[75] The first endangered the American military effort in World War I, since the authors attempted to prevent the government from amassing a fighting force. The second did not have a similar effect, since the United States was not at war with Russia.

The test for clear and present danger was grounded on a paradox that became increasingly apparent, especially as used by Brandeis in cases in the 1920s. The test began with the assumption that free speech was not an absolute right, despite the First Amendment. It endorsed governmental infringement on individual liberties in principle and tolerated specific infringements. But it also set limits on the power of a legislative majority to suppress speech and permitted the judiciary to determine those limits. A court, under the test, could take a free-speech case away from the jury if it decided that the words sought to be suppressed had not in fact created a clear and present danger to majority security. The test could thus be seen, as Brandeis said in *Schaefer v. United States*,[76] as a "rule of reason":[77] a means by which judges scrutinized the rationality of legislative acts. As a rule of reason, it could conceivably be used the way late-nineteenth-century judicial rules of reason had been used—namely, as a means of allowing the judiciary to make substantive judgments on the worth of legislation.

Here Brandeis's confidence in the inherent soundness of his own judgments prevailed over his tendency to interpret the range of judicial powers narrowly. He believed that a careful analysis of the facts of a case could lead one to truth. When the insights generated by an inquiry into facts harmonized with his own predilections, conclusions became irresistible. Once he had drawn conclusions, he was not particularly tolerant of opposing views, nor terribly anxious, as a judge, to allow them much weight. In *Schaefer* he decided that the publication of newspaper articles expressing skepticism about the professed intent of the United States to send troops to Europe was so far from being an immediate danger to the American war effort that "no jury in calmness" could find it such. Accordingly, the test for clear and present danger dictated withdrawal of the case from jury consideration.[78] Similarly, in *Pierce v. United States*,[79] after carefully studying a Socialist Party leaflet that depicted the horrors of war and asserted that the Morgan interests were behind the war effort, Brandeis concluded that it was a mere expression of opinion that had even recognized its own impotence in inducing resistance against the war.

In these cases Brandeis was making a gloss on Holmes's test that Holmes himself was not entirely prepared to accept. Brandeis was concerned not only with the close connection of the suppressed speech to the occurrence of a preventable evil, but also with the seriousness of the evil that might occur. Holmes, in the 1919 cases in which he had formulated the test, had been interested primarily in the chronological relation of the speech to the evil. Brandeis believed that mere chronological proximity was not enough. If the evil that the speech induced was relatively trivial, the speech should be protected. In *Gilbert v. Minnesota*[80] a lobbyist was convicted, under a Minnesota statute prohibiting public speeches against the war effort, for stating that conscription should be subject to popular vote and that "if they conscripted wealth like they have conscripted men, this war would not last over forty-eight hours."[81] Holmes voted to sustain the conviction and uphold the statute's constitutionality; Brandeis dissented. The statute created a blanket prohibition of public speech against enlistment or in behalf of pacificism, Brandeis maintained. No effort was made to inquire into the purpose of the speech or to ascertain whether the speaker's remarks could reasonably be expected to induce others to perpetrate truly serious evils.

As free-speech cases moved outside the context of World War I, this difference in focus between Holmes and Brandeis persisted, even though it did not again result in their casting opposing votes. In *Gitlow v. New York*,[82] a 1925 case, a Socialist was convicted under the New York Criminal Anarchy Act of 1902 for advocating mass strikes and hostile action against the bourgeoisie. Holmes, in dissenting from the Court's decision sustaining the conviction against a free-speech challenge, distinguished between the advocacy of ideas in the abstract, and concrete attempts to induce others to carry out those ideas immediately. The "redundant discourse" of Gitlow, he maintained was not "an attempt to induce an uprising against government at once," but "at some indefinite time in the future."[83]

Brandeis joined this dissent, but his subsequent concurrence two years later in *Whitney v. California*[84] indicated that he was concerned with the seriousness as well as the imminence of the resulting evil. He read the test for clear and present danger, he said, as meaning that whenever the "fundamental rights of free speech and assembly" were allegedly invaded, a defendant could raise three questions: whether "there actually did exist at the time a clear danger"; whether "the danger, if any, was imminent"; and "whether the evil apprehended was one so substantial as to justify the stringent restriction interposed by the legislature."[85] The first two questions were questions of fact, the third was a question of law. A court could determine that the evil perceived was not sufficiently serious to merit legislative interference with free speech, and so withdraw the case from the jury. The judicial deference to legislative wisdom championed by Brandeis in liberty-of-contract cases did not always apply in speech cases.

Holmes joined Brandeis in his *Whitney* concurrence, but the facts of the case qualified his support. The defendant in Whitney had been convicted under a California criminal statute for participating in the organization of a state Communist Labor Party. The statute prohibited persons from becoming members of organizations that advocated violence as a means of inducing social or political change, and thus attempted to punish those who merely associated with persons who advocated or practiced violence. A majority of the Court peremptorily sustained the statute. Brandeis, however, thought that the statute might be constitutionally defective as applied to Miss Whitney. Her association with Communists, he argued, did not by itself constitute a sufficiently imminent danger to the security of the State of California. But there was other evidence that might have suggested that Miss Whitney and her associates posed an immediate threat to California's security; and thus Brandeis tolerated her conviction. His focus, ultimately, was thus on the imminence of the danger rather than the seriousness of the perceived evil. This focus was consistent with that of Holmes in *Gitlow*.

At the very end of his career, Holmes seemed to have accepted the notion of reversing the presumption of constitutional validity in speech cases. In *Near v. Minnesota*[86] a majority of the Court invalidated a statute allowing injunctions against newspapers that had printed allegedly defamatory material. In the process, the majority, through Chief Justice Charles Evans Hughes, asserted the importance of keeping the press immune from censorship of its publications and claimed the power to weigh the serious public evil caused by authority to prevent publication against the evils suppressed by the statute.[87] In this, the last speech case decided before Holmes's retirement, he and Brandeis were both members of the majority. Whether Holmes's acquiescence stemmed from his belief that protection from "prior restraints" formed the core of the First Amendment or whether he had actually endorsed Brandeis's gloss on his original clear-and-present-danger test is unclear.

Also in 1931 came one of the last liberty-of-contract cases of the twentieth century, *O'Gorman v. Hartford Ins. Co.*,[88] in which a New Jersey statute regulating the fees paid to local agents by insurance companies was challenged as a violation of the Fourteenth Amendment's due process clause. Brandeis, in a majority opinion sustaining the statute, made the familiar analysis of evils and remedies he had made in earlier liberty-of-contract cases and then invoked the presumption of the constitutionality of legislative acts to dispose of the case. Holmes voted with the majority. The entire five-man majority of *O'Gorman*, which included Justices Holmes, Brandeis, Hughes, Stone, and Owen Roberts, adopted a rule of presumptions for liberty-of-contract cases differing from that used for speech cases. Conversely, the four dissenters in *O'Gorman*—Justices Butler, McReynolds, Sutherland, and Van Devanter—proclaimed the inviolability of freedom to contract, but, as dissenters in *Near*, argued that legislative attempts to curb speech were presumptively valid. By 1931 liberty of speech had apparently come to occupy the exalted place once reserved for liberty of contract, while liberty of contract had been discredited.

Holmes and Brandeis had played an important part in a process that ultimately led to temporary placement of First Amendment liberties in a constitutionally "preferred position" over economic liberties. This development, when it was made manifest by the Court in 1945,[89] was hailed as a victory for liberalism and a tribute to the influence of the foremost judicial liberals of the early twentieth century, Holmes and Brandeis.[90] But rather than demonstrating the compatibility of liberalism with Holmes's and Brandeis's interpretations of their office, the liberty-of-contract and speech cases had unearthed the paradoxical nature of the modern liberal blueprint for judicial performance.

V

Holmes had taught that ideas and values, whether employed by judges or by others, were not absolutes but products of changing social conditions. Brandeis had taught that the empirical indices of change could be observed and analyzed and that, by this process, public policies could be made responsive to the dictates of contemporary life. Liberalism, as it coalesced into a definable ideology, drew upon both these insights. American society after World War I was marked by a simultaneous collapse of allegedly timeless values and norms and a pervasive need for governmental policies that responded to the newly perceived facts of modern industrial life. To an extent, Holmes helped make palatable a world without consensual norms, while Brandeis sought to show how governmental institutions could intervene to make that world more livable. Each contributed to the belief of modern liberalism that an activist state could provide both security and progress.

But if some strands of the thought of Holmes and Brandeis were harmonious with liberalism, others were not. The dissonance that thus resulted highlighted the uneasy role of the appellate judiciary in the liberal state. Holmes had been a leading late-nineteenth-century intellectual radical. His quarrel with that century's faith in universal axioms had made him an early-twentieth-century juristic reformer, exposing the essential subjectivity of the oracular approach to judging. With his distaste for intuitive judicial decision-making came an exaltation of self-restraint, and in the liberal world of fragmented values judicial self-restraint seemed eminently sensible. Holmes was hence a professional judge for liberals: the "completely adult jurist," to Jerome Frank.[91] But he was no humanitarian. He not only tolerated but actually believed in the principle of majoritarian repression of minority rights. He rejected the notion that free speech was an absolute right as surely as he rejected the inalienability of a liberty to contract. He was indifferent to the civil rights of blacks, Orientals, and aliens;[92] he was often satisfied with summary forms of procedural due process. His clear-and-present-danger test cut both ways: it carved out an area of constitutionally protected speech but also justified widespread suppression of "dangerous" expression. In short, Holmes abjured close scrutiny of repressive legislation as well as of welfare legislation. Hours and wages laws were sanctioned, but so were statutes requiring the compulsory sterilization of mental defectives.

Brandeis, as well, fell short of the paradigm of a liberal judge. Sometimes, as in the wartime prohibition cases, he assumed the presence of a consensus of values on moral issues that liberalism denied, thereby reaching what were perceived as illiberal results.[93] On other occasions his deviance from liberalism exhibited itself in his methods, as in those speech cases where through his gloss on the clear and present danger test he appeared to be endorsing a subjective form of judicial decision-making that the professional canons of liberalism repudiated. Brandeis was a liberal in his result-orientation only to the extent that liberalism endorsed Brandeisian social policies; he was a liberal in methodology only to the extent that judicial self-restraint fostered results that he thought sensible.

The careers of Holmes and Brandeis hence illustrated the tension in judicial liberalism between "right" results and "right" methods. That tension had been implanted in the movement at its origin. The early-twentieth-century critics of "mechanical" jurisprudence objected not only to methods but to results as well. They disliked conservatism in the appellate judiciary as much as they disliked subjective activism. Their critiques assumed that the liberty-of-contract doctrine represented unsound social policy as well as illogical reasoning, and that assumption rested on their own strong perception of the common goals of American civilization. But as the substantive content of consensual American values became increasingly difficult to perceive after World War I, judicial self-restraint took on an expanded meaning. It was not merely a check against wrong-headed subjectivity but also a means by which the judiciary assured that the decisions of the institution best suited to discern and reflect majoritarian sentiment—the legislature—were given their proper weight. Since the state had become a substitute for value consensus, its legislative fiats should be supported as buffers against anarchy.

The concept of an expansive regulatory state rested, however, on the premise that it would be responsive to the needs of disadvantaged minorities. Otherwise the egalitarian and democratic traditions of America would vanish, and liberalism would be synonymous with totalitarianism. The state was permitted to regulate private conduct only to the extent that its regulations were fairly implemented, and also conferred benefits on the disadvantaged that outweighed the costs to everyone else. Not every manifestation of majoritarian sentiment was to be tolerated; some legislative policies were illiberal. The only institution capable of scrutinizing the fairness of legislative activity was the judiciary; hence, judges in the liberal state should use their expertise in interpreting the Constitution to undertake that scrutiny. They should presume legislation to be constitutionally valid, but be prepared to override that presumption.

The harmony of methods and results envisaged by this conception of judicial performance was fated to dissolve in instances where pressure for national solidarity clashed with pressure to vindicate minority rights. The speech cases represented one such instance in which judicial self-restraint did not produce liberal results. Holmes and Brandeis, both of whom, in varying degrees, believed in tolerating legislative judgments and in vindicating free expression, struggled with the dilemma posed by these cases. Their eventual resolution, at least in the *Near* case, appeared to subordinate a liberal methodology to the achievement of liberal results. As a result of that case and other instances in which they seemed to champion the disadvantaged, they were apotheosized as liberals. That apotheosis, however, ignored the differences between them and minimized the inherent contradictions in modern liberalism's mandate for the judiciary. The considerable skills of Holmes and Brandeis—the keenness of their minds, their capacity for eloquence, the coherence of their thought—did not make any easier for them the task of squaring approved liberal results with approved liberal methods of judging. They, at least, were acute enough to see a potential tension between methods and results. Other early-twentieth-century members of the Supreme Court, who opposed modern liberalism in any form, failed to perceive a distinction between judging and vindicating one's social or political preferences. That failure generated another threat to the independence of the American appellate judiciary.

8

Hughes and Stone: Ironies of the Chief Justiceship

The catchphrase "first among equals" both reveals and obfuscates the role of the Chief Justice of the United States Supreme Court. The Chief Justice is a person with one vote in conference and one mind with which to make his presence felt. Often, though not always, his colleagues are his intellectual superiors, and sometimes Associate Justices dominate a Court, as with the Chase Court and to a lesser extent the Waite and Fuller Courts. Relations among those who occupy the office of Supreme Court Justice are shaped by the pride in self and status that accompanies the possession of that office. No member of the Court can fairly think of another as his subordinate, nor expect to be so perceived by his colleagues. In addition, the internal rituals of the Court reflect, to an extent, an institutional attempt to foster feelings of equality. Notes and memoranda are exchanged, critical comments are made, independence is asserted, heated discussion is anticipated, strength of character and conviction is valued even among antagonists. The Chief Justice presides, to be sure, over arguments, conferences, and other functions, but he also listens and defers and yields.

The Chief Justice can thus be said to be "among equals," and members of the Court—especially Chief Justices—have suggested that the "firstness" of the office is merely perfunctory and ceremonial. But this has not been true since Marshall's tenure. The office of Chief Justice has carried with it a special influence, an extra dimension of power, added opportunities to make one's mark in history. Among the perquisites of the Chief Justiceship is the possibility of leading a Court in more than formal ways. Not all Chiefs have chosen to exercise this kind of leadership, and some have tried and failed. But the possibility remains attached to the office. Marshall not only bequeathed a general legacy of judging to the Justices that followed him, he also left a special legacy to his successor Chiefs, a legacy that included a tradition of unanimity in Court decision-making, a sense of the delicate and ambivalent political position of the Court in the processes of American government, and a custom of forceful executive leadership in the Chief Justice. Marshall had built this legacy in numerous ways, among them his substitution of an opinion by the Court for the customary seriatim opinions; his insistence that members of the Court not engage openly and actively in partisan politics; his assignment of important opinions to himself or to Story, his trusted delegate; his subterranean efforts to disseminate his ideas beyond the courtroom and to vindicate his positions against attack.[1]

I

None of Marshall's nineteenth-century successors was able to preserve intact the combination of personal and political influence he passed on to them with his office. Taney was more permissive toward dissent and somewhat less astute as a political statesman. He dominated his Court to a lesser degree than did Marshall and saw it lose stature as a repository of political wisdom. Chase was embroiled in the *Legal Tender* controversy almost immediately after taking office and failed to divorce his office from his Presidential ambitions, thereby losing the respect of his colleagues. Waite fought cheerfully and not always unsuccessfully against the apparent inevitability of Field's ideas, but became increasingly overshadowed. Fuller came to the office with ordinary intellectual talents and little professional reputation, and managed to remain obscure even though he was regularly in sympathy with the majority views of his Court.

The strong Chief Justice apparently returned with the twentieth-century appointments of White and Taft. Holmes had felt that, next to himself, White was the finest intellect on the Fuller Court.[2] Not a man to change his mind in the face of opposition, White did not shrink from attempting to exercise influence over others. Taft, for his part, came to the office with experiences and lines of communication that no previous Chief had ever had. But two changes coinciding with the advent of the twentieth century were, in separate ways, to limit the power of both White and Taft. First, the business of the Court was to grow to the point where the Chief Justice's administrative duties took on a new dimension. Second, the Court developed a reputation as a leading source of resistance to social change.

At the opening of the 1870 term the Court had 636 cases listed for decision. Five years later, Congress passed the Judiciary Act of 1875,[3] which expanded the jurisdiction of the federal courts to include "federal question" disputes and a full range of diversity-of-citizenship cases, when the alleged damages exceeded $1000. The effect of this Act was to increase greatly the Court's docket.[4] In addition, from 1866 to 1889 direct review to the Court was expanded, encompassing civil rights,[5] patents,[6] jurisdictional questions,[7] and habeas corpus petitions.[8] Furthermore, the practice of lower federal judges of certifying questions for guidance by the Court was eliminated by statute in 1872,[9] and in its place the Court was authorized to review on appeal cases in which federal circuit court judges had evidenced differing views.

In 1891 Congress passed the Everts Act,[10] which attempted to meet the problem of overcrowded Court dockets. The Act created three-judge circuit courts of appeals as intermediaries between the federal district courts and the Supreme Court, and restricted the means of appeal to the Court by introducing discretionary certiorari power, through which the Court could decline to hear selected cases if a given number of Justices felt that the case was not of sufficient importance. Denial of a certiorari petition meant that the decision of the Circuit Court was upheld. The certiorari power, however, did not extend to all cases, and between 1891 and 1925, when another Congressional statute[11] attempted to reduce the Court's workload, the docket continued to expand. Major increases in population, a more extensive governmental administrative apparatus, and other less perceptible factors accounted for this trend. By the time of Taft's tenure the certiorari power was seen as the Court's principal means of keeping abreast of its work.[12]

White's Chief Justiceship showed the increased importance of administrative ability in the Court's presiding officer. Fuller was "extraordinary" as an administrator, according to Holmes. "He had the business of the court at his fingers' ends; he was perfectly courageous, prompt, dedicated. He turned off the matters that daily call for action easily, swiftly, with the least possible friction . . . and with a humor that relieved any tension with a laugh."[13] Holmes thought these qualities helpful but trivial. Others, such as Charles Evans Hughes, found them more important.

Hughes came on the Court in 1910, at the same time that White was named Chief Justice. Later Hughes was to remember White's habits of stating cases imprecisely at conference, offering virtually no suggestions as to how to dispose of each case, and allowing discussion to ramble.[14] During White's tenure the Court was not clear about how to make use of its new certiorari power and suffered from a haphazard management of its docket. It might begin a term behind in its work, then allow more important cases to be pushed ahead, so that it often ended in June with a backlog of over a hundred undisposed cases.[15] The experience taught Hughes a lesson he was to put into practice: an efficient, well-organized Chief could not only manage his docket but increase his power in the process.

Taft succeeded at administration where White had failed. He helped push through Congress the Judiciary Act of 1925, which reorganized the federal courts and put teeth in the certiorari power. During his tenure the practice of assigning to each Justice a law clerk (first called a secretary) to help with certiorari petitions and other research was adopted generally. He pressed his colleagues to keep up with their workload. He asserted himself, in his own genial fashion, in conference. But the very sources of Taft's strength were also sources of weakness. He cajoled and pressured his brethren toward unanimity and consistency in their decisions and took pride in the regular triumph of his views, but he unwittingly painted for the nation a picture of the Court as a monolith of reaction, asserting the beliefs of the late nineteenth century in a changed world.

The leadership patterns of White and Taft indicated means by which twentieth-century Chief Justices could exercise or fail to exercise leadership. The first means, of ever increasing importance, was through administration of the Court's internal business. Faced with a massive docket, armed with a research staff and the certiorari power, entrusted with the duty of organizing and presiding over conferences, allotted the increasingly important task of summarizing the work to be taken up at a conference, the Chief Justice could shape the Court's business in a fashion convenient to himself, thereby making administration an exercise in maintaining power and perpetuating of influence. A second means was through scholarly exchange. The Chief continued to be among equals, but enjoyed the privilege of stating his views first and voting last. An accomplished administrator could combine the first two means through careful selection of items for the agenda and sophisticated presentation of viewpoints affecting each item.

The third means was through political influence. Taft had been an artist at one sort of political involvement, but other, more symbolic options were open—e.g., speeches before professional groups, cultivation of an imposing manner of presiding over the Court, development of subtle but effective lobbying with Congress for accoutrements, an interest in the response of the nation's press to Court decisions. In each of these areas the twentieth-century Chief Justice was better suited to exert influence than any of his colleagues. He stood for and could shape his Court.

In the light of such opportunities, the careers of two prominent twentieth-century Chief Justices, Charles Evans Hughes and Harlan Fiske Stone, were fraught with ironies. The ironic cast of their respective Chief Justiceships came from the fact that performance expectations engendered by the image of each man on his confirmation as Chief were unrealized. Neither Hughes nor Stone can be said to have failed as Chief Justices. Their experience simply did not materialize as they and others expected it to. Their reputations were not necessarily damaged by the experience, but they were altered. Their tenures reveal the complexity and uncertainty of the process of holding the office of Chief Justice of the Supreme Court.

In Hughes's case the central irony concerned his management of his office. It appeared at the time of his nomination that no man had ever come to the Chief Justiceship better suited to perform its duties. Hughes was the embodiment of the modern Chief Justice. He was conspiciously efficient, ideologically receptive to progress and reform, aloof from partisan politics, of immense public stature, with wide-ranging contacts in all branches of government and influential sectors of private enterprise, possessed of superior qualities as an intellectual technician, and experienced as a Supreme Court Justice. If ever an individual seemed matched to the needs of an office, it was Hughes: the modern Chief for a Court adapting itself to New Deal America. And yet under Hughes the Court first isolated itself from the mood of the nation, then painfully and embarrassingly embraced it, revealed itself as being polarized and rancorous, saw its autonomy and even its composition threatened, and lost its aloofness from politics. Hughes himself was not responsible for most of these difficulties, but he was powerless to alleviate them and may even have exacerbated them.

In the case of Stone the ironies were strikingly different. Upon his appointment to the Court as an Associate Justice, Stone became a marginal member of the Taft majority. Yet before long he found himself increasingly quarreling with that majority's premises, and, on the Hughes Court, siding with those Justices who supported New Deal experimental legislation. Eventually this group itself became a majority, one apparently committed to sympathetic treatment of the policies of the Roosevelt Administrations. In short, Stone became Chief Justice of a Court whose personnel increasingly supported positions he had held under fire and seen vindicated. Yet under Stone the new majority fell out among themselves, both personally and ideologically, so that the expectations of the nation—as expressed by the nation's press—of a new "liberal" monolith were dashed into fragments.

As in the case of Hughes, some of Stone's difficulties seemingly arose from factors over which he had no control. Fragmentation of the "liberal" Stone Court came in part from the fact that the issues confronted by the Court at the onset of the New Deal were somewhat different from those it would confront in the 1940s. Justices who agreed, for example, on the general principle of judicial permissiveness toward economic regulation might not agree on specific extensions of that principle, especially when those extensions affected institutional balances in a federalist system of government.[16] Fragmentation was related also to the consideration of altogether novel issues, such as the role of civil liberties in a society dominated as never before by statutory and administrative regulation. But it came as well from Stone's style of leadership. He was not able to coalesce his Roosevelt appointees into a majority that articulated a consistent, rounded philosophy of constitutional interpretation, although he had seemed, by reason of his acknowledged skills, his symbolic role in preceding Courts, and his strong and likable personality, eminently capable of such an achievement.

Both Hughes and Stone underwent experiences that symbolized the ironies of their tenures. The unassailable, nonpartisan Hughes went hat in hand in 1937 to argue for the perpetuation of a nine-man Court before a Senate Committee. Stone, the Justice who had seen more of his dissents become majority positions than any other Justice in the Court's history, delivered as the last opinion of his life a dissent from one of those new majority decisions.[17] The position he had once espoused and the Court now adopted was, he maintained, no longer good law.

II

Hughes was an extraordinary person, it seemed, almost from the moment he was born. As a child his health was frail and his contacts with others minimal, but his intellectual powers were fearsome. A photographic memory, combined with an internalization of his parents' maxim to "be thorough in all you undertake,"[18] enabled him to excel in undergraduate classes at Madison College (now Colgate University) and Brown University, at Columbia Law School, and on the New York State bar examination, where he received the highest possible score.[19] For all his working life Hughes retained his obsession with thoroughness and his great capacity for amassing and organizing details. During his early career as a practitioner in New York, where he entered a partnership with Walter S. Carter and Paul D. Cravath, two founding fathers of modern Wall Street practice, Hughes mastered German and the intricacies of the sugar beet industry for one case so that he could cross-examine German engineers in connection with breakdowns in the operation of a sugar beet factory designed in Germany.[20] He could, one of his law clerks said, "read a paragraph at a glance, a treatise in an evening, a roomful of papers in a week";[21] he could also retain what he read to a remarkable degree. In this respect Hughes was an ideal investigator of complex businesses, such as the New York State gas utilities and insurance industry or the aircraft industry in World War I, or the armaments industries in the 1920s.

Hughes was an ideal early-twentieth-century investigator and administrator in two other respects. Like many others who saw themselves as "progressives," Hughes made a fetish of efficiency.[22] In his view, modern America had grown complicated and technocratic almost overnight, and hence careful, thorough management of private and public enterprise was essential to prevent disorderly and wasteful growth. His zeal for efficiency harmonized with his own intellectual abilities. His talents lay in sifting, organizing, and marshaling pieces of evidence rather than in imaginative or creative thought.[23] He associated efficiency with objectivity and nonpartisanship, two qualities he and numerous others of the time valued in public service. Moreover, as he matured he saw efficient administration as a means of acquiring and holding power.

The second quality that endeared Hughes to early-twentieth-century reformers was his combination of moral fervor and personal aloofness. Hughes's strong religious antecedents survived in his adulthood as a strong sense of duty. He had been filial toward his parents, despite his not opting for the ministry, as they had wished; likewise he was loyal to the perceived obligations of the offices he held, and he invariably interpreted them in moral terms. This meant rigid nonpartisanship as referee, arbitrator, investigator, or judge; strong commitment to social justice through efficient administration as Governor of New York; a certain forced buoyancy and conviviality coupled with Calvinistic patriotism as a Presidential candidate. In playing these various roles, Hughes seemed to hold something back. To those around him he appeared unapproachable, austere, and cold, and his career as an elected official may have suffered accordingly. But despite his concern that the public regarded him "as a human icicle,"[24] his aloofness may well not have been a disadvantage. He personified the reformer who was above politics, the man immune from corruption and special influence, committed only to the ideals of honest government, efficiency, and progress. In addition, detachment from the privileges and favors of his offices allowed Hughes to appear as a genuine public servant whose constituency was not the professional politicians but the people. This was a position he took seriously and an image he thought consonant with reality. "I am," he said during his tenure as Secretary of State, "counsel for the people of this country."[25] In other roles his assumed aloofness was a positive advantage. Felix Frankfurter said of Hughes as Chief Justice that he "acted on the realization that aloofness is indispensable to the effective discharge of the Supreme Court's functions."[26]

Hughes tried to appear human, and succeeded with some of his closest acquaintances. A shipmate on a European voyage found him "friendly and genial" rather than the "cold, detached, self-centered individual" he expected;[27] Holmes thought him "funny" and not altogether rigid in his "nonconformist conscience";[28] Justice Roberts described him as "considerate, sympathetic, and responsive";[29] Frankfurter felt him whimsical, genial, and mischievous.[30] His wife and children regularly received warm tributes of admiration and affection from him.[31] Others, however, persisted in thinking him remote. Herbert Hoover, one great admirer, said that he had "no instinct for personal friendship that I ever could discover."[32]

Hughes's personal characteristics so dominated his social attitudes that his ideological views resist characterization. He joined strongly held, quasi-religious convictions with a general desire to be thought of as a political moderate. So long as he appeared consistent to himself, he was not particularly concerned with how his actions were characterized by others, caring only that his views did not isolate him. He came to the career of judging with deep beliefs about the close connection between efficiency and justice. If persons in authority performed their tasks in an impartial and careful fashion, he reasoned, they would effectively serve the welfare of their constituents. "The more we study the problems of organization and method and appreciate the necessity of improvements in these respects," he wrote in 1931, "the more sensible we are that such improvements can serve only to clear the way for the essential judicial service which no unit of mechanization can supply."[33] Effective management and organization bred stability, stability was a necessary component of progress, and "growth and progress are the law of our nature."[34]

In some respects Hughes, as a judge, appeared to be a link to the Founding Fathers.[35] He believed that the structure of American government rested on delicate balances, such as that between individual autonomy and the demands of governing institutions, that between competing sovereign powers, federal and state, that between the respective branches of government, and that between the intentions of the framers and the open-ended content of the commerce, due process, and equal protection clauses. He tried to adapt this system of balances to an industrial, urbanized, polyglot society without essentially disturbing its equilibrium. This entailed a series of trade-offs. The commerce clause need not prohibit all forms of state taxation,[36] but it did prohibit some; Congress could regulate instrumentalities not used solely in interstate commerce, so long as they affected that commerce,[37] but sometimes factual investigations revealed that they did not affect it.[38] Administrative agencies could constitutionally make an independent, final determination of facts necessary to their decisions,[39] but a court, on review, could make its own factual determinations if the agency's action had adversely affected property rights.[40] Government infringements on civil liberties should be carefully scrutinized[41] and vigorously checked,[42] but not all libertarian interests were to be protected,[43] and the due process clause gave no greater safeguards to civil liberties than it did to property rights.[44]

The theme of moderation suggests itself in Hughes's balancing efforts and in certain of his public statements, such as his insistence in 1932 that judges "escape the errors of . . . extreme constructions" in constitutional adjudication.[45] But although Hughes liked to be thought of as a moderate, he was not, either temperamentally or ideologically. He was nervous, intense, and compulsive. He took long vacations to avoid undue mental strain; he abandoned smoking and adopted a regular routine of exercise as a defense against frequent headaches. He believed that a judge should "[do] his work in an objective spirit,"[46] and, further, that a methodical analysis of the facts and issues in a case would result in an "objective" solution. When he had arrived at that solution, he regarded it not as a compromise or an exercise in political discretion, but as the correct result. He did not, in short, think of himself as being moderate, but as being right. Rightness and moderation were linked only because he perceived the Constitution's framers as having been moderates.

Yet Hughes attempted, as Chief Justice, to associate himself and his Court with the principle of moderation. He was himself inclined to strike balances and make fine factual distinctions in interpreting the Constitution, so that in being "moderate" he was often merely arguing for his own position. In addition, his Court was split into opposing factions whose presence Hughes wanted to conceal as much as possible from the public. Finally, as an administrator Hughes was committed to the principle of power maintenance through efficient and full use of management techniques, which in his case were substitutes for ideological compromises. The second and third of these comments require elaboration.

The Hughes Court was confronted with pressures for social change of an almost unprecedented magnitude. Not since the period of the Chase Court had the nation's social and economic theories been in such turmoil; not since the Taney Court had the consequences of Court involvement in political issues seemed so grave; not perhaps since the Marshall Court had the Court's future appeared so precarious. In addition, the Court's personnel appeared singularly ill-equipped to respond to these pressures beyond merely reflecting them. Between 1931, the year of Hughes's nomination, and 1937, when Van Devanter resigned, the Court's composition remained virtually fixed, Benjamin Cardozo replacing Holmes in early 1932. In the same timespan Hoover was replaced by F. D. Roosevelt, voting patterns were dramatically realigned, the capitalist system seemed close to collapse, Fascism and Communism entered expansionist phases in Europe, and the social programs of the New Deal were launched. In the midst of this turmoil stood nine Justices, only one of them under sixty when Roosevelt assumed office and only one of them graduated from law school in the twentieth century. It is remarkable that during these first six years any of the Hughes Court Justices was capable of responding sympathetically to the proposed redistributions of political and economic power that came before them. Those proposals were designed to respond to the exigencies of what to the Justices must have seemed a startlingly new world.

Brandeis and Cardozo were able to embrace some of the early New Deal schemes because their interpretation of judging was in some respects a passive one, and, to a lesser extent and in varying degrees, because they were politically sympathetic to social experimentation in behalf of disadvantaged persons. Stone's enthusiasm for the social welfare legislation was more subdued, and his conception of his office requires separate treatment. Stone's view, did, however, enable him to tolerate some New Deal legislation, even though he had once said that "abstract or social justice as a test for the correctness of judicial decisions is absolutely without value."[47] Consequently he often voted with Brandeis and Cardozo in the Hughes Court, and was perceived by others on that Court as a member of a faction, and by commentators as a "liberal" or a "Roosevelt" Justice.

For the first years of the Hughes Court, Hughes and Owen Roberts found themselves sandwiched between a phalanx of Justices: Willis Van Devanter, James McReynolds, George Sutherland, and Pierce Butler (who later came to be known as the "Four Horsemen," an allusion to the potentially apocalyptic tendency of their jurisprudence) and another group, Brandeis, Cardozo, and Stone. The Four Horsemen regularly met Friday evenings before the Court's Saturday conference to iron out collective positions on pending cases; the "Three Musketeers," as Brandeis, Cardozo, and Stone came to be called,[48] met for the same reason on Saturday mornings. The thorniest issues of the early 1930s involved the scope of Congress's commerce and taxing powers, a secondary issue being the extent to which Congress could delegate those powers to adminstrative agencies. The Four Horsemen held views on the scope of federal power and the ability of Congress to delegate its powers that were entirely consistent with late-nineteenth-century canons of constitutional interpretation. The Three Musketeers were more prepared to tolerate some expanded scope for the regulatory powers of Congress and federal agencies, although some of the legislation proposed by the first Roosevelt Administration was breathtakingly innovative in that regard.

As New Deal statutes were challenged on constitutional grounds and the challenges worked their way up to the Court, Hughes and Roberts sensed that they were being buffeted by two increasingly incompatible judicial cadres. Hughes's jurisprudential inclinations were cautious and precise: he liked splitting doctrinal hairs and fashioning distinctions that verged on unintelligibility. Those tendencies, and the fact that he was Chief Justice, inclined him to play a moderate, coalition-building role on an increasingly polarized Court. Roberts, on the other hand, seemed genuinely uncertain as to how to proceed.

Immediately after joining the Court in 1930, Roberts had shown an inclination to support state regulatory legislation. But he began to exhibit concern about comparable legislation promulgated by the federal government, and in 1935 wrote an opinion striking down, on both due process and commerce clause grounds, a proposed Congressional pension plan for railroad workers employed in interstate commerce.[49] In eighteen cases involving government regulation of the economy in the 1935 term, Roberts voted for the government's position in only three.

Roberts's railroad pension opinion, and a subsequent one in which he invalidated the Agricultural Adjustment Act on the grounds that federal taxing and spending powers did not extend to the regulation of agricultural production,[50] were attacked by commentators,[51] and contributed to the Roosevelt Administration's perception that a majority of the Court was hostile to its regulatory program. This set the stage for one of the most celebrated episodes in American constitutional history, in which, during the Court's 1936 Term, Roosevelt introduced a bill that called for additional Justices to be named to the Court if sitting Justices declined to retire at the age of seventy. The "Court-packing" bill did not pass, and it would have affected Brandeis as well as Van Devanter, McReynolds, and Sutherland, but between 1937 and 1939 the Court sustained several pieces of New Deal legislation against constitutional challenges, with Roberts and Hughes, on the whole, voting to uphold the legislation.[52]

A well-established historical narrative of the Court-packing episode has treated it as leading to a "constitutional revolution" in which entrenched doctrinal barriers to state and federal regulation were lifted, and the Court adopted a deferential attitude toward statutes regulating economic activity or redistributing economic benefits.[53] Roberts figured prominently in the narrative: he was alleged to have voted differently in two nearly identical cases, objecting to a New York compulsory minimum wage statute the term before the Court-packing plan was introduced[54] and sustaining the Washingon statute a few months after its introduction. Like most compelling historical anecdotes, the Court-packing/"constitutional revolution" story has proven too good to be true.[55] Although most historians continue to believe that the Court's constitutional jurisprudence shifted decisively in the late 1930s and 1940s, some of the changes have been shown to have been in place before the Court-packing plan was even conceived, and others to have emerged well after it was defeated.[56] Roberts himself has been given a "new trial"[57] and largely vindicated from the charge of changing his votes in response to external pressures. He had already voted to sustain minimum wage legislation, for example, before the Court-packing plan was even launched.[58]

But if Roberts was a more principled Justice than the Court-packing narrative suggested, he was not a gifted one; his somewhat unpredictable voting patterns were too often accompanied by broad, sweeping opinions that bordered on the analytically inept. He seemed, as a judge, to associate moderation with fuzzy-mindedness. In contrast, Hughes associated it with aspirations to dominance.

Immediately on becoming Chief Justice, Hughes set out to meet the problem of increasing pressure on the Court's docket. He did this primarily through skillful use of the certiorari power. When certiorari petitions came to the Court, Hughes took it upon himself to read and summarize them all, weeding out some as easily disposable. The ones so designated went on a separate list before the Saturday conference. In conference Hughes attempted to average about three and one-half minutes for discussion of each certiorari petition, and since his preparation far exceeded that of the other justices, his views on petitions were seldom challenged. The result of Hughes's use of the certiorari power was not always, however, a restriction of access to the Court. As an example, he expanded the Court's scrutiny of *in forma pauperis* petitions to the point where habeas corpus arguments by prisoners became an important portion of the Court's docket.

Hughes used similar administrative techniques in the internal consideration of major cases. He came to the Saturday conference prepared to the hilt, opened discussion of each case with a short but comprehensive review of its issues, barely tolerated debate, and actively discouraged requests for more time to study or reflect on an issue. Some of his colleagues mocked his zeal for efficiency and order; others saw his practices as attempts to impose his views on others. Brandeis recalled ironically that the Saturday conferences lasted six hours and that Hughes did all the talking.[59] In Frankfurter's opinion Hughes saw the conference not as "a debating society" but as "a place where nine men do solos."[60] Stone believed that discussion of cases on the Hughes Court should have been "much fuller and freer."[61] President Roosevelt, who had misgivings about Hughes, was reported to have believed that he used his authority to steer the course of debate in conferences for the purpose of sowing discord among New Deal sympathizers.[62]

In fact, Hughes was far more interested in preventing the exposure of divisions within the Court, and in identifying himself with the least controversial position possible, than in seeing "conservative" or "liberal" views triumph. He continually strove to maintain the appearance of unanimity and nonpartisanship in Court opinions. If he believed the sentiments he expressed in 1928 that "unanimity which is merely formal, which is recorded at the expense of strong conflicting views, is not desirable in a court of last resort,"[63] as Chief Justice he no longer believed them, or did not practice them. He took pains to assign opinions in such a way as to blunt the identification of any Justice with a partisan position. He sought to secure widespread support for moderate draft opinions. He filled his own opinions with careful distinctions intended to distinguish contrary precedents without overruling them. He rarely dissented, and he urged swift disposition of highly controversial cases, such as *Powell v. Alabama*,[64] one of the "Scottsboro Boys" cases, in order to cut down the amount of public attention focused on the Court.

The results of Hughes's drive for influence or authority through moderation were ambiguous. Despite his efforts, he was not able to influence any members of the Court to accept his jurisprudential views, with the imperfect and sporadic exception of Roberts. This was partly because Hughes's jurisprudence represented something of a balance between the Fieldian views of the

Four Horsemen and the reformist stance for the judiciary advocated, in differing ways, by the Three Musketeers. Hughes offered no real alternative to either position, but simply blended them in an *ad hoc* fashion. Thus on occasion he was more capable of securing individual votes than philosophical conversions at large. Hughes's internal influence was also lessened, paradoxically, by the strategies he used to enhance the Court's stature. One Justice found that his technique of making decisions through a meticulous comparison of the facts of the case before the Court with those of arguably applicable precedents sometimes produced meaningless distinctions.[65] Another felt that Hughes was "unduly emphasizing keeping the dockets clear as against the quality of the clearing."[66] Hughes's administrative skills were frequently employed to the disadvantage of others: Justices were asked to write on a subject they did not enjoy,[67] or to write an opinion not squarely in keeping with their general inclinations; Justices' views were summarily dismissed or suppressed in discussion; Justices' strategies were outflanked by Hughes's sheer preparedness, and forcefulness—in the words of Justice Robert Jackson, Hughes "look[ed] like God and talk[ed] like God."[68]

However much Hughes saw his task as one of minimizing and concealing tension among his colleagues, there is evidence he may have stimulated it. Though he may have tried to lead his Court on a narrow path out of the nineteenth century and not too far into the twentieth, there is evidence that the Court led him, staking out the poles as if on a magnetic field and drawing him this way and that. A dominant Chief Justice like none since Marshall, he could dominate in only minor ways. When he tried to achieve through administration what he could not through jurisprudence, he lost some of the harmony he sought.

Yet one hesitates to view Hughes as a captive or a victim of events. Another type of person fated to be Chief Justice in the Hughes Court might have accomplished far less and tarnished his reputation far more. Hughes, after all, overcame the Court-packing crisis (if he did help precipitate it), presided over a vast change in theories of constitutional adjudication without seeing his Court lose its identity, and successfully initiated administrative reforms to deal with the greatly increased business of the modern Court. Although he was not faultless as an administrator, he was far more adept than his successor, Harlan Stone. Although he had no well-rounded theory of judicial performance and no genuine consistency in his decision-making, he was dedicated to the preservation of an ideal for the Court—as a detached, impartial, efficient, dignified, and just institution—and he did not, at a time when myths were being exposed and idols shattered, make a mockery of that ideal.

III

In the last years of the Hughes Court there developed what might have seemed to the Chief Justice an example of history's perversity. Cases testing the limits of governmental control over the economy receded in importance as the Court's new majority coalesced in an unaccustomed attitude of broad tolerance toward regulatory legislation. Older suspicions of the constitutionality of administrative agencies vanished; the new major concerns of administrative law involved questions about the proper allocation of functions between courts and agencies.[69] Civil liberties issues began to receive serious attention for the first time in more than a decade, and some members of the Court began to doubt its apparent decision not to interfere with the determinations of legislatures if those determinations infringed on human rights.[70] Hughes had been least comfortable with the transition from the nineteenth century to the twentieth in the area of property rights; he could not bring himself to a ringing affirmation of the value of administrative regulation of private enterprise. But he had been a consistent supporter of civil liberties.[71] Had such cases been the meat of the New Deal Court he might have been able to exercise a Marshallian kind of substantive leadership.

As it was, the task of leading the new Court majority of the 1940s devolved on Harlan Stone. At a time when the Court was in one of its most expansive, ebullient phases, Stone was committed to a view of appellate judging that emphasized the unique role of the judiciary in American government and the limitations on judicial power implicit in that role. In a period when many members of the Court appeared to share, in a surface way, predilections and values, their Chief Justice was a man accustomed to looking beneath the surface even if the search revealed new areas for disagreement. Although changes of personnel, the impact of the Court-packing plan, and a shift of focus had produced strong expectations of a harmonious, active, reformist Court in the 1940s, the new Chief Justice was a man who, for all his personal charm, had an administrative style calculated to encourage dissent, disrupt harmony, and fragment reformist impulses.

Stone sought balance in his intellectual life as in his personal life, but sought it with a certain passion and fierceness. He had grown up in a spartan, enterpreneurial environment where economic scarcity was a fact of life, and flush times an enticing dream. Once out of that world he indulged himself in comforts of leisure, such as fine wines and the arts, while retaining a sense that affluence ought not to breed extravagance and that love of pleasure ought not intrude on good health. Unlike Hughes, Stone was not a compulsive worker, nor remote in his personal contracts, nor lacking in humility. Like Hughes, however, he was tenacious in his views and confident of his intellectual powers. He probed to the heart of issues until satisfied that he saw the value conflicts they revealed. He then refused to rest in those conflicts, but pressed on to make a choice, or to learn why he, as a judge, should not choose. In the course of these inquiries he was not distracted by those who believed the search futile or excessively time-consuming or impolitic, and he rarely abided their counsel, even though he invited it.

The coexistence in Stone of humility and pride, open-mindedness and stubbornness, intemperance and a yearning for balance made him interpret leadership roles in a distinctive way. He was impulsive and sometimes indiscreet in stating his views on issues, and might on occasion, after "sober second thought,"[72] modify his position, thereby giving a simultaneous impression of intellectual honesty and political naïveté. He was reluctant to assume leadership, declining the post of editor-in-chief of his college newspaper and even refusing to accept the deanship of Columbia Law School; but he might be persuaded to assume such leadership. He did not avoid positions of power if he felt that he could hold them and maintain his independence. He would abandon a leadership role, however, if he felt compromised on a principle. Nicholas Murray Butler, President of Columbia University in the early twentieth century, periodically attempted to influence the development of the Law School during Stone's tenure as dean (1910 to 1923). Butler's actions, such as comments in an annual report to the Board of Trustees that "legal education has fallen into ruts . . . and been treated . . . too little as a matter of education,"[73] invariably piqued Stone, who believed that Columbia Law School had gained in stature during his deanship. Finally in 1923 Stone had had enough of the ambitious Butler and "the petty bickerings which go on in the life of a university,"[74] and resigned. His primary motivation, however, was the principle of institutional autonomy: the Law School of which he was dean was not to tolerate judgments made by persons outside the legal profession.

Nonetheless, despite his independence, stubbornness, honesty, and fidelity to conviction, as Chief Justice Stone gave an impression of vacillation and indecisiveness. Two different elements of his character combined to produce this image. The first was his philosophy of judging, which, paradoxically, was more fully and carefully developed than that of any Chief Justice since Marshall. The second was his reluctance to see himself, despite his role as first among equals, as superior in any sense to his colleagues on the Court. The two elements are discussed separately.

For a man who was to become identified with the use of the judicial office to insure the continuance of social experimentation in America, Stone exhibited, in the years before his appointment to the Court, a singularly negative attitude toward that proposition. Not only did he believe, as he said in 1912, that abstract or social justice as a test for the correctness of judicial decisions was without value, he even supported attempts on the part of courts to resist experimental legislation. He defended, for example, the *Ives v. South Buffalo Ry. Co.*[75] decision, in which the New York Court of Appeals invalidated a 1910 state workmen's compensation statute, to the dismay of, among others, Roscoe Pound and Benjamin Cardozo. Stone felt, as the *Ives* Court had, that workmen's compensation should come through "the orderly process of constitutional amendment";[76] that "social justice may mean anything, and therefore, as a basis of judicial description, means nothing";[77] that "the unfit do survive in fact and perpetuate their species to become sources of weakness to the social structure";[78] and that the task of appellate judges was "to ascertain whether the facts proved in the case" were "controlled by rules of law which may be found in the precedents."[79] In taking these positions, Stone identified himself, in the eyes of a contemporary, as an opponent of "adherents of sociologic[al] jurisprudence who would make judicial decisions in regard to large public questions depend upon the fallible and sometimes hasty human sciences of sociology and economics."[80]

With time, however, Stone's resistance to the use of social theory as a test of the effectiveness of judicial decisions began to erode. During his deanship at Columbia he became involved in the early stages of the American Law Institute's promulgation of Restatements of Law, whose purpose was, he said, to "state in detail and with precision accepted rules and doctrines, eliminating or modifying the rule or doctrine not supported by reason or adapted to present-day social institutions and needs."[81] He began, at the same time, to argue that "in declaring law the judge must envisage the social utility of the rule which he creates."[82] By 1938 he was prepared to concede that he probably did not agree with much of what he had said in 1915 about the relation of courts to their social context.[83]

Yet a consistent thread ran through Stone's early-twentieth-century writings about judging. He believed that the law was an evolutionary process, that common law adjudication reflected its evolutionary character, and that therefore the common law model of decision-making, which in Stone's view produced change through continuity, and reform through order, was the single most appropriate method for the appellate judiciary. Stone had at first rejected theories of social justice as apt criteria for evaluation of judicial performance, as he found them speculative and irrelevant to the rules and doctrines judges declared. As he became persuaded that those theories did, however, play a part in determining how socially useful an existing common law doctrine was, he broadened his concept of common law adjudication to embrace them. Significantly, he looked upon currently-held beliefs not as a counterweight to adjudication but rather as part of the evidence weighed by the common law method. On the Court, he began to question altogether the idea of law declaration by judges. The common-law model, he saw, allowed some judicial law-making in the sense of making delicate political adjustments between competing social values. He thus moved from the conceptualist jurisprudence Holmes had attacked in *Lochner v. New York* to a position not unlike that of Holmes, and finally to one that went beyond Holmes in the degree of creativity and political compromise it tolerated in courts.

Stone's judicial philosophy, in its mature form, attempted to accommodate personal flexibility with institutional constraint. He believed that Supreme Court Justices, particularly but not exclusively in the area of constitutional law, should have a certain freedom to ignore or modify precedents if faced with unanticipated exigencies that made suspect the continued viability of such precedents. On the other hand, he believed that Justices should be prepared to justify their modifications by appeal to reason, so that a decision to change the state of the law appeared to have been made on other than *ad hoc* grounds. Stone's trade-off, then, was between pragmatic accommodation and fidelity to an institutional ideal of rationality, consistency, and transcendence of the immediate. Once the judiciary was given a power to interpret the Constitution, Stone believed that it necessarily had a certain freedom to change the meaning of constitutional language with time or find statutory language offensive where it had once been tolerated. But judges could not exercise such power without a sense of the institutional and intellectual limitations that accompanied it.

Stone identified these limitations primarily with certain techniques of appellate judging. He attempted, as he said, to "[mark] out, as cases arise, step by step, the line between the permitted and the forbidden, by the process of appraisal and comparison of the experiences of the past and the present."[84] This meant a search for a narrow rationale by which to distinguish a new case from a seemingly troublesome precedent, while not overruling that precedent. It also meant, however, the avoidance of *ad hoc* judgments, requiring that some rationale of intermediate generality accompany even the most delicate distinctions. Analytical techniques represented a search for the overriding purposes of laws. Purposes could be found, in cases involving statutory interpretation, in the words and actions of legislators; in constitutional cases, in the language of the Constitution itself, as disclosed through judicial interpretation;[85] and, on occasion, in an obligation in the judiciary to make delicate political choices when conditions required them and no other branch of government had made them.

Stone's effort to articulate different standards for judicial review of legislation in accordance with the character of the interest invaded was part of his general theory of judging. That effort has often been associated with a footnote in Stone's opinion in *United States v. Carolene Products,* and with his dissent in *Minersville School District v. Gobitis*. In those cases Stone suggested that the presumption of constitutionality for legislation might be given a narrow scope where civil liberties interests, as distinguished from economic interests, were infringed. This distinction, however, was only part of Stone's general attempt to identify occasions on which a legislative decision to curtail individual rights, whether economic or civil, had been made without an effective "political restraint."[86] Examples included statutes where the economic interest involved was out-of-state,[87] and statutes curtailing the civil rights of a small and powerless minority. The absence of an effective political restraint, for Stone, invited closer judicial scrutiny of legislation. In such cases the judiciary frankly placed itself in a quasi-legislative position and weighed the importance of the values protected and infringed by the legislation in question. That position he made tenable by singling out in the Constitution certain rights deserving of special protection. If the political process would not protect those rights, the judicial process should.

Stone's view of judging, for all its analytic subtlety and power, did not have a happy effect on the members of his own Court. It failed, of course, to satisfy any of the Four Horsemen so long as they remained in service. More important, it was not fully accepted, on different grounds, by any of the Roosevelt appointees. In the 1940s three issues surfaced that had not received much attention in the earlier years of Stone's tenure: legislative discrimination against the civil rights of blacks, legislative or administrative suppression of civil liberties in a wartime context, and legislative promotion or restriction of the powers of labor unions. In a loose sense, "liberalism" in the 1940s was identified with sympathy for each of the three groups whose interests were being affected. Yet the "liberal" Stone Court divided in a variety of ways on these issues.

The personnel of the Stone Court from 1941 to 1946 was heavily identified with the Roosevelt Administration, and yet revealed the diverse character of Roosevelt's political constituency. Stone, Roberts, and Harold Burton (who replaced Roberts at the very end of Stone's Chief Justiceship), were the only non-Roosevelt appointees. Three of Roosevelt's nominees were academics: Felix Frankfurter, William O. Douglas, and Wiley B. Rutledge (former dean of the State University of Iowa Law School). Two were practitioners and government servants: Stanley Reed and Robert Jackson, each of whom had been a Solicitor General under Roosevelt. Two more, Hugo Black and James Byrnes, had been senators from Southern states; and the last, Frank Murphy, had been the Governor of Michigan and a Roosevelt Attorney General. Their diverse backgrounds, when coupled with strong personal conviction, were not conducive to jurisprudential harmony, however much they might be identified with one political party or President. Stone himself noted in 1942 that "any high expectations that the Justices of the newly reorganized Court would have minds with but a single thought and hearts that beat as one were speedily dissipated."[88]

In civil rights cases involving blacks, for example, Stone ran into markedly different kinds of difficulties with his fellow judges. In a 1941 case, *United States v. Classic,*[89] Stone used his method of searching for overriding constitutional purposes to find that a primary election was an essential part of the voting process, giving voters a constitutional right to an honest count. He also found that dishonest state officials could be prosecuted under the Civil Rights Act of 1870, even though primaries were not in existence when the Act had been passed. The latter finding offended Justices Douglas, Black, and Murphy, who felt that the Act was not sufficiently specific to allow prosecution. The *Classic* case was a harbinger of things to come. Stone's protection of one set of individual rights was seen by civil libertarians on his Court as an infringement on another set.

Classic plunged Stone into difficulties of a different kind with Roberts. In *Grovey v. Townsend,*[90] a 1935 opinion written by Roberts and joined by Stone, the Court had characterized voting in a primary as a privilege of party membership rather than a constitutional right. *Classic* put that characterization in jeopardy. For Stone, precedents were persuasive only if the principles they represented were sound. He did not, however, enjoy square overrulings of recent precedents. He failed even to mention *Grovey v. Townsend* in *Classic,* although he was prepared to follow through the implications of his *Classic* opinion for it. When the case of *Smith v. Allwright,*[91] testing the constitutionality of all-white primaries in Texas, came before the Court in 1944, Stone privately took the position that *Classic* had overruled *Grovey v. Townsend,* but encouraged Justice Reed to write an opinion that stopped short of saying that.[92]

Such subtleties were too much for Roberts, who was embarrassed by the fact that he had joined Stone in *Classic.* He attacked Stone's view of precedent, maintaining that "not a fact differentiat[ed] [*Grovey*] from [*Smith v. Allwright*] except the names of the parties." The *Allwright* case, which provoked Roberts's railroad ticket analogy, symbolized his increasing dissatisfaction with Stone's philosophy of judging. For him it destroyed a sense of "consistency in adjudication"[93] and was disingenuous to boot. A year after *Allwright* came down, Roberts resigned from the Court.

Stone's attempt to strike a measured balance between flexibility and restraint in wartime civil liberties cases proved to be equally offensive to some of his colleagues. Five justices of the Stone Court—Black, Douglas, Murphy, Rutledge, and, from a different perspective, Jackson—were notably sensitive to alleged violations of civil liberties. One measure of their commitment was the belief, held by the first four, that all the procedural safeguards of the first eight Amendments to the Constitution were incorporated into the due-process clause of the Fourteenth Amendment, serving as checks against the actions of the states as well as against those of the federal government. Another example of their commitment to civil libertarianism came in cases testing the wartime scope of government power to restrict individual rights. In such cases, although they could not entirely agree among themselves, they clashed with Stone.

The wartime civil liberties cases in the Stone Court illustrate the difficulties of achieving judicial consensus on politically explosive issues. Throughout World War II Stone sought to articulate a position that tolerated discretionary decisions by the military yet protected civil liberties. He believed that the Constitution did authorize the substitution of military tribunals for civilian courts in times of national emergency, but he also believed that it underscored the importance of keeping civilian courts open and available wherever possible. The occasions on which military courts and martial law prevailed were matters for the judiciary to decide, since the Constitution allowed Congress and the Executive "to authorize martial law in appropriate cases."[94] If martial law prevailed, traditional civil liberties guarantees could be infringed. Otherwise, the guarantees applied even to wartime enemies of the nation.

Difficulties for the Stone Court congealed in *In re Yamashita,*[95] in which a military commission convicted a Japanese general for war crimes without granting him the acceptable procedural safeguards of a civilian court. Army lawyers for Yamashita, appealing on habeas corpus to the civilian courts, raised two questions: whether the power of the commission to try Yamashita was subject to judicial review, and whether the commission's mode of conducting its proceedings was similarly subject. Stone's majority opinion answered the first affirmatively and the second negatively. The second answer alienated Murphy and Rutledge. In Rutledge's view, judicial review on habeas corpus required scrutiny of possible Fifth Amendment violations by the tribunal. Murphy felt that the absence of procedural safeguards in war crimes trials required not only civilian scrutiny but even a revamping of the system of military justice.

Meanwhile Stone had run into problems in maintaining support for his views on the scope of military discretion to confine the activities of Japanese residents of the United States. Here he retained the vote of Black, who was able to subordinate his interest in fair procedure to his patriotism, but he offended, in various ways, Douglas, Murphy, Rutledge and Jackson. *Hirabayashi v. United States,*[96] a 1943 decision, tested the constitutionality, in the face of a right to travel, of a military order establishing a curfew for U.S. citizens of Japanese origins. Sustaining the order, Stone attempted, for a majority that included Black and Jackson, to distinguish between military judgments about the dangerousness of certain ethnic groups in wartime and more general ethnic discriminations. Such general discriminations were "odious to a free people whose instructions are founded upon the doctrine of equality";[97] the specific instances were justifiable if made on the reasonable belief of those "charged with the responsibility of our national defense" that a genuine threat to national security existed.

Douglas, however, suggested that disloyal Japanese, rather than all Japanese, were the objects of the curfew order, and hence some mode of judicial review should exist whereby an individual Japanese could show that he had been singled out unfairly as a threat. This position invited countless habeas corpus petitions in the federal courts and was therefore disruptive of the efficiency of the war effort. Stone could not shape his majority opinion in *Hirabayashi* to accommodate Douglas without losing other votes; Douglas ended up writing a concurrence. Meanwhile Murphy and Rutledge worried about the wide discretion given to military officials by Stone's opinion, and concurred separately.

In short, the delicate balances on which Stone's view of civil liberties in wartime rested made his approach too vulnerable to political emotions to serve as a doctrine for the Court in the 1940s. In *Korematsu v. United States,*[98] a 1944 Japanese internment case, and *Duncan v. Kahanamoku,*[99] a 1946 case testing the scope of the power of military courts in Hawaii, Jackson, Murphy, Rutledge, Douglas, and finally Black came to find Stone's flexible definition of the discretionary powers of the military too threatening. The majority opinion in *Korematsu,* written by Black and joined by Stone, justified the exclusion of Japanese from selected areas on the West Coast because the process bore "a definite and close relationship to the prevention of espionage and sabotage." For Stone and Black the test was whether an acknowledged discretionary power in the military had been reasonably exercised. Rutledge voted with the majority in *Korematsu,* but Jackson decided that wartime cases inevitably involved untoward violations of civil liberties, and suggested that the Court not entertain them.[100] Murphy called *Korematsu* a bald-faced attempt to legitimate racism.[101]

By the date of the *Kahanomoku* case Black, Douglas, Murphy, and Rutledge had decided that the time had come to impose strict limits on the war power. In an opinion declaring that civilians in Hawaii could not be tried in military courts despite the presence of martial law, those four Justices, through Black, called the American system of government "the antithesis of total military rule."[102] Stone disagreed, reaffirming his view that martial law could be applied in "those cases where it [was] needful in the interest of public safety and good order."[103]

In the wartime incarceration cases and other wartime civil liberties cases,[104] Stone repeatedly tried to decide on the narrowest possible grounds, to preserve a measure of doctrinal consistency and to face hard political decisions while seeing "that the emotions of war are kept out of the courtroom."[105] Much of the time he maintained a majority for his viewpoint, but he almost never escaped without an inflammatory concurrence or dissent. His approach conceded too much for some of his colleagues and not enough for others. It was too flexible to satisfy one set of justices and too moderate to suit another. The wartime civil liberties cases did pose problems of delicate balancing, but few of the members of Stone's Court really wanted to balance. They were either fervent patriots and warhawks or zealous defenders of minority rights or, as in the case of Black and Douglas, they were converts from the first position to the second and found it difficult to find accommodation.

If the civil liberties cases of the 1940s were a testing ground for Stone's approach to interpreting the Constitution, labor cases of the same decade tested his approach to statutory interpretation. He resolved these controversies by ascertaining the primary purposes of the relevant legislation involved. On the Hughes Court he had tolerated the presence and the potentially expansive jurisdiction of the National Labor Relations Board, but had refused to make it a foil for organized labor.[106] His primary interest was reading the National Labor Relations Act[107] so as to effectuate what he thought to be its central purpose: the creation of even-handed administrative machinery through which labor and management could negotiate their differences.

As the NLRB evolved, its rulings exhibited an increasing sympathy with the views of labor unions. This raised two difficulties for Stone. His apprehensions about unchecked union power were renewed, and he became concerned about the emergence of administrative construction of a statute, as he thought this could be used to circumvent the statute's primary purposes. As NLRB cases moved from inquiries as to whether unions possessed any power, to questions about the scope of their power, Stone sought to restrict what he thought were indiscriminately pro-union constructions of the Act on the part of the NLRB. He was somewhat frustrated in this effort by his own earlier efforts. He had been a leading supporter of labor on the Hughes Court. Now Justices on his own Court, such as Black, Douglas, and Murphy, seemed anxious to tolerate any pro-union decision. Previous suggestions by Stone[108] that Congressional statutes protected unions from unfair discrimination were converted into justifications for wide union power to coerce unsympathetic employers.[109] Once again, Stone felt, a search for moderation and restraint, based on fidelity to statutory language and a gradualist approach to change, had been converted into a politicized crusade.

Stone's theory of judicial performance was better suited to the Hughes Court than his own. It emphasized political accommodation and stressed the limitations on judicial lawmaking, allowing change while confining it. It grounded its rationale not on factual distinctions, as had the Hughes approach, but on a subtle understanding of the relations between governing institutions. As such Stone's theory enabled the Court to avoid being imprisoned by the set of social attitudes exhibited by the Four Horsemen while not appearing entirely result-oriented in its decisions. Once a new militancy emerged on the Court in the 1940s, however, Stone's view became a restraining influence, in terms of both end results and implicit assumptions about the power of judges. Those more deeply committed to substantive change than he were impatient with his belief that judicial creativity functioned only in a limited institutional ambit.

Stone's theory of judicial performance was not, however, the sole or perhaps even the primary cause of fragmentation in his Court. Of equal or possibly greater significance was his view of leadership. His humility, independence, and distaste for open personal confrontations combined to make him uncomfortable with Hughes's approach to the Chief Justiceship. Moreover, Stone was disinclined or reluctant to attempt to convert others to his views. The Stone Court was not one molded by the preferences of its Chief. Although Stone set the tone for his Court, it was a tone that deemphasized conventional leadership.

Stone's pre-Court career, especially his deanship at Columbia Law School, had suggested that he would be reluctant to assume positions of leadership, loathe to cloak himself in the status perquisites of an office, publicly deferent to the views of others, yet at the same time fiercely independent and prepared to relinquish power for the sake of a belief. In addition, those years had indicated that, when thwarted, Stone inclined to retreat from controversy, but that he nonetheless tended to communicate his antagonisms privately in a manner that was less than discreet.[110] Each of these characteristics reappeared on the Court. Once Chief Justice, Stone rapidly abandoned Hughes's practice of summary dispositions of cases in conference. As an Associate Justice he had characterized Hughes's technique as one of "greatly over-elaborating the unimportant details of [a] case and disposing, by ipse dixit, in a sentence or two, of the vital question."[111] He encouraged full discussion and debate in conference, viewing his function as not unlike his new role as chairman of the Judicial Conference of the United States: "to focus discussion . . . without being too much of a Czar."[112] He stated his own views with diffidence, allowed himself to be freely interrupted, and invariably granted extensions for more time to consider an issue.[113]

For all his open-mindedness and deference to his colleagues' views, Stone, once he had staked out his own position, was stubborn and vocal in its defense. Justice Reed recalled him as "an indefatigable proponent for the position he had reached, an ardent advocate and a forceful writer for the ground that he deemed solid."[114] Stone regarded the Court's internal debates as intellectual exercises. He found them stimulating, rarely took offense at one advocating views counter to his, borrowed ideas from others freely, and enjoyed the process of sharpening or trimming a position through the exchange of memoranda. To the extent that Hughes had identified leadership with detachment and "objectivity," Stone altered that conception. To him influence on the Court was equated with the soundness and firmness of one's intellectual views and the degree of one's persuasiveness. By this criterion, Justices as diverse as Van Devanter and Brandeis won his admiration, and others, such as Frankfurter and Rutledge, with whom he often had a sympathy of views, did not.

Stone carried over to the workings of the Court the sense of balance that marked his philosophy of judging. He traded off efficiency in the handling of the docket against "full exposition" and "painstaking consideration" of issues before the Justices. He was interested in unanimity and shaped his majority opinions to achieve it, but he believed that "differences of opinion in the court . . . should be fully expressed."[115] He felt that a Chief Justice should be "fired by a passion for the prompt and faithful performance of the work of the Court," but that he was only a "titular leader among equals."[116] He believed that conflict, paradoxically, bred detachment: "a considered and well-stated dissent" was "a manifestation in its best sense of the common effort of judges to develop law dispassionately."[117] And while he "dreaded [personal] conflict," as Jackson said, and sometimes "feared action that would bring it about,"[118] also believed that legal doctrines should "be exposed to the most searching examination and criticism."[119]

Stone's combination of personal diffidence and intellectual combativeness, when commingled with the vibrancy and contentiousness of others on his Court, formed a catalyst for divisiveness. Stone had to contend as Chief Justice with at least four Justices—Black, Douglas, Frankfurter, and Jackson—of high intellectual ability and marked strong-mindedness and persistence, and three others—Roberts, Murphy, and Rutledge—who could on occasion become perversely or militantly doctrinaire. Only in Justice Reed did Stone have a colleague amenable to persuasion and largely amiable about it.[120] During his tenure as Chief Justice, Stone endured, among other things, an early expression of the longstanding quarrel between Black and Frankfurter, in which Black wrote a concurrence whose sole purpose was to attack a Frankfurter dissent;[121] the celebrated dispute between Black and Jackson over Black's failure to disqualify himself in a case argued by his former law partner;[122] and an awkward series of internal bickerings among the Justices over the writing of a retirement letter to Justice Roberts, who had alienated almost all his colleagues by the time of his resignation in 1945.[123] Some commentators concluded that this divisiveness earned the Stone Court "less popular admiration and respect than any previous Supreme Court has enjoyed within the memory of living men."[124] Others, however, believed that the Court between 1937 and 1945 was one of the greatest in American history.[125]

IV

The office of Chief Justice of the United States Supreme Court is not that of an ordinary Justiceship, although Stone may have so conceived it. It contains an internal political dimension with which each occupant is forced to come to terms. Internal politics on the Court is not politics in the conventional sense, but it is more than mere "administration," as that word is commonly used. A Chief Justice, above all his colleagues, seeks to convey a sense, as Stone put it, that the Court is "greater than the individuals who happen for the moment to represent it."[126] He attempts to communicate to the public an impression that harmony prevails among the Justices, that intellectual honesty is admired, that reason triumphs over irrationality and partisanship, that pettiness is at a minimum and statesmanship predominant. He is forced, at the same time, to deal with personal antagonisms, political differences, disingenuousness, artifice, and estrangement.

A continually dissenting Chief Justice is not a Chief; he does not lead his Court. When he does not dissent, he must assign an opinion; no other member of the Court is faced so frequently with that delicate political exercise. When important cases are handed down, there is pressure on the Chief to speak for the Court, and additional pressure—if the case has major social ramifications—to secure unanimity or a clear majority for his viewpoint. On explosive occasions, therefore, he is put in the position of being an agent of compromise and an apostle of harmony.

The position of Chief Justice thus requires both intellectual power and political acumen, and in an abstract sense both Hughes and Stone possessed these skills. Nevertheless, because of the interaction of their personal styles with the context, both personal and historical, in which they operated, neither was able to use them to best advantage. Hughes's formidable intellect and mastery of administrative techniques appeared as arbitrariness, heavy-handedness, or pedantry. His commitment to preserving the autonomy and integrity of the Court occasionally undercut his political strength, or further polarized an easily divided Court. The remarkable subtlety and sensitivity of Stone's conception of his office sometimes created the image of one who abdicated leadership when controversies were heated, while his humanness and gregariousness served dissension and encouraged, conflict. There is much to admire in Hughes and Stone as intellects, as public officials, and as human beings. Both may have achieved a certain greatness as Chief Justice, but it was a greatness tinged with irony. Their experiences demonstrate the fortuitousness of the process of leading the Supreme Court and the potential vulnerability of any occupant of the Chief Justiceship.

9 

Personal versus Impersonal Judging: The Dilemmas of Robert Jackson

With the death of the oracular theory of judging, two emerging jurisprudential perspectives placed contradictory sets of pressures on the twentieth-century appellate judiciary. One perspective emphasized human limitations (such as irrationality and bias) on judges, assumed that judges made law, encouraged the judiciary to acknowledge candidly those "realities," and implicitly conveyed a skepticism about the permanency of values or truths, in law or elsewhere.[1] The second, building on the insights of, while responding to the potential nihilism of the first, emphasized institutional limitations. It attempted to limit the influence of judicial bias and judicial lawmaking through methodological techniques that recognized the limited and distinctive role of the American judiciary. It began with a recognition that law was not a body of discoverable truths, but nonetheless attempted to define law as more than the aggregate of the biases of officials. Ultimately, this perspective defined law as a process, with its own internal limitations on the conduct of judges and other lawmakers.[2]

The thrust of the process perspective was methodological in the sense that judges were encouraged to transcend their biases through the use of analytical reasoning. Those (primarily academicians) who shared its assumptions believed that a thorough and balanced articulation by judges of the competing issues at stake in a case would produce a rational solution whose justification lay in the technique of analysis that derived it. In the context of the 1940s and 1950s this set of beliefs had substantive ideological and political implications as well. It was designed in part as a counterweight to the implicit moral relativism of "realistic jurisprudence,"[3] which became linked with totalitarian threats to American civilization.[4] As the value of national solidarity increased in importance during World War II and the Cold War, the distinctive features and shared beliefs of American society were reaffirmed. As part of this reaffirmation, rationality, democratic ideals, and law were interfused. Judging came to be seen not only as an exercise in reason but also as a means of implementing the historic values of a democratic society, a society in which law was more than the fiats of governmental officials.[5]

The judicial career of Robert Jackson, who was appointed to the Supreme Court by Roosevelt in 1941 and remained there until his death in 1954, mirrored the contradictory jurisprudential impulses of the times. Jackson openly rejected the oracular theory and maintained a vividly personalized and "realistic" approach to judging. At the same time he strove to develop a theory of adjudication that emphasized the importance of internalized constraints on judges. He recognized the substantive implications of his approach and sought to redefine traditional American values, such as libertarianism or egalitarianism, in the light of an enhanced interest in national solidarity and security. Confronting competing pressures, he sought accommodations of one to the other. Although his solutions were idiosyncratic and not particularly influential, they helped frame central issues for the American appellate judiciary in the decade immediately after his death.

Three features of Jackson's judicial career have particular relevance to the role attributed to him above. One was his style, which was an index not simply of literary inclinations but of character traits and social values as well. Another was his efforts to redefine the proper relations between individual citizens and the state in post-war America. A third was his view of the role of law and lawyers in American society, from which he derived his attitudes toward judging.

I

"In his case," Felix Frankfurter observed in a memorial tribute, "the style was the man."[6] To a degree unusual in their profession, Frankfurter believed, Jackson's judicial writing revealed his thoughts and feelings. In contrast to

Frankfurter himself, Jackson rarely seemed to be searching for the proper "judicial" stance or tone in his opinions. Instead, he appeared capable of expanding the stylistic range of opinion writing to accommodate his human reactions. As Holmes had done, and most of his predecessors had not, Jackson entertained with his style. Quips such as "If it is interstate commerce that feels the pinch, it does not matter how local the operation which applies the squeeze"[7] filled his opinions. In such moments the distance between judges and mortals was suddenly shortened; charm became a counterweight to pomposity. The assorted "Jacksonisms"[8] of his opinions reminded his audience that, for him, judging was not sharply distinguishable from other public performances, and that in all such ventures he was to retain his individuality.

For Jackson, then, style was more than a blending of temperament with role. It was a means by which the self pierced through roles to communicate at a more personal level. This conception of uniqueness and worth in oneself was a core value for Jackson. He was, as he said repeatedly, an individualist, both temperamentally and philosophically. Individualism meant a variety of things. It was associated with a thirst for competition ("I was never a crusader. I just liked a good fight").[9] It served to identify financial security and generalist law practice with independence. It manifested itself in a flashy style of dress or in an affinity for Emerson ("Self-reliance, self-help, and independence of other people I believe to be the basis of character and essential to success").[10] It produced a small businessman-entrepreneur bias on economic issues, and was the source of dissenting views on politics ("The great difficulty with the conservative class in this country is that they've lost their guts. The American industrialist has just ceased to be an individualist. . . . Instead of an old-fashioned liberalism, the liberals have tended to collectivism and communism. . . . Both groups . . . lack imagination and constructive thinking"[11]). Individualism had been, in Jackson's eyes, the creed of his ancestors and the motif of his locality; it was a counterbalance to the mass society he saw America becoming.

Jackson's individualism decisively affected his professional relations. It motivated him to develop a law practice in Jamestown (New York) that was distinguished by the diversity of its clientele. The only corporate client that Jackson's firm persistently serviced was a locally owned business, the Jamestown Telephone Corporation, which was fighting to preserve its independence in the face of encroachments by the Bell System. Beyond that,

Jackson represented, among others, a streetcar company, a bank, striking members of a labor union, and occasional accused murderers. General practice, he believed, made lawyers "harder to dominate" and kept them from being "hired men."[12] Not one of Jackson's clients (he guessed) contributed as much as five per cent to his gross income, but his practice nonetheless "laid the foundation of financial independence which is an important asset in public office, relieving one of fear of loss of office and contributing a general sense of security."[13]

Once consulted on a problem, Jackson felt, a lawyer "usually dominated the matter, no matter who the [client] was."[14] Lawyering brought independence and power, but also a sense of self-worth. This was because law was a necessary ingredient of civilized living, a cementing force in a society of individualists. It functioned, fundamentally, as a means of accommodating competing claims and resolving disputes. A lawyer's skills were largely practical and his orientation was basically pragmatic. He succeeded in his profession primarily through careful preparation, persuasiveness, common sense, and sound judgment. But he could feel satisfaction beyond the immediate victories of his clients, in doing his part to minimize friction and to maintain order in society. Receptiveness to the needs and wants of individual citizens was essential in America; but since individual claims were so diverse, some measure of social organization was required. A good lawyer could function as an honest broker between individual persons and the institutions whose purpose it was to maintain that organization. Law was hence both a process of harmonizing competing desires and a "rule" of civilized conduct. A lawyer stood for the maintenance of both.

In fostering the latter attitude in the mind of his clients, a lawyer needed to develop within himself an impersonal, detached attitude toward potentially provocative situations. A practitioner needed to separate his sense of appropriate tactical behavior from his perception of what his clients wanted, so that he could give "sincere advice" instead of telling a client "exactly what he wanted to hear."[15] A judge, especially, ought to be "a man that didn't let the personalities on either side interfere with his deciding the case. . . . The interpretation of the law ought to be as impersonal as possible."[16] When one "[put] on a judicial robe," Jackson said, "psychological change" was required. One needed "to get into an attitude of deciding other people's controversies, instead of waging them." After being appointed to the Court he acknowledged that some judges were never able to adapt themselves to this change in perspective, and he was not sure that he had.[17]

Here as in other places Jackson understood himself. His self-esteem, zest for personal combat, ambition, and fear of being compromised—manifestations of his individualism—made his transition from private practitioner and government lawyer to judge a painful and imperfect one. He had admired or gravitated toward strong personalities—notably Hughes, Roosevelt, and Henry Morgenthau—before becoming a judge, and even his abiding ambitions could not always temper his zeal to meet strength with strength. Harold Ickes once said of Jackson that "he is far from aggressive, but disposed to accept what comes along without really fighting for a different result . . . , [and] more of a lawyer than an aggressive leader."[18] But these comments were made in the context of Jackson's apprentice relations with Roosevelt, who had in 1937 encouraged Jackson to run the next year for Governor of New York, who had appointed him Solicitor General in 1938 and Attorney General in 1940, and who had intimated that he would name him to succeed Hughes as Chief Justice.[19] While Jackson was consistently deferential to Roosevelt, he was to no one else, including Morgenthau, who had first brought him to Washington in 1934 as General Counsel to the Bureau of Internal Revenue.[20] On the Court he encountered more strong personalities, such as Stone, Douglas, and Black. Buoyed by the achievement of independence, he did not suppress his differences.

In debate Jackson utilized the talents that had made him appear to a fellow advocate in Jamestown as "wickedly brilliant."[21] He personalized issues and poked fun at opposing Justices' views;[22] he filled his opinions with devastating similes and pejorative metaphors. When pressed, he revealed the internal politics of the Court[23] and on occasion seemed to suggest that partisanship was its lifeblood. One such occasion was his impassioned attack on Justice Black in 1946. This attack, which came in the form of a cable from Nuremberg, Germany, where Jackson was serving as chief prosecutor at the war crimes trials, was the culmination of a series of earlier confrontations dating back to Jackson's appointment to the Court in 1941.

In a 1942 case, *United States v. Bethlehem Steel Corporation*,[24] Jackson, who had worked on the case as Solicitor General, disqualified himself, then saw his position repudiated by the Court in a Black opinion. In 1944 and 1945 two cases[25] came to the Court involving the effect of the Fair Labor Standards Act on contracts between mine workers and their employers. In both cases the workers were represented by Crampton Harris, a former law partner of Black's. In both instances a majority of the Court read the Act favorably for the workers. Both decisions ranged well beyond the collective bargaining context to announce a comprehensive policy with regard to overtime benefits in the mining industry. Jackson objected to the decisions as being overbroad and politically inspired.

The Jewell Ridge Coal Corporation, the defeated party in the second case, subsequently petitioned the Court for a rehearing on the grounds of Black's close connection with Harris. In June 1945, denying the petition for the Court, Jackson emphasized that disqualification questions were matters for decision by individual Justices, rather than the Court, and that this was the sole ground for denying the petition. Subsequently Jackson temporarily left the Court to participate in the Nuremberg Trials.

While Jackson was in Nuremberg a petty dispute arose among the Justices over the wording of a letter to Justice Roberts on his retirement. Stone had included in his draft of the letter (whose tone was polite but not effusive) the phrases "brings to us a profound sense of regret that our association with you in the daily work of the Court must now come to an end," and "you have made fidelity to principle your guide to decision."[26] In accordance with custom, Stone routed the draft to Black (by now the senior Associate Justice) for his signature. Black suggested deletion of the two phrases, the only ones that could be interpreted as an endorsement of Roberts's performance as a Justice. Stone responded to Black's suggestion by inviting Black to write his own draft and submit it to the remaining Justices. Black merely forwarded Stone's draft, with his deletions, adding a note that Stone "had me sign it first in order to save time."[27]

Frankfurter, who had learned of Black's objections privately from Stone, reacted by criticizing Black for implying that Stone's original draft was no different from Black's revised version. Frankfurter refused to sign the revision and pressed Stone to circulate the original draft—which Stone eventually did. Black reacted by repeating his refusal to sign the original and withdrawing his own draft. There matters stood at the end of August 1945. Meanwhile, in mid-August Jackson, who had been sent Stone's original draft and had signed it, received a letter from Stone describing Black's objections. Jackson responded by saying that "the deletions leave the letter so colorless that it would be best to omit the letter entirely," and refused to sign a letter "that deliberately omits the only sentence that credits [Roberts] with good motives."[28] A poll of the other Justices, however, revealed that all six were prepared to sign Black's version,[29] leaving only Jackson, Stone, and Frankfurter in favor of the more generous letter. Stone ultimately issued no letter at all, announcing Roberts's retirement orally in court in October 1945, with the Black draft as his text.[30]

The letter incident heightened Jackson's sense that the Court had become factionalized, with Black at the head of a faction and Frankfurter and himself in opposition. Isolated in Nuremberg, he felt vulnerable to attack from his colleagues. He had consulted none of the Justices before accepting the Nuremberg appointment and knew that Stone deeply disapproved of it. In January 1946, he offered to return temporarily to the Court in April to facilitate the discharge of business, but Stone ultimately suggested that a temporary stay would be counterproductive.[31] In the midst of this atmosphere, Stone suddenly died on April 22, 1946, and Jackson was prominently mentioned as his successor. In the last days of April President Truman consulted Hughes, then eighty-four and in the fifth year of his retirement, and Hughes apparently recommended Jackson.[32] Meanwhile some Jackson supporters, fearing that his absence from Washington would hurt his chances, suggested that he return to America for Stone's funeral. Jackson, who was at a critical stage in the Nuremberg proceedings, refused. Later he said, "I wouldn't have asked Harry Truman for a commitment as to the Chief Justiceship any more than I would cut my head off."[33] There is little doubt, however, that Jackson coveted the office and felt that he was entitled to it.

Between Hughes's meeting with Truman at the close of April and the nomination of Fred Vinson as Chief Justice on June 6 an anti-Jackson campaign was launched[34] by persons identified by Jackson with the Black faction.[35] Drew Pearson announced in a radio broadcast that Black had told Truman that he and another Justice would resign if Jackson were appointed to the Chief Justiceship.[36] On May 15, 1946, a newspaper columnist, Doris Fleeson, repeated that Black threat and revealed some of the debate in conference over the rehearing petition in the *Jewell Ridge* case. She referred to the antagonism between Black and Jackson as a "blood feud" and asserted that Black had perceived Jackson's suggestion that he disqualify himself as "an open and gratuitous insult, a slur upon his personal and judicial honor."[37] Jackson, who received notice of the Pearson and Fleeson accounts in Nuremberg, believed that the columnists' sources were members of the Court and that the purpose of the stories was to discredit his candidacy. He responded by preparing a public statement describing in detail his role in the *Jewell Ridge* disqualification controversy.

On June 10, four days after Vinson's appointment, Jackson released to the press a communication to the chairmen of the Judiciary Committees of the House and Senate. In it he characterized the Fleeson account of the *Jewell Ridge* rehearing debate as detrimental to "the reputation of the court for nonpartisan and unbiased decision," declared that insinuations that the debate represented "a mere personal vendetta among justices" were "utterly false," and insisted that his differences with Black involved questions not of "honor" but of "judgment as to sound judicial policy" in disqualification matters.[38]

Jackson then gave a full account of the *Jewell Ridge* conference debate. The question debated, he maintained, was whether the Court should summarily deny the petition for rehearing or cite its lack of power, as an institution, to pass on disqualification issues. "Justice Black," Jackson said, "insisted on a mere denial to his participation. . . . Neither I nor the other [dissenting] justices . . . wanted to lend our names to [that option]." In conference, Jackson revealed, he had argued that the Court should discuss the disqualification issue in denying the petition for rehearing, whereupon "Mr. Justice Black became very angry and said that any opinion which discussed the subject at all would mean a declaration of war." Then, Jackson continued, "I told Justice Black in language that was sharp but no different than I would use again that I would not stand for any more of his bullying and that, whatever I would otherwise do, I would now have to write my opinion to keep self respect in the face of his threats." As to the principle he regarded as being at stake in the debate, Jackson asserted that "however innocent the coincidence of these two victories at successive terms by Justice Black's former law partner, I wanted the practice stopped. If it is ever repeated while I am on the bench I will make my *Jewell Ridge* opinion look like a letter of recommendation by comparison."[39]

The attack on Black and the skirmishes that preceded it revealed the contradictions within Jackson. He was proud but ambitious, politically astute but quixotic, at times morally uncompromising, at other times pragmatic. He took the political squabbles and maneuvers of judging as a given, and yet at the same time identified the judiciary with detached nonpartisanship. He strove to impose his personal views of proper judicial behavior on his colleagues, but often these views stressed the limitations on judicial power. Jackson's interpretation of his office implied the coexistence of two sets of counteracting characteristics in appellate judges. They were human beings, capable of pride and spitefulness and arrogance and disingenuousness in their relations. But they strove to be symbols of the nobility and impartiality and transcendence of law, which was composed of more than the sum of human passions and prejudices. Jackson believed in the latter ideal of judges as much as he acknowledged the former characteristics. Yet he conveyed the humanness of himself and his colleagues so sharply that he seemed to be living proof of the unattainability of his own standards for judicial performance.

Jackson's style was a self-representation in that it conveyed a lofty vision in pungent terms. The terms themselves distracted from the vision, just as Jackson's dapper appearance distracted contemporaries from his basic indifference to social pretensions. He demythologized his office with his candor and his wit. When a Justice of the Supreme Court could announce "I have never discovered that disregard of the Nation's liquor taxes excluded a citizen from our best society and I see no reason why it should banish an alien from our worst,"[40] some of the solemnity of the appellate judiciary peeled off. When the same Justice could confess, "I see no reason why I should be consciously wrong today because I was unconsciously wrong yesterday,"[41] the mysterious art of following precedent had been given a human dimension. But when the jurisprudence of that Justice was oriented toward eventual distinctions between the behavior of judges and that of other persons, or between law and mere power, stylistic strengths became weaknesses. Candor became a counterweight to dignity; pithiness an antidote to reverence, and Jackson the man became a difficulty for Jackson the judge.

II

When Jackson joined the Court in 1941, the established tradition of judicial tolerance toward legislative attempts to regulate the economy had taken on a new meaning. The tradition had arisen in the context of state statutes affecting private economic interests. The questions debated by the White and Taft courts in this area had primarily involved largely the permissible scope of state power to regulate private enterprise in the face of the due process clause. Once the liberty-of-contract doctrine was discredited, state regulatory legislation flourished. But almost simultaneously with this development came a reorientation of the locus of economic regulation and a new spate of problems. With the New Deal the federal government emerged as a regulatory force, and after the Four Horsemen's attempts to resist this change had been overcome, two regulators—the states and the federal government—began an uneasy coexistence. The Stone Court had to address itself to the implications of this coexistence and, consequently, had to re-examine the meaning of federalism in the post-New Deal economy. An essential issue for the Stone and subsequently the Vinson Court was whether a spirit of judicial permissiveness toward state economic regulation could be maintained in the face of the increased presence of the federal government.

This issue was complicated by a potentially new meaning for the commerce clause in modern America. Marshall had used the commerce clause to create an area of plenary federal power, but Congress had generally not exercised that power, so that a judicial decision declaring that the federal government pre-empted an area of the nation's economy had usually left the area free from regulation altogether. Only in the early twentieth century did extensive federal regulation appear, in the form of directives from newly-created independent regulatory agencies; and these directives did not receive full-blown support in the courts until the Court-packing crisis. By the time of Jackson's tenure, however, recognition of federal power in a particular area implied affirmative control of the economy in that area rather than unexercised potential control. Commerce clause questions became problems in distinguishing between types of regulation as much as between regulation and its absence. Federalism, therefore, became identified with a modern rationale for a nationally oriented economy, in which attempts by states to regulate private enterprise were seen as inimical to broader national considerations.

The new meaning of federalism implicitly revived a role for the judiciary that had become increasingly dormant in the early twentieth century. Passivity toward legislative experimentation in the area of economic regulation had allowed federal appellate judges to avoid posing as advocates of any particular approach to economic questions. They were simply considering the permissible scope of state regulation, not passing on its wisdom. But the presence of an alternative federal regulatory forum not only changed the ground of constitutional debate from the due process clause to the commerce clause, it forced an evaluation of the comparative worth of nationally and locally administered regulatory systems. In considering the limits of state power to regulate the economy, judges were asked to become economic theorists. An old bugaboo for the judiciary was thus reborn. Against a legislative act was pitted open-ended constitutional language; judges were invited to give substantive content to the language by interpreting it to compel a result consistent with a particular social or economic theory. Yet the judiciary, as Holmes and his followers had believed, was a peculiarly inappropriate instrument for promulgating social and economic views.

A dilemma for the post-New Deal Court was thereby raised. How could the judiciary adopt an approach to regulatory questions consistent with increased federal participation in the economy, without putting itself back into the vulnerable position of advocating a particular point of view? Jackson faced this problem squarely in his decisions in cases involving government regulation, and attempted an ingenious solution. He conceded to the judiciary an intermediate power to interpret open-ended constitutional concepts, such as "commerce," "due process" or "equal protection," so as to achieve practical solutions to contemporary problems. Yet he insisted that judicial interpretations be sufficiently broad and general in their applicability to reflect popular sentiments rather than to attempt to influence them. For Jackson, in the area of economic regulation, as elsewhere, an appellate judge could make law, but only if in the process he conveyed his ultimate subordination to it.

As a member of the Roosevelt Administration, Jackson had labored to achieve legitimacy for the proposition that federal regulation of the economy was constitutionally permissible and desirable. His concern in that effort was with defining the scope of federal power to control private enterprise more than with marking out the precise boundaries between federal and state regulation. In an opinion written a year after his appointment, Jackson indicated that he viewed the commerce clause as giving virtually unlimited power to the federal government to regulate private economic activity.

The case (*Wickard v. Filburn*[42]) involved the constitutionality of a federal statute authorizing the Secretary of Agriculture to impose quotas on wheat production and to prescribe penalties for excesses. A penalty was imposed on Filburn, an Ohio farmer who claimed that he used his wheat crop for home consumption as well as for marketing. Counsel for the Department of Agriculture, mindful of older Supreme Court decisions defining "commerce" narrowly, argued that the statute purported to regulate only marketing. Jackson dismissed this argument. Filburn's decision to consume some of his own wheat, he maintained, affected interstate commerce in the sense that it could be said to constitute part of a collective decision by a class of persons. That decision, taken at large, had an impact on the supply of wheat; it was spurious to pretend otherwise. The statute, as applied to Filburn, was therefore a legitimate exercise of Congressional power to regulate commerce, a power extending to matters indirectly as well as directly affecting its flow.

The views Jackson expressed in *Filburn* suggested that state efforts at economic regulation whose effect was to curtail potential federal powers might prove troublesome to him. Congress, he argued, might not choose to exercise its powers in a variety of areas, thereby inviting states to fill the void. Judicial toleration of regulatory state legislation might, under such circumstances, defeat one of the purposes of the commerce clause, uniformity of economic conditions throughout the nation. If Congress took no action because state restraints were "individually too petty, too diversified and too local to get [its] attention," the "practical result" would be "the suffocat[ion], and retard[ation] and Balkaniz[ation] [of] American commerce, trade, and industry."[43] Jackson was concerned that "the reaction of [the] Court against . . . excessive judicial interference with legislative action" might lead it to "rush to other extremes,"[44] namely indiscriminate toleration of any action taken by state legislatures in the area of economic regulation. Judicial responsibility under the commerce clause, in this view, was different from that under the due process clause. "The excessive use for insufficient reason of a judicially inflated due process clause to strike down states' laws regulating their own internal affairs" was illegitimate. Invocation of the commerce clause "to keep the many states from fastening their several concepts of local 'well-being' into the national commerce" was "a wholly different thing."[45]

In taking the view that the judiciary could assess the economic impact of state regulation prior to Congressional intervention Jackson was associating himself in a limited way with a discredited view of the judiciary as a barrier against legislative excesses. In a case decided before Jackson came on the Court, Justice Black had announced his conviction that "judicial control of national commerce—unlike legislative regulations—must from inherent limitations of the judicial process treat the subject by the hit-and-miss method of deciding single local controversies upon evidence and information limited by the narrow rules of litigation."[46] The judiciary being incapable of creating "integrated national rules"[47] for the protection of interstate commerce, Black argued, the matter should be left to Congress. Premature judicial intervention only signified for Black, as he said in a 1949 dissent from a Jackson opinion, "an instinctive hostility to any governmental regulation of 'free enterprise.' "[48]

Jackson met this attack by recourse to his distinction between intermediate and ultimate judicial power. The commerce clause was capable of a variety of interpretations. It could fairly be analyzed by judges with reference to the practical results its use fostered. Deciding whether a state regulation "affected" interstate commerce, and if so, whether "directly" or "indirectly," was a traditional judicial inquiry. If it produced different results at different times, that was because economic conditions changed. Freedom in the judiciary to interpret broad constitutional language such as "commerce" to secure pragmatic accommodations to changed circumstances was not illegitimate if judges were faithful to original constitutional purposes. And Jackson saw a clear purpose for the commerce clause. "There can be no doubt," he wrote in the year of his death, "that in the original Constitution the states surrendered to the Federal Government the power to regulate interstate commerce. . . . They did so in the light of a disastrous experience in which commerce and prosperity were reduced to the vanishing point by states discriminating against each other through devices of regulation."[49] This original meaning ultimately ensured that the judiciary would in the future be unable to impose its views on the commerce clause insofar as such views ran counter to those of the framers. Ultimate impotence justified intermediate power. Since the "philosophy that the federal interstate commerce power should be strongly supported"[50] was a bedrock of the Constitution, judges in their interpretive role could flesh out the implications of the commerce clause in given situations.

Given this mandate, Jackson felt, judicial suspicion of "impingement of the states upon that commerce which moves among them"[51] was entirely warranted. Arkansas could not require a permit for the transportation of liquor through the state.[52] New York could not prevent a Massachusetts milk dealer from obtaining part of its supply from farms within New York State.[53] New Jersey could not place a tax on the storage of coal whose ultimate destination was outside the state.[54] Neither Maryland[55] nor Iowa[56] could enact compensating "use" taxes on sales by out-of-state business to local residents. Utah could not enact an inheritance tax on an out-of-state transfer of shares of stock in a railroad incorporated in the state.[57] In short, "the desire of the Forefathers to federalize regulation of foreign and interstate commerce" stood "in sharp contrast" to "their jealous preservation of the state's power over its internal affairs."[58]

Federalism, for Jackson, was thus a doctrine that could justify both local and national primacy, depending on the emphasis of the framers. In matters of economic regulation Jackson detected a firm original intention to allow Congress and individual entrepreneurs to work out their economic relations for themselves. Thus federal regulation of commerce-related matters should be anticipated and the ambit of federal regulatory power could be very broad. But the free flow of private trade and investment—the maintenance of an unrestricted "national market"—was also thought desirable. Where Congress had not acted, it had exhibited a tacit preference for the national market, not a desire to shift regulatory power to the states. This had been the original meaning of economic federalism. In the period of Jackson's tenure, with its greater emphasis on legislative regulation, that meaning had enhanced significance. "It is more important today than it was then," Jackson wrote in 1954, "that we remain one commercial and economic unit and not a collection of parasitic states preying upon each other's commerce."[59]

III

State primacy in certain areas, however, was also inherent in the framers' vision. Federalism dictated, for example, a measure of judicial deference to the states in their efforts to maintain security and order within their boundaries. Herein Jackson was faced with difficulties in the area of civil liberties. The framers, he believed, had begun with the assumption that human rights ought to be free from governmental control. But the government against which rights were held they had identified as the federal government rather than the state, and they had also recognized that on occasion human liberty had to give way to the preservation of social order. Formalized restrictions on state usurpations of individual liberties had come only with the Reconstruction Amendments. All this suggested the possibility of a double standard for protection of civil liberties, whereby the federal government was restrained to a greater degree than the states from intruding on rights. But if this were so, was not the abstract inalienability of human rights sharply reduced in practice?

In his civil liberties decisions Jackson struggled to find a set of principles that would satisfy these separate insights. He occasionally characterized Bill of Rights guarantees as absolutes. "The very purpose of a Bill of Rights," he declared in 1943, "was to withdraw certain subjects from the vicissitudes of political controversy, to place them beyond the reach of majorities and officials and to establish them as legal principles to be applied by the courts."[60] In such instances his theory of ultimate judicial impotence served him well. In protecting Bill of Rights freedoms, judges acted "not by authority of our competence but by force of our commissions"; history had "authenticate[d]" a function for the Court "when liberty [was] infringed."[61] The judiciary had only to declare the fundamentality of the right being protected and its consequent immunity from governmental infringement. In cases testing the scope of the Fourth Amendment's protection against illegal searches and seizures, Jackson expressed similar sentiments. He felt that "uncontrolled search and seizure is one of the first and most effective weapons in the arsenal of arbitrary government";[62] he found the Fourth Amendment a safeguard of human dignity and self-reliance.[63]

But Jackson was quick to emphasize the context in which usurpations of civil liberties had taken place, and mindful of countervailing values that might justify usurpations in specific instances. He tolerated restrictions on free speech if they protected tranquility[64] or prevented disorderly conduct[65] or fostered harmony in race relations.[66] He allowed members of the American Communist Party to be convicted under a criminal statute for conspiring to teach the necessity of overthrowing the United States government, even though no showing had been made that an overthrow was an imminent result of their teaching.[67] He permitted coerced confessions in major crimes,[68] indicated that he would tolerate roadblocks and searches as a means of tracking kidnapers,[69] and in general opposed attempts to use the due process clause to give criminals "new and unprecedented opportunities to re-try their cases, or to try the prosecuting attorney or their own counsel."[70] Although he once stated that "security is like liberty in that many are the crimes committed in its name,"[71] he accepted as a reasonable trade-off the denial of procedural safeguards for the criminally accused to allow the police not to be "forced to stand by helplessly while those suspected of murder prowl about unmolested."[72]

On balance, Jackson found clearer answers in the Constitution on questions of economic regulation than on issues involving government restrictions of civil liberties. Federalism, with the passage of time, seemed more intelligible as an economic philosophy than as a social one. A national free market was as meaningful in the 1950s as it apparently had been to the framers, but the language of the Bill of Rights seemed elusive in its simplicity when re-examined in the light of Reconstruction, an official police force, an international Communist conspiracy, rapidly changing attitudes toward religious privileges and race relations, an expanded governmental intelligence apparatus, and the legacy of two World Wars. The overriding constitutional principles being cloudy and double-edged, Jackson retreated in civil liberties cases to practical accommodations between the competing values of liberty and order. On the Stone Court his approach became a counterweight to militant libertarianism; on the Vinson Court it became an aid to those who tolerated curtailment of civil liberties when national security was allegedly involved.[73]

IV

In a variety of ways Jackson's views on the proper function of the judiciary ran counter to those held by the influential Justices of his tenure. To the extent that such Justices as Black and Douglas perceived an obligation in governmental institutions to aid disadvantaged persons and supported results that were consistent with that perception, Jackson's attitude diverged from theirs. He believed in "liberal legislation," he said in 1948, as long as it was "conservatively construed."[74] He did not think it appropriate for judges "to seize the initiative in shaping the policy of the law, either by constitutional interpretation or by statutory construction."[75] At the end of his life he attacked the "cult of libertarian judicial activists" on the Court whose attitude, he felt, "encourage[d] a belief that the judges may be left to correct the result of public indifference to issues of liberty."[76] In two areas especially, Jackson's differences with Black and Douglas on this point produced opposing votes: labor relations and civil liberties. Black and Douglas regularly voted to construe the Fair Labor Standards Act and the National Labor Relations Act in ways sympathetic to labor unions; Jackson frequently disagreed.[77] After World War II, Black and Douglas took a virtually uncompromising stand in behalf of protection for civil liberties against usurpations by federal and state governments;[78] Jackson's view disclaimed this stance for an approach that asked the Court to "temper its doctrinaire logic with a little practical wisdom" lest it "convert the constitutional Bill of Rights into a suicide pact."[79]

Jackson's clashes with Black and Douglas underscored the fact that his conception of appellate judging was too delicately poised between intermediate activism and ultimate restraint to satisfy his colleagues on the Stone and Vinson Courts. Stone's theory of judging rejected distinctions between intermediate and ultimate stages in judging. He simply acknowledged that the judiciary was sometimes forced to make hard choices between competing social values with no guidance from history. Stone's belief that judicial activism was permissible where an interest being invaded had no effective recourse to the political process assumed a freedom in the judiciary to decide the scope of its own power. Jackson found that assumption untenable. Frankfurter, in contrast, did not deny Jackson's belief that judges were ultimately impotent as social policy-makers, but claimed that they could not even function in a policy-making capacity at intermediate levels. When Jackson maintained in a 1942 opinion that judges could "legislate" in unraveling a "jurisdictional snarl" involving a taxation issue, Frankfurter found the remark offensive. It "disregard[ed]," he asserted, "the role of this Court in our Constitutional system since its establishment in 1789."[80] Yet Frankfurter, for all his efforts to avoid functioning as an architect of social policy, came to scrutinize the constitutionality of legislation through an accommodation process—not unlike Jackson's—in which competing interests and values were balanced. What Frankfurter could not abide was Jackson's open confession that a choice not to subordinate one's personal preferences for the judgments of a legislature was still a choice, with political implications.

The responses of Jackson's colleagues highlighted the central tension in his approach to judging. He insisted that judges could respond to the exigencies of practical problems while at the same time basing their resolutions on principles of law that transcended merely pragmatic judgments. His involvement with the Nuremberg trials reflected this dual sense. Stone and also Frankfurter criticized his participation in the trials as threatening to the stature of the judiciary. The outcome of the trials was foreordained, they argued; for Jackson to lend his office to the prosecution suggested that the Supreme Court could be identified with what Stone called a "high-grade lynching party."[81] Others on the Court were said to have expressed concern with Jackson's participation in Nuremberg for different reasons, either because he did not establish an overwhelming case against leading Nazis or because he had accepted the job of Chief Prosecutor to advance his own political career.[82]

Jackson, however, believed that Nuremberg could illustrate the capacity of law to serve as a force for social cohesiveness. The trials, if carefully conducted, could legitimate desired results—the execution of enemies to the American nation and the repudiation of a way of life they personified—and also demonstrate the inherent fairness and justice of the Anglo-American adversary system. As prosecutor, Jackson was both an advocate for the destruction of Nazism and a servant of the legal system under which that destruction was being attempted. He could not expect to achieve vindication of the positions he advocated unless the system, through its evidentiary rules and procedural safeguards, affirmed them. Trying the Nazi criminals in a court of law, Jackson felt, was worth the conceded risk of failing to convict them. "The world yields no respect to courts," he had said prior to his Nuremberg appointment, "that are merely organized to convict. . . . You must put no man on trial before anything that is called a court . . . if you are not willing to see him freed if not proven guilty."[83]

In his remarks as prosecutor, Jackson stressed the two levels of his approach. His case was "hard and uncompromising." Defendants were characterized individually as "venomous vulgarian," "half militarist and half gangster," and "the greatest and cruelest slaver since the Pharaohs of Egypt."[84] Their conduct was pictured as "a dreadful sequence of aggressions or crimes . . . the destruction of all that was beautiful and useful in so much of the world." They were "living symbols of racial hatreds, of terrorism and violence, and of the arrogance and cruelty of power."[85] Yet at the same time the task of the trial was to "draw the line" between "just and measured retribution" and "the unthinking cry for vengeance which arises from the anguish of war." The Nazis had not distinguished between law as a tool of power and law as an emblem of "the moral sense of mankind";[86] that was all the more reason for keeping that distinction sharply in focus at Nuremberg.

Jackson believed that his participation in the Nuremberg trials had been the "most important, enduring and constructive work of [his] life."[87] He took the notion of a "rule of law" seriously: properly administered, law could be a repository of "detachment and intellectual integrity" that fulfilled "humanity's aspirations to do justice."[88] It could also be a guide for practical conduct, a vehicle for facilitating business arrangements, a method of reconciling value conflicts, a forum for vindicating human rights, and a process through which the virtues of rationality and civilization could become dominant. Yet Jackson as a judge was never quite capable of conveying the sense that law could have an existence apart from the workings of its agents. As an advocate, whether in Jamestown, Washington, or Nuremberg, he had attempted to adopt partisan stances without giving the impression that he had surrendered his independence or integrity. He was a lawyer, not a hired man, and in suggesting the difference between the two he helped distinguish law from power or partisanship. But on the Court he somehow failed to personify the detachment he tried to achieve at Nuremberg. He was at his most effective as a judge, paradoxically, in the use of adversary skills, ridiculing the positions of Justices who opposed him, or restating an issue in vivid but sometimes polemical terms.

Consequently Jackson was himself a counterargument for his belief that judges could wield power at one level only to yield it at another. His puncturing of fictional doctrines, his candid discussions of his own thought processes, his recognition that judges "legislated" whether they supported or opposed the actions of legislatures, his open squabbles with his colleagues, his use of humor, sarcasm, and irony in his opinions—all these created the impression of a human being whose personal passions and prejudices had not been lessened by his becoming a judge. Yet Jackson's approach to judging rested on a premise that at some point in the decision-making process subordination of individual will to institutional imperatives was required. The approaches to economic regulation and civil liberties that he took were, in this sense, not his but those of the framers of the Constitution. They were compelled not by personal predilection but by a legacy of eighteenth-century social and economic policies. Jackson was so much the modern judge, however, breaking down the mystique of his office, that his deference to eighteenth-century views seemed out of joint. One was tempted to ask whether the framers' economic theories were not Jackson's in disguise, and whether a distinction between the intermediate and ultimate stages of judging really existed.

There were those, however, who took seriously Jackson's effort to characterize judging as an exercise of both power and humility, and who accepted his premise that law could simultaneously function as a process for adjusting conflict and a rule of civilized conduct.[89] If Jackson's influence in the Stone and Vinson courts was more that of gadfly than that of intellectual leader, his theory of judicial performance did not atrophy after his death. In a society increasingly marked by legislation, Jackson's theory freed the judiciary from an utterly passive stance toward the actions of legislatures; in times when competition between the federal government and the states had revived, it reasserted the framers' belief that American government rested on balances between the powers of the states and those of the nation; in a world where judges no longer merely discovered law, it refused to concede that law was therefore synonymous with the dictates of judges. As debates about the proper function of the judiciary focused increasingly on means to achieve a satisfactory balance between creative leadership and fidelity to institutional constraints, Jackson's view offered itself as an intellectually respectable model, made less controversial, perhaps, by its eventual dissociation from its architect.

10 

Cardozo, Learned Hand, and Frank: The Dialectic of Freedom and Constraint

Throughout the early and middle years of the twentieth century, jurisprudential dilemmas of the kind confronted by Jackson and other Supreme Court Justices were experienced also by appellate judges of the lower federal and state courts. Although lower court judges heard far more private law cases and had far fewer opportunities than Supreme Court Justices to interpret the federal Constitution, they too felt the pressures swirling about the demise of oracular judging.

Although those pressures were still unresolved and keenly felt as late as Jackson's tenure, they had originated in the late nineteenth century. As early as the 1870s a skepticism had arisen about the validity of universal principles whose truth could not be empirically demonstrated. This insight, symbolized by Holmes's *The Common Law* (1881), and first confined to a handful of intellectuals, interacted with the numbing effects of World War I, which seemed to symbolize the simultaneous collapse of "gentlemanly" codes of behavior, a hierarchical society, and the martial virtues, to produce a value crisis of major proportions.[1] One side effect of the crisis, previously discussed, was an intense questioning of the absolutist character of moral truths. Two others of a more academic nature were criticism of formalistic methodologies based on *a priori* postulates and growing intellectual support for the proposition that the only "reality" was that which was empirically observable.[2]

The attacks on and the eventual repudiation of the oracular theory of judging may be traced to the same sources. The oracular theory was challenged and eventually discarded because it assumed the existence of unverifiable fixed truths in an intellectual climate in which that assumption was no longer credible. Once a conception of judges as oracles was discarded, however, the vulnerability of the autocratic judiciary in a democratic society became evident. If judicial decisions were not merely declarations of finite truths, but were something resembling the personal views of judges, they had to be justified on different intellectual grounds.

In response to this need the jurisprudential theories previously alluded to—Sociological Jurisprudence, Realism, and Process Jurisprudence—emerged in a consecutive sequence from the 1900s through the 1950s. Sociological Jurisprudence insisted that decisions be grounded in empirical observations of changing social conditions and thereby replace pseudologic with "experience."[3] Realism, which drew on the contributions of Sociological Jurisprudence but ultimately deviated from it, assumed that judging was as illogical and idiosyncratic an exercise as any other form of decision-making by human beings and sought to reduce its irrationality by developing, through empirical observation, methods of predicting court decisions.[4] Process Jurisprudence, reacting to Realism's apparent fatalism toward unchecked judicial power, attempted to build institutional constraints back into adjudication and to identify rational judging with an awareness of the discrete functions of the judiciary and other branches of government.[5] No longer, then, was the twentieth-century appellate judge an oracle; he was, depending on the theory advanced, primarily a social engineer, or a "hunch player"[6] who understood and trusted his instincts, or a craftsman in the "reasoned elaboration"[7] of justifications for his power.

These developments, stretching over more than fifty years, produced an ambivalent stance for the twentieth-century appellate judge, a stance that reflected recognition that judges were human as well as an attendant sense of the possibility that a judge could use his office to promote values in which he believed. At the same time this stance conveyed the importance of continued identification of judging with the values of impersonality, impartiality, and rationality. A judge had opportunities for creativity; at the same time he had obligations and constraints that bound those opportunities.

Jackson's interpretation of judging centered on the question as to what extent a judge dedicated to the ideal of impersonality could personalize his office. The interpretations of Benjamin Cardozo, Learned Hand, and Jerome Frank centered on a related question raised by Hand in a 1933 radio address: How far was a judge free in rendering a decision?[8] The question was intended to incorporate the several facets of the twentieth-century judge's role: a human being, a member of contemporary American society, a representative of a special type of governing institution, an heir to a tradition of decision-making that emphasized independence and accountability, individuality and self-limitation.

During their careers, Cardozo, Hand, and Frank made prime contributions to an understanding of the dialectic of freedom and restraint in the appellate judiciary. In certain respects they were particularly well-situated to make that contribution. For the great part of their collective judicial careers, they were judges on appellate courts of intermediate status, reviewing the decisions of inferior courts in their system but bound to follow judgments of the United States Supreme Court. Cardozo served on the New York Court of Appeals for eighteen years, from 1914 to 1932. During that time he made a national reputation as a judge and wrote his most influential extrajudicial works, including *The Nature of the Judicial Process*. His short subsequent career on the Supreme Court, which ended with his death in 1939, paled by comparison. Hand served for fifteen years as a federal district court judge, then for thirty-seven on the United States Court of Appeals for the Second Circuit. Frank's only experience as a judge consisted of his sixteen years as Hand's Scond Circuit colleague. For most of their judicial lives Cardozo, Hand, and Frank wrote their opinions with the awareness that they were both free to overrule decisions that came to them yet required to have their opinions possibly subjected to further scrutiny.

Moreover, Cardozo, Hand, and Frank held judicial office during a time of profound and rapid social change, in an environment that magnified the scope and pace of that change. When Cardozo first took office, the status of the automobile industry in American society was indeterminate; Cardozo himself helped clarify it. By the time of Learned Hand's death in 1961, two world wars and a world-wide depression had been weathered, and radio, television, travel by airplane, and the computer had become features of American life, each headquartered in New York City. No judge operating in such an atmosphere could fail to perceive the implicit pressure upon the law to be responsive to changing social conditions.

The combination, perhaps, of the New York environment, the status of their courts, and their own intellectual powers moved Cardozo, Hand, and Frank to produce judicial and extrajudicial literature of considerable quality and influence. They distinguished themselves among early-twentieth-century American appellate judges in their attempts to create jurisprudential stances to accommodate the contradictory pressures of modern judging. For them judicial decision-making meant neither assuming complexities out of existence nor being defeated by them. Rather, it meant trying to unravel such complexities until the social trade-offs they represented were revealed. Each man had his own method for dealing with the necessity of balancing what Hand called "incommensurable" values.[9] Although the relative soundness of their methods is largely a question of individual taste, each man clearly distinguished himself in his effort. Together the three added a dimension of intellectual sophistication to the American judicial tradition.

I

Cardozo's family history might have been chronicled by Edith Wharton or Louis Auchincloss. His ancestors were Sephardic Jews, longtime residents of New York, successful businessmen, educators and patriots,[10] a closely knit and intermarried clan. Relatives sat on the board of Columbia University, held judgeships, were patrons of the arts and generally carried out the rituals of New York's upper class, whose anti-Semitism did not extend to prominent Sephardic Jews who could trace their American citizenship to the eighteenth century. Three years after Cardozo's birth in 1870, the position of his family was severely shaken by the implication of his father, Albert Cardozo, a judge of the Supreme Court of New York, in a probe of the Erie Railroad's bankruptcy proceedings. The elder Cardozo resigned to avoid impeachment, having apparently acted with impropriety in the appointment of a receiver for the railroad, and having, on other occasions, allowed immigrants to acquire citizenship illegally. He had also assigned a large share of his authorized appointments as a bankruptcy referee to one of his nephews. His resignation dishonored the Cardozos and created in his son Benjamin a lifetime mission of restoring the family name.[11]

Cardozo grew to maturity in an environment marked by intrafamily trials and tensions. His mother died when he was nine and his father six years later, leaving a depleted inheritance to be divided among six children, only two of whom were potential wage earners. He was raised by his sister Ellen, who combined, throughout his life, the roles of mother, confidant, and companion, and Cardozo confided once to a cousin that he would never marry because he "could never put [Ellen] in second place."[12] From his college days at Columbia, where he was described as antisocial and clannish,[13] to his years on the Court of Appeals in Albany, from which he wrote Ellen with great regularity,[14] Cardozo demonstrated a singular preoccupation with private family affairs. For over twenty years before 1913, his life consisted primarily of work with his brother Albert's law firm and its successors, and of family gatherings, at which he often played piano duets with Ellen. He appeared to some contemporaries as "congenitally shy" and "monkish in his habits."[15] Learned Hand said that he "never wanted anybody to penetrate into his inner life."[16]

Yet Cardozo's mission of restoration dictated that to some extent he seek public contacts and even covet public attention. In this task he proved remarkably adept, despite his reclusive tendencies. He continually managed to charm those with whom he came in contact. His shyness projected itself as modesty, his reserve as calmness and poise, his tendency to enjoy and indulge in flattery as graciousness and civility. He appeared, to observers, as a man of "rare courtesy," with a "nobleness and lofty exaltation of spirit," who possessed "extraordinary charm and infinite benevolence of character"; a "saintly character," who was "sweet, gentle, modest, and ever considerate."[17] Even those who displeased him were given little cause for offense. "Cardozo," maintained Learned Hand, "could handle the scalpel . . . but perfectly painlessly so that the subject would not know he was being dissected."[18]

Cardozo's self-effacement and charm masked his ambition but did not eradicate it. In 1913, after considerable success as an appellate litigator, he was proposed as a candidate for a judgeship on the New York Supreme Court. Here was a dramatic opportunity to bury his father's ghost; and although Cardozo publicly maintained that he would not participate in the campaign, he worked carefully and astutely behind the scenes[19] and was elected. A month later he was named to the Court of Appeals, and his public career was launched. While a judge, he combined a tendency to cherish his privacy with intermittent forays into the public eye, each undertaken with a certain coyness. He initially declined an invitation to give the Storrs Lectures at Yale in 1921, protesting that he had nothing to talk about, but subsequently realized that he could describe how he went about deciding cases, and produced *The Nature of the Judicial Process*.[20] He allegedly resisted pressure from those who sought to have him nominated to the Supreme Court to replace Holmes, and upon being nominated complained bitterly about having to leave Albany. Nonetheless, he did not decline the invitation when it came.

The reconciliation of Cardozo's private self with his public image was not effectuated without some strain. His unpublished college essays reveal a concern with the depersonalizing effects of thwarted aggression and repressed passions, as well as the emotional demands communal living made upon individuals.[21] Those close to him saw occasional snatches of bitterness and self-pity. Nicholas Murray Butler, one of his teachers at Columbia, referred to him as "desperately serious";[22] Learned Hand spoke of his "very deep skepticism" and tendency to "shy away from a commitment";[23] George Hellman, his authorized biographer, referred to "channels of affection, even perhaps of married love" that were "consciously barred" by Cardozo's family loyalties.[24]

Cardozo's surface affect—gentle, ethereal, humble, lavish in his praise of others—did not adequately convey his skepticism, ambition, bitterness, and tendency to evaluate others critically. To an extent he must have worn a mask in public, his graciousness and charity representing defenses against overly intimate contact with others. His judicial opinions exhibited a similar quality, and were at times close to being disingenuous. But he did not deceive himself. His theory of the proper exercise of the judicial function candidly admitted that on many occasions a judge found himself free to shape the course of the law, yet might choose to mask that freedom of choice in the traditional techniques and canons of his profession. That kind of artifice, for Cardozo, was not hypocrisy or dishonesty but simply good sense. It strengthened rather than undermined respect for the judiciary.

The state of mind in which Cardozo initiated his investigations into the nature of appellate decision-making was characteristic of his time and place. He saw the "perpetual flux" of his immediate environment; he recognized that "nothing [was] stable, [n]othing absolute, [a]ll fluid and changeable."[25] Yet at the same time he confessed to a "yearning for consistency, for uniformity of plan and structure," for "a larger and more inclusive unity in which differences will be reconciled and abnormalities vanish," finding in himself an "intellectual craving" for "symmetry of form and substance."[26] To fashion a rule that settled one case, then to expand it, through logical progressions, to the point where it covered countless similar cases was enormously satisfying. Not only was the process analytically and conceptually tidy, it gave the professional constituents of appellate judges—the bar and its clients—clear guidelines for the future conduct of their affairs.

But the law, like modern civilization, was pitted with anomalies and irregularities. Logical symmetry took a judge only so far. Historical anachronisms dominated the law of real property, their earlier logical significance obscured by time. The legal steps that created an estate in fee simple could not be distinguished from those that created a life estate by any process except an appeal to history. Yet the procedures were part of modern estate planning. Another source of logical anomalies was the incorporation into the law of the customs and practices of a trade, such as the proliferation of different types of securities, with the attendant creation of new rights and responsibilities in the law of secured transactions. In deciding a controversy involving the exchange of securities a court could not ignore the role played by custom, whatever it thought of the logic of a particular business practice. Finally, logic sometimes conflicted with equity and justice. One might begin with the traditional premise that private property rights should be protected from governmental usurpation. Expanded to its logical outcome, this premise forbade state regulation of railroad rates, since the substitution of a state-imposed rate for a "market" rate was surely an interference with the right to free enjoyment of the fruits of private ownership. In the absence of regulation, however, railroads tended to set discriminatory rates, making it more costly for certain classes of persons to use their facilities, and denying some classes the use altogether. At times the resultant inequities proved so offensive to the general public that sound policy required a partial retreat from the original premise.

For Cardozo the appellate judge's task, most broadly defined, was to seek an accommodation between the values embodied in symmetrical logic and the competing values manifested by any anomalies. In his extrajudicial writings he proposed several means by which this accommodation might be sought. One employed a distinctive methodology for appellate decision-making; another made use of a refinement of that methodology, one that emphasized the role of broad overriding purposes and goals in American society. Still another flowed from an eventual recognition of the inadequacy of any one method of decision-making in solving the complex value choices that judging required.

In *The Nature of the Judicial Process*, a work that established him as one of the leading jurists of his time, Cardozo described a method of decision-making that would enable appellate judges to respond to simultaneous pressures for continuity and change. Both stability and progress were contemporary goals, Cardozo believed, the question being how to ensure their coexistence. The answer lay in a selective use of four distinct methods: philosophy, emphasizing logical symmetry; history, anachronistic vagaries; tradition, the customs and practices of a trade or business; and sociology, the social policies behind legal rules. The first three methods were associated with particular areas of the law. Logical analysis took care of the ordinary run of appellate cases, in which matching precedents to new facts was all that was required; "a page of history was worth a volume of logic"[27] in areas (such as real property) where ancient procedures had survived; trade practices dominated the law of commercial transactions. The fourth method "was always in reserve": when other methods conflicted, it served as an "arbiter" between them. New conceptions of the responsibility of private property-holders had created "new restraints upon ancient rights"[28] in which contemporary logic clashed with history. The question in such instances was whether "a paramount public policy" prevailed over "certainty and uniformity and order and coherence."[29] Judicial appeal to contemporary social values helped resolve that question.

Cardozo's audience, mindful of the dramatic value shifts taking place in early-twentieth-century America, hopeful yet skeptical about progress, unsure of the roles history and tradition were to play in the modern world, reacted to his book with great enthusiasm. After the author's first lecture at Yale University the auditorium was overflowing; at its conclusion he received a spontaneous standing ovation.[30] The book has become a classic of legal education, and is continually recommended to aspiring law students on the perhaps dubious ground that "it still possesses the same validity and vitality . . . as it did when published."[31] The appeal of the work was that it represented a compromise between oracular and nihilistic judging. The four methods—really classification devices—retained a conceptualistic approach familiar to the late nineteenth century. At the same time, Cardozo conceded that judges made law, albeit in a limited sense. Since the methods—even that of sociology—were intended as restraints on the judge, Cardozo could face the fact that he was not an oracle without appearing to be a tyrant.

The success of *The Nature of the Judicial Process* created a market for Cardozo's further reflections on his function. In two additional series of lectures, *The Growth of the Law* (1924) and *The Paradoxes of Legal Science* (1927), he refined his thinking. *The Growth of the Law* focused on the problem of choosing between alternative methods of decision-making. In a case in which traditionally protected practices were being rescrutinized in light of a new calculus of social values, a judge had the option of employing the methods of history and custom or the method of sociology. His choice, Cardozo maintained, should rest on an understanding of the purposes each method served as well as on a determination as to which purposes more accurately approximated the current ends of society. Law, in Cardozo's view, was continually growing, and its growth was "conscious" in that it reflected "the attainment of the moral end" as embodied in "legal forms."[32] By searching for purposes in the law and testing its decisions with reference to perceived ends, judges could make a more intelligent balancing of the competing values cases presented.

The argument advanced by Cardozo in *The Growth of the Law* assumed the existence and intelligibility of shared social purposes and goals. This was a large assumption, especially in the light of the sense of value disintegration perceived by many of his contemporaries in the 1920s. With the publication of *The Paradoxes of Legal Science* Cardozo exhibited some doubts about this premise. He rejected the concept of continual progress, asserting that the law changed over time but did not necessarily grow. He rejected, in addition, two implications of his earlier works—the belief that morality could be said to have a fixed content, and the ideal of law as a science. Judicial decisions ought to reflect contemporary moral values, to be sure, but one generation's morality was not necessarily another's. A fourfold classification of methods for appellate decision-making was a helpful analytical device but not a scientific formula. The judicial calculus was "precarious," consisting of "little compromises and adjustments, the expedients of the fleeting hour."[33] No method or approach could dispel uncertainty; paradoxes lay at the heart of social organization. A judge could not achieve any ultimate reconciliation of stability with progress. His function was "not to transform civilization"[34] but to make a "timid and tentative approximation" of currently cherished values.[35]

Cardozo's interpretation of his office, then, juxtaposed a private craving for certainty and predictability against a public acceptance of the complexities of modern life. Although he believed that "where conflict exists, moral values [were] to be preferred to economic and economic to aesthetic,"[36] and that morality had a core of timeless substantive content, he stopped short of imposing these beliefs on his constituents. His style was rather to lay bare the competing elements in a case and then to make it appear as if their clash had been resolved by someone other than himself, either in principles of law laid down by his predecessors or in the actions of a legislature. He was candid in revealing the problems he faced, but in solving them he retreated behind conventional techniques of judicial subterfuge—of which he was a master. His retreat was motivated less by a desire to deceive than by a fear that if the sovereign prerogative of choice were truly his alone he would not know how to make it. The judiciary's arsenal of craft techniques was his barrier against that fear. It allowed him, said Learned Hand, to appear inflexible once he had arrived at a decision, although he had agonized in the process of reaching it.[37]

II

With Cardozo there was a continual layer of gentility between him and the contemplation of social disintegration and personal despair. If he was not completely the saintly, ethereal figure some saw him as, he had at least enough commitment to the ideals of nobility and purity to have merged those qualities in his public image. Learned Hand, by contrast, had no particular fear of the horrors and brutalities in life and no illusions about his own saintliness. At one level this made him a less artful judge and a more accessible person than Cardozo. Yet in his own fashion he was remote and distant, with his own areas of self-consciousness and self-doubt.

Throughout his life, but especially in the eminence of his later career, Hand had the gift of public charm. Like Holmes, he could inspire his professional audience with an unforgettable pithy phrase, usually a metaphor rather than a epigram. Life was "a dicer's throw"; reason "a smoky torch."[38] Hand was more versatile than Holmes in his appeal, however. He could sing a stanza of Gilbert and Sullivan, tell a ribald story, mock a dialect, or serve as the voice of God in an Archibald MacLeish play. He was a clubman, a figure on the banquet circuit, an academic lecturer, a speaker at patriotic public ceremonies, a commemorator of his fellow judges. He never failed to notice the nuances of these different roles; the tone of his remarks was always appropriate. Even on the most delicate occasions during his tenure as Chief Justice of the Second Circuit, he knew how to charm. Writing to Judge Charles Clark at a particularly trying time in the latter's career, Hand said: "We all get the feeling that we are beating our wings ineffectively in the void, and I know of no way to prevent that mood coming on us from time to time. I should like to say, however, for whatever it may be worth, that we all think of you as one of the outstanding judges on the federal or any other bench. . . . Courage, mon ami, le Diable est mort."[39]

Yet Hand's singular charm and great zest for companionship were in part products of a private tendency toward introspection and even melancholia. He did not like to be alone, an old friend once said: he was "a man of moods," and good conversation cheered him.[40] As an undergraduate at Harvard, he described himself as being "just on the fringe" socially: "all his friends got into clubs and he did not." He wondered, much later in his life, whether he had not been "kind of a sissy."[41] He was not comfortable or successful as a law practitioner, either in Albany, where he worked from 1896 to 1902, or in New York City, where he practiced until his 1909 appointment to the United States District Court for the Southern District of New York.[42] His father and grandfather had been judges; there his talents seemed best suited, he said, for he "thought with his fingers."[43]

But judging was not without its uncertainties and disappointments. First was its close identification, in early twentieth-century New York, with state and national politics. Hand owed his district judgeship to the overtures of Charles C. Burlingham, one of the kingmakers of the New York bar, who was also influential in Cardozo's campaign for the New York Supreme Court in 1913. Through Burlingham and George Wickersham, Attorney General under President Taft, Hand received his first appointment. Three years later, in the 1912 election, he publicly supported Theodore Roosevelt and the Progressive Party against Taft. In 1913, he ran for the New York Court of Appeals on the Progressive ticket, did not campaign, and was soundly defeated. The alienation of Taft produced by this series of events redounded to Hand's considerable disadvantage, for Taft (as has been noted) exercised veto power over major federal judicial appointments during the Harding and Coolidge administrations. In 1922 Hand, still a district judge, was proposed to Harding as a Supreme

Court candidate, but Taft, remembering Hand as "a wild Roosevelt man and a Progressive," suggested that he would be a divisive force on the Court.[44]

This legacy of political animosity combined with other circumstances to deny Hand a Supreme Court nomination all his life. He managed to secure promotion to the Second Circuit in 1924, again with the aid of Burlingham; but Taft's presence kept him from further consideration for the Court until 1930. He was then twice denied nomination by the fortuity of geography, two other able candidates, Cardozo and Charles Evans Hughes, also being residents of New York. By 1942, at age seventy, he seemed finally destined to succeed. Felix Frankfurter, who had lobbied long for Hand's nomination, was instructed by President Roosevelt to prepare a statement announcing it. At the last minute, however, Roosevelt backed down, embarrassed by his own Court-packing arguments, which had emphasized the advanced age of the then current justices.[45] Thus Hand, despite a growing national reputation, remained on the Second Circuit. "For about 20 years or so," he said late in his life, "every time I went to Washington . . . I said, 'Oh, wouldn't it be wonderful if I got on the Supreme Court.' "[46] By the end of his career he had put aside both the hope and the subsequent disappointments. Only vestiges of his feelings occasionally surfaced, as when he asked President Kennedy in 1961 to "promote those best qualified in the lower levels [of the federal judiciary] when you can."[47]

Despite these and other smaller frustrations, which occasionally provoked outbursts of temper in the courtroom,[48] Hand, like Holmes, had the fortune to live long enough to be made fully aware of the high esteem in which he was held. As early as the 1920s, before he joined the Second Circuit, Holmes had urged his appointment to the Supreme Court;[49] in 1925 Cardozo put Hand in "a little group of two or three" judges who were "pretty close" to "my idol" Holmes in his esteem;[50] Justice Stone lobbied for Hand's appointment to the Court in the 1930s;[51] Felix Frankfurter, a consummate promoter, boosted Hand incessantly for thirty years. In 1946 Hand was termed in *Life* Magazine "the spiritual heir of Marshall, Holmes, Brandeis and Cardozo."[52] In a tribute issue of the *Harvard Law Review* a year later he was called "unquestionably first among American judges."[53] In proceedings commemorating his fiftieth year of judicial service in 1959, Frankfurter called him "the greatest master of English speech on the bench since Holmes laid down his pen."[54] Others paid tributes to Hand, as they had to Holmes, such as are rarely paid to the dead and almost never to the living.

Yet the stature of Hand has recently been questioned. The intermediate status of his court and his "restraintist philosophy" of judicial review, it has been argued, made his impact "less than his reputation would lead us to expect."[55] His reputation has been seen as "mostly myth": "he was great because he was reputed to be great."[56] This assessment of Hand raises once more the question of the sources of an appellate judge's image in history. To an extent the reputation of an appellate judge is a function of the sociological or political implications of the results he reaches, and as such changes with time.[57] In addition, insofar as a judge reveals the philosophical foundations of his approach to decision-making he becomes vulnerable to changing fashions, since activism and self-restraint rise and fall in public esteem. Finally, the legal questions of dominant interest for most educated Americans have been constitutional questions, and the opportunities of an intermediate appellate court to render major decisions on constitutional issues are extremely limited. As Hand once wrote Stone, "The most futile job I have to do is to pass on Constitutional questions. Who in hell cares what anybody says about them but the Final Five of the August Nine of which you are one?"[58]

But the sources of Hand's eminence were more varied than those of most judges in comparable positions. His notable longevity on the bench gave him the opportunity to write in a number of areas and thereby tended to counteract the limited reach of his court. The crowded, varied docket of the Second Circuit, the skill of the New York City bar, and the high quality of his judicial colleagues resulted in the regular presentation of complex issues whose ramifications were thoroughly perceived and articulated. The economic and intellectual importance of the New York environment meant that his decisions on normally arcane subjects, such as patent law, could take on national significance. The originality and clarity of his writing style served to widen the audience for his opinions, and his versatility as a public speaker expanded his popular impact. Finally, his theory of judicial performance, imperfectly described as a "restraintist philosophy," encouraged creativity as much as it checked it. His criticism of judicial activism was reserved for constitutional cases, and his advocation of a limited interpretation of judicial power in that area associated him with an influential body of early-twentieth-century jurisprudential thinkers, including Holmes and Brandeis. Only very late in his life did his philosophy of judging appear to isolate him from current events.

Hand began thinking about the intellectual process of judging by, as he said, looking the grey rat in the eye.[59] Civilization was a thin layer covering the anarchistic and brutal tendencies of humanity. Beneath its surface "the murderer lurk[ed] always not far . . . to break out from time to time, peace resolutions to the contrary notwithstanding."[60] Social gains came "with immeasurable waste"; conflict was normal; the path of history was "strewn with carnage." And there were no eternal guiding principles for social conduct: the Absolute was mute. All man could do was grope through trial and error, trying to "shake off the brute" and keep the social order he had created from disintegrating.[61]

There was a certain comfort in this acceptance of man's limitations. Wisdom, Hand felt, emerged as the "false assurance[s]" of human omniscience and omnipotence vanished. "[G]entle irony, friendly skepticism," and open-mindedness were the appropriate moods in which to assess the worth of man's attempts to organize his society.[62] There was little hope of human perfectibility, he felt, and little assurance of progress, but some indication that, at least in democratic societies, individuals tended to tolerate each other's needs and to make accommodations with conflict rather than exacerbate it. This "spirit of moderation"[63] was not always evident, nor were attempts of accommodation always triumphs of reason, but despair was premature. So long as one did not expect too much from efforts to make life in America more civilized, one could find some solace in those efforts.

These perceptions could be useful to the work of American appellate judges, who had, Hand believed, some responsibility to contribute to "civilization" and also some power to dictate the ways in which individuals were to conduct their affairs. Judicial wisdom came, for Hand, with a dual realization. First, a judge could not ignore the powers of his office. "The law" was not always clear, and inevitably in interpreting it a judge mingled his own sense of the appropriate rules of social conduct with already existing sanctions. To the extent that his own glosses on prior cases and statutes were accepted, a judge was free to "make" law. Second, on the other hand, governing in America was a reciprocal process. Although "the law" was synonymous with the commands of government officials, those officials were charged with the duty of expressing the common will. The common will, however, was difficult to discern, largely because of the inability of human beings to articulate, or even to know, what values they shared with each other. Thus the judge was "in a contradictory position . . .

pulled by two opposite forces."[64] He had to try to interpret "the common will expressed by the government" even in those circumstances when it was virtually indecipherable, trusting that his analytical powers and instincts would produce an acceptable formulation. But he could not merely "enforce whatever he [thought] best."[65]

In walking this delicate line of creativity and restraint Hand was guided by his original judgments about mankind and civilization. He began with three paradigm situations. Where the judge had emerged as a declarer of the common will of the people, as expressed in law, ample room for judicial creativity existed; common law cases were the best example. Where the legislative branch of government had articulated the common will through a statute, the judge was bound to interpret that statute in conformity with the legislature's intentions. And where two sets of potentially conflicting declarations existed, such as a statute and the United States Constitution, or where the specific intent of a legislature could not clearly be determined, a judge was forced to balance the expertise of his office against the institutional limitations on it.

Hand refined these paradigms in the light of his social perceptions. Given that the common will was so difficult to discern and articulate, great caution had to be exercised in following its apparent mandates. The more specific the mandate, the greater the confidence one could have that it truly expressed the desires of the people. The more general it was, the less valuable it became in this capacity. In the case of specific mandates, the judge was required to "loyally enforce"[66] the dictates of the legislature. Where the only mandate that existed was that of an implicit delegation of power to judges to enact "authentic bit[s] of special legislation,"[67] the judge was only constrained by the canons of his profession, the people having agreed to be guided by judicial expertise. In the intermediate situations of statutory and constitutional interpretation, the generality of the mandate determined the appropriate judicial response.

Some provisions of the Constitution were "specific enough to be treated like other legal commands": they prescribed clear limitations on the jurisdiction of courts or the power of legislatures and were simply to be obeyed. Other provisions were of intermediate specificity. Their application to an individual case could be determined by "look[ing] to their history and their setting with confidence that these will disclose their purpose."[68] Still others, however, such as freedom of speech and freedom of press, due process of law, and equal protection of the laws, were so general that they ceased to be commands and became merely "moral adjurations."[69] "[N]ot definite enough to be guides on concrete occasions,"[70] they could only be used by the judiciary as a check on legislative activity in situations in which evidence indicated that a piece of legislation represented "nothing but the patent exploitation of one group whose interests [had been] altogether disregarded."[71] There the due process or equal protection clauses might come into play; but such occasions, Hand felt, would be very infrequent, for the fact-finding powers of courts were limited and usually not capable of amassing much evidence about internal legislative affairs. Judicial review of legislation under the general provisions of the Bill of Rights thus was extremely limited.

A comparable restraint did not always exist in situations involving statutory interpretation in the absence of a constitutional provision. If a statute was of intermediate specificity, judges should attempt to ascertain its general purposes and to reason from these assumed purposes to the specific question of application they faced. In this class of cases the judicial function was analogous to that of interpreting similar constitutional provisions. If, however, the statute was very broadly drafted, Hand viewed it as an invitation to the courts to "do what you think is right"—namely, "take the conflicting values and probabilities and make the best guess you can."[72] General statutory language thus invited judicial creativity; general constitutional language dictated restraint. In the former case the public had implicitly indicated a preference for judicial rather than legislative guidance. In the latter, it had merely made "admonitions of moderation"[73] to the legislature.

Hand's view of the proper function of the judiciary places him in an anomalous position in the history of twentieth-century jurisprudence. In the early years of the century his insistence that judges were free, within limits, to be creative identified him with Holmes, Pound, Cardozo, and other critics of both mechanical jurisprudence and what Hand called the "dictionary school"[74] of literalist statutory interpretation. At the same time his position on judicial review of the constitutionality of legislation was compatible with that advanced by Holmes and glibly identified with liberalism. But whereas his fellow members of "the race of giants"[75]—Holmes, Brandeis, and Cardozo—all died before World War II, Hand lived on into the 1960s, to confront the Warren Court and see the meaning of judicial liberalism apparently change. Suddenly, close judicial scrutiny of the impact of legislation on equal protection and due process rights became a "liberal" response. Hand saw, in the light of these developments, a virtual repudiation of his thesis by legal scholars and jurists. In 1964, three years after Hand's death, Judge Charles Wyzanski wrote that "[his] thesis has not yet been supported by a single eminent judge or professor."[76]

Believing that tolerance and moderation were virtues, Hand was well suited to bear this isolation. Believing, as well, in man's insatiable appetite for social panaceas, he may have viewed the current of opinion that rejected his positions as further evidence of man's persistent attempts to shake off the brute. If he could not accept Warren Court activism intellectually, perhaps he understood it emotionally: liberty and democracy, after all, were values he cherished despite their limitations. What he insisted upon, finally, was that judges take concepts like "equality" and "the common will," explore them, and come to see them for what they were—catchwords for a whole set of complex and ambiguous phenomena. Sometimes this process of exploration gave rise to delicate judicial choices and a balancing of values that were hard to weigh. Sometimes that choice had to be faced and made, at other times it had to be delegated to another arm of government. The process, however, was what judging was all about. Explaining it to others was the "honest craft" of his profession, in which Hand delighted.[77] Grounded in the unresolvable complexities of modern life, it yet held out a hope that the judiciary could help maintain the persistence, if not the permanence, of civilization.

III

In his discussions of freedom and restraint in the judiciary, Hand had rejected "two extreme schools"[78] of jurisprudence. One was the dictionary school, the other a school that argued, he said, "that a judge should not regard the law; that this has never really been done in the past, and that to attempt even to do it is an illusion." Rather, Hand continued, the judge according to this second school "must conform his decision to what honest men would think right, and it [was] better for him to look into his own heart to find out what that is."[79] The school thus caricatured was Realist Jurisprudence. One of its American founders, Jerome Frank, came to be Hand's colleague on the Second Circuit. Neither Hand nor Frank substantially changed his view during his tenure together, and the institutional limitations on judges so important to Hand remained partially illusory for Frank. If anything were to limit a judge's freedom to make law, Frank thought, it should be a sense of the personal sympathies and antipathies that led him to irrational conclusions, but even those, if candidly set forth, could become part of a reasoned opinion. Yet, despite this divergence of positions, Frank told Hand that "no one else I've ever known has excited in me such admiration and affection." Hand was Frank's "model as a judge":[80] to sit with him was "an inestimable privilege, a constant source of education."[81] Hand, for his part, wrote Frank's widow after his death in 1957 that "we . . . agreed about the real values of life, much as we often differed about the ways and means."[82]

The intellectual combativeness and close personal involvement manifested in his relations with Hand was characteristic of Frank's professional encounters. He was continually anxious to encounter new ideas and remarkable in the speed with which he could absorb them; and yet he greeted them with skepticism and often quickly cast them off. He relished conversation and debate and was judged by many of his acquaintances to be an exceptionally stimulating companion,[83] but he tended, especially in print, to caricature opposing positions and to engage in personal attacks on those he criticized. He was capable of undiscriminating hero worship and also of unbalanced enmity. Persons he had savagely attacked in his writings found him friendly and engaging in person. Judge Charles Clark, who clashed continually with him in correspondence during their service on the Second Circuit, said that Frank "never seemed to harbor permanent spite of any form whatsoever" and doubted if Frank "realized how heavy was the impact of his intellectual blows."[84]

The presence or absence of certain characteristics in others set off emotionally charged reactions in Frank. He could not bear intellectual dishonesty, duplicity, or self-delusion; conversely, he greatly admired skepticism, candor, and detachment. His heroes, such as Holmes, Hand, Aristotle, or Lord Halifax, took no refuge in dogma, legal or otherwise. They could face hard truths (men were not angels, legal rules were fictions, judges were inevitably biased, social conflict was inevitable) and build a philosophical stance that incorporated them instead of wishing them away. By contrast his villains, who included Edward Coke, Plato, and Christopher Columbus Langdell (Dean of Harvard Law School from 1870 to 1895 and founder of the case-method approach to legal education), were immature or unscrupulous neurotics who imposed their own obsessions on others in the form of one-sided or disingenuous theories. Coke, for example, was "a nasty, narrow-minded, greedy, cruel, arrogant, unsensitive man, a time-serving politician and a liar who, by his adulation of some crabbed medieval legal doctrines, had retarded English and American legal development for centuries."[85]

The extent to which Frank personalized his assessments of the ideas of others is illustrated by his changing attitudes toward Cardozo. In 1930 Frank published *Law and the Modern Mind*, the culmination of an intensive three-year exploration of the relations of the behavioral sciences to law, including a six-month stretch during which Frank underwent psychoanalysis. *Law and the Modern Mind* asserted, among other things, that the persistent attachment of lawyers and judges to rules or principles of law perfectly illustrated Freud's insight that a childhood desire for security and certainty was retained in adults. Legal rules and principles, Frank argued, were artificial, fungible entities manufactured for the purpose of rationalizing predetermined results. Judging, an intuitive, idiosyncratic, flexible process, was being presented as if it were systematic, depersonalized and formal. This presentation, resting upon the childish wish that law could be made certain and predictable, was wholly mythical.

At the time *Law and the Modern Mind* appeared, jurisprudence in America was in ferment. As noted, a long line of criticism of "mechanical" decision-making had appeared, and Holmes, Pound, Learned Hand, and Cardozo, among others, had made separate contributions to the development of an approach that Pound loosely termed "sociological" jurisprudence.[86] This approach emphasized the dual responsibility in judges to preserve continuity and to respond to change. Various decision-making strategies were proposed through which this responsibility could be met, including Cardozo's fourfold classification of methods.[87] In *The Paradoxes of Legal Science*, Cardozo had suggested that although the values of continuity and change still framed judicial choices, no one method of decision-making could insure success in the balancing process of adjudication. On some occasions, he conceded, the judge's choice was merely intuitive.[88] This insight found support in a 1929 article by another judge, Joseph Hutcheson, who argued that "the intuitional faculty" was "essential . . . to great judging."[89]

While drawing on the contributions of sociological jurists in *Law and the Modern Mind*, Frank dissociated himself from them. He agreed with Hutcheson, he said, that judging was largely intuitive, but he rejected any intimation of the sociological jurists that it could be made otherwise. He saw their interest in the preservation or promotion of continuity in the law as simply a manifestation of the collective desire for certainty that he was exposing. Any method directed at the attainment of that end was ill-conceived. Cardozo, then, generated an ambivalent response in Frank. "His writings [have] been of inestimable value," Frank wrote in *Law and the Modern Mind*, "in making possible realistic thinking about law." But his "yearning for the absolute" gave Frank pause.[90]

As Frank's view of the judicial function coalesced after 1930, he found himself increasingly estranged from Cardozo. Frank identified himself with Realist Jurisprudence in 1931,[91] and Cardozo openly criticized the Realists in a 1932 address to the New York State Bar Association. The crux of the quarrel was over the place of "certainty and order and rational coherence,"[92] as Cardozo put it, in the law. Cardozo read some Realists, including Frank, as saying that the elements of randomness and chance always predominated in adjudication, and that therefore principles and rules were meaningless aphorisms. If this reading was fair, Cardozo maintained, Realism was "a false and misleading cult."[93] Indeterminacy was surely present in judge-made law, he felt, but it was only one of several ingredients in the cauldron. The value of certainty was another of these ingredients, and it often prevailed, to conform the law with established customs or the plain and unquestioned dictates of contemporary morality.[94] To assert that it was merely a childish fiction was to give a distorted picture of the process of judicial decision-making.

Frank responded to Cardozo's critique in two ways. He refined his own thinking and found that in some respects he and Cardozo were not, after all, at loggerheads. In 1948, for example, he divided "realists" into two groups: "rule-skeptics" and "fact-skeptics." Rule-skeptics, he claimed, "resembled Cardozo in that they had little or no interest in trial courts, but riveted their attention largely on appellate courts and on the nature and use of the legal rules." Some rule-skeptics, however, "went somewhat further than Cardozo as to the extent of the existent and desirable power of judges to alter the legal rules." Fact-skeptics, of which he was one, were primarily interested in trial courts. They traced "the major cause of legal uncertainty to trial uncertainties." So "far as appellate courts and the legal rules are concerned," Frank argued, "the views of the fact-skeptics as to existent and desirable legal certainty approximated the views of Cardozo . . . and many others not categorized as 'realists.'"[95] This description of himself vis-à-vis Cardozo was bizarre, since he had clearly been a "rule-skeptic" in *Law and the Modern Mind* and had never at any time "approximated" Cardozo's position on legal certainty.

The other way was to attack Cardozo personally in an oblique and unfortunate fashion. In 1943, under the pseudonym "Anon Y. Mous of Middletown," Frank wrote a critique of Cardozo's style. In it he advanced the thesis that Cardozo, in response to personal pressures, had adopted the disguise of "an 18th Century scholar and gentleman" and that his style, "imitative of 18th Century English," was a manifestation of that persona. Cardozo had, Frank claimed, "translated himself into a past alien speech environment." One of Cardozo's "selves or persons," Frank surmised, "was that of an educated Englishman engaging in imaginary conversations with Charles Lamb or Dr. Johnson."[96]

Frank's perception that Cardozo's affect and manner served as devices to shield him from his public contacts was shared by others who knew Cardozo well. "Very few," Hand said of Cardozo, "have ever known what went on behind those blue eyes."[97] But Frank chose to caricature his insight. He accompanied quotations from Cardozo's opinions with editorial comments. He claimed that in using "elaborate metaphors"[98] Cardozo "was opposing the national genius of the [American] language," which "tends to the use of plainer materials and towards a simpler cut."[99] He suggested that Cardozo's "ornaments" were "annoyingly functionless," and he maintained that his style was designed to flatter his readers "that they are sharing in English upperclass virtues."[100]

The anonymous Cardozo essay was vintage Frank. His intuitions about others were often perceptive and his characterizations imaginative. But he frequently incorporated those perceptions into the set of ideas that currently interested him, so that his judgments on his contemporaries, especially in print, took on an ideological or even a polemical tone. In the Cardozo essay, for example, he began with a suggestion that Cardozo preferred to use his lawmaking powers covertly rather than openly and that this illustrated a personal use of masks and disguises in his public contacts. But he rapidly converted that suggestion into a crusade for "plainness" in judicial writing and an argument against yearning for the "unattainable . . . absolute in law."[101] The result was an effort that offended many readers of the essay and somewhat embarrassed Frank.[102] Yet Frank, characteristically, never retracted his position. The last year of his life, in an article on Learned Hand, he repeated, nearly verbatim, many of the observations he had made on Cardozo fourteen years earlier.[103]

Despite his tendency to polarize debate, caricature the views of his critics, and conduct intellectual exchange at an awkwardly personal level, Frank was a compassionate and gregarious man who enjoyed making and having friends, was sensitive to criticism, and found it difficult to view his close acquaintances with critical detachment.[104] He could, as in his relations with Charles Clark, carry on a series of correspondence debates in which his remarks were often biting, even acrimonious,[105] and then write (to Clark), "Somehow you seem to have obtained the impression that I'm antagonistic to you. Through some fault of mine, I got off on the wrong foot with you. I'd like to start again."[106] By and large, he maintained cordial relations with those whom he saw regularly on a face-to-face basis; at a greater distance he had more difficulty. His most rabid hatreds were reserved for those, like Coke, whom he never met and never could. As long as he was able to think of people as personifications of values or ideas that he found distasteful, he could criticize them with abandon; as soon as he met them, some of his intellectual anger dissipated.

The provocative tone of Frank's writings was characteristic of the jurisprudential school he helped found. The Realists, especially when they first perceived themselves as having a group identity, had the zeal and dogmatism of any collection of persons who believe they have found truth. The "realities" of lawmaking, particularly by judges, had been revealed to them; they had no patience with those who slavishly maintained the fictions of the past. They saw, as had others in the 1920s, the collapse of traditional moral values in America, but the lesson they drew was that morals and ethics were relative terms, not absolutes. They seized on Holmes's deliberately caricatured picture of law as the predictions of what courts did in fact, and used it to create a technique of "institutional analysis" through which the "real" factors controlling the decisions of governmental office could be studied empirically.[107] Stripping away the "rationalizations" in judicial opinions, they revealed the subjective values that lay beneath. In the process they perceived the manipulation of "paper" rules of law to produce desired results, and discovered the "real" rules of judicial decision-making, whose significance became clear "only after the investigation of the . . . behavior" of judges.[108] Armed with these insights, they set out to reorient American jurisprudential thought.

Frank's particular contribution to Realism was his psychoanalytic theory of the judicial function. The process of judging, he argued, began with tentatively formed conclusions rather than with the discovery of rules or principles of law. In writing an opinion the judge reasoned backward from results: legal principles served as "formal justifications—rationalizations—of [predetermined] conclusions."[109] The crucial factor in judging was the biases of the judge whose sympathies or antipathies influenced the way he heard evidence, the importance he placed on particular facts, and, eventually, his determination of the result. The "law" a judge announced was therefore "really" a manifestation of his own value judgments, concealed by "verbal contrivances" whose function was to give an illusion of harmony and continuity. Being humans, judges came to believe in their own fictions, so that they not only claimed that "announced rules" were "the paramount theory in the law," they also became convinced that the values of uniformity and certainty were of great importance and could be "procured by uniformity and certainty in the phrasing of rules."[110]

A realization of the psychological dimensions of the judging process could, in Frank's judgment, lead to a more realistic and "progressive" approach to adjudication. If judges "c[a]me to grips with the human nature operative in themselves," they could begin to abandon the fantasy of a perfect, consistent, legal uniformity for a sensible skepticism.[111] Frank suggested two devices to aid in this process—the use of experts to aid judges in their fact-finding efforts, and the use of "the best available methods of psychology"[112] as a means of revealing to judges their own biases.

Frank's insight that judicial decision-making was rooted in subjective preferences led him to argue that judges should have freedom and power to function as creative lawmakers. So long as a judge knew that he could not be detached, he did not have to be. So long as he understood that "facts" were manipulable pieces of data rather than symbols of truth, he could choose the facts he wanted to emphasize. And so long as he understood the role of value preferences in judicial decision-making, he could interpret his function as one of enlightening the public as to the importance of certain social values. In Frank's view judges, like other governmental officials, could be seen as members of an elite that drew on its special expertise to educate its constituents. If judges understood that "law" as an abstract entity neither prohibited nor required anything, they could make decisions that, for example, secured special treatment in the courts for economically or socially disadvantaged persons. Thus, skepticism could nurture paternalism, and realist jurisprudence could harmonize with the social goals of the New Deal.[113]

The jurisprudential theories of Frank and Hand, then, started with similar assumptions but ended with divergent views of the judicial function. Hand and Frank both believed that legal doctrines contained elements of myth and fiction and that these elements should be exposed; that subjectivity was an important element in the judicial process; that no aid to judging, or indeed to living, could be found in philosophical, moral, or religious absolutes; and that judging could fairly be described as an attempt to weigh unquantifiable values. But they drew different inferences from these assumptions. For Hand the presence of bias in the judge engendered a search for detachment, which he equated with wisdom. For Frank a judge did not have to be detached if he knew that detachment was ultimately unattainable. Common morality, as a workable entity, was elusive for both men, but Hand nonetheless preferred a dim approximation of it over his own intuitions, while Frank thought that it could be ignored altogether if contrary to the views of "ethical leaders."[114] In general, Hand's sense of the idiosyncratic and intuitive nature of judging engendered a conviction that judicial creativity should be curtailed as much as it was encouraged, whereas the same perception in Frank led him to believe that the primary check on the judge need only be his own self-awareness.

The iconoclastic views expressed by Frank might have seemed incompatible with judicial service. But he had been an early and enthusiastic supporter of Roosevelt and the New Deal, serving as General Counsel to the ill-fated Agricultural Adjustment Administration and later as Counsel to the Reconstruction Finance Corporation and Chairman of the Securities and Exchange Commission. In 1934 he called himself and fellow "experimental" jurisprudes "humble servants to that master experimentalist, Franklin Roosevelt."[115] Roosevelt, for his part, admired Frank and had a highly politicized view of the office of judge. Hence, when a vacancy appeared in the Second Circuit in 1941, Frank was given the appointment, which was a presidential prerogative. One commentator likened the choice of Frank to that of a heretic for a bishopric in the Catholic Church.[116]

IV

The major opportunities for Cardozo, Hand, and Frank to operationalize their respective attitudes toward freedom and restraint in judging came, of course, in the decision of cases. They were fortunate in being able to serve on courts of considerable stature and significance. To the Second Circuit and the New York Court of Appeals came significant pieces of litigation, argued by members of one of the leading bars in the nation, involving sizable sums of money and energy and reflecting the rapid pace of social and economic change in twentieth-century urban America. Like the Supreme Court, and unlike many lower appellate courts, the New York Court of Appeals and the Second Circuit provided its members with a diversity of material and abundant opportunities for visibility and prominence.

During Cardozo's eighteen years on the Court of Appeals the traditional common-law framework in which American state appellate judges made their decisions confronted the momentum of mature industrialization, which transformed economic and social relations in the early twentieth century. Older descriptions of the rights and responsibilities of participants in industrial enterprise appeared increasingly inadequate in their modern setting. The doctrine that employees assumed all the risks of dangerous jobs seemed troublesome when the employees in question had no other employment options. The theory that manufacturers of dangerous products were responsible only for the safety of persons who had contracted to buy the products appeared to make little sense if the products were regularly used by third-party consumers. As industrial enterprise expanded, millions of persons came to be affected by it, even though their connection with the actual processes of product manufacturing and distribution was peripheral or nonexistent. Once injured, either physically or economically, they came to be perceived as victims of industrial progress, a perception that generated lawsuits asking that courts expand the remedial coverage of the common law to include these new potential beneficiaries.

A conventional piece of wisdom about the common law system of adjudication is that a court may not grant an injured party relief unless it can base that result on some existing principle of substantive law. Even in a so-called case of first impression, a court, if it is to create a new remedy, must subsume that remedy under the articulation of a new common law doctrine. Thus, where social change creates grievances that a pre-existing body of legal doctrine has not anticipated, a common law court has to decide whether, reasoning by analogy, the existent body of doctrine can fairly be stretched to cover the new grievance. If it decides that the questions presented by the new grievance are too novel or unique to sustain such a stretch, it has, in the conventional view, only two options. It may announce, as a matter of substantive law, that the aggrieved party is not entitled to relief, or it may refuse to entertain the grievance by asserting that doctrinal change of such magnitude should be made by the legislature. It may not, in this view, allow the aggrieved party relief while conceding that the logic of preexisting doctrine mitigates against that result. To do so would be to replace a durable impersonal body of common law principles with intuitive individual notions of justice in a given case.

Cardozo developed his theories of judicial performance within the confines of this attitude. Believing, by and large, that common law judges were permitted to "make" law only through reasoned interpretations of previously received doctrine, he attempted to show in his opinions that any changes his court made in substantive law stemmed from the adaptability of previous common law principles to new situations. Believing also, however, that common law courts should be responsive to social or economic change, he tried to avoid denying an aggrieved party relief simply because previous generations of courts had not envisaged the complainant's predicament. The strains engendered by these simultaneous beliefs motivated Cardozo to search for a means of making novel results appear to be the logical products of established doctrines, so that changes in the common law seemed to underscore common law continuity.

Cardozo made this search his mission as a jurist and his art as a judge. His national reputation, which stemmed primarily from his common law decisions on the Court of Appeals, was founded on his ability to make his innovations seem the natural, almost inevitable consequence of past decisions. This achievement was grounded on his skill in analyzing common law precedents. Faced with a series of arguably relevant prior decisions, each with its own factual circumstances, he could extract from them a general principle of law linking them to the case before him. Often that principle allowed him to extend the common law's remedial coverage; sometimes it gave him a point where coverage could be cut off. Many times the principle was itself a distinction between some types of cases and others; where it was, the distinction invariably illuminated the position of the case he was considering. On occasion, Cardozo's analysis was not altogether candid. He could deemphasize or ignore contrary evidence and make distinctions without differences. But he was not result-oriented in his decision-making; rather, he recognized competing values and agonized over choices between them. If many of his results promoted progress, as his colleague Irving Lehman observed, his justifications for them were often, Hand noted, "tentative, at times almost apologetic."[117]

Cardozo's most influential common law opinions came in the areas of torts and contracts. The ferment in those areas during his years on the Court of Appeals symbolized the increasingly industrial and commercial character of the New York environment. The traditional negligence calculus of tort law, which conditioned liability on "fault" defined in terms of duties of reasonable care, was reexamined by Cardozo's court in the fact of changing approaches to the problem of industrial accidents. In contracts, an existing series of technical, formal requirements affecting the creation of contractual obligations was reconsidered in the context of the complicated commercial transactions taking place in twentieth-century New York.

In both areas Cardozo's opinions changed the state of the law by reshaping existing doctrines, but the changes did not appear dramatic, nor was the reshaping process easily perceived. In torts, Cardozo initiated, over a period of time, a new approach to one aspect of the negligence calculus. It was clear, as courts came to consider negligence cases in the latter half of the nineteenth century and the early twentieth, that although the violation of a standard of reasonable care was a prerequisite for liability, not every violation resulted in a holding of liability. In particular, the courts appeared reluctant to hold negligent defendants responsible for remote or bizarre consequences of their acts. Considerable difficulty had arisen, however, in converting this common-sense reluctance into doctrines of law. Courts had emphasized the closeness of the relation between the plaintiff and defendant, borrowing contract terms such as "privity," or they had asked whether the defendant's negligence "caused" the plaintiff 's injury. In both instances they encountered linguistic snarls, for some injured persons, though not in a direct contractual relation with a defendant, were known by him to be relying on his careful conduct, and, alternatively, endless chains of causation could be constructed linking remote injuries to negligent acts.

Cardozo shifted discussion in this portion of the law of negligence to inquiries about the anticipation of risks. If the result that generated a negligence suit was one that came within the foreseeable ambit of risks created by the defendant's failure to meet a standard of reasonable care, Cardozo maintained that the defendant should be found liable. The class of persons injured and the type of injury suffered were subsumed in the term "result." One asked whether the defendant could reasonably be expected to anticipate that his careless act would create a risk of this result. Using this approach, Cardozo found that a manufacturer of motor cars had a duty to make a careful inspection of the cars' wheels, and that this duty extended beyond the car dealers "in privity" with the manufacturer to the ultimate purchasers of the cars.[118]

In another case,[119] however, he used the same analysis to prevent recovery against the Long Island Railroad by a woman injured while standing on the platform of a railroad station. In that case a passenger, racing to catch a moving train, was helped onto the train by two guards employed by the railroad. In the process the guards knocked loose a package the passenger was carrying which, unbeknownst to them, contained fireworks. The package fell to the ground and exploded, setting off vibrations which caused a set of scales on the station's platform to fall on the woman, who was sitting near the scales some distance from the train tracks. In determining the railroad's liability to the woman, Cardozo stated that "the risk reasonably to be perceived" defined "the duty to be obeyed." Risk was "a term of relation": here the relation of the woman's injury to the carelessness of the guards was too remote to allow a finding that they should have anticipated that their negligence would inflict that particular injury. Cardozo sought in his analysis to relate a defendant's carelessness not only to the type of injury that had occurred but to the class of persons injured. The term "risk" encompassed both considerations.

Risk analysis did not fundamentally reorient tort law but merely shifted some of its emphasis. It invited courts to ask cost-benefit questions, considering the degree of difficulty in anticipating and preventing certain types of risks and the social desirability of various enterprises, such as railroads. These kinds of questions marked a departure from the previous metaphysical ones. Asking whether a result was within a set of risks may have seemed to be very similar to asking whether a careless act was the "proximate cause" of an injury, but there was a subtle difference. The new set of questions prepared the way for courts to consider which segments of society were best suited to bear the costs of risky enterprises. Such considerations have led to attacks on the negligence calculus itself: the fault standard, it is said, is an inefficient means of shifting or spreading costs.[120] Cardozo, however, intended to retain the fault system, merely wanting to make it more responsive to the conditions of modern industrial life.

In contracts, as in torts, Cardozo made few sudden changes in doctrine, but his opinions suggested a changed judicial perspective. He de-emphasized formalities and literal readings of contracts, finding, on occasion, implied promises where explicit ones were lacking.[121] He disregarded the requirement of consideration for a promise in certain cases in which the promise had been "justifiably" relied upon, while retaining it in general usage.[122] He scrutinized the circumstances under which contracts were made and broken to see if performance was absolute or conditional, sometimes giving greater weight to unforeseen events than to the language of the original agreement.[123] He interpreted the statute of frauds and the parol evidence rule liberally, believing that neither should "be pressed to the extreme of a literal and rigid logic."[124] In general, except perhaps for his treatment of certain consideration cases,[125] he made no innovations in the substantive law of contracts, but rather sought to induce judges to read agreements with more flexibility and common sense. "The law," he argued in one contracts case, "has outgrown its primitive stage of formalism when the precise word was the sovereign talisman, and every slip was fatal."[126]

The most intriguing aspect of Cardozo's judicial service, however, was his approach to writing opinions. Methodology was his chief concern as a jurisprude and his special art as a judge. *MacPherson v. Buick*, one of his earliest and best-known opinions, reveals the strengths and limitations of his method. The *MacPherson* case, noted earlier, presented the question whether the Buick Motor Company was liable to one Donald MacPherson for injuries he suffered when a wheel of his Buick collapsed. Buick claimed that it was not in privity with MacPherson, since he was a consumer rather than an automobile dealer. An old precedent,[127] involving a mail coach in England, had held that a supplier of coaches was not liable to third parties not in privity with it for injuries resulting from defects in the coaches caused by the supplier's negligence. But the precedent appeared shaky. New York cases had created an exception to it for "inherently dangerous" instrumentalities, scholars had attacked it, and automobiles had the potential to travel at much greater speeds and submit their occupants to much greater risks than did carriages. Despite these developments, the New York Court of Appeals had reaffirmed the "privity" rule only eight years before the *MacPherson* case was heard.

Cardozo began his opinion in *MacPherson* with a characteristic technique: statement of the operative "principle" of law that governed the case. But the principle, he found, was not that of no liability absent privity but of liability absent privity in certain circumstances. The principle, then, rested on a distinction. If the instrumentality used by the defendant was "inherently" dangerous, privity was not required; otherwise it was. The distinction was illustrated by *Thomas v. Winchester,*[128] a case imposing liability on a defendant who had carelessly mislabeled a poison bottle. *Thomas v. Winchester*, Cardozo claimed, had laid "the foundations of this branch of the law, at least in this state."[129]

A successive series of cases, Cardozo maintained, had attempted to apply the *Thomas* principle. The first two cases had held that no liability existed absent privity. They illustrated for Cardozo "a narrow construction of the [*Thomas*] rule."[130] The next two demonstrated "a more liberal spirit."[131] They had applied the *Thomas* holding against a manufacturer of an improperly constructed scaffold and against the manufacturer of a defective coffee urn, both of whom were sued in behalf of injured third parties. The court had apparently failed to distinguish between "inherently dangerous" objects and other objects, and Cardozo turned this error to his own advantage. Coffee urns and scaffolds were not inherently dangerous, as were poison bottles. They became destructive only if imperfectly constructed. Hence, the two cases might "have extended" the *Thomas* holding, Cardozo stated, to "imminently" as well as "inherently" dangerous instrumentalities. "If so," he maintained, "this court is committed to this extension."[132]

Thus *Thomas*, not the English carriage case, was transformed into the "foundation of this branch of the law" rather than being denominated a special exception of the privity rule. *Thomas v. Winchester*, Cardozo argued, "became quickly a landmark of the law . . . ; there has never in this state been doubt or disavowal of [its] principle."[133] He cited three additional cases in which the *Thomas* holding had been followed: a builder of a defective building, a manufacturer of an elevator, and a contractor who supplied a defective rope were all held liable for injuries to persons outside privity with them. These cases, Cardozo felt, demonstrated a "trend of judicial thought."[134]

Cardozo thus interpreted precedents so as to prepare the way for a further extension of the *Thomas* exception, but his goal was even more ambitious. He wanted the exception to swallow up the privity rule in *MacPherson*-type cases. To achieve this end he sought to buttress the public policy foundations of a new definition of a manufacturer's duty to persons to whom it had supplied hazardous products. Seizing on the dictum in an English opinion[135] that a duty of ordinary care, irrespective of contract, could be imposed on manufacturers, Cardozo argued that the "tests and standards" created by that dictum were, "at least in their underlying principles," the tests and standards of the common law of New York. If the nature of a product was such that it was reasonably certain "to place life and limb in peril" if carelessly made, Cardozo announced, the product was "a thing of danger." If a manufacturer of this kind of product knew that it would be used "by persons other than the [immediate] purchaser," without further tests, then the manufacturer was under a duty to make it carefully "irrespective of contract."[136]

Hence, "the principle" of *Thomas* was "not limited to poisons . . . and things of like nature."[137] It encompassed all instrumentalities that met the tests of "dangerousness" as formulated by Cardozo. The nature of automobiles "[gave] warning of probable danger if their construction [was] defective." The Buick Motor Company knew the danger, "knew that the car would be used by persons other than the buyer"[138] and was therefore liable for the damages suffered by MacPherson. As for the English carriage case, "[p]recedents drawn from the days of travel of stage coach do not fit the conditions of travel today. The principle [of "dangerousness"] does not change, but the things subject to the principle do change. They are whatever the needs of life in a developing civilization require them to be."[139]

The *MacPherson* opinion reveals the nature of Cardozo's artistry. He announced in the opinion that a definition of the duty of a manufacturer "emerge[d] from a survey of the [New York] decisions." In actuality, the definition arose from the English judge's dictum and Cardozo's unexpressed belief that the New York decisions extending *Thomas* were groping toward the position expressed in the dictum. By the time that Cardozo came to apply his definition of a manufacturer's duty to the situation in *MacPherson*, the reader had the impression that the definition had long existed in New York, even though it had not previously been articulated. But this was not the case. The *Thomas* case itself reaffirmed the privity rule, while creating a special exception; the coffee urn and scaffold cases appear to have been decided on equity grounds related to their special facts; and the Court of Appeals had followed the privity rule in a 1908 case involving an exploding glass bottle.[140] In *MacPherson* Cardozo employed the method of sociology, which underscored the "needs of a developing civilization" for a means of recourse against negligent automobile manufacturers, as a counterweight against the method of logic. He was, as he said in *The Nature of the Judicial Process*, "testing and sorting . . . considerations of analogy and logic and utility and fairness." He was assuming "the function of a law-giver,"[141] but he gave the impression that he was simply acting as a traditional common law judge, reviewing precedents and applying them to the case before him. With Cardozo the line between art and artifice was blurred. His opinions, like his public stances generally, contained levels of candor and deceptiveness. His intuitions were sound, but he rarely revealed their existence.

The period of Cardozo's tenure on the Court of Appeals marked the end, in a sense, of traditional common law adjudication in America. Since 1931, when he was appointed to the Supreme Court, even state appellate judges no longer serve primarily as interpreters of case law established solely by their predecessors. Partial codification of the common law, through federal or state statutes, has taken place in nearly all major substantive areas. In contracts decisions, courts are now aided by the Uniform Commercial Code; for questions involving property relations, state statutes or housing ordinances modify ancient common law rights; for torts questions, workmen's compensation statutes, and, increasingly, no-fault accident insurance programs prevail. The common law of crimes, of course, has been extensively altered by statutes. This codification is by no means complete, but it has significantly affected the function of the appellate judge, who now allocates a sizable portion of time to the interpretation of statutes.

While Cardozo was making a national reputation as a traditional common law judge, Learned Hand, over a similar time span, was enhancing his own reputation by pioneering the modern judicial approach to statutory interpretation. Hand recognized very early in his career[142] that although statutes would make a great impact on twentieth-century lawmaking, their presence would not necessarily restrict judicial creativity and freedom of choice.

His theory of statutory interpretation, as previously noted, rejected the view prevalent in the late nineteenth century that courts could go no farther than the "ordinary" or "plain" meaning of words in a statute, so that, for example, independent contractors were not covered by legislation directed at "employees." But it also rejected readings that substituted for "what the government did not say" things a judge thought "it ought to have said."[143] Hand's approach sought to achieve a middle ground between the perspective of mechanical jurisprudes and that of realists by use of the concept of statutory purpose. A judge began with statutory language, but refrained from interpreting it too liberally or ignoring it altogether. Instead, he examined it as a manifestation of the general purposes of the statute, the broad social policies the legislature "intended" to implement. Where specific statutory coverage of a situation was lacking, Hand deduced coverage or its absence from an application of the general statutory purposes to the particular situation.[144]

This theory assumed, of course, that a court was capable of determining the primary purposes of a statute. That assumption seems to have been easier for Hand to make than for some other judges. Although he was not indifferent to popular enthusiasms and hatreds, he was somewhat detached from them, and was neither a partisan nor an ideologue. Once he saw what a legislature wished to achieve, he was not apt to be captivated or offended by the end it sought. Conversely, he was not inclined to find a purpose where none existed, simply to protect the interests of a favored group. He believed that most legislative purposes, being accommodations of values, bore a presumption of legitimacy. So long as legislative words were capable of interpretation at all, he reasoned, a search for purpose would not be fruitless.

How did the judge proceed, then, when called on to interpret a statute? First, by looking at the language in its specific applications; then, if those seemed inappropriate, in its more general sense. When the meaning of general language in the context of the litigation before the court remained imprecise, the search for statutory purpose began.[145] In this search Hand reasoned by constructing alternative interpretations of language, each producing different results, then asking which result would best conform to the general intent of the legislature, insofar as he could determine it through examination of the statute as a whole.[146] If he could not satisfactorily determine purpose by this method, he turned to further aids, including the legislative history of the statute or administrative interpretations of it. But he did not seek out those aids without first deciding for himself which of the alternative meanings, and consequently which result, was most consistent with his impression of the general purpose. Legislative history and administrative interpretations of a statute only served to test the validity of his tentatively formulated hypotheses.[147]

Hand's theory required judges to maintain the delicate balance between creativity and restraint that he associated with wisdom in the judiciary. It not only assumed that statutory purpose could be found, but that all the intellectual ingenuity exercised in searching for purpose and applying a general intent to unanticipated specific situations could operate in the service of the legislative purpose alone. If the judge's alternative interpretations of the statute were to receive more weight than expressions by legislators or interpretations by agencies, the judge needed to remain neutral toward the political implications of the legislative purpose. Otherwise his own views on the wisdom of legislation might affect his construction of the statute, since he knew that his reading of purpose would be decisive in a doubtful case. He could be creative in interpretation, then, only to the extent that he refrained from an evaluation of the worth of legislation. Hand recognized this dilemma. "On the one hand," he wrote, the judge must not enforce what he thinks best; . . . on the other he must try . . . honestly to say what was the underlying purpose expressed." Nobody does this exactly right, Hand said; "great judges do it better than the rest of us."[148]

In his statutory interpretation decisions, Hand demonstrated that he was not merely one of "the rest of us." He twice brought maintenance workers who were not specifically designated beneficiaries of the Fair Labor Standards Act under its coverage, once where the tenants of the building in which the workers operated were manufacturers and once when they were administrators.[149] He refused to deem a corporate reorganization a "tax-exempt entity" under the Internal Revenue Code when the sole purpose of the reorganization was to reduce taxes.[150] He dismissed a literal reading of the Trading With the Enemy Act of 1917, which would have barred all creditors' claims to alien property after the outbreak of World War II.[151] And, in his next to last year on the bench, he read the federal Copyright Act as protecting textile pattern designers against "deliberate copyists" of their patterns.[152] Statutory interpretation cases did not by any means form the bulk of Hand's judicial labors; he left his impact on numerous other areas, from patent law[153] to free speech.[154] But in one sense they were his most representative, for they illustrate most clearly the theory of judging that influenced all his efforts. One of his colleagues said that he achieved "perhaps his greatest mastery"[155] in matters of statutory interpretation; "mastery" in Hand was appellate judging at its finest.

If Cardozo revealed his approach to judging most clearly in torts and contracts cases, and Hand in exercises in statutory interpretation, Frank's area of special interest and concern was criminal procedure. Here his philosophical inclinations undoubtedly stimulated his strong interest in the subject matter. He believed, in a general way, in the obligation of the state to upgrade the quality of its citizens' lives. He looked favorably on social welfare legislation; he supported direct governmental intervention to correct inequalities and promote the values of fairness and justice; he sympathized with the lot of disadvantaged persons and saw their plight as one of society's responsibilities. In addition, he felt that evidence used as an "objective" foundation for judgments by governmental officials could be manipulated; he was hence continually skeptical about the fairness of allegedly neutral and impartial procedures. His paternalism merged with his "fact-skepticism" to produce a highly charged response to cases involving the procedural rights of criminal defendants. "In all too many [criminal trials]," he maintained, "the prosecutors utilize unjust techniques to obtain convictions of men who may be innocent." To disregard "courthouse injustices to the humble, obscure man," he felt, was "to disregard that which renders a democratic society distinctly antitotalitarian."[156]

One of the questions of greatest interest for followers of Frank, after his 1941 appointment to the Second Circuit, was how his Realist stance toward judicial decision-making would affect his judicial performance. By the early 1940s he had already begun to modify some of the implications of his work in the 1930s, notably its apparently relativistic approach to morals and ethics.[157] He continued this modification in articles throughout the 1940s and 1950s, conceding that precedents and rules, especially in appellate decision-making, had more weight than he had originally ascribed to them.[158] He never, however, abandoned his commitment to the notion that judging was not a formal, detached process but an informal and impassioned one, susceptible of coloration by value judgments.

Nothing in the body of a lawsuit, then, was neutral for Frank. "Facts" were as manipulable as rules or precedents or principles. A judge's sense of justice necessarily affected his attitude toward the use of all legal procedures and processes, no matter how technical or mundane. Law enforcement techniques, rules of evidence, regulations for the incarceration of criminals were inherently susceptible of critical evaluation on ideological grounds. There were, to be sure, some institutional limitations on appellate judges. Frank accepted, for example, the canon of *stare decisis*, although he did not rigidly adhere to it.[159] But these constraints did not prevent the judge from being an uncompromising advocate of the social values he cherished, provided he acknowledged the limits on his powers and openly revealed his attitudes.

Frank therefore regarded the liberalization of rules of criminal procedure, to do justice to "humble, obscure [men]," as a legitimate performance of his function. This interpretation of his office foreshadowed an interpretation subsequently advanced by a majority of the Supreme Court during Earl Warren's tenure as Chief Justice. Under this view the appellate judiciary could closely scrutinize the conduct of law enforcement officials, both in and out of court, to determine whether the accusatory procedures they employed against criminal suspects were, in a broad sense, fair and just. The traditional deference of the judiciary to the discretionary powers of other branches of government, according to this view, vanished when constitutional guarantees of fair procedure were involved. State and federal rules of criminal procedure needed to conform to constitutional fairness and justice.[160]

Frank's approach to criminal procedure cases was not precisely like that subsequently adopted by the Warren Court majority, primarily because the expansive view of Bill of Rights freedoms developed by members of that Court was not in full-blown existence during the years of Frank's service on the Second Circuit.[161] Although Frank was concerned that criminal procedures not infringe upon the constitutional rights of defendants, his specific interest in preserving Bill of Rights freedoms was subordinated to a more general interest in preventing injustices in the process by which criminal suspects were indicted, tried, and convicted.

The central difficulty in that process, Frank felt, was that law enforcement officials possessed an ability to exercise almost complete control over the use of evidence relevant to the crimes under consideration. They could, by virtue of their power to incarcerate persons accused of crimes, deprive those persons of access to others who might help them defend themselves; they could put psychological or even physical pressure on them to reveal important information. Since Frank doubted the objectivity of "facts," this inequality of position greatly troubled him. He worried aloud[162] about criminal convictions of innocent persons; the fact that crimes had to be proven beyond a reasonable doubt did not altogether dispel this fear. As an appellate judge, operating on only a printed record, Frank felt incapable of truly understanding what had happened in a criminal prosecution. In order to "sleep well"[163] he wanted some means of satisfying himself that the process, at all stages, had been fair to the defendant.

A chronological history of Frank's criminal procedure opinions, many of which were dissents, reveals his interest in scrutinizing every instance where a law enforcement official could use his powers to manipulate evidence. One major example was the use of pressure on defendants to compel them to reveal information despite their Fifth Amendment privilege against self-incrimination.

In a 1942 case[164] Frank protested the use of the contempt power against persons who had testified as to the elements of a crime but refused to admit the details. Sentencing them to jail for this refusal, he maintained, made a mockery of the privilege by forcing the defendant to either admit incriminating evidence or go to prison, an unfair dilemma. Another example of injustice, in Frank's view, was the absence of legal representation at trial for criminal defendants. Without the advice of counsel, defendants could be tricked or bullied into incriminating themselves, or the jury could be permitted to draw dubious inferences from the evidence. Anticipating the Warren Court by twenty years, Frank declared in a 1943 case that the Sixth Amendment required trial counsel for all criminal defendants unless the right had been fairly waived.[165]

Throughout the 1940s Frank continued his search for justice in criminal proceedings. In two cases in 1945 he began a series of assaults on the use of hearsay evidence in conspiracy trials and continued an earlier attack on the so-called "harmless error" rule as employed by the Second Circuit. The out-of-courtroom testimony of one conspirator had been deemed admissible as evidence in the subsequent trial of another; Frank maintained that this violated the general prohibition against hearsay evidence. The crime of conspiracy itself, he felt, was excessively vague and "fraught with danger to the innocent." The admissibility of hearsay evidence compounded the dangers.[166]

Frank's harmless-error position in the cases was a crystallization of an insight he had first articulated in 1943: the Second Circuit was simply calling a technical deficiency in the trial proceedings "harmless" when a majority of judges felt that, on balance, the defendant was guilty.[167] The proper means of treating such deficiencies, Frank argued, was "to reverse where error [had] been committed, regardless of [the judges'] belief in guilt or innocence, unless [the judges] conclude[d] that in all probability the error had no effect on the jury."[168] Using this test for harmless error, Frank voted to reverse convictions in one case in which a defendant's Italian nationality had been commented upon in a trial that took place while the United States was at war with Italy,[169] and in another in which a prosecutor had released information to newspapers during the course of a trial.[170] The aim of Frank's test for harmless error was to reflect the more stringent standards of proof in criminal trials by foreclosing an appellate court from deciding that an error was "harmless" merely by determining that it was more probable than not that the criminal defendant was guilty. Preponderance of the evidence was a civil standard of proof; Frank felt it should not be introduced, *sub rosa*, into criminal cases.

Frank also expressed in the 1940s a concern about the extensive discretionary power given prosecutors in introducing evidence before a grand jury. A case came before the Second Circuit in which the prosecution, seeking an indictment, had presented to the grand jury a confession obtained through physical abuse. The prosecution argued that the confession, concededly inadmissible at trial, could nonetheless be used to secure an indictment. Frank called this "an astonishingly callous argument." A wrongful indictment, he felt, "often works a grievous, irreparable injury to the person indicted . . . ; [f]requently the public remembers the accusation and still suspects guilt, even after an acquittal."[171] He maintained that prosecutors should be barred from using any illegally obtained evidence in indictment proceedings.

The indictment case also illustrated Frank's interest in protecting criminal defendants from coercion or harassment by law enforcement officials. He expressed this concern in several contexts in the 1950s. Long delays before arraignment of a prisoner rendered a confession obtained during the delay inadmissible.[172] Even the slightest use of entrapment techniques by police officers was illegal.[173] The privilege of self-incrimination extended to witnesses at grand jury proceedings.[174] A witness could refuse to answer non-incriminating questions if they were interspersed with incriminatory ones.[175] The use of concealed eavesdropping devices by narcotics agents violated the Fourth Amendment's prohibition against unreasonable searches and seizures.[176] "The test of the moral quality of a civilization," Frank wrote in 1955, "is its treatment of the weak and powerless."[177]

In only one area was Frank less than passionately concerned for the rights of criminal defendants: cases involving violations of national security. Here Frank's sympathy for the disadvantaged clashed with the strident patriotism he came to advocate in the 1940s and 1950s. Frank's zealous championing of the values and institutions of American civilization was motivated partially, no doubt, by articles in the late 1930s linking realist jurisprudence with totalitarianism.[178] In attempting to refute his critics, Frank may also have set out to convince himself of his patriotism. If so, he succeeded, at least to the point of tolerating some infringement of Fifth Amendment rights in cases involving national security interests.[179]

Frank's most celebrated national security case was *United States v. Rosenberg*,[180] in which Julius and Ethel Rosenberg were convicted of violating the Espionage Act of 1917 and sentenced to death. Frank, writing for the Second Circuit, affirmed the conviction, despite his dislike of capital punishment and despite the fact that the government had, at trial, introduced evidence of the Rosenbergs' membership in the American Communist Party. One might reasonably infer, Frank wrote, that "an American's devotions to another country's welfare" might make him "more likely to spy for it than other Americans. . . . [T]he Communist label yields marked ill-will for its American wearer."[181] Thus, patriotism and the atmosphere of the 1950s helped reverse Frank's general presumption that criminal defendants tended to be treated unfairly. But the Rosenberg case remained in his consciousness. The year of his death he published a book depicting the lives of innocent persons who had been wrongly convicted of crimes.[182]

V

The experiences of Cardozo, Hand, and Frank, when added to those of the major figures on the Supreme Court from Holmes through Jackson, demonstrated the dramatic reorientation of American appellate judging in response to the intellectual and cultural ferment of the early twentieth century. Cardozo and Hand, in different ways, tried to retain and revive the longstanding canon that judges were never truly free to decide in accordance with their personal views. They converted metaphysical constraints—those derived from an eighteenth-century conception of law—to methodological constraints derived from an early-twentieth-century approach to governance. Frank's angle of vision was different still. For him freedom in judges was a profound "reality," and constraints were primarily personal rather than institutional. For him oracular judging had not died; it had only existed as a collective fantasy.

The jurisprudential ferment attendant upon the abandonment of oracular judging did not radically upset the delicate balances that had previously characterized appellate judging in America; it merely changed their intellectual context. Whether law was thought of as a brooding omnipresence, a social science, the fiats of officials, or an "on-going, functioning, purposive process,"[183] American appellate judges still functioned as autocratic officials in a democratic society; still labored to maintain an image of impartiality and detachment while operating in a highly politicized atmosphere; still looked outside themselves for justifications for their decisions, even though their decisions may have been personally motivated. Although the cultural milieu in which judging took place underwent profound changes in the twentieth century, the core elements of the tradition nonetheless endured.

11 

Rationality and Intuition in the Process of Judging: Roger Traynor

Cardozo, Hand, and Frank had spanned in their careers successive crises of legitimacy for the twentieth-century appellate judiciary. To recapitulate: the first crisis was that of "mechanical" jurisprudence, in which the oracular theory of judging was discredited by its identification with outmoded social and political attitudes. Cardozo attempted to respond to this crisis by developing a theory of judging that retained a nineteenth-century conceptual framework but made that framework responsive to social change. He employed the characteristic constructs of oracular judging—fixed principles, time-honored precedents, received doctrines—but sought to show their ability to expand or contract under the pressures of time and circumstance.

Cardozo's response, which paralleled that of Hand in his early career, was inadequate for those who were prepared to question the sanctity of any sort of conceptualist judging. If rules, principles, and doctrines were fictions, and precedents merely examples of judicial lawmaking, all vestiges of oracular judging should be eliminated and the appellate judge should start afresh, with empirical observation and a candid awareness of his own predilections serving as his only relevant source materials. But the destructive effects of Realism on surviving remnants of oracular judging precipitated a second legitimacy crisis, illustrated by the Court-packing controversy. If the "rules" of law were discredited, what was left except the arbitrary judgment of officials? How was law thus a cementing force in society, a repository of moral values or national beliefs? How, at another level, were certainty and predictability to be fostered by appellate judging? Frank grappled, not always successfully, with such questions.

In response to the second crisis a process theory of judging emerged, in which analytical reasoning and institutional self-consciousness combined to limit judicial choices to those that could be competently made and rationally justified. But despite the process theory's responsiveness to the social and intellectual climate of America in the late 1940s and the 1950s, it did not forestall the appearance of yet another potential legitimacy crisis. A central message of the process theory was that judges should confine their involvement with social issues to those areas susceptible to reasoned analysis by a court. Some social problems did not admit of rational judicial solution. They were "political" or "legislative" in their nature; no "neutral principles" existed by which they could be judicially resolved.[1] The constraints on judicial activity fashioned by the process theory suggested that explosive social issues might remain unresolved, if they were not capable of "judicial" consideration, when another branch of government did not attempt to resolve them. But when such issues were perceived as involving individual rights, the process theory appeared to clash with one of the American judiciary's historic functions: that of protector of rights and liberties. Thus, in the 1950s and 1960s pressure mounted for a judicial vindication of individual rights in cases where other governmental institutions had been indifferent to them, despite the absence of impeccably rational justifications for the vindication. An intuitive sense of fairness and justice, where individual rights were concerned, became a counterweight to rationality.[2]

Each of the twentieth-century judges thus far considered was forced to confront one or another of the above crises. Learned Hand, in the course of his fifty years as a judge, was involved with each. At various stages of his judicial life Hand was a critic of oracular judging, a skeptical observer of Realism, and a sounding board against which adherents of the process theory tested their ideas. At the very end of his career, Hand, who had always conceded the role of intuition in judging, sharply dissociated himself from efforts to make constitutional interpretation an intuitive exercise.[3] Hand's ubiquity and longevity were not typical, however; other judges, in addition to Cardozo and Frank, may be identified with one of the crisis periods. The Four Horsemen confronted the first, only suggesting the possibility of the second. Jackson functioned primarily in the context of the second. As for Hughes and Stone, the timing of their service required that they face both the first and second crises, thus adding to their already considerable burdens.

Roger Traynor, who served on the California Supreme Court from 1940 to 1970, developed his approach to judging in response to the third crisis of legitimacy. A firm advocate of the process theory, Traynor nonetheless saw its limitations as a vehicle for promoting the values of fairness and justice. Convinced that rationality was the essence of judging, Traynor nonetheless did not suppress his intuitions, believing that he could articulate reasoned justifications for them.

If New York, with its long preindustrial history, its successive waves of immigration, its tradition of commercial dominance, and its rapidly changing patterns of enterprise and communication, had invited reflection by its leading appellate judges on continuity and change in the law, California was also a source of stimulation. California, too, suggested the problem of harmonizing past with present, but more acutely, for the state had come to maturity almost overnight. The provincial state Supreme Court on which Field had served was but one step, at least in his person, from impressionistic frontier justice; Traynor's Court confronted the complex litigations of a modern industrial and commercial society. Only about seventy-five years separated the two institutions. The earlier Court bequeathed a legacy of case law to the later, dramatizing the pressure placed on *stare decisis* by rapid social change.

California's most rapid growth took place during the years after the philosophy of modern liberalism had become acceptable. Not only were economic and social discrepancies perceived as problems, affirmative governmental action to relieve them was expected. Social planners came increasingly to favor legislative solutions to the problems they perceived; statutes proliferated in California. A relatively sparse body of common law, inadequate to meet an apparent need for increased governmental planning, had created a climate favorable to legislative activity; and as legislation fostered problems in statutory interpretation, the California judiciary was forced to expand the range of its activity.

The California appellate judiciary in the years of Traynor's tenure accordingly faced the recurrent task of defining its role as a contributing institution to the "welfare state"[4] system of government. In this task, apparently, it was handicapped by the ominous contrast between its previously limited range of activity and the massive array of legal problems engendered by modern California life. The corpus of legal doctrine created by the California Supreme Court prior to 1940 had been of average size and scope for a moderately populated, predominantly rural state in an age of quiescent government; suddenly California became one of the nation's most populous and most urbanized states, with attendant growth pains. Under the prodding of the Warren Administrations from 1940 to 1952, the California legislature had responded to demographic changes with a variety of pieces of social service legislation. State agencies were created, statutes proliferated, affirmative government became a feature of modern California life.

The interaction of massive growth and affirmative governmental action altered fundamentally the character of California jurisprudence. A need was created for a body of judge-made law that could coexist with the proliferating social problems and legislative responses of the 1940s, 1950s, and 1960s. Judicial decisions, in this context, needed to be modernized, so that they could be responsive to the social conditions of contemporary California life; to be generalized, so that they could function as guidelines for conduct in an increasingly complicated world; to be synthesized, so that they could function as uniform rules rather than *ad hoc* judgments; to be deprovincialized, so that they no longer reflected the parochial anomalies of California's frontier past.

Roger Traynor's judicial career can be seen as an effort to meet the foregoing needs and thereby transform the position of the appellate judiciary in California government. In the course of this effort Traynor established a model for judicial performance that extended beyond the boundaries of his state. His model assumed that judges were lawmakers and found activist, innovative judging compatible with that assumption. It replaced traditional distinctions between branches of government with a theory of governance in which activity by one branch could stimulate activity by another. It enlarged the scope of appellate judges' prerogatives and expanded the audiences at which their opinions were directed. It emphasized the dependence of judging on rationality and disinterestedness, but stressed that making choices between conflicting social values or policies was a basic aspect of judicial decision-making.

If California was a testing ground for governmental theories of modern liberalism, Traynor was an architect of a judicial role compatible with the activities of the modern liberal state.

I

Although Traynor's most significant response to the demands of time and place came in his technique of judging, he also proved responsive in personal ways. In believing that courts had "a creative job to do" upon finding "that a rule has lost its touch with reality and should be abandoned or reformulated to meet new conditions and new moral values,"[5] Traynor was asking the judiciary to act as public spokesmen, not unlike elected officials. This posed the familiar Realist dilemma: how was bias to go unchecked in the absence of political restraints; what was to keep judicial formulations of a society's value choices from being mere statements of a judge's own inclinations? Traynor's solution was embodied in the terms disinterestedness and rationality. Judges were "uniquely situated," he felt, "to articulate timely rules of reason." They enjoyed a "freedom from political and personal pressures and from adversary bias," a "long history of high public service." Their "environment for work" was "independent and analytically objective"; their task was "keeping the underlying body of the unwritten general law . . . 'rationally consistent within itself [and] rationally related to the purposes which the social order exists to serve.' "[6] They knew that "one entrusted with decision . . . must also rise above the vanity of stubborn preconceptions . . . , that he must severely discount his own predilections," that he must "realize how essential it is . . . that he be interested in a rational outcome."[7]

To this conception of judges as aloof, independent, rational beings one might respond, as did unreconstructed Realists[8] in the years of Traynor's service, that judges could not remain immune from political pressures, that preconceptions and predilections hardened with the process of opinion-writing, that analytic objectivity was elusive, or that many "rational" outcomes were possible. Yet Traynor himself made a strong case for the proposition that disinterestedness and rationality were attainable ideals. He achieved this, primarily, by burying himself beneath a layer of official discourse, so that he could write controversial opinions in a tone of relentless impersonality or describe his objectives as a judge in a series of elusive metaphors.

An example will illustrate. In *Escola v. Coca Cola Bottling Co.*,[9] a case arising from injuries sustained by a waitress when a defective soda bottle broke as she carried it from its case to a refrigerator, Traynor suggested an innovative treatment for defective-products cases in the California common law of torts. His treatment rested on an imaginative interweaving of twentieth-century developments in torts and contracts; it relied on policy judgments rather than legal doctrines; it was original with Traynor. Yet it was presented, like Cardozo's decision in *MacPherson v. Buick*, as though it were the inevitable result of a thorough canvass of the law of defective products; an impersonal, rational solution that any "analytically objective" judge could have reached. One had the sense, on reading the opinion, that a straightforward inquiry into the economics of the soft-drink industry had revealed an obviously efficient and equitable means of allocating the costs of injuries from defective products. If absolute liability for defects were placed on the soft-drink manufacturer, the manufacturer could then insure against injuries and distribute the cost of his insurance among his consumers. Yet that allocation scheme represented a major change in the law of defective products and, once adopted, necessitated a recalculation by California manufacturers of their cost of doing business.

The primary doctrinal change made by Traynor in *Escola* was to fuse an expanded concept of negligence in the products liability area with developments in the law of sales. Cardozo and other judges in the early twentieth century had succeeded in imposing on manufacturers a duty of care for defects in their products, a duty extending beyond immediate purchasers. Ordinary users, like the waitress in *Escola*, could sue manufacturers for negligence even though they had received the product from someone else in the chain of distribution. Meanwhile, the concept of an implied warranty of fitness and merchantability had emerged in contract law. Sellers were considered to have warranted to buyers that their products would not be defective in ordinary use, and sellers could be sued for damages should the products prove unsafe. No showing of negligence on the part of the seller was necessary for the buyer to recover; in turn the seller, if a retailer, could recover against the manufacturer on a warranty theory without proving negligence.[10]

Traynor combined these two developments in *Escola* to create the doctrine of an absolute liability in tort on the part of manufacturers for injuries caused by their defective products. The doctrine represented, he maintained, a substitution of public policy imperatives for common-law fictions and gimmicks. It was "needlessly circuitous" to use exceptions to the standard negligence calculus, such as the device of *res ipsa loquitur*, which under certain conditions relieved plaintiffs of the burden of affirmatively proving negligence, to "impose what is in reality liability without negligence."[11] It was equally unnecessary to maintain the double litigation required by the warranty model. Injured consumers should be able to base their actions "directly on the manufacturer's warranty."[12] The warranty of the manufacturer to the consumer rested "on public policy," although "the courts [had] resorted to various fictions" to rationalize extending it that far.[13] Such fictions were no longer necessary once "the warranty is severed from the contract of sale between the dealer and the consumer and based on the law of torts as a strict liability."[14] Once that was done the justification for abandoning sales law and negligence theory in the defective products became clear. If defective products found their way into the market, "it is to the public interest to place the responsibility for whatever injury they may cause upon the manufacturer," since he was "best situated to afford . . . protection" against the risks of injuries.[15]

The triumph of *Escola* was the apparently irresistible simplicity of its logic. Traynor was able to convey a sense that the result was inevitable once one thought through the purposes of allocating risk-bearing among the participants in a chain of distributing merchandise from manufacturer to consumer. The party best suited to bear the risks of defective products on the market was the manufacturer, since he alone could make an empirical determination, through testing, of how risky the product was likely to be at each point in the distribution chain, and then weigh the related cost of his insurance against the financial benefits to be derived from making the product available to the general public. Strict liability made that calculus an open one, since fault was no longer an issue. The manufacturer bore the cost whether he could have prevented the risk from being created or not. With one stroke the doctrines used by sales and negligence law to extend a manufacturer's liability to remote consumers were recast: one suddenly saw that their purpose all along had been risk allocation. Traynor appeared as the objective analyst. Once the area of products liability was approached from this perspective, nearly anyone could see the rational solution. But Traynor had himself created the perspective. He had synthesized the parallel developments in sales law and negligence law; he had articulated the policy justifications for imposing absolute liability on the manufacturer; he had contrasted his social accountant's logic against the fictions of past courts; and he had reached a result that seemed intuitively just.

The *Escola* approach to products liability, which was eventually adopted by all of Traynor's colleagues,[16] was not simply an exercise in substituting one sort of reasoning for others. It asked manufacturers of potentially defective products—and as the case law developed, this included nearly any product—to reorder their thinking about liability for consumer injuries. A negligence standard invited them to plan to avoid liability by showing, in the courts, that they had not acted carelessly. This meant expert witnesses, constant litigation, release forms, investigations of the activities of victims who brought claims against them. The strict liability standard invited them to consider changing their thinking. Absent a showing that a "defective" product had been used in an unreasonable way, they were forced to bear the costs of the injuries that this product caused. Avoiding liability was thus perhaps less efficient than spreading or shifting its costs through insurance and higher wholesale or retail prices. This proposed recalculation was an extensive one, giving new meanings to what Traynor had called the "cost of doing business." Traynor had been aware of *Escola's* implications in this regard. "The manufacturer's obligation to the consumer," he commented, "must keep pace with the changing relationship between them."[17] His opinion had not merely underscored the changes in that relation, as it implied, but had stimulated them as well. He had functioned as an economist and a policymaker, although his tone suggested that he was merely an impersonal judge.

The jurisprudential point of *Escola* was to suggest that careful analysis would yield a result that could be identified not with the presuppositions of the judge who reached it but with the more dispassionate and durable values of rationality and common sense. The judge, in this view, was simply a mouthpiece for the rational policy choices of his time. Although he no longer "found" the law, he made law by "finding" public policy. Traynor recognized, however, that the process of judging was more complicated; that preconceptions interspersed themselves with logic in a way that could make one judge's "rational" solution quite different from another's. In his efforts to articulate the way he performed his function, he implicitly communicated the intuitive dimensions of judging, primarily through the use of metaphors in his descriptions of the judicial process.

In a 1961 address at the University of Chicago Law School Traynor came closest, perhaps, to an articulation of the limits of "objective analysis" in judging. Finding "acceptable rational alternatives" for the disposition of a case did not enable a judge to avoid the choice between them, Traynor said; and there was an obligation to avoid making that choice an arbitrary one. A decision would "not be saved from being arbitrary merely because [the judge was] disinterested"; he could not "remain disoriented forever, his mind suspended between alternative possible solutions." A "value judgment as to what the law ought to be" was required; an "interest in a rational outcome" at some point became channelled into "an interest in a particular result." But the result needed to be justified, and there the value of rationality became apparent. In searching to articulate his reasons, the judge drew on the aggregation of scholarship and common sense about him. Result-orientation was "no more than the final step toward reasoned judgment."[18] The judgment was the judge's, but the reasoning somehow more than his, the embodiment of the consensual attitudes of his environment.

The last step of this process was the one Traynor found hardest to describe. Indeed, he refrained from describing it with any precision. The step did not solve the problem of reconciling an obligation on the part of judges to reason their way to decisions with the necessity of making value choices, because the impression that a judgment was "reasoned" rather than "arbitrary" could be created by the judge. A result, in a close case, was not an inevitable logical necessity. Reaching it was often, as Traynor said, an exercise in "professional skill . . . and legal imagination."[19]

At this stage, then, an allegedly rational process came to be conveyed in metaphors. A judge took care "that when the chips are down, they have fallen into the right places."[20] He "looked beyond . . . disintegrating trees along judicial trails" to "the oaks from little peppercorns growing" and "placed a contemporary case within the sheltering ambit of contemporary live oaks."[21] He undertook "reclamation" of the "badlands" in a "realm of reason."[22] He attempted "careful pruning," on which the "vigorous growth"[23] of the law depended. He tried to "synchronize" into the common law "the unguided missles launched by legislatures"[24] without "shield[ing] wooden precedents from any radiations of forward-looking statutes."[25] He "work[ed] away" at "fine interweaving."[26] He performed "the close work of imposing design on fragments of litigation, dealing . . . with the bits and pieces that blow into [his] shop on a random wind."[27] In such statements Traynor communicated a sense that judging was ultimately an art, resisting precise characterization. The statements also served to distract his audience from himself to the craft of his profession. In thinking about the metaphors, one had no clearer picture of their creator. He seemed to personify the characteristics he sought in judging: detachment, intellectualism, impersonality, rationality.

II

But Traynor's judging nonetheless revealed his personal sympathies and inclinations, which were highly intellectualized. In particular, Traynor created for himself a sophisticated theory of decision-making that attempted to fuse the institutional value of rationality with his own intuitive preferences. His theory contained a reinterpretation of older characterizations of the technique of judging, the development of an alternative technique more harmonious with a model of affirmative government, and a re-evaluation of the place of the judiciary in the modern process of lawmaking in the light of that technique's implications.

Traynor began thinking about the methodology of judicial decision-making by noting the legacy of attitudes he had received on becoming a judge in 1940. Looking back over time, he noted a persistence of "formulism"—a "vision of the common law as a completed formal landscape graced with springs of wisdom that judges needed only to discover."[28] Formulism, though it had "been discredited by its cumulative inadequacies and distortions," continued "to haunt our own time."[29] Its presence was felt in two related cults of judicial behavior: reluctance to abandon precedent, and insistence on a sharp separation between the "lawmaking" functions of the legislature and the "maintenance" functions of courts. The two cults were united in the conventional belief that "whatever incidental law courts create they are bound to maintain unless the legislature undertakes to unmake it."[30] Hence, courts perpetuated "ill-conceived, or moribund, or obsolete precedents" on the ground that their action enhanced the stability or predictability of the law[31] and represented proper deference to their superiors.

Traynor's reading of history revealed, however, that those canons had not always been followed in practice. The "greatest judges of the common law" had "steadily made advances," taking "an occasional dramatic leap forward . . . in the very interest of orderly progression." Holmes and Brandeis had "cleared the way for a liquidation of ancient interpretations of freedom of contract that had served to perpetuate child labor." Cardozo had "moved the rusting wheels of *Winterbottom v. Wright* to one side to make way for *MacPherson v. Buick Motor Co.*"[32] In the realm of statutory interpretation, creativity was also discernible. Early in the history of common law, judges had coined the phrase "equity of the statute,"[33] which became a device by which they could avoid unjust results produced by a literal reading of statutory language. Moreover, judges found statutory rules "a source for analogous [common law] decisions."[34] In short, alongside the "recurring grotesqueries in the evolution of law"[35] produced by blind adherence to precedent and false distinctions between the work of courts and legislatures was a counter-tradition of significant judicial participation in lawmaking on a variety of fronts.

Buoyed by this tradition of judicial innovation, Traynor set out to identify it with order and rationality. He noted the gaps between outmoded legal rules and their application, both by courts and by juries. Courts resorted to fictions, such as lost grants, to further property settlements.[36] Juries in negligence cases imposed liability without fault through saving doctrines such as last clear chance or *res ipsa loquitur.*[37] The purpose of these efforts was to "achieve a rough justice by circumventing rules long out of tune with community values."[38] Such tendencies, though necessary, undermined respect for the process of adjudication. The solution was to reform the rules themselves. If a strict liability standard for torts was more suitable to "our ultra-hazardous age," the courts should make the change openly, and "thereby impose uniform operation of the law."[39] In lieu of "magic words"[40] that had lost their meaning, "tried and half-true formulas," or "antiquated compositions,"[41] judges should "create some fragments of legal order out of disordered masses of new data."[42] In a judicial universe where the sharpness of syllogisms was liable to rust with time, adherence to rules that had lost their practical effectiveness was foolish. In 1926, while a law student, Traynor had condemned the perpetuation of an ancient rule of property despite its being "universally condemned as entirely without reason or common sense to support it."[43] Thirty-five years later he noted that the rule "still eke[d] out a precarious existence," and likened those courts that followed it to "that pack rat who hoards what is familiar to him, regardless of its value, and spends his energies to protect it at all costs."[44]

Traynor was motivated by these occurrences to search for judge-made rules that could be based on rational grounds and applied in a uniform fashion. His search proceeded in stages: a compilation of current sources from which a rule could be derived; an attempt to articulate the rule as a principle of general applicability; finally, an assessment of the consequences of the first two stages for the place of the judiciary in the larger process of lawmaking. By the last stage Traynor was prepared to concede that although "the mechanical logic grounded in old forms of action" had ceased to be a "quality control" for judging, no "model of rational methods" had supplanted it, "a tradition of reasoning on a noble plane"[45] had not yet been achieved.

Since he believed that judicial rules could not be rationally based if they did not conform to contemporary intellectual premises and social values, Traynor sought out "environmental data"[46] to supplement the traditional source materials of his profession. Such data, which were distinguishable from "the selected litigated facts presented to the court" by necessarily partisan counsel, could be gathered "through independent research" in the customs and practices of business, in scholarly treatises and law review articles, in the recent decisions of other courts. In their marshaling of data, appellate judges ought not to be confined to the evidence supplied them by litigators. Their "very independence" developed in them an ability to "detect latent quackery in science or medicine, to edit the swarm spore of social scientists, to add grains of salt to the fortune-telling statistics of the economists." They could inform themselves on matters beyond the facts of a particular case, and, when reliable data were lacking, "construct . . . environmental assumptions."[47]

In practice Traynor relied heavily on academic theorists to supply him with supplementary insights. Academicians had "the freedom . . . to differentiate the good growth from the rubbish," to "mark for [judicial] rejection the diseased anachronism."[48] In contracts Traynor drew on Arthur Corbin[49] and Samuel Williston;[50] in torts, William Prosser;[51] in conflicts of law, Brainerd Currie;[52] for an overview of administrative law, Walter Gellhorn, Kenneth Culp Davis, and Louis Jaffe.[53] In most instances he used scholarship as authority for the proposition that an older, judge-made rule needed revision as being analytically unsound or unresponsive to current conditions.

A final source of data consisted of actions by the California legislature. Here Traynor devised an ingenious theory of the use of statutes in common-law cases. The traditional separation of legislative lawmaking from judicial interpretation, he believed, was simplistic. In actuality, courts and legislatures had a symbiotic relationship, each drawing on the actions of the other. Legislatures passed statutes whose applicability to specific situations was uncertain; courts undertook the applications; legislatures revised the courts if they found a specific application offensive. Alternatively, statutes supplied, by analogy, common-law rules: when a case was "not governed by a statute," a court was "free to copy an appropriate model in a statute."[54] For example, when the California Probate Code provided detailed rules for administration of testamentary gifts by executors, but failed to include in its coverage administration by guardians, Traynor created a common law rule for guardians by analogy to the executor provisions of the statute.[55] Once created, the judicial rule took on "a life of its own"; it could "serve as a model . . . for successive judge-made rules."[56]

Traynor's partnership theory of legislative-court interaction led him to reject some traditional maxims of statutory interpretation. Like Hand, he deplored the "dictionary" approach to statutory language: "The words of a statute . . . are no longer at rest in their alphabetical bins . . . ; they challenge men to give them more than passive reading, to consider well their context."[57] As with Hand, Traynor made his basic inquiry in statutory interpretation "What purpose did the legislature express . . . ?"[58] Courts, in his view, ought to prevent "erratic omissions or errant words"[59] from defeating legislative purpose. Legislative silence, in this vein, did not always mean approval. The maxim that the failure of a legislature to repudiate an erroneous judicial interpretation of a statute meant that the legislature had incorporated that interpretation into the statute was for Traynor a "fiction." Legislative silence was "much more likely to mean ignorance or indifference" than "applause."[60] Courts should not be barred from re-examining their own statutory interpretations merely because they had been ignored by a legislature.

Judicial reliance on unconventional source materials exposed another myth about appellate judging: that "policy" was "a matter for the legislators to decide."[61] Traynor's approach was predicated on the notion that since there was always an area not covered by legislation in which judges needed to revise old rules or formulate new ones, policy considerations were "appropriate and even . . . basic" to their decision-making. His use of extralegal materials assumed that judicial "responsibility" connoted "far more than a mechanical application of given rules to new sets of facts"; it included also "the recurring choice of one policy over another in . . . the formulation of new rules."[62] Judicial decisions were responses to current social problems; lawmakers should reflect contemporary value choices rather than isolate themselves from them. That was the whole point of searching for clues outside the law books.

Despite his skepticism about maxims, formulas, and other "magic words," Traynor did not deny that courts had an obligation to articulate their decisions in general terms. The fact that judge-made rules became obsolete was a reason to avoid their indiscriminate perpetuation, he maintained—but not a reason to avoid formulating them at all. Appellate courts needed to "frame their opinions with enough perspective to guide others in comparable fact situations."[63] They had an obligation to articulate "guiding principles."[64] Their decisions had to "allay the suspicion of any man in the street who regards knowledge of the law as no excuse for making it." They also ought to "afford conscientious lawyers an ample basis of predictability for purposes of counseling and determining when to litigate."[65]

But if rules should be grounded in the environmental conditions and assumptions of a society at a specific point in its history, and consequently might change with time, how could a judge insure that they would serve as guideposts for social planning in more than the most ephemeral sense? Here Traynor entered the "neutral principles" controversy of the 1960s, which had been stimulated by Herbert Wechsler's insistence that courts rest their decisions "on reasons . . . that in their generality and neutrality transcend any immediate result that is involved."[66] No one could quarrel, Traynor felt, with an obligation in appellate courts to generalize their results, or to base their decisions on reason. But the phrase "neutral principles" sounded "pure and simple" to "a judge who confronts problems ridden with impurities and complications." It smacked of "magic words." Such principles were "hardly to be found in briefs" and not always in academic treatises.[67]

For Traynor, however, the primary difficulty with the neutral-principles theory was not in the elusiveness of its central phrase, but in its assumption that generalized legal rules could be durable. Its advocates apparently believed that judges could "somehow walk out of themselves and record a distilled impersonal judgment yet stay close enough to common people to gain their acceptance."[68] These assumptions were sticking points for Traynor, for they ignored the inability of courts to predict the likelihood that rules they formulated would survive the moment of their articulation. In Traynor's jurisprudence judge-made rules responded to the contemporary environment; no one could tell how that environment might change. Even though it might seem reasonably clear to a court that a legal concept seemed destined to expand, judges had "no way of divining a concept's optimum tolerance for expansion at a given moment in a given situation."[69] Rules, in this sense, could never be "principles" if that term connoted permanency, any more than policy choices could ever be "neutral."

Traynor's theory of judging, in short, blended a belief that empirical observation, personal disinterestedness, and intellectual integrity could insure that appellate decisions were grounded in rationality, with a sense that those decisions, if properly made, were ultimately subservient to the dictates of history. He differed from Holmes in that he did not read the inevitability of social change as compelling fatalism in the judiciary. A competent judge's reasoning, he felt, could be more than merely an articulation of the "felt necessities" of his time; it could be a guideline for continued change. Active judicial participation in change, through an innovative reformulation of rules and doctrines, could insure that the process of lawmaking remained orderly while it evolved. Policy choices were in one sense dictated by the environment, but in another sense made by judges. The manner in which they were made could make a difference. "Well-tempered" judges could "stabilize the explosive forces of the day," do "everything within their power of reasoning to make each day in court lead constructively to the next one and to set an example approaching what a civilized day could be."[70]

Certain implications for a court's role in the process of lawmaking followed from the above. Whenever possible, Traynor preferred to retain decision-making power in courts rather than in juries, since he believed that judges had greater capacity for formulating orderly and intelligible rules. He dismissed as unrealistic the "arbitrary line" between questions of "fact" and questions of "law." The questions overlapped, he felt, and the distinction should not be used (as it had been on occasion in torts) to deny a court the power to set forth a standard for negligence or to confine appellate judicial review to matters of "law."[71] He rejected the image of the branches of government as "those of a hatrack, fixed and therefore incapable of movement."[72] Courts not only made law, they made policy; they were partners of the legislature, interacting with it in a variety of ways. Similarly, courts interacted with administrative agencies. Traynor supported active judicial review of agency decisions even if they were purportedly grounded in "expertise." Technical appraisal by an administrator in a specialized field was insulated from review, but not opinions of agency officials on matters "that should as much be within the ken of judges."[73] Finally, Traynor recognized the extent to which modern lawmaking institutions "interact[ed] in countless ways with powerful private groups."[74] Understanding the expectations and practices of these groups was another obligation of courts. This responsibility, however, gave rise to a power in judges to insure that these groups did not in their own decisions arbitrarily infringe on the rights of individuals.[75]

The accepted premise that judges made law, then, created for Traynor an obligation on their part to make law in a rational and orderly fashion, but this obligation itself conferred power on the judiciary to expand the scope of its prerogatives, since judicial decisions were a prime source of rationality in the legal process as a whole. An area illustrating this line of reasoning was the retroactive application of new judge-made rules of criminal procedure. Traynor conceded that new rules expanding protection to criminal defendants in the 1950s and 1960s had not been "discovered." They represented a policy choice to restrict the ability of law enforcement officials to abuse their discretion. Expanded procedural safeguards, however, meant increased opportunities for incarcerated criminals to challenge their confinement on the ground that they had not been afforded a full measure of protection. Retroactive application of new criminal procedure rules therefore suggested that countless criminals might be turned loose upon the public.

Traynor approached the problem by equating the automatic retroactivity of new judge-made rules of law with the oracular theory of judging. If judges merely *found* the law, "new" law was law for all time but had simply not previously been discovered, and hence, retroactive application was required. But if judges *made* the law, and especially if in the process they based their judgments on a perception of current conditions, they could adjust the retroactive scope of their decisions to meet contemporary social needs. If retroactive application of criminal procedure rule changes resulted in a wholesale freeing of incarcerated criminals, this negative value could become part of a judge's calculus. Prospective application of innovations in criminal procedure (which Traynor advocated)[76] was thus in keeping with his perception of the way judges functioned in modern America. If prospectivity suggested freedom in the judiciary to make policy choices openly, those choices, after all, were attempts to construct rational responses to the demands of the environment in which judges functioned.

The thrust of Traynor's approach to judging was thus to carve out a wide area of lawmaking power for the judiciary, but to equate effective use of that power with the constraints of rationality. The judge could substitute himself as a lawmaker for juries or legislators or administrators if he exemplified in his decisions social awareness, intellectual openness, and powers of analysis. These qualities gave his decisions the measure of rationality that they needed to be accepted. In making law the judge was synthesizing and organizing the insights of others. His primacy was justified by an exhibited dependence on outside contributions.

The delicate reciprocity between judicial power and restraint envisaged by Traynor's technique of adjudication appeared to ignore a difficulty raised earlier. If judges could, by imaginative use of extrajudicial sources, retain for themselves a number of problems traditionally entrusted to other lawmaking branches, what prevented techniques of craftsmanship from being a means of concealing bases for decision rather than of revealing them? Could not a judge decide on intuitive grounds, then express his preference in terms that suggested a greater amount of impersonality and detachment than he in fact had?

The implicit answer to this inquiry, for Traynor, was that in a sense the original motivations of the judge did not matter. If a judge took the time and effort to reason his judgments through, to justify them by means of broadly based social and intellectual appeals, his original intuitions became secondary to his own articulated reasoning processes. The significance of a result was indistinguishable from the reasons given in connection with it. If the reasons were vulnerable to attack, so was the result. Conversely, a potentially upsetting result, in the sense of one that dramatically changed the state of the law, was less troublesome if the reasons advanced for it were sound. Judicial innovations were thus no less troublesome than alterations in the law of other branches, provided they were rationally based. Reason remained for Traynor a nearly objective concept. He felt that one could easily distinguish what was rational from what was arbitrary; that one could subsume one's intuitions in an analytical exegesis.

III

The confidence that Traynor placed in the innovative capabilities of the judiciary was exemplified by his own contributions to numerous cases of substantive law. In torts—perhaps the area of his widest impact—he pioneered in the development of strict liability in defective products cases;[77] undermined the defense of immunity, whether charitable,[78] sovereign,[79] or family,[80] in negligence actions; exposed fictional distinctions in the law defining the responsibilities of a landowner for accidents on his property;[81] and helped create the new tort of intentional infliction of emotional distress.[82] In contracts he went beyond the contents of documents to gather information about and assess the practical impact of the agreements they signified, and was not deterred in his search by rules limiting a court's consideration of extrinsic evidence[83] or traditional limitations on the fact-finding abilities of courts.[84] Once having secured ample information, he attempted to piece together the reasonable expectations of the contracting parties and weigh these against the policy implications of one outcome or another.[85] He did not take literally legislative requirements that contracts be in writing,[86] nor was he reluctant to discard the formalities of offer and acceptance in allocating responsibility for business losses between general contractors and subcontractors.[87] He voided contracts, however, on occasions in which one of the parties had not been authorized by the legislature to enter into the type of agreement in question.[88] In short, his approach de-emphasized formalities in the face of immediate practical considerations.

In real property, Traynor discarded or reformulated older decisions setting forth requirements for the delivery of a deed of title,[89] adverse possession of land,[90] the recognition of security interests in real property transactions,[91] the remedies of a landlord on forcible entry of his property by a tenant,[92] and the remedies of a seller against defaulting purchasers of land.[93] The thrust of these decisions was to break down stringent rules by altering them to fit the context of particular sets of real property transactions. In civil procedure, similarly, Traynor discarded the rule of mutuality, which had insisted that when a person attempted, in a later litigation, to invoke an earlier judgment against another, he could make use of the first judgment only if he himself was bound by it.[94]

In a case where the administrator of a will attempted to sue a bank for unauthorized payment of money in the will to a beneficiary, the bank invoked an earlier judgment of a probate court that the payment was authorized by the will. The bank, however, had not been a party in the probate court, although the administrator had. The mutuality rule therefore prohibited the bank from using the probate court judgment to prevent the administrator from subsequently suing it. Traynor took the occasion to reject the mutuality rule outright and substitute a test that focused on the issues resolved in the first adjudication (were they "identical" with those presented in the second?), the occurrence of a "final judgment on the merits" in the first adjudication, and the presence of the same party or his contractee in both suits.[95]

Despite Traynor's status as a state judge, he was able to make innovations in constitutional law through his consideration of analogous issues in the California constitution and his interpretation of the implications for the states in any changes in federal criminal-procedure rules. In 1948, for example, Traynor struck down a California anti-miscegenation statute on equal protection grounds,[96] anticipating a Warren Court decision[97] by sixteen years. Two years earlier he had invalidated the California Syndicalism Act as applied against officers of the American Civil Liberties Union who had refused to swear that they were not members of subversive organizations.[98] In later cases he protested against a loyalty oath's being made a condition of tax-exempt status,[99] and Communist Party affiliation's being made the sole basis for discharge of an employee.[100]

Likewise in criminal procedure Traynor found his views congenial to the innovative stance of a majority of the Warren Court. After holding, in 1942,[101] that the Fourth Amendment's prohibition of the use of illegally acquired evidence in criminal trials did not apply against the states, Traynor reversed his position in 1955[102] and subsequently expanded protection for criminal defendants against illegal searches and seizures, including searches of a home without uncoerced consent or a warrant,[103] and searches incident to "felony" arrests where the arresting officer knew only that a felony had been committed.[104] His changes, however, were not always favorable to criminal defendants. In the course of reconsidering standards for police conduct in the late 1950s and the 1960s, he created rules that justified arrests on observation of a defendant's behavior[105] or reasonable searches even before arrests.[106] He also expanded the discovery rights of prosecutors against defendants despite the Fifth Amendment's requirement that persons accused of crimes not be compelled to incriminate themselves.[107]

Two other substantive areas deserve attention in this brief review of Traynor's innovations: conflict of laws, and taxation, both of which were fields of special interest for him. Conflict of laws, because of its abstract, conceptual character, gave Traynor a stark opportunity to criticize mechanical rules and formulate functional ones of his own; taxation offered him a chance to apply as a judge views that he had first developed as a law professor. The "conflicts" field was dominated originally by dichotomies between questions of "substance" and questions of "procedure," or by rigid rules such as the rule that territoriality defined the primacy of competing state laws.[108] After an early struggle to work within the framework of these concepts[109]—in which he increasingly questioned their usefulness—Traynor eventually abandoned them altogether, first in a contracts case[110] and then in a tort case.[111] In their place he substituted an analysis that compared and evaluated the respective interests of the states affected. Sometimes this analysis produced a bona-fide conflict between competing state interests; when this happened, another policy, such as that facilitating commercial transactions among the states, could be used to resolve the conflict.[112] On many other occasions investigation revealed no real interest on the part of one state and a substantial interest on the part of another, so that a "false conflict" could be said to exist. Interest analysis in conflicts lead ultimately to a consideration of the social policies promoted by choosing a legal rule of one state over that of another. That was the kind of inquiry Traynor attempted to make in all his decisions. Rules were meaningful only to the extent that they reflected rational policies derived from a responsiveness to social conditions.

If conflicts was perhaps Traynor's most congenial field in the latter portion of his career, taxation had originally been his compelling interest. While teaching law at Berkeley, he recognized that expansion of governmental activity required additional taxation, and that the welfare purposes of affirmative government would be subverted if tax obligations were not equitably allocated.[113] He gave particular attention to state taxation of national banks, publishing a series of articles on the subject[114] and participating in a 1933 revision of the Bank and Corporation Tax Act, which reflected his views.[115] He also sat on legislative committees to redraft tax statutes for sales, personal income, motor vehicle licensing, corporation income, and fuel consumption. He served as administrator of the California sales tax in the 1930s, and in 1937 as tax advisor to the U.S. Treasury Department. All the while he taught courses in taxation at Berkeley in which, as one of his students observed, "the quality of mercy . . . dropped as the gentle rain from heaven upon the Sahara."[116]

The function of appellate judges in tax cases often consists of supplying operational meanings, in varied contexts, to statutory language. This requires fine verbal distinctions that have practical significance. Traynor was equal to that task. The phrase "source of income" invited a distinction between a tax applied directly to net income and a tax on franchises measured by net income.[117] Lease-holds on land exempt from taxation were "real property" for the purposes of the property tax laws.[118] "Full cash value" was defined as arm's-length market value under ordinary conditions.[119] Liquor licenses were not "intangible personal property."[120] And "goods in transit," immune from taxation, embraced out-of-state goods temporarily stored in San Francisco while awaiting shipment to Hawaii during wartime.[121]

IV

Despite the continually innovative character of Traynor's judicial performance, despite his receptiveness to affirmative governmental action, and despite the fact that many of his changes in the common law of California broadened the opportunities of aggrieved persons to seek redress in the courts, conventional political characterizations are no more helpful in illuminating his stance than they are for Story, or Shaw, or Cooley, or Doe. Traynor was, though not universally, a "liberal" judge if the term signifies receptiveness to change, or interest in the plight of disadvantaged persons, or, as previously used in this study, a commitment to the management of society by professionals. But calling him a liberal does not clarify his attitude. Of greater importance is his methodological approach to judging. Traynor regarded results as simply a logical consequence of a satisfactory technique of analysis, the final steps of a reasoned judgment. In his most significant opinions, such as *Escola, Muskopf v. Corning Hospital District* (in which he discarded the doctrine of governmental immunity), or *Reich v. Purcell* (in which he abandoned the "place of the wrong" rule in multistate conflicts cases), his results were difficult to classify in ideological terms, though his methodological approach was consistent and distinctive. In each case Traynor focused on a conventional judge-made rule or doctrine, identified its working difficulties, repudiated it, and substituted for it a rule of his own derived from extrajudicial sources as well as from the ordinary materials of the appellate judge.

Traynor's technique of decision-making emphasized that judging was not an exercise in declaring rules but a process of weighing varieties of evidence in search of a rational solution. Effective judicial "laws" underscored the rationality of the process by which they were made, rather than the content of their language. Effective law-making by appellate courts gave them freedom to revise their own decisions without abandoning their allegiance to rationality. Here Traynor's starting assumptions about judging were thrown into sharp relief. The "primary internal characteristic of the judicial process" was that it was "a rational one." It was "based on reasoning and presupposed[d]—all antirationalists to the contrary notwithstanding—that its determinations [were] justified only when explained or explainable in reason."[122]

More than any appellate judge of his time, Traynor witnessed a dramatic change in the social context of his decisions. If American society in the years between 1940 and 1970 became increasingly complicated, heterogeneous, consumer-oriented, diversified, and dominated by the presence of institutions of government, California was at the crest of those trends. No state in the nation had developed so rapidly. None of comparable size and population had undergone such massive changes after omnipresent government had become tolerated in American society.

Traynor's contribution, in these terms, was to develop a theory and a technique of judging that proved responsive to the symbolic experience of California life. As the process of distributing products from manufacturers to consumers became altered with the advent of supermarket economics, Traynor reoriented tort law to reflect that alteration. As purchasing power widened so that more uneducated or uninformed persons entered into contracts, Traynor recognized that arm's-length bargaining based on complete information was often a fiction, whether in commercial ventures or in the sale of homes. As governmental institutions demonstrated their capacity to injure persons as well as to aid them, Traynor saw the undesirable consequences of immunities. As more and more persons crossed state lines in their occupational and leisured pursuits, Traynor perceived that territorially-based conflicts rules needed reexamination. And as legislatures made laws with increasing frequency, created agencies to administer them, and looked to courts to clarify their meaning in specific instances, Traynor resolved that a theory of government that emphasized rigid boundary lines between governing institutions was unrealistic.

Like other judges of his time, Traynor's perceptions of the imperatives of social change were intuitive, and doubtless the results he reached brought him emotional as well as intellectual satisfaction. But for Traynor the promotion of substantive policies in a judicial opinion was easily distinguishable, if the opinion was properly crafted, from the individual bias of the writer. The identification of law as a process and of appellate judging as an intellectual effort to keep the process in smooth working order focused discussions of judicial decision-making on reasons rather than on results. Reasons, in fact, subsumed results; process subsumed substance; result-orientation was merely one stage in the progression toward a reasoned judgment. A social policy was promoted not because of its emotional appeal to the judge but because, after careful examination, it emerged as a rational and intellectually defensible resolution of a current conflict.

In the context of American society after World War II, a society widely perceived by scholars as being unprecedented in its complexity and interrelatedness,[123] the notion of law as an integrated, impersonal, rationally-based process was appealing. Process Jurisprudence framed divisive value conflicts in an orderly institutional structure that resolved them; it allowed some freedom for governing officials to shape law to changing conditions, but confined each branch of government to the tasks it could perform most rationally. Process Jurisprudence thus suggested the restoration of balance and harmony in government at a time when extremes of behavior were out of fashion and consensual American values were being reaffirmed. It also identified law and legal institutions with the social assumptions of modern liberalism by providing an apparently nonpartisan technique of implementing affirmative governmental action.

Yet the dichotomy between the process of reasoning and the substantive results that process yielded remained a central element of American appellate judging in the 1950s and 1960s. Despite the timeliness of Traynor's approach, views such as his did not sweep the field. Pressure for legal change, especially with respect to the rights and interests of minorities, combined with inertia on the part of legislatures to create a fruitful climate for the open judicial espousal of substantive values. In their fervor to respond to this need and their sense of the importance of the values themselves, influential judges began to eschew intellectual niceties for ringing affirmations of the rights and privileges of American citizenship. In their affirmations results transcended reasons, and process was only a means of conveying substance. While in his opinions Traynor was able to achieve a delicate fusion of substantive change and methodological consistency, of intuition and rationality, in other judges those goals became self-opposing, engendering the jurisprudential controversies of the Warren Court.

12 

The Mosaic of the Warren Court: Frankfurter, Black, Warren, and Harlan

Over the course of American history, the practice of identifying an incumbent Supreme Court with the figure of its Chief Justice has produced analytical difficulties. Personifying the Court in its Chief may exaggerate the influence of certain holders of that office, as in the Chase Court. It may suggest a flavor to the Court that in fact it does not have: the Stone Court, typically, did not reflect the jurisprudential views of its Chief. It may invite political characterizations that lead to erroneous assumptions, such as that the Taney Court signified a sharp break from the Marshall Court. Or it may suggest that the Court's history falls into neat chronological phases, synonymous with each change in Chief Justice. This is often not the case: transitions from Waite to Fuller and from Fuller to White, for example, produced no major alterations in the Court's stance.

The practice has some utility, however, as a shorthand device for indicating the opportunity available to each incoming Chief Justice to encourage, through personal and intellectual leadership, the development of a collective jurisprudential viewpoint among his colleagues. No Chief, not even a Marshall, can expect to make a Court's attitude synonymous with his own; none can hope to achieve unanimity on a very high percentage of issues; none, not even a Hughes, can expect by force of personality and intellect to impose fully a style of decision-making on his fellow justices. Judging at the Supreme Court level is too individualized, independent, and prideful an activity for such expectations to be realized. Challenges nonetheless come with the succession to the Chief Justiceship, the challenge of extracting unity from diversity, that of supplying channels for intellectual energies, and that of giving a loosely identifiable cast to the institution. The designation "Warren Court" is an apt one in the sense that its Chief attempted to meet those challenges. Earl Warren invested his Court with a discernible character, if not necessarily a coherent jurisprudence.

I

The unity of the Warren Court did not suppress its diversity, but was merely superimposed upon that diversity. If one analogizes the creation of an intellectual identity for a Court to the creation of a cultural identity for a nation, the Warren Court was not a melting pot but a mosaic. Its dominant Justices retained their distinctive points of view, harmonizing with one another only sporadically and superficially. No individual emerged as its intellectual leader during the sixteen years of Warren's tenure; several powerful figures stood in trenchant opposition or in uneasy coexistence. No theory of constitutional interpretation or judicial performance captured the Court; instead, much of its energy came from a clash of competing jurisprudential attitudes.

Despite this clash, a generalized pattern of behavior came to mark the Warren Court. The pattern may be described as a momentum toward an increasingly broad definition of the rights attaching to American citizenship. It was no more precise than that. The Court, as a unit, did not draw clear distinctions as to eligibility for these rights or as to the class of government officials compelled to respect them. Abstract statements were made about the rights extending to "all Americans"; yet certain rights clearly did not so extend, and others extended beyond citizens to aliens. Similar comments were voiced about the broad responsibilities of all government officials—whether federal or state, administrators or legislators, bureaucrats or law enforcers—to protect citizenship rights, although in practice the obligations of these categories of officials were differently defined. In short, although the Warren Court as a whole revealed itself as increasingly inclined to recognize new citizenship rights or to protect those already extant, its individual Justices could not arrive at any broad collective decision about what rights they wanted protected against which sorts of persons in what specific contexts. The Warren Court's concern for rights was abstract and growing: its breadth and momentum, rather than its precise content, gave the Court its character.

The social and institutional values around which the Warren Court cohered were markedly broad and abstract. The Justices, to a man, accepted the principle that affirmative governmental action to meet the problems of disadvantaged persons was a necessity in mid-twentieth-century American society. Their quarrels were over methods of implementing the principle—especially with regard to the role of the judiciary—rather than with its general validity. The Warren Court Justices believed also in the inevitability of social change and were generally optimistic about the American people's ability to better themselves in the process of responding to changing conditions. Beyond this abstract belief, however, they rapidly diverged: some justices tended to equate "the people" with their elected or appointed representatives; others came to find representative government not always responsive to popular needs.

The Warren Court in the aggregate also accepted the notion that U.S. government was in some sense paternalistic, and they did not insist on participatory democracy in its pure forms. They quarreled, however, over the institutional implications of paternalism. In general, some held a vision of a paternalistic Court scrutinizing the other branches of government to insure that their processes afforded full protection to the people's rights; others identified paternalism primarily with other branches of government and sought to restrict the class of wards protected by the Court. Finally, the Warren Court was unified behind a broad sense of patriotism, and its participants shared a faith in the unique worth of American society and a commitment to its preservation. They differed, however, in their interpretation of the imperatives of patriotism in specific instances, some equating it with preservation of human rights more than with maintenance of national unity or security, others reversing this balance; some exhibiting a fidelity to models of government employed by the American nation at its origin, others suggesting that the American experiment implied that those models were to change with time.

Although the core values of the Warren Court were abstractions, they were not all-embracing political shibboleths. Alternative viewpoints had been articulated and widely accepted during the course of American history. The

Founding Fathers had exhibited little confidence in the ability of the masses to govern themselves; some believed that even a government made up of the people's representatives was not a sufficient buffer against the excesses of the mob. For a good part of the nineteenth century the theory that a government governs best which governs least was influential: paternalism was "odious," and affirmative government action offended against the laws of the universe. Patriotism was a recurrent value, but had in previous decades been linked with certain attitudes, such as racial and ethnic discrimination, that the Warren Court largely deplored. The shared values of the Warren Court Justices, in short, were those of modern liberalism. Life in America was assumed to be composed of complex patterns of change and affected by a loss of consensual values; victims of an industrializing society were identified, and an active, benevolent government of professionals was invested with the tasks of meeting current needs and serving as a force for social cohesiveness.

Stating the credo of modern liberalism underscored its internal ambiguities. It had, as indicated earlier, a commitment to professionalism. One of its purposes was to insure that the programs of affirmative government would be conceived and managed in a manner sufficiently sophisticated to respond to the complexities of modern life. Achievement of this goal seemed to require a careful evaluation of the roles and functions of governing institutions so that the agencies of government did not overlap one another or venture into areas where they had no expertise, and so that the decision-making procedures of the separate institutions responded to the needs of their different constituents. The logic of this approach appeared to mandate a limited role for the judiciary as an agent of affirmative government. Judges had little access to current empirical data, and the data they did receive was skewed by the adversary process. They were not, by and large, representatives of the people, and their nonpartisan status insulated them from the waves of current opinion; hence, for them to pose as social theorists raised dangerous questions of unchecked judicial tyranny. Holmes's model of a passive judiciary, refined by Brandeis and Stone to tolerate judicial involvement where expertise could be acquired or where legislative attempts at social ordering had produced woefully inefficient or unfair side effects, harmonized with this thrust of modern liberalism.

Another purpose, however, was to give aid to the casualties of industrial and urban progress. As individual initiative came to be seen as inadequate, and as social and economic powerlessness came to be perceived as threshold barriers to upward mobility, paternalistic governmental action was regarded as the chief means of ameliorating the social condition of disadvantaged persons. The "freedom" of a market economy proved to be one-sided; political action, in the form of social welfare legislation, emerged as the remedy. By accident, the Holmes model of institutional performance interacted with this humanitarian thrust of liberalism, since many of the legislative innovations he declined to scrutinize were designed to subordinate economic freedom to the needs of the disadvantaged. Brandeis's decisions exemplified more starkly the policy dimensions of a passive theory of judicial performance in the early twentieth century. On the relatively few occasions when an experimental piece of state legislation served an antihumanitarian purpose, such as suppressing the rights of expression of a political or ethnic minority,[1] Brandeis asked himself whether the evil that the legislation was designed to eradicate was sufficiently noxious to justify the statute's regressive thrust.[2] His calculus in such cases smacked of substantive due process, anathema to advocates of a passive judiciary.

In the Stone and Vinson Courts tensions between the professionalist and humanitarian impulses of modern liberalism were evident. Celebrated cases of the 1930s, 1940s, and early 1950s—such as the flag salute controversies[3] (in which the Stone Court overruled itself within a three-year time span[4]), cases involving racial discrimination in colleges,[5] in primary elections,[6] and in housing,[7] or the clashes between free speech and national security[8] after World War II—can be seen as struggles in harmonizing judicial passivity with humanitarian impulses. In those decades a shifting number of justices, despite their voiced opposition to substantive due process, came to favor judicial intervention in behalf of minorities whose civil rights and liberties had been infringed by states or the federal government. No detailed rationale for this intervention was formulated: it seemed to rest on an unexpressed commitment to substantive values. In the second flag-salute case, Justices Douglas and Black indicated that although they remained "reluct[ant] to make the Federal Constitution a rigid bar against state regulation of conduct thought inimical to the public welfare," on certain occasions the "application" of that "sound" principle was "wrong."[9]

The doctrinal struggles of the pre-Warren Court years were manifestations of a more fundamental issue: What were the costs and benefits of a substantive judicial commitment to modern liberalism? Herein lay the origins of a central theme of the Warren Court, the conflict between the professionalist and humanitarian strands of the modern liberal impulse. From one perspective the history of the Warren Court may be seen as a clash between these strands in the context of an expanding judicial definition of citizenship rights. Although the Warren Court Justices began with shared assumptions as to the role of government in modern American, as well as a generalized commitment to the social ends—efficiency, humanitarianism, equality of economic opportunity, equal treatment before the law—of modern liberalism, they soon exhibited major disagreement over the methods of achieving these ends, especially as they affected the role of the Court. In the course of the debate, professionalism and humanitarianism were expanded into jurisprudential postures that might be represented by the terms "process" and "substantive liberalism."

Process Jurisprudence, as noted above, accepted lawmaking in judges but confined it to limited areas, emphasizing the anti-democratic character of the judiciary and the inability of judges to achieve detailed technical expertise. A passive model of judicial performance was thus part of its tenets. In addition, Process Jurisprudence emphasized the complexity of post-World War II American society and the proliferation of government agencies, and attempted to match governmental institutions to the areas they were best prepared to supervise and the problems they were most suited to resolve. Lawmaking became an exercise in affirmative governmental action of a specialized and confined sort. Governing institutions could be aggressively innovative so long as they remained in their ambits of competence. Catchwords and catchphrases described specialized institutional skills: courts were "disinterested" and their judgments "reasoned"; legislatures were "representative of popular opinion" and could "canvass a wide spectrum of views"; the executive was "efficient"; administrative agencies were "flexible" and "expert." An integration of specialized governing institutions produced the hybrid, pragmatic social ordering of post-New Deal America. As new problems surfaced, their character was defined, the appropriate institution for their solution identified, the process of affirmative government set in motion, and the limitations on each unit of government once more underscored. The smooth functioning of the process became the overriding goal. The general implementation of social values transcended the particular content of the values. The process theory was hence integrated with modern liberalism: it assumed the necessity of positive governmental action and sought to provide jurisprudential guidelines to make that action effective.

The impact of process liberalism on the Warren Court was manifested primarily in a set of limitations on judicial performance. Such limitations included a requirement that the Court decide only mature and full-blown controversies; an obligation on its part to avoid deciding "political" questions; an insistence that it justify its decisions by appeal to intelligible legal principles, or, if no principles emerged, refrain from deciding altogether; an indentification on the part of Justices of their own biases, with a view to achieving the proper mood of detachment; a preliminary classification of controversies as suitable for "judicial," "legislative," "executive," or "administrative" decision, and their consequent allocation to the appropriate branches of government, with the judiciary recognizing its own limited jurisdiction. Justice Frankfurter, on his retirement in 1962, described the obligations of process liberalism for a judge. It required, he said, the "pertinacious pursuit of processes of Reason in the disposition of controversies," a pursuit identified with "intellectual disinterestedness in the analysis of the factors involved in issues that called for decision," which decision was in turn a product of "rigorous self-scrutiny" in the judge "to discover, with a view to curbing, every influence that may deflect from such disinterestedness."[10]

But what if a judge believed that some values did not compete with others, but invariably superseded them? What if he perceived American society as being grounded on fundamental guaranties of citizenship and could point to the Constitution as declaring those guaranties? What if he further believed, as had Marshall and Story, that some values were embedded in the fabric of American society in addition to being alluded to in specific constitutional provisions? Could not his balancing process regularly affirm those values against the competing claims of other values in accordance with their fundamental social importance? Could not the claims of disadvantaged persons be seen in this context, so that judicial responsiveness to them was simply a recognition of the primacy of egalitarianism and libertarianism in America, which compelled the eradication of social and economic inequalities? Was not the humanitarian impulse of modern liberalism thus part of a historic tradition in America, a tradition that defined the meaning of the nation? If so, why should this impulse be subordinated to any judicial conception of the currently appropriate process of social ordering—a conception that was, after all, itself a value judgment?

Therein lay the Warren Court's competing theories of judging: the sophisticated models of process liberalism against the straightforward imperatives of substantive liberalism. Originally conceived of only as different methodological techniques, these theories took on broader implications in the latter years of Warren's tenure. Since process liberalism fostered caution in the judiciary and deference to the judgments of other governmental institutions, it served as a brake in the momentum of substantive liberalism in areas where legislatures, agencies, and the executive were taking no action. An example was the issue of whether state legislatures should be reapportioned on a population basis. If the judiciary, terming that question "political," declined to compel reapportionment, then it allowed a system of unequally weighted representation to persist, since no other unit of government had shown an inclination to change the existing system. The demands of process liberalism thus harmonized, in this instance, with counteregalitarian values; judicial inaction perpetuated the power of rural areas in state legislatures.

As humanitarian impulses gained momentum in the Warren Court, techniques of process liberalism became vehicles for the maintenance of countervailing values, such as the autonomy of law enforcement (against increased protection for criminal suspects), freedom of association (against equal access to facilities by all races), or federalism (against uniform courtroom procedures across the nation). Since espousal of the Warren Court's humanitarianism required change in all of these areas, process liberalism became identified with political conservatism. To argue, on professionalist grounds, for confinement of the Warren Court's jurisdiction was often to advocate resistance to sweeping social change.

Seventeen justices served in the Warren Court, so that describing only a few of them as predominant invites difficulties. In terms of the themes of this chapter, however, four Justices were of special importance: Felix Frankfurter, Hugo Black, Earl Warren, and John Harlan. Frankfurter and Harlan, on one side, and Black and Warren, on the other, were the most influential representatives of the theories of process and substantive liberalism. Frankfurter and Black represented polar positions in the first stage of this controversy, which ended with Frankfurter's retirement in 1962 and in which the conflicts were more methodological than political. Harlan and Warren, along with Black, played significant roles in the second stage, which lasted until Warren's retirement in 1969 and in which the original debate metamorphosed into something resembling an ideological confrontation. At stake in the debate was more than the delineation of proper techniques of opinion-writing or even the designation of social values deserving of judicial implementation; at stake was the viability of the process theory of appellate judging.

II

An important dimension of the Warren Court was its sensitivity to the implications of status. This Court numbered among its influential Justices three men—Black, Douglas, and Warren—who had seen poverty in their youths, who identified with persons of low social and economic status, who remained indifferent to or suspicious of inherited wealth and social position, whose philosophy of government was a leveling one, and yet who were upward-mobile in their own lives and not uncomfortable with the possession or maintenance of power achieved through individual initiative. Another member—Harlan—reflected a fundamentally different perspective. He was conscious of his own elite social and intellectual status and interested in maintaining civilized standards and in protecting the social order from anarchistic impulses. Many issues considered by the Warren Court had status implications, since many of the persons whose rights the Court vindicated—prisoners, blacks, industrial laborers, migrant workers—were identified with low socioeconomic standing.

The presence of Frankfurter was richly suggestive of this theme. Frankfurter was himself upward-mobile, a German-Jewish immigrant from New York's Lower East Side with a lifelong fascination with public figures—such as Henry Stimson, Franklin D. Roosevelt, Holmes, and Hand—with aristocratic backgrounds. But Frankfurter's heritage encompassed academic and intellectual traditions, and his conspicuous success in the American educational system gave his upward mobility a special flavor. He emerged from Harvard Law School in 1906 proud of his Jewishness but determined to enter the Wasp-dominated world of Wall Street practice, a firm supporter of the democratic bias of American civilization but a member of and apologist for the Eastern intellectual meritocracy.

In his later career these patterns continued. He spoke disparagingly of special privilege and economic imperialism,[11] but limited his classes at Harvard Law

School to students of high academic standing. He participated enthusiastically in the elitist apprenticeship system of the legal profession, in which conspicuously high grades at a national law school created a series of opportunities—law review staff membership, judicial clerkships, positions on law faculties or with large urban law firms—for a narrow stratum of candidates. In the 1930s, by virtue of his numerous contacts, tireless energy, and seemingly endless capacity for promoting the candidacies of those whose qualities struck him favorably, Frankfurter was a nerve center of the apprenticeship network. He helped choose the clerks of Holmes, Brandeis, and Learned Hand; he served as a conduit between Harvard graduates and Wall Street firms or government agencies; he secured research assistantships at Harvard for Supreme Court clerks who had a potential interest in teaching; he wrote joint articles with promising law students as a means of exposing them to the process of academic publication. In his mind this patronage served a noble end, the perpetuation of an elite based on merit rather than on privilege, and hence compatible with democratic ideals.

Frankfurter reconciled intellectual elitism with democracy through the notions of paternalism and social responsibility. He believed that the masses needed opportunities to achieve elite status, but that they could recognize those opportunities only if educated by an elite. Public-mindedness was the obligation attendant on one's rise in the meritocracy. The expertise and elite status achieved in reward for surviving the competition of the educational system was to be used to prepare the way for other entrants. American citizens had the capacity for self-improvement, and even self-government, Frankfurter believed, if shown the proper techniques; those techniques were to be conveyed to them by elite leadership.

In his vision of a paternalistic, responsible, expert elite channeling the innate wisdom and virtue of the masses into constructive and noble tasks, Frankfurter was representative of a group of early-twentieth-century thinkers who called themselves "progressives" and who thought that popular sovereignty and elitism were as easily reconcilable as humanitarianism and professionalism.[12] Progressivism had its greatest meaning for Frankfurter in a concern that elites use their privileged status to further rather than block mass participation in education and politics. Out of this concern evolved his conception of the limited role of the Supreme Court.

During the first twenty years after Frankfurter's graduation from law school, while he was supporting standard Progressive policies such as scientific management,[13] organization among laborers[14] and the "Wisconsin idea" of state-university cooperation,[15] as well as championing the 1924 Presidential candidacy of Robert LaFollette,[16] the Supreme Court was demonstrating a persistent, if not universal, hostility to the kind of experimental humanitarian legislation that Progressives supported. Aroused by Court invalidation of wage-and-hour legislation, Frankfurter began to question the justifications for such power. Although he first viewed the problem as simply one of personnel, so that a "Court dominantly composed of Holmes and Brandeis and Learned Hand and Cardozo"[17] would be acceptable even if omnipotent, he came, on reflection, to frame the question in an institutional perspective. If the Court functioned as a "revisory legislative body,"[18] it sapped the independence of legislatures and "mutilat[ed] the educative process of responsibility."[19] Judicial negation of legislation under the due process clause was unsound regardless of the worth of the legislation, inasmuch as it deterred the masses from participating in government and thereby deprived them of opportunities for self-education and public service. The Court should no more attempt to "guarantee toleration"[20] by invalidating legislation with a religious bias than it should attempt to protect economic privilege by striking down minimum wage laws, since the values of humanitarianism and efficiency could be fully instilled in the population only through education and direct political participation.

Many types of elitism were possible in Frankfurter's ideal polity, but the judicial variety had to be of a peculiarly negative kind. Courts had to use their power to restrain themselves so that other branches of government, as being better forums for public education, could expand the range of their activities. A strong Presidency could provide "brave and clear-sighted leadership";[21] administrative agencies could supply necessary expertise; legislatures could serve as vehicles of "public scrutiny" and report "alert public criticism."[22] Cooperation among the branches of government and symbiosis between the intelligentsia and the masses could insure continual progress.

Such were the views Frankfurter held upon his nomination (by Roosevelt) to the Court in 1939. Two years earlier, Black had joined the Court holding remarkably similar beliefs. Although Black's boyhood environment was less intellectually charged and his professional training less formal than Frankfurter's, the two men shared a sense of the incomparable value of self-education. Frankfurter's education, although wide-ranging in its scope, had had an institutional structure and a substantive focus; Black had for the most part created his own program. He had attended college and law school in Alabama and developed an interest in history and classical civilization in addition to law, but once out of the academic situation he channeled his interests, and his reading became more systematic. Before his election to the Senate in 1926 he was said to have had nightly sessions in which he and a law partner read aloud from Gibbon;[23] to have devoured selections on Thomas Jefferson;[24] and to have devised reading lists for himself.[25] Once a Senator, his access to books widened with the proximity of the Library of Congress, and he began to follow reading programs, such as Will Durant's 1929 selection of "One Hundred Best Books."[26]

Black's reading selections indicate that he read purposively and self-consciously. He invariably preferred reacting to a book independently to accepting another's evaluation. Once a book made an impression on him, he reread it often, underlining passages, making marginal notations, and occasionally supplying his own index.[27] His selections tended to expand, but also reinforce, his own attitudes. Tacitus, Livy, and Thucydides showed him the degradation of human liberties by tyrannical governments; Plutarch, the complexities and deceptions in human relations; Macaulay, the egalitarian tradition in Anglo-American history. Edith Hamilton's *The Greek Way* described the origins of democratic thought in ancient Greece; Vernon Parrington, Charles Beard, and Claude Bowers presented American history from a perspective unsympathetic to vested privilege; Saul Padover's *To Secure These Blessings* and Leon Whipple's *Our Ancient Liberties* dramatized the exalted status of the rights codified in the American Constitution; Joseph Baldwin's *The Flush Times of Alabama and Mississippi* reminded him of the wild-and-woolly, unromantic environment of his youth.[28] For Black, education through reading meant independence, self-analysis, and finally wisdom; through reading the recurrent qualities of human nature and the inevitable links between past and present were revealed.[29] One could, through self-education, develop and distill a working philosophy.

Black's education led him to embrace, in his pre-Court career, some of the values supported by Frankfurter. One theme of his reading had been the negative effects of privileged status and concentrated power. He saw his heroes, among them Jefferson, Jackson, Lincoln, and Brandeis, as champions of the common man.[30] His law practice in Alabama had handled a significant amount of personal-injury litigation and labor disputes. He believed in the unionization of labor and welcomed the Roosevelt Administration's identification with labor movements. Consequently he regarded judicial utilization of the due process clause to nullify wage-and-hour legislation to be as inappropriate as had Frankfurter.

In 1924 Frankfurter had said that "the due process clause ought to go";[31] seven years later Black declared in a Senate speech that the Court had no power to pass on the reasonableness of state or federal legislation under the due process clause.[32] Black as a lawyer and Senator shared Frankfurter's preference for legislative over judicial solutions to social problems, since a legislature, in his view, had a better opportunity to reflect the needs of the average man. Finally, Black and Frankfurter were united in their enthusiasm for Roosevelt. Both saw the Roosevelt Administrations as progressive and humanitarian, favoring the common man over vested interests. Both strongly believed in active, paternalistic government with a leveling bias; both regarded unregulated giant industries as oppressive forces; both had a certain faith in the virtue and good sense of the mass public. Both were regarded on their appointments to the Court as "liberals" whose voting records would reflect the position of the Roosevelt Administration.

Although none of these characteristics augured the deep differences that would ultimately develop between the two men as Justices, there were other qualities that presaged the alienation to come. One was personal style. Frankfurter was a bundle of nervous energy: garrulous, effusive, intense, enthusiastic, fond of debate for its own sake. In court and in conference he lectured counsel or his colleagues, interrupted the remarks of others, and "buttressed straightforward argument [with] anger, scorn, sarcasm, and humor."[33] These qualities made him, especially to his numerous friends, a delightful conversationalist and a stimulating companion. To others he appeared pretentious, feisty, tiresome, or petty. Although generous in his appraisal of others and unabashed in his communications of friendship, Frankfurter thrived on controversy: a no-holds-barred intellectual debate, he felt, could bring the antagonists closer to one another. As a judge he felt a responsibility to submit issues to a full and thorough exploration, so that reasoned solutions might emerge. He did not believe in consensus or compromise until an issue had been thoroughly articulated and explored, and he was not interested in dispatching business promptly or in joining a majority opinion if he felt that his position had not been fully aired.

Frankfurter's impulsiveness and effusiveness sometimes made him indiscreet.[34] By contrast, although Black rivaled Frankfurter in the strength of his views, he made an effort to be diplomatic in his collegial relations. When pressed, Black did not shrink from controversy, but he avoided open confrontation where possible. During his long career he became embroiled in several incidents of public concern, of which the *Jewel Ridge* disqualification dispute with Jackson was only one, and in most instances his response to attacks on him was a calculated silence.[35] He took pains to be gracious and civil to his fellow Justices. He valued charm and kindness in acquaintances; he did not like rancor and was not easily provoked. He was quick to make up his mind on issues, and disinclined to change it. He proceeded to the solution of problems in his own idiosyncratic fashion, seeking the counsel of few save his clerks and rarely inviting debate on propositions he had thoroughly considered. Self-contained, private, impatient with detail, largely indifferent to debate as an intellectual exercise, he was, in these respects, the antithesis of Frankfurter.

The differences between Black and Frankfurter ultimately went well beyond personal characteristics. When Frankfurter was appointed to the Court he had a well-developed theory of the judicial function, seeing himself as the heir of Holmes, Brandeis, Cardozo, and Stone, the architects of a passive model of appellate judging. Frankfurter's conception of his office, however, did not precisely match the conceptions of any of the others. He was less indifferent to the substantive content of legislation than Holmes, and his self-restraint was sometimes anguished, as in the flag-salute cases. He was not so much inclined as Brandeis to give civil liberties a higher priority than economic rights; he tried to be scrupulously indifferent to the character of the interest a statute invaded. He was less openly moralistic than Cardozo, although his conscience was sometimes shocked;[36] he continually attempted to subordinate his personal sympathies and animosities to the dictates of his office. Although he recognized with Stone that the Court inescapably made choices between competing values and was thus involved in American politics, he was slow to find necessity for Court intervention even when the recourse of a minority to the political process seemed to be unavailable. By drawing on the contributions of his four precursors and developing shadings of his own, Frankfurter created a consistent and wide-ranging philosophy of adjudication: his particular version of passivity, articulated in virtually unchanging fashion during his twenty-three years on the Court.

Black brought no philosophy of such breadth and depth with him to the Court in 1937. If he did evolve a pattern in his decisions throughout the 1930s and 1940s, it was that of support for values he believed in, even in the face of apparent historical or institutional limitations. Hence, he resisted judicial scrutiny of legislation that regulated business[37] or other property rights,[38] delegated broad power to administrative agencies to oversee the securities market[39] or labor negotiations,[40] and restricted the activities of minority groups in wartime.[41] He tolerated judicial scrutiny, however, where free speech was concerned,[42] although not universally.[43] He joined a 1937 opinion holding that all the Bill of Rights guaranties did not extend as against the states,[44] and he allowed state restraint-of-trade laws to prevent picketing.[45] On the other hand, he invalidated a city ordinance prohibiting announcements from sound trucks.[46] In sum, in his early career Black balanced interests, choosing one over another on an intuitive basis.

By the late 1940s, however, Black showed signs of abandoning this stance for one revealing a more abstract and integrated philosophy of adjudication, at least in the area of constitutional law. Outside that ambit he persisted in older habits; he had been the friend of maritime and industrial workers and small businessmen before coming on the Court, and he continued to be so as a Justice, manifesting his friendship through favorable statutory construction.[47] When interpretations of the Constitution were involved, however, Black developed his own comprehensive and internally consistent theory of judging. In practice it served as an alternative to the passive model, although it was predicated on the responsibilities and duties of judges rather than on their powers.

Black's theory was uniquely his own, the culmination of his self-education. It began with the assumption (reinforced by his reading) that human nature was unchanging, and thus that principles of conduct established by one era could serve as guides for the next. Just as Plutarch yielded insights into current social relations, so could the Constitution be a guide to contemporary affairs. But the Constitution was more than a source of conduct of Americans, it was *the* source. It had been elevated to a position of dominance by the very structure of American government; it was a blueprint for all time. Its words were explicit limitations on the power of governmental institutions and explicit grants of rights against the state. Judges had a responsibility to follow its commands, but no power to make glosses on them. They were servants of the document, but their power in that subservient capacity transcended that of all other branches, for constitutional imperatives prevailed over all other lawmaking efforts. The judiciary could do no more than apply the meaning of the Constitution, and certainly could do no less.

In the intellectual context of Black's first decade on the Court, this view could be seen as purposive. Its emphasis on the literal meaning of constitutional language precluded pouring substantive content into the due process clause; indeed, Black's view apparently rendered invalid any judicial "balancing" of rights in the interpretation of a clause in the Constitution. At the same time Black's position seemed to compel a broad-ranging, "absolutist"[48] reading of the Bill of Rights provisions that conferred rights against the government. Since many of these provisions codified support for values that Black had long believed in, calling them absolutes precluded their being "balanced" against a countervailing interest, such as national security or law enforcement. The chief analytical difficulty with this position was that the Bill of Rights was directed at the federal government, not at the states, and hence its scope was relatively narrow. Black solved this problem for himself when, in a dissent in *Adamson v. California* (1947),[49] he announced that the due process clause of the Fourteenth Amendment incorporated against the states all the Bill of Rights guaranties. His reading of the Fourteenth Amendment in *Adamson* was not a gloss, he argued, but a product of historical research.[50]

Difficulties remained for Black if his theory of constitutional interpretation was viewed as a purposive enterprise. He had gone on record as deploring judicial glosses on Constitutional language; hence he seemed committed to the notion that the Constitution gave protection to individuals only in those areas where its framers had explicitly granted protection. This meant that attempts by the Court to expand the ambit of constitutional language could be viewed as intolerable usurpations of power. Certain areas, especially, presented problems: activities, such as wiretapping and eavesdropping, that could be said to come within the meaning of a Bill of Rights clause ("search and seizure") but had not been explicitly considered by the framers; activities, such as sexual relations among married couples, whose regulation by governmental institutions seemed offensive but which had received no explicit protection from regulation in the Constitution; and activities, such as poll tax requirements, which were clearly tolerated by the framers but which over time came to be perceived as inimical to egalitarian traditions in American society. These areas were troublesome for Black because they invited conflict between the specific values he wanted to protect and the superordinate value of judicial fidelity to the literal meaning of the Constitution.

Black reconciled these difficulties through two devices that came teasingly close to contradicting each other. The first device was to adopt Marshall's view of the Constitution as a document whose core meaning was not to change with time, but whose language could be interpreted as expansively as it could endure. Protected "speech" could include types of speech (broadcasts from sound trucks)[51] that the Founding Fathers had never anticipated. The "literal" words of the Bill of Rights could be given a "liberal" judicial reading. By this technique the relevance of the past to the present was underscored; an eighteenth-century document could thrive in the mid-twentieth century. The phrases of the Constitution could be read in light of its over-all design. If a particular provision was intended to reflect the original importance of a social value such as liberty or equality, a judge could anticipate that the extension of that provision's coverage to unforeseen sets of circumstances would be consistent with the original purposes of the Founders.

Black's first reconciling device was intended to give judges a small amount of freedom from history; his second was to confine them within it. The words of the Constitution, he believed, were barriers to judicial initiative. Speech, whether libelous[52] or obscene,[53] was protected to the fullest, but conduct that served a communications function, such as picketing[54] or sitting-in,[55] was not. Only unreasonable searches and seizures were constitutionally prohibited, given the language of the Fourth Amendment,[56] but the Fifth Amendment prohibited absolutely compulsory self-incrimination.[57] No right of privacy was mentioned in the Constitution; hence judges could not create one.[58] Poll taxes as prerequisites for voting, however anti-egalitarian and therefore undesirable, were not forbidden by any constitutional language.[59] Where the scope of a provision's reach was not clear, judges ought to appeal to history, not to current social impulses. If those appeals produced inconvenient answers, such as the fact that corporations were not intended to be included in the Fourteenth Amendment's definition of "persons,"[60] judges ought not to ignore or discard them. Otherwise, the supremacy of the judiciary became a surrogate for the supremacy of the Constitution.

A delicate tension between the powers and limitations of the judicial branch of government thus characterized Black's philosophy of constitutional adjudication, as it had Marshall's. Judges were permitted to scrutinize the activities of other branches of government, and to intervene to modify or abrogate governmental action, precisely because they were not acting for themselves. The duty to follow the dictates of the Constitution had become a source of power. The determination of whether that duty compelled intervention remained a judicial one, but the standards used in the determination process were so clear and straightforward that glosses could barely creep in. Only in those instances in which the meaning of a word or phrase—"liberty" in the Fourteenth Amendment, for example—was not clear from the body of the Constitution itself, thus inviting a judicial foray into history, did substantive judging re-enter Black's calculus. On these occasions he used history purposefully, to promote values in which he believed.[61] On balance, however, he was prepared to make interpretations that did not reinforce his own views—he thought birth control laws deplorable, for example, but nonetheless could not find power to invalidate them—to maintain the consistency of his theory.

As with Frankfurter, the original motivation for Black's theory of constitutional adjudication was probably a response to concrete events. Frankfurter had appropriated the passive model of judging in the context of the invalidation by the Taft Court and the Four Horsemen of legislation he supported. From the polemical position that the due process clause "ought to go," he had moved to a theory of judging designed to strip the clause of substantive content. Similarly, Black had responded negatively to the Vinson Court's apparent indifference toward government intrusions on civil liberties,[62] but felt himself precluded from reincarnating substantive judging, through the due process clause or any other means, to support the rights he thought were being unduly circumscribed. His mature philosophy of constitutional adjudication provided a solution to this dilemma: judges could protect the rights of minorities because a literal and liberal reading of the Constitution compelled it.

Black's theory, in its developed form, thus provided a full-blown alternative to that of Frankfurter. It by-passed questions about the proper allocation of power among governing institutions by simply asserting that if the Constitution had declared rights against the government, the judiciary had an obligation to enforce them. A calculus based on language replaced one based on process. Instead of asking what interests were competing in an issue of constitutional adjudication, one asked whether the rights allegedly invaded by an act of government were enumerated in the Constitution as subject to its protection.

If one answered this question affirmatively, questions of process became irrelevant. Governing institutions had to accommodate themselves to the protection of these rights, whether the task was inefficient, whether interests of their own were invaded, and regardless of the offensivenesss of the persons whose rights were invaded. Frankfurter's stress on properly limiting the reach of the antidemocratic judiciary was a matter of complete indifference to Black, since he felt that the judiciary's reach never exceeded the Constitution's. Since the Constitution was in principle a democratic document and since judges were bound by its strictures, judicial tyranny was impossible if constitutional interpretation was properly carried out. Only if what Black caricatured as the "natural law-substantive due process-fundamental fairness" school of judging prevailed could the Supreme Court become a threat to democracy.

Black's theory had bowed to process liberalism by positing that the role of the judiciary in constitutional interpretation was essentially a constrained one. But its implications pointed in another direction. By compelling judicial action where the Constitution required it, and by permitting the judiciary to determine the ambit of the Constitution's reach, Black's theory invited a renaissance of substantive judging. Black himself confined judicial involvement strictly; another judge, less interested in Black's literalism and more in his mandate for compulsory judicial action, might find Black's theory useful in other respects. A judge with those inclinations joined the Court with Earl Warren's appointment as Chief Justice in 1953.

Little in Warren's background augured his eventual prominence. His family's financial security was dependent on the whims of the Southern Pacific Railroad, which laid off Warren's father without notice. He had been encouraged to pursue an education, but had not been conspicuous in his academic performance. When he graduated from the University of California Law School at Berkeley in 1914 he did not have a wide range of employment opportunities, and his first job in law practice eventually proved unbearable. At thirty-four he was a deputy District Attorney in Alameda County. His first state-wide office was not attained until he was forty-seven, when he was elected Attorney General of California. Fifteen years later he was Chief Justice of the United States, having been a successful Governor of California, a candidate for U.S. Vice President, and a serious Presidential contender. Reminiscing, his acquaintances attributed his success to intangibles, not to the power of his intellect, the charismatic qualities of his leadership, or the adroitness of his political maneuvering. He seemed to have succeeded by virtue of characteristics long thought incompatible with public office: integrity, nonpartisanship, honesty, humanity. He appeared to have acquired prominence and power simply by being a good man.[63] It all seemed too mythic to have actually occurred.

There was, of course, more to Warren than his surface affect. He had an extraordinary ability for making people like him; he could remember names, size up acquaintances, put others at ease. He had a strong ideological distaste for influence and corruption, and thought of himself as beholden to none, his morals untarnished. He inspired others, partly through an intuitive eloquence, partly through a certain domineering attitude. He was a genial companion but did not reveal his private thoughts; he held out his hand to the world, but retained his reserve. He tolerated no disloyalty or disingenuousness in an employee, and surrounded himself with persons whom he perceived as trustworthy and dedicated. He could be stubborn and self-righteous; he was not above trapping an opponent or summarily dismissing one who had affronted him. His grudges and animosities were longstanding; he remained outwardly unmoved by public abuse but bore in his mind the images of his attackers.

He had an intuitive sense of California politics, and his ability to avoid exposing himself on controversial issues was marked. He enjoyed power and knew that its use could serve to expand its scope; he liked executive action and disliked delegating responsibility. When pressed, he resorted to face-to-face confrontation, for here his blend of geniality, stubbornness, shrewdness, and decisiveness made him a formidable opponent. He came to the Court with no judicial experience, limited exposure to the world of ideas, no easily characterizable social attitudes, and no evidence of literary talent. But he did not come, as some thought he had, to be a ceremonial, conciliatory, middle-of-the-road Chief Justice. He came, rather, imbued with self-confidence in his ability to persuade others, possessed of a strong belief in the worth of active government, secure with power and unafraid of controversy, and eager, as in the past, to make his influence felt. The fact that initially he had no well-developed philosophy of judging was in his case of no consequence; he had instead a well-developed philosophy of governing.

The atmosphere on the Court that Warren joined in the summer of 1953 was marked by two significant realities: the estrangement of the mature philosophy of Frankfurter from that of Black, and the specter of the school segregation decisions, which had first reached the Court in 1952. Internal security and criminal procedure cases of the late 1940s and the 1950s had demonstrated the incompatibility of the Frankfurter and Black positions—federalism, limitations on the scope of judicial power, and countervailing values of law enforcement or national solidarity were simply irrelevant to Black when Bill of Rights freedoms were being infringed. Black had quarreled with Frankfurter over the general incorporation of Bill of Rights guaranties in the due process clause of the Fourteenth Amendment,[64] over specific examples of incorporation in the criminal procedure area,[65] and over the availability of First Amendment protection to advocates of Communist Party doctrine.[66] In two of these cases the opinions of one Justice were directed at the views of the other. Black deplored what he called in another case "substitution of this Court's day-to-day opinion of what . . . is fair and decent for . . . Bill of Rights guaranties";[67] Frankfurter, for his part, attempted to show that his adversary was engaging in "warped construction of specific provisions of the Bill of Rights."[68]

At the core of the dispute, insofar as it had become personalized, was a memory from the past. In Black's early years on the Court, Chief Justice Stone, concerned that Black's approach to judging was too politicized, had invited Frankfurter to advise Black discreetly on the historical limitations on the judiciary. Frankfurter, never one to resist an opportunity to educate others, had complied.[69] One can imagine the effect on Black, who valued his independence, had a full measure of pride, and intended to work out his jurisprudential views for himself. By the 1950s Black had solidified his stance and become interested in converting others.[70] In his mind he had moved beyond Frankfurter's intricacies to see the mandate of the Constitution in sharp relief. He invited others to share his vision, while Frankfurter continued his own efforts at conversion. The natural beneficiary of this joint wisdom was Warren, affable and seemingly open-minded, inexperienced in the fine points of Constitutional interpretation, and potentially malleable.

The school segregation cases presented this jurisprudential controversy in terms Warren could appreciate. A special ingredient of Frankfurter's jurisprudence was cautious judicial participation in politically sensitive areas. When the Court first considered re-examining the separate-but-equal principle of *Plessy v. Ferguson*[71] in the context of public schools, Frankfurter sought to avoid a final decision; Black voted with Douglas, Burton, and Minton to overrule *Plessy*.[72] The case, *Brown v. Board of Education*, was not decided that term;

it was set down for reargument during the following term. Vinson's death and Warren's appointment in the summer of 1953 meant a new composition for the Court and the possibility of a different result in the *Brown* case. Warren was hence in a position of particular significance in the reconsideration of *Brown*. Not only was he a new member with unknown views, he was also a national politician with his fingers allegedly on the pulse of American society.

The critical political question in *Brown* was not whether the system of separate educational facilities should prevail—for all signs pointed to increasing Court animosity toward artifacts of racial segregation, especially in the area of schools.[73] The question rather was whether an adequate rationale for reversing *Plessy v. Ferguson* could be found so that the South would comply with the decision. Over this issue the Black and Frankfurter views seemed in potential conflict. For the Court to find that a system of segregated schools violated the equal protection clause, a finding was necessary that the separate sets of schools were not "equal" in fact. This involved an empirical inquiry by the Court into local "political" conditions, the very sort of practice that Frankfurter's jurisprudence cautioned against. That inquiry was justified, however, if one read, with Black, the equal protection clause as an inexorable mandate. The Constitution insisted that laws equalize educational opportunities, and the judiciary was bound to implement that principle by ascertaining whether or not it had been subverted in a given context.

The rationale for overruling *Plessy* was thus apparent: separate-but-equal schools violated the equal protection clause if they did not in fact provide equal educational opportunities. But that rationale was very broad and abstract, rested on the Court's taking notice of empirical data, and made the Court a watchguard of local conditions. Nonetheless, Warren endorsed the rationale and secured unanimity for it. Frankfurter, ultimately no less sensitive to racial discrimination than any other Justice on the Warren Court, joined the opinion in *Brown*. But he retained his concern about the political wisdom of the decision, and the phrase "all deliberate speed"—the standard for compliance with *Brown*—was his suggestion.

The *Brown* decision was a symbolic event in shaping Warren's approach to his office. If he came to the Court with a history of less than total sympathy with the interests of racial minorities,[74] he unburdened himself of that with *Brown*. His longstanding beliefs that government should be responsive to the people at large, not to special interests, was transposed into an image of an energetic court protecting the rights of all Americans, especially the downtrodden and disadvantaged. His moral indignation over corruption and dishonesty metamorphosed into an undeviating interest in the abstractions of fairness and justice, and a conception of law as inexorably linked with ethics. He retained the impatience with legislative insensitivity or inactivity that had surfaced during his gubernatorial years in California, substituting judicial action for executive action in instances in which a legislature had been indifferent or inimical to human concerns.

Warren extended the *Brown* principle of judicial intervention to support the rights of minorities in numerous other areas of American life, coming to view that extension as a mission to help the Constitution reach the people. In the course of this excursion he was continually touched by the same impulse of patriotic duty, moral outrage, pride, and compassion that had moved him in *Brown*. He was willing to face controversy and suffer abuse for the rightness of his cause; he reached beyond the academic critics of his methods to the public beneficiaries of his acts.

Like that of Black, Warren's jurisprudence gained momentum with time. If Black's overriding principle of adjudication was fidelity to his conception of the Constitution, Warren's was fidelity to his interpretation of the rights inherent in American citizenship. Warren started tentatively, his early decisions constraining such rights as much as they affirmed them.[75] After the two *Brown* cases he began to take a more expansive view. Fishing expeditions by the House Un-American Activities Committee into the private lives of persons suspected of having Communist sympathies outraged him, and he initiated what was to become a persistent practice of issuing ringing affirmations of individual freedoms and scathing condemnations of the activities of those who would infringe them.[76] Buoyed by a change in membership of the Court in the early 1960s, he expanded his horizons, encouraging judicial reform of legislative apportionment, criminal procedure, Church-State relations, antitrust laws, labor relations, and the boundaries between the federal government and the states.

Although Warren's positions dovetailed with those of Black in many areas, the views of the two Justices ultimately diverged. Black's theory allowed for some extensions of the literal commands of the Constitution, but it was essentially based on constraint. The judge could do no more than the Constitution permitted, whether he wanted to or not. Warren did not feel similarly confined. He, too, interpreted his role as that of enforcing the Constitution's mandates, but he was also prepared to enforce mandates that appeared not from a reading of the constitutional text but from analogy to it. He analogized the constitutional requirement of procedural safeguards in criminal cases to disputes between private parties,[77] and he determined that the Fifth Amendment empowered the Court to write precise codes of conduct for police in their relations with criminal suspects.[78] On occasion he also declined to confer the full protection of the Constitution on persons whose conduct outraged him, such as panderers of obscene literature[79] or gamblers.[80]

Pressed to its logical outcome, Warren's jurisprudence appeared to make the humanity and integrity of judges themselves the only check on judicial power. It de-emphasized the complexity of the process of judging and emphasized the substantive importance of values at stake in a case. Over and over again Warren stressed that the Constitution embraced the small and helpless, the disfranchised, disadvantaged, and discriminated-against. His perspective was openly humanitarian and just as openly antiprofessional, almost contemptuous of the niceties of a legal argument when fundamental American beliefs called out to be affirmed.

At the high tide of its momentum in behalf of citizenship rights, and especially in the person of its Chief Justice, the Warren Court dramatically portrayed the contrasts between process and substantive liberalism. Having once invaded an area hitherto felt to be inappropriate for judicial appraisal, the Court seemed to gain confidence, even in the face of adversity, and invaded another. In some areas, such as civil rights, it seemed in a race with Congress to outlaw notorious practices.[81] Confident of the rightness of its governing principles, it minimized or discounted analytical barriers. In the process it revealed itself as having a distinctly ideological character.

With this revelation the Warren Court majority became exposed to the ancient attack that they were simply using their office to propound their own social views. But the attack in this instance had a different slant from that made on the Four Horsemen in the 1930s. The Warren Court reforms had run with the tide of ideas in postwar America rather than against it; contemporary definitions of equality, liberty, fairness, and justice were difficult values to oppose. Hence critics of the Warren Court majority argued that the difficulty with its premises was not that they were misguided but that they were simplistic. The Court's code words, the argument ran, concealed complexities and ambiguities, thereby endangering delicate balances in the process of living and governing in modern America.

John Harlan came to personify this criticism of the Warren Court majority. In Harlan's hand the two-pronged character of the criticism became clear. It was based both on the methodological canons of process liberalism and on a substantive quarrel with the majority's value orientation. Harlan's approach did not precisely resemble that of Frankfurter, a justice to whom Harlan had ascribed "a fierce determination to keep his own ideologies and predilections out of the decision of cases."[82] Harlan did not always make a similar effort. His ideological stance, however, was a counter-stance, not so much affirming particular values as suggesting that the momentum of Warren Court egalitarianism was trampling on interests and ignoring attitudes deserving of respect. Harlan's position, in its maturity, represented a blending of standard caveats about the unrestrained exercise of judicial power that had characterized one strand of twentieth-century jurisprudence since Holmes, and his own personal suspicions of substantive liberalism. He added another dimension to the inner controversies of the Warren Court: he asked not only whether a given innovative result had been reached by proper judicial methods but also whether it was sound philosophically. His views, especially when contrasted with those of Warren, signified the eventual incompatibility of the professionalist and humanitarian impulses of modern liberalism.

The substantive dimension of Harlan's jurisprudence was shaped by his instinctive social inclinations and by the ideological atmosphere of the Warren Court. If a populist tinge marked the Warren Court's consciousness, so that legal issues came to be perceived as struggles between "haves" and "have nots" or between vested interests and the common man, then Harlan's orientation offered a stark contrast. He had been born to wealth and status, educated at Princeton and Oxford, and assimilated into the upper strata of the New York bar. If the Warren Court showed an increasing sympathy for the rights of persons accused of crimes, Harlan had seen the other side of law enforcement, serving under Emory Buckner in the U.S. Attorney's office in the 1920s and as General Counsel to the New York State Crime Commission in the 1950s. If the Warren Court could be said to be suspicious of big business, Harlan had given longstanding counsel to members of the Dupont family.[83] If the symbolic journey of certain Warren Court Justices from the environments of their youth to Washington had been filled with reminders of poverty and oppression, Harlan's had encompassed the accustomed way-stations of a respected member of an intellectual and social elite. In contrast to the other influential Warren Court Justices, Harlan could not be said to have experienced the stings of arbitrary injustice, whether based on ethnic prejudice or on the lack of family income.

Harlan's social background was not the sole determinant of his judicial vision, but it may have made him less passionate about those inequities in American life whose very presence outraged some of his fellow Justices. Thus, when the Warren Court majority embarked on its reform crusades, Harlan may have been less inclined to ignore analytical obstacles because his sympathies were enlisted less in the cause. In this vein, Harlan's stance could fairly be identified as conservative. American civilization, despite its egalitarian premises, had been fraught from its origin with social and economic inequalities and had not reflected participatory democracy in its governing institutions. The momentum of the Warren Court was toward a re-examination of practices that deviated from those egalitarian ideals; in resisting this momentum Harlan was allying himself with a longstanding tradition of resistance to mass equality. He was conservative, in the context of the Warren Court, to the extent that he embraced its humanitarian and egalitarian goals less regularly and less sweepingly than the majority.

If Harlan began his examination of the social problems coming before the Warren Court with such inclinations, he did not end the inquiry with them. Instead he created an approach that harmonized Frankfurterian assumptions about the role of the judiciary with a substantive critique of what he called "unrestrained egalitarianism."[84] Perhaps the most representative example of his approach was in his linking of the framers' theory of federalism to judicial self-restraint. That linkage required some redefinition of terms. The theory of federalism, in Marshall's day, emphasized national as opposed to state power, and Marshall had used it to justify active judicial scrutiny of the actions of state government. Marshall's interpretation resembled that of the Warren Court majority, envisioning for the national government a broad mandate that was to be implemented by the federal judiciary. The principal difference between the Marshall Court's and the Warren Court's theory of federalism was in the effects: the former served to protect private rights from any sort of governmental control, the latter, to simulate affirmative governmental action.

Harlan's federalism more closely resembled that of Holmes, Brandeis, and other architects of the passive model of judging, in that it stressed balances between state and federal sovereignties and called for judicial tolerance of experimental legislation by the states. This was, of course, the reverse of Marshall's interpretation. Judges were to suffer state regulation of private enterprise rather than actively oppose it. Federalism stood not for the primacy of national power but for emphasis on the two-tiered character of American government. In the early years of the twentieth century this version of federalism insulated state experimental legislation in economic areas; in the Warren Court years an emphasis on distinctions between state and federal government attempted to serve a different purpose, insulating the states from the increasingly stringent checks on governmental activity demanded by the Warren Court's expansive reading of the Bill of Rights.

Thus the concept of federalism, which Marshall had identified with plenary national power, Taney with concurrent sovereignty, Holmes, Brandeis, and Frankfurter with state experimental legislation, and Jackson with expanded national regulation of the economy, came to serve yet another purpose for Harlan: a justification for the preservation of values infringed by bold judicial definitions of citizens' rights. One such value was law enforcement: the application of a literalist view of Bill of Rights protections against the states hampered indigenous state efforts to prevent crime and violence. Another was grass-roots democracy: rigid mandates affecting the representativeness of local government stifled experiments in governmental organization. Still another value (and linked to the second) was that of allowing the states to function as laboratories for social planning. A fourth was the privacy and autonomy of the individual citizen, federalism serving as a barrier between such citizens and the continually expanding federal bureaucracy of postwar America by reducing units of administration and helping to keep government entirely removed from a range of private affairs. By linking federalism to these values, Harlan sought to demonstrate that the egalitarian momentum of the Warren Court was not a necessary good; that humanitarian gestures sometimes trespassed on individual rights.

Superimposed on the values that Harlan identified with federalism were all the canons of Process Jurisprudence: judicial detachment and disinterestedness;

a limited lawmaking role for the elitist judiciary; a search for "principled adjudication," which for Harlan meant an adequately broad rationale in an opinion, to serve as a clear guide in deciding future cases; a presumption in favor of adherence to precedent so as to promote clarity and stability in the law, even when a prior decision was found to be distasteful; emphasis, in opinion writing, on careful exposition of the facts, marshaling of the arguments on both sides, and full-blown statement of reasons for a decision; the fostering of harmony between lawmaking institutions by deference to the actions of administrative agencies and legislatures wherever possible; and self-conscious, methodical, and articulate balancing of competing social values in circumstances where the Constitution required such weighing. In all these respects Harlan resembled Frankfurter, but his angle of vision was somewhat different. For Frankfurter these tenets defined his role. His paramount goal as a judge was adherence to them rather than to the promotion of any set of social values. Harlan asked what results this adherence tended to produce and noted that in the context of the Warren Court it often produced resistance to judge-initiated reforms. On occasion, Harlan acknowledged that he was as comfortable with the policy implications of his stance as he was with its methodological underpinnings; in a rare instance he abandoned process liberalism altogether in order to promote substantive values; at other times, however, he complained that the dictates of process liberalism prevented him from reaching humanitarian results. In short, Harlan recognized the substantive elements of his judicial calculus and, in a small number of contexts, gave them free play.

III

Such, in rough outline, were the views of the four figures who stood out most prominently in the mosaic of the Warren Court. They can be seen as forming symbolic confrontations: Frankfurter's consummate process liberalism against Black's highly individualized blend of formalized restraint and active championing of individual freedoms; Warren's energetic substantive liberalism—in some respects a logical extension of Black's views—against Harlan's version of process liberalism, in which substantive conservative values were occasionally affirmed. The confrontations were more abstract than concrete, since heated jurisprudential debates, even among the four, were exceptional in the ordinary course of the Court's judicial business. Tendencies were nonetheless revealed in individual decisions, and it was possible to discern phases in the Court's history. In the first phase, from Warren's appointment to Frankfurter's retirement, process and substantive liberalism marked out an uneasy coexistence, their ultimate incompatibility not entirely clear. In the second phase, from Frankfurter's departure in 1962 to Warren's retirement in 1969, substantive liberalism continually gathered momentum to the point where differences between the views of Warren and Black became strikingly apparent, and process liberalism, in Harlan's hands, was seen as compatible with substantive conservatism.

Three cases serve to illustrate the first phase: *Trop v. Dulles*,[85] *Poe v. Ullman*,[86] and *Baker v. Carr*.[87] *Trop v. Dulles* was decided in the context of anti-Communist hysteria in the 1950s, which placed high priority on the values of patriotism and national solidarity. In the name of those concerns an ample degree of government scrutiny of the lives and careers of citizens had been tolerated, in the Supreme Court as well as elsewhere. In a 1954 case, for example, the Court, in a 6–3 decision, allowed New York State to suspend the medical license of a physician who declined to produce records of an anti-Fascist organization to which he belonged.[88] Warren had joined the majority in that instance, but by 1958, when *Trop v. Dulles* came down, he had become indignant at inquisitorial or repressive practices in the name of loyalty or national security.[89] The *Trop* case was for him another such example.

Trop and a companion case, *Perez v. Brownell*,[90] tested the constitutionality of sections of the Nationality Act (1940), which provided for loss of American citizenship in specified instances. In *Perez* a citizen had voted in a Mexican election; in *Trop* another citizen had deserted the Army in wartime. Both had been expatriated as a consequence. The Court split on the two cases, finding that Congress, pursuant to its implied power to regulate foreign affairs, had authority to strip away citizenship as a consequence of voting in a foreign election, but that it had no authority to expatriate for desertion. Frankfurter wrote the majority opinion in *Perez* and dissented in *Trop;* Warren dissented in *Perez* and wrote for a plurality in *Trop;* Black voted in each case with Warren, Harlan in each case with Frankfurter. *Trop* was the more significant case of the two for the breadth of Warren's opinion and the controversy it engendered.

Warren had, in his *Perez* dissent, indicated that he was not prepared to tolerate any attempts on the part of the federal government to impose loss of citizenship. He maintained that citizenship was "man's basic right," the "right to have rights," and that it was "not subject to the general powers of the government."[91] Citizenship, in his view, could be only voluntarily relinquished. The Act of 1940 had, he believed, merely attempted to describe certain acts—such as voting in a foreign election—that might give rise to the inference that a person had voluntarily relinquished his citizenship. But voting could not alone create the inference; the voting would have to be "at the behest of a foreign government to advance its territorial interests."[92] This had not been shown in *Perez* and was not actually required by the Act; hence the Act was overbroad and defective as applied to the citizen in *Perez*. For Warren the issue was crystal clear: the Court had an "imperative . . . duty" to protect "the fundamental rights" of American citizens under the Constitution.[93] By conferring citizenship on all persons residing in the United States, the Fourteenth Amendment had raised an absolute bar to governmental efforts to take away that citizenship; and the Court was compelled to enforce that bar.

The difficulty with Warren's position, in practical terms, was that only he, Douglas, and Black accepted it in its pure form. The other six Justices conceded a power, albeit limited, in Congress to expatriate under certain circumstances. The question, then, was whether desertion, the "voluntary" act in *Trop*, was sufficiently different from voting in a foreign election to preclude Congressional exercise of its authority to expatriate. Justice Whitaker, who had questioned the scope of the expatriation power in *Perez*, and Justice Brennan decided that it was, producing five votes for disallowing expatriation. Warren then sought to articulate a rationale for the decision.

Warren's opinion was characteristic of his approach. He began with an impassioned statement of what he believed to be the controlling principle in the case; the statement, taken in context, was entirely dictum. Citizenship, he declared, was "not subject to the general powers of the National Government," and therefore could "not be divested in the exercise of those powers."[94] The deprivation of citizenship was "not a weapon that the Government may use to express its displeasure at a citizen's conduct, however reprehensible that conduct may be." On "this ground alone,"[95] Warren asserted, *Trop* should be decided; but for that proposition he had only three votes.

Next, Warren confronted the critical challenge that his opinion faced—that of stating "why the action taken in [*Trop*] exceeds constitutional limits, even under the majority's decision in *Perez*."[96] Here two principal strategies were available to him, and his choice between them was revealing. One strategy was to attempt to distinguish (as Justice Brennan was to do in his concurrence) between rational governmental exercise of the power to regulate foreign affairs (which had occurred in *Perez*) and the attempted exercise of power in *Trop*. Expatriation in *Trop* was concededly based on the war power and not on the power to regulate foreign affairs. It was intended to maintain discipline in the armed forces by deterring desertion. In Brennan's view other such deterrents existed, whereas expatriation bore "only a slight or tenuous relation"[97] to the war power. Expatriation being an extraordinarily harsh remedy for desertion, and other remedies existing, it was therefore not a means "reasonably calculated to achieve [the] legitimate end" of waging war.[98] The section of the Nationality Act providing for expatriation as a consequence of desertion therefore offended the Fifth Amendment.

Warren did not choose this option, with its emphasis on technical niceties. Rather he defined the constitutional question raised by the desertion provision as being "whether or not denationalization may be inflicted as a punishment."[99] To support his position he had to show that expatriation of American citizens was different from deportation of foreign nationals, held by the Supreme Court not to constitute "punishment";[100] that the purpose of expatriation was to punish rather than merely "to prescribe rules governing the proper performance of military obligations";[101] and that expatriation for desertion was a punishment that violated the Constitution. This he did in the most sweeping and summary fashion. The deportation of aliens, he said, was incident to the government's sovereign power to regulate the naturalization of foreigners; no such sovereign power over its citizens existed, since the people were sovereign. The provision was penal rather than regulatory in that it "prescribe[d] the consequences that will befall one" who failed to abide by military regulations; thus the purpose of "taking away citizenship from a convicted deserter" was "simply to punish him."[102] The question therefore became whether this punishment was "cruel and unusual" within the meaning of the Eighth Amendment.

Here Warren faced his greatest analytical difficulty. The Court was then conceding that the death penalty was not cruel and unusual punishment: the Rosenbergs had been executed only five years previously. How was denationalization of a citizen a fate crueler than death? It was so, Warren maintained, because it involved "the total destruction of the individual's status in organized society"; it was "more primitive than torture," because it destroyed "for the individual the political existence that was centuries in the development."[103] For these and other reasons denationalization was "offensive to cardinal principles for which this Constitution stands." The Court's role in Constitutional cases of this type, Warren maintained, was clear. The meaning of the Eighth Amendment could change with "the evolving standards of decency that mark the progress of a maturing society."[104]

An interesting aspect of Warren's opinion in *Trop v. Dulles* was the extent to which it showed the influence of Black while at the same time revealing differences in focus between the two Justices. Warren's view of constitutional adjudication in *Trop* was Blackian in its assertion of the absolute primary of an enumerated constitutional right, its lack of sufferance for balancing that right against countervailing values such as national security, its impatience with fine statutory distinctions in the light of constitutional imperatives, and its posture for the judiciary of enforcing the mandates of the Bill of Rights. But there was no appeal to history. The deportation precedents were summarily dismissed, the death penalty analogy placed "to one side," the legislative history of the Nationality Act characterized as "equivocal." The emphasis was rather on the "realities" of the case. Expatriation for desertion was a punishment, not a regulation, because it occurred after the act of desertion itself; it was a "cruel" punishment because all the nations of the civilized world deplored and decried the condition of statelessness. It was, in short, a violation of the Constitution because any decent-minded, humane judge could read the Constitution and see that it was.

This judicial interest in "decency" and "progress"—at least in the type of situation raised by *Trop*—was regarded by Frankfurter as outside the scope of the Court's prerogatives. He began the relevant portions of his dissent in *Trop* with some characteristic admonitions. "Judicial power . . . must be on guard against encroaching beyond its proper bounds." Judging required "rigorous observance of the difference between limits of power and wise exercise of power." It was "not the business of the Court to pronounce policy" or to "giv[e] effect to its own notions of what is wise and politic." The Constitution had "not authorized the judges to sit in judgment on the wisdom of what Congress and the Executive branch do."[105] These caveats set the stage for an opinion deferential to the power and judgment of Congress. Congress could "deal severely with the problem of desertion from the armed forces" under its war powers; the rights and privileges of citizenship imposed correlative obligations, such as compulsory military service; there was a "rational nexus" between refusal to serve in the armed forces and Congressional withdrawal of citizenship.[106]

Warming to his task, Frankfurter quarreled with Warren's "punishment" theory of the cases. "Simply because denationalization was attacked by Congress as a consequence of conduct that it had elsewhere made unlawful," he argued, "it does not follow that denationalization is a 'punishment.' "[107] Nothing on the face of the Nationality Act or in its legislative history supported that inference. And "to insist that denationalization is 'cruel and unusual' punishment" was "to stretch that concept beyond the breaking point." Constitutional "dialectic" that "seriously urged that loss of citizenship is a fate worse than death" was "empty of reason."[108] Nor was Warren's belief that the condition of statelessness was universally deplored sound, since "many civilized nations" had imposed loss of citizenship for "indulgence in designated prohibited activities."[109] Nor were denationalized citizens necessarily subject to inhumane treatment; and in America aliens enjoyed "very substantial rights and privileges" under the Constitution. In short, "the awesome power of this Court to invalidate [Congressional] legislation" needed to be "exercised with the utmost restraint";[110] and this was a case for deference.

Two interpretations of patriotism and two approaches to constitutional adjudication clashed in *Trop*. Warren's patriotism identified American citizenship with the possession of rights against the government, the supreme right being to possess and retain citizenship status. Frankfurter's no less intense patriotism identified citizenship with obligations such as service to one's country in a time when its existence was being threatened. Warren's conviction that the right to be an American citizen was beyond the power of any government official to curtail had led him to a vigorous scrutiny of Congress and a free-wheeling use of statutory and constitutional language in support of that conviction. Frankfurter's approach had begun with an orientation toward the cautious use of judicial power rather than the impassioned vindication of human rights, and ended with a series of arguments intended to justify judicial deference to Congress in the circumstances of *Trop*. Giving substantive content to citizenship had been Warren's primary purpose; maintaining fidelity to the delicate process of constitutional adjudication had been Frankfurter's.

Harlan had silently joined Frankfurter in *Trop v. Dulles*, but *Poe v. Ullman* showed that his numerous pairings with Frankfurter concealed differences in approach. *Poe v. Ullman* attempted to test the constitutionality of a Connecticut statute prohibiting the use of contraceptive devices by married couples, even when conception could be shown to constitute a potential threat to the health or life of the woman. The issues involved were troublesome, analytically as well as politically. The statute had been passed under a police-powers rationale, that the Connecticut legislature was protecting the morals of its citizens by preventing them from interfering with the creation of human life. It was being challenged as a violation of the Fourteenth Amendment, but no clear violation of a constitutional "liberty" was apparent. The Bill of Rights said nothing about a right to bear children under the terms one wished, or a right not to bear children at all. The legislation, however, was offensive, in that it purported to regulate the private lives of married persons with regard to matters that hardly seemed the concern of government. Its enforcement raised a series of constitutional problems, since one could not easily imagine state officials making random checks in the homes of Connecticut residents to insure that contraceptives were not being used in sexual relations. Affirmance of the statute put the Court on the side of public censorship of highly private affairs; invalidation forced it to find an adequate constitutional rationale and involved it in religious controversy.

These factors suggested that the Court might be well advised not to decide the merits of the case, especially since attitudes toward the use of birth control devices were in a state of flux in the early 1960s, when *Poe v. Ullman* was argued. A way to avoid decision existed: the Connecticut statute had been enforced only once in eighty years, to compel closing of public clinics dispensing birth-control information.[111] This suggested that the persons claiming that the statute infringed their interests were in no actual peril of being prosecuted under it. Primarily on this basis a majority of the Court dismissed the case for failure to present a substantial controversy justifying the immediate adjudication of a constitutional issue. Frankfurter wrote for a plurality, which included Warren. Black dissented, stating only that he believed that the constitutional questions should be reached and decided. Harlan wrote a massive dissent in which he took issue with Frankfurter on the question of justiciability and then went on to find the statute unconstitutional as applied to married persons.

The nub of the debate centered on Frankfurter and Harlan, but the positions of Black and of Warren were not devoid of interest. Black had little patience with the web of doctrines used to avoid a full-blown decision of a constitutional issue: standing, mootness, ripeness, the "political question" doctrine, the "case and controversy" requirement, and other "passive" devices.[112] He was prepared to decide constitutional cases whenever possible, since his theory of constitutional adjudication provided him with clear and enduring solutions. Warren, often eager for an opportunity to affirm a constitutional right, was not so in *Poe v. Ullman*. He believed in government censorship of morals, as other decisions indicated; he believed also in the privacy of married life. Later he was to find the same Connecticut statute unconstitutional (and Black was to vote to sustain it).[113] But in 1961 Warren was not prepared to declare himself on the issues in *Poe v. Ullman*, and he welcomed Frankfurter's disposition.

Justiciability was an important ingredient in Frankfurter's version of process liberalism. Since the Court was compelled to write thorough, analytically sound, carefully crafted opinions, and since the process of constitutional adjudication required a delicate balancing of competing values and reasoned debate of the relevant issues, the precious time of Justices should not be wasted on trivial or abstract controversies. Frankfurter tirelessly campaigned to limit the Court's jurisdiction to a relatively few selected cases so that it could do full justice to those it decided, thereby marking out the areas of its competence with precision and giving clear guidance to the bar and the lower courts. That effort largely failing, he resorted to passive devices, which he identified with "the historically defined, limited nature and function of courts" and "the fundamental federal and tripartite character of our National Government,"[114] to keep the Court from "entertain[ing] constitutional questions in advance of the strictest necessity."[115]

In his relatively brief plurality opinion in *Poe v. Ullman*, Frankfurter simply called attention to the absence of enforcement of the birth control statute in Connecticut and then strung together previous cases denying justiciability on a variety of grounds. The only ground that seemed truly germane to the case at hand was that Connecticut had not enforced the statute, thus "depriv[ing] these controversies of the immediacy which is an indispensable condition of constitutional adjudication."[116] Of the appellants in *Poe*, the two married women were not sufficiently adversely affected by the statute to merit adjudication of their claims, and the third, a doctor who had given them birth control information, had no "realistic fear of prosecution."[117]

Harlan disagreed with Frankfurter's sense of the impact of the statute. He maintained that the plurality opinion was grounded essentially on the fact that on only one occasion in more than seventy-five years had the statute been used as a basis of prosecution, and that the other grounds asserted for limited justiciability were merely window dressing. He then argued that the one prosecution could be seen as a major deterrent to noncompliance with the statute, since the prosecutor had said in the context of that case that "any person, whether a physician or layman, who violated [the statute] must be expected to be prosecuted and punished in accordance with the literal provisions of the law."[118] The "very purpose" of that prosecution, he asserted, "was to change defiance into compliance," and the purpose "may have been successful."[119] Indeed, Harlan believed, "all that stands between [the complaining parties in *Poe*] and jail is the legally unfettered whim of the prosecutor."[120] The threat of prosecution tended to "discourage the exercise of the liberties of these appellants, caused by reluctance to submit their freedoms from prosecution . . . to the discretion of the Connecticut prosecuting authorities."[121] The deleterious effect of the statute was not "chimerical,"[122] but was "present and very real";[123] hence, the Court ought to take jurisdiction and decide the merits of the case.

Implicit in Harlan's justiciability argument was his feeling that the constitutional rights allegedly infringed in *Poe* were substantial and deserving of judicial protection. This was, he said, "the core of [his] disagreement with [the Court's] disposition"[124] of the case. Harlan's deviation from Frankfurter revealed that the canons of process liberalism, although important for Harlan, were not always ends in themselves. Where their use served as a counterweight to the affirmance of values he cared deeply about, he was occasionally prepared to abandon them. In these rare instances he was prepared to accept a role for judges as glossators of constitutional language that included giving substantive content to clauses such as the due-process clause of the Fourteenth Amendment. His opinion in *Poe v. Ullman* made ingenious use of this glossing power.

The first step in Harlan's discussion of the constitutionality of the statute challenged in *Poe* was to set forth a governing "framework of Constitutional principles" in which his reading of judicial powers and responsibility under the due process clause was made explicit. The standard for judicial review of state legislation under the clause was normally whether the legislative action could be said to have a rational basis, but where "fundamental" liberties were involved, the standard was stricter, embracing the means of implementing the legislation as well as its underlying purposes. In determining whether a legislative act had violated the due process clause, the judiciary did not limit the meaning of the clause to "a guarantee of procedural fairness,"[125] nor did it define "due process" as embodying only those specific restraints on the government enumerated prior to the passage of the Fourteenth Amendment. Due process was "a discrete concept which subsists as an independent guaranty of liberty . . . more general and inclusive than the specific provisions" of the Bill of Rights.[126] The judiciary should give a general meaning to the clause, remaining attentive to "the balance which our Nation . . . has struck between . . . liberty and the demands of organized society."[127] The term "liberty" in the due process clause was "a rational continuum" that embraced "a freedom from all substantial arbitrary impositions and purposeless restraints."[128]

The judicial obligation in *Poe v. Ullman* was therefore to weigh the substantive implications of the due process clause against the social purposes served by the implementation of the Connecticut statute. In this balance, two inquiries were essential: whether the due process clause, given its expanded meaning, embraced the conduct that Connecticut sought to regulate—namely, the use of artificial contraceptives by married couples; and whether, if that question was answered affirmatively, the Connecticut statute constituted, in its operation, a justifiable use of state police powers.

Defining the judicial task in these terms allowed Harlan to proceed to the next crucial step in his opinion, defining "liberty" in the due process clause to include the use of contraceptive devices by married couples. To create this definition he analogized from other constitutional provisions, and conceded that his finding did not rest on any explicit language in the Constitution. The "liberty" offended by the statute was "the privacy of the home in its most basic sense,"[129] a condition protected implicitly by the Third Amendment, prohibiting soldiers from being quartered in homes, and by the Fourth Amendment, forbidding unreasonable searches and seizures. From these provisions Harlan drew the meaning that the Constitution, as interpreted by the Court, protected "the privacy of the home against all unreasonable intrusions of whatever character."[130]

But could not the State of Connecticut nonetheless seek to insure the "moral soundness" of its citizens? Was not a decision by the state legislature to prevent Connecticut citizens from interfering with the process of human birth grounded on a moral choice that could be rationally justified, and thus constitutionally permissible, even though it infringed on individual rights? Here Harlan distinguished between the soundness of the moral judgment made in the statute (which judgment he conceded might withstand scutiny) and the choice of means used to implement that judgment. Connecticut, he maintained, was "asserting the right to enforce its moral judgment by intruding upon the most intimate details of the marital relation with the full power of the criminal law."[131] It had determined that it could search houses for evidence of the use of contraceptives, seize contraceptives as evidence, and require married couples "to render account before a criminal tribunal of their uses" of the intimacy of their marriage.[132] In making this judgment it had exceeded the limits "to which a legislatively represented majority may conduct . . . experiments at the expense of [individual] dignity."[133] The anti-contraceptive legislation, as applied to married persons, had thus violated the Fourteenth Amendment's due-process clause.

Harlan's dissent in *Poe v. Ullman* was remarkable in its deviation from the passive model of judging that process liberalism required. It subjected a state statute to a more rigorous than normal scrutiny merely by asserting that the rights offended by the statute were "fundamental," and it based that fundamentality not on any explicit language in the Constitution, but on judicial glosses and analogies. It openly gave substantive content to the due-process clause, and created a new area of constitutional law by defining a right, privacy, that had not previously been given constitutional protection. It reflected a distaste for legislative intrusion into "intimate details of the marital relation," permissible under the statute, and built that distaste into its decision-making calculus. It was, in short, an activist, value-oriented, free-wheeling piece of judicial lawmaking, despite its articulated support for Frankfurter's belief that "the vague contours of the Due Process Clause do not leave judges at large [to] draw on our merely personal and private notions."[134]

Poe v. Ullman was perhaps the sharpest example of the different points of emphasis in Frankfurter and Harlan. On many other occasions their views converged to such an extent that only subtle differences could be perceived. *Baker v. Carr*, in this sense, was a case more representative of the work of the

Warren Court in its first phase. Warren and Black jointly supported an expansive judicial reading of constitutional language with the aim of protecting the rights of a disadvantaged minority, whereas Frankfurter and Harlan resisted that reading and the theory of constitutional adjudication that had produced it. On examination, Frankfurter's and Harlan's perspectives in *Baker v. Carr* differed in degree, but were sufficiently similar to suggest that Harlan would perpetuate many Frankfurterian tenets of judicial performance after the latter's retirement (shortly after *Baker v. Carr* in 1962).

The familiar facts of *Baker v. Carr* need only brief exposition here. The 1950s witnessed patterns of population growth and diffusion that altered the shape and character of urban centers. Inner cities had become more ethnically and racially heterogeneous; discrete homogeneous suburbs had surrounded the inner city; the population of rural areas had declined. Those patterns often produced discernible differences in voting behavior between inner cities, suburbs, and rural areas. Existing state statutes creating voting districts on a geographical basis often did not reflect the new patterns, with the consequence that rural areas with a small population and urban or suburban areas with a huge population were treated as essentially equivalent for the purpose of electing state officials. The interaction of the existing statutes with the new demographic patterns resulted in a disproportionate increase in the political value of the votes of residents of rural districts, so that the consensus on an issue or candidate reached by a district in which 150 persons voted could offset that in which 100,000 voted. The problem was made acute by the divergence of rural and urban areas on major social issues—racial integration, the prevention of crime, tax support for welfare programs—whose ramifications were primarily felt in the cities. Rural districts in a state legislature could, through their disproportionate voting power, prevent state funds from being channeled into distinctly urban needs.

In response to this difficulty urban and suburban residents sought to challenge, as violations of the Equal Protection Clause, state statutes that apportioned voting on other than a population basis. They argued that their votes "counted less" than those of residents of rural districts, and that the equal-protection clause required that the two sets of votes "count" the same. One statute so challenged was that of Tennessee. This statute, enacted in 1901, had tied legislative representation to population patterns of that time, and since then the Tennessee legislature had undertaken no reapportionment of voting districts or seats in its general assembly. In *Baker v. Carr* the Court, in a 6–2 decision, held that allegedly underrepresented Tennessee voters had standing to challenge the statute and that their challenge presented a bona-fide constitutional claim that could be adjudicated in court.

Black and Warren both joined Justice Brennan's majority opinion in *Baker v. Carr*, but one may surmise that their perspectives on the case were not precisely the same. Black believed that the equal protection clause was an absolute bar to all state discriminatory classifications infringing Bill of Rights freedoms. But there was no mention in the Bill of Rights of a right to vote, let alone to have one's vote count equally with another's. Thus Black's support for Brennan's opinion, in terms of his own attitude toward constitutional adjudication, could be based only on an appeal to the actual design of the Constitution, which he may have read as assuming that voting rights were precious and inviolate. This was a more "liberal" reading of the constitutional text than Black had ever made. His vote in *Baker v. Carr* constituted his primary departure from literalism in constitutional adjudication; it came close to being an aberration.

Warren also came to the conclusion that equal voting representation was compelled by the Constitution. He believed, however, that the judiciary had a further obligation: to scrutinize the activities of other branches of government to insure that they were not perpetuating inequalities or injustices. In this sense he did not confine the sweep of the Court's jurisdiction to those areas explicitly covered by constitutional language. He did not see judicial activism solely as an obligation following upon a reading of the Constitution, but viewed it more positively, as an affirmative exercise in enlightened governing. In *Baker v. Carr* his position coalesced with that of Black, but the coalescence was exceptional, given the fact that a judge-made gloss on the constitutional text was required to reach the result. Normally Warren diverged from Black precisely at the point where fairness and justice could be promoted only by departures from the text. Hence Warren's position in *Baker v. Carr* was representative of his jurisprudence, and Black's was highly unrepresentative of his.

Frankfurter and Harlan were likewise paired but not indistinguishable. Frankfurter's dissent confined itself to reasons, jurisprudential and historical, why the Court should not decide the case. Harlan's separate dissent incorporated Frankfurter's views by reference but went on to find that the Tennessee statute did not violate the equal protection clause (since that clause did not impose "rigid equality"[135]) but merely prohibited state discriminatory classifications that could be shown to be arbitrary or capricious. The overlap between the two dissents was considerable. Both maintained that "continuing national respect for the Court's authority depends in large measure upon its wise exercise of self-restraint and discipline in constitutional adjudication";[136] both spoke of the value of legislative experimentation on the part of the states in a federal republic; and both argued that the framers of the Fourteenth Amendment had no intention "to fix immutably the means of selecting representatives for state governments."[137] Harlan, however, was prepared, as he had been in *Poe*, to make a more explicit statement of the substantive values underlying his approach. In protesting the decision in *Baker v. Carr*, he was doing more than decrying judicial involvement in traditionally legislative areas; he was identifying himself with a tradition of American intellectual thought that juxtaposed the ideal of equality against a discomfort with total commitment to that ideal in practice.

Baker v. Carr was something of a milestone for the Warren Court. Not only did it signify the Court's willingness to extend its scrutiny of legislative activity to areas beyond that of race, thus auguring a redefinition of the relations between legislatures, courts, and the Constitution, it also marked the last term of service for Frankfurter, whose retirement deprived the Court of a spokesman for process liberalism in its most thoroughgoing form. Although the Warren Court in its last seven years remained divided on the desirability of active judicial promotion of humanitarian causes, none of its Justices envisaged so limited a role for the Court as had Frankfurter, none maintained a jurisprudential stance in which procedural technicalities played such a dominant part, and none defined his position as a judge in so self-abnegated a fashion. Consequently, few internal brakes existed for the Court's buoyant momentum in behalf of the constitutional imperatives that it perceived.

The area in which the Warren Court in its second phase made its deepest impact and engendered the most controversy was criminal procedure. The crucial analytical step in its criminal procedure reforms was the rejection by a majority of two Frankfurterian principles; first, that, because of the federal character of the American republic, state law enforcement officials were not restricted in their activities by the Bill of Rights in the same manner in which were federal officials; second, that the due process clause of the Fourteenth Amendment protected against state infringement of "basic values implicit in the concept of ordered liberty"[138]—nothing more and nothing less. The rejection of these propositions marked a triumph for Black, albeit not a complete one, since his counterprinciple—that the due process clause incorporated against the states all the specific protections of the Bill of Rights, and nothing more—was never accepted by a Court majority. Instead the Court "selectively"[139] incorporated various Bill of Rights provisions against the states. Those making the strongest impact on state administration of criminal practice were the search-and-seizure clause of the Fourth Amendment, the self-incrimination clause of the Fifth Amendment, and the Sixth Amendment's speedy trial, confrontation, and assistance of counsel clauses.

Although most of the Court's significant criminal procedure innovations took place after Frankfurter's retirement, one of its most far-reaching decisions, *Mapp v. Ohio*,[140] had been handed down during his tenure. *Mapp* squarely raised the issue of the applicability, against the states, of the Fourth Amendment's protection against unreasonable search and seizures. The Court held that all evidence obtained by searches in violation of the Fourth Amendment was inadmissible in a criminal trial in a state court. Warren was part of the majority; Black concurred, arguing that although the Fourth Amendment alone did not prevent the admission of such evidence, that the Fifth Amendment's self-incrimination clause and the Fourth Amendment's search-and-seizure clause, taken in tandem, did; Harlan and Frankfurter dissented, affirming the values of federalism and declaring their allegiance to the "ordered liberty" doctrine of the Fourteenth Amendment rather than to the incorporation theory.

Mapp was an important case in at least two respects: not only did it signify that a majority of the Court was prepared to accept incorporation in some form; it also threatened to upset existing systems of law enforcement in the states. Convictions of thousands of criminals incarcerated in state prisons had been secured through the use of evidence that *Mapp* now declared to have been illegally obtained and therefore inadmissible at trial. Even prisoners convicted before Mapp apparently had the right to challenge their convictions on habeas corpus, by reason of the then-existing principle that judge-made changes in constitutional law were presumed to have retroactive effect. The validity of this principle, which Traynor had identified as a manifestation of a jurisprudential climate in which law was "found" and changes in legal rules were seen as discoveries of the correct rule, had never been explicitly considered by the Court because it had never before had such concrete effects. Now its application threatened to empty the state prisons.

The criminal procedure reformers of the Warren Court were thus faced with a delicate trade-off. Retroactive application of new criminal procedure rules might seriously disrupt state administration of criminal justice and create a political nightmare for the Court. On the other hand, prospective application of new rules meant that some persons would receive their benefit and others not—merely by fortuities of timing. Prospective application required the judicial imposition of a cut-off date for each new rule's effect; as the Court's criminal procedure reforms continued apace, the selection of each date would mean the difference between continued incarceration and potential freedom for countless numbers of convicts. The choice of total retroactivity might identify the Court with a mass exodus from the prisons. The choice of prospectivity suggested the kind of apparently arbitrary classifications that the Court scrutinized in legislatures.

Linkletter v. Walker,[141] a 1965 decision, represented the Court's response to this dilemma. In that case a majority opted for prospective application of *Mapp*, meaning that while the petitioner in *Mapp* received the benefit of the new rule, the petitioner in *Linkletter*, whose conviction had become finalized before the date *Mapp* was handed down, did not. In choosing prospectivity the majority traded off the seemingly arbitrary exclusion of some prisoners from the benefits of its reforms against the power to continue making criminal procedure reforms. It made an implicit political judgment that disruption of state law enforcement systems would ultimately foreclose the Court from making future rulings restraining law enforcement practices. To prevent such a checkmate, the majority was prepared to limit the number of criminals who could challenge their convictions on the basis of a new rule.

Warren was part of the majority in *Linkletter* and one of the architects of the prospectivity doctrine.[142] In subsequent cases involving the retroactivity of new criminal procedure rules, the Court showed little coherence either on rationales for prospective application or on the appropriate cut-off dates.[143] Warren, however, never failed to vote for prospective application of a new rule when that option was seriously entertained, and he showed willingness to utilize any number of analytical techniques to support his position[144]—although his calculus was in fact more pragmatic than analytical, as he indicated in a 1969 opinion, *Jenkins v. Delaware*.[145] "Incongruities" resulting from the arbitrariness of the prospectivity doctrine, he maintained in *Jenkins*, "must be balanced against the impetus the technique provides for the implementation of long overdue reforms, which otherwise could not be practicably effected."[146]

The primary value furthered by decisions supporting prospective application was, for Warren, the retention of power in the Court to continue its reformist stance. Here Warren showed how closely judicial activism and the implementation of humanitarian goals were linked in his mind. The reforms were "long overdue"; they could be "practicably effected" if they did not disrupt the law enforcement process of the states; the judiciary was in a position not only to implement the reforms but to control their effect; hence, prospectivity went hand in hand with close scrutiny of state law enforcement procedures. Justice at large transcended justice for the individual litigant. The preservation of the judicial power to keep state officials from violating the Constitution surmounted the desires of individual criminals to secure their freedom.

Black's calculus in retroactivity cases was just the reverse of Warren's. He dissented in *Linkletter* and from all subsequent Warren Court decisions giving prospective application to criminal procedure rule changes. His reasons were the same in every instance: no justification existed for singling out one of many similarly situated litigants to receive the benefit of a new rule change. Justice to individual persons outweighed the potential for justice in the abstract. Here Black again revealed the purity and rigidity of his philosophy of constitutional interpretation. The "Bill of Rights safeguards," he said in *Linkletter*, "should be faithfully enforced by the courts without regard to a particular judge's judgment as to whether more people could be convicted by a refusal of courts to enforce the safeguards."[147] Black, in constitutional law cases, was concerned more with the preservation of his theory of adjudication than with the results it produced. An expansive reading of the mandates of the Bill of Rights excluded curtailment of their scope for reasons of convenience. But if the reading itself was wrong, as in a few search and seizure cases in which Black felt that a Court majority had read the Fourth Amendment too expansively, retroactive application was wrong as well. In those instances Black reiterated his *Linkletter* position but concurred in a prospectivist result.[148]

A final revealing sidelight of these cases was Harlan's emergence as an advocate of retroactive application. In *Linkletter* Harlan was a silent member of the prospectivist majority, and he continued to support prospective application for the next four terms.[149] But in *Desist v. United States*,[150] a 1969 decision, Harlan reversed his position and announced a complicated test that was designed to keep prospective application to a minimum. He had become offended, he stated in *Desist*, by the "incompatible rules and inconsistent principles"[151] engendered by prospectivist decisions and by the "pick[ing] and choos[ing] from among similarly situated defendants"[152] that prospectivity required. He confessed that he had once welcomed prospectivity because he "thought it important to limit the impact"[153] of criminal procedure rule changes he opposed, but he could no longer "remain content with the [resulting] doctrinal confusion."[154] True to his word, Harlan opposed the next prospective application of a rule change, even though he found himself "in the uncomfortable position of having to dissent from a holding which actually serves to curtail the impact" of a decision with which he had never agreed.[155] From vastly different vantage points, he and Black had become a singular pair of allies.

Harlan's evolution from *Linkletter* to *Desist* suggests that he had self-limiting jurisprudential principles that were as strong as those of Frankfurter. Foremost among them, perhaps, was "principled adjudication," under which similarly situated litigants were to be given like treatment by a court unless principles of general applicability could be found for distinguishing between them. Harlan was prepared to subordinate his social instincts to these institutional constraints, but he found the necessity for this subordination less frequent than did Frankfurter. The retroactivity decisions showed, however, that his fidelity to what he called the "classical view of constitutional adjudication"[156] was not lip service. In this sense his approach was closer to Black's than it might have appeared, and seemingly incompatible with Warren's. The first two men built perceived constraints and obligations into their jurisprudence to a far greater extent than did the third.

As prospectivity was emerging to shield future reforms, the Court maintained its reform momentum in the criminal procedure area. Perhaps its highwater mark was *Miranda v. Arizona*,[157] in which the Fifth Amendment's privilege against self-incrimination was transposed into a set of precise guidelines for police conduct during the interrogation of suspects. In the 1960s the Court shifted its focus in coerced confession cases from the "voluntariness" requirement to the atmosphere surrounding the interrogation. The very presence of police officers in authoritarian roles, the Court reasoned, was an intimidating device that put suspects "in such an emotional state as to impair [their] capacity for rational judgment."[158] *Malloy v. Hogan*,[159] a 1964 decision, applied the Fifth Amendment's privilege against self-incrimination against the states. The Court in *Escobedo v. Illinois*,[160] decided a week later, held that a "protective device" was necessary to insure that persons being interrogated by the police would not be coerced into incriminating themselves. *Escobedo* focused on the presence of counsel for the suspect as the necessary device, and held that a request by a subject for the assistance of counsel could not be denied.

Miranda went well beyond that relatively narrow holding to build a set of judicially-created procedural safeguards into the interrogation process. Once a person was "taken into custody" or "otherwise deprived of his freedom" by the police and "subjected to questioning,"[161] the police were required to warn him that he had the right to remain silent, that any statement he made could be used against him in a trial, that he had the right to the presence of an attorney, and that if he could not afford an attorney one would be appointed for him. Questioning could not begin until those warnings had been given and the suspect's rights "knowingly and intelligently" waived. The burden of proof was on the police to show that such a waiver had taken place; a waiver could be withdrawn at any time; once a waiver had been withdrawn, even through the implicit act of silence, the interrogation was required to cease.[162] The holding in *Miranda*, said Warren, author of the majority opinion, was "not an innovation in our jurisprudence," but merely, like *Escobedo*, "an application of basic rights that are enshrined in our Constitution."[163] The judiciary had an "obligation to apply these constitutional rights."[164] It was "in this spirit, consistent with our role as judges,"[165] that *Miranda* was decided.

Of all Warren Court decisions, *Miranda* has been the most controversial in the short run. Not even the noncompliance or grudging compliance with *Brown* or with *Engel v. Vitale*[166] (the decision outlawing prayers in the public schools) rivaled the furor engendered by *Miranda*. Statistical studies attempted to demonstrate that the *Miranda* warnings were being ignored by the police or were having no real impact on the interrogation process.[167] Congress sought to legislate the warnings out of existence.[168] The Court's "coddling" of criminals became a major issue in the 1968 elections; new appointees to the Court after Warren's retirement were selected in part on their commitment to law enforcement and their hostility to "criminal forces." But the significance of the decision, for present purposes, has little to do with the outcry it engendered or the efficacy of its result. *Miranda's* importance here is as a means of identifying the character of the Warren Court at large.

Miranda symbolized the interweaving of two jurisprudential threads to produce a stance and tone that distinguished the Warren Court from any of its twentieth-century predecessors. One thread was the constitutional liberalism of Black, the other was the messianic paternalism of Warren. In *Miranda* these threads, which ran in separate paths on many other occasions, united so completely that Warren's language on the judiciary's obligation to apply basic constitutional rights perfectly expressed Black's thoughts. For Black there was no issue of judicial encroachment on the prerogatives of law enforcement officials in *Miranda*. The privilege against self-incrimination was written into the Constitution; it was to be given an expansive reading; and that reading was obligatory for the judiciary. All *Miranda* did was to conform conduct to the mandates of the Bill of Rights. The most important function of the Court was to give the language of the Constitution meaning in the context of contemporary events, and that it did in *Miranda*. No question of "activism" was involved, for the Court was restrained by the literal language of the Constitution as much as it was compelled to give meaning to that language.

In the context of *Miranda*, Warren would not have disagreed with any of these sentiments. His quarrels with Black were in those areas in which expansive but literal interpretations of the Constitution unfairly failed to prohibit activity that Warren found offensive to human rights. Warren's mission in *Miranda* and elsewhere was to suppress behavior that he found obnoxious or repressive from his perspective of deep commitment to the freedoms inherent in American citizenship. The Constitution was one source of Warren's perspective, but there were others: his instincts about what was fair and just, his humanitarian premises, his outrage at brutal or immoral acts. In *Miranda* constitutional imperatives were a means of curtailing conduct he found deplorable, but the starting place for his thinking was the character of the conduct. Black's starting place, on the other hand, was his philosophy of interpreting the Constitution.

The harmony of Black and Warren in *Miranda* symbolized the jurisprudential paradigm of the Warren Court that has most often served to identify the Court, albeit incompletely, in the minds of observers. In summary form, the paradigm was as follows. The Constitution was the supreme law of the land; its mandates displaced all competing laws, whether legislative, executive, administrative, or judicial. The judiciary, in the person of the Court, had alone been given the responsibility of being the ultimate interpreter of the Constitution. Its interpretative responsibilities amounted to duties. It was bound by its interpretations of constitutional language, and a formula existed for the process of interpretation, essentially the same formula as that employed by Marshall. One began with the literal words of the Constitution and gave those words as expansive a reading as possible within their linguistic ambit. In instances where the literal words would bear alternative readings, one turned to the words of the Founding Fathers or those of the framers of later amendments to find their meaning. This formula gave changing content to citizens' rights without disturbing their original meaning. It foreclosed the particular criticism that judges were substituting their own preconceptions for those of the framers by requiring them to work only within the original text and supplementary historical sources. It avoided all discussions of the reach of judicial power, the appropriate balance to be struck between competing values, and the proper substantive content of vague clauses like equal protection or due process. The judiciary did only what the Constitution compelled it to do, but it was faithful to that obligation in a very full sense. Its power was limited only by the boundaries of the constitutional text, and although in one sense only its members knew those boundaries, in another sense they were in plain sight for everyone to see and understand.

This was the underlying stance of one pole of the Warren Court, the justification for its substantive crusades and also its link to the American tradition of an independent yet accountable judiciary. But the mosaic of the Court did not consist of that view alone. Accompanying it was a counterview, advanced by Frankfurter and refined by Harlan, that sought to expose two crucial difficulties with the paradigm outlined above. The first difficulty, according to Frankfurter, was that constitutional interpretation was never so clear a process as the paradigm made it out to be. The literal words of the Constitution did not explicitly anticipate coverage of evolving areas in American life, and the process of inclusion or exclusion was a matter of judicial art. An expansive reading of constitutional language was not categorically mandated; at times a restrictive reading might be necessary. Hence the Court in its interpretation of the Constitution was making value choices after all. Whether contemporary acts were to receive constitutional protection was a matter, in ambiguous cases, of how much value contemporary American society placed on the protection of those acts. Since this value choice was necessary, what justified the antidemocratic, unrepresentative judicial branch of government from making it? Why should the Court not defer to the value choices of more popularly-oriented branches? From these rhetorical questions the canons of Process Jurisprudence were derived. Their purpose was to prevent value choices in constitutional adjudication from being made by the judiciary and to insure that the process of judicial balancing of competing values, where unavoidable, would be fully articulated.

Harlan, who had dissented in *Miranda* and from most of the Court's innovations in criminal procedure, focused on a second difficulty, one stemming from Frankfurter's insight that a restrictive reading of the constitutional text was as possible as an expansive one. Through a combination of historical scholarship and policy-oriented ruminations Harlan showed that courts and legislatures had chosen restrictive interpretations of constitutional clauses as often as expansive ones; that those restrictive interpretations embodied counteregalitarian and counterlibertarian values that were an equally important part of the future of American civilization; that those interpretations also affirmed other liberties, such as privacy, that competed on occasion with constitutional rights, such as freedom of speech; and that, in short, there was abundant evidence that the process of constitutional interpretation was not linear and uni-dimensional, with the Constitution itself even embracing contradictory principles such as "ordered liberty." Thus, alongside the pathbreaking jurisprudential stance of one element of the Warren Court emerged a sophisticated critique of that stance that ultimately reaffirmed the validity of an earlier twentieth-century approach to judging.

The Warren Court, viewed from this perspective, embodied the dominant features of the American judicial tradition. It offered, in separate parts, the eighteenth-century linguistics of Marshall and his bold, creative use of power; the subtle philosophical insights of Holmes, along with his fatalistic acceptance of the dictates of legislative majorities; the humanitarian impulses of modern liberalism in heaping doses; the professionalist impulses of that same ideology at the crest of their academic influence; the constant clashes in American history between egalitarian ideals and elitist practices, with their resultant dilemmas for the elitist judiciary. Yet the Warren Court also added a dimension to American jurisprudence by producing and operationalizing a theory of substantive judging that stood in opposition to the dominant, passive model of the middle twentieth century.

13 

The Anti-Judge: William O. Douglas and the Ambiguities of Individuality

He began the first volume of his autobiography with a quotation from a Persian poet: "Seek disharmony; then you will gain peace."[1] He wrote an account of his years on the Court, covering nearly all the thirty-six years of his tenure, and did not discuss one of his opinions in any detail. When asked by his principal biographer to name his most important Supreme Court decision, he shrugged and remained silent.[2] He was the only judge ever to say publicly that the job of Supreme Court Justice was a four-day-a-week job,[3] that law clerks were largely unnecessary,[4] that the minds of Justices were rarely changed by discussions in conference,[5] and that he spent most of his time during oral argument doing his own research on the case rather than listening to the lawyers' presentations.[6] "If a man does not keep pace with his companions," he quoted Thoreau in the second volume of his autobiography, "perhaps it is because he hears a different drummer."[7]

William O. Douglas's tenure on the Supreme Court has regularly been seen as a testament to his rugged individualism, as a symbolic journey of one who "dared to be different." Douglas himself enjoyed those sorts of epigraphic encapsulations: his autobiography, as will be seen in more detail, emphasized the themes of solitude, escape from civilization to the wilderness, geographic and sociological travel, and defiance of the conventions and mores of those possessed of wealth, status, and power. But Douglas's individuality—the possession he most cherished and sought to convert into an explanation for his own conduct and an instructive lesson for others—was a more complex phenomenon than he made it out to be. To understand the nature of Douglas's contribution to the American judicial tradition it is necessary, first, to consider his construction of an image of himself as an indomitable individualist; second, to explore the ramifications of that self-image for his performance as a Supreme Court Justice during a time span that included the Chief Justiceships of Stone, Vinson, Warren, and Burger; and finally, to speculate on whether Douglas's judicial life further complicates the portrait of American appellate judging being sketched in this study.

I

The publication of Douglas's two-volume autobiography, which appeared in stages, first a year before his retirement from the Court in 1975 and next in 1980, the year of his death, signified the emergence of a new genre of writing by Supreme Court Justices. While several other Justices had written partial memoirs of their lives, Douglas was the first to use the form to engage in outspoken and ostensibly candid commentary on the personalities he had encountered as a Justice. He was also the first to discuss, in any detail, the internal workings of the Court and the relations between the Justices and other actors in the political culture of Washington. Finally, he was the first Supreme Court Justice to use the autobiographical medium to talk, in an apparently candid and introspective fashion, about himself: his fears, disappointments, and neuroses as well as his achievements.

The volumes of Douglas's autobiography are useful in two distinct ways. Conventionally, they provide details about the Justice's life and his career on the bench. And, as with any autobiography, they also provide a self-generated image of the author. The most striking aspect of Douglas's autobiography lies in the interaction of factual detail with image creation: that interaction takes a deeply revealing form.

The surface narrative of Douglas's autobiography is anecdotal, with the author appearing as a raconteur, telling irreverent stories and making wry observations about the famous people he has encountered in his life. A typical episode is

Douglas's account of his first meeting with John Foster Dulles, which occurred when he interviewed for a job with Dulles's New York law firm. Douglas, in recalling the incident, writes that he was "so struck by Dulles's pomposity that when he helped me on with my coat, as I was leaving his office, I turned and gave him a quarter tip."[8] But although the breezy irreverence of the Dulles episode is characteristic of much of Douglas's autobiographical writing, another tone wells up from beneath the surface: introspective meditation and reflection on the lessons of his own life. Here is, the reader is told, a man who conquered his fears and overcame his obstacles because he remained true to his individuality. The reader is to enjoy the good stories, but not miss the moral at the end.

The first volume of Douglas's autobiography begins conventionally enough, with an account of the small town of Maine, Minnesota, in the western part of the state,[9] where Douglas was born in 1898. When Douglas was three, his father, a Presbyterian minister, took his family to Estrella, California, and subsequently to Cleveland, Washington. Douglas's father established a pastorate in Cleveland, but his tenure in the position was brief: he died, during Douglas's sixth year, from complications after an operation for stomach ulcers. The Douglas family then settled in Yakima, Washington, a few miles from Cleveland. They could not afford to return to Minnesota and a relative lived nearby Yakima. Douglas relates these incidents in a matter-of-fact tone. But then comes the account of his father's funeral:

> As I stood by the edge of the grave a wave of lonesomeness swept over me. Then I became afraid—afraid of being left alone, afraid because the grave held my defender and protector. These feelings were deepened by the realization that Mother was afraid and lonely too. . . .
>
> Then I happened to see Mount Adams towering over us on the west. It was dark purple and white in the August day and its shoulders of basalt were heavy with glacial snow. . . .
>
> As I looked, I stopped sobbing. My eyes dried. Adams stood cool and calm, unperturbed by the event that stirred us so deeply. Suddenly the mountain seemed to be a friend, a force for me to tie to, a symbol of stability and strength.[10]

Thirteen pages into the autobiography, its controlling subsurface tone and its central themes are introduced. The narrator looks to extract meaning from the events of a life; the themes are loneliness, fear, and the strengthening and calming effects of the wilderness. Douglas the child and his mother are lost and afraid; her fears reinforce his; the image of Mount Adams intervenes to give the child "stability and strength."

In the next chapter, Douglas discusses his early struggle to overcome polio, which he had contracted before moving west from Minnesota. His prognosis was gloomy. The doctor "thought I would lose the use of my legs . . . and predicted I would not live beyond forty."[11] His mother massaged his legs with warm salt water, and gradually he recovered their use. "But the ordeal," he writes, "had left its scars." His legs remained weak, and he "had no medical advice, no lay adviser, no confidant as I was growing up, who could allay some of the worries about my legs." Further, the episode had instilled "great solicitude" in his mother, who, fearful of the doctor's prediction about his lifespan, "set out to guard my health, to protect me against physical strains, to do all sorts of favors designed to save my energy."[12]

The solicitude of his mother "set up a severe reaction" in Douglas. "It seemed to me I was being publicly recognized as a puny person—a weakling," and "[g]radually there began to grow in me a great rebellion." The protest was partly against his mother, but "mostly against the kind of person I thought I was going to be." The idea "that I was a weakling festered and grew in my mind," and Douglas "grew inwardly more and more rebellious."[13] In the next paragraphs, Douglas discusses the effects of his encounter with polio:

> In retrospect, I see that this period is when I became a loner. . . . I decided to prove my superiority over my contemporaries in other ways. Even a boy with weak and puny legs can get straight A's in school, I said to myself. No one would excel me in school. So I threw myself into that endeavor, and came very close to making the perfect scholastic record which I had set as a goal.
>
> Yet even this achievement was not enough. . . .
>
> . . . I was still a cripple, unable to compete physically . . .
>
> . . . I . . . used the foothills as one uses weights or bars in a gymnasium. First I tried to go up them without stopping. When I conquered that, I tried to go up without a change of pace. When that was achieved, I practiced going up not only without a change of pace but whistling as I went.
>
> I always went alone.[14]

One night on a trek that took him up a ridge near Mount Adams, Douglas found "the germ of a philosophy of life: that man's best measure of the universe is in his hopes and his dreams, not his fears."[15] The solitary forays into the wilderness had not only enabled him to conquer his physical weaknesses, they had instilled in him the idea that striving against odds was the way to combat emotional anxiety. The lone hiker in the wilderness was on a journey to gain "stability and strength."

In 1922, Douglas headed east in the boxcar of a freight train to attend Columbia Law School. His devotion to his studies had been rewarded: he had been valedictorian of his high school class in Yakima and had won a scholarship to Whitman College. He then served briefly as a stateside Army officer in World War I, and taught English for two years in the Yakima public schools. He then resolved to study law, and chose Columbia because of a chance conversation with James T. Donald, a young practitioner in Yakima whom Douglas met at the YMCA. Douglas had applied to Harvard Law School and had been accepted, but Donald told him that Harvard was expensive and, if he planned to work his way through law school, he should go to Columbia. With seventy-five dollars in his pocket, Douglas "took an old battered suitcase with a suit and a change of clothes in it and left by the back way to the railroad yards, where I would catch a freight [east]."[16]

In his description of the journey east Douglas relates several adventures. To help pay his train fare, he took over two thousand sheep with him to Chicago. After declining to pay the conductor protection money for riding the rest of the way illegally, he was thrown off the train. Finally, he hopped another freight to New York, arriving with "six cents of my seventy-five dollars left in my pocket . . . grimy and weary, . . . [having] had no bath since Chicago, no change of clothes, and doubtless look[ing] like a bum."[17] In *Go East, Young Man*, Douglas treats the journey east as if it were an episode from a picaresque novel, but at the very end of *The Court Years* he recasts it:

> As I described in the first volume of my autobiography, while I rode the rods by day, under the car, at night I was usually in a boxcar. By dusk it would fill up with people who were not only unkempt and smelly but suspicious-looking as well. By seven o'clock each car was pretty well organized with a committee in charge. Its function was to sort out the desirable from the undesirable. The committee members

> were liable to toss out the door any brother who seemed to have money, with the result that no well-heeled traveler could ride free. I'd wake at night hearing a scream or a yell and look up to see someone—on the count of three—fly across the car through the open door, followed by another scream and a third as the poor devil hit the ground on the side of the rail line.
>
> . . . These men were all strangers to me, yet I learned from whispered conversations that they thought that I was the richest of all—apparently because I looked so clean. At times I was nervous when I went to sleep, wondering whether I would be the next one to be tossed out the side door.
>
> By the time I reached New York I felt that nothing worse could possibly happen to me in the future. The "Darest Thou" philosophy had not made my freight-car journey safe, but it gave promise of greener pastures in the days ahead and helped me through the other barriers and obstacles I was to encounter in my life.[18]

Douglas had dared to go east from Yakima; dared to go by the boxcar route; dared to arrive in New York with no money and no connections. Just as by sheer will he had climbed trails until his physical weaknesses disappeared, he had managed to travel cross-country for three weeks on seventy-five dollars and his wits. The journey was another example of triumph through individuality.

The boxcar episode occurs a little less than one-third of the way through the first volume of Douglas's autobiography: by then he is twenty-four and about to enter Columbia Law School. At this point the narrator as raconteur takes over, and Douglas races through the next twelve years of his life, telescoping them in forty pages. He treats cursorily his years in law school, where he made the law review, graduated second in his class ("to my everlasting chagrin"),[19] and was "nosed . . . out" for a clerkship with Harlan Stone. "For two weeks," Douglas writes of losing out on the Stone clerkship, "I was unspeakably depressed that for all those years and all that work, I had so little to show."[20] He barely mentions his marriage to Mildred Riddle, a Latin teacher at Yakima High School ("a quiet, retiring lady of beauty who liked to sit in green meadows besides purling waters" but who "never really enjoyed the hard exhausting journeys into the high wilderness").[21] His discussions of his brief tenure with the firm of Cravath,

Henderson and de Gersdorff, which he joined immediately after law school, are largely anecdotal. Only one episode is designed for the meditative reader: Douglas's decision to leave the Cravath firm for small-town practice in Yakima.

In that episode Robert Swaine, later to be a name partner in the Cravath firm, "took me on top of the mountain and showed me the promised land of Wall Street."[22] Douglas had nearly had to drop out of Columbia for lack of money. He was able to pay his way through law school by tutoring, saving $2000 by his second year, which he used to get married. His starting salary at Cravath was $1800 a year, and after one year, according to his account, he was earning $3600. "Now Bob Swaine came to me and offered me $5000 and a future with the firm" in response to the news that Douglas was planning to leave New York for Yakima. "You've spent your life in the second balcony," Douglas remembers Swaine saying, "and I am introducing you to the orchestra." Douglas then recounts his response:

> I was flattered and pleased. Yet I had made my decision, and it was based on other values. . . . Even those who made the top [of Wall Street practice] did not seem to have much left at sixty-five. If I walked their paths, I'd never be able to climb another mountain. . . .
>
> I looked around at the older men in my profession and I knew I didn't want to be like *any* of them. They couldn't climb a mountain . . . ; they knew nothing about the world which was closest to me, the real world, the natural world.[23]

The journey to New York was a sociological as well as a geographical excursion; it took the impoverished Yakima scholarship student from the "second balcony" to the "orchestra." Law school kept Douglas from poverty; Wall Street practice offered the prospect of making him rich. "I had the fear of being trapped into a dull and listless life,"[24] Douglas had said, explaining his original decision to leave Yakima for Columbia. Now he described his decision to leave Cravath in almost identical terms. But the similar characterization of his motivations does not obliterate the fundamental difference between leaving Yakima for New York and New York for Yakima; the first decision was a search for the "orchestra," the second a rejection of it. "Money did not seem important,"[25] Douglas says of his decision to leave Cravath. "I had gone hungry and at times was filled with despair, but that seemed far behind me . . . I did not want to be rich; I only wanted to escape dire poverty."[26] "In Yakima," he continued, "I could hike my beloved hills."[27]

But Douglas did not return to Yakima for long: by 1926 he had joined the Columbia law faculty. He remained at Columbia until 1928, when he went to Yale, where he stayed until 1934. The years between 1926 and 1934 witnessed the most dramatic changes in Douglas's professional life. He went from an obscure first-year law teacher to being a figure whom Robert Maynard Hutchins, President of the University of Chicago, could describe as "the most outstanding law professor in the nation."[28] Douglas recapitulates those years in sixteen pages of a 900-page autobiography. He characterizes his involvement with the Realist movement at Columbia, which was to affect profoundly his career as a judge, as participation in a group of "rebels" who "were dubbed the leaders of 'sociological jurisprudence.' "[29] His account of the tumultuous battle over the deanship at Columbia in 1928, which prompted Douglas's resignation after only one year on the faculty, is reduced to his observation that "[w]e wanted a dean at Columbia who would be interested in [our] approach. . . .[30] We were blunt and outspoken in our demands."[31] His explanation of his resignation is that when Nicholas Murray Butler, the President of Columbia, appointed a dean, Young B. Smith, who "was the antithesis of what we wanted: he represented the past . . . I wrote a letter to President Butler [that] said in substance, 'In view of your appointment of a dean of the Law School without consulting the faculty, I tender herewith my resignation.' "[32] After resigning from Columbia, he reports, he was awakened one morning by a call from Hutchins, then Dean at Yale Law School, informing him that "he had summoned the Yale faculty to a . . . meeting and they had elected me to the faculty." Douglas's response, he says, was to ask Hutchins where Yale was.[33]

By 1930, Douglas had become Sterling Professor of Law at Yale, one of the most prestigious and highly paid academic positions in the nation. He devotes one page of his autobiography to his meteoric rise to the Sterling Professorship, which he secured only four years after he had first entered law teaching.[34] Not only is the lack of comparative space devoted to Douglas's extraordinary professional successes striking, the accuracy of Douglas's information about his own life is highly suspect.

Accuracy was clearly not a primary concern of Douglas in writing about any portion of his life, and the years from 1924 to 1934 were no exception. In two profiles of him published shortly after he had been appointed to the

Supreme Court, he said that, rather than continuing on to New York in a boxcar from Chicago, as recounted in his autobiography, he had wired his brother to secure a one-way coach ticket.[35] In his autobiography he wrote that he had not yet entered law school when he began supporting himself by preparing a correspondence course,[36] but an account by a classmate had him beginning the course after one semester of law school.[37] He had said that the top fee he charged for tutoring was $25 an hour, an amazing sum for the 1920s, and that "to obtain my services . . . students needed to be both stupid and rich."[38] In 1939, however, he had listed his top fee as $7.50 an hour.[39] He claimed that "through my tutoring services, I struck it rich at Columbia";[40] in fact, much of his financial support during law school came from his wife Mildred's teaching job in a Bernardsville, New Jersey, high school.[41]

Inaccurate recollections permeate Douglas's descriptions of his life. The autobiography gives his second-year salary at the Cravath firm as $3600;[42] firm records list it as $3000.[43] Douglas emphasized his desire to leave Cravath for Yakima, but neglected to mention that, after eight months in Seattle and Yakima, he returned to Cravath, at a raise in salary,[44] and remained there for several months before accepting an offer from Columbia to teach full-time in the fall of 1927. "A telegram came from Columbia with an offer of a five-thousand-dollar assistant professorship for full-time teaching," Douglas remembered. "I did real soul-searching. I asked my friend Elon [Gilbert] to talk the problem out with me. We sat on a lava cliff high above town one night and discussed the matter from top to bottom. Before I returned home that night, I had made my decision to return to Columbia."[45] It seems unlikely that both a lava cliff and Elon Gilbert were in the vicinity of New York City at the time. Finally, even the Dulles incident was apparently embellished: years later, Dulles confirmed the meeting but remembered only that his firm had turned Douglas down for a job.[46]

Douglas's "photographic mind"[47] also failed him in the details of his year on the Columbia law faculty. He was not the only law professor to resign from the faculty over the deanship controversy: Professors Hessel Yntema and Herman Oliphant did as well.[48] He did not quit immediately after Young Smith was named Dean in the spring of 1928; his resignation was announced that fall, when he had already accepted the Yale offer.[49] The Yale offer from Hutchins did not come the morning after "a night in May, 1928" when Hutchins and Douglas had been drinking bootleg liquor in the locker room of a Pelham,

New York[50] country club, but after Hutchins had learned of the appointment of Young Smith and the divisions on the Columbia faculty, and secured permission from his Yale colleagues to recruit any of the Columbia malcontents.[51]

Finally, Douglas had been extraordinarily cryptic, if not precisely misleading, about the events that led to his securing the Sterling Professorship at Yale. "[B]y September, 1928," he wrote,

> I was ensconced [at Yale] as an Associate Professor of Law. In 1929 Hutchins left Yale to become president of the University of Chicago. He asked me to go with him to become dean at Chicago.
>
> The top salary in law at Chicago was $10,000. Hutchins persuaded his board of trustees to offer me two and a half times that amount. . . . [A]lthough I accepted the Chicago appointment, I never taught there. I stayed at Yale and became Sterling Professor of Law. . . .[52]

The facts of the Chicago offer and Douglas's account of it are slightly different. Hutchins offered him a professorship, not the deanship, and a salary of $20,000 rather than $25,000.[53] Douglas vacillated, then finally accepted the offer, but postponed leaving New Haven for a year, claiming that he had begun research projects that involved field work in that area. After that year Dean Charles Clark announced that Douglas had been named Sterling Professor and would remain permanently on the Yale faculty.[54] He simply told Hutchins that he "couldn't come" to Chicago after all.[55]

To be sure, the inaccuracies in Douglas's account of his years in New York and New Haven are interesting by themselves. The version of events offered by Douglas in his autobiography invariably exaggerated his importance, while remaining silent about contributions made to his welfare by others. Nonetheless, the most striking quality of his reminiscences about his early professional years is that he rapidly glossed over his accomplishments and instead dwelled upon his disappointments. More space is devoted to his loss of the Stone clerkship than to his acceptance of the Sterling Professorship; more to his negative reactions to New York and Wall Street practice than to his accomplishments as an associate at Cravath. The pattern continues in his description of his years at Yale. "My days at New Haven," he begins that account, "were happy ones,"[56] and then he mentions that he enjoyed teaching at 8 a.m. "because it left the rest of the day free."[57] But more characteristic of his account of his time on the Yale faculty is the following passage:

> By the time I had reached Yale and had time for reflection, I was, in a way, sorry that I had turned to law. I had seen enough in New York City and in the state of Washington to realize that the practice of law requires predatory qualities. There seemed to be recognized prices for nuisance value in the law—prices at which groundless suits could be settled. Finance was predatory and many men who managed it had predatory proclivities. Their lawyers took on the coloration of their clients and designed ways and means of accomplishing certain projects that should have been beyond the pale. I had seen that Wall Street had its Augean stables, and many of the caretakers were lawyers. The great names in the law were, with few exceptions, attached to men who exploited the system, but brought very few spiritual or ethical values to it. . . .
>
> At Yale, Bob Hutchins and I often sat around talking of these things. There was no one on the professional horizon whose example we wanted to emulate. . . .
>
> Teaching was only a stone's throw away. Why spend one's life teaching bright youngsters how to do things that should not be done? Why teach them to be cleverer than their fathers? Or, on the other hand, why not practice and use the new-found finesse for one's own benefit?
>
> These were problems we explored; most of us did not resolve them, but ended with doubts and misgivings about law as practice, wondering whether English literature, philosophy, or conservation might not have been a better dish. In general, during and after my days in New York, most of my friends were not lawyers but biologists, botanists, geologists, ecologists and the like.[58]

Once again an apparently brilliant success by Douglas had turned to ashes in his mouth. Law had saved him from poverty, but he was indifferent to wealth. His accomplishments as a law student had introduced him to the firms and academic institutions of the Establishment, but he found there only dried-up practitioners and "sons of the elite who . . . were waiting for someone to fill their heads with knowledge."[59] He had risen to the top echelons of his profession at thirty-two, but already had come to question the worth of the work he was doing and the audience he was reaching. It is no surprise, then, that at least eighty pages of his autobiography are not about law at all but about Douglas's struggle to find inner peace and happiness. This was a struggle he occasionally coated over with the varnish of his storyteller persona, but more often presented as the desperate search that it was.

In chapters twelve through seventeen of *Go East, Young Man*, Douglas attempts to confront the psychological themes of his life. At the close of these pages he returns to an account of his career, detailing his service on the Securities and Exchange Commission, which began in 1934 and led, five years later, to his appointment to the Supreme Court. As his narrative progresses his tone reverts to what it had been before: his voice is that of a rakish raconteur and a moralizer on his life. That voice persists for the rest of Douglas's autobiography. The interlude in chapters twelve through seventeen is strikingly, almost jarringly, different in tone.

Chapter twelve of *Go East, Young Man* discusses Douglas's psychotherapy with Dr. George Draper. Douglas suffered from upset stomachs and migraine headaches while in New York, and eventually was referred to Draper. "Draper eventually psychoanalyzed me," Douglas writes, "and helped me discover and understand the stresses and strains that produced the headaches. Once I faced up to them, the migraines disappeared."[60] Draper was, Douglas felt, "the main seminal influence in my life."[61] He helped Douglas "discover that I had been launched in life as a package of fears,"[62] and attempted to convince Douglas "that all fears were illusory."[63] Draper was "a daring intellect,"[64] a "great physician in the largest sense of the word."[65]

Having sketched Draper, Douglas then turns to Draper's contributions to Douglas's development in a chapter entitled "Fear."[66] The theme of the chapter is how Douglas, through psychoanalysis with Draper, "came to full consciousness"[67] of his fears and resolved them "by confrontation and rationalization."[68] Among Douglas's youthful fears, he tells us, were "a phobia about intestinal pains,"[69] a "very great" fear of water,[70] a fear of lightning "originating in religious dogma,"[71] a fear of "inadequacy because of my weak legs,"[72] a fear of wild animals,[73] a fear of "avalanches . . . falling trees, [and] forest fires,"[74] and finally, "the fear of death, [which] is made up of all other fears."[75] Following Draper's advice, Douglas forced himself to confront each fear. Most of the fears were associations from childhood, either from direct experiences or traumas felt vicariously through his mother. He had been "much too dependent"[76] on her after his father died; she had "pampered me during my early childhood";[77] in adolescence Douglas "was torn between wanting to be tied to her apron strings and rebelling at the very thought of it."[78] Leaving Yakima for New York and abandoning his mother filled him "with a great sense of guilt";[79] the guilt feelings manifested themselves in the recurrence of childhood fears.[80] Eventually Douglas came to believe that "the fear that is truly debilitating is the fear of the unknown in the environment around us,"[81] and that "[w]hen we rid ourselves of that fear, we are free to live and can become bold, courageous, and reliant."[82]

The overriding theme of the "Fear" chapter is Douglas's effort to control features of his environment that were "unknown" and thus anxiety-producing. If the fear was of intestinal pain, the response was to understand that Douglas's mother's younger brother had died of peritonitis;[83] if the fear was of water, the response was to embark on swimming lessons with the Yale swimming coach;[84] if the fear was of lightning, it vanished when the wing of Douglas's plane was struck, yet suffered no damage;[85] if the fear was of the dangers of the wilderness, the response was to go on backpacking trips and mountain climbs.[86] Overcoming this last fear was especially important to Douglas. In his next chapter, on conservation, he identifies himself as an opponent of all those who would pollute, despoil, or civilize the wilderness. He there prophesies that "[h]e who stands up to defend the last untouched granite cliff of Yosemite . . . , or the last acre of redwoods, or the last pristine lake in Vermont . . . , or the rolling grasslands of eastern Montana . . . will in time be denounced as un-American."[87] The wilderness became a crucible for Douglas to explore his unknown fears and reassure himself of his indomitability.

Douglas's discussion of the wilderness takes him to the next chapter in the sequence, where he tells stories about the "outdoorsmen" he has encountered in his life. Most of these tales are in the raconteurial vein, light and not invested with significance. An exception is his description of Roy Shaeffer, "[t]he man who—literally and spiritually—towered above most of the Western outdoorsmen who helped educate me."[88] Shaeffer "took out parties who wanted to fish or hunt in the high mountains—or just sit and contemplate the solitude of the wilderness."[89]

In the portrait of Roy Shaeffer one can see that Douglas associated intimacy and survival with the wilderness. The wilderness was a solitary place: one needed to respect the autonomy of its inhabitants. At the same time it was a potentially dangerous place: one needed to know how to harness its natural phenomena to one's advantage. The wilderness was an ideal backdrop to revitalize oneself because, paradoxically, it was indifferent to man. Its inhabitants, flora or fauna, survived naturally; man needed to emulate their example. Shaeffer "towered" not only because of his size and strength but because of his ingenuity and respect for the environment. He had come to "know" the unknown. The wilderness was thus an intimate place because it made one realize that one was really, in the midst of nature, alone with oneself: the natural environment was either uninterested in man or unconscious of his presence. To the extent that indifference threatened man as a visitor, learning to survive was necessary. The learning process reinforced one's sense of self. This lesson leads Douglas to a chapter on his wilderness home in Goose Prairie, Washington.

"Goose Prairie is my place," the chapter begins, "in a sense that Washington, D.C. never could be."[90] Douglas had first come to know the Goose Prairie area, about sixty miles from Yakima, "as a boy when I started backpacking."[91] He would take the train from Yakima to Naches and then a dirt road into the mountains to Goose Prairie, "3400 feet above sea level, between two mountain ranges."[92] In 1922 the original homesteader of Goose Prairie died, and his land was subdivided into one-acre lots. Several years later Douglas bought twelve acres, and "fifty years or more after my first boyhood visit"[93] he built a house in the style of a Swiss chalet, with a steep cedar-shingled roof, a large chimney, and three fireplaces.

While Goose Prairie was intended by Douglas to symbolize his recurrent journey into the wilderness to find stability, strength, and peace, it came, during his career on the Court, to represent a symbol of another kind. "[U]ltimately," Douglas's principal biographer has written of his years as a Justice,

> it was not Douglas's egocentricity . . . that galled his colleagues nearly as much as what they considered his professional irresponsibility. . . . Nothing pointed this out so clearly, or aggravated Douglas's colleagues as much, as his habit of leaving Washington for his vacation home in Goose Prairie several weeks before the end of the term.[94]

Every other Justice allegedly resented Douglas's escape to Goose Prairie, one saying that Douglas sometimes left without even telling the others of his departure and that "if every justice had done that the Court couldn't have functioned."[95] Douglas's journeys into the wilderness appeared to be compulsive. His nerves were taut; he needed solitude and repose.

After the Goose Prairie chapter, Douglas moves to a subject that combines the anecdotal and instructive modes of his autobiography: his role as a father. "It takes wisdom and courage to let the child find his own levels of interest," Douglas says in beginning his account of his relations with his daughter Millie and his son Bill, "and not force him to become this or become that according to the tastes of the parent. It takes planning to expose the child to good music, fine arts, interesting conversation, controversial ideas, the harmony and the wildness of nature without at the same time forcing a cult or idea or principle down his throat. I doubt if I rated high as a father. . . ."[96]

Douglas then describes his children exclusively in terms of his own psychological themes. He recounts Millie's near-drowning as a two-year-old and his insistence that she "reenter the water and try to swim."[97] He describes two extended efforts by Bill to catch fish without any help from his father.[98] He notes that Bill is "passionately independent"[99] and tells a story in which Bill refused to give his name or any identification to two policemen who mistakenly arrested him for vagrancy.[100] The episode, in which Bill's silence prevents the police from "knowing he was the son of a Supreme Court justice,"[101] illustrates for Douglas why "I love, admire, and respect [Bill] more than any man I ever knew."[102] "Either of my children," the chapter ends, "can be dropped by parachute anywhere in our temperate zone and survive, though there are no matches, knives, or food in their pockets."[103]

In interviews later in their lives both Millie and Bill described their father as remote, tense, and driven, his most memorable expression an icy stare.[104] But their greatest resentment emerged in comments about the gap between Douglas's storytelling and the reality of their lives. One incident is particularly representative of those comments. In his account of his children in chapter seventeen of *Go East, Young Man* Douglas recounts a horseback ride in which Millie, at the age of fifteen, was caught in a sudden snowstorm. "Her clothes were soon frozen," Douglas writes. "She stopped the packtrain, dismounted, walked to the rear where I was, and said, 'Dad, I'm only fifteen and you said I couldn't have a cocktail until I'm eighteen. But I'm almost dead of cold and I know you have a bottle in your saddlebags." "Her face was blue," Douglas comments, "and the plea was too moving to deny."[105] When *Go East, Young Man* was published, Millie was infuriated on reading Douglas's account of the incident because, as she said in an interview, it had not happened as he described it. "I was wet and miserable," she said, "but I just told him to get on with it. There was no passing of the whiskey bottle." Her father, she noted, "could not, it seemed, ever get it right, either telling stories that did not happen or not telling stories that did."[106]

Douglas suggests that he might have been less than successful as a father because of a compulsion to recreate the themes of his own life in his children. Having made that suggestion, he then gives evidence of that compulsion, telling stories the purpose of which seems to be molding his children in his own image or instructing the reader as to the value of persistent struggle against adversity. The stories, his own children reveal, are not quite true, and other true ones are omitted. Douglas embellished the horseback riding story, his daughter later said, when he could have told a story in which she raced on horseback to find a doctor to come to the aid of a companion of hers who had been thrown and kicked in the head by a horse. The stories were not about Douglas's children, but about Douglas himself.

By the middle of the first volume of Douglas's autobiography, then, there is ample material to construct, as an alternative to the image of his life that he erects, a more complicated, less flattering, and surely more believable image. At that point Douglas abandons the confessional mode and never returns to it: the remaining one and one-half volumes of autobiography are anecdotal and instructive. But by now the reader has come to doubt the validity of both those modes. Douglas has made too many factual errors and emphasized the themes of indomitability and conquest too often. The entire account, purporting to instruct the reader in the lessons to be learned from an ostensibly successful and prominent life, collapses as that kind of source, and becomes another: a description of the devices a troubled person had employed to make his own life palatable. Douglas's autobiography sets out to present us one description of a life—the triumph of a man who was true to his individuality—and ends up presenting us with quite another description, the trials of a man who could not escape his individual torment. The juxtaposition of the "two Douglases" in the autobiography helps clarify the strikingly idiosyncratic approach Douglas adopted to the role of a Justice of the United States Supreme Court, and reveals another dimension of the theme of individuality in Douglas's life.

II

"I came to the Court," Douglas noted in *Go East, Young Man*, "without personal ambition ever playing a part. I had never cast my eyes its way, never dreamed, let alone wished, that I would sit there."[108] In the same passage he said that although he was "overwhelmed by the honor," the appointment was "not in any degree a fulfillment. . . . [I]t was, in a sense, an empty achievement."[109] Douglas was not being candid about his ambition for the Court, but he may well have been so about the unfulfilling nature of the position. Few lawyers who sense that they have a serious chance of being appointed to the Supreme Court fail to lobby for their own appointment, and Douglas was no exception. He forwarded copies of his speeches to President Franklin Roosevelt; he cultivated Roosevelt's advisor Thomas Corcoran and other influential New Dealers; mindful of Roosevelt's apparent conviction that the seat (previously occupied by Brandeis) should go to a Westerner, he participated in a campaign to emphasize his Yakima origins and downplay the amount of time he had spent in New York and Connecticut. All the while he used his position as Chairman of the Securities and Exchange Commission, an office to which Roosevelt had named him in 1937, to keep his name in the limelight.[110] He was rewarded in March 1939, when Roosevelt sent his name to the Senate. "I was dumfounded,"[111] Douglas wrote in describing his reaction to the news, but he nonetheless was able to describe his "backers in the Senate" and the "spearheads of opposition" to his candidacy.[112] Confirmation came on April 4 by a vote of 62 to 4.

"At first," Douglas recalled, "I did not like the work [on the Court]; it took me a few years to accommodate myself to the daily routine. Perhaps. . . . I had too much excess energy."[113] He had "been accustomed to living on the run" for most of his life: observers regularly commented on his remarkable capacity to absorb information in a short time. The Court had a "routine of reading and research"; Douglas felt that it took him "two years or more to get used to that new workday."[114] For most Justices of the Court's modern era, the first impression of their new job has been one of constant, demanding work, more than they have previously experienced. In Douglas's case the shock seems to have come from having so little to do. "[I]t was not long before I realized," he wrote in *The Court Years*, "that the job of an Associate Justice took four days a week."[115]

In fact there was little in being a Supreme Court Justice that Douglas seems to have found fulfilling. The four to five hours a day devoted by the Court to hearing oral arguments provoked his restless temperament and quick mind: he preferred the Court's schedule in his early years as a Justice, when arguments did not begin until noon, and "one could get a day's work done" by rising early and working undisturbed until argument began.[116] Although the end of a four-hour day hearing argument "was for me an exhausting time," Douglas recalled, it was not because he was listening intently to the lawyers or his fellow Justices. "I did a lot of writing on the Bench," he noted; "[w]hen I was not writing, I was doing research in the case under argument. . . . I had a knack of following the argument with my ears as I wrote. . . ."[117]

Nor was Douglas entranced with the Court's weekly conference. "The Conference discussion sometimes changes one's view of a case, but usually not," he claimed.[118] Late in Douglas's tenure, he occasionally presided over conferences when Chief Justice Burger was absent, being the most senior Associate Justice on the Court. Justices recalled his peremptory approach to the task. "Bill didn't discuss anything," one Justice said to James Simon, Douglas's most recent biographer. "He would just say, 'This is a case involving such and such a statute. The issue is such and such. I vote to affirm.' "[119]

Douglas's view of the Court's conference was a microcosm of his general attitude toward the dimensions of Supreme Court judging that involve collegial discourse and the forging of collective positions. The principal purpose of the conference, he said, was "to discover the consensus,"[120] and Douglas was not, for most of his career, particularly interested in consensus-building. "To write for five or more men means, at times, trimming and qualifying [one's position]," he noted; he was not often motivated to "trim and qualify" his views.[121] Beyond that, he did not assume that cordiality in conference or in personal relations generally had much to do with the outcome of decisions. When commenting on a newspaper editorial suggesting that the "tact and good humor" and the "unconquerable . . . spirit of fair play"[122] that had characterized Chief Justice Taft's tenure had resulted in the smoothing out of potential differences among Justices, Douglas wrote:

> That [is] of course nonsense. Men sitting on the Court are never swayed by a smile or a slap on the back. Congenial relations in the corridors and at the luncheon table have no relationship with unanimity

> or dissent on the issues before the Court. Those issues cut too deep and mark such fundamental differences in legal philosophy ever to be erased or even conditioned by a smile or by acts of friendship from a protagonist.[123]

That statement was typical of many of Douglas's recollections of his years on the Court: overdrawn and not entirely accurate. Douglas himself was not loath to write a cordial note or make a flattering comment to a Justice whose vote he coveted.[124] But in general Douglas did not exert himself overmuch in conference discussion or in the maintenance of good relations with his colleagues. He spoke little in conference, sometimes merely saying "I affirm," or "I go the other way"; he rarely circulated his opinions; he appeared to some colleagues to be "'almost uncomfortable if anyone agreed with him'" or to wish to "'ma[ke] it impossible for you to join him.'"[125] To the extent that Douglas was an internal Court strategist, his most common technique was the threat to disclose some purported irregularity in internal procedure of which he disapproved. The threat was believable only because of the perception of Douglas's colleagues that he had no particular interest in maintaining the impression that the Court was a harmonious unit.[126]

If one associates the internal features of Supreme Court judging with collegial norms first established during Marshall's tenure—norms designed to hammer out a consensus of views and present to the outside world an appearance of internal harmony and unanimity[127]—Douglas seemed to have demonstrated an indifference to those norms almost from the beginnings of his tenure. In *Go East, Young Man* he gave an account of the emergence of this stance, which he claimed had been derived from two incidents; a case the Court had decided his first term and a conversation he had had with Chief Justice Hughes.

The case was *O'Malley v. Woodrough*,[128] raising the constitutionality of a 1932 statute making the salaries of federal judges subject to federal income tax,[129] notwithstanding Article III, Section 1 of the Constitution, which forbids Congress from reducing a federal judge's salary during the judge's term of office.[130] Douglas, along with six other members of the Hughes Court, voted to sustain the statute. In *Go East, Young Man* he discussed his interpretation of that vote:

> As I entered my vote in the docket book, I decided that I had just voted myself first-class citizenship.

> The tradition had been that Justices never even voted in public elections. . . . I took a different course. Since I would be paying as heavy an income tax as my neighbor, I decided to participate in local, state, and national affairs. . . . That meant I would register and vote; . . . that I would become immersed in conversation, opposing river pollution, advocating wildlife protection, and the like; that I would travel and speak out on foreign affairs. . . . I would exercise the rights of first-class citizenship to the fullest extent possible.
>
> Many people assume that a Supreme Court Justice should be remote and aloof from life and should play no part even in community affairs. But if Justices are to enjoy First Amendment rights, they should not be relegated to the promotion of innocuous ideas.[131]

Douglas's account of the *O'Malley* case associated participation in public affairs by Supreme Court Justices with taxpayer status, but that association was a curious one. For most of the Court's history neither Justices nor citizens at large had paid federal taxes, and yet the Court's norms had discouraged Justices from engaging openly in public life, whereas, of course, other citizens had not been subject to similar constraints. The "taxpayer" argument Douglas made in his autobiography appears to be a ruse: he had simply resolved not to let his position on the Court preclude him from participation in public issues. But in Douglas's version the *O'Malley* decision "affected [his] entire life."[132]

Douglas's second formative experience on the Court, the conversation with Hughes, was "shattering but . . . true."[133] Douglas reported that Chief Justice Hughes counseled him: " 'Justice Douglas, you must remember one thing. At the constitutional level where we work, ninety percent of any decision is emotional. The rational part of us supplies the reasons for supporting our predilections.' "[134] "Before that conversation," Douglas wrote in *The Court Years*, "I had thought of the law in the terms of Moses—principles chiseled in granite." Although he had "kn[own] judges had predilections," and that "their moods as well as their minds were ingredients of their decisions," he "had never been willing to admit to [himself] that the 'gut' reaction of a judge at the level of constitutional adjudication . . . was the main ingredient of his decision." That admission, Douglas wrote, "Destroyed in my mind some of the reverence for the immutable principles."[135]

For Douglas to suggest that in 1939 he thought of law as "principles chiseled in granite" was to invite his audience to ignore his entire career as a legal academic. Although he had not written about constitutional law, and although his scholarship had discussed legal doctrine, the entire thrust of his work was toward harmonizing legal subjects with the "realities" of contemporary business practices and social and economic conditions. Like others engaged in the exploration of the relationship of law to empirical social science in the 1920s and 1930s, Douglas believed that legal principles were not meaningful as abstractions and needed above all to be responsive to the context in which they were promulgated.[136] Although he did not style himself a "Realist" or discuss legal realism in his autobiography, he was identified by a leading spokesman of the Realist movement as one of its most dedicated proponents.[137] Given his experiences at Columbia and Yale in the twenties and thirties, it is inconceivable that he found the Hughes statement anything but a confirmation of his own views. Hughes had simply extended to constitutional decisions a proposition Douglas had already endorsed in nonconstitutional areas. The proposition was that judicial predilections preceded the formulation of legal principles; the principles were rationalizations of those predilections.

In Douglas's characterization of his early years on the Court, then, outside forces—the decision in *O'Malley* and the conversation with Hughes—led him to abandon the norm of judicial nonparticipation in public affairs and the belief that the law was a body of immutable principles. It appears, however, that Douglas went on the Court with a rather different calculus, one that rested on the assumption that because law was, at bottom, a collection of the predilections of judges, the political ideology of a Justice was the most significant dimension of his service and should not be suppressed. The remainder of Douglas's career can be seen as consistent with that assumption. Because he believed that law was, fundamentally, nothing more than politics, he took no pains to avoid open participation in public affairs unless, as he put it, "a particular issue was likely to get into the Court, and unless the activity was plainly . . . partisan."[138] Although that qualification appears to be a concession to the norms of judicial nonpartisanship, it was a concession Douglas did not make consistently. In addition, because of Douglas's Realist philosophy of judging, he did not hold the same view of the significance of legal doctrine in constitutional cases that many of his colleagues on the Stone, Vinson, Warren, and Burger Courts propounded. For Douglas, the doctrinal dimensions of constitutional adjudication were relatively insignificant; what counted were the results in cases and the political philosophies that those results signified. During his years as a Justice he gave consistent attention to the political implications of constitutional cases, consistent attention to the ideological basis on which a particular political stance rested, and relatively little attention to the doctrinal formulations advanced to justify decisions.[139]

Douglas's open revelation of his preferred emphasis was so different from that of nearly all of the Justices with whom he served as to amount to a new interpretation of the role of a Supreme Court Justice in the twentieth century. When the image of appellate judges as oracles collapsed, a new set of constraints took the place of those that had fallen. The new constraints were derived from two sources, the institutional function of the nondemocratic Supreme Court in a democratic society and the doctrinal function of the Court as interpreter of the principles of the Constitution and other acknowledged legal authorities.[140] Douglas's two formative experiences on the Court, as he described them, denied the meaningfulness of both sources of constraint. As a Supreme Court Justice, the *O'Malley* case taught him, he was no different from a legislator, a member of the executive, or any other public-minded taxpayer; as a Supreme Court Justice, the Hughes conversation taught him, he simply used the impersonal discourse of doctrine to rationalize his personal biases. He was thus not constrained either by the function of his office or by doctrinal principles; he was constrained only by the rightness or wrongness of his political philosophy. That is why he found nothing unusual in writing an autobiography of his life as a judge in which he devoted no significant attention to the doctrinal contributions of himself or any of his colleagues. That is why legions of commentators and the Justices with whom he served found him, although one of the most intellectually talented persons ever appointed to the Court, to be strangely uninterested in the doctrinal underpinnings of his opinions.

Two episodes from Douglas's career on the Court illustrate his radical indifference to the approved sources of judicial constraint during his tenure. The first, which illuminates his approach to the question of judicial involvement in issues of partisan politics, is his behavior during the Court's consideration of the case of *Rosenberg v. United States*[141] which ended with the execution of Julius and Ethel Rosenberg for treason. The second, which illustrates his approach to the doctrinal dimension of appellate judging, is the role he played in the Court's post-World War II movement to accommodate a restrictive interpretation of the due process clause of the Fourteenth Amendment with an expansive interpretation of that amendment's equal protection clause. Each of these episodes has been treated amply in the scholarly literature on Douglas; the effort here is to see them in the context of his general approach to judging and of the controlling themes of his life.

In 1950 and 1951, Julius and Ethel Rosenberg were tried for conspiracy to commit espionage under the Espionage Act of 1917,[142] convicted, and sentenced to death by District Judge Irving Kaufman. They were found to have communicated secret information about the development of atomic energy to agents of the Soviet Union.[143] Sentence was passed in March 1951, and the Rosenbergs began a series of appeals. Eleven months later the United States Court of Appeals for the Second Circuit, in a three-judge panel, unanimously affirmed the Rosenbergs' conviction, with Jerome Frank writing an opinion that invited the Supreme Court to review the case further.[144] Lawyers for the Rosenbergs then filed a petition for certiorari before the Supreme Court. The Court denied that petition and another petition for a rehearing, with Justice Black dissenting[145] and Justice Frankfurter writing a memorandum that merely disclosed that four votes were necessary to secure review of a certiorari petition.[146] After the Court's actions, Judge Kaufman set the date for execution of the Rosenbergs as the week of January 12, 1953.

The Rosenbergs' lawyers then moved for a new trial in Judge Sylvester Ryan's federal district court, claiming that one of the witnesses at their trial had committed perjury and that the prosecutor, Irving Saypol, had made inflammatory and prejudicial statements to newspapers during the trial. Ryan summarily dismissed both claims,[147] and the Rosenbergs again appealed to the Second Circuit. On December 31, 1952, three weeks after Ryan announced his decision, the Second Circuit affirmed,[148] with Judge Thomas Swan's opinion characterizing Saypol's conduct as "wholly reprehensible"[149] but finding that the Rosenbergs had not been sufficiently prejudiced by it.[150] The Second Circuit, however, stayed the Rosenberg's execution until the Supreme Court could review its decision.[151] The Rosenbergs again filed a certiorari petition before the Court, and that petition was discussed by the Justices in an April 11, 1953, conference. At that conference the Justices voted to deny the petition. Douglas, who had voted against granting certiorari on the first of the Rosenbergs' petitions, also voted to deny certiorari on the second petition.[152]

The Justices' order formally denying the Rosenbergs' second petition was delayed, however, while Frankfurter, who had voted to grant it, debated whether he would publish a dissent from the order. Eventually, on May 10, Frankfurter circulated a memorandum to the other Justices in which he declared that he believed that prosecutor Saypol had acted "inexcusable[y]," but that any dissent might encourage the Communist party or imply that the Rosenbergs had been convicted though innocent. He would not, he said, publicly dissent from the order.[153] Suddenly, on May 22, Douglas circulated a memorandum in which he stated that he would dissent from the Court's order and that his dissent would read as follows: "Mr. Justice Douglas, agreeing with the Court of Appeals that some of the conduct of the United States Attorney was 'wholly reprehensible" but, believing in disagreement with the Court of Appeals that it probably prejudiced the defendants seriously, votes to grant certiorari."[154]

Douglas's change of position did not mean, on its face, that the Court would now grant the Rosenbergs' petition, because in the April 11 discussion only two Justices, Black and Frankfurter, had been inclined to grant. But in the discussion on the Rosenbergs' first petition in December 1952, Justice Harold Burton had voted to grant, although at the same time he indicated that his position was based more on deference to the views of Black and Frankfurter than on support for the petition itself.[155] Although Burton had voted against the second petition, Frankfurter seized on Douglas's change of position to urge that the Justices discuss the *Rosenberg* case once again, and to write an impassioned letter to Burton urging him to change his vote as well.[156] Frankfurter also conferred with Justice Robert Jackson, who had previously intimated to Frankfurter that although he was disinclined to grant review, he was offended by Saypol's conduct and might join a dissent that censured Saypol.[157]

The Justices did reconsider the *Rosenberg* case, meeting on May 23. Only one account of that meeting has survived, a long memorandum by Frankfurter dated June 4, 1953, deposited in the Frankfurter Papers in the Harvard Law School Library.[158] In that memorandum Frankfurter described the May 23 conference and some events immediately preceding it. One such event was a conversation Frankfurter had with Jackson in which he had urged Jackson to consider changing his vote to a grant. Jackson responded, according to Frankfurter, by saying, "[D]on't worry, Douglas's memorandum isn't going down," and adding that Douglas's act in changing his vote on the second Rosenberg petition was "the dirtiest, most shameful, most cynical performance that I think I have ever heard of in matters pertaining to law."[159] Frankfurter went on to say that in the conference itself

> Jackson . . . said he too would now grant, because the Court, it seemed to him, was put in an impossible position by Douglas's memorandum. There were now, he said, four people who at different states had voted to grant [Black, Frankfurter, Burton, and Douglas]. . . . This, he continued, was bound to leak. Furthermore, it was now to be publicly said by a member of the Court that the Rosenbergs had not had a fair trial. It was impossible to deny under those circumstances.[160]

Frankfurter then described Douglas's response to Jackson's comments. Douglas, who by seniority would have spoken before Jackson in the conference, had at that point merely voted to grant. But after it had become clear that with Jackson's vote (added to Frankfurter's, Black's, and Douglas's) the Court now would be granting the second petition, and discussion had turned to the scheduling of argument on that petition, Douglas spoke. As Frankfurter recounted it,

> At about this time, the discussion having gone on for quite some little time, Douglas spoke up. He had been quiet since announcing that he would grant. He ought to say something, he started. What he had written was badly drawn, he guessed. He hadn't realized it would embarrass anyone. He would just withdraw his memorandum if that would help matters.[161]

Frankfurter then described Jackson's response to this statement by Douglas: "If Douglas's memorandum was withdrawn, Jackson said, we were exactly where we had been before, and there was no longer any reason for him to change his vote. . . . The petition for certiorari was thus, again, denied," Frankfurter added, "and we turned to other matters."[162]

On May 25, two days after the conference, the Court issued a formal order denying the Rosenbergs' second petition, and Douglas, alone among the Justices, registered a formal dissent. His dissent merely stated that "Mr. Justice Douglas is of the opinion that the petition for certiorari should have been granted," omitting his earlier language about the prejudicial conduct of Saypol.[163] The *Rosenberg* case then entered its next phase, in which lawyers for the

Rosenbergs scrambled desperately for some means of delaying their execution, now scheduled for June 18, 1953; the Eisenhower administration attempted to make a deal with the Rosenbergs in which their death sentence would be commuted in exchange for their confessions of guilt and their assistance with respect to other alleged spies;[164] and the Supreme Court Justices prepared to wind up their 1952 Term.[165]

In this phase of the *Rosenberg* case, which ended with the executions of the Rosenbergs on the evening of June 19, Douglas was once again involved in a controversial fashion. Among the grounds alleged by the Rosenbergs' lawyers in seeking to prevent their execution was that new evidence had surfaced indicating that the prosecution had knowingly used perjured testimony. They made a motion before Judge Kaufman for a new trial, or in the alternative, a hearing on the new evidence. Judge Kaufman, after considering the matter for two days, denied the motion. Two days later, on June 8, the Second Circuit affirmed Judge Kaufman's ruling and denied a further stay of execution.[166] On June 12, attorneys for the Rosenbergs applied to Justice Jackson for a stay, arguing that they needed additional time to prepare briefs to make a formal appeal of Kaufman's ruling. Jackson referred the matter to the entire Supreme Court, recommending that oral argument take place on the question whether a stay should be granted to allow the lawyers time to prepare. The Court voted not to grant a stay, 5-4, with Douglas voting with the majority, taking the position that he would only grant a stay to hear argument on the merits of the case.[167] The Court's formal action on Jackson's stay was announced on June 15, and the Justices prepared to adjourn and leave Washington for the summer.

At this point another unexpected development involving Douglas occurred. Having voted to deny the stay referred to the Court by Jackson, he then granted another stay on his own motion, after he was approached by Fyke Farmer, a lawyer who filed a "next friend" habeas corpus petition on behalf of Irwin Edelman, who had sought to aid the Rosenbergs' defense but had been rebuffed by the Rosenbergs' lawyers. In the petition, originally filed before Kaufman on June 14, Farmer argued that the Espionage Act of 1917 had been superseded, with respect to atomic energy espionage, by the Atomic Energy Act of 1946,[168] and that that Act permitted the death penalty in atomic energy espionage cases only when the penalty had been recommended by a jury. The Rosenbergs had continued to pass atomic secrets after 1946, the prosecution had argued in the original indictment against them, and thus were within the Atomic Energy Act's coverage.[169] When Kaufman denied Farmer's petition on June 15, Farmer went to Washington in the hope of securing a stay of execution from a Supreme Court Justice. He approached Douglas on June 16 and presented him with an application for a stay, which Douglas, after researching the Atomic Energy Act issue, granted the next day.[170] Douglas's action set the stage for an extraordinary and unprecedented special session of the Court on June 18 and 19, in which a majority of Justices, including Vinson, Minton, Jackson, Clark, and Reed, eventually overturned Douglas's stay, with Burton joining the majority only after it was clear that he would not provide their fifth vote.[171] The Court eventually issued a formal opinion, written by Vinson, stating reasons for that denial; Jackson and Clark wrote concurring opinions and Black, Douglas, and Frankfurter wrote dissents.[172] The majority opinions were not filed until July 16; the Rosenbergs were executed on June 19, the same day that the Court's decision vacating Douglas's stay was announced.

Commentators have tended to agree on the facts of Douglas's behavior in the *Rosenberg* case, but significant differences of opinion exist about the motivation for Douglas's apparently inconsistent actions. Before the question of Douglas's motivation is explored, however, it is useful to review Douglas's own account of his role in the case.

In the second volume of his autobiography Douglas discussed the *Rosenberg* case, his treatment representing the only extended attention he gave to any case from his thirty-six-year tenure on the Court. His discussion did not mention his change of vote during the Court's consideration of the Rosenberg's second petition. He confined his comments on that phase of the case to a notation that "Mr. Justice Black . . . and I [had] vot[ed] to grant [certiorari]" in the case.[173] Even that language did not make clear that he and Black had dissented on different occasions, and that only Black of all the Justices who had heard the *Rosenberg* case in all its forms had consistently and publicly supported granting them review on the merits.

Douglas spent more time on his role in granting the Rosenbergs a stay. The "key point made by Fyke Farmer" that persuaded him to grant a stay, Douglas said, was "the ambiguity in the [Atomic Energy] Act."[174] He explained this comment by stating that Jerome Frank on the Second Circuit had later told him that "if my stay had not been vacated and my ruling had reached the Court of Appeals, as it would have, there was no doubt that the Court of Appeals would have held that the imposition of the death sentence was improper."[175] He had granted the stay, Douglas said, because "[i]n the Rosenberg case the jury had made no . . . recommendation [of the death penalty]; and the trial court had proceeded on the ground that only the original [Espionage] [A]ct was applicable."[176] The "incriminating evidence against the Rosenbergs," he asserted, consisted of "events happening *after* the 1946 amendment that ameliorated the punishment."[177]

The principal purpose of Douglas's discussion of the *Rosenberg* case seemed to have been to stress the inappropriateness of the Court's special session that vacated his stay and the public hysteria surrounding the case. He declared that Vinson "had no authority to convene a Special Term of Court,"[178] that Black had "vigorously objected" to one being called without a formal vote of a majority of the Justices,[179] and that he himself "decided to waive the point" only because "a majority of the Court was clearly of a mind to ratify the action of the Chief."[180] He then suggested that the Court's precipitous handling of the stay issue was a response to "the hysteria that beset our people" because of the "threat of Communism."[181] "[T]hat hysteria touched off the Justices also," he wrote, and "they ran pell-mell with the mob in the Rosenberg case and felt it was important that this couple die that very week."[182] The *Rosenberg* case illustrated for Douglas the "serious danger to our legal system . . . when *ideological* trials take place behind the facade of *legal* trials."[183]

Douglas's version of his actions in the *Rosenberg* case thus stresses his dissent from the denial of the second certiorari petition and his granting of the stay, identifies his position as supportive of full justice for the Rosenbergs, and characterizes the case as ideological, with the majority of the Court that denied the petition and vacated his stay capitulating to the atmosphere of the Cold War. But some of the internal actions of Douglas in the case, notably his offer to withdraw his memorandum dissenting from the denial of the second certiorari petition "if that would help matters,"[184] and his two earlier votes against granting the Rosenbergs Supreme Court review, seem inconsistent with his own account. Noting these inconsistencies, commentators have advanced their own explanations.

Professor Michael Parrish, who first brought to light the internal sources on the Court's deliberations in the *Rosenberg* case, has advanced an explanation for Douglas's conduct that basically tracks that given by Jackson and Frankfurter. In a 1977 article on the *Rosenberg* case, Parrish wrote:

> The harshest interpretation, provided by Jackson through Frankfurter, suggests that Douglas did not want the case brought before the Court where he, like the others, would be forced to affirm or reverse the convictions. . . . The memorandum of May 22 provided a way out of his predicament: Douglas could dissent vigorously from the denial of certiorari, affirm his liberal credentials, yet not be required to vote on the case after full arguments. He withdrew the memorandum in the conference when it became clear that the Court, above all Jackson, preferred to hear the case rather than endure a provocative dissent. Sensing Jackson's motives, Douglas retreated, encouraged Jackson to switch his vote, and thereby killed the grant of certiorari.[185]

Parrish also argued that Frankfurter and Jackson took a similar view of Douglas's granting of the stay. "Every time a vote could have been had for a hearing," Frankfurter reported Jackson saying, "Douglas opposed a hearing in open Court, and only when it was perfectly clear that a particular application would not be granted, did he take a position for granting it."[186] Parrish concluded that "both Frankfurter and Jackson believed that Douglas had contradictory motives in the Rosenberg litigation. On the one hand, he worked to retain his image as a liberal tribune who, when necessary, fought alone on behalf of the oppressed. On the other, he thwarted collective efforts to review the case."[187]

James Simon, Douglas's principal biographer, posits an explanation not unlike that advanced by Jackson, Frankfurter, and Parrish:

> It may be true, as Douglas contended, that the new legal argument presented on behalf of the Rosenbergs on June 16 was more substantial then the earlier ones, and that that point was decisive for him. [But] [w]hat is troubling about the Douglas record [in the Rosenberg case] . . . is that his earlier negative votes seemed so inconsistent with his whole judicial approach and philosophy. . . . He had rarely based his judicial decisions on technical procedural grounds—when such grounds cut against the interests of individual defendants. . . .

> [T]here was something profoundly unsettling about Douglas' behavior. Douglas, the outspoken champion of the underdog, insisted on dealing with the Rosenberg case on his terms alone . . .
>
> In his . . . autobiography, Douglas . . . [wrote] with pride of his stay of the Rosenbergs' executions on June 17, 1953. That is the Douglas, the libertarian symbol, that he wanted the public to remember.[188]

Neither Parrish's nor Simon's explanations have satisfied Professor William Cohen, a former law clerk to Douglas. Using essentially the same evidence relied upon by Parrish and Simon, but focusing more heavily on the technical legal questions presented in the *Rosenberg* case, Cohen has concluded that Parrish and Simon "are wrong about Douglas"; that Douglas's "philosophy and actions were consistent throughout the Rosenberg saga."[189] Douglas, according to Cohen, believed that Supreme Court review should not be granted unless the Rosenbergs, or any petitioners to the court, "raised substantial questions of law, worthy of review on the merits."[190] After a detailed examination of the various stages of the *Rosenberg* case, Cohen concluded that "Douglas voted on the merits of the issues presented, without reference to the public clamor either to save the Rosenbergs or to execute them."[191] In the course of his interpretation, Cohen relies on his understanding of Supreme Court procedure, his belief that Douglas "consistently voted against plenary Supreme Court review, even in capital cases, when review would be pointless,"[192] and his conviction that "on the Court [Douglas] stated and voted his honest convictions and left the business of winning converts and votes to others."[193] For Cohen, the distinction between substantial and unsubstantial questions being raised in a review petition was a crucial one for Douglas, not only in *Rosenberg* but in other cases.[194]

The basic difference between the commentators' explanations stems from their belief or disbelief in Douglas's inclination to separate technical legal issues from larger ideological issues when considering a controversial Supreme Court case. Parrish, following Jackson and Frankfurter, suggests that Douglas was entirely prepared to manipulate technical legal procedures, such as the rule that four Justices must agree to grant certiorari for the Court to hear a case, or the rule that appeals based on technical errors in a criminal conviction must be genuinely harmful to the determination of the defendant's guilt or innocence, for his own ideological ends. Simon is not quite so skeptical, but he finds Douglas's concern with maintaining a distinction between substantial and "technical procedural" grounds for review in the *Rosenberg* case "troubling" in light of Douglas's lack of emphasis on such a distinction in other criminal cases.[195] Cohen, for his part, finds the distinction between substantial and insubstantial questions in a Supreme Court review petition a controlling feature of Douglas's stance as a judge.[196] Various images of Douglas as a Supreme Court Justice emerge from the respective explanations, varying from that of a quintessential political strategist to a loner who disdained political maneuvering and voted his own convictions.

Critical to an assessment of Douglas's motivation in the *Rosenberg* case, then, is a judgment about Douglas's conception of his job as a Supreme Court Justice: did judging involve simply an independent assessment of the legal "merits" of cases, or was it a more politicized, strategic, ideological exercise? Jackson and Frankfurter, both of whom had served on the Court with Douglas for over a decade at the time of the *Rosenberg* case, obviously believed that Douglas held the latter view of judging, as they did.[197] Parrish and Simon, on the whole, seem to share that belief.[198] Cohen, however, who clerked for Douglas only four years after the *Rosenberg* case had been decided, obviously believed that Douglas genuinely wanted to ensure that the Rosenbergs received a fair trial because he saw them as victims of Cold War hysteria. Douglas "consistently had the courage and foresight to stand up for what was right" in the Cold War period, Cohen began his account.[199] As Douglas's law clerk, Cohen had felt " 'privileged to be on the side of a man of courage who was doing the right thing.' "[200]

The portrait of Douglas thus far sketched in this chapter is not consistent with his holding a belief that judging was simply an exercise in reaching the "merits" of issues without regard for their personal or political consequences. The psychological tensions of Douglas's early years, his actions during his years on the Columbia and Yale faculties, his efforts to facilitate his nomination to the Court, and the labor he invested in his autobiography to construct an image of himself as wholly independent of political or personal pressures each suggest that strategic, consequentialist behavior was a consistent feature of his professional life. It is hard to imagine that, once appointed to the Supreme Court, Douglas suddenly became oblivious to the personal and political ramifications of his decisions.

Moreover, Douglas had been taken seriously in many quarters as Roosevelt's logical successor: indeed he had been proposed by Roosevelt himself for the Vice Presidency in 1944.[201] While publicly disclaiming any interest in that office, Douglas, according to some accounts, hoped and expected to get the nomination.[202] Four years later, Douglas was again mentioned prominently for the Vice Presidency, and this time was offered the position by President Harry Truman.[203] He declined the offer, saying in a prepared statement that "definitely and finally . . . I am not available for any public office," and writing Truman that "politics had never been my profession, and . . . I could serve my country best where I am."[204] Nonetheless his friends and advisors, such as Thomas Corcoran, Harold Ickes, the journalist Arthur Krock, and the economist and man of letters Eliot Janeway, assumed that Douglas might well try for the Presidency in 1952.[205]

But in September 1951, Douglas wrote Truman a letter, published in the *New York Times* in January 1952,[206] that stated categorically that he would remain on the Court for the balance of his public career. Numerous factors, such as the deterioration of his marriage to Mildred Riddle and the fact that his political constituency—primarily members of the Eastern liberal intelligentsia—had diminished in influence among professional Democratic politicians during Truman's presidency,[207] may have contributed to Douglas's decision. But whatever the basis of his withdrawal from national elective politics, it was not accompanied by a withdrawal from involvement with public issues. Janeway told James Simon in 1979 that in the 1950s "the Court became Douglas's power center, and it had none of the problems posed by administrative responsibilities and patronage of political office."[208]

In short, the expectations of others in the political community necessarily played a part in the shaping of Douglas's self-image. Supreme Court Justices were public figures, capable of providing leadership on social issues. Douglas did not merely travel, write, and speak out on public matters for his own pleasure; he engaged in those activities because he thought them another means of reaching a constituency.

Douglas's grant of the stay in the *Rosenberg* case thus presented no conflict with his conception of his office. He appears to have believed that Farmer's argument might be worthy of serious attention. That belief surfaced extraordinarily late in the *Rosenberg* proceedings, but that does not mean it was not genuine, especially with Douglas's being well aware of the Rosenbergs' impending execution. There is no gainsaying the fact, however, that Douglas also knew, at the time he granted the stay, that five Justices—Vinson, Clark, Reed,

Minton, and Jackson—were dead set against overturning the Rosenbergs' conviction. Thus in any instance where five Justices were required to sustain a Court action favorable to the Rosenbergs—that is, any time when the Justices were voting on any question except whether to grant certiorari—Douglas knew that a position favorable to the Rosenbergs would lose. He may have hoped to persuade others to change their minds and vote to grant his stay. But he had no history of engaging in persuasion of that kind. Thus in a sense it does not matter whether Douglas, in granting the stay, was playing to a larger political constituency or simply following his genuine belief in the merits of the statutory argument. The outcome would have been the same, and he knew it.

The decisions that produced his double change of mind on the second certiorari petition are less capable of straightforward explanation. Evidence from more than one set of internal Court papers indicates clearly that Douglas was originally disinclined to vote to grant certiorari.[209] Douglas may have been a defender of free speech during the Cold War years, but he was also a visible anti-Communist as well, writing books warning of the threat of Communist infiltration in Asia and Africa and offering advice as to how it might be countered.[210] There is no evidence suggesting that he thought the Rosenbergs innocent of the charges brought against them. When he changed his mind about the second certiorari petition, he had reason to believe that his change of mind would make no difference: his memorandum of May 22 was written in the form of a public dissent. When Jackson then changed his vote on the second certiorari petition, and the Justices began discussing the scheduling of arguments on the issues raised in that petition, Douglas knew that he would no longer be filing that memorandum as a dissent. His explanation that he was withdrawing the memorandum because it was "badly drafted" and might "embarrass" some of the other Justices made no sense, for with Jackson's change of vote he would have no need to file it. When Jackson then changed his vote back, Douglas again made his dissent public.[211]

If Douglas were genuinely convinced that a substantial legal question—the question whether Saypol's statements to the newspapers at trial had seriously prejudiced the Rosenbergs—was being raised by the second certiorari petition, it is odd that, once he had secured the votes to view that petition, he then withdrew the memorandum. Its language would not now "embarrass" anyone. If he remained convinced that the petition should have been granted, it is strange that he omitted the language about prejudice from his dissent. In short, his double change of mind on the second certiorari petition appears consistent with the strategy of a person who wanted to identify himself as a "dissenter" in the *Rosenberg* case but did not want the Rosenbergs' conviction overturned. It does not seem consistent with any other strategy, especially the strategy of a person who now believed that the Rosenbergs had been unfairly convicted and wanted their convictions reversed.

Douglas's behavior in the *Rosenberg* case also appears consistent with that of a person whose approach to the internal deliberations of the Court was designed to promote his individual goals rather than any institutional goals the Court might have had as a body. The Court in *Rosenberg* was especially concerned with creating an impression that the case was not, as Douglas was later to say, an ideological trial taking place behind the facade of a legal trial.[212] Beginning with the circulation of his May 22 memorandum, Douglas behaved in a way that effectively made it impossible for the Justices to claim that their decision in the *Rosenberg* case had been based on a unanimous finding that no substantial legal issues remained to bar the Rosenbergs' execution. His dissent from the second certiorari petition, his issuance of a stay, and his dissent from the Court majority's overturning of his stay all signified that he believed that substantial issues did remain. In his account of *Rosenberg,* he described the censure he took for issuing the stay, the political atmosphere in which the Court's deliberations took place, the "sadistic satisfaction" many people experienced on witnessing pictures of the execution,[213] and the Court majority's running "pell-mell with the mob" rather than allowing "the point of law on the legality of [the Rosenbergs'] sentence [to] be calmly considered and decided."[214] It is clear that the impression of the case he wanted to create for posterity was that of a case in which he, almost alone, stood up for the Rosenbergs in an atmosphere in which the barbarity of capital punishment coalesced with the hysteria of anti-Communism. That impression appeared designed to embarrass the Court majority and remind Douglas's public of his individuality.

If one looks at the *Rosenberg* case as an exercise in Douglas's approach to the perceived constraints imposed on Supreme Court Justices by the demands of collegiality, the appearance of disassociation from politics, and the obligation to articulate "legal" as distinguished from "ideological" reasons for decisions, Douglas's posture in the case appeared to treat none of those constraints as applying to him. To the extent that this set of institutional constraints responded to the problem of judicial bias in a society where the federal judiciary, as personified by the Supreme Court, was taken to be a counter-majoritarian and undemocratic institution, Douglas did not seem to hold a theory of judging designed to suppress the element of bias in judicial decision-making. Indeed, his behavior in the Rosenberg case appeared consistent with a theory incorporating the notion that "bias"—in the elevated sense of politically conscious ideology—should be *furthered* by the deliberative process of the Court. Alternatively, according to this view, the deliberative process of the Court was simply a vehicle for the implementation of bias in its elevated sense. The first version of Douglas's theory, in the face of mid-twentieth-century jurisprudential canons designed to curb bias, seemed deeply, almost anarchically, radical; the alternative version seemed deeply cynical. Jackson and Frankfurter, who believed that Douglas held to the latter version, used the label of cynicism to describe his performance in *Rosenberg*. Douglas, who claimed in his autobiography that "in my long service, I . . . never tried to persuade any Justice that I was right and he was wrong,"[215] would likely have described *Rosenberg,* or any other case, as simply an opportunity for the "right" values to triumph. The constraints on judges, in Douglas's theory, did not come from within institutions but from within individual judges themselves. The individual judge was constrained only to get a decision right.

Douglas's characterization of judging as getting results "right" provides an explanation not only for his indifference to the role of collegiality in Supreme Court decision-making but also for his indifference to the doctrinal underpinnings of his own opinions. No feature of Douglas's career caused more commentary from both critics and admirers than his apparent unwillingness to buttress the results he reached in cases by resorting to the common analytical techniques employed by twentieth-century Justices as justificatory devices. If a case involved textual interpretation of the Constitution or a statute, Douglas rarely engaged in extensive textual exegesis; if a body of precedent was considered applicable to the case, he rarely relied on it or took pains to distinguish it.[216] The most significant feature of his opinions was their espousal of positions that were doctrinally novel without extensive justification of the innovation or more than cursory recognition of its novelty.[217] Douglas's opinions, even his majority opinions, appeared to be almost indistinguishable from his nonjudicial writings: both were highly individualized responses to social problems. His opinions appeared to deny that there was any difference between judicial language and logic and the "ordinary" language and logic of social commentary by lay persons.

Two paradigmatic Douglas majority opinions are *Skinner v. Oklahoma*[218] and *Griswold v. Connecticut,*[219] decided twenty-three years apart. The *Skinner* and *Griswold* cases, not often linked by constitutional commentators, are remarkably similar in several respects. Both were doctrinally audacious opinions whose innovativeness was cryptically, even assertively presented; both involved detours around apparently insurmountable analytical barriers; and both touched upon a theme—the decision to procreate and thus to pass on one's legacy of individuality to one's progeny and hence to posterity—that touched deep currents in Douglas's life.

Skinner, testing the constitutionality of an Oklahoma statute providing for the compulsory sterilization of "habitual criminals," was decided in the 1942 Term, five years after the Court, in *West Coast Hotel Co. v. Parrish*,[220] had demonstrated its reluctance to use the Fourteenth Amendment's due process clause to substitute its judgments on economic issues for those of state legislatures, and fifteen years after the Court had sustained a Virginia statute authorizing the mandatory sterilization of inmates in state institutions who were found to have a hereditary form of imbecility or insanity. In that case, *Buck v. Bell*,[221] Holmes, for the majority, had not only uttered the notorious aphorism "three generations of imbeciles are enough," but had disparaged an equal protection clause argument advanced on behalf of the inmate as "the usual last resort of constitutional arguments."[222]

Douglas was thus faced with a jurisprudential atmosphere in which substantive judicial inquiries into the meaning of the due process clause had been disapproved, and equal protection arguments, in the identical context of the statute at issue in Skinner, had been ridiculed. He responded by striking down the statute on equal protection grounds. After pointing out that the statute made an exception for embezzlement, although the state provided the same criminal penalties for embezzlers as it did for those who committed grand larceny, he noted that a consequence of the statute was that while "[a] person who enters a chicken coop and steals chickens . . . may be sterilized if he is thrice convicted," a person who was asked to hold the chickens and "fraudulently appropriates" them could not be sterilized "no matter how habitual his proclivities for embezzlement are and no matter how often his conviction."[223] Douglas then continued:

> [T]he . . . legislation runs afoul of the equal protection clause, though we give Oklahoma . . . large deference [to make classifications]. We are dealing here with legislation which involves one of the basic civil rights of man. Marriage and procreation area fundamental to the very existence and survival of the race. The power to sterilize, if exercised, may have subtle, far-reaching and devastating effects. In evil or reckless hands it can cause races or types which are inimical to the dominant group to wither and disappear. There is no redemption for the individual whom the law touches. . . . He is forever deprived of a basic liberty. We mention these matters not to reexamine the scope of the police power of the States. We advert to them merely in emphasis of our view that strict scrutiny of the classification which a State makes in a sterilization law is essential, lest unwittingly, or otherwise, invidious discriminations are made against groups or types of individuals in violation of the constitutional guaranty of just and equal laws. . . . The equal protection clause would indeed be a formula of empty words if such conspicuously artificial lines could be drawn.[224]

In that paragraph Douglas had identified procreation as a "fundamental right," indicated that state legislation that had the effect of depriving persons of such rights would be subjected to "strict scrutiny" by the Court, and announced that "invidious discriminations" by state statutes in cases implicating "fundamental rights" ran afoul of the equal protection clause. He had formulated these doctrinal generalities in a case in which Chief Justice Stone authored a concurring opinion that found the equal protection clause an inappropriate basis for the judgment.[225]

Given that the case arose at a time in which the equal protection clause was virtually dormant as a basis for searching judicial review of legislative decisions, Douglas's conversion of *Skinner* into a fundamental rights-strict scrutiny equal protection case was striking. Even more startling, however, was the absence of any doctrinal basis for the general claims he advanced in his crucial paragraph. His statement that marriage and procreation were "fundamental" rights,[226] among "the basic civil rights of man,"[227] was not accompanied by any citation to a text of the Constitution giving them explicit protection.[228] He stated that the Skinner majority's view was that strict scrutiny of classifications made in sterilization laws was "essential,"[229] presumably because of the fundamentality of the rights being affected, but he did not give any reasons for why fundamentality triggered strict judicial scrutiny in the sterilization area when state deprivations of economic "liberties," a deprivation with some textual basis in the Fourteenth Amendment, did not trigger such scrutiny.[230] Finally, he announced a connection between the unequal enforcement of sterilization laws and "invidious discriminations,"[231] which he took to be the central evil the equal protection clause was designed to protect, but he gave no reasons for that connection. In sum, the three interconnected doctrinal propositions of his *Skinner* opinion were advanced without any textual or doctrinal support.

Douglas's opinion in *Griswold*, which appeared in a strikingly similar jurisprudential context, took a comparable approach. In two cases in the years between *Skinner* and *Griswold* the Court had shown a willingness to make substantive judgments in the equal protection area, tracking the analysis that Douglas had offered in *Skinner* through the same paces of fundamentality, strict scrutiny, and invidious discrimination.[232] But the Court had refrained from making comparable substantive inquiries in the due process area, mindful of its strictures in *West Coast Hotel Co. v. Parrish*.[233] *Griswold* presented a case where birth control information had been distributed to married persons in violation of a Connecticut statute prohibiting the use of contraceptive devices.[234] The case did not appear to be an equal protection case because the statute applied to "Any person."[235] It appeared to be a due process case, with the word "liberty" in that clause implicated by Connecticut's effort to restrict the choices of married persons to procreate or not.

Douglas confronted the substantive due process implications of *Griswold* in his first paragraph directed at the merits of the petitioners' claim. "W[e] are met with a wide range of questions," he announced,

> that implicate the Due Process Clause of the Fourteenth Amendment. Overtones of some arguments suggest that Lochner v. New York should be our guide. But we decline that invitation as we did in [West Coast Hotel v. Parrish]. We do not sit as a super-legislature to determine the wisdom, need, and propriety of laws that touch economic problems, business affairs, or social conditions. This law, however, operates directly on an intimate relation of husband and wife. . . .[236]

Douglas then engaged in his controversial "penumbral"[237] analysis of "specific guarantees in the Bill of Rights,"[238] designed to show that "[v]arious guarantees create zones of privacy."[239] Having extracted "emanations"[240] from the First, Third, Fourth, Fifth, and Ninth Amendments,[241] he then cited cases that "bear witness that the right of privacy which presses for recognition here is a legitimate one."[242] Prominent among such "privacy" cases was *Skinner*.[243] The right of privacy being protected in *Griswold*, he concluded, was "older than the Bill of Rights"; the "association" from which the right emanated, marriage, was "intimate to the degree of being sacred."[244] He had begun *Griswold* by emphasizing that "*married persons*"[245] had sought to receive the birth control information prohibited by the statute: it appeared that the "fundamental" quality of the right to privacy was augmented by (or perhaps derived from) its marital context.

A later decision extended *Griswold* beyond its marital setting,[246] and eventually the Court openly conceded that *Griswold* had been a substantive due process case all along; there was a difference between legislative regulation of economic affairs and legislative regulation of the non-economic liberties derived from personal autonomy.[247] But the significance of Douglas's *Griswold* opinion was not that it chose the rubric of privacy on which to justify its result, but that it responded to what appeared to be a doctrinal impasse by simply creating constitutional doctrine on the spot, as Douglas had done in *Skinner*. The impasse in *Skinner* had been the perceived weakness of the equal protection clause as a safeguard against "rational" legislative classifications. Douglas's response had been to claim that searching equal protection review was necessary where "fundamental" rights were affected, suggesting that in those instances "invidious discriminations" might be involved in the classification. The impasse in *Griswold* had been the perceived weakness of the due process clause where a legislature had made substantive judgments about how its police powers and individual liberties should be balanced; Douglas's response was to claim in *Griswold* that the "liberty" affected was the fundamental right of marital privacy. He gave no more detailed reasons for his doctrinal pronouncements in *Griswold* than he had in *Skinner;* the justification for the results was ultimately that they were overwhelmingly "right."

At bottom, *Skinner* and *Griswold* rested on two rhetorical questions that Douglas put in the course of his doctrinal analysis. The question in *Griswold* was stated explicitly: "Would we allow the police to search the sacred precincts of marital bedrooms for telltale signs of the use of contraceptives?[248] The question in *Skinner* had been posed implicitly when Douglas juxtaposed the hypothetical case of the "habitual" chicken thief and the "habitual" embezzler of chickens others had entrusted to him. "Should we allow the state of Oklahoma to sterilize the thief but not the embezzler?" was the question.[249] In both cases, the answer was an immediate and obvious no. In those questions and the answers they elicited lay the essence of the cases: *Skinner* involved a patently unfair legislative classification and *Griswold* involved a patently intrusive legislative edict. Douglas sensed that both cases were "easy" cases in that sense: he knew that the result he reached was "right." The only difficulties were analytical, created by the presence of awkward doctrinal barriers. Douglas simply disregarded those barriers and created some new doctrine.

This analysis of *Skinner* and *Griswold* emphasizes the fact that from 1942 on Douglas sensed that one of the central unarticulated problems of constitutional adjudication in a political culture in which equality and liberty were increasingly identified as core values was the interface between the equal protection and due process clauses. Douglas had come on a Court in which the due process clause was out of fashion, and the equal protection clause dormant, as judicial devices to scrutinize legislative activity. The bulk of his career was spent on a Court in which judicial scrutiny of legislatures increased, typically justified by appeal to a cluster of values in which freedom was associated with equality. In the Stone Court Douglas's *Skinner* opinion had identified him as the progenitor of substantive equal protection doctrine; in the Vinson Court he had been, at least publicly, the civil libertarian protesting against Cold War repression in First Amendment cases.[250] In the latter years of the Warren Court the momentum of egalitarianism seemed to reinforce momentum for the protection of civil liberties, and Douglas's fusion of the concept of "fundamental" rights with the concept of "invidious discrimination" became a valuable doctrinal exegesis for Warren Court majorities.

Nowhere was this fusion more evident than in *Harper v. Board of Elections*,[251] one of the most activist decisions of the later Warren Court. The question in *Harper* was whether the state of Virginia's imposition of an annual poll tax of $1.50 on all residents over twenty-one years of age as a precondition for voting in state elections violated the equal protection clause.[252] The modern Court had twice sustained poll taxes against constitutional challenges,[253] but by 1966, when *Harper* was decided, all but four states had abolished poll taxes in state elections and the Twenty-fourth Amendment had abolished them in federal elections. Poll taxes had become notorious because of their historic association with racial discrimination. As Douglas noted in a footnote in *Harper*, the "'Virginia poll tax was born of a desire to disenfranchise the Negro.'"[254] There was thus no question how the Court majority would decide the case; the question was whether it should decide it, given the fact that poll taxes seemed about to be legislatively extinguished, and what the rationale for the decision would be, in the face of contrary precedent and some apparent analytical difficulties.

There were three such analytical difficulties. First, legislative classifications based on wealth, which poll taxes amounted to on their face, had not been closely scrutinized by the modern Court under its equal protection jurisprudence.[255] Second, the Constitution had not expressly conferred any right to vote in state elections, so the constitutional violation inherent in conditioning voting in a state election on wealth or any other qualification was not immediately apparent. Third, absent any settled doctrine providing for stricter scrutiny of legislative classifications based on wealth where enumerated constitutional rights were not at stake, *Harper* amounted to a "rational basis" case. As Justice Harlen pointed out in his dissent, a state might rationally have concluded "that payment of some minimal poll tax promotes civic responsibility, weeding out those who do not care enough about public affairs to pay $1.50 or thereabouts a year for the exercise of the franchise."[256]

Douglas ignored each of these difficulties. He announced, citing the Warren Court's reapportionment decisions, that the "right of suffrage"[257] was "'a fundamental matter in a free and democratic society.'"[258] He announced that "[l]ines drawn on the basis of wealth or property, like those of race, are traditionally disfavored."[259] And he concluded that "[t]o introduce wealth or payment of a fee as a measure of a voter's qualifications is to introduce a capricious or irrelevant factor," which causes "an 'invidious' discrimination that runs afoul of the Equal Protection Clause."[260] In other words, the right to vote was "fundamental" because the reapportionment cases had held that voting power could not be diluted because of residency within a state; because the combination of a "fundamental right" and a "traditionally disfavored" basis for legislative classification reversed the presumption of constitutionality for state poll tax legislation; and because a fundamental right had been infringed upon by a traditionally disfavored classification. Conditioning voting on wealth thus caused an "invidious discrimination" and violated the equal protection clause. Douglas's last two paragraphs made this reasoning explicit:

> We had long been mindful that where fundamental rights and liberties are asserted under the Equal Protection Clause, classifications which might invade or restrain them must be closely scrutinized and carefully confined. . . .
>
> Those principles apply here. For to repeat, wealth or fee paying has, in our view, no relation to voting qualifications; the right to vote is too precious, too fundamental to be so burdened or conditioned.[261]

Douglas, mindful of the recent precedents finding poll taxes not to violate the equal protection clause, had noted along the way that that clause was "not shackled to the political theory of a particular era. . . . Notions of what constitutes equal treatment for purposes of the Equal Protection Clause *do* change."[262]

A commentator on Douglas's *Harper* opinion noted that it "expressly or impliedly repudiates every conventional guide to legal judgment."[263] By "conventional guides" the commentator meant the text of the Constitution, which nowhere contains any language about the right to vote in state elections; the practices of the framers, who permitted poll taxes; the history of judicial construction of the Constitution, which revealed no efforts to use the equal protection clause to invalidate poll taxes; and the recent reaffirmation by the Court of the validity of poll taxes in two decisions. *Harper* was thus a prototypical Douglas opinion in its defiance of "conventional guides" to constitutional adjudication in the twentieth century.

Harper was a prototypical Douglas opinion in another sense. It cited *Skinner* prominently and followed the doctrinal format announced in *Skinner*: when "fundamental" rights were at stake, and "strict" judicial scrutiny of a legislative classification was thus required, the presumption of legislative constitutionality was reversed and states needed to show something like a compelling interest in order to justify discriminations that otherwise would be characterized as "invidious." That Douglas did not mean these features of the "new" equal protection doctrine he had created in "fundamental rights" cases to emerge from conventional guides was perfectly plain. His pattern of opinion-writing from *Skinner* to *Harper* had shown that was capable of invoking or ignoring, as he saw fit, the commands of the text, precedent, settled judicial construction, and other "guides." He intended the doctrine that he had promulgated in *Skinner* to come into play when a Justice believed that the rights allegedly being infringed were fundamental, and the legislative classification infringing those rights therefore was presumptively invalid. He meant, in other words, that when a judge had searched his own values and concluded that the right was basic to this conception of enlightened society, the rest of the *Skinner* analysis naturally followed. The doctrine of *Skinner* did not come from anywhere except the judge's mind and heart. But if the insights yielded by that personal value search were "right," then that was, properly, where the doctrine should come from. The judge's individual consciousness was in this sense the conscience of the nation.

The cases in the *Skinner-Griswold-Harper* line were also significant as substantive policy statements. Together they stood for the proposition that egalitarian solutions to policy issues such as sterilization or birth control or suffrage were to be preferred to elitist solutions.[264] They also stood for the proposition that freedom of individual expression should not be limited to the areas of speech and the press: it also was implicated in areas such as the decision to procreate or not to procreate and the decision to cast one's vote regardless of one's affluence. They demonstrated the progression of Douglas's ideological views from those of an early-twentieth-century liberal pragmatist to those of an "absolutist" defender of individual freedom and equality of condition.[265] They marked the transformation from the author of *An Almanac of Liberty*,[266] with its message of Cold War liberalism, to the author of *Points of Rebellion*,[267] with its apparent embrace of late 1960s protest radicalism. Increasingly, as the momentum of egalitarianism increased during the 1960s, Douglas became more visibly and outspokenly the egalitarian activist, identifying egalitarian social policies as fostering rather than curtailing individual liberties.

In *Doe v. Bolton*,[268] a companion case to *Roe v. Wade*,[269] Douglas took the ideology of *Skinner, Griswold*, and *Harper* yet a step further. After apparently working hard to ensure that majority of the Court approved the constitutionality of a right to have an abortion,[270] Douglas wrote a concurrence in *Doe v. Bolton*. The concurrence announced that Douglas believed, after all, in substantive due process, even though he claimed that *Griswold* had "nothing to do with substantive due process."[271] The right protected in *Roe v. Wade* was part of a "catalogue of . . . customary, traditional, and time-honored rights, amenities, privileges, and immunities that come within the sweep of 'the Blessings of Liberty' mentioned in the preamble to the Constitution,"[272] many of which "come within the meaning of the term 'liberty' as used in the Fourteenth Amendment."[273] He then gave a list of those rights, in order of their strength:

> *First is the autonomous control over the development of one's intellect, interests, tastes, and personality.*
>
> *Second is freedom of choice in the basic decisions of one's life respecting marriage, divorce, procreation, contraception, and the education and upbringing of children.*
>
> *Third is the freedom to care for one's health and person, freedom from bodily restraint or compulsion, freedom to walk, stroll, or loaf.*[274]

Douglas ranged these rights on a scale from "absolute" to "fundamental"; none, he believed, could be infringed without the demonstration of a compelling state interest. His listing of the rights indicated that he had abandoned his earlier positions about the ability of government to restrict certain substantive rights on merely a showing of minimum rationality;[275] it also made clear that since *Griswold*, at least, he did not require that constitutional rights be attached to any explicit textual provisions. Above all, the "catalogue" of *Doe* demonstrated Douglas's focus on substantive values rather than traditional doctrinal sources as a basis for justifying results in constitutional cases.

The *Doe* concurrence was written in 1973; less than two years later Douglas suffered a stroke from which he was never to recover.[276] His last years were a painful testament to the fact that he was no more indomitable than other humans. He refused to accept incapacitation, struggled against the permanent loss of some of his physical and mental powers, had to be strongly urged to resign from the Court, and even believed that he could still serve as an active Justice after he had resigned.[277] He worked sporadically on the second volume of his autobiography, which appeared after his death, but his periods of full mental capacity grew shorter. In January 1980 he died, his reputation as a Justice, judging from the commentary in professional journals, still an object of controversy.[278]

III

Douglas's career presents a formidable puzzle for anyone undertaking to associate a tradition of American appellate judging with a series of constraints identified with the nature of judicial reasoning itself. The techniques employed by judges to justify their decisions have changed with time, as various analytical and doctrinal formulations have gained or lost stature. But the ebb and flow of particular justificatory devices should not imply that judicial reasoning has been perceived as indistinguishable from the reasoning of other lawmakers in American society. In particular, when constitutional issues have been raised, appellate judges have been seen as resolving issues by a process of reasoning distinct from that of legislators or members of the executive. The text of the Constitution, the "intention" of its framers, prior judicial precedent, and other sources conceived as external to a judge's personal sympathies and antipathies have commonly been expected to form the bases of an appellate judicial decision. Moreover, the opinion in which the decision is announced has commonly been expected to treat those sources as possessing far greater authority than the opinion writer's personal predilections. Indeed, the opinion has been expected to assume that its writer's politics and ideology were irrelevant to the decision.

One may choose to treat judicial deference to external sources of authority as a sham and thus characterize the problem of legitimating judgments made by an autocratic branch of government in a democratic society as a pseudoproblem, arguing that one can never know whether judicial reasoning offered as a basis of legitimating a judgment is genuine or contrived. But that is not to say that the legitimating problem does not exist; it has existed, in one form or another, since Marshall ventured to substitute the Supreme Court's judgment for that of Congress in *Marbury v. Madison*.[279] Whether or not appellate judges are constrained by an obligation to base their judgments on "authoritative" sources external to their contemporary predilections, they have had to act as if they are. Their obligations to publish the reasons for the decisions they reach, and to include among those reasons appeals to external authoritative sources, have existed since Marshall's time.

One persistent element of the American judicial tradition has thus been a relationship between what one might call the covert and overt bases of an appellate decision. "Internal" histories of appellate courts, including the Supreme Court during Douglas's tenure, have regularly suggested that the covert basis of an individual judge's decision in a case, especially a controversial case of constitutional interpretation, comes from the judge's ideological preferences.[280] In many cases, this literature suggests, that covert basis is concealed by the opinion to which the judge ultimately subscribes. That opinion offers another basis, one appealing to traditional external sources of authority. An opinion is thus simultaneously a suppression of the "real" reasons for the judge's decision and a transformation of those reasons. The overt basis of the decision becomes its justification as a legitimating device; the covert basis becomes "inside" material for students of the internal politics of the appellate judiciary.

The public statements of nearly all Douglas's fellow Justices during his tenure on the Supreme Court suggested that they gave great weight to the overt bases of decisions made by the Court, and that they regarded the covert bases of decisions as either nonexistent or having receded into insignificance once opinions had been handed down. No Justice explicitly asserted this conclusion: the Justices did not so much as admit that any distinction between the covert and overt bases of an opinion existed. Rather, this conclusion was implicit, suggested by two factors. One factor was the practice of discussing previous Court cases, however closely divided the votes in those cases, exclusively in terms of their official justificatory rhetoric and their doctrinal dimensions. No mention was made of the internal deliberations that produced the results in the cases. The other factor was the effort on the part of nearly all of Douglas's contemporaries to maintain in their own opinions the appearance of doctrinal consistency, as if to suggest that their decisions had been reached through fidelity to external authoritative sources—those sources including the proper relationship of the judiciary to other branches of government in a constitutional democracy—rather than through fidelity to their own predilections. Even in the opinions of some of Douglas's contemporaries on the Warren Court, such as Black or Warren, who showed an impatience with the prototypical analytic reasoning of their time, one can discern a search for jurisprudential orthodoxy.[281]

Douglas did not go so far as to suggest that his opinions were not based on external authoritative sources. But he treated those sources cavalierly, and adopted or discarded a particular source whimsically. Those techniques conveyed an implicit message that he did not care very much about the traditional sources of judicial authority. His opinions, I have sought to show, demonstrated that, to him, ideology and resonance to contemporary life were far more significant guides for judging than the text of the Constitution or precedent or established doctrine or dominant theories of the judicial function. The multiple grounds he advanced for the results he reached, the changes over time in his analysis of issues such as free speech or privacy, the brief and assertive tone of many of his opinions, his reluctance to engage in extended doctrinal analysis of the conventional sort, and his penchant, exemplified by *Skinner* and *Griswold*, for doctrinal analysis of the unconventional sort, all implicitly communicated a sense that derivation of the overt basis of a decision was not a task he invested with much significance. On the other hand, the passion of his language on behalf of values and goals in which he believed, his publicized involvement in public affairs and outspokenness on social issues, his continuous effort to communicate his views to the general public through his writings, even his studied effort not to discuss his opinions in his autobiography, appeared to make it clear that he regarded his task as a Supreme Court Justice to be that of translating his views of social policy into law, with "law" being the thin veneer of doctrine that somehow made those views acceptable.

In this sense Douglas was the foremost anti-judge of his time. His career took place squarely within the years in which Legal Realism had helped to expose the subjective elements of judging and blurred the distinction between judges and other lawmakers, and in which Process Jurisprudence had erected, on Realist assumptions, a set of doctrinal and institutional constraints designed to curb subjectivity and thus re-legitimate judicial lawmaking in the form of properly crafted and properly deferential judicial interpretation.[282] Douglas, nurtured on Realism, continued to act on the Court as if he believed that the Realists' characterization of doctrinal analysis as a sham and their insistence on the compelling importance of judicial predilections were still true, even when such beliefs were highly impolitic for judges to express. Moreover, Douglas's life off the Court complemented his actions as a judge: he led protest marches for environmental concerns, issued a manifesto for 1960s rebels, poked fun at his judicial colleagues in print, and revealed that he had spent several years undergoing psychoanalysis. That he chose this role for a Supreme Court Justice at the very time when judicial subjectivity had emerged as the controlling theme by which critics of the appellate judiciary in America expressed their concerns and fears testifies to the importance Douglas attached to maintaining his individuality.

By the last decade of his tenure Douglas had so established his self-image of judge as rugged individualist that it was hard to tell, in his narratives of his life and in his numerous idiosyncratic opinions, where that persona left off and its more complex creator began. Gone, at least in Douglas's public pronouncements, was any memory of the years in which he had been a conciliatory, upward-mobile careerist, a pragmatic New Deal and Cold War liberal, a regular candidate for high political office. His autobiography sought to vindicate a life supposedly governed by the principle that daring to be true to one's convictions, even in the face of social disapproval or political controversy, ensured self-fulfillment. The individuality principle, in its varnished version, lent a consistency to all of Douglas's public life. He had not made a fetish of doctrinal and institutional canons that were only designed to conceal the realities of judicial decision-making; he had not capitulated to political pressures in controversial cases such as *Rosenberg;* he had embraced the values of egalitarianism and autonomy of personal choice even if that stance made him the defender of the downtrodden and the despised. He had, in short, stood nearly alone in his refusal to wrap himself in the intellectual cloaks manufactured by those who sought to provide judges with devices to hide the ideological character of their work from the public. He had been the individualist ideologue of the successive Courts on which he had served, and he welcomed public awareness of that fact. His values, especially the overriding value of being true to oneself, were his justification.

In reality Douglas's tenure had been less consistent, and his concern for maintaining his individuality more tortured, than his retrospective version suggested. He had paid, throughout life, a heavy price for his compulsive efforts to conquer his fears and struggle against his disadvantages. The underside of his resolute individualism had been a recurrent perception by his colleagues on the Court that he was a sometimes distracted and sometimes manipulative figure, and a not dissimilar perception by members of his family that he was remote, unpredictable, and sometimes frightening. The apparent ease with which he moved in the high strata of the legal profession, his singular combination of skills as an academic and a strategist, his great intellectual versatility, and the astonishing successes of his early professional life had resulted in his being put in a position to emerge as one of the great Supreme Court Justices in history. But when he retired, reaction to his career was far more mixed and reserved in its praise.[283]

The ambiguities of Douglas's search for and investment in the individuality principle were so charged and pervasive that one has a sense that his was a life that could not have been lived in some other fashion: his dwelling on psychological themes in his autobiography was no accident. He happened, however, because of his talents, because of his ambition, and because of the vicissitudes of mid-twentieth-century liberal politics, to spend most of his professional life as an appellate judge rather than as a law professor or a cabinet member or a candidate for President. In Douglas's case the fact of his becoming an appellate judge seems to have made a great deal of difference.

The very qualities that made Douglas so conspicuous in his legal career prior to going on the Court made him a puzzling and to some a disappointing figure as a judge. He had succeeded brilliantly in law school and in legal academics because of a combination of intellectual strengths, a gift for professional strategizing, and above all, a single-mindedness. In a world that gives one room to concentrate on one's own pursuits but demands ample and visible scholarly productivity, Douglas, with his keen sense of contemporary affairs and his quick, fertile mind was ideally suited to become one of the leading contributors to the first decade of Realist scholarship.

But as an appellate judge Douglas encountered three features of a professional role that he had not had to confront as an academic, or, for that matter, as a government administrator. One was the fact that most of his decisions were collegial products. Another was that he could not, for the most part, choose the issues of social policy that he was being asked to address. Finally, he was functioning in a professional subculture in which the decisions of those persons holding positions of influence were not expected to be the product of their individual value choices. As a Supreme Court Justice in the mid-twentieth-century, Douglas, in accordance with the expectations of his profession, was implicitly asked to be collegial, "self-restrained," and deferential to doctrinal and institutional "principles." He was temperamentally disinclined—even incapable—of meeting any of those professional expectations. Indeed, his behavior on the Court conveyed the impression that he thought each of those expectations spurious.

Douglas is thus more than the archetypal anti-judge of the period from the New Deal through the Nixon Administration. Modern jurisprudential theories assume appellate judges to be not merely "finding" or "declaring" law in their decisions, but at a minimum to be "interpreting" and "applying" law (even though the "law" remains indeterminate as to content until a given judicial exegesis). Douglas's career raises the question whether such judges can truly said to be constrained. One of the enduring elements in the American judicial tradition has been the interplay of two uneasily juxtaposed values: the judge's comparative freedom to "make law," and the constraints that stem from the fact that judicial "lawmaking" must be justified in written opinions available for public criticism. During the period of Douglas's tenure, two grounds for criticism of judicial opinions surfaced as a response to the perception that judges were lawmakers of a sort. The grounds can be designated as doctrinal, focusing on the analytical rubrics offered as justifications for particular result, or as institutional, focusing on the implicit attitude toward the lawmaking power of the judiciary exhibited by a given opinion. The separate grounds were regularly fused in a critique that suggested that because the doctrinal justifications of a decision were wrongly or ineptly advanced, the decision amounted to an exercise of political power that was inappropriate for the judicial branch of government in a democracy. Such a critique was regularly leveled at Douglas's opinions during his tenure, and has persisted into the 1980s. A recent commentator, after observing that "the Court [has] frequently reached highly controversial results which it made no attempt to justify in terms of the historic Constitution or in terms of any other proffered basis for constitutional decision-making,"[284] offered as a "single example"[285] Douglas's opinion in *Harper v. Virginia Board of Elections*.[286]

The persistent critique of appellate judges for offering inadequate justifications for their decisions suggests that those judges who are chiefly concerned with reaching results consistent with their ideological affinities are constrained by an obligation to advance "adequate" justifications for the results. Douglas's career suggests, first, that he did not take either the "doctrinal" or "institutional" obligations of judging seriously; second, that he regarded ideological considerations as dispositive in the decision of cases; and, third, that he paid a price, in terms of his external reputation and possibly in terms of his internal influence on the Court, for this attitude.

One possible meaning of Douglas's career is thus that there are limits on the capacity of humans to face particularly threatening forms of truth. If judges are at bottom ideologues, and the official justifications offered for their decisions so much empty and contingent rhetoric, few people in the business of writing judicial opinions or commenting on them seem to want that fact disclosed. Better to censure Douglas than to think of judges as other than impartial propounders of doctrine. If this meaning is accepted, the idea of American judges having been "constrained" becomes problematic. In this version of Douglas's career he becomes the anti-judge in a cosmic sense: the judge who reveals what judges "really" are.

There is, however, another possible meaning to Douglas's career. Perhaps for reasons of his own he chose not to grasp or to ignore the fact that collegial decisions, collegial opinions, and the publication requirement for decisions are devices designed to ensure that the arbitrary facts of current power and influence do not become synonymous with the content of law in American culture. Ideology surely counts in judging, but not everyone's ideological affinities are the same. Supreme Court opinions are collegial products rather than seriatim offerings in recognition of that fact. Similarly, the obligation of judges to explain their votes presupposes that failure to explain would be inconsistent with a public expectation that American judges act impartially. Once an explanation is culturally required, one can see how an allied requirement rapidly surfaces: some explanations are "better" than others—better in the sense of more consistent with the impartiality principle. Doctrinally based justifications for a result are, in this vein, simply exalted versions of an implicit claim that a judge's decision deserves respect because it was "impartial" in its fidelity to something other than the judge's ideology.

At some point, then, any appellate judge, recognizing that the office can carry with it power to make final judgments on issues affecting human beings, confronts the paradox that judging *is* ideological, and because it is ideological it requires in its practitioners efforts to show that the ideological position being advanced in a given case is a position based on sources external to its author, a position others with different preconceptions can share. Those efforts are demonstrated in the reasoning accompanying a decision. It seems fair to say that although the judge is the source of such reasoning, the judge is also constrained by that reasoning, because given the expectation of impartiality and the distinction made between the fact of power and the content of law, some reasons will facilitate the sharing of an ideological position better than others.

Douglas did not seem, during his long tenure on the Court to give much attention to this paradox; perhaps he did not see it as a paradox at all. He was himself quickly partisan on issues and disinclined to attribute impartiality to his colleagues: perhaps he minimized the strength of the public expectation of impartiality and thus minimized the significance of justificatory devices designed to respond to that expectation. But the persistence of the paradox of impartiality in twentieth-century appellate judging has not been simply a result of the dilemma of judicial subjectivity exposed by Realism and addressed by Process Jurisprudence. The paradox has persisted because it touches something deep in American culture: the belief that in the modern world judging can amount to subjective, wilful shaping of the content of law by persons who happen to have the power to do it and face no boundaries on that power. Douglas's approach to judging would appear to constrain such persons only by their good instincts. Given the ambiguities of Douglas's own life, perhaps one can understand why his critics found that solution unsatisfying.

14

The Burger Court and the Idea of "Transition" in the American Judicial Tradition

The association of phases in the history of the Supreme Court of the United States with the successive tenures of Chief Justices is, of course, an exercise that invites difficulties. A given Chief Justice may not be the dominant or even a strong figure on "his" Court, witness Chase, Fuller, White, and Vinson. A Chief 's tenure may be fortuitiously short, such as Stone's, and a Chief may have made a more lasting impact as an Associate Justice, witness Stone and perhaps Hughes. Even in instances where a Chief appears to have been a significant figure, as in the case of Marshall, Taney, and Warren, too close an identification of a court with its Chief slights the contributions of other Justices and results in facile ideological labels. Was the Taney Court a Court of apologists for slavery because its Chief Justice authored *Dred Scott?* Did the Warren Court exclusively reflect the jurisprudential attitudes of Warren? Were the practice of encapsulating Courts in the names of their Chiefs not convenient, it probably would have long ago been abandoned.

The idea that Courts can be identified with the ideology of their Chiefs has given rise to another device for characterizing the history of the Supreme Court: the idea that certain periods, or even whole tenures, represent "transitions" from the ideology of one Chief to that of another. The Marshall Court, for example, is often characterized as a resolutely "nationalist" court, consistently solicitous of federal power; the Taney Court is seen as more of a "states' rights" Court, permitting inroads on federal supremacy. With these characterizations in place, the later years of Marshall's tenure, in which the marked unanimity of the Justices on constitutional questions began to break down, and the early years of Taney's tenure, in which holdover Marshall Court Justices such as Story continued to exert an influence, are described as constituting a period of "transition."[1]

The idea of transitions between Courts or between phases of a given Court thus might be said to assume the validity of single-minded ideological characterizations of Chief Justices and their Courts. This study has sought to demonstrate the futility of such characterizations, emphasizing that the contributions of individual judges often resist easy ideological characterization and that much of the jurisprudential character of given Courts comes from the clash and accommodation among individual Justices with differing points of view. The Court's history is personified in individuals in this study, but that emphasis is not intended to suggest that the Supreme Court of the United States can be reduced to a series of personages. In short, the idea of transitions between ideological reference points, when applied to the history of the Supreme Court, appears to be a most problematic concept.

All this said, it must be conceded that the years of Warren Burger's tenure as Chief Justice of the United States appear to present a fertile opportunity for the exercise of the "transition" hypothesis. If one assumes that the "character" of a given Court is a product of the interaction of the people who staffed that Court with the external culture in which the Court was situated, the Burger Court presents an intriguing case. At the time of Warren Burger's appointment to succeed Earl Warren in 1969, the Supreme Court was a decidedly "liberal" institution, however much that label may conceal complexities. By the time of Burger's retirement in 1986 the Court was discernibly more "conservative" in its viewpoint. More significant, the turnover of personnel from the Warren to the Rehnquist Court was gradual, so that by 1974 there were still more Warren Court holdovers than post-Warren Court appointees, but nonetheless marked, so that by 1986 only three Justices from the Warren years remained. The Rehnquist Court is thus clearly different from the Warren Court in its composition; such differences did not mark the Burger Court for all of its history.

Moreover, the political culture in which the successive Courts sat changed dramatically from Warren's last years to the first years of Rehnquist as Chief Justice. The last ten years of Warren's sixteen-year tenure were years in which the Democratic Party controlled the White House and, for most of that period, Congress as well; years in which the policies of the Kennedy and Johnson Administrations were based on the assumptions of welfare liberalism; and years in which democratic and egalitarian ideologies were dominant in American elite and popular culture. The years of Burger's tenure were marked by Republican control of the White House, with the exception of Carter's four-year Presidency, and, for the most part, of Congress. By the Ford and even the Carter administrations policies identified with welfare liberalism had become political liabilities, and by the time of Reagan's election in 1980 an apparently decisive mandate had been granted the Republican Party to abandon much of the egalitarian and welfarist assumptions that had characterized American political thought since the New Deal.

Finally, Republican Presidents had had ample opportunities to replace Justices appointed by Democrats or identified with welfare liberalism. The appointments made to the Court between 1969 and 1986 were made by Nixon, Ford, and Reagan: among the Justices replaced were Warren, Black, and Douglas. In the place of those Justices were named persons who were each Republican in their political identification and in some instances identified as having a strong ideological affinity for the anti-welfarist assumptions of the right wing of the Republican Party. Symbolically, the change from Warren to Rehnquist could not have been starker: a Justice who asked on his retirement that the Supreme Court during his tenure be remembered as the "people's court"[2] had, seventeen years later, been succeeded by one who as a Supreme Court law clerk had complained about the leftist tendencies of his fellow clerks.[3]

In many respects, then, it may be tempting to think of the Burger Court as having occupied a space between two discernibly ideological Courts, the egalitarian late Warren Court and the potentially anti-welfarist Rehnquist Court of the future. But the strongest argument for characterizing the Burger Court as a "transition" Court comes not from the suggestive contrasts in personnel and politics that marked its predecessor and successor. The argument surfaces rather from the Court's performance itself, especially in two respects, its internal political configurations and the pragmatic, *ad hoc* character of its constitutional jurisprudence. Accordingly, I shall be exploring the idea that the Burger Court was a "transition" Court by focusing on two of its features, the dynamics of its internal composition and the nature of its approach to constitutional issues. Along the way I will be assessing the contributions of the Burger Court's more influential Justices.

I

If the Warren Court was composed of a number of especially prominent and influential Justices, the Burger Court marked a return to the more modest composition of early-twentieth-century Courts. Part of the explanation for the presence of less visible figures on the Burger Court can be found in the altered nature of the process by which Justices were confirmed. After Warren's retirement, and the attendant debacle of Abe Fortas's nonconfirmation as Chief Justice and resignation from the Court, Senatorial scrutiny of nominees to the Court markedly increased, causing an implicit shift in the criteria employed by appointing Presidents. The early efforts of Nixon to appoint Justices constituted a challenge to and ultimately an acquiescence of the expanded role of the Senate. After the nonconfirmation of Judge John Parker for ideological reasons in 1930, Senatorial deference to Presidential appointments to the Court became the norm from the New Deal through the 1960s, resulting in the appointments of several justices, notably Black, Douglas, Frankfurter, and Warren, who had been identified with controversial groups, taken controversial positions, or lacked significant experience as lower court judges or practitioners. The enhanced scrutiny of Fortas that resulted in his nonconfirmation signaled a new role for the Senate, and the confirmation process became politicized as supporters of Fortas resolved to challenge any Nixon appointees that failed to meet the new implicit criteria of significant professional experience and noncontroversiality.

Nixon's first two confirmed appointees, Warren Burger and Harry Blackmun, met those criteria, but Nixon did not secure his appointments without difficulty. Burger, Nixon's first appointment to a position that had in effect been vacant for over a year, encountered no difficulties, being a Court of Appeals judge of relatively longstanding tenure, with a substantial enough reputation, an identification with "law and order" in criminal cases, and no history of ethically dubious conduct. Burger was known to be an ideological conservative, but the Nixon Administration, which had successfully campaigned against the alleged permissiveness of the Warren Court, had no difficulty appointing a candidate whose lower court career suggested he would be sympathetic to law enforcement officials in criminal justice cases.

The altered role of the Senate became more evident in Nixon's efforts to make a second appointment to replace Fortas. Determined to appoint a Justice from the South, Nixon proposed two candidates, Clement Haynsworth of the United States Court of Appeals for the Fourth Circuit, a native of South Carolina, and subsequently, Harold Carswell, a federal district court judge from Florida. The Senate narrowly failed to confirm both candidates, with alleged ethical improprieties looming large in Haynsworth's defeat and an undistinguished record and a prior identification with racism dooming Carswell's candidacy. In the case of Haynsworth, especially, the impact of the Fortas defeat on the confirmation process was revealed. Haynsworth was an experienced judge with a relatively moderate and fairly distinguished record whose allegedly unethical conduct consisted of failure to disqualify himself in litigation in which he had owned stock in a subsidiary of one of the litigants. Standards for judicial disqualification have never been clear-cut, and recusal has traditionally been considered a matter for individual discretion. There was no clear evidence that Haynsworth was even aware that he might be a prospective beneficiary of the litigation. His defeat was a signal that politics, disguised in neutral criteria such as ethics or experience, had re-entered the confirmation process.

Nixon's experiences with his early appointments set a pattern for Burger Court nominations, one which placed heavy emphasis on the moderation, noncontroversiality, and experience of the nominee. The Fortas seat eventually went to Harry Blackmun, a federal appellate judge whose record, while competent, was singularly free from identification with any controversial positions. Nixon's next two nominees, Lewis Powell and William Rehnquist, were also not particularly risky candidates, though for different reasons. Powell was a former President of the American Bar Association, a political moderate, and a longtime Richmond practitioner who had been active in public affairs. Rehnquist, an Assistant Attorney General in the Justice Department, was known to hold more decisively ideological views, but was also possessed of outstanding professional qualifications, having been first in his class at Stanford Law School and a former law clerk to Justice Jackson. Rehnquist also had the good fortune to be nominated before the Watergate scandal broke: his immediate superior and close friend, Richard Kleindienst, was implicated in that affair. Despite Rehnquist's strong qualifications, he was attacked by liberals in the Senate, and at one point his nomination seemed in jeopardy when it was revealed that he had written a memo to Jackson that argued for upholding the segragationist precedent, *Plessy v. Ferguson*, in the Court's internal discussions of *Brown v. Board of Education*. Rehnquist's nomination was saved when a fellow clerk revealed that Jackson had asked his clerks to prepare separate memos urging that the *Plessy* precedent be followed or overruled.[4]

President Ford, himself in a shaky political position, followed the new criteria for nominees when he had an opportunity to make an appointment to the Court following Douglas's resignation in 1975. His choice, John Paul Stevens, was, like Blackmun, a respected and noncontroversial federal court of appeals judge, and, like Rehnquist, a former Supreme Court law clerk. One message of the new confirmation process was that such appointees were confirmed overwhelmingly, and Stevens was no exception. The effect of the Senate's enhanced role in the confirmation of nominees to the Court, then, had been the appointment of three Justices—Blackmun, Powell, and Stevens—whose jurisprudential views appeared to be firmly moderate—and two Justices—Burger and Rehnquist—who more closely approximated the ideological positions of the Presidents who appointed them. The process thus helped retard a significant ideological swing from the Warren to the Burger Courts by producing more moderate nominees than an earlier, more deferential process might have; it also implicitly discriminated against prospective nominees, such as visible lower court judges or academics, whose jurisprudential views had been more firmly staked out.

The last appointment to the Burger Court, Sandra Day O'Connor, can also be seen as responsive to the new implicit criteria employed by Presidents after Nixon. O'Connor's status as a woman, at a time in which the inclusion of women on the Court was perceived as an idea whose time had surely come, ensured a certain groundswell for her confirmation, but in choosing O'Connor President Reagan again invoked the criteria of impressive professional credentials (O'Connor had been a member of the Stanford Law Review with Rehnquist) and relatively obscure or noncontroversial performance (O'Connor was an Arizona state appellate court judge without a particularly visible record). Although the Reagan Administration may have believed that O'Connor would eventually emerge as a right-wing ideologue, her previous judicial career had not given much evidence of that inclination.

The O'Connor appointment was at the same time a harbinger of a more decisively idiological slant to nominees. The next three nominees, none to the Burger Court itself, were persons whose views were far more visible and less moderate than any of the Burger Court nominees. As such they stimulate a comparison between the largely ideological nominees of the late Warren Court—Goldberg, Fortas, and Marshall—and the far less discernibly ideological nominees of the Burger Court. Rehnquist, nominated as Chief Justice, Judge Antonin Scalia, and Judge Robert Bork were known entities with respect to their political and jurisprudential views in a way that none of the Burger Court nominees were, with the possible exception of the Chief Justice. Rehnquist, Scalia, and Bork were each experienced and talented judges with distinguished professional records, but they were far more outspoken in their views than the Burger Court nominees. The role of ideology in a Supreme Court nominee became a major public issue in the debate over Bork's nomination, which was eventually rejected, 58–42, by a Democratically controlled Senate. Bork's candidacy lost simply because he could not convince enough Senators that, despite his outstanding professional credentials, he was "in the mainstream" of constitutional jurisprudence. Particularly telling was Bork's opposition, over a sixteen-year period, to all of the Burger Court's visible "privacy" decisions, including the right on the part of individuals to have access to birth control pills. The defeat of Bork piqued the Reagan Administration to nominate another right-wing ideologue, Judge Douglas Ginsburg of the U.S. Court of Appeals for the District of Columbia circuit. But Ginsburg, the first Supreme Court nominee to be born after the Second World War, was revealed to have used marijuana as a college student and a young lawyer, and eventually withdrew his nomination after that revelation embarrassed the Reagan Administration, which had campaigned vigorously against drug use. Reagan's next nominee, Judge Anthony Kennedy of the U.S. Court of Appeals for the Ninth Circuit, appeared to be a throwback to the Burger Court type, a moderate conservative with a noncontroversial record. The success of Kennedy's nomination suggests that the moderation of the Burger Court nominees may have been more than an outcome of the confirmation process;

it may have been a more representative jurisprudential posture of the years between the late 1960s and the 1980s, years in which one set of ideological presuppositions was only gradually and irregularly replaced by another. With this last supposition we reach the possibility that the very lack of ideological coherence on the Burger Court may have been a reflection of the larger political culture in which that Court functioned. But that possibility requires further exploration, which should be postponed until the internal consequences of the new confirmation process are examined.

The late Warren Court was dominated by a shifting "liberal" majority of justices whose increasingly activist and egalitarian dispositions of issues were successively self-reinforcing. After the retirements of Frankfurter and Whittaker in 1962, we have seen, a new phase of Warren Court jurisprudence began. While the new liberal majority sometimes numbered as many as seven justices (including Justices Black, Brennan, Douglas, Goldberg or Fortas, Marshall, occasionally White, and Warren) at its core, as internal forces, were four of those Justices—the formidable ideologues Black and Douglas, the doctrinal strategist Brennan, and the redoutable emotional leader, Warren. Characteristic of this phase of the Warren Court were free-swinging and openly ideological opinions, strong internal debate, and determined activism on the part of the Chief Justice and his confederates.

With Warren's retirement and the loss of Fortas's vote the decisive Warren Court majority was eliminated, and the votes of Justices only marginally identified with Warren Court jurisprudence, White and Stewart, took on increased significance. In this atmosphere a new Chief Justice, apparently committed to reversing some to the trends of the later Warren Court, assumed his post, and with it the procedural powers of the Chief Justiceship: speaking first and supposedly voting last in conference and assigning opinions when he was in the majority. In the first two years of Burger's tenure, faced with the presence of Warren Court holdovers such as Black, Brennan, and Harlan, and sensing the possibility of forming a new "anti-Warren Court" majority, the new Chief Justice seems to have developed a unique style of leadership, one with which he was to be associated through the balance of his tenure.

During Warren's Chief Justiceship the formal practice of Justices speaking in order of seniority and then subsequently voting in reverse order had been replaced with a more informal version, in which each Justice stated his views on the case and concluded by saying how he would vote.[5] Burger, realizing that many cases would be closely decided on the newly composed Court that he headed, began a practice of deferring his vote on cases that he sensed were close so as to give him the opportunity to be the last member of a five-man majority and thus be able to assign the opinion in the case. On some occasions he reportedly changed his vote after the conference, joined the majority, and sought to assign the opinion, even though it previously had been assigned by the senior Associate Justice who had originally voted with the majority. On others he declined to vote at all and then subsequently emerged as a member of the majority, circulating memos announcing his vote and the assignment of the opinion.[6] Other justices speculated that Burger attempted to manipulate the voting and assignment procedure on the average of about one case per conference.

It became apparent to other members of the Court that Burger's interests as Chief Justice did not lie in marshaling an internal consensus or in writing opinions. He spent long amounts of time on ceremonial functions, lobbying for appropriations for the Court, renovating the Supreme Court building, and devising plans for the administration of the lower federal courts. In perhaps the most politically charged case of his tenure, the Watergate tapes case, he rebuffed a suggestion from other Justices that a *per curiam* opinion be issued that each of the Justices signed individually, assigning the Court's opinion to himself. The draft opinion that he circulated was reportedly so poorly received by the other Justices that several formed a cabal to produce an alternative draft, assigning separate sections to individual Justices. When the Chief Justice circulated his draft, individuals responded by saying that they would like the suggestions embodied in an alternative draft incorporated or simply that they preferred the alternative. Eventually an opinion was issued that bore the Chief Justice's name but which other Justices had authored.[7]

Burger's apparent manipulation of the assignment procedure, lack of interest in the intellectual features of his job, and inadequacies as an opinion writer facilitated a lack of respect among the other Justices who served with him and created a leadership void on the Burger Court. At the same time, the new composition of the Court meant that those Warren Court holdovers who had been accustomed to providing leadership, such as Black and Brennan, could no longer count on majoritarian support for their positions. After Nixon's appointments, the Court settled into a configuration in which three holdover Warren Court liberals, Brennan, Douglas, and Marshall, and two conservative ideologues, Rehnquist and the Chief Justice, competed for the votes of four centrists, White, Stewart, Powell, and Blackmun. The centrist role was a familiar one for White and Stewart, who had occupied it to a lesser extent on the Warren Court, and for Powell, who was temperamentally and jurisprudentially inclined toward moderation. Blackmun's centrist posture represented something of an evolution: his first term he voted so regularly with the Chief Justice that commentors dubbed the two Justices "The Minnesota Twins." But for a variety of reasons, including his personal discomfort with Burger[8] and his increased contact with Brennan,[9] Blackmun's voting pattern became less predictable as he spent more time on the Court.

Given the fact that neither wing of the Burger Court could command a majority without the presence of centrist Justices, the tenor of opinions began to change from the broad, sweeping declarations that had marked the later Warren years. The leading activist opinion of the early Court, the abortion case of *Roe v. Wade*, illustrates this shift. The abortion decision was authored by Blackmun, writing for a majority that included Brennan, Douglas, Marshall, Stewart, Powell, and the Chief Justice. But Douglas, Stewart, and Burger wrote separate concurrences which revealed that their views on the doctrinal foundations of the opinions were very far apart. The opinion itself represented a compromise solution to the abortion problem, permitting unrestricted abortion decisions in a limited time frame and requiring medical approval for abortions performed beyond the first trimester. The Court was also cautious about the constitutional foundations for its decision, mentioning precedents allegedly establishing a constitutional right of privacy but ultimately grounding the outcome on the Due Process Clause of the Fourteenth Amendment. In concurrences Stewart rejected the privacy rubric and Douglas the substantive due process rubric; Blackmun's opinion simply listed both as possible bases for his conclusion. The internal deliberations on the abortion cases had been marked by the virtual withdrawl of Burger from a leadership role once it became apparent that he could not muster a majority for declaring abortions as having no constitutional sanction. Burger eventually joined the majority at the last minute; his concurrence read more like a dissent.[10]

The appointment of Stevens served to reinforce the Court's centrist posture. Stevens rapidly revealed himself to follow an idiosyncratic voting pattern, taking positions that were unpredictable and sometimes grounded on arguments other Justices thought inapplicable to the case.[11] He welcomed his independence and did not seem intimidated by more experienced Justices; his vote became another one to be courted. With Douglas gone, the new composition was more firmly centrist, with only two Justices on either ideological wing and the remainder capable of forming a majority in themselves. In the 1976 death penalty cases, a centrist trio of Justices, Stewart, Powell, and Stevens, managed to convert a majority opinion to a plurality by using an "alternative draft" technique similar to that which had been employed in the tapes cases.[12]

Thus personnel changes and the Chief Justice's inability to assume a leadership position, resulted, by 1975, in the Burger Court's becoming dominated by a shifting majority of centrists who preferred, for the most part, narrow and cautious dispositions of issues. This alteration in the Court's character had two principal effects. First, it changed the roles of certain holdover Warren Court Justices, whose careers took new and perhaps unexpected directions. Second, it had a visible effect on certain areas of constitutional law. The remainder of this section is devoted to altered roles for Justices; the next section considers changes in constitutional doctrine.

On the Warren Court, William Brennan, shortly after his appointment in 1956, became a member of a group of four Justices, including Black, Douglas, and Warren, who favored activist solutions to social issues, inclined toward federal supremacy in conflicts between federal and state powers, and were sympathetic to the rights of minorities. Until 1962 this group of Justices was not always in the majority, but with the retirements of Frankfurter and Whitaker in that year, and the eventual appointment of Abe Fortas and Thurgood Marshall to the Court, decisive support for Brennan's positions was secured. In the later years of the Warren Court, where liberal, activist results were relatively easy to come by but unanimous rationales more difficult to obtain, Brennan functioned as a moderate craftsman, whose carefully constructed majority opinions were subscribed to by Justices with diverse jurisprudential perspectives. Examples were *Baker v. Carr*,[13] where Brennan somehow managed to secure Black's vote even though the text of the Constitution said nothing about a right to have one's vote counted equally, and *New York Times v. Sullivan*,[14] where Brennan unified First Amendment "absolutists" such as Black and Douglas and "balancers" such as Warren and Potter Stewart with an opinion that advanced multiple theories of the "core" of First Amendment protection.

By the mid-point of the Burger Court, with Marshall the only other Warren Court liberal remaining, Brennan had ceased to write many majority opinions, and the tone of his dissenting opinions was noticeably more strident. In his dissent in *National League of Cities v. Usery*, for example, he called the majority opinion, which found that the Tenth Amendment placed some substantive limits on Congress's power to regulate wages and hours in the states, a "patent usurpation of the role reserved for the political process," and "abstraction without substance . . . having . . . profoundly pernicious consequences," and "a transparent cover for invalidating a congressional judgement with which they disagree."[15] Only occasionally, as in his influence in encouraging Justice Blackmun to disassociate himself from Chief Justice Burger and to take a more centrist posture,[16] did Brennan play the role of internal strategist that he had occupied on the later Warren Court.

If the shift in Brennan's roles was evidence of his diminished influence, changes in the roles performed by two of his Warren Court colleagues, Stewart and Byron White, pointed in the opposite direction. Stewart, who in the first years of his tenure had occupied a centrist position on the early Warren Court, became one of the principal dissenters during Warren's later years, often joined only by Justice John Harlan. Stewart was particularly loath to join the Warren Court's efforts to reform constitutional doctrine in the area of criminal procedure, but he also dissented in the Court's reapportionment cases, school prayer cases, and right of privacy cases.[17] By the early 1970s, however, he had reoccupied the centrist role that he found most compatible with his temperament. An example was *Harris v. McRae*,[18] in which Stewart, who had dissented in the right of privacy case *Griswold v. Connecticut* but concurred in *Roe v. Wade*, held for a five-person majority that Congress could prohibit the use of federal funds to assist indigents who sought abortions except where the life of the mother was endangered or rape or incest had taken place. One of the themes of *The Brethren*, which purported to give an "inside" account of the first six terms of Burger's Chief Justiceship, was the role of Stewart and other Justices in developing a centrist coalition of justices that held the balance of internal power in the absence of leadership from the Chief.

Another member of that centrist coalition was Byron White, whose jurisprudential style seemed far better suited for the Burger Court than its predecessor. White's voting record on the Warren Court had been difficult to characterize politically: he joined the liberal majority on civil rights and reapportionment cases but was a consistent dissenter in criminal justice cases and took a more modest view of First Amendment rights and federal power than did the majority Justices. His preference was for narrowly gauged, pragmatic, fact-specific opinions, a preference that better suited the jurisprudence of the later Burger Court. Two White opinions from the Burger Court that demonstrated his style and influence were *Cox Broadcasting v. Cohn*, a 1975 decision, and the 1986 case of *Bowers v. Hardwick*. The question in *Cox Broadcasting*, potentially, was whether the First Amendment privilege to report news permitted a newspaper to disclose true but "private" facts about a person who sought to shield them from public scrutiny. The case involved disclosure of the name of a rape victim who had not survived the attack, and White took advantage of the fact that the names of victims of crimes would be in the public record to limit the constitutional privilege to a "public records" context. Similarily in *Bowers*, a case in which a person was prosecuted for engaging in consensual homosexual sex in private, the potential constitutional issue was whether states could prevent consenting adults from privately engaging in sodomitic conduct in light of the Fourteenth Amendment's guarantee of "liberty" in its Due Process Clause. White framed the issue in *Bowers* as being limited to consensual sex engaged in by homosexuals, thus leaving open the more momentous question of whether consenting heterosexuals could have their private sexual conduct regulated by the state.

The altered roles for Brennan, Stewart, and White demonstrated the significance of a "fit" between an individual's temperamental and jurisprudential inclinations and the internal demands of a particular Court as an element of influence in a Supreme Court Justice. For most of Brennan's tenure on the Warren Court his engaging style, flexible temperament, and ability to accommodate potentially clashing positions in judicial language made him an ideal "spokesman" for that Court's highly individualistic group of liberal Justices. During most of the Burger Court's tenure Brennan had no comparable opportunity to exercise those skills. For much of Stewart's tenure as a judge, he was able to occupy a position that he coveted: the cautious, prudent "swing man," neither readily characterizable as a liberal or a conservative, intimately involved in the internal politics of hammering out decisions. For a brief interval in the Warren Court his politics did not put him in the center of his colleagues, and he was reduced to the role of the irate dissenter, one with which he was not particularly comfortable. White's narrow, fact-specific jurisprudence was out of place on the late Warren Court, whose majorities preferred bold innovations and broad prophylactic constitutional rules. The more closely divided Burger Court and the implicit bias of the new confirmation process toward centrist appointees meant that broadly based innovations were less likely to be attractive, hence White's approach became better suited to the narrow, *ad hoc* decisions of Burger Court majorities. No better measure of the change from the Warren to Burger Courts could be found than this transformation of the skills associated with internal influence. Few observers of the late Warren Court would have predicted that six years after Warren's retirement both Stewart and White would have surpassed Brennan as influential figures. The evolution of roles for those three Justices reminds us that distinction in a judicial career is a function of opportunities as much as of intellectual talents.

II

When Burger replaced Warren, and particularly when Nixon was able to name four new Justices two terms after Warren's retirement, several commentators predicted the emergence of a "Nixon Court," which would soon produce a dramatic reversal of Warren Court doctrines.[19] In fact the years of Burger's tenure were more notable for changes in the form and style of opinions than for changes in substantive doctrine. Three areas have been chosen as illustrative: gender discrimination, defamation, and substantive due process.

The Warren Court's approach to gender discrimination cases reflected the slow surfacing of gender consciousness in modern American liberal thought. The same Justices who had broken ground in race, reapportionment, criminal procedure, and religion were confronted with almost no cases involving gender discrimination, and in those cases exhibited attitudes that reflected traditional and stereotyped views on gender roles. In *Hoyt v. Florida*, a 1961 decision, for example, a Florida jury selection system that excluded women from jury service unless they affirmatively signified an interest in serving was challenged on equal protection grounds. The Court sustained the statute, adopting as a standard for scrutiny of legislative activity in the area of gender discrimination the conventional "rational basis" standard, in which a state need only demonstrate that its legislation rests on some rational ground. "[W]oman is still regarded as the center of home and family life," Justice Harlan wrote for the Court. "We cannot say that it is constitutionally impermissible for a State, acting in pursuit of the general welfare, to conclude that a woman should be relieved from the civic duty of jury service unless she herself determines that such service is consistent with her own special responsibilities."[20]

Decisions such as *Hoyt* reflected the fact that the revolution in gender consciousness which surfaced in the late 1960s did not penetrate the Warren Court. By 1971, however, a major equal protection challenge to gender-based legislation was heard, and the Court showed signs of becoming responsive to stereotypes. In *Reed v. Reed*, an Idaho statute that established a preference hierarchy for persons entitled to administer the estate of a person who had died without making a will was challenged. The statute, after prescribing that parents would take preference over children and children over siblings, then specified that if two persons were of the same entitlement class, preference would be given to the male. The justification for the preference was reducing the work of state probate courts by eliminating a potential series of controversies where two or more persons, of equal priority under the statutory hierarchy, sought to administer an estate.

In a unanimous opinion, the Court found that the statute violated the equal protection clause. Employing a rational basis standard that required a statutory classification to bear some "fair and substantial relation to the object of the legislation,"[21] the Court concluded that giving a mandatory preference for members of one sex bore no rational relationship to the objective of reducing the workload of probate courts. The decision, although cryptically justified, was significant in two respects: first because the Court had employed a rational basis standard with some "bite," and second because to find the Idaho statute "arbitrary" the Court needed to assume that there was no rational relationship between gender and competency to administer an estate. This last assumption suggested that the Court may have believed that the classification was based on outmoded stereotypes about the involvement of men and women in business affairs.

The next Burger Court gender discrimination case, *Frontiero v. Richardson*, suggested that the Court might rapidly elevate gender to a "suspect" classification such as race. The case was a particularly attractive one for a strong statement against gender discrimination because the classification under constitutional attack burdened men as well as women. Strictly speaking, the case was not an equal protection case but a due process case, since it involved a Congressional statute regulating medical and dental benefits for military personnel.

The statute provided that male servicemembers could claim their wives as "dependents," for the purpose of receiving additional medical and dental benefits, without any showing that the wives were in fact dependent upon them for one-half of their support. Women in the services, however, were not permitted to claim their husbands as dependents absent such a showing. Sharron Frontiero, a lieutenant in the Air force, challenged the statute as "unjustifiable discrimination" under the due process clause, the equivalent of an equal protection challenge. Since the statute in question was clearly an effort to encourage persons to remain in the armed services by in effect increasing their pay through supplemental benefits, the case amounted to an "equal pay for equal work" case, with women seeking the same automatic benefits as men. As such a ruling for Frontiero not only seemed to strike at what many opponents of gender discrimination regarded as its least defensible aspect, unequal pay scales for men and women performing similar functions, but it also benefited not only women in the service but also their working husbands, who now could expect the fringe benefits from the service regardless of their incomes.

Sensing the strength of Frontiero's claim, Justice Brennan sought to use the case as an opportunity to make gender a suspect classification. He read *Reed v. Reed* as representing a "departure from traditional rational basis analysis" since the Court had treated Idaho's interest in achieving administrative efficiency in the disposition of estates as "not without some legitimacy," but had nonetheless invalidated the statute. The reason, Brennan suggested, was that the *Reed* Court had recognized that the Idaho statute was based on "gross, stereotyped distinctions between the sexes" which had "the effect of invidiously relegating [an] entire class of females to inferior legal status without regard to the actual capabilities of . . . individual members."[22] Thus *Reed*, taken together with other evidence that Congress and other institutions had become aware "that the sex characteristic frequently bears no relation to ability to perform or contribute to society,"[23] suggested to Brennan that classifications based on gender should "be subjected to strict judicial scrutiny."[24]

Brennan was, however, only able to muster four votes for his strict scrutiny analysis, those of Douglas, Marshall, and White in addition to his own. Four other Justices concurred in the result in *Frontiero*, Stewart because he felt that the statute made an "invidious discrimination" under the due process clause, and Powell, Blackmun, and Burger because they found *Reed* controlling and felt it was unnecessary to elevate gender to the status of a suspect classification. Ironically,

Powell's concurrence, joined by the other Justices, advanced as a reason for delaying that elevation the Equal Rights Amendment, whose language clearly made discrimination on gender grounds inherently suspect. The Amendment provided an opportunity for an even broader mandate against gender discrimination, Powell argued, and the Court should not interfere. The Amendment, of course, failed to achieve the requisite number of states ratifying it, and the Court has not yet made gender a suspect category.

Indeed the next important gender discrimination case,[25] *Craig v. Boren*, suggested that Brennan, the erstwhile architect of strict scrutiny in gender cases, had abandoned that stance in order to secure a heightened standard of review that did not approximate strict scrutiny but went beyond a rational basis analysis. Like *Frontiero, Craig* was an attractive case for a strong statement on gender discrimination since the petitioners in the case were men, who claimed that an Oklahoma statute permitting females between the ages of 18 and 21 to drink 3.2 percent beer but denying that permission to males of the same age violated the equal protection clause.

Brennan, for the majority, reminded his audience that *Reed* was controlling, but restated the *Reed* standard. "To withstand constitutional challenge," he announced, "classifications by gender must serve important governmental objectives and must be substantially related to achievement of those objectives." He suggested that "previous cases [had] establish[ed]" that standard of review, but his language marked a departure from *Reed* and *Stanton v. Stanton*, and no majority had embraced his heightened scrutiny standard in *Frontiero*. "Important governmental objectives" were a far cry from the requirement in *Reed* that a classification be "reasonable, not arbitrary," although requiring a "substantial relationship" to those objectives was similar to language in *Reed*. Brennan also read *Reed, Frontiero*, and *Stanton* as rendering "archaic and overbroad" generalizations about gender traits suspect and requiring that "loose-fitting characterizations" about such traits "be premised on their accuracy." The result was a suggestion that classifications based on gender stereotypes would rarely provide evidence of an "important governmental objective." Even Powell's concurrence in *Craig*, which complained that it was "unnecessary to *Reed* as broadly as some of the [majority's] language may imply," conceded that "*Reed* and subsequent cases make clear that the Court subjects [gender] classifications to a more critical examination than is normally applied," and that "candor compels the recognition that the relatively deferential 'rational basis' standard of review normally applied takes on a sharper focus when we address a gender-based discrimination."[26]

The "intermediate scrutiny" analysis developed by Brennan in *Craig*, together with the suggestion that classifications based on outmoded gender stereotypes carried a heavy burden of justification, appeared firmly in place by 1979, when in *Orr v. Orr* a six-man majority, headed by Brennan, invalidated an Alabama statute requiring husbands but never wives to pay alimony. At one point in his opinion Brennan noted that "[l]egislative classifications carry the inherent risk of reinforcing stereotypes about the 'proper place' of women and their need for special protection." Even statutes "purportedly designed to compensate for and ameliorate the effects of past discrimination," Brennan said, "must be carefully tailored."[27]

But in the 1980 Term the Court appeared to be pulling back even from the suggestion that gender discrimination triggered heightened scrutiny. In two cases, *Michael M. v. Superior Court* and *Rostker v. Goldberg*, explicit gender discriminations were sustained. *Michael M.* involved a challenge to a California "statutory" rape law that made it a crime for males to engage in sexual relations with females under the age of majority, but not for females to engage in sexual relations with underage males. Rehnquist, for a plurality of the Court, held the statute constitutional and along the way announced that statutes burdening males but not females did not attract "the special solicitude of the courts."[28] The statute could be justified, he found, as a device for deterring teenage pregnancy and encouraging underage women to report sexual encounters. Males and females were not "similarly situated with respect to the problems and the risks of sexual intercourse," and the state could take those differences into account. The *Michael M.* plurality ignored the fact that the statute seems to have been based originally on stereotyped notions that young women were particularly in need of protection from sexual encounters, to which they were deemed incapable of consenting, and the fact that the state's asserted purpose of deterring teenage pregnancies could have been better served by a gender-neutral statute, which would have created greater incentives for young women not to engage in sexual activity. The plurality status of the *Michael M.* opinion suggests that the case may not be regarded as having much general significance.

Similarly, *Rostker v. Goldberg* might be regarded as a case decided on special circumstances. There a majority held constitutional a Congressional statute requiring men, but not women, to register for the draft. Rehnquist's opinion, this time for a majority, stressed the considerable deference given Congressional exercise of powers related to military affairs and argued that the principal purpose of the draft was to develop a pool of combat-eligible troops, whereas women were not eligible for combat. Brennan, White, and Marshall, in dissent, suggested that there was no substantial relation between the objective of developing a pool of combat troops and the means chosen by Congress, which was to exclude all women from the draft. Women could serve in other military positions, and it was hard to imagine how having women in the draft pool would frustrate the purpose of developing a combat-ready force. The case can be read as a departure from the Court's prior insistence, in cases such as *Craig* and *Stanton*, that gender-based classifications be carefully tailored to fit a state's objectives, but it is also possible to see *Rostker* as a "military affairs" case, with the Court relaxing its heightened scrutiny in an area where, as Rehnquist put it, "the scope of Congress" constitutional power is broad, [and] the lack of competence on the part of the courts is marked."[29]

An interpretation that sees *Michael M.* and *Rostker* as cases without much general significance for the Court's gender discrimination decisions might be reinforced by the Court's decision in the 1982 case of *Mississippi University for Women v. Hogan*. There a male applicant to a state nursing school was rejected on the basis of gender, and challenged the exclusion of men from nursing schools. The Court, 5–4, held that single-sex nursing schools violated the Equal Protection Clause. Along the way O'Connor's opinion reaffirmed the heightened standard of review for gender discrimination cases, explicitly taking back any suggestion in *Michael M.* that heightened scrutiny was not required where a statute discriminated against males, restating its sense of the illegitimacy of gender-based statutes premised on "fixed notions concerning the roles and abilities of males and females," or "archaic and stereotypic notions," leaving open the question whether classifications based on gender were inherently suspect.[30] The *Hogan* decision, which employed an antidiscrimination perspective even stronger than that of *Craig*, raised the possibility that all state single-sex education institutions might be found unconstitutional. The decision indicated that the Court saw its opinions from *Reed* through *Frontiero* to *Craig* and beyond as having a cumulative effect.

In one sense the Burger Court's gender discrimination decisions were truly revolutionary, marking a significant change in the posture of the Court from that suggested in *Hoyt v. Florida*, jeopardizing all state-supported single-sex education institutions, and exposing gender-based "stereotypes" that only a decade ago had been deeply embedded in American Culture. The impact of the decisions becomes less significant, however, if one emphasizes the narrow majorities on which most of them rested, the zig-zag pattern of decisions, the reluctance of a majority of the Court to embrace a strict scrutiny standard or to cast the impact of any one decision broadly, and the dramatic changes in women's roles and consciousness of women's rights that took place in American society after 1970. The Court certainly did not play a leadership role in fostering altered attitudes toward women comparable to its role in gender relations after *Brown v. Board*, but it was not unresponsive to those altered attitudes. A decision like *Frontiero*, with its discussion of " 'romantic paternalism' which, in practical effect, put women, not on a pedestal, but in a cage," would have been unthinkable ten years earlier.

For all their innovativeness, the gender discrimination decisions of the Burger Court were modest in their doctrinal stance. The *Frontiero* exchange between Brennan and Powell revealed that a significant phalanx of Justices on the Court were reluctant to engage in the kind of prophylactic doctrinal formulations that had characterized the later Warren Court. At least five Justices—Powell, Blackmun, Stevens, Stewart, and White—demonstrated their reluctance to cast doctrinal pronouncements broadly and their tendency to frame decisions in a narrow compass. Powell and Stevens both took occasion in the gender discrimination cases to reveal their opposition to "multiple-standard" equal protection review, preferring to adopt a general rational basis standard that they varied in intensity depending on the character of the discrimination and perhaps the facts of a case. It was not clear that the reluctance of a majority to commit to a strict scrutiny standard for gender cases made any difference in terms of results, for *Reed, Frontiero, Craig*, and *Hogan* all invoked a standard of review with considerable "bite," and may have survived even strict scrutiny. But a majority of Justices' reluctance to embrace *any* broad propositions in the gender discrimination area, save the proposition that such cases triggered some form of "heightened" scrutiny, was a clue to the differences in jurisprudential style between the Warren and Burger Courts. In its arguably most "liberal" and innovative line of cases, the Burger Court nonetheless attempted to stress its jurisprudential moderation.

One area in which the character of the late Warren Court had been conspicuously revealed was that of defamation. Despite nearly two hundred years of permitted coexistence between the First Amendment and the common law of libel and slander, the Court discovered, in the 1964 case of *New York Times v. Sullivan*,[31] that the two regimes were largely incompatible. False and defamatory statements about "public officials" made in the press were privileged by virtue of the First Amendment: they could only be made the basis of a libel action if they were intentionally false or had been made with a reckless disregard for the truth. The effect of the *New York Times* decision was virtually to insulate the press against libel suits by public officials.

The *New York Times* decision was characteristic of the late Warren Court in its doctrinal novelty, the breadth of its application, and its controversiality. Moreover, the Court quickly extended the *Times* analysis to other false statements with a "public" component, concluding, in *Curtis Publishing Co. v. Butts* and *Associated Press v. Walker*,[32] that the First Amendment privilege applied to suits by "public figures" as well. One commentator suggested that "the invitation to follow dialectic progression from public official to government policy to public policy to matters in the public domain, like art, seems to me to be overwhelming."[33] An early Burger Court decision appeared to be following that progression. In *Rosenbloom v. Metromedia*,[34] a plurality of the Court extended the *Times* privilege to false statements made in connection with a "matter of public concern." The plurality was composed of Brennan, the author of *New York Times*, and two less likely Justices, Blackmun and Burger. The *Rosenbloom* case was an oddity in several respects. Only one of the Court's two "absolutists" on First Amendment issues, Justice Black, participated in the case, concurring in the result as he had in all defamation cases that held false commentary was privileged but that the privilege was not absolute. Since Douglas did not participate, the Court's fifth vote for protecting the publication was provided by White, who took the narrow ground that since the alleged defamation of a private person occurred in the context of a broadcast on a police raid, there was a privilege "to report and comment upon the official actions of public servants."[35] Harlan, Stewart, and Marshall dissented, believing that the decision represented an unsupportable extension of the *Times* privilege.

While *Rosenbloom* may have appeared to represent a logical culmination of *New York Times*, suggesting that the Court would find that the First Amendment cut deeper and deeper into the law of defamation, the fractionalized line-up of votes in the case and the odd configuration of Justices in the plurality augured future difficulties. And just three years after the *Rosenbloom* decision the Court, now with two new Justices, granted certiorari in a case seemingly controlled by *Rosenbloom*: false statements of fact made about an attorney representing the family of a youth killed by a Chicago police officer. Since the statements were made in context of a "matter of public concern," the Court's decision to hear the case suggested a lack of consensus for the *Rosenbloom* standard. And when the Court's opinion in the case, *Gertz v. Robert Welch, Inc.*, was issued, the constitutional law of defamation had been substantially recast.

Powell's opinion for the Court, a five-man majority composed of Marshall, Stewart, Rehnquist, and Blackmun in addition to himself, abandoned the *Rosenbloom* standard and established the touchstone for a *New York Times* privilege as whether the defamed plaintiff was a "public figure," as distinguished from a "private citizen." Public officials were subsumed in the category of public figures, but the status of the plaintiff was determinative, not whether the context of the defamation was a matter of public concern. The *Gertz* majority did not stop there, however. It declared that the First Amendment prohibited the states from imposing strict liability for defamation where a "publisher or broadcaster" defamed a private individual.[36] It also held that First Amendment concerns prevented states from imposing punitive damages on a publisher or broadcaster who defamed a private citizen absent a showing of recklessness or malice. The decision thus appeared to create bright-line categories of defamation actions, varying with the status of the plaintiff, the status of the defendant ("publishers and broadcasters" apparently being treated differently from nonmedia defendants), and the presence or absence of the kind of malice in a defendant that would forfeit the privilege under *New York Times.* The *Times* rule was retained for "public figure" cases, but the visibility of the plaintiff in *Gertz* (he was a member of numerous boards and commissions and the author of several books) suggested that the Court would read the "public figure" category narrowly.

As stated, the *Gertz* decision appeared to clear up a good deal of the confusion resulting from the accommodation of traditional concepts of state defamation law with the First Amendment. One member of the majority, Blackmun, expressly indicated that despite having joined the *Rosenbloom* plurality he was prepared to join *Gertz* so that the Court could "come to rest in the defamation area" and "have a clearly defined majority position."[37] But the *Gertz* consensus concealed some significant divisions beneath the surface. First, the five Justices who composed the majority had quite different views on how First Amendment concerns should be balanced against the interest in reputation, ranging from Blackmun, who admitted that he would otherwise have adhered to his *Rosenbloom* view, to Rehnquist, who was subsequently to reveal a position much less solicitous of First Amendment protections. Second, the dissenters in *Gertz* also expressed a variety of positions, from Burger and White, who would have reinstated the jury verdict on behalf of attorney Elmer Gertz and thus held that presumed or punitive damages could still be imposed against media defendants, to Douglas, who would have found the reports absolutely privileged, to Brennan, who continued to adhere to the *Rosenbloom* solution. This line-up suggested that only one or possibly two Justices continued to believe that the *New York Times* privilege should be extended beyond "public figures," but beyond that nothing was very clear.

Two years after *Gertz* the Court took another step in curbing the scope of the *Times* privilege. In *Time Inc. v. Firestone*[38] a magazine reported that a member of "one of America's wealthier industrial families" had received a divorce because of his wife's adultery. The actual divorce decree was not clear about the reasons for divorce, but only "extreme cruelty" and "lack of domestication" were mentioned.[39] The wife sued *Time* for defamation, claiming that her divorce had been negligently reported. For her to recover she would have to establish that she was not a *Gertz*-type public figure, since such persons could only recover on a showing of constitutional malice. The Court, with Rehnquist writing for the majority, held that Mrs. Firestone was not a public figure, even though her name had regularly appeared in local newspapers and she had held several press conferences, and that she had not become a public figure merely by being involved in a litigation.

The trend toward narrowing the class of public figures continued in *Wolston V. Reader's Digest*[40] and *Hutchinson v. Proxmire*,[41] two cases decided in 1979. In *Wolston* a person who had been convicted of contempt of court in 1958 for failing to appear before a grand jury investigating Soviet espionage was listed in a 1974 book as one of a number of "Soviet agents identified in the United States" who had been "convicted of espionage or falsifying information . . . or who field to the Soviet bloc to avoid prosecution." The petitioner in Wolston had been the subject of extensive newspaper coverage at the time of his contempt conviction in 1958, but the coverage ceased in a few weeks and he had not been in the public eye since. A majority of the Court held him not to be a "public figure" under *Gertz* because he had not voluntarily "thrust" himself into the forefront of any controversy surrounding his contempt citation. His subsequent actions of filing a defamation action did not make him a public figure either.[42]

In *Hutchinson* a research scientist had received grants from various federal organizations to support his research on certain behavior patterns in animals, such as the clenching of jaws in primates. Senator William Proxmire issued a press release and newsletters giving a "Golden Fleece" award to the agencies who had supported the scientist, saying, among other things, that they had "made a monkey's uncle out of the taxpayers." The scientist sued for defamation, claiming that Proxmire's statements had distorted the substance of his research. The Court, in a majority opinion written by Burger, held that Hutchinson was not a public figure merely by having written several specialized publications and did not become one by responding to the caricaturing of his work in the "Golden Fleece" award.

The cases from *Gertz* through *Hutchinson* suggest a consistent narrowing trend with respect to First Amendment privileges in the defamation area, reversing the expansive trend signified by the *New York Times-Butts* and *Walker-Rosenbloom* sequence. But then came an astonishing decision in 1985, *Dun & Bradstreet v. Greenmoss Builders*,[43] which seemingly threw the entire area of defamation back into confusion. The case involved two related aspects of *Gertz*, the limitation of damages in defamation claims to "actual damages," a category that excluded presumed and punitive damages, in the absence of constitutional malice; and the applicability of *Gertz* to nonmedia defendants.

In *Dun & Bradstreet* a crediting reporting agency field an incorrect report about the financial condition of a construction contractor to five of its subscribers. The report was confidential, but one of the subscribers told the contractor's president about it, and the contractor became aware of its erroneous nature. The contractor demanded a correction and asked for the name of the subscribers who had received the report. The agency wrote the subscribers that the contractor "continued in business as usual" (the earlier report had indicated that it had filed a voluntary petition for bankruptcy) but refused to identify the subscribers. The contractor sued for defamation and was awarded both compensatory and punitive damages, and the credit agency appealed on the ground that *Gertz* required that punitive damages be applied only where constitutional malice had been shown.

The *Dun & Bradstreet* case seemed an ideal opportunity for the Court to clarify the range of *Gertz*. The Vermont Supreme Court, from which the case had been certified, had decided that *Gertz* was inapplicable to nonmedia defendants and that a credit agency supplying confidential information to specified private parties was not a media defendant. In the Court's plurality opinion, however, Justice Powell, writing for Rehnquist and O'Connor in addition to himself, stated the question before the Court to be whether *Gertz* applied "when the false and defamatory statements do not involve matters of public concern."[44] Powell then proceeded to read all the Court's cases from *New York Times* through *Gertz* as involving "expression on a matter of undoubted public concern." Thus the statements made in *Gertz* about the unconstitutionality of presumed or punitive damages absent a showing of constitutional malice only referred to cases where the defamatory statements involved issues of public concern. The plurality then held that when the speech that formed the basis of a defamation action involved no matters of public concern, states could allow a finding of presumed or punitive damages even absent a showing of constitutional malice.[45]

In short, the *Dun & Bradstreet* plurality declined to attach any significance to the distinction made in *Gertz* between media and nonmedia defendants and appeared to revive the "matter of public concern" standard the Court had abandoned in *Gertz* as a significant analytical category in defamation actions. Burger and White concurred in the judgments in *Dun & Bradstreet*, but their opinions made it clear they were simply taking the opportunity to limit the range of *New York Times* as far as possible. Brennan, Marshall, Blackmun, and Stevens, dissenting, argued that the plurality had confused *Gertz*, resurrected a criterion they had abandoned in *Gertz*, and significantly limited the effect of *Gertz* in the process. Indeed it was hard to know what was left of the *Gertz* criteria after *Dun & Bradstreet*. The endorsement of "matter of public concern" as a significant test for whether presumed or punitive damages could lie appeared to cloud the meaning of the Court's earlier inquiries, summarized in *Gertz*, as to whether the plaintiff was a public figure or private citizen. The *Dun & Bradstreet* plurality did not make it clear whether that inquiry was retained to determine the extent of the privilege afforded to the defendant in a defamation action, but not to determine the permissibility of damages once the question of privilege had been resolved, or whether some other analytical approach was to be adopted. The only thing one could say with confidence about *Dun & Bradstreet* was that it did not command a majority of the Court.

From another perspective, however, *Dun & Bradstreet* continued a trend on the Burger Court of increased solicitude for the rights of persons whose reputations had allegedly been damaged by the false statements of others. *New York Times* and its progeny, with their emphasis on a wide definition of "public official" and "public figure," had suggested that the day was near when most defamations, being on "matters of public concern," would be privileged and virtually immune from attack. In *Rosenbloom* that day nearly arrived, but changes in Court personnel brought a halt to the progression. *Gertz, Firestone, Wolston* and *Hutchinson* had begun another progression, this time in the opposite direction: the effect of those cases had been to widen the range of "private citizen" defamation actions permissible under the Constitution. But all those cases retained *Gertz*'s conclusion that even private citizen plaintiffs could not recover anything except "actual" damages unless they could succeed in the very difficult task of proving constitutional malice. *Dun & Bradstreet* abandoned that requirement for those defamatory actions brought by private citizen plaintiffs whose subjects did not involve matters of public concern. As one example in the *Dun & Bradstreet* opinions put it, after that decision a female private citizen of impeccable reputation whose jealous neighbor called her a whore would be able to recover damages without any showing of actual injury.

Dun & Bradstreet is thus explicable as a continued cutting back on the reach of *New York Times* protection in defamation actions. Doctrinally the case is far less explicable. While the Court's disinclination to seize upon the distinction between media and nonmedia defendants can be understood as a reluctance to grant to media speakers any stronger degree of First Amendment protection than to other speakers, there was no language in *Gertz* or any of the subsequent cases suggesting that the *Gertz* requirements were limited to "matter of public concern" cases. It was odd, in fact, that criteria similar to the "matter of public concern" criterion were used by the Court in *Firestone, Wolston, Hutchinson* and *Gertz* itself to *limit* the range of *New York Times*: in none of those cases was the plaintiff held to have thrust himself into the vortex of public controversy. Yet in *Dun & Bradstreet* the plurality concluded that, after all, those cases were "matter of public concern" cases.

In short, the Burger Court's defamation decisions can be reconciled only by their results: a shifting majority of Justices continually cut back on the reach of *New York Times*, first at the level of privileges, finally at the level of damages. The *Gertz* opinion, in retrospect, can be seen as atypical for the Court in its effort to "come to rest" in prophylactic rules for privileges, standards of liability, and damages. But having done that, the Court then retreated from all of those rules, narrowing the privileges by reading "public figure" narrowly in *Firestone, Wolston*, and *Hutchinson*, resurrecting strict liability for defamation in *Dun & Bradstreet*, and allowing other than "actual damages" for private citizen plaintiffs in that case even where no constitutional malice had been shown. It was as if having tried a "Warren Court" doctrinal solution to defamation problems, the Court became uncomfortable with its breadth and returned to the *ad hoc* style with which it was seemingly comfortable.

The modern era of substantive due process began in the Warren Court with a decision that explicitly rejected the idea that the Due Process Clause of the Fourteenth Amendment could be given substantive content. In *Griswold v. Connecticut*[46] two officials of the Planned Parenthood League of Connecticut were prosecuted for giving birth control information to married couples under a Connecticut statute prohibiting any person from using "any drug, medicinal article or instrument for the purpose of preventing conception."[47] They claimed that the statute violated constitutional rights of married persons to make decisions affecting their family, arguing that such decisions were an exercise of "liberty" under the Due Process Clause. Douglas, for the Court, "decline[d] [the] invitation" to read the Due Process Clause substantively. Nonetheless he concluded that the Connecticut statute was unconstitutional. The reason was that it infringed on a "right of privacy," nowhere mentioned in the Constitution but inferable from "penumbras and emanations" of specific Bill of Rights guarantees, such as the First Amendment's right of association, the Fourth Amendment's protection from unreasonable searches and seizures, and the Fifth Amendment's self-incrimination clause. Privacy was a background right, a "zone" created by the above guarantees. The idea of police "search[ing] the sacred precincts of marital bedrooms for the use of contraceptives" was "repulsive to the notions of privacy surrounding the marriage relationship."[48]

Griswold was an example of a "hard" case that made bad law. The case was "hard" only because the Court had gotten itself into a doctrinal straightjacket by rejecting the idea that the Due Process Clause could have substantive content in the aftermath of its abandonment of the "liberty of contract" doctrine installed in *Lochner v. New York*. By abandoning *Lochner* it had apparently abandoned substantive due process altogether: Douglas announced in *Griswold* that "we do not sit as a super-legislature to determine the wisdom, need, and propriety of laws. . . ."[49] And since privacy was not mentioned anywhere in the Constitution, this left the Court in the awkward position of having to return to a version of *Lochner* or sustain what Stewart called "an uncommonly silly law."[50] Douglas attempted to avoid either of those options by creating "penumbral" or background rights in the Constitution, but that methodology was nearly unprecedented[51] and the Court has never again employed it. These features of *Griswold* made it a "bad" decision, although the result—as suggested by Douglas's rhetorical question about police searches of marital bedrooms—was surely correct.

If *Griswold* was a "privacy" decision, did the "privacy" protected inhere in the marital relationship? The Burger Court answered that question in *Eisenstadt v. Baird*,[52] where a Massachusetts statute prohibiting the distribution of birth control information and contraceptives was successfully challenged by a single person. "It is true," Brennan wrote for the Court, "that in *Griswold* the right of privacy in question inhered in the marital relationship." But "if the right of privacy means anything, it is the right of the *individual*, married or single, to be free from unwarranted governmental intrusion into matters so fundamentally affecting a person as the decision whether to bear or beget a child."[53]

While *Eisenstadt* used the "privacy" rhetoric of *Griswold*, it was not a "privacy" case in the sense of raising issues related to the intrusion into some "sacred" private sphere. The statute did not prevent the use of contraceptive devices, only their distribution to unmarried persons. When the Court spoke of the "privacy" rights of individuals implicated by the statue, then, it meant something like the right to make decisions about one's sexual conduct, a right better captured by the label "autonomy" or perhaps "liberty." That "privacy" had come to subsume a bundle of rights not precisely associated with freedom from intrusion was made clear by the Court's next "privacy" case.

That case was *Roe v. Wade*,[54] perhaps the most famous of all the Burger Court's cases, in which a 7–2 majority of the Court declared a limited right for a woman to have an abortion. Like *Eisenstadt, Roe v. Wade* was not a privacy case in the *Griswold* sense; going to a hospital to have an abortion was a semi-public act. The choice being protected in an abortion decision was one to escape the burdens of pregnancy or one to choose whether or not to bear children, a choice, like that in *Eisenstadt*, based on autonomy or liberty concerns. Nonetheless, Blackmun, for the majority, used the "privacy" language, citing *Griswold* and noting that "a right of personal privacy, or a guarantee of certain areas or zones of privacy, does exist under the Constitution.[55] Blackmun went on, however, to suggest that privacy subsumed a series of "fundamental" rights, such as procreation, contraception, family relationships, child rearing, and education. The right of privacy, he concluded, was "founded in the Fourteenth Amendment's concept of personal liberty."[56]

At this point Blackmun converted *Roe v. Wade* into a "fundamental rights" case, drawing on the doctrinal evolution of that concept in the Court's equal protection decisions, and began "balancing" state interests in restricting the "liberty" to have an abortion against the right itself. He assumed that the right infringed by anti-abortion legislation was a "fundamental" one, and therefore that the state had to show a "compelling" interest in restricting it. This analytic framework was borrowed from the Court's equal protection cases: Douglas had announced it, thirty years earlier, in *Skinner v. Oklahoma.* Blackmun did not discuss why "fundamental rights" analysis was appropriate in the due process area, or why the right to have an abortion was "fundamental." He concluded that the state interest in preserving the health of the mother or the potential viability of the fetus became "compelling" after the first trimester of pregnancy, so that up to that point the state could not restrict abortions at all.

Roe v. Wade thus set the stage for modern substantive due process analysis, in which older notions of "fundamentality," reflected in the Vinson and Warren Courts' decisions incorporating some Bill of Rights provisions against the states through the Due Process Clause of the Fourteenth Amendment, were revived,[57] and the Due Process Clause was openly given substantive content. *Roe* has thus spawned a number of other cases that would originally have been included under the rubric of "privacy," such as state withdrawals of funds for nontherapeutic abortions,[58] federal limitations on the use of Medicaid Funds for abortions,[59] state efforts to regulate abortion procedures,[60] spousal consent for abortion decisions,[61] parental consent for abortion decisions by minors[62] parental notification for abortion decisions by minors,[63] and minors' access to contraceptives.[64] In addition, the

Court considered some cases where the "liberties" asserted against governmental regulation were closely related to privacy in the expanded sense of personal autonomy. A pair of cases, *Village of Belle Terre v. Boraas*[65] and *Moore v. City of East Cleveland*,[66] raised the question whether municipalities could restrict the choice of individuals to live together. In the latter case the Court, in a plurality opinion authored by Powell, identified "the freedom of personal choice in matters of marriage and family life" as "one of the liberties protected by the Due Process Clause of the Fourteenth Amendment," and said that while "there are risks when the judicial branch gives enhanced protection to certain substantive liberties without the guidance of the more specific protections of the Bill of Rights," the "history of the *Lochner* era . . . counsels caution and restraint, [b]ut it does not counsel abandonment."[67] In *Belle Terre* the Court found that a city could restrict the kinds of individuals living together in dwelling units so long as it allowed all who were related by "blood, adoption, or marriage" to live together. In *Moore* the city of East Cleveland had defined "family" for dwelling purposes more narrowly, excluding some related members. The Court treated the liberty of family choice as "fundamental" in both cases, and held that the narrow definition of "family" in *Moore* made that effort at state restriction impermissible.

The substantive due process analysis reintroduced in *Griswold* and made explicit in *Roe* suggested that the Court might begin a logical progression of substantive "liberties" in the area of privacy or autonomy comparable to that which it had begun in the area of First Amendment privileges for defamatory "speech." Two commentators suggested in 1977 that the "privacy," "family," and sexual conduct cases were part of a larger trend toward constitutional protection for personal "lifestyle choices" under the Due Process Clause.[68] Among the choices eligible for protection, they argued, were those involving sexual activity, appearance, and domestic companionship. Particularly singled out for substantive due process treatment were laws restricting sodomitic conduct among consenting adults and laws dictating uniform hair styles.[69] The Court, however, perhaps mindful of the earlier difficulties it had encountered in following the logic of its own precedents in the defamation area, used substantive due process methodology to restrict choices in the area of appearance and sexual conduct. In *Kelley v. Johnson*[70] it had held that the "liberty" interest claimed by a policeman in maintaining his hair at a chosen length despite department regulations was "distinguishable" from that raised by the *Eisenstadt-Roe* line of cases. Those cases had involved "a substantial claim of infringement on the individual's freedom of choice with respect to certain basic matters of procreation, marriage, and family life," the *Kelley* Court said: freedom to wear one's hair at the length one chose was of a different order. Indeed the Court in *Kelley* permitted the regulation because it was not "irrational," suggesting that it did not even recognize the asserted interest as "fundamental."[71]

In the area of sodomitic conduct the Court apparently went even further. In a 1976 decision, *Doe v. Commonwealth's Attorney*,[72] the Court had summarily affirmed a three-judge district court's conclusion that a Virginia antisodomy statute, which applied to heterosexuals as well as homosexuals and to consenting adults, was constitutional. The panel's decision had ignored *Eisenstadt* and held that the right of "privacy" was confined to a married heterosexual context, in an action brought by homosexuals to avoid prosecution for private consensual acts.[73] The Court's summary affirmance, with three Justices dissenting, meant that all antisodomy statutes, even those reaching private consensual conduct by married heterosexuals, remained in force. As the Court declined to entertain any further challenges to antisodomy legislation in the next several years, commentators assumed that eventually a challenge would be successful. One suggested in 1980 that "within a few years fornication and sodomy laws will be found unconstitutional, on something [like the] right of consenting adults to control their own sex lives."[74]

Eventually, in the 1985 Term, a challenge came. In *Bowers v. Hardwick*[75] a Georgia antisodomy statute was attacked on substantive due process grounds by a male homosexual who had been prosecuted for engaging in private consensual sexual activities. He argued that the *Griswold* line of cases had established a constitutional "liberty" to engage in sexual practices free from state interference. A majority of the Court rejected his argument. White's opinion, for O'Connor, Rehnquist, and himself, with Burger and Powell joining its crucial findings, confined the holding to homosexual sexual practices but held flatly that there was no constitutional right to engage in homosexual conduct in private. Homosexual conduct was not "implicit in the concept of ordered liberty," it was not a liberty "deeply rooted in . . . history and tradition," and it had not been given constitutional protection by the Court's earlier substantive due process decisions, which dealt with rights pertaining to the family, marriage, or procreation. There was, in short, no "fundamental right" to engage in homosexual conduct, whether private and consensual or not. Indeed the "liberty" to engage in such conduct was sufficiently lacking in constitutional stature as to be capable of being regulated simply on grounds of morality. A state might merely believe that homosexual conduct was "immoral" to proscribe it.

Bowers thus threw the substantive due process cases on the Burger Court into disarray. One commentator, proclaiming that *Bowers* heralded the "second death of substantive due process," noted that *Griswold, Eisenstadt*, and *Roe*, taken together, had established a fundamental right in an individual to engage in procreative or nonprocreative sexual relations. Moreover, *Roe* had affirmed a version of that right in the face of a strong state interest in protecting fetal offspring, whereas there was no interest of similar strength asserted in *Bowers.*[76] *Bowers* and the earlier cases were thus "inconsistent and irreconcilable."[77] It is also worth noting that while the majority in *Bowers* specifically limited their holding to homosexual conduct, the statute upheld did not merely prohibit sodomitic sexual activity between homosexuals, but extended to consenting married heterosexuals as well. If the rhetorical question put by Douglas in *Griswold* retained its power, one could ask the majority in *Bowers* whether they would allow the police to search the sacred precincts of marital bedrooms for telltale signs of the practice of sodomy.

It is, however, possible to see *Bowers* as a "homosexual" case, and in that sense representative of the Burger Court's style of constitutional adjudication. After the *Griswold* line of cases, plus *Stanley v. Georgia*,[78] a firm residue of protection for consensual sexual activity practiced in private seemed to be in place. *Stanley* had afforded protection to activities, such as viewing pornographic movies, that were engaged in in one's home even if the activities would have been illegal in the outside. That suggested that the Court recognized an enhanced First Amendment right to view even unprotected materials when the viewing took place in private. The *Griswold* line and *Stanley* suggested comparable protection for consensual sexual activities that might be illegal when engaged in in public, and the emphasis in *Griswold* and the "family privacy" cases on the sanctity of marriage suggested that the level of protection might be even higher where married persons were concerned.

Given, then, the very high degree of solicitude for consensual heterosexual conduct performed in private, the apparent explanation for the *Bowers* majority's different treatment of private consensual homosexual conduct was that homosexuals were "different." That interpretation is reinforced by the majority's easy assumption that Georgia could justify proscribing such conduct on grounds of morality. Would the court have accepted similar rationale for discriminations against blacks or women or disabled persons? The case was perceived by the majority as a "homosexual case": a case where the result was dictated by the fact that the interest at stake in the case was not that of a more abstract liberty or privacy, but that of homosexuals to engage in intimate conduct with persons of the same gender. The decision thus did not fit with the Court's other substantive due process cases because it was an *ad hoc* decision, similar to the Court's decisions in the defamation or gender discrimination cases. The surprising feature of *Bowers* was that it appeared to be a sharp deviation from a logical doctrinal progression that had begun with *Griswold* and appeared to culminate with the declaration in *Bowers* that sodomy (and probably adultery and fornication) laws were unconstitutional. But there never had been any such progression: there had only been successive majorities for successive cases. When a majority refused to take a further step on behalf of homosexuals, the progression suddenly resembled that in the defamation and gender discrimination areas: zig-zag patterns rather than "progressions" at all. Thus the floating, centrist character of the Burger Court, whose majorities varied from case to case and from fact situation to fact situation, can be seen in constitutional doctrine as well as in the internal dynamics of the Justices.

III

Despite the piecemeal character of the Burger Court's decision-making style and its shifting doctrinal patterns, there was abundant evidence that in the years of Burger's tenure another phase in the history of the American appellate judiciary had begun. No better evidence of the emergence of that phase was the dissolution on the Burger Court of the jurisprudential controversy at the very heart of Warren Court decision-making: process versus substantive liberalism. We have seen that some of the great cases of Warren's tenure—*Brown v. Board of Education, Baker v. Carr, Griswold v. Connecticut*—were conceived by the justices as conflicts between a jurisprudential liberalism that emphasized the deference of courts to legislatures, especially where less than fully entrenched textually protected rights were being curtailed, and a jurisprudential liberalism that emphasized the promulgation of values that were allegedly embedded in the structure of the Constitution, such as liberty or equality.

"Process liberals" such as Frankfurter or Harlan reminded their colleagues of the obligation of the judiciary to defer to more democratic institutions of government in order to preserve the credos of a democratic society; substantive liberals such as Warren stressed the fundamentality of the values being affirmed in the face of legislative resistance. The central jurisprudential debates of the Warren Court were not cast in terms of results but in terms of methodologies, with cases such as *Brown* or *Griswold* spawning controversy not over the value of opposing racial segregation or protecting privacy but over the methodology employed to achieve that end or the policymaking competence of the institution seeking to achieve it.

It is interesting that none of the major Burger Court cases, such as *Reed, Gertz*, or *Roe*, represented debates of this kind. No Justice suggested in *Reed* that the Court was an inappropriate institution to be giving substantive content to the equal protection clause or interfering with a state's administration of its probate courts. No Justice argued that the Court's wholesale restriction in *Gertz* of the states' power to set damages or standards of liability in defamation cases was a usurpation of a legislative function. And no Justice in *Roe* argued that in light of the lack of precise textual support for a right to have an abortion, and in light of renewed legislative interest in the abortion decision, state legislatures were the appropriate forum to strike the balances between the autonomy of the mother and the potential viability of the fetus. Any debates that existed in these cases were debates about the substantive strength of the constitutional right being advanced. Those Justices who opposed the Court's decisions in the cases did so because they felt that greater protection needed to be given to statements on matters of public concern, because they found no constitutional protection for the choice to have an abortion, or because they elevated fetus viability rights to a position of considerable strength. The Burger Court's debates, in short, were debates about substance, not debates pitting substance against process.

The Burger Court's response to the accountability quotient of appellate judging thus both paralleled that of the Warren Court and departed from it. Some Warren Court members believed that certain of its decisions had not paid sufficient heed to the accountability priniciple because they were neither grounded in appropriate constitutional analysis or predicated on an appropriate theory of institutional functions. To this criticism Warren Court majorities responded that the decisions were justifiable because they were substantively right: they affirmed values to which the American public subscribed. In a sense the debate during much of the Warren Court's tenure was about whether, if a decision is overwhelmingly "right," it needs to be properly crafted or institutionally sensitive.

When that debate ceased during the Burger Court, the problem of accountability remained. Americans remained divided on the necessity of eradicating greater discrimination, the limits of protection for speech, the legitimacy of abortion. The Court's approach to those areas reflected those divisions. But the Court's awareness that the issues it was deciding were divisive did not take the form of a withdrawal from the role of decision-maker in favor of a more democratic substitute, but rather took the form of making decisions that were themselves substantive compromises. Gender discrimination triggered an intermediate level of scrutiny; false and defamatory statements were given constitutional protection in some areas and not others; abortions were permitted in some phases of pregnancy and forbidden in others. The Burger Court's version of accountability was to recognize the divisive character of the issues it was addressing by deciding them in a pragmatic, *ad hoc*, and compromised form, in contrast to the broad, sweeping ideological pronouncements of the Warren Court. As one commentator has said of the Burger Court, its "distinctive hallmark" had been a "powerful aversion to making fundamental value choices"; its "efforts have been inspired almost exclusively by discrete, pragmatic judgments regarding how a moderate, sensible judicial accommodation might help to resolve a potentially divisive public controversy."[79]

Here, finally, another sense emerges in which the Burger Court may eventually come to be thought of as a "transitional" Court. Part of the difference between the ideological context in which the Burger and Warren Courts functioned was the apparent ability for certain arguments from principle to serve as "trumps" in the years of the Warren Court, and the inability of those arguments to serve the same function in the Burger years. One can take nearly any major area of Warren Court doctrinal innovation and see this phenomenon at work. In race relations the trump of equality of educational opportunity has yielded to the more complex notion of affirmative action. In reapportionment a similar trump, the idea that one person, one vote is the only method of apportionment that will satisfy the equality principle, has yielded to distinctions between "individual" and "proportional" representation that permit the practical dilution of voting power.[80] In establishment of religion cases the concept of a "wall" between church and state, an important justification for Warren Court decisions in school-prayer cases,[81] has been replaced by fungible criteria for an "establishment" of religion that permit cities to display creches[82] but forbid state legislatures from authorizing moments of silence in the public schools.[83] A similar pattern has been noted in the defamation cases, with the trump of liberty, dominant in *New York Times*, giving way to the accommodations of *Gertz* and *Dun & Bradstreet*.

The primacy of "trump" arguments is not just a function of the ability of the Justices making those arguments. It is also a function of the ideological culture of a given Court. The later Warren Court years represented a period in which Americans were seemingly confronted with the primacy of certain powerful moral truths, such as the belief that all persons should in fact be treated equally, skin color not withstanding, or the belief that the state should not interfere with harmless conduct simply because some people found it offensive. These beliefs gave new force to the principles of equality and liberty and invested them with the status of trumping arguments. In their engagement with the renewed force of the equality and liberty principles, Americans of the late sixties tended to minimize countervailing values, or to ignore the fact that sometimes the elevation of equality meant the suppression of liberty, or vice versa. In the years of the Burger Court such complexities came once more to the fore, spelling, among other things, reduced influence for the reflexive liberalism that had dominated American politics since the New Deal. Nowhere was this more evident than in the contrast between the Warren Court racial discrimination cases from *Brown* through *Green v. County School Board*,[84] all unanimous decisions and all based on the equality principle, and *Regents of the University of California v. Bakke*,[85] a decision in which the equality principle competed with itself and a decision in which no clear majority existed.

The Burger Court was different from the Warren Court, then, not only because of changes in personnel but because of changes in the ideological context in which its decisions were set. The differences reflected, in important part, the evolution of American liberal politics from a messianic to a tempered phase, a period of transition, to paraphrase Holmes, from an era of creative transformation to solvent philosophical reaction. What remains unclear is whether the reaction will come in the years of the Rehnquist Court and what form it will take. All that one can say at this point is that there are contradictory signs. The election of Ronald Reagan for two terms appeared to signal a decisive shift in political ideology in America: the end of the welfarist, egalitarian political consciousness of the New Deal and its replacement with a more libertarian, antiwelfarist ideology. With Reagan's retirement approaching, the shift appears less clear. What is not apparent is whether candidates whose partisan affiliation is in the tradition of Roosevelt, Kennedy, and Johnson will wrap themselves in the rhetoric and embrace the assumptions of that tradition, or whether they will decisively reject it, as has Reagan. There are two significant elements to the liberal political tradition, an emphasis on welfarist policies and an emphasis on human rights, and even antibureaucratic Democrats such as Carter embraced at least one of those elements. Were a "free market," libertarian Democrat to win the party's nomination, a political transformation would clearly have taken place. That prospect is by no means clear.

Should such a transformation come to pass, the ideological culture of the Rehnquist Court might well be different from that of the Burger Court. New trumps might appear, most particularly the trumps of liberty and autonomy, and a new majority might come into being that discarded the *ad hoc* centrism of the Burger Court for a more sweeping prophylactic style of decision-making, albeit one that reached results quite incompatible with those reached by the Warren Court. Continued personnel changes make the surfacing of such a majority—potentially composed of Chief Justice Rehnquist and Justices White, O'Connor, Scalia, and Kennedy—possible. But prophylactic decision-making is hardly Justice White's style, and Justice Scalia's and Kennedy's tenures have just begun. Regardless of what style of decision-making or ideological inclination surfaces on the Rehnquist Court, it will be different from that of the Burger Court because the context of the Court's decisions, the personnel, and the issues the Court faces will all be different. Should the Rehnquist Court become the reverse mirror image of the later Warren Court, the Burger Court "transitional" role will be easily apparent. But even if the Rehnquist Court takes a much less ideologically discernible form it will not resemble its predecessor; transitions will have occurred. Of all the generalizations one might advance about the tradition of appellate judging in America, the easiest is that the style and substance of judging will change as American culture changes. If the latter form of change is inevitable, so is the former. The American judicial tradition has important elements of continuity, but its predominant feature is that of a reflection of cultural change.

15

The Unexpectedness of the Rehnquist Court

An observer of the process by which Justices were nominated to the Court in the late twentieth century might have anticipated, on noticing the partisan affiliations of nominating Presidents, that the Rehnquist Court's constitutional law decisions would take a sharp turn from their dominant character in the Warren and even in the Burger years. Between 1970 and 1992 all of the Presidents who nominated Justices were Republicans. One of those, Ronald Reagan, was a different sort of Republican from his predecessors: an outspoken critic of expansive government who hoped to dismantle much of the regulatory apparatus inspired by the New Deal. Reagan served for two terms and had four Court appointments. His Vice President, George H. W. Bush, served an additional term and had two more. The sole Democratic President to serve in that time frame, Jimmy Carter, had no opportunity to make an appointment.

Moreover, Reagan's and Bush's appointees were, at the time of their nominations, perceived as distinctly rightward leaning. Two were comparative unknowns, Sandra Day O'Connor in 1981 and David Souter in 1990, but nothing in their records indicated a sympathy toward New Deal–inspired liberalism. Three others, Antonin Scalia, Clarence Thomas, and William Rehnquist, were perceived as the equivalent of in-your-face right-wingers: Scalia as an outspoken critic of a "living Constitution" approach to constitutional interpretation; Thomas, an African American, as hostile to affirmative action; and Rehnquist, dubbed the "Lone Ranger" for his repeated dissents from Burger Court decisions tolerating expansive governmental power or extending protection for civil rights, as the quintessential New Right judge. By the time Reagan nominated Robert Bork to the Court in 1987, ideology had come to be perceived as a decisive criterion in the nominating process, and Anthony Kennedy, whom Reagan appointed after ideological opponents defeated Bork, was initially thought by some observers to be nearly as right of center as Bork himself.[1]

Thus, between 1986 and 1992, with Rehnquist installed as Chief Justice, and the Court's membership coming to include only one Justice—the far from stereotypically liberal Byron White—who had been nominated by a Democratic President, commentators waited for the Court to, as one put it, "turn right."[2] Three lines of decisions associated with the Warren and Burger Courts seemed particularly vulnerable. The first, which tended to overshadow all other issues in the nominations from O'Connor's on, was the line of substantive due process holdings that culminated in *Roe v. Wade*'s determination that women had a limited right to choose to terminate pregnancies. The second was affirmative action: commentators expected new majorities on the Rehnquist Court to be less receptive than their predecessors to the proposition that race could be taken into account in the admissions programs of state educational institutions or the awarding of government licenses or contracts. Finally, the Warren Court's prophylactic rules governing police conduct in the arrest and detention of criminal suspects, exemplified by the *Miranda* decision, were thought to be unattractive to many Rehnquist Court Justices, several of whom had been appointed by Presidents associated with "law and order" values.

None of those lines were disturbed in the first six years of Rehnquist's tenure. In fact, by the time of his death in 2005, each had been reinvigorated. Putative characterizations of the Rehnquist Court now needed to acknowledge that it had established a new rationale for affirmative action programs in higher education,[3] explicitly reaffirmed the *Roe*[4] and *Miranda*[5] decisions, and extended constitutional protection to consensual sexual activity engaged in by members of the same sex.[6] Commentators who were inclined to think of the Rehnquist Court as turning rightward needed to look elsewhere.

This is not to say that in 2005 the Rehnquist Court was approximately in the same place, in its constitutional decisions, as its two predecessors. But no one should have expected that. Constitutional law invariably changes as altered circumstances contribute to the emergence of new social issues that find their way to the Court. The blithe dismissal by a unanimous Warren Court, in 1961, of a challenge to jury selection on gender lines[7] would have been thought inconceivable by the Courts that struck down gender-based standards for giving young people access to alcohol[8] and declined to allow the state of Virginia to exclude women from a college with a tradition of preparing its members for the military.[9] A cursory endorsement of the criminalization of intimate homosexual liaisions made by a Court majority in 1986[10] was overruled by another majority in 2003.[11] What had changed, in both instances, was not merely Court personnel but attitudes toward gender equality and discrimination on the basis of sexual preference. Such changes are the norm in constitutional law, and as a result Courts never simply reaffirm the decisions of their predecessors.

Even against this backdrop, however, the outstanding characteristic of the Rehnquist Court was its unexpectedness. But the nature of that unexpectedness has not been fully grasped. A Court with Rehnquist as its Chief Justice, staffed mainly by Justices nominated by Republican Presidents, was expected to depart significantly from the signature decisions of its predecessors, and, on the whole, did not. The reasons for that relative jurisprudential stasis are not easily found in factors habitually offered as explanations for judicial decisions: judicial ideology and external politics.

For one thing, the internal atmosphere of the Rehnquist Court was unexpectedly harmonious. This was largely due to two factors: the continuity of the Court's personnel, which remained constant from 1994 to 2005 (the second longest period in the history of the Court) and the metamorphosis of an Associate Justice who had played the role of loner ideologue on the Burger Court into a collegial, gregarious, non-confrontational Chief. This meant that when the Court came to reconsider its past decisions, especially during the later stages of Rehnquist's tenure, they were sometimes confronting decisions authored by Justices who were still sitting. Overruling opinions written by one's colleagues is never pleasant, especially when the collegial group is, on the whole, getting along well.

But the most unexpected feature of the Rehnquist Court was not its sometimes surprising continuity with its predecessors's decisions. It was the dramatic shift in its jurisprudential culture. For several decades, beginning in the early 1940s, debates in American constitutional jurisprudence had centered on the issue of reconciling aggressive judicial review of legislation with the "undemocratic" character of the judicial branch of government. Justices and commentators asked whether a degree of "judicial activism" was necessary in order to protect the rights of minorities against discriminatory policies imposed by legislative majorities, or whether judges should "restrain" themselves from substituting their views on the meaning of open-ended constitutional provisions for those of the more "democratic" branches of government. In short, the role of judges as constitutional interpreters was described as embodying a tension between judicial activism and judicial restraint.

That description of the judicial role was not central to the Rehnquist Court. That Court's jurisprudence cannot be fairly described as a clash between judicial activists and advocates of a restrained review posture. Instead of focusing on institutional considerations, such as whether courts or legislatures were better suited to protect the rights of minorities, jurisprudential debates on the Rehnquist Court focused directly on questions of constitutional interpretation. In particular, they focused on two sets of interpretive questions. One was the extent to which history, as embodied in the texts of constitutional provisions and the "understandings" of those texts by their framers and contemporaries, should control the interpretation of the Constitution by subsequent generations of judges. The other was whether the "meaning" of the Constitution—the judicial application of its provisions to new cases and controversies—changed over time.

Placing those questions at the center of jurisprudential debates meant that the locus of meaningful constraints on judges as constitutional interpreters had shifted. Neither side in the debate was interested in whether the "countermajoritarian" judiciary ought to defer to the judgments of more popularly elected branches. Instead each side assumed that the obligation to define the meaning of the Constitution fell on the judiciary and asked how that meaning should be supplied as new cases appeared. Both sides might be thought of as reviving the older idea of foundational constraints on judges as interpreters that had been associated with oracular jurisprudence. For Rehnquist Court Justices attracted to what has come to be called "originalism," the concept of historical understandings serving as a constraint on judges was an echo of Marshall's distinction between the will of the law and the will of the judge. And non-orginialists on the Rehnquist Court believed in a set of constraints as well: the obligation of judges, as they interpreted an evolving Constitution, to unearth the foundational principles that undergirded constitutional provisions and ensure that they be given continuing effect.

For all its affinity with the oracular era, however, the constitutional jurisprudence of the Rehnquist Court was a product of a modern jurisprudential sensibility, in which judges were taken to be a species of lawmakers and the role of human agency in constitutional interpretation was taken as paramount. Nonetheless, the shift from institutionally derived constraints on judges as constitutional intepreters to historically and linguistically derived constraints may well have ushered in a new stage in the history of the American judicial tradition. If that turns out to be the case, perhaps the most unexpected feature of the Rehnquist Court will be its radical jurisprudential character.

I

Fourteen justices served on the Rehnquist Court. The careers of three are better understood as identified with other Courts. Lewis Powell overlapped with Chief Justice Rehnquist only one Term, and Powell's blend of personal grace and consensual, centrist inclinations was a welcome antidote to the fractionalized atmosphere of the Burger Court, which often seemed one step from disintegrating into polarized chaos.[12] William Brennan had been a highly influential member of both the Warren and Burger Courts, serving as something of a campaign manager for Warren and his cohorts' efforts to make constitutional law comport more closely with their sense of fairness and justice, and skillfully preserving and extending Warren Court jurisprudence in the face of skepticism from some of his Burger Court colleagues. Thurgood Marshall had been a regular member of the phalanx of Warren Court Justices dedicated to extending the reach of the Constitution into the nooks and crannies of American life, but he was far less interested than Brennan in the intricacies of fostering or preserving jurisprudential majorities, and he increasingly slid into the role of impassioned dissenter as his career drew to a close. Five years after Rehnquist replaced Burger, all three had retired.

Byron White, appointed in 1961 by Kennedy, remained until 1993. His jurisprudential posture remained constant throughout his tenure, making him, on whatever Court he served, strongly deferential to Congress and the Executive on questions involving the exercise of national powers, opposed to racial segregration and its vestiges but otherwise lukewarm on civil rights issues, sympathetic to law enforcement values, and disinclined to conceptualize constitutional rights broadly when more narrow, pragmatic formulations would suffice. This posture made him, in the eyes of some commentators, a "liberal" on some Courts and a "conservative" on others, but it was the issues, rather than White, that had changed. As the Rehnquist Court, in its early years, came to be associated with forms of social conservatism, such as opposition to abortion rights or affirmative action, White signaled that he was comfortable with those developments. But on other issues, notably separation of powers and federalism, he retained his deference to federal executive and legislative policies. His role on the early Rehnquist Court approximated his role on the Burger Court: that of a Justice whose vote was available to prospective majorities on either end of the Court's jurisprudential spectrum, depending on the issues in question.[13]

When John Paul Stevens was appointed to the Court in 1975, commentators predicted that he would be a "centrist" judge,[14] somewhat in the manner of White, and Stevens shared with White a theoretical commitment to judicial deference and an idiosyncratic approach to constitutional interpretation.[15] But as new Justices joined the Court in the 1980s and 1990s, Stevens's posture tended to align him more frequently with Justices perceived as "liberals" than with those perceived as "conservatives." His voting patterns in cases in the 1990s regularly diverged from those of Rehnquist, Scalia, and Thomas and tracked those of Ruth Bader Ginsburg, Stephen Breyer, and the unexpectedly "liberal" Bush appointee David Souter.[16] On the most visible social issues of that decade Stevens remained less than stereotypically progressive, generally, but not universally, supporting abortion rights,[17] affirmative action,[18] and equal protection challenges to legislation making distinctions on gender[19] or sexual preference,[20] but resisting libertarian interpretations of First Amendment rights.[21] But on the sorts of issues that were perceived as distinguishing late-twentieth-century liberalism and conservatism, such as support for criminal defendants, the separation of church and state, campaign finance reform, and support for the powers of the national government vis-à-vis those of the states, Stevens was almost invariably on the liberal side.[22]

The sharp divergence in Stevens's and Rehnquist's voting patterns, coupled with Stevens's status as senior Associate Justice for the entire duration of the Rehnquist Court's second phase, resulted in Stevens's acquiring the assignment power in some visible cases in which Rehnquist found himself in dissent. In one such instance Stevens revealed himself as something of a strategist.[23] Although he had tended to support equal protection challenges in gender discrimination cases, Stevens had not committed himself to a standard of heightened review in such cases, preferring to decide each on its facts. In *United States v. Virginia*[24] the constitutionality of the refusal of the Virginia Military Institute (VMI) to admit women to its student body was challenged. The Institute argued that its primary educational purpose was to train students for careers in the military, and that in pursuit of that purpose it had created a mentally and physically rigorous "adversative" program under which incoming students were repeatedly subjected to demands by upperclassmen. The program involved versions of physical and mental harrassment that VMI argued would be inappropriate for female students.

The VMI case was argued early in Ginsburg's tenure on the Court. She had been a celebrated advocate for gender equality before her appointment, known for her dogged, if politic, efforts to analogize classifications based on gender to those based on race, which when challenged on constitutional grounds received a very high level of scrutiny from the Court.[25] Ginsburg produced an opinion in the VMI case that, by summarizing the Court's prior gender discrimination decisions as requiring that any statute making classifications on gender grounds rest on an "exceedingly persuasive" justification, under which the government needed to show "at least that [the classification served] important governmental objectives" and that it was not based on "overbroad generalizations about the different talents, capacities, or preferences of males and females," in effect placed future gender discrimination cases in a "strict scrutiny" category.[26] After *United States v. Virginia*, it was hard to imagine any single-sex state educational institution surviving a constitutional challenge.

The progression of Stevens's role on the Court illustrates the importance of context in the shaping of judicial careers. Stevens's voting patterns and jurisprudential posture bear a resemblance to those of Frankfurter, who by the time of his retirement was generally thought of as a judicial "conservative." On constitutional issues, Stevens's votes have diverged from Frankfurter's primarily in criminal procedure cases, where Frankfurter was less inclined to be solicitous of the rights of defendants. On free speech and equal protection issues both Justices were relatively cautious balancers; both believed in a wall between church and state; both were sympathetic to federal power; both tended to be deferential to Congress and the Executive; both were advocates of case-by-case adjudication and subscribed to the rhetoric of judicial restraint. Those positions, taken cumulatively, have placed Stevens close to the left end of the Rehnquist Court's jurisprudential spectrum; they placed Frankfurter to the right of center in the Warren Court.

If Stevens may have found that his jurisprudence was perceived as drifting leftward over time despite the overall consistency of his positions, Harry Blackmun actually moved leftward during his tenure. The evolution of Blackmun's views illustrates how the accident of a Justice being decisively involved in a visible, controversial opinion of the Court can have implications that extend well beyond the case generating that opinion. In Blackmun's instance, the opinion, *Roe v. Wade*, came comparatively early in his tenure, and his being assigned the option was comparatively fortuitous.

To understand the pivotal importance of Blackmun's *Roe v. Wade* opinion in the subsequent development of his career, it is necessary to recall that when *Roe* was decided, it was not primarily perceived of as a "women's rights" case. *Roe*, challenging a Texas statute prohibiting abortion under all circumstances except when "saving the life of the mother" was involved, and a companion case, *Doe v. Bolton*, directed at a Georgia statute with somewhat broader exceptions, first came to the Court in the 1971 Term, when the Court had not yet extended the idea of a constitutional right to make intimate sexual or reproductive choices beyond the marital context.[27] The primary concern with the abortion statutes challenged in *Roe* and *Doe* was that by providing criminal penalties for doctors who performed unauthorized abortions, and limiting authorized procedures to situations in which a mother's "health" was threatened, they were unconstitutionally vague, failing to give physicians precise enough notice of the circumstances in which abortions were not unlawful.[28]

Blackmun and several of his colleagues may have thought, at the time *Roe* was decided, that controversies over abortion would quickly recede. Several states in the early 1970s were in the process of modifying or repealing their statutes criminalizing abortion. Not only were physicians vulnerable to prosecution under such statutes but also a complete ban on abortions had obvious health implications to pregnant women. Finally, the logic of subsuming an abortion decision, which self-evidently involved intimate personal and procreational choices, in the line of constitutional "privacy" and "liberty" cases stretching from *Griswold* through *Eisenstadt*, seemed compelling. Few of the Justices who signed on to Blackmun's opinion in the *Roe* and *Doe* cases (six in all, Burger concurring in the results, with White and Rehnquist dissenting) could have predicted the magnitude or duration of the controversy it produced.

Indeed it does not seem too much to say that the remainder of Blackmun's career, which stretched through the 1993 Term, was dominated by his identification with *Roe* and the abortion controversy. Throughout the 1970s a majority of Justices continued to support *Roe*'s conceptualization of abortion as a "fundamental" right, but Blackmun's opinion, which keyed the weight given to abortion decisions to the trimesters of pregnancy, was subjected to withering academic criticism,[29] and national politicians regularly denounced the decision and declared themselves supporters of a "right to life." By the early 1980s, speculation, fueled by the electoral triumph of the Reagan Adminstration and the retirement of Stewart, became rife as to which new Justice would provide the vote to overrule *Roe*. The speculation began with O'Connor's appointment in 1981, even though a clear majority—Brennan, Marshall, Stevens, and Powell, in addition to Blackmun—still existed in support of the decision. Opinions O'Connor wrote in 1983 and 1985 revealed her disatisfaction with *Roe*'s trimester framework, and with Kennedy's replacement of Powell in 1987, the speculation increased. Next came two cases in which a new majority of the Court, while stopping short of overruling *Roe*, appeared to be poised to do so.[30] Nor were the retirements of Brennan in 1990 and Marshall the next year any comfort to Blackmun. Three times between 1989 and 1992 he wrote draft dissents predicting the overruling or expressing concern that it had occurred.[31] He was unexpectedly saved from confronting the demise of *Roe* in 1992, but the years of waiting for the shoe to drop had had their effect.

As *Roe* came to be seen as a "culture wars" case, and a "women's rights" case, Blackmun's identification with it, and his symbolic role in debates about the Court, helped shape his jurisprudential sensibility. So did his increasing estrangement from Burger. He and Burger had been intimate friends, their association dating back to kindergarten in St. Paul, Minnesota, but soon after Blackmun joined Burger on the Court those feelings evaporated. Blackmun's innate decency and graciousness to his colleagues enabled him to build relationships among them that the more obtuse and distant Burger could not. After two early Terms in which his voting record closely paralleled that of Burger's, Blackmun began to detach himself, and by the summer of 1974, when the Court decided the Nixon Administration "tapes" case,[32] he and Burger were no longer on comfortable terms.[33] Burger had assigned the opinion in the tapes case to himself, but other Justices, operating under the perception that Burger was close to incompetent as a legal analyst and opinion writer, conspired to replace each portion of his draft with their own versions. Blackmun himself participated in the exercise, rewriting Burger's garbled statement of the facts of the case.[34]

It may have been coincidental that on virtually every area of constitutional law in which Burger had staked out a visible position—the death penalty, abortion, affirmative action, restrictions on lawyer advertising—Blackmun eventually ended up taking an opposing view.[35] By the time Burger retired in 1986 Blackmun, who had clearly been seen as among the "conservatives" Nixon had appointed with a view toward reversing the direction of the Warren Court,[36] was now seen as one of the Court's "liberals."[37] And this alteration of Blackmun's image was not a function of changed personnel or circumstances. At the time of his appointment to the Court Blackmun had been a supporter of the death penalty, unsympathetic to constitutional "privacy" rights, largely oblivious to issues of gender discrimination, inclined to disfavor race-conscious remedial measures, and cautious about the reach of the First Amendment outside the area of political speech. By his retirement he had changed his mind on all of those issues. When he left the Rehnquist Court in 1993 he was near the left edge of his spectrum of opinion in constitutional cases.

In contrast to Stevens and Blackmun, Sandra Day O'Connor had no difficulties with the issue of ideological drift. From her appointment in 1981 to her "retirement" in 2005—she returned to the Court after having conditioned her leaving on a successor's being confirmed, and Samuel Alito's confirmation did not occur until January 2006—O'Connor self-consciously staked out positions that gave her a maximum amount of doctrinal and institutional flexibility. She often provided the fifth vote for majorities, and the doctrinal tests and standards she proposed in constitutional cases were designed to permit incremental progressions, or retreats, from the Court's previous decisions.[38] The result was that O'Connor occupied a centrist position on the Burger Court in the early 1980s and continued to occupy that position through the last years of Rehnquist's tenure.[39]

Reagan's criteria for his first appointment to the Court had not been particularly ideological. The outstanding feature of O'Connor's candidacy was that she was a woman with an excellent law school record. Although she had been a state appellate judge, most of her experience in the public sector had been as a legislator, and in neither forum had she displayed much of an ideological cast. Although she was a Republican, and was thought to have "conservative" instincts, her views on such issues as abortion, gender discrimination, and affirmative action were essentially unknown. The O'Connor nomination thus formed a marked contrast to Reagan's other Court nominations.[40]

In 1986 and 1987 Reagan had opportunities to name three additional justices. Burger's retirement presented him with one, and Reagan created another for himself by nominating Rehnquist, whose confirmation signified the first time a Chief Justice had been chosen from the sitting Court since 1940.[41] When Reagan chose to fill the slot he had created by nominating Judge Antonin Scalia from the D.C. Circuit, it was clear that ideology was now driving his choices.[42] Rehnquist had been an outspoken dissenter for much of his career on the Burger Court, differing with a majority of colleagues on issues ranging from federalism[43] to free speech.[44] Scalia, for his part, had been a visible proponent of judicial deference to other branches of government, judicial accommodation of religion, and enhanced constitutional protection for private property.[45] Although he had not had much occasion to decide abortion or affirmative action cases, he was regarded as an opponent of abortion rights and affirmative action policies.

Scalia's candidacy received little attention during the confirmation process. His nomination was submitted in tandem with that of Rehnquist, and opponents of the Chief Justice–designate had fourteen years of service on the Court to criticize. Although the memorandum Rehnquist had presented to Jackson in connection with the arguments on *Brown v. Board of Education* in the 1952 again surfaced, and twenty-eight Senators voted against his confirmation, in a Republican-controlled Senate, it was never in doubt. The attention paid to Rehnquist nonetheless distracted potential critics of Scalia, who was also advantaged by the fact that as a law professor at Virginia and Chicago, and as a circuit judge, he had not taken public positions on constitutional issues that were contentious at the time of his nomination. Most of his scholarship, and many of his opinions, had been in the area of administrative law.

The confirmation image of Scalia as a gregarious, accessible man with a large family—the Reagan Administration made much of the fact that he was the first person of Italian heritage to be named to the Court—belied the fact that few Justices had come to the Court with as extensive a substantive and methodological agenda. Many years of law teaching, government service, and judging had combined with a voracious appetite for the intellectual dimensions of law to result in Scalia's having a considered position on a great many legal issues. Several of his views, moreover, were heterodox. He was a strong supporter of a unitary Executive, despite the burdens created by the Nixon Administration's machinations for advocates of executive power.[46] He believed that race-conscious policies, however beneficent their goals, were a version of racism.[47] And perhaps most significantly, he would come to hold a view of constitutional interpretation that no one on the Court had maintained since at least the 1940s. Provisions of the Constitution, Scalia argued, should be interpreted in conformity with their "original meaning."[48] This meant, in many cases, that the views of the framers of a constitutional provision should be followed by judges, even if those views had long gone out of fashion.

In the early years of Scalia's tenure it appeared as if the broadly and deeply grounded character of his jurisprudence, his rhetorical skills, and some personnel changes on the Court might well propel him to a position of considerable influence. The first two years of the 1990s produced two more Court vacancies, and on their appointments both David Souter and Clarence Thomas were expected to add to a "conservative majority" on the Court that would now include Rehnquist, White, O'Connor, and Kennedy as well as Scalia.[49] Moreover, Thomas and perhaps Rehnquist were thought by some commentators to be attracted to Scalia's version of revisionist constitutional jurisprudence. A scenario in which the Court invalidated affirmative action programs, overruled *Roe*, and increasingly accommodated religion in government programs was anticipated by potential critics.

None of that scenario came to pass, nor did Scalia's anticipated influence emerge. Prior to the Souter and Thomas appointments he found that his model of a unitary Executive, emphasizing a broad interpretation of presidential powers, with limits on those powers being based only on express constitutional provisions, and clear judicial rules marking the boundaries between the branches of government, did not appeal to any of his colleagues.[50] By the 1992 Term Souter, O'Connor, and Kennedy had signaled that they were not attracted to originalist jurisprudence, not prepared to abandon the Court's existing doctrinal framework in establishment clause cases, which Scalia had attacked, and not ready to overrule *Roe*.

Part of Scalia's difficulty may have centered in his rhetorical style, which featured vivid, acerbic attacks on Justices who disagreed with his positions. His dissenting opinion in *Casey*, for example, said that the plurality opinion authored by Justices Anthony Kennedy, O'Connor, and Souter had merely "rattle[d] off a collection of adjectives that . . . decorate a value judgment and conceal a political choice." "It is not reasoned judgment that supports the Court's decision," he maintained, "only personal prediliction."[51] When Kennedy and O'Connor, who had previously expressed dissatisfaction with *Lemon v. Kurtzman*,[52] a 1971 decision outlining a test for determining whether a statute had "established" religion, declined to overrule *Lemon* in 1993 and 1994 cases,[53] Scalia made fun of Kennedy's approach[54] and called O'Connor's an effort to replace *Lemon* "with nothing."[55] And in a 1996 dissent he wrote that "[t]he Court must be living in another world. Day by day, case by case, it is busy designing a Constitution for a country I do not recognize."[56]

One commentator suggested that "Scalia isn't as smart as he thinks he is." "The vocal admiration Scalia received from conservative legal activists and the politicians they influenced," the commentator thought, "unfortunately reinforced [Scalia's] sense of his superior abilities."[57] Rehnquist, Stevens, Breyer, Souter, and Ginsburg were Scalia's intellectual equals, he believed, and in addition Scalia "came up short . . . [o]n [the] score [of] good judgment." His opinions repeatedly suggested that he was "[t]ough, smart, and honest, in contrast with his opponents, who were . . . weak, dumb, and dishonest."[58] That approach was certain to reduce Scalia's influence.

The example of Scalia reveals that Justices with considerable intellectual talent do not necessarily wield influence among their colleagues.[59] The example of Justice Anthony Kennedy, appointed by Reagan in 1987 after the Bork nomination debacle, illustrates that sometimes Justices with less talent find themselves in influential positions. In Kennedy's case influence has been connected to his disinclination to align himself consistently with either of the groups of Justices clustering on the left or right wings of the Rehnquist

Court's ideological spectrum. When the Court began chipping away at the post–New Deal legacy of federalism jurisprudence in the 1990s, occasionally concluding that federal regulatory statutes had unconstitutionally infringed on the reserved powers of the states, Kennedy joined some of those opinions.[60] But at the same time he rejected originalist readings of the Fourteenth Amendment, joining Stevens, Souter, Ginsburg, and Breyer in gender discrimination cases[61] and signaling in a 1989 case that he was prepared to find the due process clauses a source of unenumerated constitutional rights.[62] And he wrote the majority opinions for the Court in *Romer v. Evans*,[63] striking down a provision in the Colorado constitution banning any state efforts to prohibit discrimination on the basis of sexual preference, and *Lawrence v. Texas*,[64] finding a constitutional right in consenting adults to engage in intimate homosexual practices.

At the same time, despite his participation in the joint opinion in *Casey v. Planned Parenthood*[65] that preserved *Roe v. Wade*, Kennedy was not a strong supporter of abortion rights. He signaled early in his tenure that he was dissatisfied with the framework of the *Roe* opinion[66] and would be receptive to sustaining statutes requiring that parents be notified before minors could have abortions.[67] After *Casey* he dissented in a case striking down a state's effort to regulate so-called partial birth abortions, ones that occurred in the second trimester of pregnancy.[68] He was, in short, not a predictable vote in a range of cases in which majorities could be expected to be narrow.

This resulted in Kennedy regularly being identified, along with O'Connor, as a "swing" vote on the Rehnquist Court. But unlike O'Connor, who seemed to structure her jurisprudential posture around the "swing Justice" role, demonstrating an instinct for doctrinal approaches that emphasized the balancing of competing interests and enhanced the opportunities of judges to proceed on a case-by-case basis, Kennedy's centrist position on the Court seemed more ideological than jurisprudential. When he wrote opinions endorsing "liberal" or "conservative" outcomes, they tended to be broad and sweeping, far more reminiscent of the perfectionist style of Warren Court justices than O'Connor's studied moderation.[69] Kennedy, in short, became an influential Justice on the Rehnquist Court simply because his voting patterns were unpredictable.

The culture of Supreme Court appointments ushered in by Fortas's resignation and Nixon's difficulties with his early appointments had resulted in the archetypal nominee, after the 1970s, being an experienced lower court judge. Blackmun, Stevens, Scalia, and Kennedy had been in that category, and O'Connor's appointment was regarded as exceptional because of her gender. In contrast, George H. W. Bush's first appointment was a virtual unknown. David Souter had been a state Attorney General, a trial judge, and a state Supreme Court judge in New Hampshire from 1968 to the spring of 1990, when, on the recommendation of New Hampshire Senator Warren Rudman, his former boss in the Attorney General's office, he had had been nominated to the U.S. Court of Appeals for the First Circuit, which sits in Boston.

Although Souter's judicial appointments in New Hampshire had been made by two conservative Republican governors, Meldrim Thomson and John Sununu, his chief patron, Rudman, was in the more liberal wing of the party. Other than the party affiliation of his sponsors, there was very little in Souter's record to predict his stance as a Supreme Court Justice, or even to suggest that he might surface as a candidate. But Rudman's assiduous support had resulted in Souter's coming to Reagan's attention at the time Kennedy was nominated, and when Brennan retired after a stroke in 1990, Rudman put Souter's name before Bush. There were apparently four candidates on Bush's initial list, and after a successful interview, Souter emerged as the nominee, apparently because Bush, mindful of midterm elections, did not want a partisan battle over the seat.[70] Souter made a good impression in his confirmation hearings and was overwhemingly confirmed, but his views remained largely obscure.

Close students of the Souter hearings might have drawn attention to three Supreme Court Justices he mentioned in his testimony. One was Holmes, on whom he had written an honor's thesis as an undergraduate at Harvard College.[71] Another was John Harlan II, whom he singled out as a exemplary Justice.[72] The third was the retiring Brennan, whose record Souter praised in terms that went beyond the conventionally polite encomiums nominees paid to their predecessors.[73] None of those Justices could have been identified with New Right jurisprudence.[74] Those who feared that Souter might provide a fifth vote to overrule *Roe* should have noticed that he endorsed Harlan's view that an "unenumerated" right of constitutional privacy could be extracted from the due process clause of the Fourteenth Amendment, and that he maintained that overruling the Court's prior decisions raised the potential of "great hardship" to citizens who had "relied on [them] in their own planning."[75]

The fact was that Souter came to the Court with very little experience in deciding high-profile constitutional cases. In his first Term he proceeded cautiously, writing comparatively few opinions and tending to vote with conservative majorities, mainly in criminal procedure cases.[76] But in the 1992 Term he began to take an independent stance, joining a 5–4 majority to invalidate a nondenominational prayer at a middle school graduation[77] and, as noted, being one of the authors of the plurality opinion that reaffirmed *Roe*. By the mid-1990s it had become clear that, far from being a confederate of Rehnquist, Scalia, and Thomas, Souter was not even a centrist of the Kennedy or O'Connor stripe. His approach to constitutional issues would place him closer to Stevens than to any of the other Reagan or Bush appointees.[78]

With the appointments of Clarence Thomas in 1991, Ruth Bader Ginsburg in 1993, and Stephen Breyer in 1994 the Rehnquist Court assumed a shape it would hold for the next twelve years. Unlike Blackmun or Souter, none of those three Justices underwent a substantial evolution of their views or postures during the remainder of Rehnquist's tenure. Thomas, himself a beneficiary of affirmative action programs, was chiefly known at the time of his appointment for being one of the few prominent African American lower court judges—after being chairman of the Equal Employment Opportunities Commission (EEOC) during Reagan's presidency, he had been appointed to the United States Court of Appeals for the District of Columbia Circuit—who opposed affirmative action. Ginsburg had herself served on the D.C. Circuit for twelve years, and before that had been a law professor and advocate for gender equality. Her reputation was that of an ideologically moderate, cautious judge. Breyer, another former law professor who was on the First Circuit at the time of his appointment, had a comparably moderate, if somewhat more adventurous, judicial reputation.

Observers of the nominees expected Ginsburg's and Breyer's voting patterns to more approximate those of Stevens and Souter than the Court's other Justices, and Thomas's to mirror those of Scalia. With some exceptions, those predictions turned out to be accurate. Perhaps because of a brutal confirmation hearing in which he was accused of having sexually harassed a co-worker of his at the EEOC, Anita Hill, Thomas, after narrowly surviving the process, isolated himself from the public, surrounding himself with clerks and friends he considered ideologically sympathetic, making inspirational speeches at all-black colleges, and determinedly going his own way as a constitutional interpreter.[79]

By the mid-1990s he had endorsed a version of originalism in constitutional interpretation that stressed that the original intentions of the framers should be understood against a background of natural law.[80]

Although Thomas often voted with Rehnquist and Scalia in constitutional cases, he wrote comparatively few constitutional law majority opinions. This may have been because his originalism made him a doctrinal revisionist in many areas of constitutional law, leading him to place far less weight on the Court's accumulated precedents than many of his colleagues. Rehnquist, who controlled the assignment of constitutional cases when he and Thomas were members of a majority, may have thought that Thomas's opinions would be too idiosyncratic to retain the other members, or Thomas may have been unwilling to temper his analysis to hold a majority coalition together. The result was that most of Thomas's opinions for the Court were on nonconstitutional issues.[81] But when he expressed his opinions in constitutional cases, often writing only for himself, he revealed himself to be the most deeply committed originalist on the Rehnquist Court.[82]

In contrast, Ginsburg and Breyer tended to eschew comprehensive theories of constitutional interpretation. Outside the area of gender discrimination, which she had helped develop as a scholar, Ginsburg's opinions have tended to be cautious and narrow, although her voting patterns, outside the area of criminal law, have been consistent with predictions at the time of her appointment that she would tilt toward the left in the Court's ideological continuum.[83] She identified as a "judicial hero" Justice John Harlan II, who resisted the sweeping perfectionism of later Warren Court majorities.[84] Breyer, in a book published in 2005,[85] identified himself as primarily interested in determining the "purposes" of constitutional provisions and assessing the consequences of particular applications.[86] He disclaimed any overarching approach to constitutional interpretation,[87] and his opinions have tended to balance competing interests and give attention to institutional considerations.[88] At the same time his voting pattern has identified him as committed to maintaining the edifice of New Deal federalism and the Warren Court's solicitude for civil liberties.[89]

In this mix of Justices the figure of Rehnquist as Chief turned out to have considerable significance. When Rehnquist became Chief Justice in 1986 only three Justices on the Court had served with Warren, and by 1992 all of those had retired. Only two Justices, Stevens and O'Connor, had been on the Burger Court to witness Rehnquist in his role as "the Lone Ranger," writing solitary dissents in which he identified his differences with his colleagues.[90] Of the six new colleagues who joined Rehnquist between 1986 and 1993, none had the memory of Burger, let alone of Warren, with which to contrast their Chief.

But it was clear that Rehnquist would become a very different Chief Justice from either of his two predecessors. Unlike Warren, who believed in promoting the solidarity of the Court in cases he believed to be important, and who accordingly worked hard to forge majorities and to suppress concurrences and dissents,[91] Rehnquist did not believe in trying to persuade others holding different views, nor did he take offense when sharp criticism was directed at him. In one sequence of commercial speech cases he wrote an opinion for the Court asserting that a state's unquestioned power to ban gambling within its borders yielded a lesser power to prevent advertisements for casinos from appearing in magazines distributed within the state.[92] Ten years later a new Court majority concluded that the power to ban an activity could not, consistent with the First Amendment, be made a justification for prohibiting commercial speech about that activity, and overruled the earlier decision. Rehnquist joined the new majority.[93]

The result was that Rehnquist was a far less hands-on Chief than Warren, and far less strategic in conducting conferences than Burger.[94] One of the features of Burger's Chief Justiceship that did not endear him to his colleagues was his tendency to delay taking a definitive position on cases whose outcome he expected to be close. By the Warren and Burger Courts the Justices were discussing cases in order of seniority in the conference, so that the vote, as well as the views, of the Chief Justice would be given first. By declining to reveal his vote, Burger gave himself the opportunity to be the decisive vote in a divided Court, or to join a majority that had already formed by the time he was ready to vote. Joining that majority allowed him, rather than the next senior Associate Justice, to assign the opinion of the Court in the case.[95]

There is no evidence that Rehnquist behaved in a comparable fashion, or that he approached the Court's conference strategically. His primary concern appeared to be with dispatching the Court's business efficiently and with distributing assignments on as equal a basis as possible. He valued colleagues who turned out their opinion assignments with dispatch and chafed when opinions were delayed, but his first principle was to afford his colleagues an equal share of the workload. He may well have assigned opinions, as other Chiefs had, with the goal of preserving majorities, especially when they were narrow, and when he took on an opinion, and found that a particular line of argument was not registering well with others who had voted with him, he was not at all loath to discard it. He did not worry overmuch about overarching theories of interpretation or even doctrinal consistency; as Chief he was mainly concerned with keeping majorities together and deciding cases in a timely fashion.

He did not discourage dissents or concurrences, and apparently did not regard an occasional sharp exchange between colleagues holding different positions as unseemly, although he very rarely advanced open criticism of positions with which he disagreed. He did not work an excessively long day, kept his weekends for family matters, and did not immerse himself in the pomp or ceremony of his office. At the same time he enjoyed, and encouraged, social gatherings among the Justices and their clerks. When he was first appointed to the Court, he had proposed to Burger that the Justices and the clerks meet for informal parties at the end of a workday, with refreshments and casual chat. Burger wrote back that he would be unlikely to attend such gatherings, and doubted whether many of the other judges would.[96] When Rehnquist succeeded Burger, he initiated the custom of an end-of-Term party in which law clerks provided satirical sketches of the Justices, and he played a prominent role in the Court's annual Christmas party, leading the attendees in Christmas carols, in defiance of those who thought that the practice linked a governmental institution too closely with religion.

Rehnquist's values as Chief had some direct effects on the Court over which he presided. A striking feature of the Rehnquist Court was the decline in the number of cases it annually decided. In the Burger Court the number of cases decided by full opinions ranged between approximately 140 and 160. This represented an increase from the number decided by the Warren Court, which decided between approximately 90 and 120 cases between 1954 and 1970. At the opening of Rehnquist's tenure in 1986 the Court was still deciding over 140 cases, but that number fell precipitiously between 1986 and 1994, leveling out to an average of about 80 cases a year between 1994 and 2005.[97]

Moreover, despite some impressions to the contrary, this decline in the number of cases decided was not accompanied by an increase in the number of separate opinions, or by an increase in decisions accompanied by plurality opinions, commanding less than a majority of the Justices. The ratio of majority opinions to all opinions remained approximately constant from the Warren through the Rehnquist Courts; the number of separate opinions, which had dramatically increased from the Warren to the Burger Courts, declined, on the Rehnquist Court, as sharply as had the output of opinions; and the number of plurality opinions also declined.[98] Moreover, the pattern of decline of separate opinions almost perfectly tracked that of opinions themselves, falling sharply from 1986 to 1994 and then remaining at a roughly constant level from that year until 2005. In the 1994 to 2005 period the number of plurality opinions declined, and at the same time the number of 5–4 decisions increased.[99]

In short, the Rehnquist Court, in its last decade, decided comparatively few cases, issued fewer fragmented opinions than in its early history, and decided progressively more cases by a 5–4 margin. And in that decade its personnel remained constant.

When these internal features of the Rehnquist Court are arranged alongside one another, it seems evident that there were two discernible phases in the Court's history during Rehnquist's tenure. In the first phase, from 1986 through 1993, the Court's docket declined but the number of separate and plurality opinions it issued remained comparatively high: in the 1988 Term, thirteen percent of the opinions issued by the Court were plurality opinions.[100] In the second phase, from 1994 through 2005, the Court's docket leveled off, and its separate and plurality opinions declined. In the same time interval the number of its 5–4 opinions increased.

When one considers the fact that the Court's current internal deliberative process places a very high emphasis on give and take among Justices who evaluate, join, or decline to join the opinions of their colleagues, and also enables the Justices to control, through the certiorari power, the scope and content of the Court's docket, one can readily see that there are strong incentives for Justices to become acquainted with the jurisprudential tendencies of those who sit on the Court with them. In the two processes of decision that are arguably most central to the work of the Justices—that of granting or denying certiorari and that of joining or not joining a draft opinion of the Court—the views of judicial colleagues form an essential part of a Justice's calculus. A Justice considering whether to grant or deny certiorari needs to take into account his or her colleagues's potential views on the merits of the case in question, and how those views might square with his or her own. A Justice drafting a majority opinion likewise has to consider the reaction of colleagues to prospective rationales for the opinion's result.

The more contact a Justice has with colleagues, the more likely he or she is to gain an understanding of their jurisprudential tendencies. Although the proliferation of law clerks and computers, which has enabled Justices to exchange written communications with one another far more readily than their predecessors, may have reduced the Justices' informal oral contacts, being a Supreme Court Justice is still a job in which one is regularly exposed to the ideas of one's colleagues. Indeed one might say that everything a Justice does, from attending oral arguments to participating in conference to writing or reacting to draft opinions, is done in the company of the other members of the Court. This constant exposure is bound, over time, to give Justices a strong sense of the sensibilities of their peers.[101]

The cumulative impression of the Rehnquist Court, especially in its second phase, which featured a constancy of personnel, was that of a Court that was comfortable deciding cases raising highly visible and controversial public issues and that did not seem troubled about the increasing number of its decisions featuring 5–4 divisions. In addition, despite occasionally acerbic language in contesting opinions, the Rehnquist Court Justices gave an impression, particularly in the decade beginning in 1995, of being comfortable with one another. This characteristic may have been a result of the common experiences most of the Rehnquist Court Justices had shared: seven of its nine members had been lower federal court judges before being appointed. But it may also have been a reaction to the low-key, unpretentious, gregarious, thick-skinned style of its Chief.

II

Three lines of cases can serve to illustrate the Rehnquist Court's general tendencies in constitutional interpretation.[102] The first line was unenumerated rights, including abortion rights and the potential extension of the due process clause of the Fourteenth Amendment to choices not previously accorded constitutional protection, such as the choice to engage in assisted suicide and the choice to have intimate sexual relations with a person of the same sex.[103] Although the Court came to an unexpected resolution of the abortion debate in

1992, resulting in the virtual disappearance of abortion cases from that point to the close of Rehnquist's tenure and the preservation of *Roe v. Wade* as a precedent, that development did not mark its withdrawal from unenumerated rights cases altogether, and its contributions to the continued development of unenumerated rights jurisprudence were striking.

The second line was federalism cases, where the Court seemingly began a campaign to undermine the edifice of post–New Deal jurisprudence, in which the federal government had been treated as having nearly limitless regulatory power over "local" activities. Although the campaign received a fair amount of attention from commentators and revealed that some justices were prepared to revive much older theories of the proper constitutional balance between the federal government and the states, in the end it did not amount to a major doctrinal change.

The third line was cases involving the establishment and free exercise clauses. There Court majorities showed a clear inclination to move away from the Warren Court's religious clauses jurisprudence, which emphasized the "wall of separation" between church and state in establishment clause cases and the need to accommodate religious beliefs in free exercise cases. The Rehnquist Court abandoned much of the Warren Court's legacy in the area of state aid to religious education and seemed at one point to be abandoning that Court's insistence that on some occasions the state needed to accommodate the religious beliefs and practices of minorities. But it drew back from that posture, and at the same time continued to exhibit a suspicious attitude toward the display of government symbols or practices that appeared to entangle the state with religion.

O'Connor's appointment to the Court signaled that a new attitude toward abortion cases might be taking hold.[104] In the first abortion case she considered during her tenure, *Akron v. Akron Center for Reproductive Health*,[105] O'Connor indicated that she disagreed, in two respects, with the conceptualization of abortion rights outlined by the Court in *Roe v. Wade*. First, O'Connor suggested, *Roe*'s assumption that a right to terminate an abortion extended throughout the first trimester of pregnancy was based on a rigid, and possibly outdated, conception of viability. Fetuses might be viable earlier in a pregnancy, and in any event *Roe*'s association of abortion rights with stages in a pregnancy was clumsy. In addition, O'Connor claimed, abortion cases were not about any "rights" in physicians, which *Roe* had suggested; they were about balancing a woman's constitutional right to choose to terminate a pregnancy against the state's interest in the preservation of life.[106] O'Connor was attracted to the evaluative standard for balancing those interests proposed by the Reagan Administration in its *Akron* brief: whether a particular regulation restricting a woman's choice imposed an "undue burden" on pregnant women.[107]

O'Connor's decision not to join the majority in *Akron*, and also in a 1986 case, *Thornburgh v. American College of Obstetricians*,[108] was not crucial to the outcome of those or to the Court's continued preservation of abortion rights. Between the year O'Connor joined the Court and 1988, at least five votes, those of Justices Brennan, Marshall, Blackmun, Powell, and Stevens, could be counted on to maintain the essential holding in *Roe v. Wade*. Nor did O'Connor's dissents in *Akron* and *Thornburgh*, in which she again signaled that she favored the "undue burden" standard for evaluating abortion cases, indicate that she was prepared to overrule *Roe*. But when Kennedy replaced Powell in 1987 and the Court granted certiorari in another abortion rights case, it appeared that O'Connor's vote might be pivotal. If Kennedy were regarded as not favorably disposed toward *Roe*, there were now four opponents of that decision—Rehnquist, Scalia, and White being the others—and four supporters. O'Connor was the ninth justice.

The case, *Webster v. Reproductive Health Services*,[109] involved a Missouri statute that prevented abortions from taking place in public facilities or state employees from performing them. It also required prenatal testing for viability if a physician determined that a pregnancy had existed for at least twenty weeks. The Eighth Circuit Court of Appeals had invalidated all of those provisions.[110] In conference discussion[111] Rehnquist proposed that the Missouri provisions be upheld without revisiting *Roe*, and O'Connor agreed. White, Scalia, and Kennedy were prepared to accept that disposition but would have preferred to, as Kennedy put it, "alter the method and structure of *Roe*."[112] Rehnquist's draft opinion, however, maintained that any regulation that "reasonably furthers the state's interest in protecting potential human life" should be upheld, even if it restricted choices prior to viability, effectively overruling *Roe*. O'Connor declined to accept that formulation, and prepared a separate opinion that, although sustaining all the provisions of the Missouri statute, explicitly preserved *Roe*. This sufficiently provoked Scalia that he filed a concurrence stating that the Court might as well overrule *Roe* directly.[113]

Difficulties for abortion rights advocates apparently continued to mount after the *Webster* case was decided. In 1990 and 1991 Souter and Thomas joined the Court, replacing Brennan and Marshall. Neither of the new appointees was expected to be a proponent of *Roe*, which both Brennan and Marshall had supported. When the Court granted certiorari in *Planned Parenthood v. Casey,* a case from Pennsylvania challenging a statute with two provisions—a required twenty-four-hour waiting period before an abortion and a requirement that the person seeking an abortion give "informed consent" to the procedure—that it had previously invalidated,[114] the decision was taken as a signal that a newly constituted majority wanted to overrule *Roe*. That inference was reinforced by the opinion of the U.S. Court of Appeals for the Third Circuit in the case. The Third Circuit had upheld those provisions of the statute but struck down another that required that the husband of a woman seeking an abortion be notified before the procedure was undertaken. In the process the Third Circuit concluded that after *Webster*, O'Connor's "undue burden" test now commanded a majority, and that test did not have the effect of subjecting statutes restricting abortion decisions to strict scrutiny.[115]

Both sides in *Casey* urged the Court squarely to affirm or to overrule *Roe*. The Justices rephrased the questions in the certiorari petition, limiting them to whether the Third Circuit had erred in uphold the waiting period and informed consent provisions and invalidating the spousal notice provision. After conference, it appeared that there was a majority to uphold the first two provisions, and possibly the spousal notice provision as well. Rehnquist assigned the opinion to himself and produced a draft upholding all three provisions. Although the draft did not overrule *Roe*, it announced that "[t]he Court was mistaken in *Roe* when it classfied a woman's decision to terminate her pregnancy as a 'fundamental right' that could be abridged only in a manner which withstood 'strict scrutiny.'" The future standard for abortion cases, the draft announced, would be whether a state regulation restricting the choice to have an abortion was "rationally related to a legitimate state interest."[116]

O'Connor had now reached a point in abortion cases where her "undue burden" approach, and her critique of the *Roe* decision's rigid trimester test for determining the level of scrutiny, were about to become accepted by a majority of the Court. But with that prospect in sight, she backed off from abandoning *Roe*. After Rehnquist circulated his majority opinion she began discussions with Kennedy and Souter about the possibility of an alternative opinion that might overrule *Akron* and *Thornburgh* but retain *Roe*'s "essential holding." When those Justices eventually circulated a joint opinion a week after Rehnquist's had appeared, both Blackmun and Stevens agreed to join the portions of it that reaffirmed *Roe*. The result was that a majority existed for upholding the Third Circuit's disposition of the statute's provisions, in which *Akron* and *Thornburgh* were scuttled, but another majority existed for retaining *Roe* as a precedent.[117]

Those developments placed O'Connor precisely where she liked to be in considering constitutional issues: applying an evaluative standard that provided her and her fellow Justices with maximum flexibility to decide cases on fact-specific grounds, and thereby develop constitutional doctrine on an incremental basis. The *Casey* decision,[118] coupled with the advent of two new Justices, Ginsburg and Breyer, who were relatively sympathetic to abortion rights, ushered in a lengthy interval in which the Court decided no additional abortion cases. It was not until 2000 that it took up one of the most divisive issues in the abortion controversy, the so-called partial birth abortion procedure, in which a fetus in the second trimester was aborted because of complications in the pregnancy that threatened the health of the mother. Several states had statutes prohibiting abortions beyond the first trimester, and some had no maternal health exceptions. A majority of the Court, in *Stenberg v. Carhart*,[119] invalidated one such statute.

The Court's composition in *Stenberg* illustrated the determinedly centrist position in which O'Connor had established herself. Breyer wrote an opinion for the Court, joined by Stevens, Souter, Ginsburg, and O'Connor. Rehnquist, Scalia, Thomas, and Kennedy dissented. All the Justices except Souter wrote separate opinions. O'Connor's opinion stressed the general legitimacy of statutes barring post-viability abortion procedures, but retaining the principle that not having a maternal health exception limited a woman's fundamental freedom to make reproductive choices. Kennedy's dissent in *Stenberg* suggested that his participation in the joint opinion in *Casey* had primarily been based on institutional considerations. Not so in O'Connor's case: the *Casey/Stenberg* sequence revealed that O'Connor simply wanted to apply her "undue burden" test to all abortion cases, balancing reproductive rights against state interests on a fact-specific basis. That sort of approach was characteristic of her approach to constitutional issues generally.

By essentially taking abortion cases off the Court's agenda after 1992, the *Casey* plurality opinion enabled the appointment process to help solidify its preservation of the core holding of *Roe.* With the departure of White, and the appointments of Ginsburg and Breyer, a new five-justice majority was in place that favored the constitutionalization of some form of abortion rights. Stevens had long been pro-choice, and both Ginsburg and Breyer supported *Roe*, as did Souter. O'Connor's interest in seeing that her "undue burden" standard eventually became the evalutive test for abortion cases meant that she would not vote to overrule *Roe*. And Kennedy, despite being prepared to go rather far to restrict abortion choices, was hardly going to depart from the justifications for retaining *Roe*'s essential holding that he had advanced in *Casey*. Rehnquist's tenure ended with *Roe* still viable, and with abortion cases having been relegated to a secondary concern of the Court.

By the *Casey* decision it had become clear that abortion cases were seen as having implications that went well beyond the actual decision of a woman to terminate a pregnancy. Not only were they perceived of as "women's rights" cases, they were perceived of as "privacy" cases. The unsuccessful nomination of Robert Bork in 1987 had made that clear. Bork was an opponent of abortion rights, but primarily on constitutional as opposed to ideological grounds. He believed that there simply was no constitutional protection for unenumerated "rights." In his hearings he made it clear that he thought that not only *Roe* but *Griswold* and *Eisenstadt* had been wrongly decided, because the term "liberty" in the due process clauses could not be stretched to cover intimate personal choices not mentioned in the constitutional text and because there was no justification for deriving constitutional rights from the "penumbras" and "emanantions" of specific textual provisions, as Douglas had done in *Griswold*. Although those were respectable views on constitutional interpretation, and Bork was hardly alone in expressing them,[120] they were disastrous for Bork's nomination. His opponents quickly portrayed him as an opponent not just of abortion rights but of all privacy rights, and the negative fallout this produced among members of the Senate indicated that by 1987 many Americans had come to believe that the Constitution protected their "privacy," by which they meant the freedom to make a number of intimate personal choices free from governmental interference.[121]

So the Rehnquist Court abortion cases were not just about the continuing legacy of *Roe* as a precedent. They were also about the future scope of unenumerated rights. If "liberty" in the due process clauses protected more choices than the one to terminate a pregnancy, what were those choices? And if Bork's attack on the methodology of modern substantive due process cases was regarded as unpersuasive, what methodology should govern their analysis?

In his portion of the *Casey* plurality opinion Kennedy had resurrected the approach to due process cases taken by Harlan in a dissenting opinion in *Poe v. Ullman.*[122] Harlan's approach treated "liberty" in the due process clauses as a "continuum" potentially embracing a number of "fundamental" rights and evolving over time. He acknowledged that protection for decisions about sexual intimacy and procreation by married couples had not previously been deemed a due process liberty, but argued that such decisions implicated the "privacy of the home in its most basic sense."[123] Kennedy identified *Roe* with the same line of argument: an abortion decision involved a sphere of privacy that the state had only limited power to invade.[124]

How far would that sphere extend? In 1998 the Court considered a challenge to a Washington statute making it a felony to assist someone in attempting suicide.[125] The Ninth Circuit Court of Appeals had found the statute unconstitutional as a violation of Fourteenth Amendment "liberties."[126] The Rehnquist Court unanimously reversed, distinguishing between a right to refuse life-saving medical treatment[127] and one to participate in assisted suicide. Despite the unanimity, the case revealed deep divisions among the Justices on the appropriate methodology in modern due process cases.

In a 1986 decision, *Bowers v. Hardwick*,[128] the Burger Court had rejected a challenge by consenting homosexuals to a state law criminalizing sodomy. White's opinion for the Court, in the process of concluding that no constitutional right to engage in consensual homosexual sex existed, had identified two governing approaches in due process cases: "history and tradition," emphasizing the extent to which the "right" had previously been regarded as protected, and "ordered liberty," focusing on a determination of whether the right involved could be said to be foundational in the Anglo-American system of constitutional jurisprudence.[129] Neither approach, White reasoned, justified the constitutionalization of a right to engage in intimate consensual homosexual activity. Statutes criminalizing such activity were longstanding, and the comparably longstanding belief that intimate homosexual liaisions were immoral was inconsistent with treating intimate homosexual activity as foundational.[130]

Rehnquist's opinion for the Court in *Washington v. Glucksberg*, the assisted suicide case, revived White's approach, although it did not mention *Bowers*. In fact Rehnquist seemed to go further than White, suggesting that for a right to be "fundamental," for the purposes of due process analysis, it had to be *both* "deeply rooted in . . . history and tradition" and "implicit in the concept of ordered liberty."[131] Interestingly, after finding that a right to engage in assisted suicide met neither of those criteria, Rehnquist went on to make a more searching analysis of the Washington statute than had been made in *Bowers*, and conceded that the Court's decision "[did] not absolutely foreclose" future challenges to assisted suicide laws.[132]

All those features of Rehnquist's opinion seemed strategic. The omission of a reference to *Bowers* may have been to placate Kennedy, who in 1996 had written an opinion for the Court in *Romer v. Evans*,[133] invalidating an amendment to the Colorado constitution designed to prevent the category of sexual preference from being included in antidiscrimination legislation. In that case Kennedy had stated that the amendment seemed "inexplicable by anything but animus" against homosexuals, and was thus unjustifiable under the equal protection clause.[134] *Bowers*, in contrast, had suggested that one of the permissible justifications for discriminating against homosexuals was moral disapproval of their conduct. Kennedy joined Rehnquist's opinion.

Rehnquist's more searching inquiry into the Washington statute consisted of a recital of reasons why a legislative ban on assisted suicide was a response to public health concerns, such as the difficulties created by allowing physicians to administer lethal injections to persons suffering from temporary depression. It stressed that factual findings about the health concerns had motivated the legislature, and thus the statute was reasonably related to "important and legitimate" state interests.[135] All of this seemed unnecessary in light of *Bowers*, where the finding that there was no fundamental right to engage in same-sex sodomy obviated any inquiry into the factual basis of the legislation. In fact there had been no comparable health findings justifying the legislation in *Bowers*, nor even any findings that same-sex sodomy between consenting adults undermined public morals. It had been enough for the Court in that case that some people thought same-sex sodomy immoral. Surely that was also the case with assisted suicide, but Rehnquist's analysis took a harder look at the statute.

A possible explanation for that feature of the opinion, and for Rehnquist's footnote suggesting that *Glucksberg* had not foreclosed the possiblity of future challenges to assisted suicide laws, can be found in O'Connor's concurrence, which provided Rehnquist with a fifth vote for his approach. The rest of O'-Connor's concurring opinion seemed to suggest that she had a more expansive view of unenumerated rights than Rehnquist and would accordingly take a searching look at legislation that allegedly infringed upon them.[136] She also made it explicit that she might recognize a fundamental right in mentally competent persons to end their lives when suffering great pain.[137] That issue did not arise for her in *Glucksberg* because Washington allowed such persons to obtain medication that alleviated suffering, but it could in another case. O'Connor's approach to unenumerated rights cases was perceived to be so different from that employed in the majority opinion that Breyer concurred in her opinion "except insofar as it joins the opinion of the Court."[138] The remaining justices, Stevens, Souter, and Ginsburg, concurred only in the result in *Glucksberg.*

The course of unenumerated rights decisions from *Casey* through *Glucksberg* had been unusual. In *Casey,* O'Connor, Kennedy, and Souter had identified themselves with language stating that "our law affords constitutional protection to personal decisions relating to marriage, procreation, contraception, family relations, and education" and that "[t]hese matters involve the most intimate and personal choices a person can make in a lifetime, choices central to personal dignity and autonomy, and central to the liberty protected by the Fourteenth Amendment."[139] That was a clear statement that protection for a choice to terminate a pregnancy was part of a larger bundle of due process "liberties." In *Romer* the Court had indicated that there was no apparent justification for denying such liberties to persons simply on the basis of sexual preference. And although the majority in *Glucksberg* appeared to retreat from an expansive definition of unenumerated rights, on closer scrutiny that feature of it appeared to be only endorsed by four justices, with Kennedy's endorsement, in light of the *Casey* language, seeming particularly odd. One of the Justices separating themselves from Rehnquist's opinion in *Glucksberg*, Souter, had explicitly revived Harlan's *Poe v. Ullman* approach for unenumerated rights cases, stating that *Casey* had relied upon it.[140] Souter also made it clear that the course of unenumerated rights could not be determined exclusively by "history and tradition" because the "continuum of rights to be free from 'arbitary impositions' and 'purposeless restraints'" might change over time.[141]

Thus when the Court took up a challenge to Texas's sodomy law in the 2002 Term, strikingly different approaches to unenumerated rights cases had developed. In the case, *Lawrence v. Texas*,[142] three factors combined to produce a decisive 6–3 majority to invalidate the law and overrule *Bowers*. One was Kennedy's earlier association with a broad conception of unenumerated rights and his conviction, expressed in *Romer*, that laws discriminating on the basis of sexual preference were primarily based on negative stereotypes and taboos. A second was O'Connor's attraction for a seemingly efficient way to invalidate same-sex sodomy legislation without needing to expand the category of unenumerated "fundamental rights," namely reliance on the equal protection clause.[143] O'Connor's strategy did not fully accomplish the finesse she intended, because, under conventional equal protection analysis, her conclusion that the Texas statute was a violation of equal protection presupposed that a "fundamental right" to engage in adult consensual sex existed, triggering an inquiry into the legislative justifications for criminalizing homosexual but not heterosexual sodomy.

The third factor was the acceptance by Stevens, Souter, Ginsburg, and Breyer of some version of the *Casey* formulation of unenumerated rights. This became apparent in the broad language of Kennedy's majority opinion, which did not cite *Glucksberg* and announced that "[a]s the Constitution endures, persons in every generation can invoke its principles in their search for greater freedom."[144] That statement was endorsed by Stevens, Souter, Ginsburg, and Breyer. Kennedy's approach was also denounced by Scalia, in an opinion joined by Rehnquist and Thomas, for departing from *Glucksberg*.[145] Thus the Rehnquist Court ended with a bare, and sometimes wavering, majority supporting an expanding definition of unenumerated rights, and with a clash between deeply discordant analytical approaches to the issue.

The Court's post–New Deal federalism jurisprudence had been one of the most consistent and resilient elements of twentieth-century constitutional law. From the early 1940s, Congress was treated as having substantial power to regulate activities that affect states and localities, primarily under the commerce clause. By the 1970s it appeared that the Court was prepared to allow Congress to regulate nearly anything it chose to, even if the connection between the activity and interstate commerce was not obvious.[146] Two principal rationales had emerged in support of the vast reach of Congress's regulatory powers: the increasingly interstate character of the American economy and a rationale captured in the phrase "the political safeguards of federalism."[147] The latter rationale emphasized that Congress was composed of representatives from the states, who were capable of protecting their own interests in the process of legislation.

In a 1975 dissent Rehnquist signaled that he was not prepared to embrace so sweeping a view of federal power. In *Fry v. United States*,[148] the issue was whether Congress could impose federal floors and ceilings on the wage levels of state employees. Rehnquist distinguished between federal regulations affecting private persons or enterprises and those seeking to control "the State itself." Wages and hours, he felt, were "closely allied with traditional state functions."[149] Rehnquist thought that preserving those functions from federal oversight was necessary to achieve an appropriate balance between federal and state spheres of influence.

To the surprise of many commentators,[150] Rehnquist's view commanded a majority of the Court a year later. In *National League of Cities v. Usery*,[151] Congress sought to amend the Fair Labor Standards Act to bring most employees of states and cities within its wages and hours limitations. Rehnquist, for the Court, held that the amendment infringed on the residuum of state power anticipated by the Tenth Amendment because it was "directed, not to private citizens, but to the States as States." Because compelling states and cities to conform to federal wages and hours requirements would "significantly alter or displace [their] abilities to structure employer-employee relations in such areas as [police protection and fire prevention], the amendment "interfered directly with "the States' freedom to structure integral operations in areas of traditional state functions."[152] He was able to get Burger, Stewart, and Powell to join his opinion, and Blackmun concurred, suggesting that the opinion "adopts a balancing approach" to federalism issues.[153]

The revival of federalism augured by *Usery* did not initially materialize. In a series of decisions between 1981 and 1983 the Court struggled to define "traditional state functions" under *Usery*, upholding the application of federal statutes to the operation of strip mines within a state,[154] the collective bargaining requirements of a state-owned railroad,[155] rate levels imposed by stsate utilities commissions,[156] and age discrimination policies for state employees.[157] Although the Court outlined criteria for determining whether a state activity was immune from federal regulation in one of those cases,[158] by 1985 a new majority had concluded that the criteria were "unworkable" and overruled *Usery.*

The case, *Garcia v. San Antoinio Metropolitan Transit Authority,*[159] involved an effort to apply the Fair Labor Standards Act to a county mass transit agency in Texas. Blackmun's opinion for the Court concluded that the "traditional governmental functions" test was not one that judges could easily administer, and "inevitably invites an unelected federal judiciary to make decisions about which state policies it favors and which it dislikes." Reviving the "political safeguards" rationale, he concluded that "State sovereign interests . . . are more properly protected by procedural safeguards inherent in the structure of the federal system than by judicially created limitations on federal power."[160]

As Rehnquist succeeded Burger as Chief Justice, the future of the *Garcia* approach to federalism cases was uncertain. O'Connor, who had dissented in *Garcia*, and Rehnquist remained interested in developing substantive limitations on the powers of Congress, and Kennedy and Scalia were thought to be potentially sympathetic to that position. But a five-justice majority of Brennan, White, Marshall, Stevens, and Blackmun supported *Garcia*, and in 1988 only O'Connor dissented when the Court allowed Congress to remove the exemption from federal income tax for certain bonds issued by South Carolina.[161] The majority reasserted *Garcia*'s insistence that "[s]tates must find their protection from congressional regulation through the national political process, not through judicially defined spheres of unregulable state activity."[162]

Four years later, however, O'Connor was able to command a majority, which included not only Rehnquist, Scalia, and Kennedy but new arrivals Souter and Thomas, for a long-neglected proposition in federalism jurisprudence, the "anti-commandeering principle." The case involved a 1985 Congressional statute that sought to create incentives for the states to dispose of low-level radioactive waste generated within their borders.[163] One of those incentives was embodied in a provision that declared that if a state was unable to provide for disposal of its own waste by 1996, it would be obliged to take title to the waste. The state of New York challenged the constitutionality of the statute as an impermissible encroachment on state powers. Citing one of the Court's post-*Usery* decisons as standing for the proposition that Congress could not "commandeer the legislative processes of the States by directly compelling them to enact and enforce a federal regulatory program," O'Connor invalidated the "take title" incentive provision, stating that the Tenth Amendment forbade the federal government from "compel[ling] the States to enact or administer a federal regulatory program."[164]

The case ushered in a period in which new majorities on the Court handed down some federalism decisions that would not have been contemplated two decades earlier or anticipated by the post-*Garcia* majority. In addition to the anti-commandeering principle, which was reasserted in a 1997 decision,[165] the Court revived the Eleventh Amendment, codifying the sovereign immunity of the states, as a potential barrier to Congress when it seeks to compel states to acquiesce in federal regulations.[166] And in two decisions in which the scope of Congress's regulatory power under the commerce clause was directly challenged, 5–4 majorities actually found that two Congressional statutes enacted on the basis of the commerce power, one prohibiting the possession of guns in local schools[167] and the other providing a federal civil remedy for women attacked on the basis of their gender, were unconsititutional on federalism grounds.[168]

Those cases, together with some other decisions in which the Court sided with states or localities when Congress sought to compel them to conform to federal laws or policies,[169] have tempted some commentators to claim that a "federalism revolution" was instituted on the Rehnquist Court.[170] But the nature of that "revolution" is far from clear. Just as the Court seemed poised to use its revitalized Eleventh Amendment jurisprudence to exempt the states possibly even from Title VII of the 1964 Civil Rights Act,[171] it pulled back in *Nevada Dept. of Human Resources v. Hibbs*, a 2003 decision,[172] which held that Congress could compel the states to conform to the provisions of the Family Medical Leave Act as part of its power to abolish unjustifiable gender discrimination under Section Five of the Fourteenth Amendment. Further, although the Rehnquist Court, in contrast to its immediate predecessors, recognized that some substantive limits on the scope of federal power exist, and did not invariably follow the suggestion in *Garcia* that it mainly leave federalism issues to the national political process, it also largely left standing the doctrinal edifice of the Court's post–New Deal federalism decisions.

To get a sense of how far from "revolutionary" the Rehnquist Court's federalism decisions were, one can consider a case from its 2004 Term, and contrast the perspective on federalism issues exhibited by the majority in that case with the approach of Thomas toward federalism cases. Thomas would revive the "compact theory" of sovereignty that attracted critics of the Marshall

Court, maintaining that "[w]here the Constitution is silent about the exercise of a particular power, the Federal Government lacks the power and the States enjoy it."[173] He would abandon the "substantial effects" test for determining the scope of federal government's power to regulate "local" activities under the commerce clause.[174] He would exempt "wholly intrastate, point-of-sale transactions" from the reach of the federal commerce power,[175] and he would abandon the Court's role in "negative commerce clause" cases, in which a state regulation affecting interstate commerce can be invalidated in the absence of any federal legislation governing the area.[176] His approach would revive much of the Court's pre–New Deal federalism jurisprudence.

Thomas's approach seems to have no appeal, at this point, to any of his fellow Justices on the Court. That would seem clear from the 2004 case of *Gonzales v. Raich*.[177] The *Raich* case also illustrates that at least five Justices on the Court, despite its flurry of federalism decisions since *Lopez,* seem very far from abandoning the established liberal interpretation of the scope of Congress's regulatory powers.

In *Raich* two women, Angel Raich and Diane Manson, were ingesting marijuana as pain relief for serious medical conditions. Their use of marijuana for medical purposes was authorized by physicians pursuant to the California Compassionate Use Act of 1996, which permits "seriously ill" persons to have access to the drug under the supervision of a physician, and creates exemptions from criminal liability for physicians prescribing marijuana and patients or caregivers cultivating it. Manson cultivated her own marijuana; Raich relied on caregivers to provide her with it and prepare it in forms for injesting. In 2002 agents of the federal Drug Enforcement Administration visited Manson's home along with county police officers, and even though the county officials certified that Manson's use of marijuana was legal under the Compassionate Use Act, the federal agents seized and subsequently destroyed all of Manson's cannabis plants.[178] Their authority to do so was based on the Controlled Substances Act, a section of the Comprehensive Drug Abuse Prevention and Control Act of 1970,[179] which makes it unlawful to possess or manufacture a variety of controlled substances, including marijuana.

Raich and Manson brought a preliminary injunction against enforcement of the Controlled Substance Act against them, citing the California Compassionate Use Act and arguing that the Controlled Substance Act, as applied to the intrastate, noncommercial use of marijuana for medical purposes, was a violation of the commerce clause. A panel of the U.S. Court of Appeals for the Ninth Circuit, reversing a federal district court that had denied the injunction, agreed. The Court granted certiorari and reversed in an opinion authored by Stevens and joined by Kennedy, Souter, Ginsburg, and Breyer, with Scalia concurring. O'Connor wrote a dissent, portions of which were joined by Rehnquist and Thomas, and Thomas dissented separately.

Crucial to Stevens's opinion in *Raich* was his claim that the Controlled Substance Act was unlike the statutes struck down in *Lopez* and *Morrison*. He gave two reasons in support of that claim. One was that the use of drugs such as marijuana was a "quintessentially economic" activity,[180] for which there was a substantial market. In contrast, the statute struck down in *Lopez*, making it a crime for an individual to possess a gun in a school zone, "did not regulate any economic activity."[181] Nor did the statute invalidated in *Morrison*, creating a federal civil remedy for the victims of gender-motivated crimes of violence, regulate economic activity.[182]

The other was that the Controlled Substance Act, unlike the statutes in *Lopez* and *Morrison*, was a "comprehensive regulatory regime" designed to regulate economic activity that substantially affected interstate commerce.[183] It was like the statute in the New Deal case of *Wickard v. Filburn*, which Stevens characterized as a comprehensive attempt to regulate the market in wheat.[184] The statutes in *Lopez* and *Morrison* were different: the former was a "brief, single-subject statute,"[185] and the latter was not directed at economic activity.[186] Thus the Controlled Substances Act met the Court's criteria for legislation properly based on the federal government's commerce power: it was a regulation of economic activity that had a substantial effect on interstate commerce.

Along the way Stevens noted that under the Court's traditional posture in Commerce Clause cases, "we need not determine whether [Raich's and Manson's] activities, taken in the aggregate, substantially affect interstate commerce in fact, but only whether a 'rational basis' exists for so concluding."[187] He noted that evidence submitted by Raich and Manson that the consumption of marijuana was effective in controlling pain and in reducing nausea and vomiting "would cast serious doubt on the accuracy of the findings" that had caused Congress to list marijuana in a category of drugs that were proscribed for any purpose. "But the question of whether [marijuana] might be reclassified in the future," Stevens maintained, "has no relevance to the question of whether Congress may now regulate its production and distribution."[188]

All in all, the *Raich* decision revealed that a majority of the Court was very far from leading a "revolution" in the jurisprudence of federalism. In addition to reaffirming *Wickard v. Filburn*, a classic case of judicial deference to a Congressional judgment (Congress had concluded that regulating the home consumption of wheat by one farmer had a substantial effect on interstate commerce), the *Raich* opinion appeared to confine *Lopez* and *Morrison* to a potentially small category of cases in which Congress had made the mistake of trying to regulate an activity that was not "economic." Moreover, Scalia's concurrence maintained that Congress's power to regulate activities that "substantially affect interstate commerce" also derived from the necessary and proper clause, which he believed allowed Congress even to regulate activities that did not have a substantial effect on interstate commerce "[w]here necessary to make a regulation of interstate commerce effective."[189]

The message to Congress, based on Stevens's and Scalia's opinions in *Raich*, was clear. All Congress had to do was to enact a comprehensive regulation of "economic" activity, and it could then sweep nearly any category of that activity into the regulation, whether it affected interstate commerce or not. The only requirements were that the activity be "economic" and that the regulation be "comprehensive," and the definition of an economic activity apparently gave little concern for the actual use of the activity. Even though Raich and Manson had simply consumed home-grown cannabis for medical purposes, the fact that there was a "market" in marijuana for recreational use of the drug made their consumption "economic." Under Stevens's and Scalia's reasoning, Congress could have barred the possession of guns in schools simply by enacting a "comprehensive regulation" of the gun industry.

O'Connor, Rehnquist, and Thomas protested against the Court's approach to federalism issues in *Raich*, but the differences in the first two justices's perspectives from that of Thomas were apparent. O'Connor and Rehnquist attacked the *Raich* majority's analysis as encouraging Congress to evade federalism limitations by "packaging regulation of local activity in broader schemes,"[190] called its definition of economic activity "breathtaking,"[191] and suggested that it had allowed Congress to sweep the private use of home-grown marijuana into the category of activities having a substantial effect on interstate commerce without any findings of that effect.[192] They also stated that Scalia's invocation of the necessary and proper clause as a justification for allowing the regulation of intrastate activity that had no substantial effect on interstate commerce was inconsistent with the Tenth Amendment.[193] O'Connor's and Rehnquist's position indicated that at least some Justices on the Rehnquist Court thought that *Wickard* should mark the outer limits of judicial tolerance for federal regulation of local activities.

For Thomas, *Wickard* and a large number of the Court's post–New Deal Commerce Clause decisions had been wrongly decided. His argument was as follows. The original meaning of the commerce clause was that the federal government should have power to regulate interstate "commerce," not manufacture or other activities related to Congress.[194] The appropriate question in commerce clause cases was thus not whether an activity had "substantial effects" on interstate commerce but whether it *was* interstate commerce.[195] Nor did the necessary and proper clause allow Congress to regulate activities that had "substantial effects" on interstate commerce, because that clause was only designed to allow the federal government to enact laws that were "necessary and proper" to enforce its enumerated powers.[196] Since it had no enumerated power to regulate activities that were not part of interstate commerce, the necessary and proper clause was no help in *Raich*. The approach in *Raich*, in conclusion, was designed to gut the powers of the states.[197]

Stevens's opinion pointed out, properly, that Thomas's position "would turn the Supremacy Clause on its head," would "resurrect limits on congressional power that have long since been rejected," and would "have far-reaching implications beyond the facts of [*Raich*].[198] Under Thomas's reasoning, Stevens noted, "Congress would be equally powerless to regulate, let alone prohibit, the intrastate possession, cultivation, and use of marijuana for *recreational* purposes." Thomas's rationale "seemingly would require Congress to cede its constitutional power to regulate commerce whenever a state [chose to exercise its police powers.]"[199] These implications of Thomas's opinion illustrated how far he stood from the rest of the Court on federalism issues. He, and he alone, was the true revolutionary on those issues on the Rehnquist Court.

The line-up of Rehnquist Court Justices in religion cases, after the Court's personnel became constant after 1993, may have been the most consistent with ideological stereotyping of any of the Court's constitutional areas. Three Justices, Stevens, Souter, and Ginsburg, revealed themselves to be supporters of the Warren Court's suspicion of entanglements between governmental institutions and religion and of its interest in accommodating the religious beliefs of minority sects. Three other Justices, Breyer, O'Connor, and Kennedy, found themselves in the center of the Court's decision-making spectrum in religion clause cases, either because they showed an interest in balancing competing concerns or because, in Kennedy's case, they seemed uncertain about their posture. Three Justices, Rehnquist, Scalia, and Thomas, were generally opposed to the Warren Court legacy, either because they thought it inconsistent with a historical understanding of the religion clauses, because they approved of an infusion of religion into American public life, or because they thought that both religious entanglements and the beliefs of minority religious sects were not worth taking overly seriously.

The early years of the Rehnquist Court, in which Brennan, Marshall, and Blackmun remained active, produced an establishment clause decision that reflected the continuing influence of the Warren Court's jurisprudential legacy. In that decision, *County of Allegheny v. American Civil Liberties Union*,[200] the Court split a number of ways in concluding that the display of some religious symbols during the Christmas holidays was constitutionally permissible and the display of others amounted to an endorsement of religion. In an earlier case,[201] a majority of the Burger Court had upheld the display of a creche, in connection with that of a Christmas tree and a Santa Claus house, by the city of Pawtucket, Rhode Island. Burger's opinion, in concluding that there was a secular purpose for the display of the creche, emphasized that the display was limited to the holiday season and that any benefit to a particular religion, or religion generally, was "indirect, remote, and incidental."[202] He was joined by White, Powell, and Rehnquist. O'Connor concurred, signaling that she regarded the central inquiry in establishment clause cases as whether the government had "endorsed" religion.[203] Brennan, joined by Marshall, Blackmun, and Stevens, dissented, arguing that the creche was not only a religious symbol but a sectarian one, and that displaying it represented a "coercive . . . step toward establishing the sectarian preferences of the majority at the expense of the minority."[204]

When the *Allegheny County* case came before the Court five years later, divisions among the Justices were even more apparent. Allegheny County in Pennsylvania displayed a nativity scence on the main staircase of its courthouse, and also placed, next to its Christmas tree, a menorah and a "salute to liberty" banner. Six Justices voted to allow the menorah and banner. Blackmun, writing for one majority, stated that the menorah was not an exclusively religious symbol.[205] O'Connor, concurring in the judgment, stated that the menorah's placement "sends a message of pluralism and freedom to choose one's own beliefs,"[206] and Rehnquist, White, Scalia, and Kennedy, also concurring, concluded that none of the symbols represented direct aid to religion or an effort to coerce citizens to adopt particular religious preferences.[207] Brennan, Marshall, and Stevens dissented on the ground that both the menorah and the nativity scence were religious symbols.[208] Blackmun's opinion used a test O'Connor had proposed in the earlier display case, asking whether the government had "endorsed" religion,[209] but only O'Connor's opinion accepted that test, Brennan, Marshall, and Stevens preferring a more demanding standard for religious displays and Kennedy, in an opinion joined by Rehnquist, White, and Scalia, maintaining that the "no-endorsement" test "reflects an unjustified hostility toward religion."[210]

By 1992 a different configuration of Justices produced a different debate about the establishment clause. In *Lee v. Weisman,*[211] a Providence, Rhode Island, middle school offered a nondenominational prayer at its graduation ceremony. Although there were repeated references to "God" and "the Lord" in the prayer, its remaining religious content was minimal. The parents of a middle school student challenged the practice of having prayers at graduation ceremonies. A five-justice majority held the practice unconstitutional, Kennedy's opinion emphasizing that students and their families were coerced into attending the ceremony, which, although it was voluntary, was so important a social event that few graduating students or parents would not attend.[212] Blackmun, Stevens, O'Connor, and Souter provided the additional four votes for invalidating the prayer, with Blackmun and Souter writing concurring opinions. Rehnquist, White, Scalia, and Thomas dissented.

Lee v. Weisman indicated that by the early 1990s history had become the principal interpretive battleground for establishment clause cases. In his dissenting opinion Scalia argued that prayers were a common feature of public occasions at the time of the framing and that the purpose of the establishment clause was to prevent the government from establishing churches or compelling citizens to adopt particular religious beliefs, not to prevent it from giving aid to religion generally. He also argued that although evidence of coercion would trigger an establishment clause violation, no meaningful coercion had taken place in *Weisman*.[213] Souter, concurring, sharply disagreed with Scalia on both points. He reviewed the historical evidence, concluding that the framers were intending to prevent nonpreferential as well as preferential aid to religion, a proposition he found buttressed by the Court's 1947 decision in *Everson v. Board of Education*,[214] which had stated that the establishment clause prevented state practices that "aid all religions." Finally, he maintained that coercion was not a prerequisite for an establishment clause violation: the question was whether the government practice could be thought of as endorsing religion.[215]

Souter's views were shared, for the most part, by Blackmun, Stevens, and O'Connor. Blackmun wrote a separate concurrence in which he stated that "our decisions have gone beyond prohibiting coercion," a point Souter had also made.[216] Stevens and O'Connor joined that opinion, and also joined Souter's. So it appeared, after *Lee v. Weisman*, that at least three Justices were interested in maintaining the Warren Court's rigid separation between governmental practices and religion, O'Connor was suspicious of any practice that looked like a governmental "endorsement," and Kennedy, and possibly the dissenters in *Weisman*, insisted on "coercion" being shown to make out an establishment clause violation.

The replacement of Marshall, White, and Blackmun by Thomas, Ginsburg, and Breyer resulted in a larger majority of Justices being inclined to find violations when governmental institutions engaged in symbolic endorsements. A 2000 case[217] involving the delivery of a prayer at a Texas high school football game illustrated that development. The school district involved had instituted a policy of authorizing students to vote on whether to open games with "invocations" and to choose who would deliver them. Stevens, in an opinion joined by O'Connor, Kennedy, Souter, Ginsburg, and Breyer, held that the policy was "coercive" because some students, such as members of the team and cheerleaders, were required to attend the games, and the social importance of the games resulted in many other students feeling pressure to attend them. The prayer opening the game was hence the equivalent of the prayer in *Weisman*.[218]

Outside the area of symbolic endorsements, however, the Rehnquist Court was less concerned than its immediate predecessors about facially neutral governmental programs that incidentally aid religion. The most common example was state subsidies to educational institutions that had the effect of benefiting religious schools. In a series of decisions extending from 1968 to 1986, the Court invalidated some programs that resulted in aid to religious schools or parents with children in those schools and upheld others.[219] The cases seemed to turn on whether the benefits were directly conferred on religious schools or on parents who sent their children to the schools, as opposed to being conferred on all schools, all parents, or prospective enrollees in religious schools. Shifting majorities in the cases regarded establishment clause concerns as being satisfied if the programs did not single out religious institutions for government largesse, but other Justices repeatedly expressed concerns that the programs symbolically identified the state with religion or religious worship.

Those perspectives were carried over into two Rehnquist Court decisions in the 1990s. In the first, a school district paid the salaries of sign-language interpreters for deaf students attending schools within the district.[220] A student attending a parochial high school paid for the services of an interpreter. A majority upheld the program as a general disbursement of funds to aid disabled students that conferred no direct benefit on religious schools and created no financial incentive for parents to send their children to such schools.[221] Blackmun and Souter dissented, emphasizing the symbolic aspects of a government employee "participat[ing] directly in religious indoctrination" in the capacity of an interpreter.[222]

The second case resulted in a more closely divided Court. It involved the distribution by the University of Virginia of payments from a mandatory student activities budget to printers associated with a student-run religious magazine.[223] The majority, in an opinion by Kennedy, described the payments as reimbursements for the provision of "secular services for secular purposes on a religion-neutral basis," stressing that printing was "a routine, secular, and recurring attribute of student life." The student activities fees, Kennedy maintained, were dispersed to both secular and sectarian groups on an even-handed basis.[224] That was not enough for four dissenters, Stevens, Souter, Ginsburg, and Breyer. They described the program as "direct public funding of core sectarian activities," a classic establishment clause violation.[225]

The different approaches were maintained in cases decided in 1997 and 2000. The 1997 case involved a New York City program in which public school employees would make unannounced monthly visits to parochial schools to help with remedial training.[226] The program also provided training in public schools. A five-justice majority upheld the program, overruling an early decision invalidating "direct" aid to parochial schools. The majority argued that there was no reason to believe that because teachers providing remedial services were entering some parochial school classrooms, they were engaging in religious instruction, or that the mere presence of the teachers in parochial schools constituted a "symbolic union" between the state and religion.[227] Stevens, Souter, Ginsburg, and Breyer, in dissent, emphasized that the program provided direct subsidies to religious institutions, which could reasonably be seen as an endorsement of religion.[228]

The 2000 case[229] produced a somewhat similar breakdown, with the difference that Thomas's opinion for the Court provoked O'Connor and Breyer into disassociating themselves from it. The program in question lent computers and library books to nonpublic schools, including some religious schools, with the amount of aid being determined by each school's enrollment. It was challenged on the ground that the computers and books might be used for religious instruction. Thomas claimed that so long as government aid did not itself have any religious content, the fact that it might be diverted for religious purposes was irrelevant.[230] That was too much for O'Connor and Breyer, who concurred on the ground that although the aid was "direct," the evidence that it would actually be diverted for religious purposes was minimal.[231] Stevens, Souter, and Ginsburg were not even satisfied by that finding: for them any direct governmental aid to religious institutions violated the establishment clause.[232]

The latter case paved the way for the Court's endorsement of school voucher programs, which came in *Zelman v. Simmons-Harris*, a 2002 decison.[233] The state of Ohio issued a voucher program for school districts that had been designated as "failing" and placed under state control. Under the program, certain students in the Cleveland city school district were given tuition aid that they could use to attend other private schools or public schools who chose to participate in the program, or to remain in the district schools and receive tutoring. The schools identified as options by the program were "community" public schools, which were run by their own school boards, "magnet" public schools, emphasizing particular subject matter areas, and participating private schools. In the 1999–2000 school year, eighty-two per cent of the private schools participating in the Cleveland program had a religious affiliation, no adjacant public schools participated, and ninety-six per cent of the students participating enrolled in religiously affiliated private schools.[234]

Once again a narrow majority upheld the voucher program on the grounds that public as well as private schools were included in the alternatives to "failed" public schools, that the vouchers were paid to parents, who could then make choices, rather than directly to any religious schools, and that there were no financial incentives for the parents to choose private schools, because the vouchers covered only a portion of their tuition. The program was "neutral," the majority claimed, with respect to the religious affiliation of schools participating in it.[235] Stevens, Souter, Ginsburg, and Breyer maintained that this "neutrality," and the majority's emphasis on the "private choice" of parents, were, as Souter put it, "nothing but examples of verbal formalism."[236] Given the fact that a very large proportion of the families applying voucher parents used them for private religious schools, that vouchers could not be used for regular public schools, and that many designated public schools chose not to participate in the program, they thought that the voucher scheme represented "substantial" aid to religious institutions.

It is clear that the Rehnquist Court's establishment clause cases, taken together, represented a substantial modification of earlier precedents, at least with respect to facially neutral governmental programs aiding religious institutions. By the voucher cases a majority of the Court was prepared to uphold programs that had the practical effect of encouraging parents and students to seek out religious education, and the case involving the University of Virginia indicated that a state university's direct support of a student organization expressing a religious viewpoint did not run afoul of the establishment clause. When juxtaposed with the Court's posture in "symbolic endorsement" cases, those results seem to have resulted in a jurisprudence that remains suspicious of government association with symbolic activites whose religious content is arguably de minimus, such as invocations at athletic contests or nativity scenes displayed during the Christmas holidays, but at the same time is prepared to tolerate direct governmental subsidies to educational activities and institutions with a religious affiliation. The cases also reveal that at least four Justices remain on the Court who retain something of the earlier hostility toward government entanglements with religion, whether symbolic or real.

In free exercise clause cases a similar pattern of partial detachment from perspectives associated with the Warren Court can also be discerned. Such cases group themselves roughly into "mandatory accommodation" and "permissible accommodation" clusters, the former cluster composed of cases testing whether the government is required to accommodate the religious preferences of an individual, the latter of cases raising the question whether a government attempt to make such an accommodation sufficiently entangles the state with religion so as to violate the establishment clause. *Sherbert v. Verner*,[237] a 1963 decision, represents a paradigmatic Warren Court response to the mandatory accommodation issue.

In *Sherbert* a member of the Seventh-Day Adventist sect was fired from her job because her religious beliefs forbade her from working on Saturdays. When she was unable to find work in her Alabama community because of her unwillingness to work Saturdays, she filed for state unemployment benefits. Although the unemployment benefit programs of several states treated the refusal of workers to work on particular "Sabbaths" as "good cause" for refusing employment, Alabama's program did not. A five-justice majority of the Court held that the denial of benefits imposed an impermissible burden on Sherbert's exercise of her religion. By forcing her to choose between receiving no unemployment benefits or violating one of the precepts of her religion by accepting work, Brennan wrote for the Court, Alabama's practice put "the same kind of burden upon the free exercise of religion as would a fine imposed upon [Sherbert] for her Saturday worship."[238]

In the two decades following *Sherbert* the Court invalidated a handful of additional state statutes on the ground that they imposed an impermissible burden on the exercise of religion. Three of the examples involved unemployment compensation.[239] A fourth case concerned the refusal of a member of the Old Order Amish to send his children to Wisconsin public schools after the eighth grade.[240] The two children involved in that case were fourteen and fifteen; Wisconsin had a law mandating school attendance until the age of sixteen. The Old Order Amish sect objected to high school for their children because they wanted them to live in a "church community separate and apart from the world," and felt that high school introduced Amish children to "competitiveness, worldly success, and social life with other students."[241] Balancing the state's interest in educating its citizens against the Amish sect's beliefs, a majority of the Court concluded that the additional benefits to Amish children from one or two years of high school, given the Amish's "long history as a successful and self-sufficient segment of American society," were minimal.[242]

After those decisions, however, the Court began to move away from requiring mandatory accommodations to religious beliefs. A claim by a member of the Old Order Amish to be exempt from Social Security taxes on religious grounds was denied on the basis that exceptions from taxation for religious belief would undermine the comprehensiveness of the tax system, which was deemed essential to its viability.[243] An orthodox Jewish member of the air force was denied a request to wear a yarmulke indoors as an exception to a general regulation prohibiting the wearing of headgear.[244] A prison regulation preventing Muslim prisoners from attending a weekly religious service was upheld as necessary to maintain the prison's security.[245] Applicants for Social Security benefits who sought an exemption, on religious grounds, from the requirement that they provide administrators with Social Security numbers failed to gain such an exemption.[246] And Indian tribes were unsuccessful in their efforts to prevent the construction of a road in a national forest preserve on the ground that the road would disrupt areas traditionally regarded as sacred places for religious rituals.[247]

The above cases, decided between 1982 and 1988, set the stage for *Employment Division v. Smith,*[248] in which the petitioner was fired from his job at a private drug rehabilitation clinic in Oregon because he had consumed a drug, peyote, as part of a religious ritual sponsored by the Native American Church. Oregon listed peyote as among the "controlled substances" it made illegal to possess or use, and did not provide an exemption for the consumption of peyote for religious purposes. After being fired the petitioner applied for unemployment benefits, and was denied on the ground that he had been fired for work-related misconduct. The Oregon Supreme Court concluded that criminalizing the consumption of peyote for religious purposes violated the free exercise of religion, and the petitioner was therefore entitled to unemployment compensation.

A majority of the Court, in an opinion by Scalia, reversed the Oregon Supreme Court. Scalia took the opportunity to reframe the Court's mandatory accommodations jurisprudence, asserting that *Sherbert*'s requirement that a state needed to demonstrate a "compelling interest" in restricting religious practices did not apply when a "generally applicable" law incidentally burdened religious expression.[249] In *Smith* the law in question was one criminalizing the possession or use of certain controlled substances, and was not specifically directed at religious practices. Scalia read the Court's prior mandatory accommodations cases as only applying the *Sherbert* test to unemployment compensation. He asserted that the Court had never held that "an individual's religious beliefs excuse him from compliance with an otherwise valid law prohibiting conduct that the State is free to regulate."[250] He distinguished *Yoder* on the grounds that it was not just a free exercise case but a free speech case, because it involved the rights of parents to direct the education of their children.[251]

The Court's line-up in *Smith* was somewhat unusual for its religion clause cases, with not just Rehnquist and White but also Kennedy and Stevens joining Scalia's opinion. O'Connor's concurrence assumed that the "compelling interest" test remained applicable every time a regulation was challenged on free exercise grounds, but she believed that the test had been satisfied in *Smith* because of the state's overriding interest in restricting harmful drug use and the administrative difficulties produced by giving exemptions.[252] Brennan, Marshall, and Blackmun also applied the *Sherbert* test, concluding that an exemption for the consumption of peyote for religious purposes was not administratively burdensome because of the drug's bitter taste, and that the consumption was clearly part of a religious ritual, akin to the sacramental use of wine.[253]

Only three years after *Smith* was decided, Scalia's opinion seemed in jeopardy. Although all of the three dissenters in *Smith* had left the Court, neither Souter, Ginsburg, or Breyer showed an attraction for *Smith*, and O'Connor had never been a supporter. In *Church of the Lukuni Babalu Aye v. City of Hialeah*,[254] a municipality had imposed a ban on the "ritual slaughter" of animals in connection with religious services. The Santeria sect, which used the slaughtering practice as part of its traditional religious ceremonies, challenged the ordinance as discriminating against them. A unanimous Court struck down the ban after finding that, among other things, it excluded almost all secular killings of animals and was unconnected to the objectives of protecting animals from inhumane slaughter or preventing the unhealthy disposal of animal carcasses.[255] In concurring opinions Scalia and Souter advanced differing interpretations of the effect of *Lukumi* on *Smith*. Scalia maintained that the problem with the statute in *Lukumi* was that its purpose was to interfere with religious practices; a general ban on animal sacrifices that had the incidental effect of restricting such practices would be permissible.[256] Souter, in contrast, suggested that *Smith* represented a departure from the Court's prior free exercise decisions, was inconsistent with the history of the free exercise clause, and should be overruled.[257] O'Connor was subsequently to endorse that position.[258]

The Court's decisions from *Sherbert* through *Lukumi* have thus left mandatory accommodations doctrine in an uncertain state. If *Smith* is still good law, it would appear that the only instances in which governments are required to accommodate religion are where their policies directly burden the exercise of religious beliefs, either by forcing believers to choose between their religious faith and governmental benefits (*Sherbert* and the other unemployment compensation cases) or by imposing burdens on a particular sect's practices (*Yoder* and *Lukumi*). It would still seem possible for a governmental unit to incidentally burden the exercise of religion in the form of a generally applicable law, although *Yoder* fits uneasily with *Smith* on that issue. By the close of Rehnquist's tenure the future course of mandatory accommodations remained unclear.

Both mandatory and permissible accommodations of religious beliefs and practices highlight a potential tension between the Constitution's religion clauses. To the extent that the government accommodates religion, it runs the risk of establishing it; and to the extent that any entanglements between government and religion are consitutionally disapproved, the free exercise of religion may be thwarted. The Warren Court's solution, embodied in the juxtaposition of its school prayer cases and *Sherbert*, was to disfavor symbolic entanglements between the state and religion but to be supportive, on free exercise grounds, of governmental programs that created exemptions to adminstrative schemes burdening members of particular religious faiths.

As the Rehnquist Court began to permit more facially neutral state programs that incidentally benefited religion, the question was raised as to whether such programs amounted to a tolerance on the Court for the advancement of religious beliefs and practices. The various instances in which the Court had tolerated indirect state aid to religious schools could be seen, in that vein, as permissible accommodations of religion. If that were the case, the next question was how far government could go in those accommodations. An early Rehnquist Court decision had identified one limit: states could not directly exempt religious publications from taxation. In a 1989 case striking down a Texas statute providing that religious publications were not subject to the state's sales tax, Brennan, for the Court, distinguished between a general sales tax incidentally burdening religious publications, which he believed would be constitutional, and a direct subsidy to religious organizations. The latter scheme, he asserted, burdened secular competitors of the organizations and was not required by the free exercise clause because the religious groups could still communicate their messages.[259]

In 1994 a differently composed Court considered another possible limitation on state accommodation of religion: the creation by the New York legislature of a special school district to accommodate the concerns of the Satmar Hasidim, a group of Orthodox Jews.[260] The group resembled the Old Order Amish in seeking to avoid contacts with society at large, and typically educated their children in religious schools. An earlier decision of the Court had invalidated the state's provision of remedial services to students in private schools as an impermissible entanglement,[261] and pursuant to that decision New York had declined to provide education for handicapped students attending religious schools. This resulted in handicapped Satmar children being sent to neighboring public schools for remedial education, a process that their parents found traumatic. In response to their complaints, the New York legislature designated the village of Kiryas Joel, where the Satmar community lived, as a special school district.

A majority of the Court found that the legislature's action was not a permissible accommodation of the Satmars. Souter, for the Court, reasoned that it was not clear that the creation of a special legislative district was necessary to alleviate the concerns of the Satmars, or whether other groups with their own concerns about the education of their children would be similarly accommodated. Further, the legislation singled out a particular religious group for benefits.[262] Scalia, Thomas, and Rehnquist dissented, treating the legislature's accommodation to the Satmars as simply the outcome of a particular group's effective lobbying and suggesting that the accommodation was not so much toward Satmar religious practices as toward their "cultural peculiarities."[263]

The *Kiryas Joel* case indicated that a majority of the Court believed that a some point state aid to religious institutions or communities, however couched, might constitute an establishment clause violation. But there was a flip side to that issue: to what extent was a general scheme of state aid to private and public, religious and non-religious educational institutions *required* to accommodate religious concerns? Commentators had identified this issue after the Court's decision in *Zelman*, the Ohio school vouchers case.[264] If facially neutral government programs providing indirect funding to religious schools satisfied the establishment clause, could the government exclude religious alternatives to those programs? The Court took up that issue two years after deciding *Zelman*.

Washington state had a program providing merit- and income-based scholarships to students attending public and private colleges within the state, including religious colleges. Students attending religious colleges, however, were ineligible for the program if they majored in devotional theology, sometimes a requirement for preparation for a career in the ministry. The denial of funding to such students was justified because of a Washington state constitutional provision allegedly mandating a very firm separation of church and state. The denial of funding to theology students was challenged, in *Locke v. Davey*, as a violation of the free exercise clause.[265]

In a 7–2 decision written by Rehnquist, the Court upheld the denial of funding. Rehnquist's opinion distinguished between a discretionary state decision to include indirect funding for theology candidates and programs, which he found constitutionally permissible under *Zelman*, and a requirement that states include such candidates and programs in a general funding scheme. He cited a historical opposition within some states for taxpayer support of the clergy, and asserted that "there is room for play in the joints" between the establishment and free exercise clauses.[266] The implications of a decision the other way in the Washington case would have been quite significant: general public funding of educational institutions would have had to include religious instruction. On the other hand, the decision was interpreted by lower courts as permitting states to decide not to include religious schools in general voucher programs.[267] That suggests that although indirect state aid to religious institutions is constitutionally permitted, whether or not it occurs can be determined by the political process. This arguably makes the entire line of Rehnquist Court cases involving "indirect" aid to religious schools less epochal than initially thought, since although states and cities can establish programs that eventually funnel resources to schools and colleges, they are not required to, and their doing so or not doing so isn't likely to raise constitutional issues. Nonetheless, the contrast with the Warren Court and even the late Burger Court, where even a minimal association of the government with religious institutions was thought to give rise to a constitutional violation,[268] seems very marked.

III

The influence of the Chief Justice on the Rehnquist Court's internal atmosphere has been noted. One might note as well his influence in bringing unenumerated rights, federalism, and religion clause issues to the forefront of the Court's constitutional jurisprudence. His participation in all three sets of issues was persistent since he first came to the Court in 1971, and he gradually saw his position move from that of a decided outsider to one of influence. He started out one of only two dissenters in *Roe*, and by *Webster* and *Casey* he was poised to overrule *Roe* as a precedent. He never endorsed any broad view of unenumerated rights, and by *Glucksberg* he was able to claim, without too much stretching, that the Court's mainstream approach to those "rights" was to test them against history, tradition, and the "ordered liberty" criterion. He lost in *Casey*, and lost again in *Lawrence*, and had he stayed on the Court, he might have lost in some additional unenumerated rights cases. But he took essentially the same position toward unenumerated rights expressed by Bork in his unsuccessful confirmation hearings, occasionally tempered it at the edges, and made it part of the Court's mainstream jurisprudence.

His contribution to the Court's federalism jurisprudence was even more marked. He began, in *Fry*, as a lone voice on a Court reflexively endorsing the idea of judicial deference to virtually unlimited federal regulatory power. He authored a temporary qualification of that posture in *Usury*, only to see it taken back in *Garcia*, but he remained interested in reviving the idea of reserved state powers. In *Lopez*, *Morrison*, and the Eleventh Amendment cases he found some allies, and made the most of it, his own opinions serving to significantly constrain the force of Congress's commerce and Section Five enforcement powers. By the end of his tenure his project had hit something of a wall, and he joined the opposition in *Hibbs*, if not in *Raich*. Despite Stevens's language in *Raich*, the Court's posture toward its post–New Deal heritage of federalism cases was far different in 2005 from the rubberstamping of Congress's authority that had marked the Court Rehnquist joined. If "traditional state powers and functions" were to be taken seriously by the Court once again, Rehnquist could take substantial credit for that development.

Likewise in religion clause cases Rehnquist persistently moved the Court away from the mainstream jurisprudence of the Warren and Burger Courts. As the Rehnquist Court chipped away at the "wall of separation" in aid to education cases, Rehnquist consistently voted with those doing the chipping. In the space of two decades the jurisprudence of establishment clause cases moved from a position of virtually no toleration for entanglements between the state and private religious schools to one that endorsed voucher payments from public funds that could be applied to religious school tuition. Rehnquist would have gone further, allowing the state to display symbols with religious content and to retain prayers at school graduations, but he nonetheless made considerable progress. Once again, near the end of his tenure, his project hit a wall in the case testing whether the use of public grants for religious purposes was not just constitutionally permitted but constitutionally required, and once again he joined the opposition, and backed off from the logic of his own position. When Rehnquist's tenure ended, he had become not merely one of the more successful but one of the most influential Chief Justices in the Court's history.[269]

Taken as a group, the Rehnquist Court's most representative lines of constitutional cases had evolved in unexpected ways. The fears aroused by Bork's nomination centered on a concern that he and other originalists would usher in a new jurisprudence of indifference to civil rights and liberties. Not only had Bork denied that the Constitution protected a right of privacy, he had advanced as a reason for that belief the lack of enumerated support for that "right" in the Constitution's text. If originalism captured the Court, the theory—on which a fair amount of Warren Court constitutional jurisprudence had been erected—that the Constitution encompassed protection for some foundational, "unwritten" rights seemed destined for the scrapheap. Not only would the use of contraceptive devices or the choice to terminate a pregnancy lack constitutional protection, constitutional "liberties" could not encompass homosexual, or for that matter heterosexual, sodomitic conduct. But by Rehnquist's death the Court's unenumerated rights cases had moved in just the opposite direction. Birth control, abortion, intimate homosexual conduct, a right to refuse life-saving medical treatment, and possibly same-sex marriage had received constitutional protection.

The federalism cases were unexpected in a different way. After the *Usery*/*Garcia* sequence in the Burger Court, it appeared as if the New Deal orthodoxy on federalism issues—whatever Congress chooses to regulate, it can—was even more firmly in place, because *Usery*'s concept of "traditional state functions" had been deemed "unworkable,"and the "political safeguards of federalism" rationale had provided another reason why Congressional supremacy was really not synonymous with the eradication of state power. Then came the first unexpected turn, as a narrow Court majority began to revive federalism-based limits on Congress's regulatory power. By the twenty-first century some commentators were raising the possibility of a Rehnquist Court–led demolition of New Deal orthodoxy. Just at that point the Court decided *Hibbs* and *Raich*, and the second unexpected turn occurred: suddenly the anticipated "federalism revolution"of the Rehnquist Court seemed much less likely to occur. Still, the very possibility that a twenty-first-century Court would contain some Justices who were more attracted to pre–New Deal understandings of the relationship between federal and state powers than to long-established New Deal–inspired understandings was surprising and significant.

If the evolution of religion clauses jurisprudence on the Rehnquist Court was less unexpected from the standpoint of judical ideology, it was a major surprise from another point of view. Modernity in twentieth-century America, and the development of a modernist consciousness that accompanied it, had emphasized the secularization of higher learning. Religious attendance and religious practice had steadily declined in the United States in the first three-quarters of the twentieth century. The Court's decisions outlawing mandatory prayer in the public schools can be seen, from one perspective, as illustrative of a perfectionist reading of the establishment clause, but they can also be seen as the acknowledgment that atheistic beliefs had gained a foothold in modern America. It seems unlikely that on Warren's retirement many commentators would have predicted that for the remainder of the century, and beyond, religious beliefs in America would proliferate and grow in intensity. But instead of religion becoming increasingly less relevant in a modern, secular state, it became increasingly more relevant. In that sense the Rehnquist Court's continued sensitivity to the impact of religious symbols, and also its increasing tolerance for governmental accomodations of religious beliefs and practices, can be seen as a response to the growing importance of religion in late-twentieth- and twenty-first-century American culture. That growing importance had itself been unexpected.

But in the long run the unexpectedness of the Rehnquist Court may not primarily lie in the surprising success of its Chief Justice, or the direction of its major lines of constitutional decisions. At some point in the future the Rehnquist

Court may be best known as the locus of a major change in the jurisprudence of constitutional interpretation. To understand the nature of that change, consider the interpretive debates that took place on the Rehnquist Court in unenumerated rights cases, federalism cases, and religion clause cases, and contrast them with the debates that took place in those areas on the Warren and Burger Courts.

Warren Court unenumerated rights cases, such as *Poe v. Ullman* and *Griswold*, were debated within an interpretive framework centering on the "countermajoritarian difficulty," the perceived inconsistency of "lawmaking" by an unelected Court in a majoritarian democracy. *Poe* came to the Court two years before its declaration, in *Ferguson v. Skrupa*,[270] that "liberties"in the due process clauses should be confined to matters of procedure. Although this repudiation of "substantive"judicial readings of "liberty"in due process cases was not as thoroughgoing as it sounded—the Court continued to engage in substantive readings of the Fourteenth Amendment's due process clause in a line of Fourteenth Amendment "incorporation" cases, which Harlan invoked as the source of his conclusion in *Poe* that certain liberties connected to individual privacy and dignity were "fundamental"—it reflected the widely held jurisprudential assumption that unconstrained constitutional interpretation invited inappropriate judicial lawmaking. The issue in *Poe* was thus not whether the government's intrusion into the procreation decisions of married couples should be tolerated. It was whether the Court, as opposed to a more democratic branch of government, should correct the situation.

History was not part of the debate in *Poe* between judges who believed that the Court should avoid deciding the issue and Harlan. Harlan's derivation of the "fundamental" nature of the right to make procreational decisions had been based on the Court's comparatively recent "ordered liberty" glosses in incorporation cases. History would not have been particularly helpful to either side in the debate because the contraceptive devices involved in *Poe* and *Griswold* were twentieth-century innovations. But history was not invoked in the debate because both sides implicitly adopted a "living Constitution" theory of constitutional interpretation. Harlan's opinion assumed that the meaning of "liberty" in due process cases could change over time, and so did the majority. Harlan openly declared that the tradition of ordered liberty was a "living thing,"[271] but the majority also assumed that the meaning of constitutional provisions was capable of changing. That assumption, process theorists argued, actually reinforced judicial deference where open-ended constitutional provisions were concerned, because there was always a risk that judges would try to conform the meaning of those provisions to their current value preferences.

By the *Glucksberg* case the debate over unenumerated rights, as reflected in Rehnquist's and Souter's opinions, had taken on a quite different cast. Rehnquist claimed that "history and tradition," into which he folded the Court's line of "ordered liberty" cases, should be controlling in unenumerated rights cases; Souter adopted Harlan's approach in *Poe*, emphasizing the "living" dimension of the concept of "ordered liberty."[272] By 1998 both sides were well aware what those two points of interpretive emphasis signified. Rehnquist was associating himself with a view of constitutional interpretation, originalism, that confined judicial interpretations of constitutional provisions to the "original understanding" of those provisions and that objected to the "living Constitution" approach. Rehnquist had registered his objections to "living Constitution" jurisprudence as early as 1976,[273] but originalism had not emerged as an influential theory of constitutional interpretation on the Court until the late 1980s and early 1990s, when first Scalia and then Thomas identified themselves as originalists.

In the meantime the process perspective reflected in Frankfurter's opinion in *Poe* and in influential academic commentary in the late 1950s and 1960s had become increasingly less visible in the Court's interpretive debates in the 1970s and 1980s. The Court's last important constitutional opinion resting on the comparative institutional competence of courts and the political branches was arguably *Garcia*. By the 1990s debates in federalism cases featured contrasts between "original understandings" of the reach of federal and state powers and the Court's battery of post–New Deal precedents that had largely abandoned those understandings. The evolution from the *Usury/Garcia* sequence to *Raich* was instructive: in the former sequence of cases Blackmun argued that the "traditional state functions" Rehnquist had rediscovered as substantive constitutional limits on federal power were best understood as operating as "political safeguards" in Congress; in *Raich* Stevens, confronted with two post-*Garcia* "substantive limits" cases, *Lopez* and *Morrison*, invoked the precedent of *Filburn* to suggest that extensive federal regulatory power was still the norm. Stevens did not advance a *Garcia*-style institutional competence argument, and Thomas's dissent found the whole line of post–New Deal federalism cases wrongly decided on originalist grounds.

A comparable debate took place in the Court's religion cases. Both Scalia and Souter invoked history to argue for particular approaches to the establishment clause, but Souter indicated that weight should be given to the Court's recent precedents even if they were not necessarily reconcilable with historical evidence.[274] And since the *Smith* decision represented a departure from the Court's earlier free exercise decisions, both Souter and O'Connor attempted to undermine it with investigations into the "original meaning" of the free exercise clause.[275]

In short, the interpretive debates among Rehnquist Court justices in the Court's most distinctive constitutional law areas were not the "countermajoritarian" debates of earlier Courts. They pitted history, in the service of originalist theories of interpretation, against recent precedent, in the service of "living Constitution" theories. As such they arguably represented a relocation of the locus of constraints on judges as constitutional interpeters in the American judicial tradition. Instead of contraints being located in deference by a countermajoritarian body to the more democratic institutions of American governance, constraints are located in the text of the Constitution, history, and the concept of "original meaning." This relocation of constraints has the potential to change the meaning of judicial activism, as that term was understood throughout most of twentieth-century constitutional history.

Judicial activism, and its counterpart, judicial restraint, were postures that emerged from a jurisprudence in which judges were assumed to be a species of lawmakers and in which the meaning of the Constitution was assumed to change over time. The *Carolene Products* regime of judicial review was designed to mark out the appropriate areas for activism and restraint. Aggressive or deferential review in designated areas was designed to foster democratic values. Hence the Court should generally defer to legislatures when they sought to regulate the economy or redistribute benefits, because legislatures were more accountable to the citizenry at large, but could be less deferential where legislatures specifically contravened enumerated constitutional rights, blocked the channels of political change by catering to established interest groups, or discriminated against powerless minorities. The stances of judicial activism and restraint were thus tied to democratic theory and the countermajoritarian difficulty. An entire corpus of twentieth-century constitutional law was developed along the axes of *Carolene Products* review.

The primary constraints on judges as constitutional interpreters in the *Carolene Products* regime were the institutional constraints of democratic theory. History played a comparatively small role in the regime because robust versions of democratic theory did not develop in American constitutionalism until the early twentieth century, so the "original meaning" of many constitutional provisions had not been articulated against a backdrop in which the judiciary was regarded as an anti-democratic force. For the framers of many of the Constitution's provisions, there was no "countermajoritarian difficulty." The judiciary was regarded as an openly countermajoritarian institution, checking the tendencies of legislatures to infringe on the fundamental rights of individual citizens. *Carolene Products* review was also consistent with a "living Constitution" theory of constitutional interpretation. It was intended to be a check on the tendency of judges to conform the meaning of open-ended constitutional provisions to current social priorities. That task, advocates of *Carolene Products* review believed, was primarily for legislatures. Modern legislatures could experiment with reform legislation that had hitherto been thought to trespass on individual rights because changing social conditions demanded that response; courts should, in most cases, allow legislatures to perform that function.

The Warren Court's constitutional decisions were made within the framework of *Carolene Products* jurisprudence. The controversial decisions of that Court were those in which critics felt that it had usurped legislative priorities in areas where democratic theory called for deference, either because the Court had been overly suspicious of the motives of legislatures or because it had taken too perfectionistic a view of constitutional rights. Examples ranged from the reapportionment cases through the school prayer cases and the criminal procedure cases. The Court was not criticized for adopting modern perspectives toward the effects of legislative districts apportioned on a basis other than population, or toward the emergence of secular opposition to traditional religious practices, or toward the practical consequences of police interrogation of criminal suspects. It was criticized for insisting that those matters raised constitutional issues that required its intervention.

The dynamic of jurisprudential debate within the Rehnquist Court in its last decade was strikingly different. Those insisting that the constitutional text and history should constrain judges are not doing so on the basis of democratic theory, or of institutional competence. Not only is the "original meaning" of most constitutional provisions largely uninformed by modern democratic theory, originalists have no difficulty with the judiciary's taking on a countermajoritarian role, since that role was consistent with most framers' understanding of American constitutionalism. The reason that originalists insist on the text and history as constraints is to forestall judicial interpretation based on a "living Constitution" model. The constraints are designed to be interpretive, not institutional.

In contrast, those who opposed originalism on the Rehnquist Court did not do so on the ground that historical analysis is inappropriate. Indeed the emergence of originalist Justices on the Rehnquist Court resulted in an increase in historical inquiry by their nonoriginalist counterparts. Nor did nonorginalists reject the proposition that the language of the constitutional text should play an important part in constitutional interpretation. The debate between originalists and nonoriginalists on the Rehnquist Court was primarily about the sources of meaning for constitutional provisions. Originalists insisted that their emphasis on historical "understandings" as the primary source of the meaning of constitutional language was another way of asserting that the meaning of that language did not change with time. It was that proposition about constitutional interpretation that gave originalism its sometimes deeply revisionist character.

In contrast, nonoriginalists are "living Constitution" interpreters, who assume that the meaning of constitutional language necessarily changes with time. If one makes that assumption, the Court's successive glosses on a constitutional provision—its conclusions that "liberty" in the due process clauses now embraces consensual homosexual sodomy or that the Fourteenth Amendment's equal protection clause now prohibits most forms of gender discrimination—are treated as changing the provision's meaning. This means that a line of Supreme Court glosses—the line of unenumerated rights cases invoked by the plurality in *Casey* or the line of post–New Deal federalism decisions invoked by Stevens in *Raich*—can be seen as evidence of what a provision currently "means." Originalists see such lines as much less weighty, indeed as having no weight if they offend against original understandings of the provision.

Thus the center of jurisprudential debates on the Rehnquist Court moved from issues of democratic theory and comparative institutional competence to issues of history and theories of constitutional interpretation. At first blush this change might not seem particularly momentous, since implicit and explicit theories of constitutional interpretation are necessary features of the Court's constitutional law cases and issues of history, democratic theory, and comparative institutional competence have been part of the discourse of commentary on Supreme Court opinions for several decades. But from another perspective the evolution from the Warren Court's jurisprudential emphasis on democratic theory and comparative institutional competence to the Rehnquist Court's emphasis on history and interpretive theory may end up having significant substantive consequences.

The *Carolene Products* regime dominated American constitutional law for at least four decades. The framework of *Carolene Products* review encouraged the Court to derive a series of doctrinal justifications for aggressive or deferential review. Those justifications were primarily implemented in the form of levels or tiers of judicial scrutiny of legislation challenged on constitutional grounds. Between the 1940s, when it first identified the mode of "strict" scrutiny in cases involving racial discrimination, and the 1980s, at which time it had developed a complex web of scrutiny levels, ranging from a supine form of "rational basis" review through more searching forms of that review through "intermediate" levels of scrutiny to strict scrutiny, the "scrutiny decision," often made by the Court without comment, let alone justification, became a crucial organizing feature of the Court's corpus of constitutional law doctrine.[276]

Scrutiny levels in the *Carolene Products* regime tracked the assumptions about democratic theory, institutional competence, and the countermajoritarian difficulty that had caused the regime to come into being. Deferential review was appropriate when the constitutional challenges involved issues, such as the regulation of economic activity or the redistribution of economic benefits, that seemed well suited for disposition by the popularly elected branches and were not directly governed by constitutional provisions. More searching review was reserved for legislative actions that affected underrepresented minorities, blocked the channels of potential political change, or were in direct contravention of language in the Constitution. With its paradigms for deferential scrutiny and heightened scrutiny in mind, the Court, in the latter half of the twentieth century, developed an intriciate corpus of scrutiny levels jurisprudence, ranging over a variety of constitutional issues.

Recent commentators have noted that the Court's scrutiny levels jurisprudence has become intricate to the point of unintelligibility.[277] Part of the difficulty may come from uncertainty about a core assumption of the *Carolene Products* regime: that one can easily discern which issues are suitable for resolution by the popularly elected branches and which are not. To the extent that the *Carolene Products* review framework is designed to identify the branch most competent to govern a particular subject matter, the framework may seem less workable where institutional competence is less clear. Discrimination on the basis of gender or sexual preference provides just one example. If such legislation is based on archaic or overbroad stereotypes, who is to say that such stereotypes are more likely to be eroded in popularly elected forums? Alternatively, who is to say that courts are competent to determine when a stereotype distorts reality?

In any event, jurisprudential debates on the Rehnquist Court seem to be focusing progressively less on institutional competence issues and more on history and theories of constitutional interpretation. The new focus might end up having significant effects on the *Carolene Products* review framework. Consider commerce power cases. Since those cases typically involve the regulation of economic activity, *Carolene Products* review places them in a category of deferential review, and the Court, from the 1940s through *Raich*, has rarely disturbed Congressional decisions about whether a particular activity has a "substantial effect on interstate commerce." That deference has followed from a judgment that legislatures are more competent than courts to fashion economic policy. But if the focus shifts to history and theories of interpretation, the issues in cases such as *Raich* become centered in the meaning of "commerce," and of "interstate commerce," and the potential for a different sort of analysis emerges. That analysis, as Thomas's dissent in *Raich* suggests, is far less interested in questions of comparative institutional competence than in questions about the meaning of constitutional language and whether that meaning can change over time.

At the close of Rehnquist's tenure Thomas's view of commerce clause or federalism cases was quite far from commanding a majority of the Court. But the shift away from institutional competence analysis to issues of history and interpretation was nonetheless apparent. This may mean that in the future cases that previous Courts classified in the terms of *Carolene Products* review will no longer be reflexively categorized in that fashion. If so, the whole edifice of constitutional tests and standards established within the *Carolene Products* regime may begin to crumble.

At that point, from a perspective some time in the future, the Rehnquist Court may emerge as the place where one longstanding approach to constitutional law issues collapsed of its own weight and another approach began to emerge. Although the unexpectedness of the Rehnquist Court should by now be apparent, its potentially revolutionary place in the American judicial tradition may take some more time to be understood.

16

The Tradition and the Future: A Summary

A prime concern of this study has been to describe the elements of a tradition of appellate judging in America, and simultaneously to explore its meaning. One area of emphasis has been the special set of freedoms and limitations that have defined the office of judge since Marshall. Because appellate judging has often been defined by judges and commentators in terms of constraints, one may incline to underemphasize its freedoms, which are worthy of recapitulation. First among them is the power to declare, in a final sense, what "the law" is. American judges function as the primary interpreters of the meaning of the Constitution or a statute, until the sovereign people, through their legislative representatives, choose to change that meaning. That is no minor perquisite, constitutional amendments being rare and statutes invariably being open to further interpretation. It was not always identified with the judiciary in America; it is not thought to be fully possessed by judges in other common-law nations.[1] Judges in America can declare and thereby make law. If one takes seriously the notion of law as a set of guidelines for social conduct, American appellate judges have had abundant opportunities to establish those guidelines.

Federal appellate judges and many state appellate judges have also had the freedom of life tenure. That freedom has been minimized by the oracular theory of the nineteenth century and by twentieth-century theories of judicial self-restraint. It has meant, however, that one holding the office of judge is beholden to far fewer persons than are other occupants of comparably powerful offices. Nowhere, perhaps, but on the United States Supreme Court could governing officials as powerful, independent-minded, and outspoken as Harlan the Elder, Jackson, or Douglas remain relatively insulated from direct political pressures. American appellate judges have been allowed to make decisions affecting fundamentally the lives of others with (in most cases) minimal fear of having those decisions rebound to their personal disadvantage. In America few offices with such power have had such relatively low personal visibility.

These freedoms in the judiciary, we have seen, have continually interacted with equally important constraints. If judges make decisions of such importance, if their decisions are exercises of power rather than of mechanical logic, and if so few checks exist on the character of their performance, how is their presence tolerated in a democracy? Numerous explanations have been offered over time in response to this query, among them responses that would invest the judiciary with a guardianship of antidemocratic and antiegalitarian prerogatives. But the response most regularly accepted has been one emphasizing the distinctive technical skills of judges. The judiciary is allegedly entrusted with power because its representatives alone understand the intricacies of the law and can make them intelligible to laymen.

The attractiveness of this explanation has been its confining effect. The power of judges pertains only to those matters peculiarly "legal," as distinguished from political. Outside their field of competence judges become mere citizens and thus as subject to the whims of public opinion as anyone else. Part of the burden of judicial opinion-writing, then, has been to show that a decision has not been grounded on other than "legal" considerations, and that within that ambit it analyzes legal issues in an intelligible fashion. The legitimacy of a judicial decision in America is somehow linked with the degree to which it meets this requirement.

Were the lines between the "legal" and "political" spheres hard and fast, the foregoing explanation might be more satisfactory. But the history of American government suggests that questions of law, especially constitutional law, have been so intermingled with questions of politics as to often be indistinguishable. In reality, judges are not asked to refrain from deciding political questions at all; rather they are asked to refrain from deciding political questions in too openly partisan a fashion. Judges cannot become so isolated from contemporary conditions that their views are obsolescent. On the other hand, they cannot reveal by their opinions too passionate a concern with partisan issues or too strong an interest in passing on orthodox political questions. Paradoxically, the effectiveness of an appellate judicial decision is related to its ability to transcend mere partisanship; and yet the more effective a decision, the wider its political impact.

But if the judiciary has functioned as a political force, its decisions have resisted characterization in conventional political terms. Throughout American history judging has taken place against a backdrop of changing ideological currents; yet those currents, insofar as they themselves are capable of characterization, have not often proved to be fruitful vehicles for analyzing the performance of individual justices. To call Marshall a "Federalist," Taney a "Jacksonian," Holmes a "liberal," or Harlan II a "conservative" not only lends a false unity to the terms, it distorts the thrust of the individual contributions of those justices.

The view of appellate judging on which this book rests emphasizes, rather than political characterizations, the changing constraints on judges as lawmakers. Judges, we have seen, were originally pictured as being not only bound to follow the dictates of "the law," but also as free to declare what those dictates were. As the oracular theory of judging disintegrated with time, its conception of the judicial function as independent but constrained has remained. All the twentieth-century jurisprudential theories described in this study, including Realism, have assumed that judges make law, but have continued to associate judging with a perception of limitations on the lawmaking power of judges. Some limitations have been intellectual (an obligation to give adequate reasons for results), some institutional (an obligation to defer to the power of another branch of government), some political (a need to avoid involvement in hotly partisan issues), some psychological (a need to recognize the role of individual bias in judicial decision-making), some historical or linguistic (a need to adhere to the text of the Constitution as it was originally understood). Emphasis on one or another set of limitations has varied with the theory of judging propounded. All the theories, however, have implicitly given the appellate judiciary a limited mandate to dispense justice as it sees fit.

"Activism" and passivity—or "self-restraint"—have sometimes been the terms employed to describe judicial responses to the above mandate. But, as indicated throughout this study, activism in the judiciary has not always been compatible with liberalism, nor have passivity and conservatism always harmonized. Marshall took an expansive view of his powers, and used them to further the interests of selected established propertyholders. But Warren adopted an equally expansive approach toward the pursuit of very different substantive ends. His activism stimulated change and favored disadvantaged persons. Brandeis, Frankfurter, and Harlan II, in varying degrees, were apostles of judicial self-restraint. It does not capture the essence of any of those last three judges to designate them "liberals" or "conservatives" without further refinement of terms. American appellate judges have had to ask themselves not simply what social goals they believe in but also whether current perceptions of the office of judge are compatible with a judicial implementation of those goals. Because they have had to ask this additional question, their decisions, in some instances, have constituted a deviation from or a subordination of their social views. Orthodox political characterizations do not ordinarily address this institutional dimension of appellate judging.

A second distinctive aspect of appellate judging has been the presence of a professional constituency of courts that can be said to differ, both in composition and in expectations, from the constituencies of other governmental branches. To recapitulate: in handing down their opinions, appellate courts are communicating to at least two differing sets of audiences—the public at large, whose lives may be influenced in a general sense by the impact of their decisions, and a professional constituency, including the lower courts, similarly situated potential litigants, and counsel for those litigants, which is influenced by a decision in a much more specific sense. An appellate opinion can be a clear signal to a select group of persons that their conduct must be adjusted in accordance with the decision, or, alternatively, that it need not be so adjusted. It functions, at this level, to give specialized guidance to other courts and private persons on particular legal questions.

These two constituencies of a top-level appellate court need not always be on the same side of a conflict. Thus, in cases such as the *Gold Clause* cases of 1935, in which a decision is both a generalized response to a political controversy—the soundness of the existing monetary system—and a specialized directive to a defined class of persons—holders of United States bonds—innovation by a court may be politically satisfying in the general sense and yet highly disruptive of existing expectations in the class of persons it directly affects. From this perspective, judicial innovation often clashes with the values of certainty and predictability, and service to a professional constituency becomes a counterweight to change. If a judge believes that appellate courts have an obligation not to upset drastically the expectations of their professional public, he or she may decline to implement a change in the law, even though welcoming that change as a political response. In that case the judge's calculus again contains a dimension that standard political characterizations cannot easily portray.

Finally, the relation between ideas and judicial decisions is more complex than the conventional terms representing ideological postures would seem to suggest. The ideological terms used in this study—e.g., federalism, paternalism, liberalism, conservatism—have had different meanings at different times, and have been identified with judicial responses pointing in a variety of directions. Complexities arise partially from the ambivalent character of the terms themselves. Federalism may connote either strength in the national government or a balance of strength between that government and the states. Paternalism can embrace both active participation by the judiciary in behalf of disadvantaged persons or tolerance by judges of the social welfare schemes of legislatures. Liberalism contains within itself mutually contradictory impulses. Complexities arise also from the adversary nature of appellate decision-making, which emphasizes ambivalences and invites the use of a single rationale to justify opposite results. Terms such as federalism may become tools in the hands of lawyers and judges: they may be perceived as being capable of pointing in more than one direction, but employed without clarification of their ambiguities. All this makes the characterization of judges as representatives of varieties of social thought a difficult and dangerous enterprise. The relation between ideological change and appellate adjudication is not a linear one.

If one accepts the thesis that the American judicial tradition has been composed of certain core elements, will those elements continue to remain relatively constant in the future? Some observations are suggested by the experience of the past. Political controversies have a way of infiltrating the courts, and no theory of judicial performance, however confining, can prevent the courts from eventually passing upon sufficiently serious and divisive issues, provided that an adequate doctrinal framework exists for their consideration.

The delicate relation between the judiciary and politics seems destined to endure, and highly charged "political" issues such as the constitutionality of "benign" racial quotas in public education or of policies forbidding same sex marriages will continue to require resolution. Various "passive" devices exist to enable the judiciary to postpone the time of decision, but not the ultimate responsibility.[2] Many such issues will be divisive, as were those in *Charles River Bridge, Brown* v. *Board of Education,* or *Griswold* v. *Connecticut,* because they represent clashes between cherished values rather than between one desirable and one obnoxious set of attitudes. The Constitution, like other sources of law in America, embodies contradictory principles. Free speech may clash with privacy, egalitarianism with racial justice, liberty with patriotism, freedom to hold property with freedom to acquire it. Appellate courts will have to make hard, temporary choices between those values.

In the process of making such decisions the independence of the judiciary will continue to manifest itself individually, unless the future of appellate judging in America differs markedly from the past. Personal skills of persuasion and expression can affect the content of a decision and can give an opinion a more secure place in history. The influence of a person in a leadership position at a given time can make subtle alterations in the course of legal development, as in the cases of Marshall, Warren, and Rehnquist. Appellate judicial decision-making is small-group decision-making; the process makes heavy use of the written opinions of individual judges in the past; judges are insulated to an important extent from outside pressures, although never immune from them. In that context individual presences will continue to make themselves felt. The judges in this study upon whom one might wish to confer the label of greatness were more than simply suited to their times or to the dictates of their office. They gave a new dimension to judging in America, stretching its meaning a little to accommodate their own convictions.

Yet the intellectual options of individual judges will remain limited by time and place. Influence in an American appellate judge has not been solely a product of the force of personality; it has required a certain conformity to currently acceptable standards of institutional performance. Marshall could not have advanced the theory that judges openly "made" law and retained his intellectual respectability. Conversely, no justice on the Warren Court could have seriously maintained, with Kent, that the judiciary's primary function was that of a buffer against democratic excesses. The tolerated limits on judicial use of power have varied over time, but a rough conformity to the predominantly accepted limit has been essential. Although one may not be able to discern in advance the boundaries of respectability, they nonetheless exist.

Finally, a mode of minimally acceptable professional competence has followed the judiciary through time, despite changes in the styles and forms of opinions.[3] Oracular and mechanical jurisprudence have given way to various twentieth-century theories, but analytical soundness, intelligibility, and rationality have been continuously associated with competent judging. These minimum requirements have been transcended in the great appellate opinions of American history, opinions in which judging has resembled high art and statecraft; yet they have thus far not been abandoned. They will remain in the future unless the appellate judiciary adopts an approach in which institutional power utterly replaces rational analysis, the euphemism becomes the sole means of communication, and the tension between independence and accountability accordingly evaporates. At that point the American judicial tradition will have lost its meaning.

Appendix

Chronology of Judicial Service

Note: This Chronology includes lower court service only for certain Supreme Court Justices.

John Marshall	1801–35
James Kent	1798–1823
Joseph Story	1811–45
Lemuel Shaw	1830–60
Roger Taney	1836–64
Thomas Cooley	1865–85
Charles Doe	1859–74, 1876–96
John Harlan I	1877–1911
Oliver Wendell Holmes	1882–1902 (Supreme Court of Massachusetts) 1902–32 (U.S. Supreme Court)
Louis Brandeis	1916–39
Charles Evans Hughes	1910–16 (Associate Justice, U.S. Supreme Court) 1930–41 (Chief Justice, U.S. Supreme Court)
Harlan Fiske Stone	1925–46
Robert Jackson	1941–54

Benjamin Cardozo	1914–32 (New York Court of Appeals) 1932–38 (U.S. Supreme Court)
Learned Hand	1909–23 (U.S. District Court for the Southern District of New York) 1923–61 (U.S. Court of Appeals for the Second Circuit)
Jerome Frank	1941–57
Roger Traynor	1940–70
Felix Frankfurter	1939–62
Hugo Black	1937–71
Earl Warren	1953–69
John Harlan II	1955–71
William O. Douglas	1939–75
Warren Burger	1969–86
Potter Stewart	1957–80
Lewis Powell	1971–86
William Brennan	1956–1990
Byron White	1962–1993
Thurgood Marshall	1967–1991
Harry Blackmun	1967–1992
William Rehnquist	1971–86 (Associate Justice) 1986–2005 (Chief Justice)
Sandra Day O'Connor	1980–2005
John Paul Stevens	1975–
Antonin Scalia	1986–
Anthony Kennedy	1987–
Paird Souter	1990–
Clarence Thomas	1991–
Ruth Bader Ginsberg	1992–
Stephen Breyer	1993–

Notes

PREFACE TO THE THIRD EDITION

1. "[A]ny idea that has been in the world for twenty years and has not perished has become a platitude although it was a revelation twenty years ago." O. W. Holmes, Jr., introduction to J. H. Wigmore and A. Kocourek, *Rational Basis of Legal Institutions*, 11 Modern Legal Philosophy Series 30 (1923).
2. On the distorted historiography of the "Four Horsemen," see G. E. White, *The Constitution and the New Deal* 3, 297 (2000); Barry Cushman, "The Secret Lives of the Four Horsemen," 83 Va. L. Rev. 559 (1997). The best overview of revisionist scholarship on late-nineteenth-century constitutional jurisprudence is Charles W. McCurdy, "The Liberty of Contract Regime in American Law," in Harry Scheiber, ed., *The State and Freedom of Contract* 161–97 (1998). The revisionist work on late-nineteenth- and early-twentieth-century constitutional history is of a piece in its dissolution of the anachronistic political categories employed by mid-twentieth-century historians to describe judicial perspectives in those periods. For more detail, see White, *The Constitution and the New Deal*, 13–32.
3. See the bibliographical essay.
4. The chapter on Kent, Story, and Shaw is organized around a distinction between "static" and "dynamic" conceptions of property rights that originated in the work of Willard Hurst. See Hurst, *Law and the Conditions of Freedom in United States History* (1956); M. Horwitz, *the Transformation of American Law* 31 (1977);

L. Friedman, *A History of American Law* 235–36 (2d ed. 1985). As Charles McCurdy has put it, Hurst's approach assumed that "[t]he idea of progress permeated the legal system; as a result, whole domains of law tended to favor 'dynamic rather than static property, property in motion or at risk rather than property secure and at rest.'" McCurdy's work on New York law and politics in the years between 1839 and 1865 demonstrates that Hurst's conceptualization may well be anachronistic. See C. W. McCurdy, *The Anti-Rent Era* xiv (2001).

5. *Osborn v. Bank of the United States*, 9 Wheat. 738, 866 (1824).
6. See chapter 6.
7. See G. E. White, *The Marshall Court and Cultural Change* 656–73 (1988).
8. For a fuller discussion of changing attitudes toward the locus of causal agency in the late nineteenth and early twentieth centuries, see White, *The Constitution and the New Deal*, supra note 2, at 5–10.
9. For more detail, see id. at 193–97, 205–10.
10. For more detail, see id. at 246–53.
11. For more detail on the transformation of American constitutional theory in the late nineteenth century, and on the relationship of the concept of a "countermajoritarian difficulty" to that transformation, see White, "The Arrival of History in Constitutional Scholarship," 88 Va. L. Rev. 488, 526–41 (2002).
12. 304 U.S. 144 (1938).
13. See the essays in V. Blasi, *The Burger Court* (1983). The phrase "rootless activism" was Blasi's: see id. at 217.
14. For discussions of the originalism of Justices Scalia and Thomas, see R. A. Rossum, "Text and Tradition: The Originalist Jurisprudence of Antonin Scalia," and M. A. Graber, "Clarence Thomas and the Perils of Amateur History," in E. M. Maltz, *Rehnquist Justice* 46–57, 87–90 (2003).
15. 505 U.S. 833 (1992).

INTRODUCTION

1. R. Pound, *The Formative Era of American Law* 82 (1938).

CHAPTER I

1. See generally R. Ellis, *The Jeffersonian Crisis* 5–6 (1971). On Massachusetts, see Nelson, "The Legal Restraint of Power in Pre-Revolutionary America," 18 Am. J. Legal Hist. 1 (1974).
2. Nelson, *supra* n: 1 at 13–26. See generally W. Nelson, *Americanization of the Common Law* (1975).
3. See J. Goebel, 1 *History of the Supreme Court of the United States: Antecedents and Beginnings to 1801* 662–793 (1971); E. Corwin, *John Marshall and the Constitution* 15–24 (1919).

4. Corwin, *supra* n.3 at 20–23.
5. The Judiciary Act of February, 1801 reduced the Court to five members. Thomas Jefferson, on assuming the Presidency in March of that year, resolved to repeal the Act, and succeeded in 1802. The new Act postponed the opening of the Supreme Court until February 1803 and increased the size of the Court to six.
6. 2 Dall. 419 (1793).
7. For the political overtones of judicial activity in this period, see R. Ellis, *supra* n.1. See generally Wheeler, "Extrajudicial Activities of the Early Supreme Court," 1973 Sup. Ct. Rev. 123.
8. Quoted in Corwin, *supra* n.3 at 23–24.
9. 1 Cranch 137 (1803).
10. 4 A. Beveridge, *The Life of John Marshall* 321 (4 vols., 1919). At one time in the writing of his biography, Beveridge was given to serious doubts about Marshall's character. His preliminary research into the Marshall family's purchase of portions of the Fairfax Estate in the Northern Neck region of Virginia, described below, suggested that Marshall may have had a conflict of interest in the cases of *Fairfax's Devisee v. Hunter's Lessee,* 7 Cranch 625 (1813) and *Martin v. Hunter's Lessee,* 1 Wheat. 317 (1816), which grew out of a controversy over the disposition of title to sections of that estate. At one time Beveridge wrote Edward Corwin that he suspected that Marshall had done "some crooked work" in connection with the cases. Beveridge to Corwin, March 12, 1919, quoted in J. Braeman, *Albert J. Beveridge* 264 (1971). Subsequent research revealed for Beveridge that Marshall had no financial interest in the sections of the estate whose ownership was under dispute. See Braeman at 264–65.

    Marshall continued to maintain an interest in the disposition of *Martin v. Hunter's Lessee* after that care was brought to the Supreme Court of the United States in 1816. Although Marshall had officially recused himself from participating in *Martin,* he actually drafted the petition for a writ of error that was presented to the Court after the Virginia Court of Appeals ruled against Marshall's side in the litigation. Constructing the petition was difficult because the Virginia Court of appeals had not made an official record of its decision. Marshall apparently self that the petition's drafting was too delicate a matter to be left to the attorneys representing his side. For the details of Marshall's intervention, which he kept secret, see G. E. White, *The Marshall Court and Cultural Change* 165–173 (1988).
11. Quoted in Corwin, *supra* n.3 at 223.
12. William Wirt, in W. Wirt, *The Letters of the British Spy* 110 (1831).
13. 2 Beveridge, *supra* n.10 at 168.
14. Quoted in 3 J. Dillon, *John Marshall* 363 (1903).
15. 2 Beveridge, *supra* n.10 at 194, 177.
16. Wirt, *supra* n.12 at 112.

17. Charles Campbell, quoted in L. Baker, *John Marshall* 709 (1974).
18. F. Gilmer, *Sketches, Essays and Translations* 23 (1828); 3 F. La Rochefoucauld-Liancourt, *Travels Through the United States of North America* 120 (4 vols., 1800).
19. Marshall notebook, Library of Congress.
20. 2 Beveridge, *supra* n.10 at 180.
21. Quoted in Corwin, *supra* n.3 at 116.
22. Wirt, *supra* n.12 at 113.
23. Rutherford B. Hayes reported hearing this anecdote from Story while a law student in one of Story's classes at Harvard. See C. Williams, 1 *Diary and Letters of Rutherford Birchard Hayes* 116 (5 vols., 1922).
24. La Rochefoucauld-Liancourt, *supra* n.18 at 347.
25. See generally Corwin, *supra* n.3 at 198–99.
26. 2 C. Warren, *The Supreme Court in United States History* 273n (3 vols., 1922).
27. Federal Judicial Center, *Report of the Study Group on the Caseload of the Supreme Court* A7 (1972). It is difficult, however, to make meaningful comparisons between the output of opinions produced by the Court in the nineteenth century and that of twentieth-century Courts. Prior to the second decade of the twentieth century, Court opinions, once assigned to a Justice, were not circulated among the Justices prior to being delivered and published. This made it much easier for opinions to be issued, and made it possible for an individual Justice to with a good many opinions in a term if he were so inclined.
28. 3 Beveridge, *supra* n.10 at 239–41.
29. 3 Beveridge, *supra* n.10 at 226.
30. Id. at 227.
31. Two recent discussions of the ambivalent meaning of the term "sovereignty" in Revolutionary America are Kettner, "The Development of American Citizenship in the Revolutionary Era," 18 Am. J. Legal Hist. 208 (1974), and Reid, Book Review, N.Y.U. L. Rev. (1974).
32. See, e.g., *United States v. Wiltberger*, 5 Wheat. 76 (1820); *Meade v. Deputy Marshal*, 1 Brock. 324 (1815); *Fletcher v. Peck*, 6 Cranch 87 (1810).
33. See 2 J. Marshall, *The Life of George Washington* 447 (1803–5).
34. See, e.g., 2 Marshall, *supra* n. 33 at 68.
35. See generally R. Faulkner, *The Jurisprudence of John Marshall* 19ff. (1968).
36. See *Johnson and Graham's Lessee v. McIntosh*, 8 Wheat. 543, 591 (1823).
37. See generally 4 Beveridge, *supra* n.10 at 472–79; Faulkner, *supra* n.35 at 51.
38. *Fletcher v. Peck, supra* n.32 at 139.
39. 9 Wheat. 1 (1824).
40. 4 Wheat. 316 (1819).
41. 12 Wheat. 419 (1827).
42. *Gibbons v. Ogden, supra* n.39.
43. *Willson v. Black Bird Creek Marsh Co.,* 2 Pet. 245 (1829).

44. Initially by Chief Justice John Bannister Gibson of the Supreme Court of Pennsylvania in *Eaken v. Raub*, 12 Sergeant & Rawle 330, 347–48 (1825) (dissent).
45. See generally Goebel, *supra* n.3 at 338. It was not, however, a dominant one. See Nelson, "Changing Conceptions of Judicial Review," 120 U. Pa. L. Rev. 1166, 1168 (1972).
46. See generally G. Wood, *The Creation of the American Republic* (1969).
47. 3 Beveridge, *supra* n.10 at 585; see generally C. Magrath, *Yazoo* (1966).
48. This tactic was also employed by Marshall in *Marbury v. Madison*, where he used the occasion of confining the jurisdictional reach of the Court in a particular instance to assert a far broader judicial power in the abstract.
49. 6 Cranch at 133–34.
50. Id. at 135.
51. Id. at 137.
52. Id. at 139.
53. Jefferson to William Johnson, June 12, 1823, quoted in Baker, *supra* n.17 at 413.
54. E.g., 4 Beveridge, *supra* n.10 at 290.
55. 4 Wheat. at 405–06.
56. Id. at 406–07.
57. Id. at 408.
58. Id. at 421.
59. Id. at 426.
60. Id. at 436.
61. Quoted in 1 Warren, *supra* n.26 at 517.
62. See generally G. Gunther, *John Marshall's Defense of McCulloch v. Maryland* (1969).
63. See 2 Warren, *supra* n.26 at 72–80.
64. *Livingston v. Van Ingen*, 9 Johns. 507 (1812).
65. 9 Wheat. at 187–88.
66. Id. at 190–93.
67. Id. at 193–96.
68. Id. at 203–4, 205–6.
69. Id. at 221.
70. Id. at 272.
71. Quoted in 2 Warren, *supra* n.26 at 71–72.
72. Quoted in Corwin, *supra* n.3 at 124.

CHAPTER 2

1. *Osborn v. Bank*, 9 Wheat. 738, 866 (1824).
2. J. Horton, *James Kent: A Study in Conservatism* 55 (1939).
3. Harrison Gray Otis to Robert Goodloe Harper, April 19, 1807, quoted in 1 S. Morison, *Life and Letters of Harrison Gray Otis* 283 (2 vols., 1913).

4. Quoted in J. Loring, *The Hundred Boston Orators* 375–76 (1852).
5. See generally Horton, *supra* n.2 at 52–60.
6. James Kent to Moss Kent, Aug. 20, 1790, quoted in Horton, *supra* n.2 at 47.
7. See generally Horton, *supra* n.2 at 99–108.
8. See I. Browne, *Short Studies of Great Lawyers* 232 (1878).
9. See Roper, "Justice Smith Thompson: Politics and the New York Supreme Court in the Early Nineteenth Century," 51 N.-Y. Hist. Soc. Q. 128 (1967).
10. See Cassoday, "James Kent and Joseph Story, 12 Yale L. J. 146, 152 (1903).
11. Quoted in 1 W. W. Story, *Life and Letters of Joseph Story* 333 (2 vols., 1851).
12. G. Dunne, *Justice Joseph Story* 20 (1970).
13. Quoted in Dunne, *supra* n.12 at 33.
14. Story to Harrison Gray Otis, Dec. 27, 1818, quoted in 1 Morison, *supra* n.3 at 122–23.
15. Story to Ezekiel Bacon, Aug. 3, 1828, quoted on 1 Story, *supra* n.11 at 538.
16. G. Dunne, *supra* n.12 at 328.
17. See *Ramsay v. Allegre*, 12 Wheat, 611, 626–38 (1827) (Johnson, J., concurring); G. Dunne, *supra* n.12 at 263–65.
18. G. Dunne, *supra* n.12 at 364–65.
19. Henry Wheaton to Eliza Lyman, May 14, 1837, quoted in E. Baker, *Henry Wheaton* 131 (1937).
20. Quoted in 1 Story, *supra* n.11 at 185.
21. See generally L. Levy, *The Law of the Commonwealth and Chief Justice Shaw* 10–20 (1957).
22. "Memorandum," Shaw Papers, Massachusetts Historical Society, quoted in Levy, *supra* n.21 at 20.
23. See Levy, *supra* n.21 at 16.
24. Quoted in Levy, *supra* n.21 at 23, 20.
25. See generally F. Chase, *Lemuel Shaw* 275–85 (1918).
26. Shaw to Lemuel Shaw, Jr., March 5, 1853, quoted in Levy, *supra* n.21 at 27.
27. Quoted in Chase, *supra* n.25 at 286; quoted in Levy, *supra* n.21 at 27.
28. Shaw, "A Sketch of the Life and Character of the Hon. Isaac Parker," 9 Pick. 577 (1830), quoted in Levy, *supra* n.21 at 24.
29. See generally Horwitz, "The Emergence of an Instrumental Conception of American Law, 1780–1820," in D. Fleming and B. Bailyn, *Law in American History* 287 (1971).
30. R. Pound, *The Formative Era of American Law* 8 (1938).
31. John Dudley, quoted in D. Boorstin, *The Americans: The Colonial Experience* 201 (1958).
32. Kent to Thomas Washington, Oct. 6, 1828, quoted in Horton, *supra* n.2 at 154.
33. Erastus Root in N. Carter and W. Stone, *Reports of the Proceedings and Debates of the Convention of* 1821 616 (1821).

34. *Packard v. Richardson*, 17 Mass. 121 (1821).
35. Quoted in Horton, *supra* n.2 at 211.
36. Dunne, *supra* n.12 at 199, 200.
37. See 1 Story, *supra* n.11 at 283.
38. See Dunne, *supra* n.12 at 169.
39. Story to Henry Wheaton, April 11, 1816, quoted in Dunne, *supra* n.12 at 149.
40. Wheaton to Story, April 19, 1816, quoted in Dunne, *supra* n.12 at 149–50.
41. Quoted in P. Miller, *The Life of the Mind in America* 225 (1966).
42. Quoted in Miller, id.
43. J. Kent, 4 *Commentaries* 20 (1832).
44. Id. at 19.
45. Kent, 2 *Commentaries* 319–28 (1832).
46. See generally Kent, 2 *Commentaries* 338ff (1832).
47. *Livingston v. Van Ingen*, 9 Johns. 507 (1812).
48. E.g., *Croton Turnpike Co. v. Ryder*, 1 Johns. Ch. 611 (1815).
49. See generally Kent, 3 *Commentaries* 459 (1832).
50. Kent in Carter and Stone, *supra* n.33 at 221.
51. Kent, "The Law of Corporations," 1 Law Reporter 57, 58 (1838).
52. Kent, 2 *Commentaries* 271 (1832).
53. See generally Kent, 2 *Commentaries* 272ff. (1832).
54. Quoted in H. S. Commager, "Joseph Story," in *Gaspar Bacon Lectures on the Constitution of the United States* 33, 57 (1953).
55. Quoted in id. at 58.
56. Quoted in Miller, *supra* n.41 at 226.
57. *Wilkinson v. Leland*, 2 Pet. 627, 657 (1829).
58. *Dartmouth College v. Woodward*, 4 Wheat. 518 (1819); *Green v. Biddle*, 8 Wheat. 1 (1823).
59. *Society for the Propagation of the Gospel v. Wheeler*, 22 Fed. Cas. 756 (1814).
60. *Terrett v. Taylor*, 9 Cranch 43 (1815).
61. See generally L. Friedman, *A History of American Law* 174–75 (1973).
62. See generally Scheiber, "The Road to *Munn:* Eminent Domain and the Concept of Public Purpose in the State Courts," in Fleming and Bailyn, *supra* n.29 at 329.
63. 4 Wheat. at 638–40 (1819).
64. See generally A. Beveridge, 4 *John Marshall* 276–81 (4 vols., 1919).
65. 4 Wheat at 669–71, 708.
66. See J. Hurst, *Law and the Conditions of Freedom* 27, 66–70 (1964 ed.).
67. *Proprietors of the Charles River Bridge v. Proprietors of the Warren Bridge*, 11 Pet. 420 (1837).
68. Story to Mrs. Joseph Story, Feb. 14, 1837, quoted in 2 Story, *supra* n.11 at 268; Kent to Story, June 23, 1837, quoted in Horton, *supra* n.2 at 294.
69. 11 Pet. at 552.

70. *Hazen v. Essex Co.*, 12 Cush. 475, 477–78 (1853).
71. See Kent, 2 *Commentaries* 275 (1832).
72. 16 Pick. 512 (1835); 18 Pick. 472 (1836).
73. *Boston Water Power Co. v. Boston and Worcester R.R.*, 23 Pick. 360 (1839).
74. *Boston and Lowell Railroad v. Salem & Lowell Railroad*, 2 Gray 1 (1854).
75. Id. at 28.
76. *Inhabitants of Springfield v. Connecticut River R.R.*, 4 Cush. 63 (1849).
77. *Dodge v. County Commissioners of Essex*, 3 Metc. 380 (1841).
78. See, e.g., *Inhabitants of Worcester v. Western R.R.*, 4 Metc. 564 (1842); *Lexington & West Cambridge R.R. v. Fitchburg R.R.*, 14 Gray 266 (1859).
79. *Fisher v. McGirr*, 1 Gray 1 (1854); *Commonwealth v. Murphy*, 10 Gray 1 (1857); *Commonwealth v. Howe*, 13 Gray 26 (1859).
80. Shaw in *Commonwealth v. Alger*, 7 Cush. 53, 85 (1851).
81. Id. at 84–85.
82. *Davidson v. B & M R.R.*, 3 Cush. 91 (1849).
83. *Wellington v. Petitioners*, 16 Pick. 87 (1834).
84. *Commonwealth v. Blackington*, 24 Pick. 352 (1837).
85. *Commonwealth v. Farmers and Mechanics Bank*, 21 Pick. 542 (1839).
86. *Commonwealth v. Alger, supra* n.80.
87. *Commonwealth v. Howe, supra* n.79.
88. *Norway Plains Co. v. Boston & Me. R.R.*, 1 Gray 263, 267 (1854).
89. Id.
90. See generally *Wellington v. Petitioners, supra* n.83.
91. *Commonwealth v. Proprietors of New Bedford Bridge*, 2 Gray 339 (1854); *Commonwealth v. Essex Co.*, 13 Gray 239 (1859); *Central Bridge Corp. v. Lowell*, 15 Gray 106 (1860).
92. *Commonwealth v. Proprietors of New Bedford Bridge, supra* n.91.
93. *Commonwealth v. Essex Co., supra* n.91; *Central Bridge Co. v. Lowell, supra* n.91.
94. See Miller, *supra* n.41, at 148–55.
95. Quoted in Levy, *supra* n. 21 at 335.

CHAPTER 3

1. *Dred Scott v. Sandford*, 19 How. 393 (1857).
2. E.g., C. Swisher, *Roger B. Taney* 115 (1935); Harris, "Chief Justice Taney: Prophet of Reform and Reaction," 10 Vand. L. Rev. 227 (1957).
3. Quoted in D. Martin, *Trial of the Rev. Jacob Gruber* 43–44 (1819).
4. Swisher, *supra* n.2 at 94.
5. Quoted in id. at 154, 158.
6. John H. B. Latrobe, quoted in J. Semmes, *John H. B. Latrobe and His Times* 202 (1917).

7. Story to Charles Sumner, Jan. 25, 1837, quoted in 2 W. Story, *The Life and Letters of Joseph Story* 266 (1851).
8. Quoted in C. Fairman, *Mr. Justice Miller and the Supreme Court* 52 (1939).
9. See C. Swisher, *The Taney Period* 17 (1972).
10. *New York v. Miln*, 11 Pet. 102 (1837); *Briscoe v. Bank of the Commonwealth of Kentucky*, 11 Pet. 257 (1837).
11. *Proprietors of the Charles River Bridge v. Proprietors of the Warren Bridge*, 11 Pet. 420 (1837).
12. Taney to Andrew Jackson, Aug. 5, 1833 in 5 J. Bassett, *Correspondence of Andrew Jackson* 147 (7 vols., 1926–35).
13. *Dred Scott v. Sandford, supra* n.1.
14. See Swisher, *supra* n.2 at 571–72.
15. C. Warren, 2 *The Supreme Court in United States History* 250 (1922).
16. 11 Pet. at 547–48.
17. *Philadelphia, W & B R.R. v. Maryland*, 10 How. 376 (1850); *Ohio Life Ins. Co. v. Debolt*, 16 How. 416 (1854).
18. *West River Bridge Co. v. Dix*, 6 How. 507 (1848).
19. *Bronson v. Kinzie*, 1 How. 311 (1843).
20. *State Bank of Ohio v. Knoop*, 16 How. 369 (1854).
21. 9 Wheat. 1 (1824).
22. *Supra*, n.10.
23. 5 How. 504 (1847).
24. *The Passenger Cases*, 7 How. 283, 464 (1849) (dissent).
25. *Pennsylvania v. Wheeling and Belmont Bridge Co.*, 13 How. 518, 627 (1852) (dissent).
26. *Almy v. California*, 24 How. 169 (1861).
27. *Cook v. Moffat*, 5 How. 295 (1847).
28. *Prevost v. Greneaux*, 19 How. 1 (1857).
29. *Propeller Genesee Chief v. Fitzbugh*, 12 How. 443 (1852).
30. *Swift v. Tyson*, 16 Pet. 1 (1842).
31. *Louisville, C & C R.R. v. Letson*, 2 How. 497 (1844).
32. See *Ohio Life Ins. Co. v. Debolt, supra* n.17; *State Bank of Ohio v. Knoop, supra* n.20.
33. *Bank of Augusta v. Earle*, 13 Pet. 519 (1839).
34. *Bronson v. Kinzie, supra* n.19.
35. *Ohio Life Ins. Co. v. Debolt, supra* n.17 at 428.
36. *Ableman v. Booth*, 21 How. 506, 521 (1859).
37. Id.
38. *Luther v. Borden*, 7 How. 1 (1849).
39. *Kennett v. Chambers*, 14 How. 38 (1852).
40. *Rhode Island v. Massachusetts*, 12 Pet. 657, 752 (1838) (dissent).
41. *United States v. Ferreira*, 13 How. 40 (1852).

42. *Gordon v. United States*, 2 Wall. 561 (1864); Taney's opinion was reported in 117 U.S. 697 (1886).
43. 16 Pet. 1 (1842).
44. J. Wallace, *The Want of Uniformity in the Commercial Law between the Different States of Our Union* 27 (1851).
45. 15 Pet. 449 (1841).
46. 15 Pet. at 503ff. See generally 2 Warren, *supra* n.15 at 346.
47. 16 Pet. 539 (1842).
48. Andrew P. Butler of South Carolina, quoted in 2 Warren, *supra* n.15 at 497.
49. See 2 Warren, *supra* n.15 at 498.
50. 10 How. 82 (1850).
51. See generally 3 Warren, *supra* n.15 at 5–6.
52. 5 J. Richardson, *A Compilation of the Messages and Papers of the Presidents* 431 (20 vols., 1917).
53. 19 How. at 404–7.
54. See 3 Warren, *supra* n.15 at 25.
55. 19 How. at 446–50.
56. See citations in 3 Warren, *supra* n.15 at 28–31.
57. Id. at 30.
58. Id. at 29.
59. Id. at 32.
60. *New York Tribune*, March 17, 1857, quoted in id. at 41.
61. Timothy Farrar, "The Dred Scott Case," 85 North American Review (1857), quoted in id. at 38.
62. Taney to Franklin Pierce, Aug. 29, 1857, quoted in Swisher, *supra* n.1 at 518–19. The dispute between Taney and Curtis that led to Curtis's resignation illustrates the Court's then existing practice of not circulating opinions among the Justices. Curtis published his dissent in *Dred Scott* as a Boston newspaper before Taney's "opinion of the court" had been released. Taney took the occasion of the publication of Curtis's dissent to revise his opinion, and then declined to give Curtis access to it. A rule of the court required that opinions, once delivered in court (as Taney's had been) be filed with the Court's Clerk but Taney insisted that this did not mean anyone else, including Justices, could have access to them. For more detail on the episode, see Swishes, *supra* n.9, at 632–637.
63. See generally Swisher, *supra* n.2 at 571–72.

CHAPTER 4

1. See Jones, "Thomas M. Cooley and the Michigan Supreme Court: 1865–1885," 10 Am. J. Legal Hist. 97 (1966).
2. See Horwitz, "The Emergence of an Instrumental Conception of American Law," in D. Fleming and B. Bailyn, eds., *Law in American History* 287 (1971);

Nelson, "The Impact of the Antislavery Movement Upon Styles of Judicial Reasoning in Nineteenth Century America," 87 Harv. L. Rev. 513 (1974); White, "From Sociological Jurisprudence to Realism," 58 Va. L. Rev. 999 (1972).

3. See generally E. Kirkland, *Business in the Gilded Age* (1952); R. Wiebe, *The Search for Order* (1967).
4. H. Hutchins, "Thomas McIntyre Cooley," in 7 W. Lewis, *Great American Lawyers* 440 (8 vols., 1909).
5. Hutchins in Lewis, *supra* n.4 at 444.
6. Id. at 455.
7. Vander Velde, "Thomas McIntyre Cooley," in E. Babst and L. Vander Velde, *Michigan and the Cleveland Era* 92 (1948).
8. See Cooley, "The Next Half-Century," *Michigan Expositor*, April 8, 1851.
9. B. Twiss, *Lawyers and the Constitution* 18 (1942). See also M. Bernstein, *Regulating Business by Independent Commission* (1955). My discussion of Cooley complements interpretations advanced in Jones, "Thomas M. Cooley and 'Laissez-Faire' Constitutionalism: A Reconsideration," 53 J. Am. Hist. 751 (1967), and Paludan, "Law and the Failure of Reconstruction: The Case of Thomas Cooley," 33 J. Hist. Ideas 597 (1972).
10. Two recent overviews of the Jacksonians are E. Pessen, *Jacksonian America* (1969), and F. Gattel, *Essays on Jacksonian America* (1970).
11. T. Cooley, *A Treatise on Constitutional Limitations* 355 (1868).
12. 20 Mich. 452 (1870).
13. See generally C. Goodrich, *Government Promotion of American Canals and Railroads 1800–1890* (1960).
14. Cooley, *supra* n.11 at 488ff.
15. *People v. Salem, supra* n.12 at 487.
16. See, e.g., *East Saginaw Manufacturing Co. v. City of East Saginaw*, 19 Mich. 259 (1869).
17. *Gale v. Kalamazoo*, 23 Mich. 344 (1871).
18. *Flint & Fentonville Plank Road Co. v. Woodbull*, 25 Mich. 99 (1872).
19. *Sutherland v. Governor*, 29 Mich. 320 (1874).
20. *Benjamin v. Manistee River Improvement Co.*, 42 Mich. 628 (1880).
21. *State of Michigan v. Iron Cliffs Co.*, 54 Mich. 350, 361 (1884).
22. Compare *Constitutional Limitations* 356 (1868):

    > When the government . . . interferes with the title to one's property . . . and its action is called in question as not in accordance with the law of the land, we are to test its validity by those principles of civil liberty and constitutional protection which have become established in our system of laws, and not generally by rules that pertain to forms of procedure merely.

    with *Weimer v. Bunbury*, 30 Mich. 201, 214 (1874):

> Administrative process of the customary sort is as much due process of law as judicial process. . . . To [hold otherwise] would be to give the judiciary a supremacy in the state and seriously to impair and impede the efficiency of executive action.

23. See Cooley, "Limits to State Control of Private Business," 1 Princeton Review 233 (1878).
24. See remarks of Charles A. Kent, quoted in 7 Lewis, *supra* n.4 at 483.
25. Judge John Dudley, quoted in D. Boorstin, *The Americans: The Colonial Experience* 201 (1958).
26. Doe to Wigmore, July 9, 1889 quoted in J. Reid, *Chief Justice* 176 (1967).
27. See generally Reid, *supra* n.26 at 82–84.
28. *Lisbon v. Lyman*, 49 N.H. 533, 602 (1870).
29. *Stebbins v. Lancashire Ins. Co.*, 59 N.H. 143 (1879).
30. *Lisbon v. Lyman, supra* n.28.
31. *Haverbill Iron Works v. Hale*, 64 N.H. 426 (1887).
32. *Darling v. Westmoreland*, 52 N.H. 401 (1872).
33. *State v. Pike*, 49 N.H. 399, 427 (1870) (dissent).
34. *Brown v. Collins*, 53 N.H. 442 (1873).
35. *Brown v. Bartlett*, 58 N.H. 511 (1879).
36. *Edgerly v. Barker*, 66 N.H. 434 (1891).
37. *Wooster v. Plymouth*, 62 N.H. 193 (1882).
38. *Opinion of the Justices*, 66 N.H. 629 (1891).
39. *Orr v. Quimby*, 54 N.H. 590, 640 (1874) (dissent).
40. *State v. U.S. & Canada Express Co.*, 60 N.H: 219, 246 (1880) (concurrence).
41. *Boston, Concord & Montreal Railroad v. State*, 60 N.H. 87 (1880).
42. Doe to John M. Shirley, undated, quoted in Reid, *supra* n.26 at 250.
43. *Dow v. Northern R.R.* 67 N.H. 1 (1886).
44. Doe to Shirley, quoted in Reid, *supra* n.26 at 263.

CHAPTER 5

1. In *Adamson v. California*, 332 U.S. 46, 62 (1947).
2. Watt and Orlikoff, "The Coming Vindication of Mr. Justice Harlan," 44 Ill. L. Rev. 13 (1949).
3. *New York Times*, May 23, 1954, §4, p. 10E, cols. 1, 2.
4. See A. Dunham and P. Kurland, *Mr. Justice* (1964).
5. See Blaustein and Mersky, "Rating Supreme Court Justices," 58 A.B.A.J. 1183 (1972).
6. That characterization of Harlan has been attributed to Justice David P. Brewer. See, e.g., Waite, "How 'Eccentric' Was Mr. Justice Harlan?" 37 Minn. L. Rev. 173, 181 (1953).

7. 16 Wall. 36 (1873).
8. 94 U.S. 113 (1877).
9. 109 U.S. 3 (1883).
10. 118 U.S. 557 (1886).
11. Harlan, "Address," 134 U.S. 751, 755 (1890).
12. For newspaper accounts of these speeches, see Hartz, "John M. Harlan in Kentucky," 14 Filson Club Hist. Q. 17 (1940). Harlan's reference to the Reconstruction Amendments is quoted at 31.
13. Quoted in id. at 34.
14. Quoted in id. at 39.
15. Harlan, "The Know-Nothing Organization," reprinted in 46 Ky. L. J. 321, 332 (1958).
16. Malvina Shanklin Harlan, "Some Memories of a Long Life," reprinted in id. at 329.
17. Quoted in Westin, "John Marshall Harlan and the Constitutional Rights of Negroes," 66 Yale L. J. 637, 639n (1957).
18. Quoted in Hartz, *supra* n.3 at 34.
19. See, e.g., Civil Rights Cases, *supra* n.9 at 33–59.
20. See *Clyatt v. United States*, 197 U.S. 207, 222 (1905) (dissent). A possible exception is *Cumming v. Board of Education*, 175 U.S. 528 (1899), where Harlan, for the majority, sustained a Georgia state court's finding that Richmond County's failure to maintain a high school for blacks did not violate the equal protection clause of the Fourteenth Amendment. *Cumming* needs to be read in its context. The black petitioners asked for an injunction closing the white high school in Richmond County; the Georgia court found only that injunctive relief was improper because the County Board of Education, in temporarily closing the black high school "for economic reasons," had not abused its discretion. Id. at 545. The precise question before the Supreme Court was whether the state court's action constituted "a clear and unmistakable disregard" of Fourteenth Amendment rights. Harlan held only that the state court's action did not, on its face, violate the Amendment. He expressly left open the question whether sanction of an affirmative refusal by the Richmond County Board to establish and maintain a black high school would violate the Fourteenth Amendment. *Cumming*, of course, appeared three years after *Plessy v. Ferguson*, in which "separate but equal" facilities were held to satisfy the equal protection clause. See discussion *infra*, text accompanying notes 88–92.
21. E.g., *United States v. Clark*, 96 U.S. 37, 44, 47 (1877) (dissent); *Standard Oil Co. v. U.S.*, 221 U.S. 1, 82 (1911) (dissent).
22. *Smyth v. Ames*, 169 U.S. 466, 527–28 (1898).
23. E.g., *Geer v. Connecticut*, 161 U.S. 519, 542 (1896) (dissent).
24. E.g., *Adair v. U.S.*, 208 U.S. 161 (1908).

25. *Atkin v. Kansas*, 191 U.S. 207, 223 (1903).
26. *Adair v. U.S.*, *supra* n.24 at 180.
27. Quoted in Abraham, "John Marshall Harlan," 41 Va. L. Rev. 871, 876 (1955).
28. White, "Proceedings on the Death of Mr. Justice Harlan," 222 U.S. xxvii (1912).
29. See *New York Sun*, May 21, 1895, p. 1, col. 7; *New York Tribune* May 21, 1895, p. 1, col. 5.
30. See Farrelly, "Harlan's Dissent in the *Pollock* Case," 24 S. Cal. L. Rev. 174, 179 (1951).
31. *Supra* n.21.
32. *U.S. v. American Tobacco Co.*, 221 U.S. 106 (1911).
33. *Northern Securities Co. v. U.S.*, 193 U.S. 197 (1904).
34. *Supra* n.21 at 104–5.
35. White, *supra* n.28 at xxvi.
36. A. Kelly and W. Harbison, *The American Constitution* 585 (1963).
37. G. Myers, *History of the Supreme Court* 678n (1912).
38. Westin in Dunham & Kurland, *supra* n.4 at 118, attributing characterization to "most commentators."
39. Westin, *supra* n.17 at 697.
40. M. Porter, "John Marshall Harlan and the Laissez-Faire Court," 1 (doctoral dissertation, University of Chicago, 1971).
41. Harlan to Augustus Willson, June 1, 1895, quoted in Westin, *supra* n.4 at 121.
42. Cf. R. Bremner, *From the Depths* (1956).
43. E.g., *Taylor v. Ypsilanti*, 105 U.S. 60 (1882); *Thompson v. Perrine*, 106 U.S. 589 (1883); *Brenham v. German-American Bank*, 144 U.S. 173, 189 (1892) (dissent).
44. E.g., *Stone v. Farmers' Loan & Trust Co.*, 116 U.S. 307, 337 (1886) (dissent).
45. *Plaquemines Tropical Fruit Co. v. Henderson*, 170 U.S. 511 (1898).
46. *Macon v. Atlantic Coast Line*, 215 U.S. 501, (511) (1910) (dissent); *Tennessee v. Union Planters' Bank*, 152 U.S. 454, 464 (1894) (dissent).
47. *Smyth v. Ames*, *supra* n.22.
48. E.g., *Hooper v. California*, 155 U.S. 648, 659 (1895) (dissent).
49. *County of Tipton v. Locomotive Works*, 103 U.S. 523 (1880); *Concord v. Robinson*, 121 U.S. 165 (1886).
50. *Mugler v. Kansas*, 123 U.S. 623 (1887); *Powell v. Pennsylvania*, 127 U.S. 678 (1888).
51. *Hennington v. Georgia*, 163 U.S. 299 (1896); *Lake Shore & Michigan South Ry. v. Ohio*, 173 U.S. 285 (1899); *Northern Pacific v. Dustin*, 142 U.S. 492, 509 (1892) (dissent).
52. *Adair v. U.S.*, *supra* n.24.
53. *Lochner v. New York*, 198 U.S. 45, 65 (1905) (dissent); *Atkin v. Kansas*, *supra* n.25.
54. *Standard Oil Co. v. U.S.*, *supra* n.21 at 83.
55. *Texas & Pacific Ry. Co. v. ICC*, 162 U.S. 197, 239 (1896) (dissent); *ICC v. Alabama Midland Ry. Co.*, 168 U.S. 144, 176 (1897) (dissent); *Harriman v. ICC*, 211 U.S. 407, 423 (1908) (dissent).

56. *Standard Oil Co. v. U.S.*, *supra* n.21 at 82 (dissent).
57. *U.S. v. E. C. Knight Co.*, 156 U.S. 1, 18 (1895).
58. *Pollock v. Farmers' Loan & Trust Co.*, 157 U.S. 429, 652 (1895) (dissent).
59. Harlan to Augustus Willson, June 1, 1895, quoted in Westin, *supra* n.4 at 121.
60. Harlan to Willson, Dec. 1, 1905, quoted in id. at 120.
61. *International Postal Supply Co. v. Bruce*, 194 U.S. 601, 606 (1904) (dissent).
62. *Adair v. U.S.*, *supra* n.24.
63. *Lochner v. New York*, *supra* n.53.
64. See cases cited at n.43 *supra.*
65. E.g., *Galveston, Harrisburg & San Antonio Ry. Co. v. Texas* (Texas Gross Receipts Tax Case), 210 U.S. 217, 228 (1908) (dissent).
66. Cf. O. W. Holmes, "The Path of the Law," in *Collected Legal Papers* 184 (1920).
67. *Supra* n.9 at 53.
68. E.g., *Murray v. Louisiana*, 163 U.S. 101 (1896); *Thomas v. Texas*, 212 U.S. 278 (1909).
69. *Strauder v. West Virginia*, 100 U.S. 303 (1880).
70. *Virginia v. Rives*, 100 U.S. 313 (1880).
71. *Ex parte* Virginia, 100 U.S. 339 (1880).
72. *Neal v. Delaware*, 103 U.S. 370 (1881). See also *Cumming v. Board of Education*, *supra* n.20.
73. *Bush v. Kentucky*, 107 U.S. 110 (1883); *Williams v. Mississippi*, 170 U.S. 213 (1898).
74. *Carter v. Texas*, 177 U.S. 442 (1900); *Rogers v. Alabama*, 192 U.S. 226 (1994).
75. *Smith v. Mississippi*, 162 U.S. 592 (1896); *Brownfield v. South Carolina*, 189 U.S. 426 (1903); *Thomas v. Texas*, *supra* n.68.
76. *In re* Wood, 140 U.S. 278 (1891); *Gibson v. Mississippi*, 162 U.S. 565 (1896).
77. 110 U.S. 651 (1884).
78. 190 U.S. 127 (1903).
79. 189 U.S. 475 (1903).
80. Id. at 493, 503–4.
81. *Clyatt v. U.S.*, *supra* n.20 (dissent).
82. *Hodges v. U.S.*, 203 U.S. 1, 20 (1906) (dissent).
83. *Bailey v. Alabama*, 211 U.S. 452, 455 (1908) (dissent).
84. *Robertson v. Baldwin*, 165 U.S. 275, 288 (1897) (dissent).
85. Id. at 301. Italics in original.
86. *Bailey v. Alabama*, 219 U.S. 219 (1911).
87. *Supra* n.9 at 47.
88. 133 U.S. 587 (1890).
89. *Hall v. DeCuir*, 95 U.S. 485 (1878).
90. *Supra* n.88 at 594–95.
91. 163 U.S. 537 (1896).
92. Id. at 560 (dissent).

93. See Westin, *supra* n.17 at 702.
94. Id. at 704–5.
95. *Elk v. Wilkins*, 112 U.S. 94, 110 (1884) (dissent).
96. *Baldwin v. Franks*, 120 U.S. 678, 694 (1887) (dissent).
97. *O'Neil v. Vermont*, 144 U.S. 323, 366, 370 (1892) (dissent).
98. *Hurtado v. California*, 110 U.S. 516, 538 (1884) (dissent); *Baldwin v. Kansas*, 129 U.S. 52, 57 (1889) (dissent); *O'Neil v. Vermont*, *supra* n.97; *Boln v. Nebraska*, 176 U.S. 83 (1900); *Maxwell v. Dow*, 176 U.S. 581, 605 (1900) (dissent); *Twining v. New Jersey*, 211 U.S. 78, 114 (1908) (dissent).
99. Brewer, "The Movement of Coercion," 1893 address before the New York State Bar Association, quoted in R. Gabriel, *The Course of American Democratic Thought* 233 (1940).

CHAPTER 6

1. Cf. C. Hughes, *The Supreme Court of the United States* 50 (1928). Hughes listed *Pollack v. Farmers Loan & Trust Co.*, invalidating the income tax, as a third such "wound." Id. at 53.
2. For an elaboration of this observation, see White, Book Review, 59 Va. L. Rev. 1130 (1973).

CHAPTER 7

1. See generally L. Hartz, *The Liberal Tradition in America* (1955).
2. The discussion to follow draws on insights in H. May, *The End of American Innocence* (1959); R. Wiebe, *The Search for Order* (1967), and P. Conkin, *The New Deal* (1967).
3. E.g., H. Laski, *Authority in the Modern State* (1919).
4. No effort is made here to deny the possibility of a divergence between the publicly expressed and the privately held views of supporters of either populism or progressivism. Both movements attracted persons from a variety of social and economic backgrounds, and various theories have been advanced as to their collective motivations for reform. Compare J. Chamberlain, *Farewell to Reform* (1932), with R. Hofstadter, *The Age of Reform* (1955), and G. Kolko, *The Triumph of Conservatism* (1963). In contrast to that of the New Dealers, the rhetoric of populists and progressives appears laden with moral appeals and visions of an idyllic society. For an expression of the contrasting tone taken by liberals, see T. Arnold, *The Symbols of Government* (1935). These different angles of vision may have reflected fundamentally different social perspectives. See H. Graham, *Encore for Reform: The Old Progressives and the New Deal* (1967).

5. For the late-nineteenth-century version of this view, see J. Sproat, *The Best Men* (1971). See generally White, "The Social Values of the Progressives: Some New Perspectives," 70 South Atlantic Quarterly 62 (1971).
6. See, e.g., Pound, "Mechanical Jurisprudence," 8 Colum. L. Rev. 605 (1908); Dodd, "Social Legislation and the Courts," 28 Pol. Sci. Q. 1 (1913).
7. Examples of the two schools in the period discussed are Pound, "The Theory of Judicial Decision," 36 Harv. L. Rev. 641, 802, 940 (1923); Oliphant, "A Return to Stare Decisis," 14 A.B.A.J. 71, 159 (1928). See generally White, "From Sociological Jurisprudence to Realism," 58 Va. L. Rev. 999 (1972).
8. E.g., R. Jackson, *The Struggle for Judicial Supremacy* 312 (1941): "Holmes and Brandeis have not only furnished the highest expression but they have been the very source and the intellectual leaders of recent liberalism in the United States."
9. See White, "The Rise and Fall of Justice Holmes," 39 U. Chi. L. Rev. 51, 56 (1971).
10. O. W. Holmes, Sr., 3 *The Complete Writings of Oliver Wendell Holmes* 59, 142 (13 vols., 1900).
11. William James, Oct. 2, 1869, quoted in R. Perry, 1 *The Thought and Character of William James* 307 (2 vols., 1935).
12. Holmes to Felix Frankfurter, June 26, 1928, in Holmes Collection, Harvard Law School.
13. Holmes, "Notes on Albert Dürer," 7 *Harvard Magazine* 41, 43–44 (October 1860).
14. Holmes, "The Path of the Law" (1896), reprinted in *Collected Legal Papers* 167, 172 (1920).
15. Holmes, "Law in Science and Science in Law" (1899), reprinted in id. at 210, 242.
16. See discussion of free-speech cases *infra*.
17. *Buck v. Bell*, 274 U.S. 200 (1927).
18. *Patsone v. Pennsylvania*, 232 U.S. 138 (1914).
19. Holmes to Harold Laski, in M. Howe, ed., 1 *Holmes-Laski Letters* 217 (2 vols., 1953).
20. Holmes, "Law in Science and Science in Law," *supra* n.15 at 239.
21. Id.
22. See Holmes to Harold Laski, January 13, 1923, in 1 Howe, ed., *supra* n.19, at 473–74.
23. Holmes to Sir Frederick Pollock, in M. Howe, ed., 2 *Holmes-Pollock Letters* 22 (2 vols., 1961).
24. Holmes to Pollock, in 1 Howe, ed., *supra* n.23 at 163.
25. Quoted in H. Pringle, 2 *The Life and Times of William Howard Taft* 969 (2 vols., 1939).
26. Charles G. Ross, *St. Louis Post-Dispatch*, quoted in I. Dillard, ed., *Mr. Justice Brandeis, Great American* 14 (1941).

27. Brandeis to Otto Wehle, March 12, 1876, in *Public Papers of Louis D. Brandeis*, U. Louisville Law School.
28. A. Mason, *Brandeis: A Free Man's Life* 42 (1946).
29. See id. at 103.
30. Brandeis to Charles Nagel, July 12, 1879, in *Public Papers*, *supra* n.27.
31. Brandeis to Amy Brandeis Wehle, Jan. 2, 1881, in id.
32. Brandeis to Alice Goldmark, quoted in Mason, *supra* n.28 at 75.
33. Testimony before the Committee of the Board of Aldermen in the Case and Management of Public Institutions, 3 *Report* 3631–32 (1874).
34. L. Brandeis, *Business—A Profession* 321 (1914).
35. See generally A. Link, *Wilson: The New Freedom* (1956).
36. Brandeis, "A Call to the Educated Jew," 1 *Menorah Journal* 15 (1915).
37. Brandeis to Alfred Brandeis, June 18, 1907 in *Public Papers*, *supra* n.27.
38. Brandeis, *Business—A Profession*, *supra* n.32, at liv–lvi.
39. Brandeis, "The Living Law," to Ill. L. Rev. 461, 465 (1916).
40. 244 U.S. 590 (1917).
41. Id. at 597, 600 (dissent).
42. Holmes wrote Laski that on one occasion he had told Brandeis that the latter was "letting partisanship disturb his judicial attitude." 1 M. Howe, ed., *supra* n.19 at 128.
43. *Duplex Co. v. Deering*, 254 U.S. 443, 479, 488 (1921) (dissent).
44. E.g., *In re* Jacobs, 98 N.Y. 98 (1885); *Millett v. People*, 117 Ill. 294 (1886); *Godcbarles v. Wigeman*, 113 Pa. 431 (1886).
45. *Powell v. Pennsylvania*, 127 U.S. 678, 687 (1888) (Field, J., dissenting); *Hooper v. California*, 155 U.S. 648, 659 (1895) (Harlan, Brewer, Jackson, JJ., dissenting); *Frishie v. United States*, 157 U.S. 160 (1895); *Allgeyer v. Louisiana*, 165 U.S. 578 (1897); *Holden v. Hardy*, 169 U.S. 366 (1898).
46. E.g., *Lochner v. New York*, 198 U.S. 45 (1905); *Adair v. United States*, 208 U.S. 161 (1968); *Adkins v. Children's Hospital*, 261 U.S. 525 (1923).
47. Theodore Roosevelt, *Autobiography* (1919), reprinted as *The Autobiography of Theodore Roosevelt* 334 (1958).
48. Pound, "Liberty of Contract," 18 Yale L. J. 454, 462 (1909).
49. Id. at 464.
50. 187 U.S. 606 (1903).
51. Id. at 608–9.
52. Holmes to Laski, in 1 Howe, ed., *supra* n.19 at 51.
53. Id. at 42.
54. Holmes, *Collected Legal Papers*, *supra* n.14 at 306.
55. *Lochner v. New York*, *supra* n.46 at 75 (dissent).
56. *Adair v. United States*, *supra* n.46 at 191 (dissent).
57. Holmes to Laski, in 1 Howe, ed., *supra* n.19 at 21.

58. 236 U.S. 1 (1915).
59. Id. at 26, 27 (dissent).
60. *Adams v. Tanner, supra* n.40.
61. *Truax v. Corrigan*, 257 U.S. 312, 354 (1922) (dissent).
62. *Burns Baking Co. v. Bryan*, 264 U.S. 504, 517 (1924) (dissent).
63. Brandeis, "The Anti-Bar Law," address before the Joint Committee on Liquor Law of the Massachusetts Legislature, Feb. 27, 1891, in *Public Papers, supra* n.27.
64. *Hamilton v. Kentucky Distilleries Co.*, 251 U.S. 146 (1919).
65. *Jacob Ruppert v. Caffey*, 251 U.S. 264 (1920).
66. *United States v. One Ford Coupe*, 272 U.S. 321 (1926).
67. *Lambert v. Yellowley*, 272 U.S. 581 (1926).
68. Holmes to Laski, in 1 Howe, ed., *supra* n.19 at 8.
69. *Abrams v. United States*, 250 U.S. 616, 630 (1919) (dissent).
70. Id.
71. 205 U.S. 454 (1907).
72. 236 U.S. 273 (1915).
73. 249 U.S. 47 (1919).
74. Id. at 52. For a discussion of the evolution of Holmes's views on the constitutional status of the free speech clause of the First Amendment between *Fox v. Washington* and *Schenck*, and between *Schenck* and *Abrams*, see G. E. White, *Justice Oliver Wardell Holmes: Law and the Innerself*, 413–436 (1993).
75. *Abrams v. U.S., supra* n.69 at 624 (dissent).
76. 251 U.S. 466 (1920).
77. Id. at 482 (dissent).
78. Id. at 482–83.
79. 252 U.S. 239, 253 (1920) (dissent).
80. 254 U.S. 325 (1920).
81. Quoted in Z. Chafee, *Free Speech in the United States* 290 (1941).
82. 268 U.S. 652 (1925).
83. Id. at 673 (dissent).
84. 274 U.S. 357 (1927).
85. Id. at 372, 379 (concurrence).
86. 283 U.S. 697 (1931).
87. Id. at 708.
88. 282 U.S. 251 (1931).
89. *Thomas v. Collins*, 323 U.S. 516 (1945).
90. See generally R. Cushman, "Clear and Present Danger in Free Speech Cases," in M. Konvitz and A. Murphy, *Essays in Political Theory* 311 (1948).
91. J. Frank, *Law and the Modern Mind* 253 (1930).
92. See generally Rogat, "Mr. Justice Holmes: A Dissenting Opinion," 15 Stan. L. Rev. 3, 254 (1963).

93. E.g., Mason, *supra* n.28 at 567: Brandeis's "stand in [cases involving] 'moral' issues" was "strangely out of key with his customary liberalism."

CHAPTER 8

1. See, e.g., G. Gunther, ed., *John Marshall's Defense of McCulloch v. Maryland* (1969).
2. Oliver Wendell Holmes to Sir Frederick Pollock, Sept. 24, 1910, in 1 *Holmes-Pollock Letters* 170 (M. Howe ed., 1961).
3. 18 Stat. 470.
4. F. Frankfurter and J. Landis, *The Business of the Supreme Court* 60 (1928).
5. Act of April 9, 1866, 14 Stat. 27; Act of April 20, 1871, 17 Stat. 13.
6. Act of Feb. 18, 1861, 12 Stat. 130.
7. Act of Feb. 25, 1889, 25 Stat. 693.
8. Act of Feb. 5, 1867, 14 Stat. 385; Act of March 3, 1885, 23 Stat. 437.
9. Act of June 1, 1872, 17 Stat. 196.
10. 26 Stat. 826.
11. Act of Feb. 13, 1925, 43 Stat. 936.
12. C. Hughes, *The Autobiographical Notes of Charles Evans Hughes* 164–65 (D. Danelski and J. Tulchin, eds., 1973). See generally H. Hart and H. Wechsler, *The Federal Courts and the Federal System*, 36–41 (2d ed., 1973).
13. Quoted in Putnam, "Recollections of Chief Justice Fuller," 22 Green Bag 526, 529 (1910).
14. Hughes to Merlo J. Pusey, May 15, 1946, quoted in 1 M. Pusey, *Charles Evans Hughes* 283 (1951).
15. Hughes, *supra* n.12 at 164.
16. See generally Dunham, "Mr. Chief Justice Stone," in A. Dunham and P. Kurland, eds., *Mr. Justice* (1964).
17. *Girouard v. United States*, 328 U.S. 61 (1946). The earlier case which the *Girouard* majority disapproved was *United States v. Macintosh*, 283 U.S. 605 (1931).
18. Mary Connelly Hughes to Charles Evans Hughes, quoted in 1 Pusey, *supra* n. 14 at 39.
19. McElwain, "The Business of the Supreme Court as Conducted by Chief Justice Hughes," 63 Harv. L. Rev. 5, 6 (1949).
20. Id. at 9.
21. Id.
22. See generally S. Haber, *Efficiency and Uplift* (1964).
23. Chafee, "Charles Evans Hughes," 93 Proceedings of the American Philosophical Society 267, 279 (1949); Danelski and Tulchin in Hughes, *supra* n.12 at xv.
24. Quoted in 1 Pusey, *supra* n.14 at 377.
25. Quoted in B. Glad, *Charles Evans Hughes and the Illusions of Innocence* 121 (1966).
26. F. Frankfurter, in *Of Laws and Men* 147 (P. Elman, ed., 1956).

27. C. Hyde, "Charles Evans Hughes," in 10 S. Bemis, ed., *The American Secretaries of State and Their Diplomacy* 327–28 (1929).
28. Holmes to Pollock, June 12, 1916, in 1 *Holmes-Pollock Letters, supra* n.2 at 237.
29. *Proceedings of the Bar and Officers of the Supreme Court of the United States in Memory of Charles Evans Hughes* 127 (1950).
30. Frankfurter, *supra* n.26 at 147–48.
31. E.g., Hughes to Antoinette Carter Hughes, Aug. 8, 1894, Papers of Charles Evans Hughes, Library of Congress.
32. Quoted in Glad, *supra* n. 25 at 109.
33. Hughes, 9 *Proceedings of American Law Institute* 44, 49 (1931).
34. C. Hughes, *Addresses 1906–1916* 247 (1916).
35. In this vein Paul Freund's "unperceptive" and "unfriendly" critic who said that Hughes "possessed one of the finest minds of the eighteenth century" was perhaps not so blind, if unsympathetic. See Freund, "Mr. Justice Brandeis," in A. Dunham and P. Kurland, *supra* n.16 at 177.
36. *Minnesota v. Blasius*, 290 U.S. 1 (1933).
37. *Minnesota Rate Cases*, 230 U.S. 352 (1913); *Houston & Texas Ry. v. United States* (Shreveport Case), 234 U.S. 342 (1914).
38. *Schechter Corp. v. United States*, 295 U.S. 495 (1935).
39. *Crowell v. Benson*, 285 U.S. 22 (1931).
40. *St. Joseph Stock Yards Co. v. U.S.*, 298 U.S. 38 (1936).
41. *Bailey v. Alabama*, 219 U.S. 219 (1911); *Norris v. Alabama*, 294 U.S. 587 (1935); *United States v. Macintosh, supra* n.17.
42. *Stromberg v. California*, 283 U.S. 359 (1931); *Near v. Minnesota*, 283 U.S. 697 (1931).
43. *Minersville School District v. Gobitis*, 310 U.S. 586 (1940); *Cox v. New Hampshire*, 312 U.S. 569 (1941).
44. *St. Joseph Stock Yards Co. v. U.S., supra* n.40.
45. Hughes, Address to the Federal Judges of the Fourth Circuit at Asheville, N.C. (1932), quoted in 2 Pusey, *supra* n.14 at 693.
46. Id. quoted in 2 Pusey, *supra* n.14 at 691.
47. Stone, "The Tenement House Decision," quoted in A. Mason, *Harlan Fiske Stone* 117 (1956).
48. See Learned Hand to Harlan Fiske Stone, May 29, 1930, Stone Papers, Library of Congress.
49. Railroad Retirement Board v. Alton Railway Co., 295 U.S. 330 (1935).
50. United States v. Butler, 297 U.S. 1 (1936).
51. See, e.g., Charles Collier, "Judicial Bootstraps and the General Welfare Clause," 4 Geo. Wash. L. J. 211 (1936); Henry M. Hart, "Processing Taxes and Protective Tariffs," 49 Harv. L. Rev. 610 (1936).
52. For an overview of the events typically treated as constituting the Court-packing/"constitutional revolution" episode, see B. Cushman, *Rethinking the New*

Deal Court 11–23 (1998). The decisions conventionally identified as initiating the "revolution" are West Coast Hotel v. Parvish, 300 U.S. 379 (1937), upholding a Washington state minimum wage statute; five cases sustaining the constitutionality of the National Labor Relations Act, 301 U.S. 1, 49, 58, 102, and 142 (1937); and three cases upholding the Social Security Act, 301 U.S. 495, 548, and 601 (1937). The decision in *Parvish* was handed down on March 29, 1937; the National Labor Relations Act cases on April 12, and the Social Security cases on May 24. See Cushman, 18–22.

53. For illustrations of the "conventional account" or Court-packing and the "constitutional revolution," see G. E. White, *The Constitution and the New Deal* 16–20 (200).
54. Morehead v. New York ex rel Tipaldo, 298 U.S. 587 (1936).
55. Historians continue to debate the larger questions of historical causation raised by the shifts in the Court's constitutional jurisprudence in the late 1930s and early 1980s, particularly the question of how much judicially imposed changes in constitutional law are a reflection of external events. See Forum, The Debate over the Constitutional Revolution of 1937, 110 Am. Hist. Rev. 1046ff (articles by Alan Brinkley, Laura Kalman, William E. Leuchtenburg, and G. Edward White).
56. See the evidence collected in White, *The Constitution and the New Deal*, 33–163.
57. Cushman, *Rethinking the New Deal Court*, 45–105.
58. The Court's Conference on *Parvish* took place on December 19, 1936. The Court-packing plan was not announced until more than six weeks later, and its identity was kept secret until the last minute. See id., 45.
59. Freund, Book Review, 65 Harv. L. Rev. 370 (1951).
60. Quoted in Mason, *supra* n.47 at 789.
61. Stone to John Bassett Moore, May 17, 1932, Papers of Harlan Fiske Stone, Library of Congress.
62. See 2 H. Ickes, *The Secret Diary of Harold L. Ickes* 552 (1953).
63. C. Hughes, *The Supreme Court of the United States* 67 (1928).
64. 287 U.S. 45 (1932).
65. Attributed to Stone by Mason, *supra* n.47 at 488.
66. Unidentified Justice to Stone, quoted in id. at 794.
67. Hughes told Merlo Pusey that he felt that "every Justice should have a chance to demonstrate through the writeup of opinions the wide range of his reasoning powers and not be kept before the public as an extremist or specialist working in one particular groove." Hughes to Pusey, May 28, 1947, quoted in Pusey, "Charles Evans Hughes" in Dunham and Kurland, *supra* n.16 at 161.
68. Quoted in E. Gerhart, *America's Advocate* 165 (1958).
69. See, e.g., *United States v. Morgan*, 307 U.S. 183 (1939).

70. E.g., *South Carolina Highway Department v. Barnwell Bros.*, 303 U.S. 177 (1938); *United States v. Carolene Products Co.*, 304 U.S. 144 (1938); *Minersville School District v. Gobitis*, 310 U.S. 586 (1940).
71. See, e.g., *Bailey v. Alabama, supra* n.41; *Frank v. Mangrum*, 237 U.S. 309, 345 (1915) (dissent); *Stromberg v. California, supra.* n.42; *United States v. Macintosh, supra* n.42; *Near v. Minnesota, supra* n.42; *Brown v. Mississippi*, 297 U.S. 278 (1936); *Lomax v. Texas*, 313 U.S. 544 (1941).
72. Cf. Stone, "The Common Law in the United States," 50 Harv. L. Rev. 4, 25 (1936).
73. [N. Butler], *Annual Report of the President of Columbia University* 27–28 (1922).
74. Stone to John Bassett Moore, April 24, 1923, Stone Papers.
75. 201 N.Y. 271 (1911).
76. H. Stone, *Law and Its Administration* 152 (1915).
77. Quoted in Mason, *supra* n.47 at 116.
78. Stone, "Introduction," in T. Beale, ed., *Man versus the State* (1916), quoted in Mason, *supra* n.66 at 119.
79. Stone, *supra* n.76 at 43–44.
80. [Morris Cohen], Book Review, 11 New Republic 227 (1917).
81. Stone, "Some Aspects of the Problem of Law Simplification," 23 Colum. L. Rev. 319, 334 (1923).
82. Id. at 328.
83. Stone to Beryl H. Levy, Oct. 1, 1938, Stone Papers.
84. Stone, *supra* n.72 at 23.
85. E.g., *United States v. Classic*, 313 U.S. 299 (1941).
86. Cf. Dunham in A. Dunham and P. Kurland, *supra* n.16 at 242.
87. *South Carolina Highway Department v. Barnwell Bros., supra* n.70.
88. Stone, Address to Twelfth Annual Judicial Conference of the Fourth Circuit, June 19, 1942, quoted in Mason, *supra* n.47 at 591.
89. *Supra*, n.85.
90. 295 U.S. 45 (1935).
91. See Smith v. Allwright, 321 U.S. 649, 666, 669 (1944) (dissent).
92. See Mason, *supra* n.47 at 615–16.
93. *Supra* n.91 at 670 (dissent).
94. Stone to Hugo L. Black, Jan. 17, 1946, Stone Papers.
95. 327 U.S. 1 (1945).
96. 320 U.S. 81 (1943).
97. Id. at 100.
98. 323 U.S. 214 (1944).
99. 327 U.S. 304 (1946).
100. 323 U.S. 214, 242 (dissent).
101. Id. at 233 (dissent).

102. 327 U.S. 304, 322.
103. Stone to Black, Stone Papers, *supra* n.94.
104. *Viereck v. United States*, 318 U.S. 236 (1943); *Schneiderman v. United States*, 320 U.S. 118 (1943); *Baumgartner v. United States*, 322 U.S. 655 (1944); *Hartzel v. United States*, 322 U.S. 680 (1944); *Cramer v. United States*, 325 U.S. 1 (1945); *Keegan v. United States*, 325 U.S. 478 (1945).
105. Quoted in A. Mason, *supra* n.47 at 684.
106. *N.L.R.B. v. Fainblatt*, 306 U.S. 601 (1939); *N.L.R.B. v. Fansteel Metallurgical Co.*, 306 U.S. 240, 263 (1939) (partial concurrence).
107. 49 Stat. 449.
108. *Apex Hosiery Co. v. Leader*, 310 U.S. 469 (1940).
109. *Allen Bradley Co. v. Brotherhood of Electrical Workers*, 325 U.S. 797 (1945).
110. See generally Mason, *supra* n.47 at 131–38.
111. Quoted in id. at 401.
112. Stone to D. Lawrence Groner, Aug. 17, 1941, quoted in P. Fish, *The Politics of Federal Judicial Administration* 259 (1973).
113. Mason, *supra* n.47 at 791. Frankfurter privately referred to "the habit of Stone . . . of carrying on a running debate with any Justice who expresses views different from his," which Frankfurter felt produced "an inevitable dragging out of the discussion." Diary, Jan. 9, 1943, Frankfurter Papers, Library of Congress.
114. Quoted in Mason, *supra* n.47 at 792.
115. Stone to Joseph Strauss, May 5, 1937, Stone Papers.
116. Stone, "The Chief Justice," 27 A.B.A.J. 407, 408 (1941).
117. Quoted in Mason, *supra* n.47, at 591.
118. Quoted in id. at 769.
119. Quoted in id. at 627.
120. See, e.g., id. at 616.
121. *Mercoid Corp. v. Mid-Continent Investment Co.*, 320 U.S. 661, 672 (1944). By 1943 Frankfurter was referring to "the earlier days here when Black talked more freely to me." He complained to Jackson that "every time we have that which should be merely an intellectual difference [it] gets into a championship by Black of justice and right and decency and everything and those who take the other view are impliedly always made out to be the oppressors of the people and the supporters of some exploiting interest." Diary, January 30, 1943, *supra* n.118.
122. *Jewell Ridge Coal Corp. v. United Mine Workers of America*, 325 U.S. 161 (1945).
123. The details of the Roberts letter incident are described in chap. 11.
124. *Houston Post*, quoted in Mason, *supra* n.47 at 624.
125. Sears, "The Supreme Court and the New Deal—An Answer to Texas," 12 U. Chi. L. Rev. 140, 176 (1945).
126. Stone, *supra* n.116 at 408.

CHAPTER 9

1. See generally W. Twining, *Karl Llewellyn and the Realist Movement* (1973); E. Purcell, *The Crisis of Democratic Theory* (1973).
2. The relation of Process Jurisprudence to Realism is discussed in Ackerman, Book Review, 103 Daedalus 119 (1974), and White, "The Evolution of Reasoned Elaboration," 59 Va. L. Rev. 279 (1973). In the latter article I used the term "reasoned elaboration" primarily to denote an aspect of the general perspective I am now characterizing as Process Jurisprudence. "Reasoned elaboration" most accurately refers to an approach to the writing of judicial opinions; it is a particular canon of a larger "process" theory. But portions of my article suggested also that "reasoned elaboration" could be used to designate a school of jurisprudence. I now withdraw that suggestion.
3. The phrase was coined by Karl Llewellyn in "A Realistic Jurisprudence—The Next Step," 30 Colum. L. Rev. 431 (1930). For a fuller discussion of Realism see chap. 13.
4. Purcell, "American Jurisprudence Between the Wars," 75 Am. Hist. Rev. 424 (1969); White, *supra* n.2.
5. For examples see L. Fuller, *The Law in Quest of Itself* (1940); Fuller, "Reason and Fiat in Case Law," 59 Harv. L. Rev. 376 (1943); H. Hart and A. Sacks, *The Legal Process* (tent. ed., 1958).
6. Frankfurter, "Mr. Justice Jackson," 68 Harv. L. Rev. 937, 938 (1954).
7. *United States v. Women's Sportswear Mfg. Assn.*, 336 U.S. 460, 464 (1949).
8. A collection is found in E. Gerhart, *Lawyer's Judge* 121–38 (1961).
9. Jackson to Eugene C. Gerhart, Oct. 8, 1948, quoted in E. Gerhart, *America's Advocate* 36 (1958).
10. Quoted in id. at 62.
11. R. Jackson, "Reminiscences," Columbia University Oral History Project, quoted in Kurland, "Robert H. Jackson," 4 L. Friedman and F. Israel, *The Justices of the United States Supreme Court* 2543 (4 vols., 1969).
12. Quoted in Gerhart, *supra* n.9 at 63.
13. Quoted in Kurland, *supra* n.11 at.
14. Quoted in Gerhart, *supra* n.9 at 63.
15. Quoted in Gerhart, *supra* n.9 at 63.
16. Quoted in Kurland, *supra* n.11 at 2563.
17. Quoted in ibid.
18. H. Ickes, 3 *The Secret Diary of Harold L. Ickes* 267 (3 vols., 1954).
19. See generally Gerhart, *supra* n.9 at 229–31.
20. See Kurland, *supra* n.11 at 2547–48.
21. Quoted in Gerhart, *supra* n.9 at 41.
22. Gerhart, *supra* n.11 at 241.

23. Arthur Krock to Eugene Gerhart, May 7, 1949, quoted in Gerhart, *supra* n.11 at 242.
24. 315 U.S. 289 (1942).
25. *Tennessee Coal, Iron & R.R. Co. v. Muscoda Local 123*, 321 U.S. 590 (1944); *Jewell Ridge Coal Corp. v. United Mine Workers of America*, 325 U.S. 161 (1945).
26. The full text of the letter is quoted in A. Mason, *Harlan Fiske Stone* 765–66 (1956).
27. Hugo Black to Stanley Reed, Aug. 20, 1945, quoted in id. at 766.
28. Jackson to Stone, Sept. 8, 1945, Stone Papers, Library of Congress.
29. See A. Mason, *Harlan Fiske Stone* 768 (1956).
30. Id. at 769.
31. Stone to Jackson, March 1, 1946, Stone Papers.
32. Gerhart, *supra* n.9 at 280.
33. Jackson to Eugene C. Gerhart, Oct. 8, 1948, quoted in Gerhart, *supra* n.9 at 278.
34. Rodell, "Supreme Court Postcript," 10 Progressive 5 (May, 1946).
35. Jackson to Eugene C. Gerhart, Oct. 25, 1949, cited in Gerhart, *supra* n.9 at 493n–94n.
36. Gerhart, *supra* n.9 at 494n.
37. *Washington Evening Star*, May 16, 1946, p. 15.
38. *New York Times*, June 11, 1946, p. 2.
39. Id.
40. *Jordan v. DeGeorge* 341 U.S. 223, 241 (1951).
41. *Massachusetts v. United States*, 333 U.S. 611, 635, 639–40 (1948) (dissent).
42. 317 U.S. 111 (1942).
43. *Duckworth v. Arkansas*, 314 U.S. 390, 397, 400 (1941) (concurrence).
44. Id. at 401.
45. Id.
46. *McCarroll v. Dixie Greybound Lines, Inc.*, 309 U.S. 176, 183, 188–89 (1940) (dissent).
47. Id., at 189.
48. *H. P. Hood & Sons, Inc. v. DuMond*, 336 U.S. 525, 545, 554 (1949) (dissent).
49. R. Jackson, *The Supreme Court in the American System of Government* 66–67 (1955).
50. Id. at 67.
51. Id.
52. *Duckworth v. Arkansas, supra* n.43.
53. *H. P. Hood & Sons, Inc. v. Dumond, supra* n.48.
54. *Independent Warehouses Inc. v. Scheele*, 331 U.S. 70 (1947).
55. *Miller Bros. Co. v. Maryland*, 347 U.S. 340 (1954).
56. *General Trading Co. v. State Tax Comm'n*, 322 U.S. 335 (1944).
57. *State Tax Comm'n v. Aldrich*, 316 U.S. 174, 185 (1942) (dissent).
58. *H. P. Hood & Sons, Inc. v. DuMond, supra* n.48 at 533–34.
59. Jackson, *supra* n.49 at 67.

60. *West Virginia State Bd. of Educ. v. Barnette*, 319 U.S. 624, 638 (1943).
61. Id. at 640.
62. *Brinegar v. United States*, 338 U.S. 160, 180 (1949) (dissent).
63. *Harris v. United States*, 331 U.S. 145, 195 (1947) (dissent); *McDonald v. United States*, 335 U.S. 451, 457 (1948) (concurrence). But see *On Lee v. United States*, 343 U.S. 747 (1952).
64. *Saia v. New York*, 334 U.S. 558, 566 (1948) (dissent).
65. *Terminello v. Chicago*, 337 U.S. 1, 13 (1949) (dissent).
66. *Beauharnais v. Illinois*, 343 U.S. 250, 287 (1952) (dissent). Jackson's dissent in the case, in which an Illinois statute providing criminal penalties for slanderous remarks based on race was sustained as applied against a white resident of Chicago who had distributed racist leaflets, did not quarrel with the majority's holding that such forms of speech could be adjudged criminal offenses.
67. *Dennis v. United States*, 341 U.S. 494, 561 (1951) (concurrence).
68. *Watts v. Indiana*, 338 U.S. 49, 58 (1949) (concurrence).
69. *Brinegar v. United States, supra* n.62 at 183.
70. *Price v. Johnston*, 334 U.S. 266, 295, 301 (1948) (dissent).
71. *United States ex rel. Knauff v. Shaughnessy*, 338 U.S. 537, 550, 551 (1950) (dissent).
72. *Watts v. Indiana, supra* n.68 at 61–62.
73. See generally C. Pritchett, *Civil Liberties and the Vinson Court* (1954).
74. Jackson to Eugene C. Gerhart, Oct. 8, 1948, quoted in Gerhart, *supra* n.8 at 304.
75. Jackson, *supra* n.49 at 79.
76. Id. at 57–58.
77. *Jewell Ridge Coal Corp. v. United Mine Workers, supra* n.25 at 170 (dissent); *Wallace Corp. v. NLRB*, 323 U.S. 248, 257 (1944) (dissent); *Farmers Reservoir & Irrigation Co. v. McComb*, 337 U.S. 755, 770 (1949) (dissent).
78. With the exception of certain wartime cases involving persons of Japanese or German ancestry. See discussion above, chap. 10.
79. *Terminello v. Chicago, supra* n.65 at 37.
80. *State Tax Comm'n v. Aldrich, supra* n.57 at 185.
81. Stone to Sterling Carr, Dec. 4, 1945, Stone Papers.
82. See Gerhart, *supra* n.9 at 256–57.
83. Jackson, "The Rule of Law among Nations," 39 Am. Soc'y Int'l L. Proc. 10, 15–16 (1945).
84. 19 International Military Tribunal, *Trial of the Major War Criminals* 400, 415–17 (42 vols., 1947).
85. 2 id. at 155, 99.
86. 2 id. at 101, 155.
87. Jackson, Introduction, in W. Harris, *Tyranny on Trial* xxvii (1954).
88. 2 International Military Tribunal, *Trial of the Major War Criminals* 101.
89. E.g., Hart and Sacks, *supra* n.5.

CHAPTER 10

1. See generally E. Purcell, *The Crisis of Democratic Theory* (1973).
2. W. Twining, *Karl Llewellyn and the Realist Movement* 10–55 (1973); Purcell, *supra* n.1 at 3–11.
3. Examples are Pound, "The Scope and Purpose of Sociological Jurisprudence," 24 Harv. L. Rev. 591 (1911), and Pound, "The Theory of Judicial Decision," 36 Harv. L. Rev. 641, 802, 940 (1923).
4. A "representative" example of the multifaceted theory of judging articulated by Realists is more difficult to set forth. Articles illustrating various aspects of the theory are Moore, "Rational Basis of Legal Institutions," 23 Colum. L. Rev. 609 (1923); Cook, "Scientific Method and the Law," 13 A.B.A.J. 303 (1927); Llewellyn, "Realistic Jurisprudence—The Next Step," 30 Colum. L. Rev. 431 (1930); and Frank, "Realism in Jurisprudence," 7 Am. L. School Rev. 1063 (1934).
5. E.g., Bickel and Wellington, "Legislative Purpose and the Judicial Process: The *Lincoln Mills* Case," 71 Harv. L. Rev. 1 (1957); H. Hart and A. Sacks, *The Legal Process* (tent. ed., 1958); Wechsler, "Toward Neutral Principles of Constitutional Law," 73 Harv. L. Rev. 1 (1959).
6. Hutcheson, "The Judgment Intuitive: The Function of the 'Hunch' in Judicial Decision," 14 Corn. L. Q. 274 (1929).
7. Hart and Sacks, *supra* n.5 at 161ff; see above, chap. 11, n.2.
8. Hand's address was delivered on May 14, 1933. It has been reprinted in I. Dilliard, ed. *The Spirit of Liberty: Papers and Addresses of Learned Hand* 103 (1952). Hereafter cited as Hand, *Spirit of Liberty.*
9. Hand, *Spirit of Liberty, supra* n.8 at 178.
10. Among members of Cardozo's family was the author of the words on the base of the Statue of Liberty. See generally Kaufman, "Benjamin Nathan Cardozo," in A. Dunham and P. Kurland, eds., *Mr. Justice* 251 (1964).
11. G. Hellman, *Benjamin N. Cardozo* 10–11, 23 (1940); Kaufman, *supra* n.10 at 252.
12. Cardozo to Aline Goldstone, quoted in Hellman, *supra* n.11 at 49.
13. See Columbia College Yearbook, Cardozo Papers, Rare Book and Manuscript Library, Columbia University. Hereafter cited as Cardozo Papers.
14. Rabbi Stephen S. Wise, a close friend of Cardozo for many years, referred a year after Cardozo's death to "very, very intimate and personal letters exchanged between Cardozo and Ellen. Wise was uncertain whether the letters ought to be published. They are not included in the Cardozo Papers. Wise to George S. Hellman, Jan. 16, 1939, Cardozo Papers, id.
15. Lloyd Stryker, Wall Street Journal, July 12, 1938, Cardozo Papers.
16. Hand orally to Hellman, Nov. 15, 1938. A memorandum of the conversation is in the Cardozo Papers.

17. The comments, in order, are from Wise, New York Times, May 23, 1930; William Lyon Phelps to Hellman, Dec. 14, 1938, Cardozo Papers; Stryker, *supra* n.15; and Judge Ferdinand Pecora, Wall Street Journal, July 12, 1938, Cardozo Papers.
18. Hand to Hellman, *supra* n.16.
19. Kaufman, *supra* n.10, at 254.
20. Corbin, "The Judicial Process Revisited: Introduction," 71 Yale L. J. 195, 197 (1961).
21. See Cardozo, "The Altruist in Politics" (1889) and "Communism" (1889), Cardozo Papers.
22. Butler to Hellman, quoted in Hellman, *supra* n.11 at 21.
23. Hand to Hellman, *supra* n.16.
24. Memorandum, Cardozo Papers.
25. B. Cardozo, *The Nature of the Judicial Process* 28 (1921).
26. Id. at 35–36.
27. Cardozo borrowed this quote from Holmes's "Path of the Law." See id. at 54–55.
28. Id. at 96, 98.
29. Id. at 67.
30. See description in Corbin, *supra* n.20 at 197–98.
31. Kaufman, *supra* n.10 at 260.
32. Cardozo, *supra* n.25 at 105; B. Cardozo, *The Growth of the Law* 50 (1924).
33. B. Cardozo, *The Paradoxes of Legal Science* 135 (1928).
34. Id. at 59.
35. Cardozo, "Law and Literature," 52 Harv. L. Rev. 471, 477 (1939).
36. Cardozo, *supra* n.33 at 57.
37. Hand, "Mr. Justice Cardozo," in Hand, *supra* n.8 at 129, 131.
38. Hand, *supra* n.8 at 122.
39. Hand to Clark, Feb. 23, 1950, quoted in M. Schick, *Learned Hand's Court* 304 (1970).
40. Charles C. Burlingham, "Judge Learned Hand," 60 Harv. L. Rev. 330, 331 (1947).
41. Quoted in H. Shanks, ed., *The Art and Craft of Judging* 6 (1968).
42. Shanks, id. at 7–8.
43. Quoted in id. at 9.
44. Taft to Harding, Dec. 4, 1922, William Howard Taft Papers, Library of Congress.
45. See M. Freedman, *Roosevelt and Frankfurter* 671–76 (1967).
46. Quoted in Shanks, *supra* n.41 at 13.
47. The letter was reprinted in the *New York Times*, June 18, 1961.
48. See Chief Judge J. Edward Lumbard's remarks in 33 N.Y.S. B.J. 410 (1961).
49. Holmes to Frederick Pollock in 2 M. Howe, ed. *Holmes-Pollock Letters* 114 (1961).
50. Cardozo to Peter B. Olney, Feb. 7, 1925, reprinted in Learned Hand Centennial Exhibit, Harvard Law School, Sept. 5–Nov. 5, 1972, p. 7.

51. See A. Mason, *Harlan Fiske Stone* 335 (1956).
52. Hamburger, "The Great Judge," 21 Life 116 (Nov. 4, 1946).
53. Burlingham, "Judge Learned Hand," *supra* n.40 at 332.
54. "Proceedings in Commemoration of Fifty Years of Federal Judicial Service," 264 F. 2d 6, 20 (1959).
55. M. Schick, *supra* n.39 at 155.
56. Id. at 12n, 156.
57. See generally White, "The Rise and Fall of Justice Holmes," 39 U. Chi. L. Rev. 51 (1971).
58. Hand to Stone, February 6, 1934, quoted in Mason, *supra* n.51 at 384.
59. Quoted in Shanks, *supra* n.41 at 14.
60. Hand, *supra* n.8 at 101.
61. Id.
62. Id.
63. Id. at 181.
64. Id. at 109.
65. Id.
66. Id. at 174.
67. L. Hand, *The Bill of Rights* 26 (1958).
68. Hand, "A Plea for the Open Mind and Free Discussion," in I. Dilliard, *The Spirit of Liberty* 274 (1960 ed.).
69. Hand, *supra* n.8 at 180.
70. Hand, *supra* n.67, at 34.
71. Hand *supra* n.8, at 178.
72. Hand, "Proceedings," *supra* n.54, at 28.
73. Hand, *supra* n.68, at 278.
74. Hand, *supra* n.8, at 107.
75. Wyzanski, "Judge Learned Hand's Contributions to Public Law," 60 Harv. L. Rev. 348, 349 (1947).
76. Wyzanski, "Introduction," in L. Hand, *The Bill of Rights* viii (1964 ed.).
77. Hand, "Presentation to the Harvard Law School of a Portrait of Mr. Justice Holmes," quoted in Pepper, "The Literary Style of Learned Hand," 60 Harv. L. Rev. 333 (1947).
78. Hand, *supra* n.8 at 107.
79. Id. at 108.
80. Frank, "Some Reflections on Learned Hand," 24 U. Chi. L. Rev. 666, 668 (1957).
81. *United States v. Rubenstein*, 151 F.2d 915, 919, 920 (2d. Cir., 1945) (dissent).
82. Hand to Mrs. Jerome N. Frank, Jan. 20, 1957, quoted in Schick, *supra* n.39 at 245.
83. See comments by Rebecca West and others, quoted in id. at 34.
84. Clark, "Jerome N. Frank," 66 Yale L. J. 817, 818 (1957).

85. Frank, *supra* n.80 at 666.
86. Pound apparently first used the term in "The Need of a Sociological Jurisprudence," 19 Green Bag 607 (1907).
87. See, e.g., Hand, "The Speech of Justice," 29 Harv. L. Rev. 617 (1916); Pound, "The Theory of Judicial Decision," 36 Harv. L. Rev. 641, 802, 940 (1923).
88. *Supra* n.33 at 60.
89. Hutcheson, *supra* n.6.
90. J. Frank, *Law and the Modern Mind* 239 (1930).
91. See Llewellyn, "Some Realism about Realism," 44 Harv. L. Rev. 1222 (1931), an article identifying and describing leading Realists. Frank had contributed heavily to the article.
92. Cardozo, untitled address, 55 Report of the New York State Bar Association 263, 290 (1932).
93. Id. at 272.
94. Id. at 288–90.
95. Frank, "Cardozo and the Upper Court Myth," 13 Law & Contemp. Prob. 369, 384 (1948).
96. [Frank], "The Speech of Judges: A Dissenting Opinion," 29 Va. L. Rev. 625, 620–32 (1943).
97. Hand to Andrew Kaufman, quoted in Kaufman, *supra* n.10 at 253.
98. *Supra* n.96 at 634.
99. Id. at 636.
100. Id. at 634.
101. Id. at 637.
102. Professor Philip Kurland, who clerked for Frank during the 1944 term, has said in conversation that Frank subsequently regretted the anonymity of the essay. Walton Hamilton, in a eulogy of Frank in 1957, maintained that Frank had nonetheless told him that he "had a hell of a good time" writing the essay. See Hamilton, "The Great Tradition—Jerome Frank," 66 Yale L. J. 821, 822 (1957).
103. See Frank, *supra* n.80 at 672–74.
104. Professor Kurland has maintained that Frank "found it next to impossible to dislike anyone whom he got to know at all well." Kurland, "Jerome N. Frank: Some Reflections and Recollections of a Law Clerk," 24 U. Chi. L. Rev. 661, 663 (1957).
105. See generally Schick, *supra* n.39 at 219–23, and correspondence there cited.
106. Frank to Clark, June 1, 1950, quoted in id. at 219.
107. See, e.g., Yntema, "The Hornbook Method and the Conflict of Laws," 37 Yale L. J. 468 (1928); Moore and Hope, "An Institutional Approach to the Law of Commercial Banking," 38 Yale L. J. 703 (1929).
108. Llewellyn, *supra* n.4 at 444.
109. Frank, *supra* n.90 at 130.

110. Id. at 154.
111. Id. at 147.
112. Id. at 147n.
113. See Frank, "Realism in Jurisprudence," *supra* n.4.
114. See the debate between Hand and Frank in *Repouille v. United States*, 165 F.2d 152 (2d Cir., 1947), where an alien who had administered euthanasia to his monstrously deformed son was denied citizenship on the ground of his "moral character."
115. Frank, "Realism in Jurisprudence," *supra* n.4.
116. Seagle, Book Review, 29 Va. L. Rev. 664 (1943).
117. Lehman, "Judge Cardozo in the Court of Appeals," 52 Harv. L. Rev. 364, 371 (1939); Hand, "Mr. Justice Cardozo," 52 Harv. R. Rev. 361, 362 (1939).
118. *MacPherson v. Buick Motor Co.*, 217 N.Y. 382 (1916).
119. *Palsgraf v. Long Island R.R.*, 248 N.Y. 339 (1928).
120. See generally G. Calabresi, *The Cost of Accidents* (1970).
121. *Sundstrum v. State of New York*, 213 N.Y. 68 (1914); *Wood v. Lucy, Lady Duff-Gordon*, 222 N.Y. 88 (1917).
122. *DeCicco v. Schweizer*, 221 N.Y. 431 (1917); *Allegheny College v. National Chataugua County Bank*, 246 N.Y. 369 (1927).
123. *Helgar Corp. v. Warner's Features*, 222 N.Y. 449 (1918); *Holden v. Efficient Craftsman Corp.*, 234 N.Y. 437 (1923).
124. *Marks v. Cowden*, 226 N.Y. 138, 144 (1919): see *Imperator Realty Co. v. Tull*, 228 N.Y. 447, 453 (1920) (concurrence); *Saltzman v. Barson*, 239 N.Y. 332 (1925).
125. E.g., *DeCicco v. Schweizer, supra* n.122, where he enforced an informal promise without any consideration. This decision was reflected in the first edition of the Restatement of Contracts, § 90 (1932).
126. *Wood v. Lucy, Lady Duff-Gordon, supra* n.121 at 91.
127. *Winterbottom v. Wright*, 10 M. & W. 109 (1842).
128. 6 N.Y. 397 (1852).
129. *MacPherson v. Buick Motor Co., supra* n.118 at 385.
130. Id. at 386.
131. Id.
132. Id. at 387.
133. Id. at 385.
134. Id. at 387.
135. Brett, J. (Lord Esher) in *Heaven v. Pender*, 11 Q.B.D. 503, 510 (1883).
136. *MacPherson v. Buick Motor Co., supra* n.118 at 389–90.
137. Id. at 389.
138. Id. at 391.
139. Id. at 391.
140. *Torgeson v. Schultz*, 192 N.Y. 156 (1908).

141. Cardozo, *supra* n.25 at 165.
142. Hand, "The Speech of Justice," *supra* n.87.
143. Hand, *supra* n.8 at 109.
144. *Lehigh Valley Coal Co., v. Yensavage*, 218 F.547 (E.D. N.Y., 1914).
145. Hand, *supra* n.8 at 108: see *Borella v. Borden Co.*, 145 F.2d 63 (2d. Cir., 1944).
146. Hand, *supra* n.8 at 181.
147. E.g., *Massachusetts Fire & Marine Ins. Co. v. Commissioner*, 42 F.2d 189 (2d. Cir., 1930); *Niagara Falls Power Co. v. FPC*, 137 F.2d 787 (2d Cir., 1943).
148. Hand, *supra* n.8 at 109.
149. *Fleming v. Arsenal Building Corporation*, 125 F.2d 278 (2d. Cir., 1933); Borella v. Borden Co., *supra* n.142.
150. *Helvering v. Gregory*, 69 F.2d 809 (2d Cir., 1934).
151. *Cabell v. Markham*, 148 F.2d 737 (2d Cir., 1945).
152. *Peter Pan Fabrics, Inc. v. Martin Weiner Corp.*, 274 F.2d 487 (2d Cir., 1960).
153. E.g., *Yale Electric Corporµation v. Robertson*, 26 F.2d 972 (2d Cir., 1928); *American Chicle Co. v. Topps Chewing Gum, Inc.* 208 F.2d 560 (2d Cir., 1953).
154. E.g., *Masses Publishing Co. v. Patten*, 244 F.535 (S.D. N.Y., 1917); *United States v. Dennis*, 183 F.2d 201 (2d Cir., 1950).
155. Friendly, "Learned Hand: An Expression From the Second Circuit," 29 Brooklyn L. Rev. 6, 12 (1962).
156. Frank, "On Holding Abe Lincoln's Hat," in B. Kristein, ed., *A Man's Reach* 3, 7 (1965).
157. Frank, "Red, White and Blue Herring," 214 Saturday Evening Post 9 (Dec. 6, 1941); J. Frank, *If Men Were Angels* (1942).
158. E.g., "Cardozo and the Upper Court Myth," *supra* n.95; Frank, " 'Short of Sickness and Death': A Study of Moral Responsibility in Legal Criticism," 26 N.Y.U. L. Rev. 545 (1951).
159. See discussion in J. Frank, *Courts on Trial* 266–80 (1950).
160. For some Warren Court decisions illustrating this view, see *Mapp v. Ohio*, 367 U.S. 643 (1961); *Gideon v. Wainwright*, 372 U.S. 335 (1963); *Miranda v. Arizona*, 384 U.S. 436 (1966).
161. The first expansive reading of the guaranties of the Bill of Rights after World War II came in Justice Black's dissent in *Adamson v. California*, 332 U.S. 46, 68 (1947). No majority of the Warren Court ever adopted Justice Black's position that all of the Bill of Rights was incorporated into the due process clause of the Fourteenth Amendment. But Black's dissent set the stage for the "selective" incorporation of portions of the First, Fourth, Fifth, and Sixth Amendments in the 1950s and 1960s. The subject is considered in more detail in chap. 12.
162. E.g., *United States v. Eheling*, 146 F.2d 254, 257, 258 (2d Cir., 1944) (dissent).
163. Id. at 258.
164. *United States v. St. Pierre*, 132 F.2d 837, 840 (2d. Cir., 1942) (dissent).

165. *United States v. Mitchell*, 137 F.2d 1006, 1011 (2d Cir., 1943) (dissent).
166. *United States v. Ausmeier*, 152 F.2d 349, 356 (2d Cir., 1945).
167. *United States v. Liss*, 137 F.2d 995, 1001 (2d Cir., 1943) (dissent).
168. *United States v. Rubenstein*, 151 F.2d 915, 919, 924 (2d Cir., 1945) (dissent).
169. *United States v. Antonelli Fireworks Co., Inc.*, 155 F.2d 631, 642 (1946) (dissent).
170. *United States v. Leviton*, 193 F.2d 848, 857 (1951) (dissent.)
171. *In re* Fried, 161 F.2d 453, 457, 458–59 (2d Cir., 1947).
172. *United States v. Leviton, supra* n.170; *United States ex rel. Caminito v. Murphy*, 222 F.2d 698 (1955).
173. *United States v. Masciale*, 236 F.2d 601, 604 (2d Cir., 1956) (dissent).
174. *United States v. Scully*, 225 F.2d 113, 116 (2d Cir., 1955) (concurrence).
175. *United States v. Gordon*, 236 F.2d 916 (2d Cir., 1956).
176. *United States v. On Lee*, 193 F.2d 306, 311 (2d Cir., 1951) (dissent).
177. *United States ex rel. Caminito v. Murphy, supra* n.172 at 706.
178. E.g., Harris, "Idealism Emergent in Jurisprudence," 10 Tul. L. Rev. 169 (1936); Mechem, "The Jurisprudence of Despair," 21 Iowa L. Rev. 669 (1936). These sentiments were expressed also in two books published in 1940: E. Bodenheimer, *Jurisprudence*, and L. Fuller, *The Law in Quest of Itself*.
179. E.g., *United States v. Ullmann*, 221 F.2d 760 (2d Cir., 1955).
180. 195 F.2d 583 (2d Cir., 1952).
181. Id. at 595–96.
182. J. Frank and B. Frank, *Not Guilty* (1957).
183. H. Hart and A. Sacks, *supra* n.5 at iii.

CHAPTER II

1. For examples, see H. Hart and A. Sacks, *The Legal Process* (tent. ed., 1958); Wechsler, "Toward Neutral Principles of Constitutional Law," 73 Harv. L. Rev. 1 (1959).
2. See Miller & Howell, "The Myth of Neutrality in Constitutional Adjudication," 27 U. Chi. L. Rev. 661 (1960); Clark, "A Plea for the Unprincipled Opinion," 49 Va. L. Rev. 660 (1963). A fuller discussion of the controversy appears in White, "The Evolution of Reasoned Elaboration," 59 Va. L. Rev. 279 (1973).
3. L. Hand, *The Bill of Rights* (1958). Hand's views on constitutional interpretation were more restrictive than those of leading adherents of the process theory. See Wechsler's comments on *The Bill of Rights* in Wechsler, *supra* n. at 2–13.
4. Traynor, "Law and Social Change in a Democratic Society," 1956 U. Ill. L. F. 230, 231.
5. Id. at 232.
6. Traynor, "Badlands in an Appellate Judge's Realm of Reason," 7 Utah L. Rev. 157, 167, 168 (1960).

7. Traynor, "La Rude Vita, La Dolce Giustizia; Or Hard Cases Can Make Good Law," 29 U. Chi. L. Rev. 223, 234 (1962).
8. E.g., Arnold, "Professor Hart's Theology," 73 Harv. L. Rev. 1298 (1960).
9. 24 Cal. 2d 453 (1944).
10. *Goetten v. Owl Drug Co.*, 6 Cal. 2d 683 (1936); *Ward v. Great Atlantic & Pacific Tea Co.*, 231 Mass. 90 (1918), cited in *Escola v. Coca Cola Bottling Co., supra* n.8 at 464.
11. 24 Cal. 2d at 463. Res ipsa loquitur (literally, "the thing speaks for itself") is a doctrine that shifts the burden of proof to tort defendants having sole control over relevant evidence.
12. Id. at 464.
13. Id. at 465.
14. Id. at 466.
15. Id. at 462.
16. *Greenman v. Yuba Power Products, Inc.*, 59 Cal. 2d 57 (1963).
17. 24 Cal. 2d at 467.
18. Traynor, *supra* n.7 at 234.
19. Id. at 235.
20. Id. at 234.
21. Traynor, *supra* n.6 at 163.
22. Id. at 170, 157.
23. Traynor, *supra* n.4 at 236.
24. Traynor, "Statutes Revolving in Common-Law Orbits," 17 Cath. U. L. Rev. 401, 402 (1968).
25. Id. at 402.
26. Traynor, "Reasoning in a Circle of Law," 56 Va. L. Rev. 739, 742 (1970).
27. Id. at 751.
28. Traynor, *supra* n.25 at 402.
29. Id. at 403.
30. Traynor, *supra* n.6 at 164.
31. Id.
32. Traynor, *supra* n.26 at 743.
33. Traynor, *supra* n.23 at 403.
34. Id. at 405.
35. Traynor, *supra* n.6 at 165.
36. Traynor, *supra* n. 25 at 406.
37. Traynor, "Fact Skepticism and the Judicial Process," 106 U. Pa. L. Rev. 635, 638 (1958).
38. Id.
39. Id. at 638, 639.
40. Traynor, "No Magic Words Could Do It Justice," 49 Calif. L. Rev. 615, 622 (1961).

41. Traynor, "Better Days in Court for a New Day's Problems," 17 Vand. L. Rev. 109 (1963).
42. Id.
43. Comment, "Real Property: Landlord and Tenant: The Rule in Dumpor's Case," 14 Calif. L. Rev. 328, 333 (1926).
44. Traynor, *supra* n.40 at 622.
45. Traynor, *supra* n.26 at 753.
46. Traynor, *supra* n.40 at 627.
47. Id. at 627, 628, 629.
48. Traynor, *supra* n.4 at 233.
49. *Freedman v. The Rector*, 37 Cal. 2d 16, 21 (1951); *Barkis v. Scott*, 34 Cal. 2d 116, 122 (1949).
50. *Escola v. Coca Cola Bottling Co., supra* n. 9 at 466.
51. *Seely v. White Motor Co.*, 63 Cal. 2d 9, 15 (1965).
52. *Bernkrant v. Fowler*, 55 Cal. 2d 588, 595, 596 (1961).
53. Traynor, *supra* n.41 at 115n.
54. Traynor, *supra* n.25 at 425.
55. *In re* Estate of Mason, 62 Cal. 2d 213 (1965).
56. Traynor, *supra* n.23 at 419.
57. Traynor, *supra* n.26 at 747–48.
58. Id. at 747.
59. Id. at 748.
60. Id. at 749.
61. Id.
62. Id. at 749, 750, 751.
63. Traynor, *supra* n.37 at 636.
64. Traynor, *supra* n.40 at 628.
65. Id. at 621, 623.
66. Wechsler, *supra* n.1 at 19.
67. Traynor, *supra* n.40 at 624, 625.
68. Id. at 624.
69. Traynor, *supra* n.41 at 121–22.
70. Id. at 124.
71. Traynor, *supra* n.6 at 169. See *Startup v. Pacific Elec. Ry. Co.*, 29 Cal. 2d 866, 872 (1947).
72. Traynor, *supra* n.40 at 616.
73. Traynor, *supra* n.41 at 115.
74. Id. at 112.
75. Id. at 119–21.
76. See generally Traynor, "*Mapp v. Ohio* at Large in the Fifty States," 1962 Duke L. J. 319.

77. *Escola v. Coca Cola Bottling Co., supra* n.9; *Greenman v. Yuba Power Products Co., supra* n.16; *Vandermark v. Ford Motor Co.*, 61 Cal. 2d 256 (1964); *Elmore v. American Motors Corp.*, 70 Cal. 2d 578 (1969).
78. *Malloy v. Fong*, 37 Cal. 2d 356 (1951).
79. *Muskopf v. Corning Hospital Dist.*, 55 Cal. 2d 211 (1961).
80. *Emery v. Emery*, 45 Cal. 2d 421 (1955).
81. *Knight v. Kaiser Co.*, 48 Cal. 2d 778 (1957) (dissent).
82. *State Rubbish, Etc. Ass'n v. Siliznoff*, 38 Cal. 2d 330 (1952).
83. *Laux v. Freed*, 53 Cal. 2d 512, 525 (1960) (concurrence); Estate of Rule, 25 Cal. 2d 1, 17 (1944) (dissent).
84. *Union Oil Co. v. Union Sugar Co.*, 31 Cal. 2d 300 (1948).
85. *Gelhaus v. Nevada Irr. Dist.*, 43 Cal. 2d 779 (1955); *Quader-Kino A. G. v. Nebenzal*, 35 Cal. 2d 287, 297 (1950) (dissent).
86. *Monarco v. Lo Greco*, 35 Cal. 2d 621 (1950).
87. *Drennan v. Star Paving Co.*, 51 Cal. 2d 409 (1958).
88. *Lewis & Queen v. N. M. Ball & Sons*, 48 Cal. 2d 141 (1957); *Fewel & Dawes, Inc. v. Pratt*, 17 Cal. 2d 85 (1941).
89. *Osborn v. Osborn*, 42 Cal. 2d 358 (1954).
90. *Sorenson v. Costa*, 32 Cal. 2d 453 (1948).
91. *Coast Bank v. Minderhout*, 61 Cal. 2d 311 (1964).
92. *Jordan v. Talbort*, 55 Cal. 2d 597 (1961).
93. *Barkis v. Scott, supra* n.49.
94. *Bernhard v. Bank of America*, 19 Cal. 2d 807 (1942).
95. Id. at 813. Abandonment of mutuality was not original with Traynor. See *Coca Cola Co. v. Pepsi Cola Co.*, 36 Del. 124 (1934). Traynor's innovation was to foreswear deciding *Bernhard* through use of a widely recognized exception to mutuality in cases involving derivative liability and to face the mutuality doctrine head-on.
96. *Perez v. Sharp*, 32 Cal. 2d 711 (1948).
97. *McLaughlin v. Florida*, 379 U.S. 184 (1964).
98. *Danskin v. San Diego Unified School District*, 28 Cal. 2d 536 (1946).
99. *Speiser v. Randall*, 48 Cal. 2d 903, 904 (1957) (dissent).
100. *Black v. Cutter Laboratories*, 43 Cal. 2d 788, 809 (1955) (dissent).
101. *People v. Gonzales*, 20 Cal. 2d 165 (1942).
102. *People v. Cahan*, 44 Cal. 2d 434 (1955).
103. *Castenda v. Superior Court*, 59 Cal. 2d 439 (1963); *People v. Gorg*, 45 Cal. 2d 776 (1955).
104. *People v. Brown*, 45 Cal. 2d 640 (1955).
105. *Willson v. Superior Court*, 46 Cal. 2d 291 (1956).
106. *People v. Simon*, 45 Cal. 2d 645 (1955).
107. *Jones v. Superior Court*, 58 Cal. 2d 56 (1962).

108. See generally *Pennoyer v. Neff*, 95 U.S. 714 (1878); *Restatement of Conflict of Laws* (1934).
109. *Grant v. McAuliffe*, 41 Cal. 2d 859 (1953); *Emery v. Emery*, 45 Cal. 2d 421 (1955).
110. *Bernkrant v. Fowler, supra* n.52.
111. *Reich v. Purcell*, 67 Cal. 2d 551 (1967).
112. *Bernkrant v. Fowler, supra* n.52.
113. Traynor and Surrey, "New Roads Toward the Settlement of Federal Income, Estate and Gift Tax Controversies," 7 Law & Contemp. Prob. 336 (1940).
114. Traynor, "National Bank Taxation in California," 17 Calif. L. Rev. 83, 232, 456 (1929).
115. See Traynor and Keesling, "Recent Changes in the Bank and Corporation Franchise Tax Act," 21 Calif. L. Rev. 543 (1933), 22 Calif. L. Rev. 499 (1934), 23 Calif. L. Rev. 51 (1934).
116. Ratner, "Reflections of a Traynor Law Clerk," 44 S. Cal. L. Rev. 876A (1971).
117. *West Publishing Co. v. McColgan*, 27 Cal. 2d 705 (1946).
118. *Forster Shipbuilding Co. v. County of Los Angeles*, 54 Cal. 2d 450 (1960).
119. *De Luz Homes, Inc. v. County of San Diego*, 45 Cal. 2d 546 (1955).
120. *Roehm v. County of Orange*, 32 Cal. 2d 280 (1948).
121. *Von Hamm-Young Co. v. San Francisco*, 29 Cal. 2d 798 (1947).
122. Traynor, quoting Justice Charles D. Breitel in Traynor, *supra* n.23 at 402n.
123. See, e.g., Fuller, "Reason and Fiat in Case Law," 59 Harv. L. Rev. 376, 393–94 (1946); R. Dahl, *Who Governs?* (1961); H. Hart and A. Sacks, *The Legal Process, supra* n.1.

CHAPTER 12

1. See, e.g., Meyer v. Nebraska, 262 U.S. 390 (1923); Gitlow v. New York, 268 U.S. 652 (1925); Whitney v. California, 274 U.S. 357 (1927).
2. See above, chap. 8.
3. *Minersville School District v. Gobitis*, 310 U.S. 586 (1940); *West Virginia Board of Education v. Barnette*, 319 U.S. 624 (1943).
4. In Justice Frankfurter's Diary for March 12, 1943, the following alleged colloquy between Frankfurter and Justice Douglas is recorded: "Douglas said, 'Hugo [Black] would now not go with you in the Flag Salute Case.' I said, 'Why, has he reread the Constitution during the summer?' Douglas replied, 'No, but he has read the papers.' " Felix Frankfurter Papers, Library of Congress.
5. *Sweatt v. Painter*, 339 U.S. 629 (1950); *McLaurin v. Oklahoma State Regents*, 339 U.S. 637 (1950).
6. *Smith v. Allwright*, 321 U.S. 649 (1944); *Terry v. Adams*, 345 U.S. 461 (1953).
7. *Shelly v. Kraemer*, 334 U.S. 1 (1948); *Hurd v. Hodge*, 334 U.S. 24 (1948).

8. E.g., *Dennis v. United States*, 341 U.S. 494 (1951).
9. 319 U.S. at 643.
10. 371 U.S. x (1962).
11. See, e.g., "Why I Shall Vote For La Follette—VI," 40 New Republic 199 (1924).
12. See generally R. Wiebe, *The Search for Order* (1967); White, "The Social Values of the Progressives," 70 South Atlantic Quarterly 62 (1971).
13. Frankfurter, "The Manager, the Workman, and the Social Scientist," 3 Bull. Taylor Soc'y 8 (1917).
14. Frankfurter, "Law and Order," 9 Yale Rev. 225 (1920).
15. See Levinson, "The Democratic Faith of Felix Frankfurter," 25 Stan. L. Rev. 430, 433 (1973).
16. Frankfurter, *supra* n.11.
17. Frankfurter to Learned Hand, April 6, 1921, quoted in Levinson, *supra* n.15 at 439.
18. Frankfurter to Learned Hand, June 5, 1923, quoted in id. at 440.
19. [Frankfurter], "The Supreme Court as Legislator," 46 New Republic 158 (1926).
20. Frankfurter, "Can the Supreme Court Guarantee Toleration," 43 New Republic 85 (1925).
21. Frankfurter to Charles P. Howland, June 10, 1932, Frankfurter Papers, Library of Congress.
22. F. Frankfurter, *The Public and Its Government* 159 (1964 ed.).
23. V. Hamilton, *Hugo Black: The Alabama Years* 46 (1972).
24. Durr, "Hugo L. Black: A Personal Appraisal," 6 Ga. L. Rev. 1, 6 (1971).
25. J. Frank, *Mr. Justice Black* 46 (1949).
26. D. Meador, *Mr. Justice Black and His Books* 2 (1974).
27. Id. at 9–11.
28. Id. at 13–29.
29. Id. at 14.
30. Id. at 13–29.
31. Frankfurter, "The Red Terror of Judicial Reform," 40 *New Republic* 110, 113 (1924).
32. Frank, "Hugo L. Black," in 3 L. Friedman & F. Israel, *The Justices of the United States Supreme Court* 2321, 2330 (1969).
33. Sacks, "Felix Frankfurter," in 3 id. at 2401, 2403.
34. Frankfurter's Diary, in the Frankfurter Papers in the Library of Congress, is filled with characterizations of his fellow justices that could not have been calculated to win their admiration.
35. A notable exception was Black's nation-wide radio address in 1939 admitting but downplaying his membership in the Ku Klux Klan. That information had become public knowledge during the confirmation proceedings pursuant to his nomination to the Court. See generally J. Frank, *supra* n.25.
36. E.g., *Rochin v. California*, 342 U.S. 165 (1952).
37. *McCart v. Indianapolis Water Co.*, 302 U.S. 419, 423 (1938) (dissent).

38. *Indiana ex rel. Anderson v. Brand*, 303 U.S. 95, 109 (1938) (dissent) (academic tenure holders); *Wood v. Lovett*, 313 U.S. 362, 372 (1941) (dissent) (purchasers of homes).
39. *SEC v. Chenery Corp.*, 318 U.S. 80, 95 (1943) (dissent).
40. *NLRB v. Columbian Enameling & Stamping Co.*, 306 U.S. 292, 301 (1939) (dissent).
41. *Hirabayshi v. United States*, 320 U.S. 81 (1943); *Korematsu v. United States*, 323 U.S. 214 (1944), discussed above, chap. 10.
42. *Bridges v. California*, 314 U.S. 252 (1941).
43. *Milk Wagon Drivers Union v. Meadormoor Dairies*, 312 U.S. 287, 299 (1941) (dissent); *Cox v. New Hampshire*, 312 U.S. 569 (1941).
44. *Palko v. Connecticut*, 302 U.S. 319 (1937).
45. *Giboney v. Empire Storage & Ice Co.*, 336 U.S. 490 (1949).
46. *Kovacs v. Cooper*, 336 U.S. 77, 98 (1949) (dissent).
47. E.g., *Schulz v. Pennsylvania R.R.*, 350 U.S. 523 (1956); *Allen Bradley v. Local No.* 3, 325 U.S. 797 (1945).
48. Cf. Cahn, "Justice Black and First Amendment 'Absolutes,'" 37 N.Y.U.L. Rev. 549 (1962).
49. 332 U.S. 46, 68 (1947) (dissent).
50. Black's interpretation of history was challenged in Fairman, "Does the Fourteenth Amendment Incorporate the Bill of Rights?" 2 Stan. L. Rev. 5 (1949).
51. *Kovacs v. Cooper, supra* n.46.
52. *New York Times Co. v. Sullivan*, 376 U.S. 254, 293 (1964) (concurrence).
53. *Ginzburg v. United States*, 383 U.S. 463, 476 (1966) (dissent).
54. *Cox v. Louisiana*, 379 U.S. 536, 575 (1965) (partial dissent).
55. *Brown v. Louisiana*, 383 U.S. 131, 151 (1966) (dissent).
56. *Berger v. New York*, 388 U.S. 41, 70 (1967) (dissent).
57. *Schmerber v. California*, 384 U.S. 757, 773 (1966) (dissent).
58. *Griswold v. Connecticut*, 381 U.S. 479, 507 (1965) (dissent).
59. *Harper v. Virginia Board of Elections*, 383 U.S. 663, 670 (1966) (dissent).
60. *Connecticut Gen. Life Ins. Co. v. Johnson*, 303 U.S. 77, 83 (1938) (dissent).
61. E.g., in *Adamson v. California, supra* n.49.
62. See Reich, "Mr. Justice Black and the Living Constitution," 76 Harv. L. Rev. 673, 694–700 (1963).
63. See generally Symposium, 58 Calif. L. Rev. 1 (1970).
64. *Adamson v. California, supra* n. 49.
65. *Foster v. Illinois*, 332 U.S. 134 (1947) (assistance of counsel in state proceedings).
66. *Dennis v. United States*, 341 U.S. 494 (1951).
67. *Foster v. Illinois, supra* n.65 at 140.
68. *Adamson v. California, supra* n. 49 at 67.
69. See A. Mason, *Harlan Fiske Stone* 469 (1956).

70. Justice Douglas said that Black was "an ardent proselytizer of his constitutional views, seeking to convert any 'wayward' Brother on the Court." W. Douglas, *Go East, Young Man* 452 (1974).
71. 163 U.S. 537 (1896).
72. Douglas, *supra* n.70 at 451; R. Kluger, *Simple Justice* 586–616 (1976).
73. As exemplified in *Missouri ex rel. Gaines v. Canada*, 305 U.S. 337 (1938); *Sipuel v. Board of Regents*, 332 U.S. 631 (1948); *Sweat v. Painter, supra* n.5; *McLaurin v. Oklahoma State Regents, supra* n.5.
74. Lewis, "Earl Warren," in 4 L. Friedman and F. Israel, *supra* n.32 at 2721, 2728–29.
75. *Irvine v. California*, 347 U.S. 128 (1954); *Barsky v. Board of Regents*, 347 U.S. 442 (1954).
76. *Watkins v. United States*, 354 U.S. 178 (1957); *Sweezy v. New Hampshire*, 354 U.S. 234 (1957).
77. *Greene v. McElroy*, 360 U.S. 474 (1959).
78. *Miranda v. Arizona*, 384 U.S. 436 (1966), discussed below.
79. *Ginzburg v. United States, supra* n.53.
80. *Marchetti v. United States*, 390 U.S. 39, 77 (1968) (dissent).
81. E.g., *Harper v. Virginia Board of Electors, supra* n. 59, outlawing poll tax requirement for voting in the face of a pending constitutional amendment; *Jones v. Alfred H. Mayer Co.*, 392 U.S. 409 (1968), reviving an 1866 Civil Rights Act prohibiting racial discrimination in the sale of housing in the context of a proposed Congressional open-housing statute.
82. Harlan, "The Frankfurter Imprint as Seen by a Colleague," 76 Harv. L. Rev. 1, 2 (1963).
83. See D. Shapiro, *The Evolution of a Judicial Philosophy* xvii (1969).
84. *Harper v. Virginia Board of Elections, supra* n.59 at 686 (dissent).
85. 356 U.S. 86 (1958).
86. 367 U.S. 497 (1961).
87. 369 U.S. 186 (1962).
88. *Barsky v. Board of Regents, supra* n. 75.
89. See *Watkins v. United States and Sweezy v. New Hampshire, supra* n.76.
90. 356 U.S. 44 (1958).
91. 356 U.S. at 64–65.
92. Id. at 76.
93. Id at 78.
94. Id. at 92.
95. Id. at 93.
96. Id.
97. Id. at 110.
98. Id. at 107.
99. Id. at 94.

100. Id. at 98.
101. Id. at 97.
102. Id.
103. Id. at 101.
104. Id.
105. Id. at 119–20.
106. Id. at 121–22.
107. Id. at 124.
108. Id. at 125.
109. Id. at 126.
110. Id. at 128.
111. *State v. Nelson*, 126 Conn. 412 (1940).
112. Cf. Bickel, "The Passive Virtues," 75 Harv. L. Rev. 40 (1961).
113. *Griswold v. Connecticut, supra* n.58.
114. 367 U.S. at 503.
115. Id.
116. Id. at 508.
117. Id.
118. Id. at 532.
119. Id. at 534.
120. Id. at 537.
121. Id. at 538–39.
122. Id. at 508 (Frankfurter's phrase).
123. Id. at 538.
124. Id. at 536.
125. Id. at 540.
126. Id. at 542.
127. Id.
128. Id. at 543.
129. Id. at 548.
130. Id. at 550.
131. Id. at 548.
132. Id. at 553.
133. Id. at 555.
134. Id. at 544.
135. 369 U.S. at 334.
136. Id. at 340.
137. Id. at 333–34.
138. Harlan in *Griswold v. Connecticut, supra* n.58, quoting Cardozo for the Court in *Palko v. Connecticut*, 302 U.S. 319, 325 (1937).

139. "Selective incorporation," as a doctrine, has not been expressly accepted by a majority of the Court, although it has been practiced. See D. Shapiro, *supra* n. 83 at 26n.
140. 367 U.S. 643 (1961).
141. 381 U.S. 618 (1965).
142. E.g., *Johnson v. New Jersey*, 384 U.S. 719 (1966); *Jenkins v. Delaware*, 395 U.S. 213 (1969).
143. Compare *Linkletter v. Walker, supra* n. 141, with *Johnson v. New Jersey, supra* n. 142, and *Desist v. United States*, 394 U.S. 244 (1969).
144. Compare *Johnson v. New Jersey, supra* n. 142 with *Jenkins v. Delaware, supra* n. 142.
145. *Supra* n. 142.
146. *Supra* n. 142 at 218.
147. 381 U.S. at 640, 650 (dissent).
148. See *Desist v. United States, supra* n. 143 at 254; *United States v. White*, 401 U.S. 745, 754 (1971).
149. E.g., *Teban v. Shott*, 382 U.S. 406 (1966); *Stovall v. Denno*, 388 U.S. 293 (1967); *De Stefano v; Woods*, 392 U.S. 631 (1968).
150. *Supra* n. 143.
151. 394 U.S. at 258.
152. Id. at 259.
153. Id. at 258.
154. Id.
155. *Jenkins v. Delaware supra* n. 142 at 222.
156. 394 U.S. at 258.
157. 384 U.S. 436 (1966).
158. Id. at 465 (Warren, C. J.).
159. 378 U.S. 1 (1964).
160. 378 U.S. 478 (1964).
161. 384 U.S. at 478.
162. Id. at 444, 467–79.
163. Id. at 442.
164. Id. at 443.
165. Id. at 444.
166. 370 U.S. 421 (1962).
167. E.g., Note, "Interrogations in New Haven: The Impact of *Miranda*," 76 Yale L. J. 1519 (1967); Seeburger and Wettick, "*Miranda* in Pittsburgh—A Statistical Study," 29 U Pitt. L. Rev. 1 (1967).
168. Omnibus Crime Control and Safe Streets Act, 82 Stat. 197 (1968).
169. For only some examples, see *Weber v. Aetna Casualty & Surety Co.*, 406 U.S. 164 (1972); *Roe v. Wade*, 410 U.S. 113 (1973); *Cleveland Board of Education v.*

LaFleur, 414 U.S. 632 (1974); *Memorial Hospital v. Maricopa County*, 415 U.S. 250 (1974).

CHAPTER 13

1. W. Douglas, *Go East, Young Man* vii (1974).
2. J. Simon, *Independent Journey: The Life of William O. Douglas* 5 (1980).
3. W. Douglas, *The Court Years* 4 (1980).
4. Id. at 172.
5. Id. at 34.
6. Id. at 41.
7. Id. at vii.
8. W. Douglas, supra note 1, at 150.
9. Id. at 4.
10. Id. at 13.
11. Id. at 32.
12. Id. at 33.
13. Id.
14. Id. at 35.
15. Id. at 39.
16. Id. at 127.
17. Id. at 134.
18. Douglas, supra note 3, at 394.
19. Douglas, supra note 1, at 148.
20. Id. at 148–49.
21. Id. at 144.
22. Id. at 156.
23. Id.
24. Id. at 128.
25. Id. at 157.
26. Id.
27. Id.
28. Id. at 164; see also J. Simon, supra note 2, at 109–10 (describing Hutchins's opinion of Douglas).
29. Douglas, supra note 1, at 160.
30. Id.
31. Id.
32. Id. at 161. For an account of the Columbia deanship controversy of 1928, see J. Goebel, Jr., *A History of the School of Law, Columbia University* 272–305 (1955).
33. See W. Douglas, supra note 1, at 160.
34. See id. at 163.

35. See Alexander, "Washington's Angry Scotsman," *Saturday Evening Post*, Oct. 17, 1942, at 9; *St. Louis Post-Dispatch*, Apr. 2, 1929 (cited in J. Simon, supra note 2, at 63).
36. Douglas, supra note 1, at 134–36.
37. See J. Simon, supra note 2, at 65.
38. Douglas, supra note 1, at 140.
39. See *St. Louis Post-Dispatch*, supra note 35 (cited in J. Simon, supra note 2, at 88).
40. Douglas, supra note 1, at 144.
41. Martha Douglas Bost to James Simon, Aug. 31, 1976 (quoted in J. Simon, supra note 2, at 74).
42. Douglas, supra note 1, 156.
43. Records, Cravath, Henderson & de Gersdorff (quoted in J. Simon, supra note 2, at 82).
44. John M. McCloy to James Simon, Aug. 11, 1977 (quoted in J. Simon, supra note 2, at 88).
45. Douglas, supra note 1, at 158.
46. See L. Mosley, *Dulles* 76 (1978).
47. Douglas attributed this quality to himself. See W. Douglas, supra note 1, at xi.
48. See Minutes of the Faculty of Law, Columbia University, June 1, 1928 (cited in J. Simon, supra note 2, at 98).
49. See Minutes of the Faculty of Law, Columbia University, June 1, 1928, and Oct. 11, 1928 (cited in J. Simon, supra note 2, at 99).
50. Douglas, supra note 1, at 163.
51. Young Smith was appointed Dean of Columbia Law School on May 7, 1928. On May 10, at a Yale Law School faculty meeting, Dean Hutchins suggested that he might be able to recruit disaffected members of the Columbia faculty, naming Douglas, Yntema, and Underhill Moore. He secured permission from the faculty "to proceed to negotiate for any one or more of the men suggested." Minutes of the Faculty of Law, Yale University, May 10, 1928 (quoted in J. Simon, supra note 2, at 102). A letter from Robert Hutchins to James R. Angell, the President of Yale, indicates that two weeks after that meeting Hutchins was planning to offer Douglas a position at Yale but had not done so. R. Hutchins to J. Angell, May 24, 1928 (cited in Schlegel, "American Legal Realism and Empirical Social Science: The Singular Case of Underhill Moore," 29 Buffalo L. Rev. 195, 213 n. 100 (1980)).
52. W. Douglas, supra note 1, at 163–64.
53. Compare W. Douglas, supra note 1, at 163–64, with Robert Hutchins to James Simon, Mar. 1, 1977 (quoted in J. Simon, supra note 2, at 110) (Douglas reporting salary offer of $25,000 at Univ. of Chicago; Hutchins confirming offer to Douglas of $20,000).
54. See J. Simon, supra note 2, at 110 (citing C. Clark, Dean's Report, Yale Law School, 1930–31).
55. See J. Simon, supra note 2, at 110–11.

56. Douglas, supra note 1, at 164.
57. Id.
58. Id. at 165–66.
59. Id. at 164.
60. Id. at 178.
61. Id. at 182.
62. Id.
63. Id.
64. Id.
65. Id.
66. Id. at 183.
67. Id.
68. Id.
69. Id. at 184.
70. Id.
71. Id. at 189.
72. Id.
73. Id.
74. Id. at 193.
75. Id. at 197.
76. Id. at 183–84.
77. Id. at 184.
78. Id.
79. Id.
80. Id.
81. Id. at 202.
82. Id.
83. Id. at 184.
84. Id. at 188.
85. Id. at 189.
86. Id. at 189–97.
87. Id. at 216.
88. Id. at 233.
89. Id.
90. Id. at 237.
91. Id.
92. Id. at 238.
93. Id.
94. Simon, supra note 2, at 432.
95. Id. at 432–33.
96. W. Douglas, supra note 1, at 249.

97. Id. at 250.
98. Id. at 252–53.
99. Id. at 253.
100. See id. at 254.
101. Id.
102. Id.
103. Id. at 255.
104. See J. Simon, supra note 2, at 232–38.
105. Id. at Douglas, supra note 1, at 251.
106. Interview with Millie Douglas Read (quoted in J. Simon, supra note 2, at 234).
107. See id.
108. W. Douglas, supra note 1, at 465.
109. Id.
110. See J. Simon, supra note 2, at 190–94.
111. W. Douglas, supra note 1, at 463.
112. Id.
113. Id. at 465.
114. W. Douglas, supra note 3, at 4.
115. Id.
116. Id. at 5.
117. Id. at 41.
118. Id. at 34.
119. J. Simon, supra note 2, at 431.
120. W. Douglas, supra note 3, at 34.
121. Id.
122. Id. at 36.
123. Id. at 36–37.
124. The authors of *The Brethren*, a source on the internal history of the Burger Court that needs to be used with great care, give as an example Douglas's efforts to flatter Justice Harry Blackmun in order to maintain the latter's position in favor of declaring anti-abortion legislation unconstitutional in the deliberations on Roe v. Wade, 410 U.S. 113 (1973). See B. Woodward and S. Armstrong, *The Brethren* 184–85, 231 (1979).
125. J. Simon, supra note 2, at 353 (quoting an unidentified Justice).
126. In the internal deliberations on Roe v. Wade during the 1971 Term, which resulted in a decision on the abortion cases being postponed for a year, Douglas reportedly circulated a memorandum attacking Chief Justice Burger's assignment of the opinion in the cases when he was not a member of the majority. The memorandum stated, "[W]hen a Chief Justice tries to bend the Court to his will by manipulating assignments, the integrity of the institution is imperilled." Douglas threatened to publish the memorandum as a dissent from any order of the

Court postponing the cases, which he believed had been decided, 5–4, in favor of a limited constitutional right to have an abortion. He eventually agreed not to publish the memorandum, but only after raising considerable turmoil within the Court. The story, based on confidential sources, is told in B. Woodward and S. Armstrong, supra note 124, at 187–89.

127. See White, "The Working Life of the Marshall Court," 1815–35, 70 Va. L. Rev. 1 (1984).
128. 307 U.S. 277 (1939).
129. The Revenue Act of 1932, ch. 209,]] 22, 47 Stat. 169, 178.
130. U.S. Const. art III,]] 1.
131. W. Douglas, supra note 1, at 466–68.
132. Id. at 466.
133. W. Douglas, supra note 3, at 8.
134. Id.
135. Id.
136. See, e.g., Clark, Douglas and Thomas, "The Business Failures Project—A Problem in Methodology," 39 Yale L.J. 1013 (1930); Douglas, "Some Functional Aspects of Bankruptcy," 41 Yale L.J. 329 (1932); Douglas, "Vicarious Liability and the Administration of Risks" (pts. 1 and 2), 38 Yale L.J. 584, 720 (1929).
137. See Llewellyn, "Some Realism About Realism—Responding to Dean Pound," 44 Harv. L. Rev. 1222, 1227 (1931).
138. W. Douglas, supra note 1, at 466.
139. I surveyed fifteen Douglas majority opinions in constitutional cases between the 1939 and 1945 Terms. The opinions were chosen from a sample in *Douglas of the Supreme Court* (V. Countryman, ed., 1959), a volume which seeks to reprint opinions that one of his former law clerks and academic supporters found valuable. Of those opinions I found two, Sunshine Anthracite Coal Co. v. Adkins, 310 U.S. 381 (1940), and Murdock v. Pennsylvania, 319 U.S. 105 (1943), in which Douglas engaged in extensive and significant doctrinal analysis. *Sunshine Anthracite* sustained the validity of a congressional statute regulating the bituminous coal industry (an earlier effort by Congress had been struck down by the Court in Carter v. Carter Coal Co., 298 U.S. 238 (1936)) against a variety of constitutional challenges. Douglas's treatment of the commerce clause and due process issues was thorough and detailed.

    Murdock held unconstitutional on First Amendment grounds a Pennsylvania statute imposing a license on members of the Jehovah's Witnesses sect, who sought to distribute religious pamphlets. The delivery of the pamphlets amounted to protected expression rather than commerce, Douglas held, and a tax on the Witnesses overburdened religious freedom. *Murdock* can be regarded as a clarification of the meaning of religious freedom under the First Amendment, and Douglas's analysis made some effort to distinguish expression protected in *Murdock* from religious ventures for commercial purposes.

In none of the other sampled opinions written by Douglas between 1939 and 1949 did his analysis match the sustained doctrinal analysis of *Sunshine Anthracite* or *Murdock*. His analysis more resembled that of Skinner v. Oklahoma, 316 U.S. 535 (1942), discussed infra notes 216–31 and accompanying text, in being sketchy, assertive, and inclined to mention emotion-laden facts in the case. The other opinions selected were State Tax Commissioner of Utah v. Aldrich, 316 U.S. 174 (1942); *Skinner;* Bowles v. Willingham, 321 U.S. 503 (1944); Ex parte Endo, 323 U.S. 283 (1944); Screws v. United States, 325 U.S. 91 (1945); Hannegan v. Esquire, Inc., 327 U.S. 146 (1946); Girouard v. United States, 328 U.S. 61 (1946); United States v. Causby, 328 U.S. 256 (1946); Ballard v. United States, 329 U.S. 187 (1946); Haley v. Ohio, 332 U.S. 596 (1948); McDonald v. United States, 335 U.S. 451 (1948); and Terminiello v. Chicago, 337 U.S. 1 (1949).

140. See G. E. White, *Patterns of American Legal Thought* 142–50 (1978).

141. 344 U.S. 838 (denying cert. to 195 F.2d 583 (2d Cir.)), reh'g denied, 344 U.S. 889 (1952), stay vacated, 345 U.S. 965 (vacating stay imposed by 200 F.2d 666 (2d Cir. 1952)), subsequent stay vacated, 346 U.S. 273 (vacating stay imposed by Justice Douglas), stay denied, 346 U.S. 322 (denying application for a stay to be imposed by the Supreme Court as a whole), reconsideration denied, 346 U.S. 324 (1953) (denying motion for reconsideration of the Court's authority to vacate the stay imposed by Justice Douglas).

142. Ch. 30, 40 Stat. 217 (codified in relevant part at 18 U.S.C.A.]]]] 793–794 (West 1976 & Supp. 1987)).

143. See R. and M. Meeropol, *We Are Your Sons* (1975); R. Radosh and J. Milton, *The Rosenberg File* (1983); W. and M. Schneir, *Invitation to an Inquest* (1965); Cohen, "Justice Douglas and the *Rosenberg* Case: Setting the Record Straight," 70 Cornell L. Rev. 211 (1985); Parrish, "Cold War Justice: the Supreme Court and the Rosenbergs," 82 Am. Hist. Rev. 805 (1977).

144. See United States v. Rosenberg, 195 F.2d 583 (2d Cir.), cert. denied, 344 U.S. 838 (1952). Judge Frank's opinion in that the United States Court of Appeals for the Second Circuit was the first appellate disposition of the *Rosenberg* "case." *Rosenberg*, however, literally consisted of a series of "cases," each with its own technical issues, but each related to the original conviction and sentencing. Judge Frank appeared to invite Supreme Court review of the matter. See Parrish, supra note 144, at 815–16. His opinion affirmed the conviction of the Rosenbergs, but appeared to question the appropriateness of the death sentence imposed upon them. See *Rosenberg*, 195 F.2d at 604–07. Although noting (apparently with some regret) the then-prevailing doctrine that a federal appellate court was powerless to modify a sentence imposed upon convicted defendants by a trial court, Judge Frank also observed that the Supreme Court could abandon

that doctrine, reinterpret the statute under which the doctrine had arisen, and modify the Rosenbergs' death sentences. See id. at 606. For convenience I refer to the *Rosenberg* "case" in the text; several different dispositions of its legal issues are cited in subsequent notes.

145. See Rosenberg v. United States, 344 U.S. 838 (Black, J., dissenting from denial of cert.), reh'g denied, 344 (U.S. 889 (1952).
146. See Rosenberg v. United States, 344 U.S. 889 (1952) (Frankfurter, J., dissenting mem.).
147. See United States v. Rosenberg, 108 F. Supp. 798 (S.D.N.Y.), aff'd, 200 F.2d 666 (2d Cir., 1952), cert. denied, 345 U.S. 965 (1953).
148. United States v. Rosenberg, 200 F.2d 666 (2d Cir. 1952), cert. denied, 345 U.S. 965 (1953).
149. Id. at 670.
150. Id.
151. See Rosenberg v. United States, 345 U.S. 965, 965–66 (1953) (vacating unreported order of Second Circuit, dated Feb. 17, 1953, granting Rosenbergs stays of execution).
152. Votes of the Justices in passing on certiorari petitions are normally not disclosed unless a Justice chooses to make public a dissent. Douglas's votes are revealed in two internal Court documents. The first of these is a memorandum on the *Rosenberg* case written by Justice Felix Frankfurter on June 4, 1953, and deposited in the Felix Frankfurter Papers, Harvard Law School Library, Box 65, file 1 (hereinafter Rosenberg Memorandum). The second is a June 19, 1953, memorandum of Justice Harold Burton, deposited in the Harold Burton Papers, Library of Congress. Frankfurter wrote an addendum to his June 4 memorandum on June 19, 1953 (hereinafter Rosenberg Memorandum—Addendum); this addendum is also deposited in the Frankfurter Papers.
153. Frankfurter, Memorandum for the Conference, May 20, 1953, Frankfurter Papers, supra note 153 (quoted in Parrish, supra note 144, at 823–24).
154. Douglas, Memorandum to the Conference, May 22, 1953, Burton Papers, supra note 153 (quoted in Parrish, supra note 144, at 823–24).
155. Burton's position is summarized in F. Frankfurter, Rosenberg Memorandum, supra note 1153 at 1–2 (cited in Parrish, supra note 144, at 824).
156. See F. Frankfurter to H. Burton, May 23, 1953, Frankfurter Papers, supra note 153 (cited in Parrish, supra note 144, at 824).
157. See F. Frankfurter, Rosenberg Memorandum, supra note 153, at 6–9 (cited in Parrish, supra note 144, at 824–25).
158. See supra note 153.
159. Id. at 6–7 (quoted in Parrish, supra note 144, at 825).
160. Id. at 7 (quoted in Parrish, "Justice Douglas and the *Rosenberg* Case: A Rejoinder," 70 Cornell L. Rev. 1048, 1052 (1985)).

161. Id. at 8 (quoted in Parrish, supra note 161, at 1052–53).
162. Id. (quoted in Parrish, supra note 161, at 1053).
163. Rosenberg v. United States, 345 U.S. 965, 966 (1953).
164. See Parrish, supra note 144, 827–28.
165. See id. at 827–34.
166. United States v. Rosenberg, 204 F.2d 688 (1953) (per curiam).
167. See Rosenberg v. United States, 345 U.S. 989, 989 (1953).
168. See Atomic Energy Act of 1946, Pub. L. No. 79–585, 60 Stat. 755, 766–67 (1946) (codified as amended at 42 U.S.C.]]]] 2274–2276 (1982)).
169. See Cohen, supra note 144, at 244–45.
170. See Rosenberg v. United States, 346 U.S. 273, 313 (1953).
171. See id. Burton's posture is described in Frankfurter, Rosenberg Memorandum—Addendum, supra note 153, at 6 (cited in Parrish, supra note 144, at 836–37), and Burton, Conference Notes on Douglas's Stay, Hugo Black Papers, Library of Congress (cited in Parrish, supra note 144, at 836–37).
172. See Rosenberg v. United States, 346 U.S. 279 (1953).
173. W. Douglas, supra note 3, at 79.
174. Id.
175. Id.
176. Id. at 80.
177. Id.
178. Id. at 81.
179. Id.
180. Id.
181. Id. at 83.
182. Id.
183. Id. at 84.
184. See F. Frankfurter, Rosenberg Memorandum, supra note 153, at 8 (quoted in Parrish, supra note 144, at 825).
185. Parrish, supra note 144, at 826.
186. Id. at 833.
187. Id.
188. Simon, supra note 2, at *312–13*.
189. Cohen, supra note 144, at 213.
190. Id.
191. Id. at 250.
192. Id. at 219.
193. Id. at 236.
194. See id. at 217–18. Cohen singled out Chessman v. Teets, 354 U.S. 156 (1957), a case decided in the term during which Cohen was Douglas's law clerk "Throughout the *Chessman* case," Cohen noted, "[Douglas] maintained the consistent position

that there was no point in reviewing even a case in which a life was at stake unless the case presented some legal issue that could arguably provided basis for action by the Court." Cohen, supra note 144, at 217.

195. J. Simon, supra note 2, at 312.
196. See Cohen, supra note 144, at 213, 250.
197. For Frankfurter's and Jackson's views of Douglas's politicized and strategic activities as a Supreme Court Justice, see notes 107–10 and 123–25 and accompanying text; see also Parrish, supra note 144, at 819, 823–26, 833 (describing Douglas's contradictory actions, and Frankfurter's and Jackson's opinions about his actions, in *Rosenberg*).

To be sure, Justice Douglas was not alone on the Supreme Court in engaging in extra judicial manipulation in order to secure some judicial result. Among Parrish's findings about the *Rosenberg* case was a set of documents, compiled by the FBI, in the papers of Judge Irving Kaufman, reporting that Justice Jackson arranged a meeting with Chief Justice Vinson and Attorney General Herbert Brownell to discuss the most effective means of vacating Douglas's stay should Douglas grant it. The meeting took place on June 16, 1953, a day before Douglas announced he had granted a stay based on Farmer's statutory argument. This information came from a June 17 letter from A. H. Belmont to D. M. Ladd (both of whom were officials of the FBI). Belmont learned of the meeting from Judge Kaufman himself, who had found out about it from an assistant United States attorney in New York (who, in turn, presumably had been told of the meeting by Attorney General Brownell). See id. at 835 n.83.

Frankfurter's strategic maneuverings during his tenure on the Supreme Court have repeatedly been documented. See e.g., R. Kluger, *Simple Justice* (1976) (discussing Frankfurter's behind-the-scenes activity in Brown v. Board of Education, 347 U.S. 43 (1954)).

198. See Parrish, supra note 144, at 826 ("Douglas's [conduct] remains inexplicable in view of his own later apparent interest in the *Rosenberg* case"); J. Simon, supra note 2 at 312–13.
199. Cohen, supra note 144, at 211.
200. Id. at 212 n.5 (quoting Justice Hans Linde) (quoted in J. Simon, supra note 2, at 298).
201. Recollections of George E. Allen in an oral history transcript in the Harry S. Truman Library, Independence, Missouri, cited in Simon, supra note 2, at 262.
202. Eliot Janeway to James Simon, May 28, 1979, quoted in id. at 266–67.
203. Id. at 273, quoting Robert Donovan, *Conflict and Crisis* 183 (1977).
204. *New York Times*, July 11, 1948; William O. Douglas to Harry S. Truman, July 31, 1948, Truman Library, Independence, Mo., quoted in Simon, supra note 2, at 273–74.
205. Simon, supra note 2, at 274–75.
206. *New York Times*, January 14, 1952: see Simon, supra note 2, at 275.

207. Simon, supra note 2, at 275; Thomas Corcoran to James Simon, December 20, 1976, quoted in Simon, supra note 2, at 275.

208. Janeway to Simon, supra note 202, quoted in Simon, supra note 2, at 275.

209. See J. Simon, supra note 2, at 300–301.

210. See, e.g., W. Douglas, *North from Malaya* (1953); W. Douglas, *Strange Lands and Friendly People* (1951).

211. There is, of course, the possibility that Frankfurter's account of the May 23 conference in his memoranda of June 4 and June 19, supra note 153, was erroneous. There is support in the papers of Justices Burton, Black, and Jackson for the fact that Douglas circulated his May 22 memorandum, and in the Burton Papers for that fact that at one point in the May 23 conference the Justices believed they were going to hear argument on the Rosenbergs' petition. But the Frankfurter memoranda are the only source for Douglas's withdrawal of his dissent and his accompanying explanation. Moreover, the Frankfurter memorandum of June 4 begins with the statement, "I have a strong feeling that history also has its claims, which should be respected," Frankfurter, Rosenberg Memorandum, supra note 153, at 6, and bears signs of careful editing, as if it was a document being created for posterity.

Those inclined to doubt the authenticity of Frankfurter's account of Douglas's actions in the May 23 conference might consider this passage from the June 4 memorandum:

> [Hugo Black] told me that he had had a visit from Douglas and that Douglas had told him that the reason he, Douglas, had withdrawn his memorandum was that it was becoming evident from the discussion that the hearing the Court was preparing to give the Rosenbergs was to be on the issue of whether their petition for certiorari should be granted rather than a hearing on the merits of the petition, subsequent to an outright grant. It did not seem worthwhile, Douglas had said to Black, to have such a hearing and then deny certiorari anyway; so he withdrew his memorandum.

Id. at 9. This passage suggests that at a minimum, Douglas withdrew his May 22 memorandum at the May 23 conference, which left him in the posture he had previously taken—that of denying certiorari—at least as far as the internal votes on the second petition were concerned. Douglas would hardly have given Black, who was not present at the conference, an explanation of his withdrawal of the memorandum if he had not withdrawn it. Thus whether or not Douglas accompanied his withdrawal with a statement about his memorandum being "badly drafted," it seems clear that the withdrawal took place.

212. W. Douglas, supra note 3, at 84. For evidence of concern on the parts of other justices that *Rosenberg* not be viewed as an ideological trial, see Parrish, supra note 144, at 816–19.

213. W. Douglas, supra note 3, at 82.

214. Id. at 83.

215. Id. at 88.
216. See, e.g., Harper v. Virginia Board of Elections, 383 U.S. 663 (1966).
217. See, e.g., Griswold v. Connecticut, 381 U S. 479 (1965); Skinner v. Oklahoma, 316 U.S. 535 (1942).
218. 316 U.S. 535 (1942).
219. 381 U.S. 479 (1965).
220. 300 U.S. 379 (1937).
221. 274 U.S. 200 (1927).
222. Id. at 207–8.
223. *Skinner*, 316 U.S. at 539.
224. Id. at 541–42.
225. See id. at 543–45 (Stone, C. J., concurring).
226. Id. at 541.
227. Id.
228. See id. at 541–42. Although Douglas cited no constitutional text, he did attempt to analogize to some case authority suggesting the special invidiousness of racial classifications. Id. at 541 (citing Gaines v. Canada, 305 U.S. 337 (1938); Yick Wo v. Hopkins, 118 U.S. 356 (1886)).
229. *Skinner*, 316 U.S. at 541.
230. See id.
231. Id.
232. See Douglas v. California, 372 U.S. 353 (1963) (requiring states to appoint counsel for indigent defendants' initial appeals); Griffin v. Illinois, 351 U.S. 12 (1956) (requiring that indigent defendants be furnished with trial transcripts).
233. 300 U.S. 379 (1937).
234. See Griswold v. Connecticut, 381 U.S. 479 (1965).
235. Id. at 480 (quoting Conn. Gen. Stat. 53–32, 54–196 (1958)).
236. Id. at 481–82.
237. Id. at 484.
238. Id.
239. Id.
240. Id.
241. See id. at 482–85.
242. Id. at 485.
243. Id. (citing Skinner v. Oklahoma, 316 U.S. 535 (1942)).
244. Id. at 486.
245. Id. at 480.
246. See Eisenstadt v. Baird, 405 U.S. 438 (1972).
247. See Roe v. Wade, 410 U.S. 113 (1973). The Court, through Justice Blackmun, held that the "right of privacy [was] founded in the Fourteenth Amendment's concept of personal liberty." Id. at 153.

248. *Griswold*, 381 U.S. at 485.
249. See *Skinner*, 316 U.S. at 538–39.
250. See Poulos v. New Hampshire, 345 U.S. 395, 422 (1953) (Douglas, J., dissenting); Dennis v. United States, 341 U.S. 494, 581 (1951) (Douglas, J., dissenting); Terminiello v. Chicago, 337 U.S. 1 (1949).
251. 383 U.S. 663 (1966).
252. See id. at 664 n.1.
253. See Butler v. Thompson, 341 U.S. 937 (1951) (per curiam); Breedlove v. Suttles, 302 U.S. 277 (1937).
254. *Harper*, 383 U.S. at 666 n.3 (quoting in Harman v. Forssenius, 380 U.S. 528, 543 (1965)).
255. For a review of the Court's actions, see Winter, "Poverty, Economic Equality, and the Equal Protection Clause," 1972 Sup. Ct. Rev. 41.
256. *Harper*, 383 U.S. at 684–85 (Harlan, J., dissenting).
257. Id. at 667.
258. Id. (quoted in Reynolds v. Sims, 377 U.S. 533, 561–62 (1964)).
259. Id. at 668.
260. Id.
261. Id. at 670.
262. Id. at 669.
263. Cox, "The Supreme Court, 1965 Term—Foreword: Constitutional Adjudication and the Promotion of Human Rights," 80 Harv. L. Rev. 91, 95–96 (1966).
264. By "egalitarian," Douglas meant policies that treated human beings equally because of their common humanity, as distinguished from policies that reflected the majoritarian judgments of a relatively "egalitarian" institution such as a state legislature. His view was that many majoritarian views could be anti-egalitarian.
265. See Powe, "Evolution to Absolutism: Justice Douglas and the First Amendment," 74 Colum. L. Rev. 371 (1974).
266. W. Douglas, *An Almanac of Liberty* (1954).
267. W. Douglas, *Points of Rebellion* (1970).
268. 410 U.S. 179 (1973).
269. 410 U.S. 113 (1973).
270. See B. Woodward and S. Armstrong, supra note 125, at 184–87.
271. *Doe*, 410 U.S. at 212 n.4 (Douglas, J., concurring).
272. Id. at 210 (Douglas, J., concurring).
273. Id. at 210–11 (Douglas, J., concurring).
274. Id. at 211–13 (Douglas, J., concurring).
275. See Hartzel v. United States, 322 U.S. 600 (1944); Prince v. Massachusetts, 321 U.S. 158 (1944); Minerville School Dist. v. Gobitis, 310 U.S. 586 (1940).
276. See J. Simon, supra note 2, at 446–54.
277. See B. Woodward and S. Armstrong, supra note 125, at 389–400.

278. See Glancy, "Getting Government off the Backs of the People," 21 Santa Clara L. Rev. 1047 (1981); Dworkin, "Dissent on Douglas" (Book Review), N.Y. Rev. Books, Feb. 19, 1981, at 3.
279. 5 U.S. (1 Cranch) 137 (1803).
280. For examples, see B. Schwartz, *Inside the Warren Court* (1983); B. Woodward and S. Armstrong, supra note 125; Hutchinson, "Unanimity and Desegregation," 68 Geo. L. J. 1 (1979).
281. With respect to Black, see G. Dunne, *Hugo Black and the Judicial Revolution* (1977); with respect to Warren, see G. E. White, *Earl Warren: A Public Life* (1982).
282. The relationship of Legal Realism to Process Jurisprudence is explained in White, "The Evolution of Reasoned Elaboration," 59 Va. L. Rev. 279 (1973).
283. See, e.g., Lewin, "Vacancy on the Court," The New Republic, Nov. 29, 1975, at 7; Lewis, "Mr. Douglas: 36 Years Out on the Frontier," N.Y. Times, Nov. 16, 1975, 4, at 2, col. 4.
284. Robert Bork, Foreword to G. McDowell, *The Constitution and Contemporary Constitutional Theory*, vii (1985).
285. Id.
286. 383 U.S. 663 (1966).

CHAPTER 14

1. See K. Newmyer, *The Supreme Court from Marshall to Taney* (1968).
2. Quoted in Lewis, "A Talk with Warren About Crime, the Court, the Country," *New York Times Magazine*, Oct. 19, 1969.
3. Rehnquist, "Who Writes Decisions of the Supreme Court?," *U.S. News & World Report*, Dec. 13, 1957.
4. For the details, see R. Kluger, *Simple Justice* 605–9 (1976).
5. See B. Woodward and S. Armstrong, *The Brethren* 417 (1979).
6. For examples, see id., at 170–72, 179–81, 417–22, 435–38.
7. Id. at 314–35.
8. Id. at 173.
9. Id. at 362.
10. Id. at 236.
11. Id. at 428.
12. Id. at 436–41.
13. 369 U.S. 186 (1962).
14. 376 U.S. 254 (1964).
15. 426 U.S. 833, 858, 860, 867 (1976).
16. Woodward and Armstrong, supra note 5, at 224–26, 362–63.
17. See e.g., Engel v. Vitale, 370 U.S. 421 (1962); Reynolds v. Sims, 377 U.S. 533 (1964); Griswold v. Connecticut, 381 U.S. 479 (1965).

18. 448 U.S. 297 (1980).
19. See, e.g., L. Levy, *Against the Law: The Nixon Court and Criminal Justice* (1974).
20. 368 U.S. 57, 62.
21. Reed v. Reed, 404 U.S. 71, 76, quoting Royster Guano Co. v. Virginia, 253 U.S. 412, 415 (1920). The choice of the *Royster* version of the rational basis standard of review suggested that the Court was requiring more than a showing that the statutory preference embodied in the classification was not arbitrary, another possibility under rational basis review. See, e.g., Williamson v. Lee Optical, 348 U.S. 483 (1955).
22. 411 U.S. 677, 684, 686.
23. Id. at 686.
24. Id. at 688.
25. Between *Frontiero* and *Craig v. Boren* was the 1975 case of *Stanton v. Stanton*, where the Court, 8–1, invalidated a Utah statute making a distinction between male and female minors for the purpose of child-support payments. Blackmun, for the Court, held that extending the period of minority for male supportees to 22 and terminating it at 18 for female supportees rested on "old notions" that women tended to mature and marry earlier than males. "No longer is the female," Blackmun wrote, "destined solely for the home and the rearing of the family, and only the male for the marketplace and the world of ideas." 421 U.S. 7, 14–15. The case, after *Reed*, was an easy one, and the Court treated *Reed* as controlling, declined an invitation to find classifications based on gender inherently suspect, and concluded that the Utah statute was unconstitutional "under any test." Id. at 17.
26. 429 U.S. 190, 210–11 (1976).
27. 440 U.S. 268, 283 (1979).
28. 450 U.S. 464, 476 (1981).
29. 453 U.S. 57, 64–65 (1981).
30. 458 U.S. 718, 724–25 (1982).
31. Supra note 14.
32. Curtis Publishing Co. v. Butts and Associated Press v. Walker, 388 U.S. 130 (1967).
33. Kalven, "The New York Times Case," 1964 Sup. Ct. Rev. 191, 221 (1964).
34. 403 U.S. 29 (1971).
35. 403 U.S. at 62.
36. 418 U.S. 323, 340–41 (1974).
37. 418 U.S. 354.
38. 424 U.S. 448 (1976).
39. Id. at 450, 458–59.
40. 443 U.S. 157 (1979).
41. 443 U.S. 111 (1979).
42. 443 U.S. at 135.

43. 472 U.S. 749 (1985).
44. Id. 751.
45. Id. at 763.
46. Supra note 17.
47. Id. at 480.
48. Id. at 485–86.
49. Id. at 482.
50. Id. at 527.
51. In NAACP v. Alabama, 357 U.S. 449 (1958), Harlan, for the Court, referred to a "vital relationship between freedom to associate and privacy in one's associations," suggesting that privacy might be an "indispensable" background right.
52. 405 U.S. 438 (1972).
53. Id. at 453.
54. 410 U.S. 113 (1973).
55. Id. at 152.
56. Id. at 152–53.
57. For example, see Adamson v. California, 332 U.S. 46 (1947); Duncan v. Louisiana, 391 U.S. 145 (1968); Benton v. Maryland, 395 U.S. 784 (1969).
58. Maher v. Roe, 432 U.S. 464 (1977).
59. Harris v. McRae, 448 U.S. 297 (1980).
60. City of Akron v. Akron Center for Reproductive Services, 462 U.S. 416 (1983).
61. Planned Parenthood of Central Missouri v. Danforth, 428 U.S. 52 (1976).
62. Bellotti v. Baird, 443 U.S. 622 (1979); Planned Parenthood Association of Kansas City v. Ashcroft, 462 U.S. 476 (1983).
63. H. L. v. Matheson, 450 U.S. 398 (1981).
64. Carey v. Population Services International, 431 U.S. 678 (1977).
65. 416 U.S. 1 (1974).
66. 431 U.S. 494 (1977).
67. Id. at 499, 502.
68. Wilkinson and White, "Constitutional Protection for Personal Lifestyles," 62 Corn. L. Rev. 563 (1977).
69. Id. at 592–600, 603–8.
70. 425 U.S. 238 (1976).
71. Id. at 248–49.
72. 425 U.S. 901 (1976).
73. See 403 F. Supp. 1199 (E. D. Va. 1975).
74. Grey, "Eros, Civilization, and the Burger Court," 43 L. & Contemp. Probs. 83, 97 (1980).
75. 106 S.Ct. 2841 (1986).
76. Conkle, "The Second Death of Substantive Due Process," 62 Ind. L.J. 213, 232–42 (1987).

77. Id. at 242.
78. 394 U.S. 557 (1969).
79. Blasi, "The Rootless Activism of the Burger Court," in V. Blasi, *The Burger Court* 216 (1983).
80. City of Mobile v. Bolden, 446 U.S. 55 (1980), permitting at-large elections in the city of Mobile, Alabama, that had the effect of preventing black candidates from being elected city commissioners.
81. See, e.g., Engel v. Vitale, supra note, 17.
82. Lynch v. Donnelly, 465 U.S. 668 (1984).
83. Wallace v. Jaffree, 472 U.S. 38 (1985). Professor Yale Kamisar, in reading an earlier draft of this chapter, pointed out that a similar analysis could be made of criminal procedure decisions in the Warren and Burger Courts. Compare, for example, Mapp v. Ohio, 367 U.S. 643 (1961), with Tennessee v. Garner, 471 U.S. 1 (1985), and Michigan v. Summers, 452 U.S. 692 (1981). In the latter two cases the Court speaks of "balancing the nature and quality of the [police] intrusion . . . against the importance of the governmental interests alleged to justify the intrusion." 471 U.S. at 8. *Mapp*, by contrast, is a case in which Fourth Amendment rights are taken as "trumping" law enforcement concerns. See generally Kamisar, "The Warren Court, . . . the Burger Court, . . . and Police Investigatory Practices," in Blasi, supra note 79, at 62.
84. 391 U.S. 430 (1968).
85. 438 U.S. 265 (1978).

CHAPTER 15

1. See Kamen, "Kennedy Moves Court to Right," Washington Post, April 11, 1989, at A1.
2. David G. Savage, *Turning Right: The Making of the Rehnquist Supreme Court* (1992).
3. *Grutter v. Bollinger*, 539 U.S. 306 (2003). A 5–4 majority of the Court held, in an opinion by Justice Sandra Day O'Connor, that race-based affirmative action programs in higher education should be subjected to strict scrutiny under the equal protection clause, but that the achievement of racial and ethnic diversity in the student body was a sufficiently compelling state interest to justify racial preferences in admissions. Id. at 307. The "diversity" rationale had not been identified as a justification for affirmative action programs in the Court's previous decisions.
4. *Planned Parenthood v. Casey*, 505 U.S. 833 (1992).
5. *Dickerson v. United States*, 530 U.S. 428 (2000).
6. *Lawrence v. Texas*, 539 U.S. 558 (2003).
7. *Hoyt v. Florida*, 368 U.S. 57 (1961).
8. *Craig v. Boren*, 429 U.S. 190 (1976).
9. *United States v. Virginia*, 518 U.S. 515 (1996).

10. *Bowers v. Hardwick*, 478 U.S. 186 (1986).
11. *Lawrence v. Texas*, supra note 6.
12. This impression of the Burger Court is captured by two quite different books, B. Woodward and S. Armstrong, *The Brethren* (1979), and V. Blasi, *The Burger Court* (1981).
13. For details on White's judicial posture, see Symposium, "Justice White and the Exercise of Judicial Power," 75 U. Colo. L. Rev. 1425ff (2003).
14. See, e.g., Oelsner, "Ford Chooses a Chicagoan for Supreme Court Seat," N.Y. Times, Nov. 29, 1975, at 1; F. X. Beytagh, Jr., "Mr. Justice Stevens and the Burger Court's Uncertain Trumpet," 51 Notre Dame L. Rev. 946 (1976).
15. See John Paul Stevens, "The Life Span of a Judge-Made Rule," 58 N.Y. U. L. Rev. 1 (1983).
16. In a 1995 article on the Court's voting patterns, Linda Greenhouse identified Stevens as being on the left edge of the Court's voting spectrum. L. Greenhouse, "Farewell to the Old Order in the Court," N.Y. Times, July 2, 1995, at E1.
17. Compare *Planned Parenthood of Central Missouri v. Danforth*, 428 U.S. 52, 102 (Stevens, J., dissenting), where Stevens maintained that a state could require that a doctor receive the consent of one parent of a minor before performing an abortion, with *Hodgson v. Minnesota*, 497 U.S. 417 (1990), where Stevens joined the majority invalidating a Minnesota statute that required that both parents of minors be notified.
18. Compare *Regents of the University of California v. Bakke*, 438 U.S. 265 (1978), and *Fullilove v. Klutznick*, 448 U.S. 448 (1980), where Stevens upheld affirmative action programs, with *Wygant v. Jackson Board of Education*, 476 U.S. 267 (1986), and *Adarand Constructors v. Pena*, 515 U.S. 200 (1995), where he voted to invalidate them.
19. Compare *Califano v. Goldfarb*, 430 U.S. 199 (1977) and *Michael M. v. Superior Court*, 450 U.S. 464 (1981) (Stevens, J., dissenting), where Stevens voted to strike down state laws challenged on gender discrimination grounds, with *Miller v. Albright*, 523 U.S. 420 (1998), where Stevens upheld a statute that imposed greater burdens in citizenship cases on children born out of wedlock to American fathers and foreign mothers than on children born to American mothers and foreign fathers.
20. Stevens dissented in *Bowers v. Hardwick*, 478 U.S. at 199, supra note 10, and joined the majority opinions in *Romer v. Evans*, 517 U.S. 620 (1996), and *Lawrence v. Texas*, supra note 6. Those cases are discussed below, pp. 433–36.
21. Compare two opinions authored by Stevens for the Court in cases involving the regulation of "indecent" speech, *FCC v. Pacifica Foundation*, 438 U.S. 726 (1978), upholding the regulation of indecency on network broadcasting, and *Reno v. ACLU*, 521 U.S. 844 (1997), striking down a federal statute regulating it on the internet.
22. See, e.g., *Rose v. Lundy*, 455 U.S. 502 (1982), dissenting from an opinion restricting the availability of habeas corpus relief in the federal courts; *Employment*

Division v. Smith, 494 U.S. 872 (1990), dissenting from an opinion upholding a federal statute that declined to grant an exemption for the use of the drug peyote in connection with religious rituals; *Santa Fe Independent School District v. Doe*, 530 U.S. 290 (2000), joining a majority opinion concluding that a student-selected prayer before a high school football game improperly "coerced" members of the student body into participating in the ceremony; *McConnell v. Federal Election Campaign Commission*, 540 U.S. 93 (2003), voting to uphold the Bipartisan Campaign Reform Act of 2002 against a First Amendment challenge; *United States v. Lopez*, 514 U.S. 549, 602 (1995) and *United States v. Morrison*, 529 U.S. 598 (2000), dissenting in cases where the Court invalidated federal legislation as improperly treading on state prerogatives. See also Stevens's opinion for the Court in *Gonzales v. Raich*, 125 S.Ct. 2195 (2004), discussed pp. xxx–xx.

23. For more detail, see L. Greenhouse, *Becoming Justice Blackmun* (2005).
24. 518 U.S. 515 (1996).
25. See, e.g., R. B. Ginsburg, "Sexual Equality under the Fourteenth and Equal Rights Amendments," 1979 Wash. U. L. Q. 161 (1979); R. B. Ginsburg, "Sex Equality and the Constitution," 52 Tulane L. Rev. 451 (1978). Ginsburg also argued all of the important Burger Court gender discrimination cases. See J. Baer, *Ruth Bader Ginsburg*, in E. M. Maltz, *Rehnquist Justice* 217–18 (2003).
26. 518 U.S. at 532–33.
27. *Eisenstadt v. Baird*, making that extension, was not decided until 1972.
28. See L. Greenhouse, *Becoming Justice Blackmun*, supra note 23, at 80. Greenhouse's account of the Court's internal deliberations in *Roe v. Wade* is based on material in Blackmun's papers.
29. Beginning with John Hart Ely, "The Wages of Crying Wolf: A Comment on *Roe v. Wade*," 82 Yale L. J. 920 (1973).
30. See *Harris v. McRae*, 448 U.S. 297 (1980), upholding a statute excluding abortion from federally provided medical services to indigent women; *Webster v. Reproductive Health Services*, 492 U.S. 490 (1989), upholding a statute preventing privately funded abortions from taking place in public health facilities.
31. See Greenhouse, supra note 23, at 190–203.
32. In *United States v. Nixon*, 418 U.S. 683 (1974) a unanimous Court, with Rehnquist recusing himself, denied Nixon's claim that taped conversations he had secretly recorded at the White House could be withheld, on the ground of executive privilege, from a grand jury investigating the Watergate scandal.
33. See id. at 8–12, 19–29, 35–48, 185–88.
34. See id. at 123.
35. On the death penalty, see *Callins v. Collins*, 510 U.S. 1141 (1994); on affirmative action, see Blackmun's dissent in *University of California v. Bakke*, 438 U.S.265 (1978); on lawyer advertising, see *Ohralik v. Ohio State Bar*, 436 U.S. 447 (1978).
36. See J. Simon, *In His Own Image* (1973).

37. *See* T. E. Yarbrough, *The Rehnquist Court and the Constitution* 30–31 (2000).
38. The best known examples were her "undue burden" test in abortion cases, first articulated in *City of Akron v. Akron Center for Reproductive Health*, 462 U.S. 416 (1983), and her "endorsement" test in establishment clause cases, first announced in *Lynch v. Donnelly*, 465 U.S. 668 (1984).
39. For more detail, see J. Biskupic, *Sandra Day O'Connor* (2005).
40. For more detail on O'Connor's appointment, see Yarbrough, supra note 37, at 14–15.
41. President Johnson had nominated Associate Justice Fortas to the Chief Justiceship in 1968, but, as we have seen, the nomination was successfully filibustered in the Senate.
42. Ideology continued to drive Reagan's third nomination, when he named Judge Robert Bork of the D.C. Circuit, perhaps the most visible and outspoken right-wing constitutional theorist in the judiciary. Bork's defeat in the Senate represented a watershed in the twentieth-century process of confirming nominees to the Court: he was the first nominee defeated solely on the basis of his ideological views. There was no dispute about Bork's competence, and he was not identified with any ethical transgressions.
43. Rehnquist had written the majority opinion in *National League of Cities v. Usery*, 426 U.S. 833 (1976), unexpectedly reviving the concept of "traditional state functions" as a limit on the scope of the federal government's commerce power. When the Court overruled *Usery* in *Garcia v. San Antonio Metropolitan Transit Authority*, 469 U.S. 528 (1985), Rehnquist dissented, predicting that the *Usury* "principle will . . . in time again command the support of a majority of this Court." Id. at 580.
44. One of the interesting dimensions of Rehnquist's free speech jurisprudence during his tenure as an Associate Justice was his reluctance to grant protection to commercial speech. See, e.g., his dissent in *Virginia State Board of Pharmacy v. Virginia Citizens Consumer Council*, 425 U.S. 748 (1976). Rehnquist would subsequently revise that view. See, in particular, his votes in *44 Liquormart Inc. v. Rhode Island*, 517 U.S. 484 (1996), and *Lorillard Tobacco Co. v. Reilly*, 533 U.S. 525 (2001), both of which involved governmental efforts to limit advertising about products with health risks. Rehnquist's dissent in *Virginia Pharmacy* had objected to broad protection for commercial speech precisely because he believed that government could engage in such efforts.
45. For an analysis of Scalia's opinions on the District of Columbia Circuit, see R. A. Brisbin, Jr., *Justice Antonin Scalia and the Conservative Revival* 34–58 (1997).
46. Id., 39–42.
47. See A. Scalia, "The Disease as the Cure," 1979 Wash. U. L. Q. 147 (1979).
48. Scalia did not hold this view until the late 1980s. See A. Scalia, "Originalism: The Lesser Evil," 57 U. Cinn. L. Rev. 854 (1989).

49. For a discussion of expectations about Souter and Thomas at the time of their nominations, see Yarbrough, supra note 37, at 19–27. The following comment from a 1994 book on the Rehnquist Court might be taken as reflecting those expectations:

> With the departure of Justice William Brennan from the Supreme Court during the summer of 1990, a new era—one that was inaugurated at least half a decade earlier—has taken on an aura of reality. . . . President George Bush's subsequent nomination of David Souter to replace Justice Brennan promised to solidify the new voting bloc. . . . More recently, with the retirement of Justice Thurgood Marshall, another acknowledged conservative, Clarence Thomas, joined the Court. . . . The Rehnquist Court, then, has come to represent a working coalition of six or seven members who, more often than not, share common public policy goals.
>
> (S. H. Freidelbaum, *The Rehnquist Court: In Pursuit of Judicial Conservatism* xiii–xiv [1994])

50. See, e.g., *Morrison v. Olson*, 487 U.S. 654, 697 (1988) (Scalia, J., dissenting).
51. 505 U.S. 833, 984 (1992).
52. 403 U.S. 602 (1971). O'Connor had criticized *Lemon* in *Lynch v. Donnelly*, 465 U.S. 668 (1984), and Kennedy had done so in *County of Allegheny v. American Civil Liberties Union*, 492 U.S. 573, 655–56 (1989)
53. *Lamb's Chapel v. Center Moriches Union Free Sch. Dist.*, 508 U.S. 384 (1993); *Board of Educ. of Kiryas Joel v. Grument*, 512 U.S. 687 (1994).
54. *Lamb's Chapel*, 508 U.S. at 397–401 (Scalia, J., concurring in the judgment)
55. *Kiryas Joel*, 512 U.S. at 732–52 (Scalia, J., dissenting).
56. *Bd. of County Comm'rs v. Umbehr*, 518 U.S. 668, 711 (1996) (Scalia, J., dissenting).
57. M. Tushnet, *A Court Divided* 147 (2005).
58. Id. at 147, 149.
59. Felix Frankfurter's career provides another example. See chapter 12.
60. See, e.g., *United States v. Lopez*, 567 U.S. 49 (1995); *Alden v. Maine*, 527 U.S. 706 (1999); *United States v. Morrison*, 529 U.S. 598 (2000). For a fuller discussion of Kennedy's federalism opinions, see E. M. Maltz, "Justice Kennedy's Vision of Federalism," 31 Rutgers L. J. 761 (2000).
61. *United States v. Virginia*, supra note 9; *J. E. B. v. Alabama ex rel T.B.*, 511 U.S. 127 (1994).
62. See *Michael H. v. Gerald D.*, 491 U.S. 110 (1989).
63. 518 U.S. 620 (1996).
64. Supra note 6.
65. Supra note 4.
66. *Webster v. Reproductive Health Services*, 452 U.S. 450 (1989); *Hodgson v. Minnesota*, 497 U.S. 417, 501(1990) (dissent).
67. *Ohio v. Akron Reproductive Health Center*, 497 U.S. 502, 520 (1990) (concurrence); *Hodgson v. Minnesota*, supra note 66.

68. *Stenberg v. Carhart*, 530 U.S. 914 (2000) (dissent).
69. See discussion in Tushnet, *A Court Divided*, supra note 57, at 178, suggesting that Kennedy resorts to "rhetoric alone" to make up for his confused jurisprudential orientation. See also Rosen, "The Agonizer," New Yorker, Nov. 11, 1996, at 82.
70. See Tushnet, *A Court Divided*, supra note 57, at 58–59. For details on Souter's nomination, see Yarbrough, supra note 37.
71. Nomination of David H. Souter to Be Associate Justice of the Supreme Court of the United States, 101 Cong., 2d Sess. 305 (1991). Hereafter cited as Souter Hearings.
72. Souter Hearings, 140–41, 196–202.
73. "Justice Brennan is going to be remembered as one of the most fiercely principled guardians of the American Constitution that it has ever had and ever will have." Souter Hearings, 186.
74. For one columnist who seems to have paid close attention, see L. Greenhouse, "No One Is Sure of Souter," N.Y. Times, Sept. 23, 1990, sec. 4, at 5.
75. Souter Hearings, 54, 68, 140, 189.
76. See Keck, "David H. Souter," in Maltz, supra note 25, at 188–89. The criminal procedure cases included *Arizona v. Fulminate*, 499 U.S. 279 (1991); *McCleskey v. Zant*, 499 U.S. 467 (1991); *California v. Acevedo*, 500 U.S. 565 (1991); and *Florida v. Bostick*, 501 U.S. 429 (1991).
77. *Lee v. Wiseman*, 505 U.S. 577 (1992).
78. See the chart in Greenhouse, "Farewell to the Old Order," supra note 16, at E4.
79. The most balanced work on Thomas's career and approach is S. D. Gerber, *First Principles: The Jurisprudence of Clarence Thomas* (1999). For more detail on Thomas's pre-Court career, see A. P. Thomas, *Clarence Thomas, A Biography* (2001).
80. For a discussion of Thomas's perspective on constitutional interpretation, see Tushnet, supra note 57, at 89–103 (citing Thomas's opinions in *Hudson v. McMillan*, 503 U.S. 1 (1992), *United States v. Fordice*, 505 U.S. 717 (1992); *Missouri v. Jenkins*, 515 U.S. 70 (1995); and *Lawrence v. Texas,* supra note 6).
81. See Tushnet, supra note 57, at 85–88.
82. See Thomas's approach to commerce clause and federalism issues, discussed below, pp. 439–43.
83. See, e.g., her votes in *Capital Square v. Pinetti*, 515 U.S. 753 (1995) (dissent); *Romer v. Evans*, supra note 20; *Santa Fe Independent School District v. Doe*, supra note 22; (establishment clause applied to prayer at football game), as well as her consistent support for an extension of federal regulatory power in commerce clause and federalism cases. For a review, see Judith Baer, "Ruth Bader Ginsburg and the Limits of Formal Equality," in Maltz, supra note 25, at 216.
84. See T. J. Ellington, *Ruth Bader Ginsburg and John Marshall Harlan: A Justice and Her Hero*," 20 U. Haw. L. Rev. 797 (1998).

85. S. Breyer, *Active Liberty* (2005).
86. Id. at 115–18.
87. Id. at 7.
88. See Kersch, "The Synthetic Progressivism of Stephen G. Breyer," in Maltz, supra note 25 at 241, 249–50.
89. See id. at 253–64, citing cases.
90. For evidence of Rehnquist's tendency to dissent during his tenure as an Associate Justice, see L. Epstein, *The Supreme Court Compendium* (1996); K. E. Whittington, "William H. Rehnquist," in Maltz, supra note 25 at 8, 12–13. For some examples of Rehnquist dissenting in that period, see *Wallace v. Jaffree*, 472 U.S. 38, 91 (1985); *Ramah Navajo Sch. Bd. v. Bureau of Revenue of New Mexico*, 458 U.S. 832, 847 (1982); *McCarty v. McCarty*, 453 U.S. 210, 236 (1982); *Nixon v. Administrator of General Services*, 433 U.S. 425, 545 (1977). For a portrait of Rehnquist in that period, see S. Davis, *Justice Rehnquist and the Constitution* (1989).
91. In his memoirs, Warren wrote that "there was but one event that greatly disturbed us in my tenure" on the Court. It was when Frankfurter, after proposing that all the Justices sign their individual names to the Court's opinion in *Cooper v. Aaron* [358 U.S. 1 (1958)], the case in which the Court insisted that Arkansas state officials had an obligation to enforce *Brown v. Board of Education*'s mandate to integrate the public schools, then wrote a separate concurrence. "[S]ome of the Justices stated," Warren said in recalling the incident, "that they would never permit a Court opinion in the future to be made public unless it was certain that the views of all were announced simultaneously." E. Warren, *The Memoirs of Earl Warren* 298–99 (1977). By "some of the Justices," Warren meant himself.
92. *Posadas de Puerto Rico Assoc. v. Tourism Co. of Puerto Rico*, 478 U.S. 328 (1986).
93. *44 Liquormart v. Rhode Island*, supra note 44.
94. For a contrast between Burger's and Rehnquist's approaches toward the Chief Justiceship, see Greenhouse, "How Not to Be Chief Justice: The Apprenticeship of William H. Rehnquist," 154 U. Pa. L. Rev. 1365 (2006).
95. See id. at 105, citing evidence in Woodward and Armstrong, *The Brethren*, supra note 12, at 417–18.
96. The story, based on material in Blackmun's papers, is told in Greenhouse, *Becoming Justice Blackmun*, supra note 23, at 103.
97. See the tables cited in Posner, "Foreword—A Political Court," 119 Harv. L. Rev. 31, 67–69 (2005).
98. See Posner, supra note 97, at 68–69. On the decline of plurality opinions, see Merrill, "*The Making of the Second Rehnquist Court: A Preliminary Analysis*," 47 Wash. U. L. J. 569, 590 (2003).
99. See Posner, supra note 97, at 68–69; Merrill, supra note 98, at 588–60. The average length of Court opinions also increased from 1986 to 1994 and then began to decline. *See* Posner, supra note 97, at 69.

100. Merrill, supra note 98, at 589.
101. See O'Hara, "Social Constraint or Implicit Collusion": Toward a Game Theoretic Analysis of Stare Decisis," 24 Seton Hall L. Rev. 736 (1993).
102. I have emphasized these lines of cases because I think that they provide the clearest cumulative impression of the Rehnquist Court's distinctive approach to constitutional law issues. There were other decisions, notably those in *Bush v. Gore*, 531 U.S. 98 (2000), and *Dickerson v. United States*, 530 U.S. 428 (2000) (the latter affirming the Court's long-besieged decision in *Miranda v. Arizona*, 384 U.S. 436 (1966)), which were clearly of great interest. But *Bush v. Gore*, which the Court was clearly reluctant to decide at all and which generated no discernible principle of equal protection, separation of powers, or federalism, seems best understood as the equivalent of the Electoral Commission of 1877's resolution of another contested presidential election: a decision overwhelmed by its political circumstances. And commentators have argued that the significance of *Dickerson* may well have been reduced by the Court's subsequent decision, *United States v. Patane*, 542 U.S. 630 (2004). See Kamisar, "Dickerson v. United States," in C. Bradley, *The Rehnquist Legacy* 124–28 (2005).
103. "Unenumerated rights" is now regarded as a convenient label for a line of cases that has been described in various ways, such as constitutional "privacy" cases, "freedom of intimate association" cases, "personhood" cases, and "new substantive due process" cases. The decisions in the line, which goes back to *Skinner v. Oklahoma*, 316 U.S. 535 (1942), have advanced a variety of justifications for protecting "rights" not singled out in the constitutional text. At this point the principal justification seems to be that the term "liberty" in the due process clauses incorporates protection for a set of intimate personal choices that are not explicitly mentioned but can be seen as embodying foundational constitutional principles. "Unenumerated rights" cases are efforts to determine which intimate personal choices qualify for constitutional protection.
104. For more detail on the Rehnquist Court's abortion cases, see Johnson, "Abortion: A Mixed and Unsettled Legacy," in Bradley, *The Rehnquist Legacy*, supra note 103, at 301–26.
105. 462 U.S. 416, 452 (1983) (dissent).
106. Id. at 456–59.
107. See Greenhouse, *Becoming Justice Blackmun*, supra note 23, at 142–44.
108. 476 U.S. 747 (1986).
109. 492 U.S. 490 (1989).
110. See Greenhouse, *Becoming Justice Blackmun*, supra note 23, at 190 (citing *Reproductive Health Service v. Webster*, 851 F.2d 1071 (1988)).
111. My discussion of the Court's internal deliberations in the *Webster* and *Casey* cases relies on material in the Blackmun Papers made use of by Greenhouse, supra note 23, at 190–206. Where I include quotations from internal Court

documents I list the pages in Greenhouse, *Becoming Justice Blackmun*, where they are cited.

112. Blackmun Papers, quoted in Greenhouse, supra note 23, at 19.
113. The story is told in id., 191–94, quoting from Blackmun Papers.
114. The provisions had been invalidated in the *Akron* decision, supra note 38, and *Thornburgh v. American College of Obstetricians and Gynecologists*, 476 U.S. 747 (1986). *Casey* also raised the constitutionality of a third provision of the Pennsylvania statute, requiring spousal notification as a prerequisite to an abortion procedure.
115. See, e.g., *Planned Parenthood of Southeastern Pennsylvania v. Casey*, 947 F.2d 682 (3d Cir. 1991). Judge Samuel Alito, a member of the Third Circuit panel, also employed the undue burden test in his opinion, but dissented, believing that all the provisions of the Pennsylvania statute were unconstitutional under that test.
116. See Greenhouse, *supra* note 23, at 203, based on correspondence in Blackmun Papers.
117. For details of the appearance of the joint plurality opinion in *Casey*, see id. at 203–6, citing material in the Blackmun Papers. The effect of the plurality opinion on *Roe*'s characterization of abortion as a "fundamental right" was not initially clear. The plurality opinion did not characterize the right to have an abortion as "fundamental," and employed O'Connor's "undue burden" standard for evaluating legislation restricting the choice to have an abortion. Since the Court has continued to use the "undue buden" standard for abortion cases since *Casey*, however, it would seem that the "undue burden" standard extends throughout pregnancy. There is thus no time when the choice to have an abortion is entirely free from state interference. This does not seem consistent with *Roe*'s "fundamental rights" characterization.
118. *Planned Parenthood v. Casey*, supra note 4.
119. 530 U.S. 914 (2000).
120. Criticism of the *Griswold* opinion, and of its claim that the Constitution protected unenumerated "privacy" rights, had surfaced after *Griswold* was decided. See, e.g., Kauper, "Penumbras, Peripheries, Emanations, Things Fundamental and Things Forgotten," 64 Mich. L. Rev. 235 (1965); Henkin, "Privacy and Autonomy," 74 Colum. L. Rev. 1410 (1974).
121. For more detail on the Bork nomination, see E. Bronner, *Battle for Justice: How the Bork Nomination Shook America* (1989).
122. 367 U.S. 497 (1961).
123. Id. at 548–49.
124. See *Casey*, 505 U.S. at 849.
125. *Glucksberg v. Washington*, 521 U.S. 702 (1997)
126. *Compassion in Dying v. Washington*, 79 F. 3rd 790 (9th. Cir. 1996) (en banc)
127. See the companion case to *Glucksberg*, *Vacco v. Quill*, 521 U.S. 793, where the Court sustained a New York statute allowing the refusal of medical treatment.

128. 478 U.S. 186 (1986).
129. Id. at 191–92.
130. Id. at 193–95.
131. 521 U.S. at 720–21 (1997).
132. Id. at 735 n. 24.
133. 517 U.S. 620 (1996).
134. Id. at 632.
135. *Glucksberg*, 521 U.S. at 704.
136. Id. at 737–38.
137. Id. at 736–37.
138. Id. at 736.
139. *Casey*, 505 U.S. at 851.
140. *Glucksberg*, 521 U.S. at 762–63.
141. Id. at 765. Souter employed the same analysis in *Troxel v. Granville*, 530 U.S. 57 (2000), striking down a Washington statute requiring divorced parents to give grandparents visitation access to their children as a violation of the "fundamental right of parents to make decisions concerning the care, custody, and control of their child." Id. at 66.
142. Supra note 6.
143. O'Connor's concurring opinion in *Lawrence* relied on the equal protection clause to invalidate the Texas sodomy statute. 539 U.S. at 579.
144. Id.
145. Id. at 591–92.
146. See, e.g., *Katzenback v. McClung*, 379 U.S. 294 (1964), where the Court applied the Civil Rights Act of 1964, prohibiting racial discrimination by hotels, to a Georgia restaurant with a primarily local clientele that served African American customers only at a take-out counter. The rationale for the Civil Rights Act was partially based on the commerce power, and in *McClung* the Court found a connection between racial discrimination and the shipment of goods in interstate commerce.
147. The rationale was first supplied by Herbert Wechsler in "The Political Safeguards of Federalism," 54 Colum. L. Rev. 534 (1954).
148. 421 U.S. 542 (1975).
149. Id. at 558 (Rehnquist, J., dissenting).
150. Several commentators professed astonishment that Rehnquist's opinion in *Usery* would treat the Tenth Amendment as imposing substantive limitations on Congress's regulatory power, and others saw it as the possible reemergence of "dual federalism," an approach apparently abandoned by the Court in the 1940s. See, e.g., Barber, "National League of Cities v. Usery: New Meaning for the Tenth Amendment," 1976 Sup. Ct. Rev. 161; Lofgren, "National League of Cities v. Usery: Dual Federalism Reborn," 4 Claremont J. Pub. Affairs 19 (1977).

151. 426 U.S. 833 (1976).
152. *Usery*, 426 U.S. at 852.
153. Id. at 856.
154. *Hodel v. Virginia Surface Mining Association*, 452 U.S. 264 (1981)
155. *United Transportation Union v. Long Island Railroad*, 455 U.S. 678 (1982).
156. *Federal Energy Regulatory Commission v. Mississippi*, 456 U.S. 742 (1982)
157. *EEOC v. Wyoming*, 460 U.S. 226 (1983).
158. *Hodel*, supra note 154, at 287–88.
159. 469 U.S. 528 (1985).
160. Id. at 546.
161. *South Carolina v. Baker*, 485 U.S. 505 (1988).
162. Id. at 512.
163. *New York v. United States*, 505 U.S. 144 (1992).
164. Id. at 170, 188.
165. *Printz v. United States*, 521 U.S. 98 (1997).
166. See, e.g., *Seminole Tribe v. Florida*, 517 U.S. 44 (1996); *Florida Prepaid Postsecondary Education Expense Board v. College Savings Bank*, 527 U.S. 627 (1999); *Alden v. Maine*, 527 U.S. 796 (1999); *Kimel v. Florida Board of Regents*, 528 U.S. 62 (2000).
167. *United States v. Lopez*, 514 U.S. 549 (1995).
168. *United States v. Morison*, 529 U.S. 598 (2000).
169. See, e.g., *Board of Trustees of the University of Alabama v. Garrett*, 531 U.S. 536 (2001).
170. See J. T. Noonan, Jr., *Narrowing the Nation's Power* (2002); M. Tushnet, *A Court Divided* 249–50 (2005); Greenhouse, "Federalism: States Are Given New Legal Shield by Supreme Court," N.Y. Times, June 24, 1999, at A1.
171. See Post, "The Supreme Court, 2002 Term—Foreword, Fashioning the Legal Constitution," 117 Harv. L. Rev. 4 (2003)
172. 538 U.S. 721 (2003).
173. *U.S. Term Limits v. Thornton*, 514 U.S. 779, 848 (1995) (dissent).
174. *United States v. Lopez*, supra note 167, at 599–600 (dissent).
175. *Printz v. United States*, 521 U.S. 898, 937 (1997) (concurrence).
176. *Camps Newfound Owatonna v. Town of Harrison*, 520 U.S. 564, 611 (1997) (dissent).
177. 125 S.Ct. 2195 (2004).
178. Id. at 2199–2201.
179. Cal. Health & Safety Code Ann. sec. 11362.5 (West Supp. 2005).
180. Id. at 2211.
181. Id. at 2209.
182. Id. at 2210.
183. Id. at 2211.
184. Id. at 2197.
185. Id. at 2209.
186. Id. at 2210.

187. Id. at 2197.
188. Id. at 2211 n. 37.
189. Id. at 2217.
190. Id. at 2222.
191. Id. at 2224.
192. Id. at 2227.
193. Id. at 2226.
194. Id. at 2230.
195. Id. at 2235.
196. Id.
197. Id. at 2238.
198. Id. at 2213 n. 38.
199. Id.
200. 492 U.S. 573 (1989)
201. *Lynch v. Donnelly*, supra note 52.
202. Id. at 683.
203. Id. at 690.
204. Id. at 725.
205. 492 U.S. at 582.
206. Id. at 634.
207. Id. at 663–64.
208. Id. at 637.
209. Id. at 604.
210. Id. at 655.
211. 505 U.S. 577 (1992).
212. Id. at 594–95.
213. Id. at 636–37.
214. 330 U.S. 1 (1947).
215. Id. at 609–10.
216. Id. at 606.
217. *Santa Fe Independent School District v. Doe*, supra note 22.
218. Id. at 311–12.
219. *Board of Education v. Allen*, 392 U.S. 236 (1968); *Lemon v. Kurtzman*, supra note 52); *Levitt v. Committee for Public Education*, 413 U.S. 472 (1973); *Committee for Public Education v. Nyequist*, 413 U.S. 756 (1973); *Sloan v. Lemon*, 413 U.S. 825 (1973); *Wolman v. Walter*, 433 U.S. 229 (1977); *Committee for Public Education v. Regan*, 444 U.S. 646 (1980); *Mueller v. Allen*, 463 U.S. 388 (1983); *Aquilar v. Felton*, 473 U.S. 402 (1985); *Witters v. Washington Department of Services for the Blind*, 474 U.S. 481 (1986).
220. *Zobrest v. Catalina Foothills School District*, 509 U.S. 1 (1993).
221. Id. at 8.

222. Id. at 18.
223. *Rosenberger v. Rector and Visitors of the University of Virginia*, 515 U.S. 819 (1995).
224. Id. at 844.
225. Id. at 878.
226. *Agostini v. Felton*, 521 U.S. 203 (1997).
227. Id. at 223.
228. Id. at 240–41.
229. *Mitchell v. Helms*, 530 U.S. 793 (2000).
230. Id. at 822.
231. Id. at 837–38.
232. Id. at 867–68.
233. 536 U.S. 639 (2002).
234. Id. at 643–48.
235. Id. at 651–52.
236. Id. at 688–89.
237. 374 U.S. 398 (1963).
238. Id. at 404.
239. *Thomas v. Review Board*, 450 U.S. 707 (1981); *Hobbie v. Unemployment Appeals Commission*, 480 U.S. 136 (1987); *Frazee v. Illinois Deparment of Employment Security*, 489 U.S. 829 (1989).
240. *Wisconsin v. Yoder*, 406 U.S. 205 (1972).
241. Id. at 210–11. The Old Order Amish did not object to basic education for their children because they felt it prepared them to "read the Bible [and] to be good farmers and citizens." Id. at 212.
242. Id. at 235.
243. *United States v. Lee*, 455 U.S. 252 (1982).
244. *Goldman v. Weinberger*, 475 U.S. 503 (1986).
245. *O'Lone v. Estate of Shabazz*, 482 U.S. 342 (1987).
246. *Bowen v. Roy*, 476 U.S. 693 (1986).
247. *Lyng v. Northwest Indian Cemetery Protective Assoction*, 485 U.S. 439 (1988).
248. 494 U.S. 872 (1990).
249. Id. at 885 n.3.
250. Id. at 878–79.
251. Id. at 881.
252. Id. at 904–05.
253. Id. at 913 n. 6.
254. 508 U.S. 520 (1993).
255. Id. at 535–36.
256. Id. at 557.
257. Id. at 559.
258. *City of Boerne v. Flores*, 521 U.S. 507, 544–45 (1997).

259. *Texas Monthly v. Bullock*, 489 U.S. 1, 14–15 (1989).
260. *Board of Education of Kiryas Joel Village School District v. Grumet*, 512 U.S. 687 (1994).
261. *Aguilar v. Felton*, supra note 219.
262. *Kiryas Joel*, 512 U.S. at 708–09.
263. Id. at 732.
264. E.g., McGinnis, "Continuity and Coherence in the Rehnquist Court," 47 St. Louis U. L. J. 875 (2003).
265. *Locke v. Davey*, 540 U.S. 712 (2004).
266. Id. at 718–19.
267. See, e.g., *Eulitt v. Maine*, 386 F. 3d 344 (1st Cir.2004); *Bush v. Holmes*, 886 So. 2d 340 (Fla. Dist. Ct. App 20004), upholding state exclusions of religious schools from voucher programs.
268. *Aguilar v. Felton*, supra note 219, in which the Court found an establishment clause violation when public school teachers provided remedial instruction, under a general program, to students in parochial schools, represents that attitude. *Aguilar's* overruling in *Agostini v. Felton*, supra note 226, signaled the changing perspective.
269. Linda Greenhouse argued in her foreword to Bradley, *The Rehnquist Legacy*, supra note 104, at xiii–xxi, that "there was the unmistakable indication in the Court's [2003 and 2004 terms] that Chief Justice Rehnquist no longer [spoke] for a majority of the Court on many of the docket's most important issues." She cited a number of decisions from which Rehnquist dissented in those terms. But at the same she concluded that "[h]istory will evaluate the Rehnquist Court in all its phases, and I would be very surprised if the ambiguity of this final phase serves to cast doubt on the effectiveness or impact of a man who is already being proclaimed as one of the great Chief Justices." Id. at xxi.
270. 372 U.S. 726 (1963).
271. 367 U.S. at 541.
272. 521 U.S. at 721; id. at 765 (Souter, J., dissenting).
273. See Rehnquist, "The Notion of a Living Constitution," 54 Tex. L. Rev. 693 (1976).
274. *Rosenberger v. University of Virginia*, supra note 223, at 876.
275. *City of Boerne v. Flores*, supra note 258, at 548–49, 565.
276. For more detail, see White, "Historicizing Judicial Scrutiny," 57 S. C. L. Rev. 1 (2005).
277. See Shaman, "Cracks in the Structure: The Coming Breakdown of the Levels of Scrutiny," 45 Ohio State L. J. 161 (1984); Kelso, "Filling Gaps in the Supreme Court's Approach to Constitutional Review of Legislation," 33 S. Tex. L. Rev. 493 (1992); Massey, "The New Formalism: Requiem for Tiered Scrutiny?" 6 U. Pa. J. Const. L. 945 (2004).

CHAPTER 16

1. See L. Jaffe, *English and American Judges as Lawmakers* (1969).
2. In *DeFunis v. Odegaard*, 416 U.S. 312 (1974), the Court postponed decision on the constitutionality of minority admissions programs in state law schools by invoking the requirement that a controversy not be moot by the time it reaches the Court. Four dissenters said that the *DeFunis* issues "must inevitably return . . . in this Court." Id. at 350.
3. K. Llewellyn, *The Common Law Tradition* (1960), and J. Welter, *The Styles of Appellate Judicial Opinions* (1960), discuss changing modes of opinion-writing over time. Llewellyn's "grand" and "formal" styles are as much prescriptive as descriptive: see W. Twining, *Karl Llewellyn and the Realist Movement* 203–69 (1973).

Bibliographical Note

A variety of primary and secondary source materials forms the basis for my assessment of the judges portrayed in this study. A fuller listing of sources appears in the notes. This essay comments briefly on some of the principal sources. Since the appearance of the second edition, scholarship on judges, hitherto a comparatively limited enterprise, has proliferated. Many more recent secondary works on some of the judges in this book could have been listed; I have included ones I think readers will find particularly helpful. In addition, the primary sources related to the careers of some judges have dramatically increased as previously unpublished letters have appeared in print. Despite those developments, the relevant sources on notable American judges remain in an uneven state.

Of the nineteenth- and early-twentieth-century writings on Marshall, some stand out. Marshall's *Autobiographical Sketch* (John S. Adams, ed., 1937), originally written in the 1830s, is a detailed account of his early years. His *The Life of George Washington* (1805–7) contains numerous comments on the political and jurisprudential climate in which the Constitution was framed. Albert Beveridge's four-volume *Life of John Marshall* (1919) remains the liveliest account of Marshall's career; both Edward Corwin's *John Marshall and the Constitution* (1919) and Robert Faulkner's *The Jurisprudence of John Marshall* (1968) are more revealing of Marshall's thought and his approach to judging. Frances Mason's *My Dearest Polly* (1961), a collection of letters from Marshall to his wife, also provides a social history of Richmond at the time of Marshall and some anecdotes about the Marshall family. Melville Jones edited a valuable collection of essays on various aspects of Marshall's thought, *Chief Justice John Marshall, A Reappraisal* (1956). William Winslow Crosskey has provocative comments on Marshall in his *Politics and the Constitution in the History of the United States* (1953) and in "Mr. Chief Justice Marshall," in Allison Dunham and Philip Kurland, eds., *Mr. Justice* (1964). Gerald Gunther discovered and published Marshall's extrajudicial *Defense of McCulloch v. Maryland* (1969). Charles Warren's *The Supreme Court in United States History* (3 vols., 1922) is a good source for public reaction to Marshall's decisions.

The Institute of Early American History and Culture at the College of William and Mary has published, at this writing, 12 volumes of *The Papers of John Marshall,* under the current editorship of Charles Hobson. That collection, whose annotation is consistently of high quality, is an indispensable starting place for work on Marshall's life and career.

Three recent biographies of Marshall are worth consulting. Charles Hobson, *The Great Chief Justice* (1996), and Herbert Johnson, *The Chief Justiceship of John Marshall* (1897), are comparatively brief overviews written by specialists on Marshall and the Marshall Court. Kent Newmyer, *John Marshall and the Heroic Age of the Supreme Court* (2001), is a more complete treatment, the best biography of Marshall yet to appear. Two works on the Marshall Court are George Haskins and Herbert Johnson, *Foundations of Power*, volume 2 of the *Oliver Wendell Holmes Devise History of the Supreme Court of the United States* (1981), which covers the period 1801–1815, and G. Edward White, *The Marshall Court and Cultural Change* (1988), volumes 3–4 of the Holmes Devise history, which covers the years between 1815 and 1835. The best source on Marshall's early life and career is David S. Robarge, *John Marshall and His Times* (1995). Two symposia on Marshall containing several useful articles are in 33 John Marshall L. Rev. 743 ff (2000) and 43 Wm. & Mary L. Rev. 1321ff (2002). G. Edward White, "Reassessing John Marshall," 58 Wm. & Mary Q. 673 (2001), proposes a framework for revisionist scholarship on Marshall and the Marshall Court.

James Kent's papers and journals are in the Library of Congress. His son William Kent edited the *Memoirs and Letters of James Kent* (1898). Holmes's edition of Kent's *Commentaries on American Law* was published in four volumes in 1873. The fullest treatment of Kent's life remains John Horton's *James Kent: A Study in Conservatism* (1939). Joseph Dorfman's effort to relate Kent's decisions and writing to the economic context of his time, "Chancellor Kent and the Developing American Economy," 61 Colum. L. Rev. 290 (1961), remained the standard perspective on Kent for many years. Lawrence Friedman's comments on Kent in his *A History of American Law* 331–333 (2d ed., 1985) recognize that Kent was a more complex figure than traditionally portrayed.

From the late 1980s on Kent scholarship has become more revisionist. Notable examples are David W. Raack, " 'To Preserve the Best Fruits': The Legal Thought of Chancellor James Kent," 33 Am. J. Legal Hist. 320 (1989); John H. Langbein, "Chancellor

Kent and the History of Legal Literature," 93 Colum. L. Rev. 547 (1993); and Carl F. Stychin, "The Commentaries of Chancellor James Kent and the Development of an American Common Law," 37 Am. J. Legal Hist. 440 (1993). The largest concentration of revisionist work appears in Symposium, 74 Chicago-Kent L. Rev. 1ff (1999).

Story's continuous concern with putting his views on paper has resulted in several primary source collections, including a set of papers in the Massachusetts Historical Society, one in the Clements Library at the University of Michigan, one in the Library of Congress, one in the University of Texas Library, and one in the Essex Institute in Salem, Massachusetts. Story also published a collection entitled *The Miscellaneous Writings of Joseph Story* (1852), which contains an "Autobiography." His son William Story produced a *Life and Letters* of his father (1851) that is a source of correspondence, as is Charles Warren's *The Story-Marshall Correspondence* (1942). As judicial biography became launched in the 1970s, two books on Story appeared, Gerald Dunne's *Justice Joseph Story and the Rise of the Supreme Court* (1970) and James McClellan's *Joseph Story and the American Constitution* (1971). They had been preceded by two important treatments of Story, Henry Steele Commager's "Joseph Story" in the *Gaspar Bacon Lectures on the Constitution of the United States* (1953) and Perry Miller's *The Life of the Mind in America* (1965). Morton Horwitz's "The Conservative Tradition in the Writing of American Legal History," 17 Am. J. Legal Hist. 275 (1973), a review of McClellan, signaled the emergence of a new perspective on Story and other early-nineteenth-century judges that identified them as "instrumentalist" policy-makers interested in the perpetuation of the interests of legal and mercantile elites.

Revisionist work on Story began in the 1980s, encapsulated by R. Kent Newmyer, *Supreme Court Justice Joseph Story: Statesman of the Old Republic* (1985), which associated Story more with the republican ideology of the framers than antebellum elites. That theme, and Story's effort to infuse American constitutional law with natural law principles, were pursued in Alfred S. Konefsky, "Law and Culture in Antebellum Boston," 40 Stan. L. Rev. 1119 (1988); Calvin Woodard, "Joseph Story and American Equity," 45 W. & L. L. Rev. 623 (1988); and Christopher Eisgruber, "Justice Story, Slavery, and the Natural Law Foundations of American Constitutionalism," 55 U. Chi. L. Rev. 273 (1988).

The Shaw papers are in the Massachusetts Historical Society and Boston Social Law Library. Two interesting contemporary accounts of Shaw's life are found in volumes of the Massachusetts Reports 15 Gray 599 (1860) and 16 Gray 598 (1861). In Frederic Chase's biography entitled *Lemuel Shaw* (1918), the last chapter has some observations on Shaw's character and personality. Leonard Levy's *The Law of the Commonwealth and Chief Justice Shaw* (1957) is a thorough account of the corpus of Shaw's decisions. Robert M. Cover's *Justice Accused* (1975) treats Shaw's slavery opinions with imagination and insight. A revealing source of Shaw's thought before his appointment to the

Massachusetts Supreme Court is an address he delivered to the Suffolk Bar in 1827, reprinted as "Profession of the Law in the United States," 7 *American Jurist and Law Magazine* 56 (1832).

Very little work has appeared on Shaw since the first edition of this book. Two important articles are Kenneth S. Lynn, "Lemuel Shaw and Herman Melville," 5 Const. Comm. 411 (1988); and Alfred S. Konefsky, " 'As Best to Subserve Their Own Interests': Lemuel Shaw, Labor Conspiracy, and Fellow Servants," 7 Law and Hist. Rev. 219 (1989).

Taney's own account of his youth, entitled "Early Life and Education," appeared in Samuel Tyler's *Memoir of Roger Brooke Taney* (1872). There is a collection of Taney papers at the Maryland Historical Society. Taney's account of his role as Secretary of the Treasury during the Jackson Administration's attack on the National Bank of the United States is in a collection of his papers in the Library of Congress. Letters from Taney to Jackson are found in John S. Bassett, ed., *Correspondence of Andrew Jackson* (6 vols., 1926–34).

Taney has not received much scholarly attention for many years. The best biography remains Carl B. Swisher's *Roger B. Taney* (1935); the best short account of his career, Robert J. Harris's "Chief Justice Taney: Prophet of Reform and Reaction," 10 Vand. L. Rev. 227 (1957); and the best history of the Taney Court, Swisher's monumental *The Taney Period*, vol. 5 of the *Holmes Devise History of the Supreme Court of the United States* (1974). For an overview of Taney's career, see William Wiecek, "Roger Brooke Taney," in Leonard Levy, Kenneth Karst, and Daniel Mahoney, eds., *Encyclopedia of the American Constitution* (4 vols., 1986), 4, 1857. Hereafter cited as *Encyclopedia*, with volume and page numbers. On the *Dred Scott* case, see Don E. Fehrenbacher's influential treatment, *The Dred Scott Case* (1978).

No biography of Cooley exists; his papers are in the University of Michigan Historical Collections. At the time of the appearance of the first edition Cooley had been treated in four specialized studies: Philip S. Paludan, *A Covenant with Death* (1975); Sidney Fine, *Laissez-Faire and the General Welfare State* (1956); Clyde E. Jacobs, *Law Writers and the Courts* (1954); and Benjamin Twiss, *Lawyers and the Constitution* (1942). The most revealing articles on Cooley as a commentator and a judge in the 1960s were Alan Jones, "Thomas M. Cooley and the Michigan Supreme Court: 1865–1885," 10 Am. J. Legal Hist. 97 (1966); Jones, "Thomas M. Cooley and 'Lassez Faire Constitutionalism': A Reconsideration," 53 J. Am. Hist. 759 (1967); and Paludan, "Law and the Failure of Reconstruction: The Case of Thomas Cooley," 33 J. Hist. Ideas 597 (1972). Those articles traced the roots of Cooley's thought, up to that point caricatured as a blend of social Darwinism and laissez-faire economic conservatism, to free-labor antebellum ideologies. For an excellent overview of the connections between antebellum and late-nineteenth- and early-twentieth-century legal thought, see Charles W. McCurdy,

"The Liberty of Contract Regime in American Law," in Harry Scheiber, ed., *The State and Freedom of Contract* (1998).

Recent scholarship has shown comparatively little interest in Cooley. Exceptions are two articles by Paul W. Carrington, "Law as 'The Common Thoughts of Men': The Law Teaching and Judging of Thomas McIntyre Cooley," 49 Stan. L. Rev. 495 (1997) and "Law and Economics in the Creation of Federal Administrative Law: Thomas Cooley, Elder to the Republic," 83 Iowa L. Rev. 363 (1998); David J. Barron, "The Promise of Cooley's City," 149 U. Pa. L. Rev. 487 (1999); and James W. Ely, Jr., "Thomas Cooley, 'Public Use,' and New Directions in Takings Jurisprudence," 14 Mich. State L. Rev 845 (2004).

Piecing together information from the Doe Collection in the New Hampshire Historical Society, the Doe Papers at the Supreme Court of New Hampshire, and various other contemporaneous documents, John Reid produced a biography of Doe, *Chief Justice* (1967), which is a classic of its kind. Among the sources Reid relied on were Elmer Doe, *The Descendants of Nicholas Doe* (1917); Jeremiah Smith, *Memoir of Hon. Charles Doe* (1897); Joshua Hall, "Memoir of Hon. Charles Doe," 2 Proc. So. N.H. Bar Ass'n 84 (1896); Crawford D. Hening, "Charles Doe," in 8 W. D. Lewis, ed., *Great American Lawyers* 241 (1909); and Note, "Doe of New Hampshire: Reflections on a Nineteenth Century Judge," 63 Harv. L. Rev. 513 (1950). For a collection of observations by contemporaries, see 2 Proc. So. N.H. Bar Ass'n 84 (1896). The success of Reid's biography and the apparent lack of any connection between Doe's career and contemporary legal issues has resulted in virtually no scholarly attention to Doe in recent decades. The one exception tends to prove the rule: it has been a review of Reid's book, Stuart Schiffman, "Chief Justice: The Judicial World of Charles Doe," 39 Judges Journal 39 (2000).

At the time of the first edition no full-length scholarly biography of Harlan the Elder had appeared, and Harlan's papers, some of which are deposited at the Library of Congress and others at the University of Louisville Law School, were in a disorganized state, partly because Alan Westin had planned to write an authorized biography and abandoned the project. A study of Harlan's decisions, Floyd B. Clark's *The Constitutional Doctrines of Justice Harlan* (1915), badly needed updating. The best source on his early years at the time of the first edition was Louis Hartz, "John M. Harlan in Kentucky, 1855–1877," 14 Filson Club Historical Quarterly 17 (1940). Some Harlan speeches and personal anecdotes were reprinted in 46 Ky. L. J. 321ff (1958).

Nonetheless, some important articles on Harlan began to appear from the mid-1950s on. Those included Loren Beth, "Justice Harlan and the Uses of Dissent," Am. Pol. Sci. Rev. 1085 (1955); Alan Westin, "John Marshall Harlan and the Constitutional Rights of Negroes," 66 Yale L. J. 637 (1957); and Westin, "Mr. Justice Harlan," in Allison Dunham and Philip Kurland, eds., *Mr. Justice* (1964).

In 1999 Linda Przybyszewski's *The Republic According to John Marshall Harlan* appeared. This was the first full-length biography of Harlan, making use of previously unpublished documents, including the constitutional law lectures Harlan gave at George Washington University during his tenure on the Supreme Court and a memoir by Harlan's wife, Malvinia Shanklin Harlan. Using these sources and others, Przybyszewski fashioned a thoroughly revisionist portrait of Harlan, emphasizing the close connections between his religious views and his constitutional jurisprudence. Harlan's judicial perspective was seen as blend of antebellum attitudes toward political economy, a midlife conversion on race relations, and his version of religious orthodoxy. The caricature of Harlan as a visionary on civil rights and a baffling figure in all other respects was rounded out.

Despite Przybyszewski's contributions, the focus of much recent scholarship on Harlan has continued to be on his dissent in *Plessy v. Ferguson* and race relations. Representative articles include those by T. Alexander Aleinikoff, "Re-reading Justice Harlan's Dissent in *Plessy v. Ferguson*," 1992 U. Ill. L. Rev. 961 (1992); Nathaniel R. Jones, Earl M. Maltz, and Nelson Lund in Symposium: *Plessy v. Ferguson* after One Hundred Years," 12 Georgia State L. Rev. 951, 973, 1129 (1996); Molly Townes O' Brien, "Justice John Marshall Harlan as Prophet," 6 Wm. & Mary Bill of Rights J. 753 (1998); Gabriel J. Chin, "The First Justice Harlan by the Numbers: Just How Great Was the 'Great Dissenter?'" 32 Akron L. Rev. 629 (1999); and Frederic Rogers, "'Our Constitution Is Color Blind': Justice John Marshall Harlan and the *Plessy v. Ferguson* Dissent," 43 Judges Journal 15 (2004).

At the time of the first edition Holmes had already been written on extensively, and there were two successful biographies with different perspectives, Catherine Drinker Bowen's *Yankee from Olympus* (1943), an undocumented popular treatment that emphasized his family relations, and Mark de Wolfe Howe's *Justice Oliver Wendell Holmes: The Shaping Years* (1957) and *Justice Oliver Wendell Holmes: The Proving Years* (1963), which stressed the development of his ideas. Among the best early articles were Walton Hamilton, "On Dating Justice Holmes," U. Chi. L. Rev. I (1941); Daniel Boorstin, "The Elusiveness of Mr. Justice Holmes," 14 New England Q. 478 (1941); Yosal Rogat, "The Judge as Spectator," 31 U. Chi. L. Rev. 213 (1964); and Robert Faulkner's appendix comparing Holmes with Marshall in his *The Jurisprudence of John Marshall* (1968). For a compilation and evaluation of this literature, see G. Edward White, "The Rise and Fall of Justice Holmes," 39 U. Chi. L. Rev. 51 (1971).

Harvard Law School acquired the Holmes papers after Felix Frankfurter selected Mark Howe to write an authorized biography of Holmes and Howe joined the Harvard law faculty after World War II. After Howe's untimely death in 1967, with a substantial portion of the biography left to complete, Holmes's literary executors decided to appoint Grant Gilmore, then on the Yale law faculty, to complete the biography. Gilmore had custody of the Holmes papers until his death in 1982 but did not produce a manuscript. Eventually, in 1985, Harvard and Holmes's executors resolved to allow the collection of Holmes's papers, which mainly consisted of letters, to be microfilmed and made available generally to scholars.

During the course of Howe's work on the biography he edited two collections of Holmes's letters, *Holmes–Pollock Letters* (1941, 2d ed. 1961), consisting of correspondence over seven decades between Holmes and his longtime friend Frederick Pollock, and *Holmes–Laski Letters* (2 vols., 1953), an even more voluminous correspondence between Holmes and the British political theorist Harold Laski, whom Holmes first met in 1916. Eventually other letter collections in the Holmes papers were published, including James B. Peabody, ed., *The Holmes–Einstein Letters* (1964), which covered Holmes's correspondence between 1903 and 1935 with the British diplomat Lewis Einstein; David M. Burton, ed., *Holmes–Sheehan Correspondence* (1976), letters between Holmes and his friend the Irish parish priest Patrick Augustine Sheehan; and Robert M. Mennel and Christine L. Compston, eds., *Holmes and Frankurter, Their Correspondence 1912–1934* (1996), covering the correspondence between Holmes and Felix Frankfurter. In addition Howe edited a diary and letters Holmes had written during his service in the Civil War, *Touched with Fire* (1946). The result was that even while the Holmes papers remained closed, scholars had considerable access to his correspondence, and since 1985 the entire body of Holmes's private letters and documents has been available.

Scholarship on Holmes, which has been voluminous, has been significantly affected by the availability of his private papers. In the years after Howe's death, as Gilmore was working on the biography, scholarship on Holmes continued at a comparatively brisk pace. H. L. Pohlman published a book in 1984, *Justice Oliver Wendell Holmes and Utilitarian Jurisprudence*, that attempted a revised understanding of Holmes's legal thought. Important essays by Benjamin Kaplan, "Encounters with O. W. Holmes, Jr.," Patrick Atiyah, "The Legacy of Holmes Through English Eyes," and Jan Vetter, "The Evolution of Holmes: Holmes and Evolution," appeared in a volume entitled *Holmes and the Common Law: A Century Later* (1983). Saul Touster, "Holmes a Hundred Years Ago," Robert Gordon, "Holmes's *Common Law* as Legal and Social Science," and G. Edward White, "The Integrity of Holmes's Jurisprudence," appeared in a symposium on Holmes in 10 Hofstra L. Rev. 633ff (1982). Frederic R. Kellogg's *The Formative Essays of Justice Holmes* (1984) treated Holmes's early undergraduate and legal essays. For an overview of recent scholarship on Holmes, see G. Edward White, "Looking at Holmes in the Mirror," Law and History Rev. 439 (1986). An essay by G. Edward White, "Oliver Wendell Holmes," in 2 *Encyclopedia* 920, summarizes the state of scholarship on Holmes in the mid-1980s.

The microfilming of the Holmes papers and the opening up of the Harvard collection to scholars resulted in a flurry of biographical studies on Holmes in the late 1980s and early 1990s. The first of those to appear was John S. Monagan's *The Grand Panjandrum: The Mellow Years of Justice Holmes* (1998), which focused on Holmes's personal life in his later years. Monagan's research in the Holmes papers resulted in his discovery of the relationship between Holmes and an Irishwoman, Clare Fitzpatrick, Lady Castletown, whom Holmes had first met on a trip to England in 1889. After returning to England in 1896 and spending time with Clare Castletown in London and one of her estates in Ireland, Holmes returned home smitten with Clare, who was married to Bernard Castletown, a Member of Parliament. In a series of letters to Clare, only some of which have survived, Holmes discussed a variety of topics, including the state of his feelings. He destroyed nearly all the letters Clare wrote to him. The letters, which mainly covered the years from 1896 to 1899, were secured from Doneraile, a Castletown family estate, by the wife of Mark Howe in the 1940s. They remained in the custody of Mark Howe and then of Grant Gilmore, who did not publicize their existence, until the Holmes papers were returned to Harvard Law School. Monagan published an account of the letters in "The Love Letters of Justice Holmes," Boston Globe Magazine, March 24, 1985, 15.

The opening up of the Holmes papers also resulted in the appearance of two trade biographies, Sheldon Novick's *Honorable Justice* (1989) and Liva Baker's *The Justice from Beacon Hill* (1991). Both were primarily centered on Holmes's personal life, and discussed the Castletown relationship. Meanwhile scholars began a reassessment of Holmes's career as a judge and legal scholar. Three works in the early 1990s reflected that trend: a collection of essays edited by Robert W. Gordon, *The Legacy of Oliver Wendell Holmes, Jr.* (1992), Michael Hoffheimer, *Justice Holmes and the Natural Law* (1993), and G. Edward White, *Justice Oliver Wendell Holmes: Law and the Inner Self* (1993). In addition Richard A. Posner edited a one-volume collection of Holmes's writings, *The Essential Holmes* (1992), which surpasses an earlier compendium by Max Lerner, *The Mind and Faith of Justice Holmes* (1943). Sheldon Novick has undertaken an edition of Holmes's collected works, encompassing his "complete public writings and selected judicial opinions." Three of five planned volumes have currently appeared. See Novick, ed., *The Collected Works of Justice Holmes* (1995).

In addition, several short biographical treatments of Holmes have appeared since the opening of the Holmes papers. They include Gary J. Aichele, *Oliver Wendell Holmes: Soldier, Scholar, Judge* (1989); David H. Burton, *The Political Ideas of Justice Holmes* (1992); Raymond S. Morris, *Supreme Court Justice Oliver Wendell Holmes Jr.* (1995); and G. Edward White, *Oliver Wendell Holmes, Jr.* (2006). Recent specialized works on Holmes include H. L. Pohlman, *Justice Oliver Wendell Holmes: Free Speech and the Living Constitution* (1991) and David Rosenberg, *The Hidden Holmes: His Theory of Torts in History* (1995). Albert W. Alschuler's *Law Without Values* (2000) is a witty, sometimes devastating critique of Holmes's jurisprudence. Louis Menand has a trenchant analysis of Holmes in *The Metaphysical Club* (2001).

Since the late 1980s articles on Holmes have also proliferated. The following are particularly useful: Robert A. Ferguson, "Holmes and the Judicial Figure," 55 U. Chi. L. Rev. 506 (1988); Michael H. Hoffheimer, "Justice Holmes: Law and the Search for Control," 1989 Supreme Court Historical Society Yearbook 98 (1989); Thomas C.

Grey, "Holmes and Legal Pragmatism," 41 Stan. L. Rev. 787 (1989); Michael H. Hoffheimer, "The Early Critical and Philosophical Writings of Justice Holmes," 30 B. U. L. Rev. 1221 (1989); Patrick J. Kelley, "Was Holmes a Pragmatist?" 14 Southern Ill. L. Rev. 427 (1990); Neil Duxbury, "The Birth of Legal Realism and the Myth of Justice Holmes," 20 Anglo-American L. Rev. 81 (1991); David Luban, "Justice Holmes and the Metaphysics of Judicial Restraint," 44 Duke L. J. 449 (1994); Robert Brauneis, " 'The Foundation of Our Regulatory Takings Jurisprudence': The Myth and Meaning of Justice Holmes's Opinion in *Pennsylvania Coal Co. v. Mahon*," 106 Yale L. J. 613 (1996); David J. Seipp, "Holmes's Path," 77 B. U. L. Rev. 515 (1997); Anne C. Dailey, "Holmes and the Romantic Mind," 48 Duke L. J. 429 (1998); I. Scott Messinger, "The Judge as Mentor: Oliver Wendell Holmes Jr. and his Law Clerks," 11 Yale J. Law & Humanities 119 (1999); Patrick J. Kelley, "A Critical Analysis of Holmes's Theory of Contract," 75 Notre Dame L. Rev. 1681 (2000); G. Edward White, "Hiss and Holmes," 28 Ohio Northern L. Rev. 231 (2002); and Vincent Blasi, "Holmes and the Marketplace of Ideas," 2004 Sup. Ct. Rev. 1 (2004).

Finally, three symposia, all generated by the centennial of Holmes's essay "The Path of the Law," should be consulted: "The Path of the Law After One Hundred Years," 110 Harv. L. Rev. 989ff (1997); "The Path of the Law One Hundred Years Later," 63 Brooklyn L. Rev. 1ff (1997); and "The Path of the Law Today," 78 B. U. L. Rev. 717ff (1998).

Alpheus Mason was Brandeis's authorized biographer, and produced *Brandeis: A Free Man's Life* (1946), and two earlier analytical studies of Brandeis's ideas, *Lawyer and Judge in the Modern State* (1933), and *The Brandeis Way* (1938). All of those works suffered from a lack of critical distance; Mason's best work on Brandeis is found in his essay "Louis D. Brandeis," in 4 Leon Friedman and Fred Israel, eds., *The Justice of the United States Supreme Court* 2043 (1969). Alexander Bickel's *The Unpublished Opinions of Mr. Justice Brandeis* (1957) contains some valuable insights on Brandeis's approach to the collegial dimensions of Supreme Court judging. Louis Jaffe's "Was Brandeis an Activist? The Search for Intermediate Premises," 80 Harv. L. Rev. 986 (1966), undertakes to evaluate Brandeis's contributions in the light of process-inspired criticism of the Warren Court. Melvin Urofsky's *A Mind of One Piece: Brandeis and American Reform* (1971) is an excellent brief overview of Brandeis's ideas. Two studies assessing Brandeis's distinctive legacy to administrative law are Jaffe, "The Contributions of Mr. Justice Brandeis to Administrative Law," 18 Iowa L. Rev. 213 (1933), and G. Edward White, "Allocating Power Between Agencies and Courts: The Legacy of Justice Brandeis," 1974 Duke L. J. 195 (1974). Collections of Brandeis papers are held at the law schools of the University of Louisville and Harvard University.

A flurry of interest of Brandeis in the early 1980s produced Allon Gal, *Brandeis of Boston* (1980), on Brandeis's early life and career; Bruce Allen Murphy, *The Brandeis/Frankfurter Connection* (1982), unearthing and discussing a secret arrangement between Brandeis and Frankfurter when the former was a Supreme Court Justice and the latter a law professor at Harvard, and Philippa Strum, *Louis D. Brandeis* (1984). Strum has continued work on Brandeis, producing *Brandeis: Beyond Progressivism* (1993) and *Brandeis on Democracy* (1994). Two particularly illuminating studies of Brandeis are Stephen Baskerville, *Of Laws and Limitations: An Intellectual Portrait of Louis Dembitz Brandeis* (1994), and Edward A. Purcell, *Brandeis and the Progressive Constitution* (2000). Melvin Urofsky has an edition of letters Brandeis wrote to Frankfurter, *"Half Brother, Half Son"*: The Letters of Louis D. Brandeis to Felix Frankfurter (1991).

Helpful articles on Brandeis that have appeared since the mid-1980s are Vincent Blasi, "The First Amendment and the Ideal of Civic Courage," 29 Wm. & Mary L. Rev. 653 (1988); Robert C. Post, "Rereading Warren and Brandeis; Privacy, Property, and Appropriation," 41 Case Western Reserve L. Rev. 647 (1991); Daniel A. Farber, "Reinventing Brandies—Legal Pragmatism for the Twenty-first Century," 1995 Ill. L. Rev. 163 (1995); Clyde Spillenger, "Elusive Advocate," 105 Yale L. J. 1445 (1996); and Christopher Bracey, "Louis Brandeis and the Race Question," 52 Alabama L. Rev. 859 (2001).

The Cardozo papers, deposited in the Columbia University Library, were severely edited at one time by friends of Cardozo, and are in consequence not particularly revealing. George Hellman, a family friend, published an undocumented biography, *Benjamin N. Cardozo*, in 1940. Hellman's notes are in the Columbia University collection. The best early work on Cardozo included a collection of essays in 52 Harv. L. Rev. 261ff (1939)—especially those by Irving Lehman, Arthur Corbin, and Warren Seavey; and Andrew L. Kaufman's two essays, "Mr. Justice Cardozo," in Dunham and Kurland, *supra*, and "Benjamin Cardozo," in Friedman and Israel, *supra*. G. Edward White, *Tort Law in America: An Intellectual History*, 114–38 (1980), has a chapter on Cardozo's torts opinions.

After nearly a decade of neglect, Cardozo scholarship underwent a significant revival in the 1990s. Not only were early biographies of Cardozo and his books of essays reprinted but also two major biographies appeared, as did Richard A. Posner's *Cardozo: A Study in Reputation* (1990). Posner's quite favorable portrait of Cardozo as a judge was rounded out by Richard Polenberg's *The World of Benjamin Cardozo* (1997) and Andrew L. Kaufman's *Cardozo* (1998). The Polenberg volume concentrated on Cardozo's intellectual and political attitudes; the Kaufman volume was an exhaustive treatment, based on years of research, of Cardozo's life and career.

Perhaps because of the high quality of the Polenberg and Kaufman biographies, comparatively few illuminating articles on Cardozo appeared in the same time period. Examples were John C. P. Goldberg, "Community and the Common Law Judge," 65 N. Y. U. L. Rev. 1324 (1990); William H. Manz, "Cardozo's Use of Authority: An Empirical Study," 32 Cal. Western L. Rev. 31 (1995); Mike Townsend, "Cardozo's *Allegheny College* Opinion," 33 Houston L. Rev. 1103 (1996); Richard Polenberg, "The 'Saintly' Cardozo: Character and the Criminal Law," 71 U. Colo. L. Rev. 1311 (2000); William H. Manz, "*Palsgraf:* Cardozo's Urban Legend?" 107 Dick. L. Rev. 785 (2003); and Curtis Bridgeman, *Allegheny College* Revisited, 39 U. Cal. Davis L. Rev. 149 (2005). Kaufman's "Cardozo and the Art of Biography," 20 Cardozo L. Rev. 1245 (1999) is an interesting discussion of the author's longtime engagement with his subject. Dan Simon, "The Double Consciousness of Judging: The Problematic Legacy of Cardozo," 79 Ore. L. Rev. 1033 (2000) is a more critical treatment of Cardozo's judicial approach. See also Symposium, Judges as Tort Lawmakers, 49 DePaul L. Rev. 281ff (1999).

During the time of first two editions the Learned Hand papers were in the possession of Gerald Gunther, who was preparing an authorized biography. Work on Hand in that period was affected by Gunther's exclusive access to the Hand papers, although some useful books and articles appeared. Marvin Schick, *Learned Hand's Court* (1970), is an account of the inner workings of the Court of Appeals for the Second Circuit while Hand was its Chief Justice, and Kathryn Griffith, *Judge Learned Hand and the Role of the Federal Judiciary* (1973) is an analysis of his jurisprudence. Both works suffer from the absence of a detailed treatment of Hand's judicial decisions. A student of Gunther's, Michael A. Kahn, used the Hand papers in "The Politics of the Appointment Process: An Analysis of Why Learned Hand Was Never Appointed to the Supreme Court," 25 Stan. L. Rev. 251 (1973). The two best treatments of Hand to appear in the mid–twentieth century were Philip Hamburger's "The Great Judge," 21 Life 116 (1946), and Hershel Shanks's introduction to *The Art and Craft of Judging: The Decisions of Judge Learned Hand* (1968). Some articles of interest are collected in 60 Harv. L. Rev. 325ff (1947). Hand contributed some extrajudicial writing of his own in the 1950s: his *Spirit of Liberty* (1953) is a revealing collection of essays, and his *The Bill of Rights* (1958) contains his advocacy of a limited judicial review of constitutional cases.

In 1994 Gunther's *Learned Hand: The Man and the Judge* appeared, dwarfing previous work on Hand in the same fashion as Kaufman's biography of Cardozo. Gunther emphasized Hand's close connection to early-twentieth-century Progressive politics, drawing on Hand's private papers. The book is consequently as much a study of urban reform in the twentieth century as of Hand's judicial career. Gunther's great affection for his subject, and his orientation toward public law, shaped his perspective on Hand, resulting in a lighter treatment of Hand's private law decisions than might have been expected and the absence of a critical stance toward some of Hand's constitutional law opinions. Nonetheless, Gunther's biography remains the starting place for information about Hand.

Gunther's limited emphasis on Hand's private law decisions has been redressed, to some extent, by several illuminating articles on Hand's famous decision in the admiralty case, *United States v. Carroll Towing Co.*, in which he offered an economic formula for determining negligence. See Matthew P. Harrington, "The Admiralty Origins of Law and Economics," 7 George Mason L. Rev. 105 (1998); Daniel Q. Posen, "The Error of the Coarse Theorem: Of Judges Hand and Posner and *Carroll Towing*," 74 Tulane L. Rev. 629 (1999); Richard W. Wright, "Hand, Posner, and the Myth of the Hand Formula," 4 Theoretical Inquiries in Law 145 (2003); and Allen M. Feldman and

Jeonghyun Kim, "The Hand Rule and *United States v. Carroll Towing* Reconsidered," 7 Am. Law & Econ. Rev. 523 (2005).

For more on Hand's constitutional opinions, see Vincent Blasi, "Learned Hand and the Self-Government Theory of the First Amendment," 61 U. Colo. L. Rev. 1 (1990); Bernard Schwartz, "Holmes v. Hand," 1994 Sup. Ct. Rev. 209 (1994); and Geoffrey R. Stone, "Judge Learned Hand and the Espionage Act of 1917: A Mystery Unraveled," 70 U. Chi. L. Rev. 335 (2003). Two reflections on Hand's judicial persona are Carl Landauer, "Scholar, Craftsman, and Priest: Learned Hand's Self-Imaging," 3 Yale J. Law & Humanities 231 (1991); and Kenneth Lloyd Port, "Learned Hand's Trademark Jurisprudence: Legal Positivism and the Myth of the Prophet," 27 Pacific L. J. 221 (1996). For an interesting exchange between Gerald Gunther and some critics of his biography, see Symposium, National Conference on Judicial Biography, 70 N. Y. U. L. Rev. 697–729 (1995), which is a good general source for work on several of the Justices in this study.

Comparatively little scholarship on Jerome Frank has appeared since Robert Jerome Glennon's biography, *The Iconoclast as Reformer* (1985). Three book-length works on Frank had appeared by the 1970s, none of them particularly illuminating: Julius Paul, *The Legal Realism of Jerome N. Frank* (1959), J. Mitchell Rosenberg, *Jerome Frank: Jurist and Philosopher* (1970), and Walter E. Volkomer, *The Passionate Liberal: The Political and Legal Ideas of Jerome Frank* (1970). Several perceptive articles appeared in 1957, the year of Frank's death, among them Thurman Arnold, "Judge Jerome Frank," 24 U. Chi. L. Rev. 633 (1957); Charles E. Clark, "Jerome N. Frank," 66 Yale L. J. 817 (1957); Sidney M. Davis, "Jerome Frank—Portrait of a Personality," 24 U. Chi. L. Rev. 627 (1957); and Philip B. Kurland, "Jerome N. Frank: Some Reflections and Recollections of a Law Clerk," 24 U. Chi. L. Rev. 661 (1957). Wilfred Rumble discussed of Frank's ideas in "Jerome Frank and His Critics: Certainty and Fantasy in the Judicial Process," 10 J. Pub. Law 125 (1961). Frank's own essay, "Some Reflections on Judge Learned Hand," 24 U. Chi. L. Rev. 66 (1957) is a better source for Frank's ideas than for Hand's. William Twining has some interesting comments on Frank in *Karl Llewellyn and the Realist Movement* (1973). The Oral History Project at Columbia University contains a memoir by Frank.

The best of the few more recent articles on Frank are Neil Duxbury, "Jerome Frank and the Legacy of Legal Realism," 18 J. Law and Society 175 (1991); Morris D. Bernstein, "Learning from Experience: Jerome Frank and the Clinical Habit of Mind," 25 Capital U. L. Rev. 517 (1996); and Kent Greenawalt, "Variations on Some Themes of a 'Disporting Gazelle' and His Friend: Statutory Interpretation as Seen by Jerome Frank and Felix Frankfurter," 100 Colum. L. Rev. 176 (2000).

Hughes is overdue for a new biography. The Hughes Papers, in the Library of Congress, should be supplemented by the David Danelski and Joseph Tulchin edition of *The Autobiographical Notes of Charles Evans Hughes* (1973). Hughes's notes are deliberately official and ponderous but revealing nonetheless. The introduction by Danelski and Tulchin is the finest single piece on Hughes. Merlo Pusey's two-volume biography, *Charles Evans Hughes* (1951), is thorough, but the fact that it is authorized makes it somewhat less than detached.

Several early works on Hughes are still useful. See Edwin McElwain, "The Business of the Supreme Court as Conducted by Chief Justice Hughes," 63 Harv. L. Rev. 5 (1949); Samuel Hendel, "The 'Liberalism' of Chief Justice Hughes," 10 Vand L. Rev. 259 (1959); F. D. G. Ribble, "The Constitutional Doctrines of Chief Justice Hughes," 41 Colum. L. Rev. 1190 (1941); and Paul Freund, "Charles Evans Hughes: Chief Justice," 81 Harv. L. Rev. 4 (1967). Michael E. Parrish's entry, "Charles Evans Hughes," 2 *Encyclopedia* 930, is a good overview.

Although recent scholars have occasionally written on Hughes himself (see, for example, Samuel R. Olken, "Charles Evans Hughes and the *Blaisdell* Decision," 72 Ore. L. Rev. 513 (1993)), most of the attention of recent scholars has centered on the Hughes Court rather than Hughes, particularly the dramatic changes in constitutional jurisprudence that took place in the 1930s and early 1940s, and have been claimed by some historians to be a response to the Roosevelt Administration's introduction of a bill to change the composition of the Court in the spring of 1937. For a statement of the long-established view that the Hughes Court "switched" its stance in political economy cases in response to the "Court-packing" plan, see William E. Leuchtenburg, *The Supreme Court Reborn* (1995). For a revisionist view, emphasizing that the Court's decision in *West Coast Hotel v. Parrish*, often singled out as illustrative of its "switch," had taken place before the introduction of the Court-packing plan, and that two justices, Willis Van Devanter and George Sutherland, actually delayed their retirements once the plan was announced, see Barry Cushman, *Rethinking the New Deal Court* (1998).

Revisionist work on the Hughes Court has precipitated a broader debate centering on the extent to which factors "internal" or "external" to the decision-making process of Supreme Court Justices precipitate changes in the Court's constitutional jurisprudence. Related to that debate is the question whether the accommodation of the Hughes Court to modern social and economic legislation furthered or retarded the "liberal" trajectory of American politics. On the former issue, Barry Cushman has been the leading "internalist." See Cushman, "The Hughes Court and Constitutional Consultation," 1998 J. Sup. Ct. Hist 79 (1998); "Lost Fidelities," 41 Wm. & Mary L. Rev. 95 (1999); "Formalism and Realism in Commerce Clause Jurisprudence," 67 U. Chi. L. Rev. 1089 (2000); "Mr. Dooley and Mr. Gallup: Public Opinion and Constitutional Change in the 1930s," 50 Buff. L. Rev. 7 (2002). See also William E. Leuchtenburg, "Franklin D. Roosevelt's Court 'Packing' Plan: A Second Life, a Second Death," 1985 Duke L. J. 673 (1985); Richard D. Friedman, "Switching Time and Other Thought Experiments: The Hughes Court and Constitutional Transformation," 142 U. Pa. L. Rev. 1891 (1994); Laura Kalman, "Law, Politics, and the New Deal(s)," 108 Yale L. J. 101 (1999); G. Edward White, *The Constitution and the New Deal* (2000);

William E. Leuchtenburg, "Charles Evans Hughes: The Center Holds," 83 N. C. L. Rev. 1187 (2005); Forum, "The Debate over the Constitutional Revolution of 1937," 110 Am. Hist. Rev. 1046ff (articles by Alan Brinkley, Laura Kalman, William E. Leuchtenburg, and G. Edward White). On the latter issue, see the Symposium in 26 Law & Hist. Rev. 115ff (2006) (articles by James A. Henretta, Daniel T. Rodgers, William E. Forbath, William J. Novack, and Risa L. Goluboff).

Alpheus Mason's *Harlan Fiske Stone* (1956) surpasses his biography of Brandeis and is one of the fine judicial biographies. Mason had access to Stone's personal correspondence during his incumbency on the Court, and the yield was a wealth of normally unrevealed information. The best brief essay on Stone remains Allison Dunham's "Mr. Justice Stone," in Dunham and Kurland, *supra.* Other helpful early works are Noel T. Dowling's "Mr. Justice Stone and the Constitution," 36 Colum. L. Rev. 351 (1936); Dowling's "The Methods of Mr. Justice Stone in Constitutional Cases," 41 Colum. L. Rev. 1160 (1941); John P. Frank, "Harlan Fiske Stone: An Estimate," 9 Stan. L. Rev. 621 (1957); Herbert Wechsler, "Stone and the Constitution," 46 Colum. L. Rev. 793 (1946); and Learned Hand, "Chief Justice Stone's Conception of the Judicial Function," 46 Colum. L. Rev. 696 (1946), the last as much for what it says about the author as for the subject. Stone's classic essay, "The Common Law in the United States," appeared in 50 Harv. L. Rev. (1936).

There has been a surprisingly little amount of scholarship on Stone since the 1970s, especially because of the great interest in his opinion in *United States v. Carolene Products Co.* as a charter for modern constitutional review. Three articles in the mid-1990s addressed *Carolene Products*: Peter Linzer, "The Carolene Products Footnote and the Preferred Position of Individual Rights," 12 Const. Comm. 277 (1995); Miriam Galston, "Activism and Restraint: The Evolution of Harlan Fiske Stone's Judicial Philosophy," 70 Tulane L. Rev. 137 (1995); and Matthew Perry, "Justice Stone and Footnote 4," 6 George Mason University Civil Rights L. J. 35 (1996). The Linzer article is particularly illuminating. Melvin Urofsky's *Division and Discord: The Supreme Court Under Stone and Vinson* (1997), a brief overview, illustrates the current tendency of historians to think of the period between 1941 and 1953, combining the two comparatively brief Chief Justiceships of Stone and Fred Vinson, as representing a distinctive phase in twentieth-century constitutional history. For a more detailed recent treatment, including portraits of Stone and several of the other justices featured in this study, see William M. Wiecek, *The Birth of the Modern Constitution* (2006).

Jackson still lacks an adequate biography. His papers are now at the Library of Congress, and they are a comparatively rich source. In addition, the Oral History Project at Columbia University has an extensive collection of interviews with Jackson, which Philip Kurland used in an interesting sketch, "Robert H. Jackson," in Friedman and Israel, *supra.* Eugene Gerhart's authorized biography of Jackson, *America's Advocate,* appeared in 1958; Gerhart's brief analysis of his decisions, *Lawyer's Judge*, in 1961. The single most illuminating analysis of Jackson remains Louis Jaffe's "Mr. Justice Jackson," 68 Harv. L. Rev. 940 (1955). Other important early articles are Paul Freund, "Individual and Commonwealth in the Thought of Mr. Justice Jackson," 8 Stan. L. Rev. 9 (1955); Charles Fairman, "Robert H. Jackson," 55 Colum. L. Rev. 445 (1955); Felix Frankfurter, "Mr. Justice Jackson," 68 Harv. L. Rev. 937 (1955); Warner Gardner, "Robert H. Jackson, 1892–1958—Government Attorney," 55 Colum. L. Rev. 438 (1955); and Telford Taylor, "The Nuremberg Trials," 55 Colum. L. Rev. 488 (1955). Jackson contributed three works of his own: *The Struggle for Judicial Supremacy* (1941), *Full Faith and Credit: The Lawyer's Clause of the Constitution* (1946), and *The Supreme Court in the American System of Government* (1955). Michael E. Parrish's overview, "Robert H. Jackson," 3 *Encyclopedia* 1006, is useful.

William Domnarski has a portrait of Jackson and his relations with some of his judicial colleagues in *The Great Justices, 1941–1954: Black, Douglas, Frankfurter and Jackson in Chambers* (2006). Although Domnarski has a good sense of Jackson's often ambivalent posture toward being a Supreme Court Justice, the book lacks analytical depth, although it is superior to another group portrait, Jeffrey D. Hockett's *New Deal Justice: The Constitutional Jurisprudence of Hugo L. Black, Felix Frankfurter, and Robert H. Jackson* (1996).

The numerous articles on Jackson that have appeared since the mid-1980s give testimony to the continuing interest in his life and career. Particularly helpful are Dennis Hutchinson, "The Black–Jackson Feud," 1988 Sup. Ct. Rev. 203 (1988); Bernard Schwartz, "Chief Justice Rehnquist, Justice Jackson, and the *Brown* Case," 1988 Sup. Ct. Rev. 245 (1998); Jeffrey D. Hockett, "Justice Robert H. Jackson, The Supreme Court and the Nuremberg Trial," 1990 Sup. Ct. Rev. 257 (1990); Stephen R. Alton, "Loyal Lieutenant, Able Advocate: The Role of Robert H. Jackson in Franklin D. Roosevelt's Battle with the Supreme Court," 5 Wm. & Mary Bill of Rights J. 527 (1997); Gregory S. Chernack, "The Clash of Two Worlds: Justice Robert H. Jackson, Institutional Pragmatism, and *Brown*," 72 Temple L. Rev. 59 (1999); Dennis J. Hutchinson, "The 'Achilles Heel' of the Constitution: Justice Jackson and the Japanese Exclusion Case," 2002 Sup. Ct. Rev. 455 (2002); and Patrick Schmidt, " 'The Dilemma to a Free People': Justice Robert Jackson, Walter Bagehot, and the Creation of a Conservative Jurisprudence," 20 Law & Hist. Rev. 517 (2002). There are two symposia on Jackson in 68 Albany L. Rev. 1ff (2004) and 531ff (2005).

The most revealing writing on Traynor is his own, in the numerous law-review articles cited in the notes for chapter 13. Three symposia contain most of the significant scholarly analyses of Traynor: 13 Stan. L. Rev. 717 (1961), 53 Calif. L. Rev. (1965), and So. Calif. L. Rev. 876 (1971). See especially Walter V. Schaefer, "Justice Roger J. Traynor," 13 Stan. L. Rev. 717; Brainerd Currie, "Justice Traynor and the Conflict of Laws," 13 Stan L. Rev. 719; Wex S. Malone, "Contrasting Images of Torts—The Judicial Personality of

Justice Traynor," 13 Stan. I. Rev. 779; Stewart Macaulay, "Justice Traynor and the Law of Contracts," 13 Stan. L. Rev. 812; Robert B. McKay, "Constitutional Law: Ideas in the Public Forum," 53 Calif. L. Rev. 67; Barbara N. Armstrong, "Family Law: Order Out of Chaos," 53 Calif. L. Rev. 121; James E. Sabine, "Taxation: A Delicately Planned Arrangement of Cargo," 53 Calif. L. Rev. 173; Harry Kalven, "Torts: The Quest for Appropriate Standards," 53 Calif. L. Rev. 189; Leonard G. Ratner, "Reflections of a Traynor Law Clerk," So. Calif. L. Rev. 876A; Geoffrey C. Hazard, Jr., "Res Nova in Res Judicata," So. Calif. L. Rev. 1036; and Page Keeton, "Roger Traynor and the Law of Torts," So. Calif. L. Rev. 1045.

For a series of tributes to Traynor on his death in 1983, see 71 Calif. L. Rev. 1037ff (1983) and 69 Va. L. Rev. 1351 (1983). I have a chapter on Traynor's decisions in the area of tort law in *Tort Law in America* at 180–219. Many of Traynor's extrajudicial writings are collected in *The Traynor Reader* (1987). A few articles have appeared on Traynor since the mid-1980s. See John W. Poulos, "The Judicial Philosophy of Roger Traynor," 46 Hast. L. J. 1643 (1995); Alfred S. Konefsky, "Freedom and Interdependence in Twentieth-Century Contract Law: Traynor and Hand and Promissory Estoppel," 65 U. Cinn. L. Rev. 1169 (1997; James R. McCall, "Thoughts About Roger Traynor and Learned Hand," 65 U. Cinn. L. Rev. 1243 (1997); and Stephen J. Lubben, "Chief Justice Traynor's Contract Jurisprudence and the Free Law Dilemma," 7 So. Cal. Interdiscliplinary L. J. 81 (1998).

With Frankfurter, as with Marshall, Story, and Holmes, a problem of selectivity arises. In addition to the Frankfurter Papers at the Library of Congress, there is an edition of Frankfurter's correspondence with Franklin Roosevelt (Max Freedman, ed., *Roosevelt and Frankfurter, Their Correspondence 1928–1945* [1967]); three volumes of essays and reminiscences, *Of Law and Men* (Philip Elman, ed., 1956), *Felix Frankfurter Reminisces* (Harlan Philips, ed., 1962), and *Of Law and Life and Other Things That Matter* (Philip Kurland, ed., 1965); several books, among them *The Public and Its Government* (1930), *The Commerce Clause under Marshall, Taney, and Waite* (1937); *Mr. Justice Holmes and the Supreme Court* (1938), and *The Case of Sacco and Vanzetti* (1962 ed.); and numerous articles and essays, both scholarly and otherwise. Five biographies have appeared: Helen Thomas, *Scholar on the Bench* (1960); Liva Baker, *Felix Frankfurter* (1969); H. N. Hirsch, *The Enigma of Felix Frankfurter* (1981); Michael E. Parrish, *Felix Frankfurter: The Reform Years* (1982); and Melvin Urofsky, *Felix Frankfuter: Judicial Restraint and Individual Liberties* (1991), as well as James F. Simon's *The Antagonists* (1989), an analysis of Frankfurter's relationship with Justice Hugo Black. Of those Hirsch's volume is the most perceptive on Frankfurter's personality and his unexpectedly ineffective internal presence on the Court, Parrish's is an excellent account of Frandkfuter's early life and career, and Urofsky's a useful brief overview. See also the essays on Frankfurter and other Warren Court justices in Mark Tushnet, ed., *The Warren Court in Historical and Political Perspective* (1993).

Wallace Mendelson's edited volume, *Felix Frankfurter, A Tribute* (1964), contains an important essay by Alexander Bickel: "Applied Politics and the Science of Law Writings of the Harvard Period." Albert Sacks's "Felix Frankfurter" in Friedman and Israel, *supra*, is a perceptive overview. The best source of Frankfurter's early years is Sanford V. Levinson's note, "The Democratic Faith of Felix Frankfurter," 25 Stan. L. Rev. 430 (1973). Louis Jaffe's "The Judicial Universe of Mr. Justice Frankfurter," 62 Harv. L. Rev. (1949), remains the best single analysis of Frankfurter's thought, even though it was written in the middle of Frankfurter's judicial career. I have some comments on Frankfurter's role during the New Deal in "Felix Frankfurter, the Old Boy Network, and the New Deal," Ark. L. Rev. 633 (1986).

Important articles on Frankfurter that have appeared since the mid-1980s include Richard L. Aynes, "Charles Fairman, Felix Frankfurter, and the Fourteenth Amendment," 70 Chi.-Kent L. Rev. 1197 (1995); William M. Wiecek, "Felix Frankfurter, Incorportation, and the Willie Francis Case," 26 J. Sup. Ct. Hist. 53 (2001); Philip Elman, "The Solicitor General's Office, Justice Frankfurter, and Civil Rights Litigation 1946–1960: An Oral History," 100 Harv. L. Rev. 817 (1987); Melvin Urofsky, "Conflict Among the Brethren: Felix Frankfurter, William O. Douglas, and the Clash of Personalities and Philosophies on the United States Supreme Court," 1988 Duke L. J. 71 (1988); Melvin Urofsky, "The Failure of Felix Frankfurter," 26 U. Rich. L. Rev. 175 (1991); Mary Brigid McManamon, "Felix Frankfurter: The Architect of 'Our Federalism,'" 27 Georgia L. Rev. 697 (1993); and David M. Siegel, "Felix Frankfurter, Charles Hamilton Houston, and the 'N-Word,'" 7 So. Cal. Interdisciplinary L. J. 317 (1998); and John D. Fassett, "The Buddha and the Bumblebee: The Saga of Stanley Reed and Felix Frankfurter," 20 J. Sup. Ct. Hist. 165 (2003). For an interesting exchange on the question of whether Frankfurter might have written a memorandum, allegedly prepared by Owen Roberts, justifying Roberts's different votes in the apparently similar *Tipaldo* and *Parrish* cases, see Michael A. Ariens, "A Thrice-Told Tale, or Felix the Cat," 107 Harv. L. Rev. 620 (1994), and Richard D. Friedman, "A Reaffirmation: The Authenticity of the Roberts Memorandum, or Felix the Non-forger," 142 U. Pa. L. Rev. 1985 (1994).

The Hugo Black papers have now been made available in the Library of Congress, but do not appear to be complete. Virginia V. Hamilton, *Hugo Black: The Alabama Years* (1972), is an account of his background; another revealing source is Clifford Durr, "Hugo Black, Southerner," 10 Am. U. L. Rev. 27 (1961). Charles Reich's "Mr. Justice Black and the Living Constitution," 76 Harv. L. Rev. 673 (1963), is an imaginative attempt to describe the development of Black's philosophy of constitutional adjudication. Edmund Cahn, "Justice Black and First Amendment 'Absolutes,'" 37 N. Y. U. L. Rev. (1962), constitutes an interview with Black and Cahn's comments, which are of interest. Sylvia Snowiss, "The Legacy of Justice Black," 1973 Sup. Ct. Rev. 187, is a perceptive overview of Black's thought. Daniel P. Meador's *Justice Black and His Books* (1974) lists the sources of Black's reading, along with an illuminating introduction.

Two rewarding contributions by Black himself are "Reminiscences," 18 Ala. L. Rev, 3 (1968), and *A Constitutional Faith* (1968). A brief memoir of Black appears in Elizabeth Black, *Mr. Justice and Mrs. Black* (1986).

Several books on Black have appeared since the mid-1980s. Tony Allan Freyer, *Justice Hugo Black and Modern America* (1985) and Howard Ball and Philip Cooper, *Of Power and Right: Hugo Black, William O. Douglas, and America's Constitutional Revolution* (1992), emphasize the "liberal" dimensions of Black's jurisprudence. Ball's *Hugo Black: Cold Steel Warrior* (1996), attempts to relate Black's liberalism to the anti-totalitarianism of the years encompassing World War II and its aftermath. Roger Newman's *Hugo Black, A Biography* (1994), is a more complete portrait, based on voluminous sources, but does not attempt a detailed analysis of Black's judicial decisions. Tinsley E. Yarbrough, *Mr. Justice Black and His Critics* (1988), discusses the reaction of commentators to Black's unorthodox approach to constitutional interpretation.

Useful articles on Black since the mid-1980s include Peter B. Edelman, "Free Press v. Privacy: Haunted by the Ghost of Justice Black," 68 Texas L. Rev. 1195 (1990); Michael J. Gerhardt, "A Tale of Two Textualists: A Critical Comparison of Justices Black and Scalia," 74 B. U. L. Rev. 25 (1994); John P. Frank, "The Shelf Life of Justice Hugo L. Black," 1997 Wisc. L. Rev. 1 (1997); and Akhil Reed Amar, "Hugo Black and the Hall of Fame," 53 Alabama L. Rev. 1221 (2002).

Warren's papers have been deposited, with restrictions, in the Earl Warren Oral History Center at the University of California at Berkeley. *The Public Papers of Chief Justice Earl Warren* (1959), are largely unrevealing. Warren's memoirs, *The Memoirs of Chief Justice Earl Warren* (1977), were unfinished at his death in 1974 and were published posthumously: only occasionally do they transcend the conventional memoirs of public figures. John D. Weaver and Louis Katcher completed biographies of Warren in 1967, both of which emphasized his political career. (Weaver, *Warren: The Man, the Court, the Era;* Katcher, *Earl Warren—A Political Biography*). Two symposia contain pieces on Warren. The first is in 67 Mich. L. Rev. 219 (1968), especially A. Kenneth Pye, "The Warren Court and Criminal Procedure," at 249; Harry Kalven, "A Note on Free Speech and the Warren Court," at 289; John P. MacKenzie, "The Warren Court and the Press," at 303; Thomas E. Kauper, "The 'Warren Court' and the Antitrust Laws," at 325; and Philip B. Kurland, "Earl Warren, The 'Warren Court,' and the Warren Myths," at 353. The second is 8 Calif. L. Rev. 1ff (1970), which contains a series of reminiscences of Warren by persons associated with him during his career. Two additional helpful articles are Archibald Cox's brief treatment, "Chief Justice Earl Warren," 83 Harv. L. Rev. 1 (1969), and especially Anthony Lewis, "Earl Warren," in Friedman and Israel, *supra.* See also Anthony Lewis, "Earl Warren," in 4 *Encyclopedia* 2019. I have a discussion of the Warren Court in 4 *Encyclopedia* 2023.

More detailed books on Warren and the Warren Court began to appear in the 1980s. Two early treatments were Bernard Schwartz, *Super Chief* (1983), and G. Edward

White, *Earl Warren: A Public Life* (1982), the former more of an analysis of the internal workings of the Warren Court than a biography. Tushnet's edited collection of essays, *The Warren Court in Historical and Political Perspective*, appeared in 1993, and Bernard Schwartz edited another collection, *The Warren Court: A Retrospective*, in 1996. Morton Horwitz's *The Warren Court and the Pursuit of Justice* (1998), based on lectures to Harvard undergraduates, is a brief, impressionistic study. Ed Cray's *Chief Justice: A Biography of Earl Warren* (1997) is directed at a trade audience. L. A. Powe's *The Warren Court and American Politics* (2000) skillfully details the close connections between the Court's decisions and the policies of other governmental branches. Michael Belknap's *The Supreme Court Under Earl Warren* (2004) is a fine general overview.

Maxwell Bloomfield's "The Warren Court in American Fiction," 1991 Sup. Ct. Hist. J. 86 (1991) is an interesting popular culture study. John Frank and Julie Zatz, "The Appointment of Earl Warren as Chief Justice of the United States," 23 Arizona State L. J. 725 (1991), adds no new information but is an accessible account. Mark Tushnet and Katya Levin, "What Really Happened in *Brown v. Board of Education*," 91 Colum. L. Rev. 1867 (1991) offers a persuasive, but short of authoritative, explanation of the Warren Court's internal deliberations in *Brown*. Lawrence Fleisher's "Thomas Dewey and Earl Warren: The Rise of the Twentieth-Century Urban Prosecutor," 28 Calif. Western L. Rev. 1 (1991), makes interesting connections between two men who ran on the same Republican ticket in 1944. In a symposium, Defining Democracy, in the March, 1997 Vanderbilt Law Review, Suzanna Sherry contributed "All the Supreme Court Really Needs to Know It Learned from the Warren Court," 50 Vand. L. Rev. 487 (1997), which provoked responses from Rebecca L. Brown, "Formal Neutrality in the Warren and Rehnquist Courts," 50 Vand. L. Rev. 487, Barry Friedman, "Neutral Principles: A Retrospective," 50 Vand. L. Rev. 503, and John C. P. Goldberg, "On the Merits," 50 Vand. L. Rev. 537. Corrina Barrett Lain, "Countermajoritarian Hero or Zero?" 152 U. Pa. 1361 (2004), reinterprets the Warren Court's criminal procedure decisions. See also Symposium, The Jurisprudential Legacy of the Warren Court, 59 Wash. & Lee L. Rev. 1055ff (2002).

David Shapiro's *The Evolution of a Judicial Philosophy: Selected Opinions and Papers of Justice John M. Harlan* (1969) contains a brief biographical essay as well as selections from Harlan's opinions and extrajudicial writings. Among the writings those of greatest interest are "The Frankfurter Imprint as Seen by a Colleague," 76 Harv. L. Rev. 1 (1963); "Thoughts at a Dedication: Keeping the Judicial Function in Balance," 49 A. B. A. J. 943 (1963); "The Bill of Rights and the Constitution," 50 A. B. A. J. 918 (1964); and introduction to Justice Potter Stewart's "Robert H. Jackson's Influence on Federal–State Relationships," 23 Rec. Ass'n of the Bar of the City of New York (1968). In addition to Shapiro's introduction, the following early articles shed light on Harlan as a person or a judge: Whitney North Seymour, "John Marshall Harlan," 1 N.Y. Law Forum 1 (1955); Norman Dorsen, "The Second Mr. Justice Harlan: A Constitutional Conservative," 44 N. Y. U. L. Rev. 249 (1969); J. Harvie Wilkinson, "Justice John M. Harlan and the

Values of Federalism," 57 Va. L. Rev. 1185 (1971); Gerald Gunther, "In Search of Judicial Quality on a Changing Court: The Case of Justice Powell," 24 Stan. L. Rev. 1001, 1004–14 (1972); Nathan Lewin, "Justice Harlan: The Full Measure of the Man," 58 A. B. A. J. 579 (1972); and Henry Friendly, "Mr. Justice Harlan as Seen by a Friend and Judge of an Inferior Court," 85 Harv. L. Rev. 382 (1971).

Tinsley E. Yarbrough, *John Marshall Harlan: Great Dissenter of the Warren Court* (1992) is the only biography of Harlan yet to appear. It is a competent study, but specialist audiences would profit from a more intensive analysis of Harlan's opinions. Since the early 1990s several law review articles have attempted that task, paying special attention to Harlan's methodology in due process cases. See Norman Dorsen, "John Marshall Harlan and the Warren Court," 1991 J. Sup. Ct. Hist. 50 (1991); Anthony C. Cirica, "A Wolf in Sheep's Clothing? A Critical Analysis of Justice Harlan's Substantive Due Process Formulation," 64 Fordham L. Rev. 2241 (1996); J. Richard Broughton, "Unforgettable Too: The Jurisprudential Legacy of the Second Justice Harlan," 10 Seton Hall Const. L. J. 57 (1999); and Andrew B. Schroeder, "Keeping Police out of the Bedroom: Justice John Marshall Harlan, *Poe v. Ullman*, and the Limits of Conservative Privacy," 86 Va. L. Rev. 1045 (2000).

The most extensive work on Harlan is in the essays in Centennial Conference in Honor of Justice John Marshall Harlan, 36 New York L. S. L. Rev. 1ff (1991). For connections between the judicial approach of Harlan and that of Justice Ruth Bader Ginsburg, see Toni J. Ellington, "Ruth Bader Ginsburg and John Marshall Harlan: A Justice and Her Hero," 20 University of Hawaii L. Rev. 797 (1998).

Any examination of Douglas's career should begin with his two remarkable autobiographical volumes, *Go East, Young Man* (1974), and *The Court Years* (1980), which, while they can not be regarded as an accurate description of events, provide a revealing commentary on the attitudes and perceptions of their author. Douglas has not fared particularly well with biographers. James Simon's *Independent Journey* (1980) is readable and balanced, but not particularly analytical, and Bruce Alan Murphy's *Wild Bill* (2003) is a single-minded effort to make Douglas into a nearly pathological prevaricator. Although Douglas was surely self-preoccupied and inclined to distort and exaggerate his life experiences, Murphy starts with the premise that Douglas systematically lied about every feature of his life and career, and makes no distinction between trivial and more serious inaccuracies. The result is that a reader cannot grasp how Douglas came to be such a professional success, or how he could have been liked and admired by people who knew him.

Among the variety of articles on Douglas's contribution to substantive legal areas, the most illuminating treatments are Hans Linde, "Justice Douglas on Freedom in the Welfare State," 39 Wash. L. Rev. (1964); Kenneth Karst, "Invidious Discrimination: Justice Douglas and the Return of the Natural Law Due Process Formula," 16 U.C.L.A. Law Rev. 716 (1969); L. A. Powe, Jr., "Evolution to Absolutism: Justice Douglas and the First Amendment," 74 Colum. L. Rev. 347 (1974); Dorothy Glancy, "Getting Government off the Backs of the People: The Right of Privacy and Freedom of Expression in the Opinions of Justice William O. Douglas," 21 Santa Clara L. Rev. 1047 (1981); L. A. Powe, Jr., "Justice Douglas After Fifty Years: The First Amendment, McCarthyism, and Rights, 6 Const. Comm.267 (1989); Melvin Urofsky, "Dear Teacher: The Correspondence of William O. Douglas and Thomas Reed Powell," 7 Law & Hist. Rev. 331 (1989); Melvin Urofsky, "Justice Douglas and His Clerks," 3 Western Legal Hist. 1 (1990); Melvin Urofsky, "William O. Douglas as a Common Law Judge," 41 Duke L. J. 133 (1991); Stephen A. Smith, "Justice Douglas and the Death Penalty: A Demanding View of Due Process," 20 Am. J. Crim. L. 135 (1992); Howard Ball and Philip J. Cooper, "Fighting Justices: Hugo L. Black and William O. Douglas and Supreme Court Conflict," 38 Am. J. Legal Hist. 1 (1994); Laura Krugman Ray, "Autobiography and Opinion: The Romantic Jurisprudence of William O. Douglas," 60 U. Pitt. L. Rev. 707 (1999); Peter Manus, "Will Bill Douglas's Last Stand: A Retrospective on the Supreme Court's First Environmentalist," 72 Temple L. Rev. 111 (1999); and Mary E. Fairhurst and Andrew T. Braff, "William O. Douglas, The Gadlfy of Washington," 40 Gonzaga L. Rev. 259 (2005).

Remarkably little has been written on Stewart. There is no biography. Two short overviews exist, Leon Friedman, "Potter Stewart," in Friedman and Israel, *supra,* and Monroe E. Price, "Potter Stewart," *Encyclopedia* 1768. On Stewart's early career, see Joel Jacobson, "Remembered Justice: The Background, Early Career, and Judicial Appointments of Justice Potter Stewart," 35 Akron L. Rev. 227 (2002). Barnett Meresman, "A Lawyer's Lawyer, a Judge's Judge," 51 U. Chi. L. Rev. 509 (1982), is an analysis of Stewart's Fourth Amendment opinions. Byron White, "Dedication," 92 Yale L. J. 407 (1983) is a brief discussion of Stewart's internal influence on the Court. See also Gayle Binion, "Justice Potter Stewart: The Unpredicatable Vote," 1992 J. Sup. Ct. Hist. 99 (1992); Stephen V. Monsma, "Justice Stewart on Church and State," 36 J. Church and State 557 (1994); William W. Greenhalh and Mark J. Yost, "In Defense of the *Per Se* Rule: Justice Stewart's Struggle to Preserve the Fourth Amendment's Warrant Clause," 31 Am. Criminal L. Rev. 1013 (1994); and Paul Gewirtz, "On 'I Know It When I See It,'" 105 Yale L. J. 1023 (1996).

Two collections of essays have thus far appeared on the Burger Court, Vincent Blasi, *The Burger Court: The Counter-revolution That Wasn't* (1983), and Herman Schwartz, *The Burger Years: Rights and Wrongs in the Supreme Court 1969–1986* (1987). Many of the essays in those volumes are successful treatments of Burger Court decisions in substantive areas of law. Earl M. Maltz, *The Chief Justiceship of Warren E. Burger* (2000), and Bernard Schwartz, *The Ascent of Pragmatism: The Burger Court in Action* (1990), are overviews of Burger's tenure. An allegedly "inside history" of the first seven terms of the Burger Court is Bob Woodward and Scott Armstrong, *The Brethren* (1979). See also A. E. Dick Howard, "The Burger Court," 1 *Encyclopedia* 176.

Since the mid-1980s comparatively little has appeared on Burger or the Burger Court. Useful articles include Stephen P. Magowan, "Interpreting the Ratifiers' Intent: The Burger Court's Eleventh Amendment Jurisprudence Reconsidered in Light of *Erie Railroad v. Tompkins*, 66 Wash. U. L. Q. 135 (1988); Mark Kohler, "Compromise and Interpretation: A Case Study of the Burger Court and the Religion Clauses," 23 Tulsa L. J. 379 (1988); George Steven Swan, "The Political Economy of the Burger Court," 7 St. Louis U. Public L. Rev. 359 (1988); Joseph F. Koblyka, "Leadership on the Supreme Court of the United States: Chief Justice Burger and the Establishment Clause," 42 Western Pol. Q. 545 (1989); Lino Graglia, "The Burger Court and Economic Rights," 33 Tulsa L. J. 41 (1997). See also Symposium, The Jurisprudence of Chief Justice Warren E. Burger, 45 Okla. L. 1ff (1992).

Lewis Powell's papers have been deposited in the Washington and Lee Law School library: they represent a quite ample source of data in excellent working condition. For a description, see John N. Jacob, "The Lewis F. Powell, Jr. Archives and the Contemporary Researcher," 49 W. & L. L. Rev. 3 (1992). John Calvin Jeffries, Jr., a former Powell clerk, produced a biography, *Justice Lewis F. Powell, Jr.* (1994), which should be treated as authoritative. Powell represents one of those judicial subjects whose private life pales in comparison to his public career, but within those limitations Jeffries's portrait is searching.

Articles on Powell in the early portions of his tenure include Gerald Gunther, "In Search of Judicial Quality on a Changing Court: The Case of Justice Powell," 24 Stan. L. Rev. 1001 (1972); A. E. Dick Howard, "Mr. Justice Powell and the Emerging Nixon Majority," 70 Mich. L. Rev. 445 (1972); and two symposia, 11 Rich. L. Rev. 259ff (1977) and 68 Va. L. Rev. 161ff (1982). Later articles include Leslie Bender, "The Powell–Stevens Debates on Federalism and Separation of Powers," 15 Hastings. Con. L. Q. 549 (1988); Mark D. Loftis, "Implied Rights of Private Action Under Federal Statutes: The Continuing Influence of Justice Powell's *Cannon* Dissent," 5 J. Law & Politics 349 (1989); Craig Evan Klafter, "Justice Lewis F. Powell Jr.: A Pragmatic Relativist," 8 B. U. Pub. Int. L. J. 1 (1998); Adam C. Pritchard, "*United States v. O'Hagan*: Agency Law and Justice Powell's Legacy for the Law of Insider Trading," 31 Securities L. Rev. 325 (1999); Adam C. Pritchard, "Justice Powell and the Counterrevolution in the Federal Securities Laws," 52 Duke L. J. 841 (2003); and Paul R. Baier, "Of *Bakke*'s Balance, *Gratz,* and *Grutter*: The Voice of Justice Powell," 78 Tulane L. Rev. 1955 (2004). The most important symposium on Powell is Contemporary Challenges to Judging, 49 Wash. & Lee L. Rev. 1ff (1992).

Of Brennan's own writings the most revealing are "The Bill of Rights and the States," 36 N. Y. U. L. Rev. 761 (1961); "The Supreme Court and the Meiklejohn Interpretation of the First Amendment," 79 Harv. L. Rev. 1 (1965); "State Constitutions and the Protection of Individual Rights," 90 Harv. L. Rev. 489 (1977); and "Constitutional Adjudication and the Death Penalty: A View from the Court," 100 Harv. L. Rev. 313 (1986).

No adequate biography of Brennan has yet appeared. Kim Isaac Eisler, *A Justice for All: William J. Brennan Jr. and the Decisions That Transformed America* (1993) is a largely surface treatment. Peter H. Irons, *Brennan v. Rehnquist: The Battle for the Constitution* (1994) oversimplifies both of his subjects' jurisprudence. Stephen J. Wermeil has an authorized biography in process; for a sample of Wermeil's approach, see Stephen J. Wermeil, "The Nomination of Justice Brennan," 11 Const. Comm. 515 (1994); Stephen J. Wermeil, "Law and Human Dignity: The Judicial Soul of Justice Brennan," 7 Wm. & Mary Bill of Rights J. 223 (1998). A good discussion of Brennan's early years is Francis P. McQuade and Alexander T. Kardos, "Mr. Justice Brennan and His Legal Philosophy," 33 Notre Dame Lawyer 321 (1958). Stephen J. Friedman, "Mr. Justice Brennan: The First Decade," 80 Harv. L. Rev. 7 (1966), summarizes Brennan's first ten years on the Court. Edward V. Heck, "Justice Brennan and the Heyday of Warren Court Liberalism," 20 Santa Clara L. Rev. 841 (1980), describes Brennan's "centrist" role on the Warren Court. An effective overview of Brennan's jurisprudence is Robert C. Post, "William J. Brennan," 1 *Encyclopedia* 148.

The number of articles to appear on Brennan since the mid 1980s is very large. Those worth consulting include Laura Krugman Ray, "Justice Brennan and the Jurisprudence of Dissent," 61 Temple L. Rev. 307 (1988); Stanley H. Feidlebaum, "Justice Brennan and the Burger Court," 19 Seton Hall L. Rev. 188 (1989); Robert C. Post, "Justice Brennan and Federalism," 7 Const. Comm. 227 (1990); Robert C. Post, "Justice Brennan and the Warren Court," 8 Const. Comm. 11 (1991); Owen M. Fiss, "A Life Lived Twice," 100 Yale L. J. 1117 (1991); Kermit L. Hall, "Justice Brennan and Cultural History," 27 Cal. Western L. Rev. 339 (1991); Michael S. Ariens, "On the Road of Good Intentions: Justice Brennan and the Religion Clauses," 27 Cal. Western L. Rev. 311 (1991); Rebecca Korzec, "Justice Brennan's Gender Jurisprudence," 25 Akron L. Rev. 315 (1991); Frank I. Michelman, "Super Liberal: Romance, Community, and Tradition in William J. Brennan Jr.'s Constitutional Thought," 77 Va. L. Rev. 1261 (1991); Edward deGrazia, "Freeing Literary and Artistic Expression During the Sixties: The Role of Justice William J. Brennan, Jr.," 13 Cardozo L. J. 103 (1991); Joel E. Friedlander, "Constitution and Kulturkampf: A Reading of the Shadow Theology of Justice Brennan," 140 U. Pa. L. Rev. 1049 (1992).

See also B. Glenn George, "Visions of a Labor Lawyer: The Legacy of Justice Brennan," 33 Wm. & Mary L. Rev. 1123 (1992); Rodney A. Grunes, "Justice Brennan and the Problem of Obscenity," 22 Seton Hall L. Rev. 789 (1992); and Kevin O'D. Driscoll, "The Origins of a Judicial Icon: Justice Brennan's Warren Court Years," 54 Stan. L. Rev. 1005 (2002). The influence of Brennan on commentators can be seen in the number of law journal symposia dedicated to him. See Symposium, Reason, Passion, and Justice Brennan, 10 Cardozo L. Rev. 25ff (1988); Symposium, The Jurisprudence of Justice Brennan, 139 U. Pa. L. Rev. 1319ff (1991); Symposium, Brennan and Democracy, 86 Calif. L. Rev. 399 (1998); Symposium, Reason, Passion, and the Progress of the Law, 43 New York L. S. L. Rev. 1ff (1999); Symposium, The Brennan Legacy: The Art of Judging, 32 Loyola of Los Angeles L. Rev. 655ff (1999).

Marshall's importance as a civil rights litigator before his appointment to the Court, and the significance of his being the first African American Justice, have resulted in a bibliographical file that differs prominently from those of most other Justices. It includes biographies, such as Juan Williams, *Thurgood Marshall: American Revolutionary* (1998), Howard Ball, *A Defiant Life: Thurgood Marshall and the Persistence of Racism in America* (1999), and Carl Thomas Rowan, *Dream Makers, Dream Breakers: The World of Thurgood Marshall* (2002), that are more concerned with the sweep of Marshall's career than his judicial decisions. It also includes books, such as Mark Tushnet's two volumes, *Making Civil Rights Law: Thurgood Marshall and the Supreme Court, 1936–1961* (1994) and *Making Constitutional Law: Thurgood Marshall and the Supreme Court, 1961–1991* (1997), that are more about Marshall the litigator than Marshall the justice. Richard Kluger, *Simple Justice* (1976) provides a striking portrait of Marshall as civil rights litigator. Two interesting analyses of episodes in Marshall's pre-Court career are Richard L. Revesz, "Thurgood Marshall's Struggle," 68 N. Y. U. L. Rev. 237 (1993) (about Marshall's nomination to the United States Court of Appeals for the Second Circuit), and Donald K. Hill, "Social Separation in America: Thurgood Marshall and the Texas Connections," 28 Thurgood Marshall L. Rev. 177 (2003).

There have been a strikingly small number of substantive analyses of Marshall's jurisprudence, especially given that he served on the Court for twenty-four years. See Jonathan Weinburg, "Thurgood Marshall and the Administrative State," 38 Wayne L. Rev. 115 (1991); Bruce A. Green, " 'Power, Not Reason': Justice Marshall's Validictory and the Fourth Amendment in the Supreme Court's 1990 Term," 70 N. C. L. Rev. 373 (1992); Tracey Maclin, Justice Thurgood Marshall: Taking the Fourth Amendment Seriously," 77 Cornell L. Rev. 723 (1992); Jordan Streiker, "The Long Road up from Barbarism: Justice Marshall and the Death Penalty," 71 Texas L. Rev. 1131 (1993); Mark V. Tushnet, "The Jurisprudence of Thurgood Marshall," 1996 Ill. L. Rev. (1996); Melvin Guttermann, "The Prison Jurisprudence of Justice Thurgood Marshall," 56 Maryland L. Rev. 149 (1997); Richard H. W. Maloy, "Thurgood Marshall and the Holy Grail–The Due Process Jurisprudence of a Consummate Jurist," 26 Pepperdine L. Rev. 289 (1999). Symposia and tribute issues have been very frequent. See A Tribute to Justice Thurgood Marshall, 6 Harv. Blackletter J. 1ff (1989); Thurgood Marshall Commemorative Issue, 35 Howard L. J. 1ff (1991); Special Issue: A Tribute to Justice Thurgood Marshall, 44 Stan. L. Rev. 1213ff (1992); Symposium, Honoring Justice Thurgood Marshall, 80 Geo. L. J. 2003ff (1992); Symposium, The Life and Jurisprudence of Justice Thurgood Marshall, 47 Oklahoma L. Rev. 1ff (1994); and Symposium, Justice Thurgood Marshall: The Legacy of His Jurisprudence, 26 Ariz. State L. Rev. xff (1994).

The best work on Blackmun comes from two sources. One is Linda Greenhouse's *Becoming Justice Blackmun* (2005), which is less a full-scale biography than a penetrating narrative of Blackmun's Court career based on her access to Blackmun's Court papers, which reflect his meticulous sense for detail. Blackmun was fortunate to have a sympathetic and knowledgable author build a narrative of his career from his papers, although there is room for a more detailed biographical treatment. The other source consists of the multiple articles precipitated by symposia and tribute issues honoring Blackmun. Many of the contributors to those issues were former clerks of Blackmun who might not have chosen to analyze aspects of his jurisprudence in another setting.

Two articles in the earlier stages of Blackmun's career noticed his decisive shift to a more independent stance and the relationship of *Roe v. Wade* to that shift: David Fuqua, "Justice Harry A. Blackmun: The Abortion Decisions," 34 Ark. L. Rev. 276 (1980) and Note, "The Changing Social Vision of Justice Blackmun," 97 Harv. L. Rev. 717 (1983). For Blackmun's own perspective on the changes in his jurisprudence, see Philippa Strum, "Change and Continuity on the Supreme Court: Conversations with Justice Harry A. Blackmun," 34 Rich. L. Rev. 285 (2000). Other useful non-symposium articles include Stephen L. Wasby, "Justice Harry A. Blackmun in the Burger Court," 11 Hamline L. Rev. 183 (1988); D. Grier Stephenson, Jr., "Justice Blackmun's Eighth Amendment Pilgrimage," 8 B. Y. U. J. Public L. 271 (1994); Martha J. Dragich, "Justice Blackmun, Franz Kafka, and Capital Punishment," 63 Missouri L. Rev. 853 (1998); Mark C. Rahdert, "A Jurisprudence of Hope: Justice Blackmun and the Freedom of Religion," 22 Hamline L. Rev. 1 (1998); and Peter Manus, "The Blackbird Whistling–The Silence Just After: Evaluating the Environmental Legacy of Justice Blackmun," 85 Iowa L. Rev. 429 (2000).

Of the variety of symposia and tribute issues, the following are most useful: Special Issue: A Tribute to Justice Harry A. Blackmun, 97 Dickinson L. Rev. 421ff (1993); Justice Harry A. Blackmun: Recollections, Jurisprudence, Real World Relections, 71 North Dakota L. Rev. 3ff (1995); and Symposium, The Jurisprudence of Justice Harry A. Blackmun, 26 Hastings Con. L. Q. 5ff (1998).

White's sparse selection of extrajudicial writings does not contain any particularly revealing entries. The most ambitious is "Supreme Court Review of Agency Decisions," 26 Ad. Law Rev. 49 (1974). Dennis J. Hutchinson's *The Man Who Once Was Whizzer White* (1998) is a good biography, written by one of White's law clerks without much cooperation from the subject. (See Martha Neil, "Justice an Uncooperative Witness for Biographer," Chicago Daily Law Bulletin, August 28, 1998, p. 3.) White drew some attention from commentators early in his career. The best early treatments are Anthony Lewis, "Byron White Gets Whittaker's Seat on Supreme Court," New York Times, March 31, 1962; Alfred Wright, "A Modest All-American Who Sits on the Highest Bench," Sports Illustrated, December 10, 1962; Lance Liebman, "Swing Man on the Supreme Court," New York Times Magazine, October 8, 1972; and Murray Kempton, "Code Duello," 31 National Review 754 (1979). Nathan Lewin, "White's Flight," 191 New Republic 17 (August 27, 1984), discusses White's changing role on the Burger Court. Michael J. Armstrong, "A Barometer of Freedom of the Press," 8 Pepperdine L. Rev. 157 (1980), and Pierce O'Donnell, "Justice Byron White: Leading from the

Center," 72 A. B. A. J. 24 (June 15, 1986), are mid-career sketches of White's jurisprudential attitudes. See also Jonathan D. Varet, "Byron White," 4 *Encyclopedia* 2048.

Since the mid-1980s, commentary on White has increased. See Mary Christine Hutton, "The Unique Perspective of Justice White," 40 Admin. L. Rev. 377 (1988); Allan Ides, "The Jurisprudence of Justice Byron White," 103 Yale L. J. 419 (1993); Ralph Ruebner, "Police Interrogation: The Privilege Against Self-Incrimination, The Right to Counsel, and the Incomplete Metamorphosis of Justice White," 48 Miami L. Rev. 511 (1994); and Dennis J. Hutchinson, "'The Ideal New Frontier Judge,'" 1997 Sup. Ct. Rev. 373 (1997). Three symposia are especially useful: see Symposium, 1994 Brigham Young L. Rev. viiiff (1994); Symposium, 55 Stan. L. Rev. 1ff (2002); Symposium on the Life and Work of Justice Byron R. White, 52 Catholic U. L. Rev. 883ff (2002); and Symposium, Justice White and the Exercise of Judicial Power, 74 U. Colo. L. Rev. 1283ff (2003).

A stereotype of Rehnquist was in place during his years as an Associate Justice (1971–1986): that of an ideological conservative who, apparently paradoxically, opposed extensions of the power of the federal government but supported virtually all efforts to enforce governmental policies that allegedly infringed on civil rights. That stereotype was captured in David L. Shapiro, "Mr. Justice Rehnquist: A Preliminary View," 90 Harv. L. Rev. 293 (1976). For an effort to link Rehnquist's posture to the ideology of the framers, see H. Jefferson Powell, The Compleat Jeffersonian: Justice Rehnquist and Federalism," 91 Yale L. J. 1317 (1982). See also Sue Davis, *Justice Rehnquist and the Constitution* (1989). For a more sympathetic portrait of Rehnquist as he was appointed Chief Justice, see Frank H. Easterbrook, 3 *Encyclopedia* 1533.

After Rehnquist's succession to the Chief Justiceship, scholarly attention to him and the Rehnquist Court dramatically increased, reaching a crescendo around the turn of the twenty-first century. The result is that there are several worthwhile books and numerous articles on both topics. The best overview is Tinsley Yarbrough, *The Rehnquist Court and the Constitution* (2000), although it does not take into account some of the pivotal developments near the close of Rehnquist's tenure. Mark Tushnet's *A Court Divided* (2005), aimed at a general audience, attempts to distill the perspectives of Rehnquist Court Justices and describe the Court's principal areas of disagreement. Of the four collections of essays on the Rehnquist Court, the most useful are Martin H. Belsky, ed., *The Rehnquist Court: A Retrospective* (1992); Earl M. Maltz, ed., *Rehnquist Justice: Understanding the Court Dynamic* (1993); and Craig M. Bradley, ed., *The Rehnquist Legacy* (2006). Herman Schwartz, ed., *The Rehnquist Court* (2002), is a less balanced treatment. The same lack of balance appears in two earlier books, Stanley H. Friedelbaum, *The Rehnquist Court: In Pursuit of Judicial Conservatism* (1994), and Stephen E. Gottlieb, *Morality Imposed: The Rehnquist Court and Liberty in America* (2000). Thomas M. Keck, *The Most Activist Supreme Court in History: The Road to Modern Judicial Conservatism* (2004), makes an argument, increasingly prominent in the last five years of Rehnquist's tenure, that the Court's approach to constitutional issues amounted to "judicial sovereignty." There is currently no biography of Rehnquist that covers his entire judicial tenure.

Articles worth consulting include Bernard Schwartz, "Chief Justice Rehnquist, Justice Jackson, and the *Brown* Case," 1988 Sup. Ct. Rev. 245 (1988), discussing the controversial memorandum Rehnquist wrote on *Plessy v. Ferguson* when he was law clerk to Jackson in the 1952 Term; Andrew Jay McClurg, "Logical Fallacies and the Supreme Court: A Critical Examination of Justice Rehnquist's Decisions in Criminal Procedure Cases," 59 U. Colo. L. Rev. 741 (1988); Nat Stern, "State Action, Establishment Clause, and Defamation: Blueprints for Civil Liberties in the Rehnquist Court," 57 U. Cinn. L. Rev. 1175 (1989); Erwin Chemerinsky, "Foreword: The Vanishing Constitution," 103 Harv. L. Rev. 43 (1989); Alan I. Bigel, "William H. Rehnquist on Capital Punishment," 17 Ohio Northern L. Rev. 729 (1991); Alfred P. Levitt, "Taking on a New Direction: The Rehnquist/Scalia Approach to Regulatory Takings," 66 Temple L. Rev. 197 (1993); Bryce M. Baird, "Federal Court Abstention in Civil Rights Cases: Chief Justice Rehnquist and the New Doctrine of Civil Rights Abstention," 42 Buff. L. Rev. 501 (1994); Jeanmarie K. Grubert, "The Rehnquist Court's Changed Reading of the Equal Protection Clause in the Context of Voting Rights," 65 Fordham L. Rev. 1819 (1997); Calvin Massey, "Federalism and the Rehnquist Court," 53 Hastings L. 431 (2002); Thomas W. Merrill, "The Making of the Second Rehnquist Court: A Preliminary Analysis," 47 St. Louis U. L. J. 569 (2003); Linda Greenhouse, "The Last Days of the Rehnquist Court: The Rewards of Patience and Power," 45 Ariz. L. Rev. 251 (2003); and Mark V. Tushnet, "Understanding the Rehnquist Court," 31 Ohio Northern L. Rev. 197 (2005). See also the responses to Thomas Merrill by Erwin Chemerinsky, Eric R. Claeys, Alan J. Howard, Richard J. Lazarus, and John O. McGinnis in 47 St. Louis U. L. J. 659ff (2003), Symposium, The Rehnquist Years: A Supreme Court Retrospective, 22 Nova L. Rev. 695ff (1998), and Symposium, Perspectives on Chief Justice Rehnquist, 25 Rutgers L. J. 557ff (1994).

O'Connor's status as the first female Justice, coupled with the pivotal role she came to play on the Rehnquist Court and her accounts of her early life and career, have resulted in a great deal of attention from commentators, much of it not directly concerned with her jurisprudence. O'Connor has written one autobiographical volume and one general account of her views, *Lazy B: Growing Up on a Cattle Ranch in the American Southwest* (2002) and *The Majesty of the Law: Reflections of a Supreme Court Justice* (2003). Several biographies have appeared, all but one while O'Connor was still active. They are of varying quality. Nancy Maveety, *Justice Sandra Day O'Connor: Strategist on the Supreme Court* (1996), and Robert W. Van Sickel, *Not a Particularly Different Voice: The Jurisprudence of Sandra Day O'Connor* (1998), are concerned with two elements of O'Connor's posture as a judge, her inclination to take centrist positions on visible issues and her muted approach to some issues associated with a gender consciousness. Of the two Maveety's is the more successful effort. Ann Carey McFeaters,

Justice in the Balance (2005), covers much the same ground as Maveety. Joan Biskupic, *Sandra Day O'Connor* (2005) is the most compelling biography to date, making skillful use of O'Connor's autobiographical writing.

An early overview of O'Connor's jurisprudence is Richard A. Cordray and James T. Vradlis, "The Emerging Jurisprudence of Justice O'Connor," 52 U. Chi. L. Rev. 389 (1985). Other useful articles include Benjamin D. Feder, "And a Child Shall Lead Them: Justice O'Connor, The Principle of Religious Liberty, and Its Practical Application," 8 Pace L. Rev. 249 (1988); George C. Thomas III, "An Elegant Theory of Double Jeopardy," 1988 U. Ill. L. Rev. 827 (1988); Susan R. Estrich and Kathleen M. Sullivan, "Abortion Politics: Writing for an Audience of One," 138 U. Pa. L. Rev. 119 (1989); Thomas R. Haggard, "Mugwump, Mediator, Machiavellian, or Majority? The Role of Justice O'Connor in the Affirmative Action Cases," 24 Akron L. Rev. 47 (1990); David B. Anders, "Justice Harlan and Black Revisited: The Emerging Dispute Between Justice O'Connor and Justice Scalia over Unenumerated Fundamental Rights," 61 Fordham L. Rev. 895 (1993); Michael E. Solimine and Susan E. Wheatley, "Rethinking Feminist Judging," 70 Indiana L. J. 891 (1995); Justin Schwatz, "A Not Quite Color Blind Constitution: Racial Discrimination and Racial Preference in Justice O' Connor's 'Newest' Equal Protection Jurisprudence," 58 Ohio State L. J. 1055 (1997); Jennifer R. Byrne, "Toward a Colorblind Constitution: Justice O'Connor's Narrowing of Affirmative Action," 42 St. Louis U. L. J. 619 (1998); and Jesse H. Choper, "The Endorsement Test: Its Status and Desirability," 18 J. Law & Politics 499 (2002). Two symposia are The Jurisprudence of Justice Sandra Day O'Connor, 13 Women's Rights Law Reporter 53ff (1991) and Justice O'Connor: Twenty Years of Shaping Constitutional Law, 32 McGeorge L. Rev. 823ff (2001).

The remaining Justices discussed in this book are still active, which has limited the opportunities of commentators to generalize about their careers, even though the tenures of some have been lengthy. Stevens's idiosyncratic approach has made him a difficult subject for commentators: no biography has yet appeared. For descriptions of Stevens's appointment to the Court, see David M. O'Brien, "Filling Justice William O. Douglas's Seat," 1989 Sup. Ct. Hist. Soc. Yearbook 20 (1989) and Victor A. Kramer, "The Case of Justice Stevens," 7 Const. Comm. 5 (1990). Stewart Abercrombie Baker, "John Paul Stevens," 4 *Encyclopedia* 1764, is a mid-career assessement. The best single work yet to appear on Stevens is Ward Farnsworth's essay, "Realism, Pragmatism, and John Paul Stevens," in Maltz, ed., *Rehnquist Justice*, 157–84.

Other useful articles on Stevens include Paula C. Arledge, "John Paul Stevens: A Moderate Justice's Approach to Individual Rights," 10 Whittier L. Rev. 563 (1989); William D. Popkin, "A Common Law Lawyer on the Supreme Court," 5 Duke L. J. 1087 (1989); Diane L. Hughes, "Justice Stevens' Method of Statutory Interpretation," 19 Harv. Environmental L. Rev. 493 (1995); and Robert F. Nagel, "Six Opinions by Mr. Justice Stevens: A New Methodology for Constitutional Cases," 78 Chi.-Kent L. Rev.

509 (2003). See also Symposium, Perspectives on Justice John Paul Stevens, 27 Rutgers L. J. 521 (1996).

In contrast to Stevens, Scalia's career on the Court has precipitated a large volume of commentary, doubtless responsive to the originality of his interpretive approach and his tendency to engage in colorful rhetoric. Scalia has also published an overview of his approach to constitutional cases, *A Matter of Interpretation* (1997). Three intellectual biographies have appeared: Richard A. Brisbin, *Justice Scalia and the Conservative Revival* (1997); James Brian Staab, *The Political Thought of Justice Antonin Scalia* (1998) and Ralph A. Rossum, *Antonin Scalia's Jurisprudence: Text and Tradition* (2006). George Kannar, "The Constitutional Catechism of Antonin Scalia," 99 Yale L. J. 1297 (1990) is a brilliant analysis of the intellectual sources of Scalia's judicial perspective.

Articles on Scalia abound. Among the most useful are Richard J. Pierce, Jr., *Morrison v. Olson*, "Separation of Powers, and the Structure of Government," 1988 Sup. Ct. Rev. 1 (1988); Michael Patrick King, "Justice Antonin Scalia: The First Term on the Supreme Court," 20 Rutgers L. J. 1 (1988); Daniel N. Riesman, "Deconstructing Justice Scalia's Separation of Powers Jurisprudence," 53 Albany L. Rev. 49 (1988); Arthur Stock, "Justice Scalia's Use of Sources in Statutory and Constitutional Interpretation," 1990 Duke L. J. 160 (1990); William N. Eskridge, Jr., "The New Textualism," 37 U.C.L.A. L. Rev. 621 (1990); Richard B. Collins, "Justice Scalia and the Elusive Idea of Discrimination Against Interstate Commerce," 20 New Mexico L. Rev. 555 (1990); Christopher E. Smith, "Justice Scalia and the Institutions of American Government," 25 Wake Forest L. Rev. 783 (1990); Bryan H. Wildenthal, "The Right of Confrontation, Justice Scalia, and the Power and Limits of Textualism," 48 Wash. & Lee L. Rev. 1323 (1991); Richard A. Brisbin, Jr., "'Administrative Law Is Not for Sissies': Justice Antonin Scalia's Challenge to American Administrative Law," 44 Ad. L. Rev. 107 (1992); Steven G. Gay, "Justice Scalia's Death Penalty," 20 Florida State U. L. Rev. 67 (1992); Timothy L. Rashcke, "Justice Scalia's Due Process Methodology," 65 So. Cal. L. Rev. 2743 (1992); Christopher E. Smith, "Justice Antonin Scalia and Criminal Justice Cases," 81 Kentucky L. J. 187 (1992); David A. Schultz, "Justice Antonin Scalia's First Amendment Jurisprudence," 9 J. Law & Politics 515 (1993); Gene R. Nichol, Jr., "Justice Scalia, Standing, and Public Law Litigation," 42 Duke L. J. 1141 (1993); Frank L. Michelman, "Property, Federalism, and Jurisprudence: A Comment on *Lucas* and Judicial Conservatism," 35 Wm. & Mary L. Rev. 301 (1993); and Eric J. Segall, "Justice Scalia, Critical Legal Studies, and the Rule of Law," 62 Geo. Wash. L. Rev. 991 (1994).

See also Bernard Schwartz, "Shooting the Piano Player? Justice Scalia and Adminstrative Law," 47 Ad. L. Rev. 1 (1995); David A. Schultz, "Scalia, Property, and *Dolan v. Tigard*: The Emergence of a Post–*Carolene Products* Jurisprudence," 29 Akron L. Rev. 1 (1995); Gene R. Nichol, Jr., "Justice Scalia and the *Printz* Case: The Trials of an Occasional Originalist," 70 U. Colo. L. Rev. 953 (1999); David M. Zlotnick, "Battered Women and Justice Scalia," 41 Arizona L. Rev. 847 (1999); James B. Staab, "The Tenth

Amendment and Justice Scalia's 'Split Personality,'" 16 J. Law & Politics 231 (2000); and Bret C. Birdsong, "Justice Scalia's Footprints on the Public Lands," 83 Denver U. L. Rev. 259 (2005). Three symposia are The Jurisprudence of Justice Antonin Scalia, 12 Cardozo L. Rev. 1583ff (1991), Reflecting on Justice Antonin Scalia's Religion Clauses Jurisprudence, 22 U. Hawaii L. Rev. 385ff (2000), and Justice Antonin Scalia Symposium, 34 Toledo L. Rev. 425ff (2003).

Comparatively little has been written on Kennedy. There is no biography, although three efforts have been made to analyze Kennedy's jurisprudence: Lisa Kay Parshall, *The Constitutional Jurisprudence of Supreme Court Justice Anthony Kennedy* (2001), Frank J. Colucci, *The Jurisprudence of Justice Anthony Kennedy* (2004), and Susika Fay, *Justice Anthony Kennedy, Pragmatic Conservative on the Rehnquist Court* (2004). The best general treatments of Kennedy yet to appear are Earl M. Maltz, "Anthony Kennedy and the Jurisprudence of Respectable Conservatism," in Maltz, ed., *Rehnquist Justice*, 140–56, and Mark Tushnet's chapter, "Anthony Kennedy and Gay Rights," in *A Court Divided*, 156–79. See also Jeffrey Rosen, "The Agonizer," New Yorker, November 11, 1985.

Useful articles on Kennedy are Christopher E. Smith, "Supreme Court Surprise: Justice Anthony Kennedy's Move Towards Moderation," 45 Oklahoma L. Rev. 459 (1992); Lawrence M. Friedman, "The Limitations of Labeling: Justice Anthony M. Kennedy and the First Amendment," 20 Ohio Northern L. Rev. 225 (1993); Akhil Reed Amar, "Justice Kennedy and the Idea of Equality," 28 Pacific L. J. 515 (1997); Earl M. Maltz, "Justice Kennedy's Vision of Federalism," 31 Rutgers L. J. 761 (2000); Louis D. Bilionis, "Grand Centrism and the Centrist Judicial Personam," 83 N. C. L. Rev. 1353 (2005); and Lisa Kay Parshall, "Redefining Due Process Analysis: Justice Kennedy and the Concept of Emergent Rights," 69 Albany L. Rev. 237 (2005).

Not much has been written on Souter, although Tinsley Yarbrough has produced a study, *David Hackett Souter: Traditional Republican on the Rehnquist Court* (2005), that attempts to link Souter to a tradition of twentieth-century "liberal" Republican justices, such as Warren, Harlan, and Stewart, who, despite being associated with Republican politics on their apppointments, exhibited a sympathetic attitude toward at least some civil liberties claims. Yarbrough's book is particularly good on Souter's nomination, which contained some information that hinted at his future course on the Court. The Souter nomination hearings are available as *Nomination of David H. Souter to Be Associate Justice of the Supreme Court of the United States: Hearings Before the Committee on the Judiciary, United States Senate, 101st. Cong., 2d. Sess.* (Government Printing Office, 1991). Thomas M. Keck has a useful treatment of Souter, "David H. Souter: Liberal Constitutionalism and the Brennan Seat," in Maltz, ed., *Rehnquist Justice*, 185–215.

Articles on Souter include Liza Weiman Hanks, "Justice Souter: Defining 'Substantive Neutrality' in an Age of Religious Politics," 48 Stan. L. Rev. 903 (1996) and Liang Kan, "A Theory of Justice Souter," 45 Emory L. J. 1373 (1996).

The Thomas nomination hearings were so visible and controversial that for several years impressions generated by them dominated commentary on Thomas. Books such as Jane Mayer and Jill Abramson, *Strange Justice: The Selling of Clarence Thomas* (1994), Sandra L. Ragan, *The Lynching of Language: Gender, Politics, and Power in the Hill-Thomas Hearings* (1996), and Jane Flax, *The American Dream in Black and White: The Clarence Thomas Hearings* (1998), focused on the hearings, and the irreconcilable testimony of Thomas and Anita Hill, as a cultural event. The hearings also prompted a symposium, Gender, Race, and the Politics of Supreme Court Appointments, 65 So. Cal. L. Rev. 1283ff (1992). It was not until nearly a decade after Thomas's confirmation that books assessing his perspective as a judge began to appear. Of those two, Scott Douglas Gerber, *First Principles: The Jurisprudence of Clarence Thomas* (1999) and Christopher E. Smith and Joyce Baugh, *The Real Clarence Thomas* (2000) are serious, if premature, efforts, although the former volume is quirky and the latter polemical. Mark Tushnet's chapter, "Clarence Thomas's Constitution," in *A Court Divided*, 71–103, gets beyond stereotyped reactions to Thomas.

Through the mid-1990s articles on Thomas continued to be dominated by the memory of his confirmation hearings. Eventually some substantive treatments began to appear. See David N. Mayer, "Justice Thomas and the Supreme Court's Rediscovery of the Tenth Amendment," 25 Capital U. L. Rev. 339 (1996); Scott Douglas Gerber, "Clarence Thomas and the Jurisprudence of Race," 25 Southern U. L. Rev. 43 (1997); Kirk A. Kennedy, "Reaffirming the Natural Law Jurisprudence of Justice Clarence Thomas," 9 Regent U. L. Rev. 33 (1997); Christopher E. Smith, "Clarence Thomas: A Distinctive Justice," 28 Seton Hall L. Rev. 1 (1997); Eric L. Muller, "Where, But for the Grace of God, Goes He? The Search for Empathy in the Criminal Jurisprudence of Clarence Thomas," 15 Const. Comm. 225 (1998); Mark Tushnet, "Clarence Thomas's Black Nationalism," 47 Howard L. J. 323 (2004); Nathan Dean, "The Primacy of the Individual in the Political Philosophy and Civil Rights Jurisprudence of Clarence Thomas," 14 George Mason U. Civil Rights L. J. 27 (2004); Tomiko Brown-Nagin, "The Transformative Racial Politics of Clarence Thomas?" 7 U. Pa. J. Const. L. 787 (2005). Two additional symposia on Thomas are A Tribute to Justice Clarence Thomas, 12 Regent U. L. Rev. 329ff (1999), and Clarence Thomas After Ten Years, 12 Am. U. J. Gender, Social Policy, and the Law 315 (2002).

Scholarship on Ginsburg has been affected by her pre-Court status as a prominent advocate for gender equality. All the books that have currently appeared on Ginsburg, some of which were prompted by her nomination to the Court in 1992, focus on her association with gender issues. The most analytical treatment is Melanie K. Morris, *Crafting a Constitutional Rationale: Ruth Bader Ginsburg and Gender-Based Equality* (2001). See also Chris W. Bonneau, *Justice Ruth Bader Ginsburg and the Feminine Voice* (1998), Jenifer M. Esquivel-Parker, *A Foundation for Feminism: A Study of Justice Ruth Bader Ginsburg's Feminist Jurisprudence* (1999), and Anastasia Wade, *Supreme Court Justice*

Ruth Bader Ginsburg (2004). The best overview of Ginsburg's career yet to appear is Judith Baer, "Advocate on the Court: Ruth Bader Ginsburg and the Limits of Formal Equality," in Maltz, ed., *Rehnquist Justice*, 216–40.

Articles on Ginsburg have been relatively sparse. See Joyce Ann Baugh, Christopher E. Smith, Thomas R. Hensley, and Scott Patrick Johnson, "Justice Ruth Bader Ginsburg: A Preliminary Assessment," 26 U. Toledo L. Rev. 1 (1994); Sheila M. Smith, "Justice Ruth Bader Ginsburg and Sexual Harassment Law," 63 U. Cinn. L. Rev. 1893 (1995); Amy Walsh, "Ruth Bader Ginsburg: Extending the Constitution," 32 John Marshall L. Rev. 197 (1998); and Laura Krugman Ray, "Justice Ginsburg and the Middle Way," 68 Brooklyn L. Rev. 629 (2003). Two symposia contain much of the most useful work on Ginsburg: A Tribute to Justice Ruth Bader Ginsburg, 20 Hawaii L. Rev. 583ff (1993), and especially Celebration of the Tenth Anniversary of Justice Ruth Bader Ginsburg's Appointment to the Supreme Court of the United States, 104 Colum. L. Rev. 1ff (2004).

Before Breyer was appointed to the Court he taught and wrote in the fields of antitrust and administrative law, producing an administrative law casebook, *Administrative Law and Regulatory Policy*, which has gone through four editions between 1992 and 2006, and a book on antitrust policy, *Breaking the Vicious Cycle: Toward Effective Risk Regulation* (1993). Since joining the Court he has written a brief overview of his approach toward constitutional interpretation, *Active Liberty* (2005). At present no biography has appeared. The best overall assessment of Breyer is Ken I. Kersch, "The Synthetic Progressivism of Stephen G. Breyer," in Maltz, ed., *Rehnquist Justice*, 241–76.

Other than assessments of his contribution to antitrust and administrative law, scholarship on Breyer has been extremely limited. For reviews of *Breaking the Vicious Cycle,* see David A. Dana, 74 B. U. L. Rev. 365 (1994), Craig Gannett, 107 Harv. L. Rev. 1095 (1994), Barry Sullivan, 89 Northwestern L. Rev. 166 (1994), Lisa Heinzerling, 62 U. Chi. L. Rev. 449 (1995), Stephen F. Williams, 93 Mich. L. Rev. 1498 (1995), David A. Wirth and Ellen K. Silbergeld, 95 Colum. L. Rev. 1857 (1995), and a symposium in 25 Antitrust Law & Economics Rev. 1ff (1994). For a symposium on Breyer and administrative law, see Justice Stephen Breyer's Contribution to Administrative Law, 8 The Administrative Law Journal of the American University 721ff (1995). Assessments of Breyer as a Justice include Walter E. Joyce, "The Early Constitutional Jurisprudence of Stephen G. Breyer," 7 Seton Hall Const. L. J. 149 (1996); Gordon R. Shea, " 'Gatering His Beams with a Crystall Glasse': The Intellectual Property Jurisprudence of Stephen G. Breyer," 2 Marquette Intellectual Property L. Rev. 195 (1998); and Lillian R. BeVier, "The First Amendment on the Tracks: Should Justice Breyer Be at the Switch?" 89 Minn. L. Rev. 1280 (2005).

Index

This index includes cases discussed in the text; for other case references, consult the notes.